THE EVOLVING GOVERNANCE OF EU COMPETITION LAW IN A TIME OF DISRUPTIONS

This book develops a timely analysis of the complex trends and transformations emerging in EU competition law in the current turbulent times.

Repeated economic crises, the climate emergency, digitalisation, and geopolitical and democratic threats are all having profound societal and economic effects on the EU. In light of its fundamental role in the Treaties, EU competition law has been called upon to play an important role in responding to this state of 'turbulence'. This brings about significant governance and constitutional challenges, firstly by questioning how the governance of EU competition law is being transformed to respond and adapt. Secondly, these crisis-induced transformations probe the logic and constitutional limits of EU competition law within the framework of EU law.

This collection brings together EU institutional and competition lawyers to reflect on the governance and constitutional challenges emerging from the post-modernisation evolution of EU competition law against the backdrop of the recent multiple crises in the EU. The essays focus on the substantive and procedural developments across the three main policy areas of EU competition law: antitrust, merger control and State aid. EU constitutional and competition lawyers will be interested in this important new collection.

Volume 119 in the Series Modern Studies in European Law

Modern Studies in European Law

Recent titles in this series:

Responsive Human Rights: Vulnerability and the ECtHR
Corina Heri

The Architecture of Fundamental Rights in the European Union
Šejla Imamovic

The EU and its Member States' Joint Participation in International Agreements
Edited by Nicolas Levrat, Yuliya Kaspiarovich, Christine Kaddous and Ramses A Wessel

The UN Convention on the Rights of Persons with Disabilities and the European Union: The Impact on Law and Governance
Carmine Conte

EU Criminal Law, Second Edition
Valsamis Mitsilegas

The EU as a Global Digital Actor: Institutionalising Global Data Protection, Trade, and Cybersecurity
Elaine Fahey

Exporting the European Convention on Human Rights
Maria-Louiza Deftou

Judicial Authority in EU Internal Market Law: Implications for the Balance of Competences and Powers
Vilija Velyvyte

The Changing European Union: A Critical View on the Role of Law and the Courts
Edited by Tamara Capeta, Iris Goldner Lang and Tamara Perisin

The Structural Transformation of European Private Law: A Critique of Juridical Hermeneutic
Leone Niglia

The Future of EU Constitutionalism
Edited by Matej Avbelj

The Changing Role of Citizens in EU Democratic Governance
Edited by Davor Jancic

The EU and the Baltic Sea Area
Edited by Allan Rosas and Henrik Ringbom

The Evolving Governance of EU Competition Law in a Time of Disruptions: A Constitutional Perspective
Edited by Carlo Maria Colombo, Kathryn Wright and Mariolina Eliantonio

For the complete list of titles in this series
see www.bloomsbury.com/uk/series/modern-studies-in-european-law/

The Evolving Governance of EU Competition Law in a Time of Disruptions

A Constitutional Perspective

Edited by
Carlo Maria Colombo
Kathryn Wright
and
Mariolina Eliantonio

•HART•
OXFORD • LONDON • NEW YORK • NEW DELHI • SYDNEY

HART PUBLISHING

Bloomsbury Publishing Plc

Kemp House, Chawley Park, Cumnor Hill, Oxford, OX2 9PH, UK

1385 Broadway, New York, NY 10018, USA

29 Earlsfort Terrace, Dublin 2, Ireland

HART PUBLISHING, the Hart/Stag logo, BLOOMSBURY and the Diana logo are trademarks of Bloomsbury Publishing Plc

First published in Great Britain 2024

A catalogue record for this book is available from the British Library.

A catalogue record for this book is available from the Library of Congress.

Library of Congress Control Number: 2023948757

ISBN: HB: 978-1-50995-179-6
ePDF: 978-1-50995-181-9
ePub: 978-1-50995-180-2

Typeset by Compuscript Ltd, Shannon

FOREWORD

In his 1997 book *The Innovator's Dilemma*, Harvard Business School professor Clayton Christensen famously theorised what he termed 'disruptive innovation'.[1] Disruptive technologies, he argued, overtook market leaders by eschewing traditional approaches, creating new markets by introducing novel products that appeal to a new set of customers. While mainstream customers initially perceive disruptive innovations as less attractive than the products of the dominant incumbents, disruptors rapidly shift the status quo to displace traditional market leaders.[2]

A generation on, disruptions continue to challenge conventional conceptions of competition. In some cases, radical transformations to existing markets have been driven by rapid company-led innovation (think of the digital economy). In other cases, transformative innovation has been provoked by forces external to the market but which have profound implications for it (think of the climate crisis). In both cases, disruptions can force us to reexamine how we set the rules of the marketplace including, potentially, the competition law framework.[3]

In the case of EU competition law, this has reignited the long-running debate over whether competition law and governance can properly have regard to broader developments and trends in our society and economy. While the early phase of EU competition law suggested an openness to taking broader social and economic issues into account within the competition analysis, the Commission's position changed in the early 2000s.[4] Since then, it has been commonly considered that competition regulators should focus purely on issues of economic efficiency and eliminating market distortions, to the exclusion of other public interest factors, which, it is argued, are a matter for the democratically elected legislature (beyond, of course, the fundamental public interest aim of controlling private market power).[5] On this thinking, competition policy should leave it to the legislator to

[1] C Christensen, *The Innovator's Dilemma: When New Technologies Cause Great Firms to Fail* (New York, Harper Business, 1997).

[2] A classic example is the salutary tale of Netflix which, from its initial position as a marginal player offering DVDs by mail order, rapidly outpaced traditional physical video rental stores (such as Blockbusters in the US) to become the global phenomenon familiar to many of our living rooms.

[3] On the regulatory challenges posed by disruptive technologies, see A Taeihagh, M Ramesh and M Howlett, 'Assessing the Regulatory Challenges of Emerging Disruptive Technologies' (2021) 15 *Regulation & Governance* 1000.

[4] This shift can be seen, for instance, in the Commission Guidelines on the Application of Article 81(3) of the Treaty OJ 2004 C 101/97. For an overview of these developments, see C Townley, *Article 81 EC and Public Policy* (Oxford, Hart Publishing, 2009).

[5] For a forceful account of this argument, see, eg, G Amato, *Antitrust and the Bounds of Power: The Dilemma of Liberal Democracy in the History of the Market* (Oxford, Hart Publishing, 1997).

regulate broader societal concerns (such as sustainability, data privacy and the broader societal and economic impacts of digital technologies), and competition authorities should not get involved.

As the contributions to this fascinating book explore, the profound challenges raised by certain societal disruptions – in particular the climate crisis and the digital transformation – have prompted a partial reassessment. In some cases, the technologically novel nature of the market raises questions of competition analysis that have simply never previously arisen. Twenty years ago, for instance, an attempt to broach the problem of algorithmic collusion, discussed by Van Cleyenbreugel in his contribution, would most probably have been met with a quizzical eye. In the case of the climate crisis, the existential nature of the societal challenge has led to a general consensus that action must enlist 'all sectors of the society and the economy, including industry'.[6] This has led to calls for a rethink of the relationship between economic and environmental policies at the highest political level. Within the EU, this is reflected in the European Green Deal, discussed by Sikora-Kalėda in her contribution. The European Green Deal is founded on an all-economy approach to environmental protection, demanding 'deeply transformative policies' underpinned by an economic model that properly values environmental and natural resources.[7]

At a basic level, a competition policy that ignores such profound societal transformations would risk being considered out of touch and as impeding the achievement of the EU's core aims. As a matter of EU law, a further dimension is added to the debate by the fact that EU competition policy is embedded in a constitutional framework and is indissociable from that framework. Thus, unlike certain other competition regimes, the EU competition rules form part of a constitutional framework that mandates a proportionality-based balancing of, for instance, the achievement of 'technical and economic progress' against the aims of protecting effective competition. In the case of anti-competitive agreements, this balancing clause is provided in Article 101(3) TFEU which, as noted above, may reasonably be interpreted as extending to environmental improvements. The CJEU has in the past held that the Commission 'is entitled to base itself on considerations connected with the pursuit of the public interest' in granting exemptions under Article 101(3) TFEU.[8] It has also held that objectives of a 'different nature' to those of competition law may justify competitive restrictions,

In the US, this approach is typically associated with the Chicago School approach to antitrust economics, whereby consumer welfare, interpreted narrowly as consumer surplus, is largely focused on effects on prices or output to the exclusion of other impacts on human well-being. See, eg, Y Brozen, 'Competition, Efficiency and Antitrust' (1969) 3 *Journal of World Trade Law* 65; R Bork, *The Antitrust Paradox: A Policy at War with Itself* (New York, Basic Books, 1978); R Posner, 'The Chicago School of Antitrust Analysis' (1979) 127 *University of Pennsylvania Law Review* 974.

[6] European Parliament resolution of 28 November 2019 on the climate and environment emergency (2019/2930(RSP)) [2021] OJ C232/28.

[7] Commission, 'Communication from the Commission, The European Green Deal' COM(2019) 640 final, Section 2.1.

[8] Case T-112/99 *Métropole Télévision* [2001] EU:T:2001:215, para 118.

if proportionate.[9] Thus, for instance, it is settled case law that market integration objectives are relevant in interpreting the EU competition rules.[10] In *TeliaSonera*, for instance, the CJEU expressed the function of the competition rules referenced in Article 3(1)(b) TEU as:

> precisely to prevent competition from being distorted to the detriment of the public interest, individual undertakings and consumers, thereby ensuring the well-being of the European Union (see, to that effect, Case C-94/00 Roquette Frères [2002] ECR I-9011, paragraph 42).[11]

This might suggest, therefore, that the principal objective of the EU competition rules is the protection of competition, viewed however from the perspective of not only undertakings and consumers, but also the public interest.

Other cross-cutting fundamental constitutional obligations may also be relevant to competition analysis. As Cseres emphasises in her contribution, after the General Court's judgment in *Sped-Pro*,[12] it is clear that rule of law considerations cannot be ignored where relevant to competition analysis. The relevance of the fundamental right to data protection was considered by the Court of Justice in the *Meta* case,[13] discussed in Monti's contribution. And in the case of environmental protection, Article 37 of the Charter of Fundamental Rights and Article 11 TFEU each constitutionally oblige the integration of a 'high level of environmental protection and the improvement of the quality of the environment' into competition policy.[14] As Colombo and Bonelli highlight in their contribution, these articles have been applied by the CJEU to require, for instance, the Commission to check compliance with EU environmental law when assessing the compatibility of Member States' grant of State aid with the internal market.[15] Indeed, as the Commission's newly amended Horizontal Cooperation Guidelines illustrate, it is perfectly possible to integrate sustainability concerns into competition analysis, including by employing valuation techniques derived from environmental economics, encompassing non-use value and collective

[9] Case 75/84 *Metro II* [1986] EU:C:1986:399.

[10] See, for instance, Joined Cases C-501/06 P, C-513/06 P, C-515/06 P and C-519/06 P *GlaxoSmithKline* [2009] EU:C:2009:610.

[11] Case C-52/09 *TeliaSonera* [2011] EU:C:2011:83, para 22.

[12] Case T-791/19 *Sped-Pro* [2022] EU:T:2022:67.

[13] Case C-252/21 *Meta Platforms* [2022] EU:C:2022:704.

[14] Article 37 of the Charter of Fundamental Rights provides, 'A high level of environmental protection and the improvement of the quality of the environment must be integrated into the policies of the Union and ensured in accordance with the principle of sustainable development.'

[15] See Case C-594/18 P *Austria v Commission (Hinkley Point C)* [2020] EU:2020:742, para 100. See similarly, Case T-101/18 *Austria v Commission* [2022] EU:T:2022:728, para 70. This examination does not, however, need to go further and include, as part of the assessment of whether the aid affects trading conditions 'to an extent contrary to the common interest' within the meaning of Article 107(3)(c), a more general assessment of potential negative environmental impacts of the aid going beyond EU law requirements: judgment in *Hinkley Point C*, para 101.

benefits. Announcing the new Guidelines, Commissioner Vestager described them as 'a key tool to push forward the green and digital transitions'.[16]

Delimiting the boundaries of when, and how, broader constitutional obligations should be taken into account in competition analysis is, of course, no easy task. It is critical that competition policy continues to perform its essential function of protecting competition; competition policy cannot become unadministrable; sufficient legal certainty must be maintained despite the rapid pace of regulatory and technological developments; and, as the Digital Markets Act demonstrates, ex ante regulation may often be necessary alongside competition enforcement. As Wright and Monti explain in their contributions, such disruptions may also have significant governance implications: it is national competition authorities, not the Commission, which have been the first movers in publishing guidance on the relevance of sustainability for competition analysis, for instance.[17]

These complex challenges underscore the need for thoughtful and rigorous debate of these crucial issues, which go to the core of our social market democracy. I commend the editors for stepping up to the plate with this important contribution.

Suzanne Kingston
General Court of the European Union
Luxembourg, June 2023

[16] European Commission Press Release, 'Antitrust: Commission adopts new Horizontal Block Exemption Regulations and Horizontal Guidelines', 1 June 2023: https://ec.europa.eu/commission/presscorner/detail/en/ip_23_2990.

[17] In particular, the Dutch and Greek competition authorities initially took the lead.

CONTENTS

Foreword v
Suzanne Kingston

List of Contributors xi
Abbreviations xiii
Table of Cases xvii
Table of Commission Decisions and Decisions of National Competition Authorities xxv
Table of Legislation xxix

Introduction 1
Carlo Maria Colombo, Kathryn Wright and Mariolina Eliantonio

PART I
POWERS AND AIMS OF EU COMPETITION LAW

1. *EU Competition Law and Democracy in the Shadow of Rule of Law Backsliding* 19
   Katalin J Cseres

2. *Digital Technology Disruptions and Competition Law: A Stress Test for the Existing Governance and Enforcement Frameworks?* 45
   Pieter Van Cleynenbreugel

3. *A Clash of Titans: EU Competition and State Aid Law and the Impact of the European Green Deal* 65
   Alicja Sikora

4. *From Crisis Cartels to COVID-19 State Aid and Cooperation: The Non Exceptionality of Crisis Management by EU Competition Law* 83
   Francisco Costa-Cabral

PART II
ACTORS AND DYNAMICS IN EU COMPETITION LAW

5. *Levelling the Playing Field: EU Regulatory Extension Through Technocratic Cooperation* 113
   Kathryn Wright

6. *Shaping the EU's Competition Law and Policy: Space for Multiple Actors?*....133
Giorgio Monti

7. *The Role of Companies in the Strategic Turn of EU Competition Law*...........153
Fernando Pastor-Merchante

8. *The Response of EU Courts to Society's Digital and Green Challenges in the Field of Competition and State Aid*........173
Phedon Nicolaides

PART III
INSTRUMENTS AND PROCEDURES IN A MULTILEVEL COMPETITION LAW LANDSCAPE

9. *Repurposing Administrative Procedures to Meet Novel Challenges in EU Competition Law*........195
Filipe Brito Bastos

10. *Soft Law in EU Competition and State Aid: An Imperfect Solution to Grand Regulatory Challenges*........213
Oana Ştefan

11. *Unpacking Multilevel Elements in Digital Markets: Informing Effective Enforcement and Remedial Design in EU Competition Law*........233
Maria Ioannidou

12. *Governing the Green Transition Through State Aid Control*........253
Carlo Maria Colombo and Matteo Bonelli

13. *Creative Compliance and the Politicisation of EU State Aid Implementation in Times of Crisis*........275
Nicole Lindstrom

Conclusions........293
Carlo Maria Colombo, Kathryn Wright and Mariolina Eliantonio

Index........311

LIST OF CONTRIBUTORS

Matteo Bonelli is an Assistant Professor of European Union law at the Faculty of Law of Maastricht University.

Filipe Brito Bastos is an Assistant Professor at NOVA School of Law.

Pieter Van Cleynenbreugel is a Professor of Law at the Faculty of Law, Political Science and Criminology of the University of Liège.

Carlo Maria Colombo is Marie Skłodowska-Curie Fellow at Sciences Po, France, and Assistant Professor of Administrative Law at Maastricht University, the Netherlands.

Francisco Costa-Cabral is a Fellow at the Tilburg Law and Economics Center (TILEC), Tilburg Law School.

Katalin J Cseres is an Associate Professor of Law at the Amsterdam Centre for European Law and Governance of the University of Amsterdam.

Mariolina Eliantonio is a Professor in European and Comparative Administrative Law and Procedure at Maastricht University.

Maria Ioannidou is a Senior Lecturer in Competition Law at the School of Law, Queen Mary, University of London.

Nicole Lindstrom is a Senior Lecturer in Politics at the University of York.

Giorgio Monti is a Professor of Competition Law at Tilburg Law School.

Phedon Nicolaides is a Professor at the University of Maastricht and at the University of Nicosia.

Fernando Pastor-Merchante is an Associate Professor of Law at IE University.

Alicja Sikora is a Senior Lecturer at the Faculty of Law of the Jagiellonian University, as well as a Legal Adviser to the Council of the European Union and the European Council.

Oana Ştefan is a Reader at The Dickson Poon School of Law, King's College London.

Kathryn Wright is a Senior Lecturer in Law at the University of York.

ABBREVIATIONS

ACCC	Aarhus Convention Compliance Committee
ACM	Authority for Consumers and Markets
AG	Advocate-General
CAP	Common Agricultural Policy
CBAM	Carbon Border Adjustment Mechanism
CEEC	Central and Eastern Europe
CEEAG	Climate, Environmental Protection and Energy
CFR	Charter of Fundamental Rights
CJEU	Court of Justice of the European Union
DCFTA	Deep and Comprehensive Free Trade Area
DFP	DoubleClick For Publishers
DG	Directorate-General
DG COMP	Directorate-General for Competition
DMA	Digital Markets Act
DNSH	Do No Significant Harm
EAW	European Arrest Warrant
EC	European Community
ECJ	European Court of Justice
ECN	European Competition Network
ECN+	European Competition Network Plus
EEA	European Economic Area
EEC	European Economic Community
EGD	European Green Deal
EHB	European Hydrogen Bank

ESI	European Union Structural and Investment
ETS	Emission Trading Scheme
EU	European Union
EUGB	European Green Deal
EUMR	European Union Merger Regulation
FBA	Fulfilment by Amazon
FDI	Foreign Direct Investment
FSR	Foreign Subsidies Regulation
FTA	Free Trade Agreement
GAFA	Google, Amazon, Facebook and Apple
GBER	General Block Exemption Regulation
GC	General Court
GDP	Gross Domestic Product
GDPR	General Data Protection Regulation
GHG	Greenhouse Gas
GVH	Hungarian Competition Authority
GWB	Gesetz Gegen Wettbewerbeschränkungen
HCC	Hellenic Competition Commission
ICA	International Competition Network
IPCEI	Important Projects of Common European Interest
MEIP	Market Economy Investor Principle
MS	Member State
OECD	Organisation for Economic Co-operation and Development
NCA	National Competition Authority
NCT	New Competition Tool
NGEU	NextGenerationEU
P2B	Platform-to-Business
RDI	Research, Development and Innovation
RRF	Recovery and Resilience Facility

RRP	Recovery and Resilience Plan
SAAP	State Aid Action Plan
SAM	State Aid Modernisation
SGEI	Services of General Economic Interest
TCA	Trade and Cooperation Agreement
TEU	Treaty on the European Union
TF	Temporary Framework
TFEU	Treaty on the Functioning of the European Union
TPR	Trade Policy Review
UK	United Kingdom
UN	United Nations
UNCTAD	United Nations Conference on Trade and Development
UNECE	United Nations Economic Commission for Europe
WTO	World Trade Organization

TABLE OF CASES

EU Cases

General Court

Case T-24/90 *Automec Srl v Commission* [1992] EU:T:1992:97. 167
Case T-112/99 *Métropole Télévision (M6) v Commission* [2001] EU:T:2001:215. .... vi, 179
Case T-65/98 *Van den Bergh Foods Ltd v Commission* [2003] EU:T:2003:281. 179
Case T-158/99 *Thermenhotel Stoiser Franz and Others v Commission* [2004] EU:T:2004:2. 264
Case T-328/03 *O2 v Commission* [2006] EU:T:2006:116. 179
Case T-210/02 *British Aggregates v Commission* [2006] EU:T:2006:253. 186
Case T-289/01 *Der Grüne Punkt – Duales System Deutschland v Commission* [2007] EU:T:2007:155 180
Case T-396/08 *Freistaat Sachsen v Commission* [2010] EU:T:2010:297. 188
Case T-419/03 *Altstoff Recycling Austria v Commission* [2011] EU:T:2011:102. 180–81
Case T-304/08 *Smurfit Kappa v Commission* [2012] EU:T:2012:351. 187
Case T-226/09 *British Telecommunications v Commission* [2013] EU:T:2013:466. 188
Case T-79/10 *Colt Télécommunications France v Commission* [2013] EU:T:2013:463. 188
Case T-468/08 *Tisza Erőmű v Commission* [2014] EU:T:2014:235. 209
Case T-362/10 *Vtesse Networks v Commission* [2014] EU:T:2014:928. 188
Case T-402/13 *Orange v Commission* [2014] EU:T:2014:991. 209
Case T-57/11 *Castelnou Energía SL v Commission* [2014] EU:T:2014:1021. .... 190, 262, 264
Case T-251/11 *Austria v Commission* [2014] EU:T:2014:1060 .... 186, 188
Case T-462/13 *Comunidad Autónoma del País Vasco v Commission* [2015] EU:T:2015:902. 188
Case T-76/14 *Morningstar v Commission* [2016] EU:T:2016:481. 178
Case T-712/14 *CEAHR v Commission* [2017] EU:T:2017:748 105
Case T-325/16 *České dráhy v Commission* [2018] EU:T:2018:368 209
Case T-705/14 *Unichem Laboratories v Commission* [2018] EU:T:2018:915. 181

Case T-330/18 *Carvalho and Others v Parliament and Council* [2019] EU:T:2019:324. 72
Case T-20/17 *Hungary v Commission* [2019] EU:T:2019:448. 290
Case T-778/17 *Autostrada Wielkopolska v Commission* [2019] EU:T:2019:756. 187
Case T-417/16 *Achemos Grupė v Commission* [2019] EU:T:2019:597....189
Case T-429/18 *BFR and SHP Comercio e Industria de Alimentos v Commission* [2020] EU:T:2020:322....197
Case T-778/16 *Ireland v Commission* [2020] EU:T:2020:338. 289
Case T-814/17 *Lietuvos geležinkeliai v Commission* [2020] EU:T:2020:545. 183
Case T-238/20 *Ryanair v Commission* [2021] EU:T:2021:91. 228
Case T-259/20 *Ryanair v Commission* [2021] EU:T:2021:92. 91–93
Case T-379/20 *Ryanair v Commission* [2021] EU:T:2021:195. 228
Case T-465/20 *Ryanair v Commission (TAP; Covid-19)* [2021] EU:T:2021:284. 166
Case T-643/20 *Ryanair v Commission (KLM; Covid-19)* [2021] EU:T:2021:286. 166
Case T-665/20 *Ryanair v Commission (Condor)* [2021] EU:T:2021:344. 166
Case T-604/18 *Google v Commission* (*Google Android*) [2022] EU:T:2022:541. .... 47, 184
Case T-19/21 *Amazon v Commission* [2021] EU:T:2021:730. 243
Case T-612/17 *Google v Commission* (*Google Shopping*) [2021] EU:T:2021:763. ....47, 166, 168, 184
Case T-678/20 *Solar Electric and Others v Commission* [2021] EU:T:2021:780. 266
Case T-263/15 *Gmina Miasto Gdynia v Commission (RENV)* [2021] EU:T:2021:927. 187
Case T-799/17 *Scania and Others v Commission* [2022] EU:T:2022:48. 181
Case T-791/19 *Sped Pro v Commission* [2022] EU:T:2022:67.... vii, 24, 40, 42, 301
Case T-363/19 *UK v Commission* [2022] EU:T:2022:349....188
Case T-235/18 *Qualcomm v Commission* [2022] EU:T:2022:358. 183–85
Case T-101/18 *Austria v Commission* (*Paks II*) [2022] EU:T:2022:728. .... vii, 190, 263–64
Case T-334/19 *Google and Alphabet v Commission* (pending)....47

Court of Justice

Case 25/62 *Plaumann v Commission* [1963] EU:C:1963:17....267
Case 56/64 *Consten and Grundig v Commission* [1966] EU:C:1966:41....70
Case 127/73 *BRT v SABAM* [1974] EU:C:1974:25....136
Case 17/74 *Transocean Marine Paint Association v Commission* [1974] EU:C:1974:106. 196

Case 33/76 *Rewe-Zentral AG v Landwirtschaftskammer für das Saarland* [1976] EC:C:1976:188. .... 39, 114
Case 74/76 *Iannelli and Volpi v Meroni* [1977] EU:C:1977:51 262
Case 78/76 *Steinike und Weinlig v Germany* [1977] EU:C:1977:52. 267
Case 27/76 *United Brands v Commission* [1978] EU:C:1978:22. 98
Case 106/77 *Amministrazione delle Finanze dello Stato v Simmenthal* [1978] EU:C:1978:49 145
Case 85/76 *Hoffmann-La Roche and Co Ag v Commission* [1979] EU:C:1979:36. 196
Case 120/78 *Rewe-Zentral AG v Bundesmonopolverwaltung für Branntwein* [1979] EU:C:1979:42 114
Joined Cases 253/78 and 1 to 3/79 *Procureur de la République v Giry and Guerlain* [1980] EU:C:1980:188 227
Case 99/79 *SA Lancôme v Etos and Albert Heijn* [1980] EU:C:1980:193. 227
Case 730/79 *Philip Morris Holland BV v Commission* [1980] EU:C:1980:209. 91
Case 84/82 *Germany v Commission* [1984] EU:C:1984:117. 279
Case 40/85 *Belgium v Commission* [1986] EU:C:1986:305. 266
Case 25/88 *Criminal proceedings against Esther Renée Bouchara, née Wurmser, and Norlaine SA* [1989] EU:C:1989:187. 202
Case C-41/90 *Klaus Höfner and Fritz Elser v Macrotron GmbH* [1991] EU:C:1991:161. 45
Case C-5/94 *The Queen v Ministry of Agriculture, Fisheries and Food, ex parte Hedley Lomas (Ireland)* [1996] EU:C:1996:205. 202
Case C-282/95 P *Guérin automobiles v Commission* [1997] EU:C:1997:159. 167
Joined Cases C-279/96, C-281/96 and C-281/96 *Ansaldo Energia SpA v Amministrazione delle Finanze dello Stato* [1998] EU:C:1998:403 114
Case C-7/97 *Bronner v Mediaprint Zeitungs* [1998] EU:C:1998:569. 52
Case C-119/97 P *Ufex and Others v Commission* [1999] EU:C:1999:116. 105
Joined Cases T-132/96 and T-143/96 *Freistaat Sachsen v Volkswagen* [1999] EU:T:1999:326. 95
Case C-104/97 P *Atlanta AG and Others v Commission* [1999] EU:C:1999:498. 156
Case C-344/98 *Masterfoods Ltd v HB Ice Cream Ltds* [2000] EU:C:2000:249. 142
Case C-379/98 *PreussenElektra v Schhleswag AG* [2001] EU:C:2001:160 186
Case C-453/99 *Courage Ltd v Bernard Crehan* [2001] EU:C:2001:465. 41
Case C-309/99 *Wouters v Algemene Raad van de Nederlandse Orde van Advocaten* [2002] EU:C:2002:98. 106–07
Joined Cases C-74/00 and 75/00 *Falck SpA and Acciaierie di Bolzano SpA v Commission* [2002] EU:C:2002:524. .... 160, 209
Case C-409/00 *Spain v Commission* [2003] EU:C:2003:92. 188

Case C-198/01 *CIF v Autorità Garante della Concorrenza e del Mercato* [2003] EU:C:2003:430 .... 107, 145
Case C-170/02 P *Schlüsselverlag J S Moser and Others v Commission* [2003] EU:C:2003:501 167
Joined Cases C-2/01 and C-3/01 *BAI and Commission v Bayer AG* [2004] EU:C:2004:2. 53
Joined Cases C-204/00 P, C-205/00 P, C-211/00 P, C-213/00 P, C-217/00 P and C-219/00 P *Aalborg Portland and Others v Commission* [2004] EU:C:2004:6. .... 162, 246
Case C-418/01 *IMS health v NDC Health* [2004] EU:C:2004:257. 54
Case C-110/03 *Belgium v Commission* [2005] EU:C:2005:223. 188
Joined Cases C-189/02 P, C-202/02 P, C-205/02 to C-208/02 P and C-213/02 P *Dansk Rørindustri and Others v Commission* [2005] EU:C:2005:408. 227
Cases C-276/03 P *Scott v Commission* [2005] EU:C:2005:590. .... 160, 209
Case C-78/03 P *Commission v Aktionsgemeinschaft Recht und Eigentum* [2005] EU:C:2005:761 267
Joined Cases C-346/03 and 529/03 *Atzenis v Regione autonoma della Sardegna* [2006] EU:C:2006:130 .... 91–92, 96
Case C-519/04 P *Meca-Medina and Majcen v Commission* [2006] EU:C:2006:492. 106–07
Case C-238/05 *Asnef-Equifax, Servicios de Información sobre Solvencia y Crédito, SL v Asociación de Usuarios de Servicios Bancarios (Ausbanc)* [2006] EU:C:2006:734. 179
Opinion of Advocate General Mengozzi in Case C-487/06 P *British Aggregates Association v Commission* [2008] ECLI:EU:C:2008:419. 159
Case C-390/06 *Nuova Agricast Srl v Ministero delle Attivitá Produttive* [2008] EU:C:2008:224 .... 69, 262
Joined Cases C-39/05 P and C-52/05 P *Sweden and Maurizio Turco v Council* [2008] EU:C:2008:374. .... 115, 129
Case C-413/06 P *Bertelsmann AG and Others v Commission* [2008] EU:C:2008:392. 162
Case C-487/06 P *British Aggregates Association v Commission* [2008] EU:C:2008:419. 259
Case C-521/06 P *Athinaïki Techniki AE v Commission* [2008] EU:C:2008:422. 167–68
Case C-75/05 P *Germany v Kronofrance and Commission* [2008] EU:C:2008:482. .... 187, 189
Case C-209/07 *Competition Authority v Beef Industry Development Society Ltd and Barry Brothers Meats Ltd* [2008] EU:C:2008:643 .... 85, 101–02
Case C-333/07 *Régie Networks v Direction de contrôle discal Rhône-Aples bourgogne* [2008] EU:C:2008:764 226
Case C-429/07 *Inspecteur van de Belastingdienst v X BV* [2009] EU:C:2009:359. 41

Case C-385/07 P *Der Grüne Punkt – Duales System Deutschland v Commission* [2009] EU:C:2009:456. 180
Case C-519/07 P *Commission v Koninklijke Friesland Campina NV* [2009] EU:C:2009:556. 266
Case C-501/06 P *GlaxoSmithKline Services v Commission* [2009] EU:C:2009:610. ....vii, 179
Cases C-441/07 P *Commission v Alrosa Company* [2010] EU:C: 2010:377 174
Case C-439/08 *Vlaamse federatie van verenigingen van Brood- en Banketbakkers, Ijsbereiders en Chocoladebewerkers (VEBIC) v Belgium* [2010] EU:C:2010:739. ....41, 144
Case C-52/09 *Konkurrensverket v TeliaSonera Sverige AB* [2011] EU:C:2011:83. ....vii, 147
Case C-375/09 *Prezes Urzędu Ochrony Konkurencji i Konsumentów v Tele2 Polska sp. z o.o. devenue Netia SA* [2011] EU:C:2011:270. 140
Case C-360/09 *Pfleiderer AG v Bundeskartellamt* [2011] EU:C:2011:389....41
Case C-17/10 *Toshiba Corporation and Others v Úrad pro ochranu hospodàrské souteze* [2012] EU:C:2012:72. 246
Case C-226/11 *Expedia Inc v Autorité de la concurrence and Others* [2012] EU:C:2012:795....228
Case C-204/12 *Essent Belgium v Vlaamse Reguleringsinstantie voor de Elektriciteit* [2013] EU:C:2013:294. 67
Case C-681/11 *Schenker and Others v Bundeswettbewerbsbehörde* [2013] EU:C:2013:404. ....41, 144
Case C-310/12 *Commission v Hungary* [2013] EU:C:2013:556....32
Case C-418/11 *Texdata Software v Landesgericht Innsbruck* [2013] EU:C:2013:588. 209
Case C-67/13 P *CB v Commission* [2014] EU:C:2014:2204. ....98, 103
Opinion 2/13 of the Court of Justice of the European Union [2014] EU:C:2014:2454. 39
Case C-431/14 P *Greece v Commission* [2016] EU:C:2016:145. 92
Case C-230/14 *Weltimmo SRO v Nemzeti Adatvédelmi és Inofrmációszabadság Hatóság* [2015] EU:C:2015:639. 197
Joined Cases C-404/15 and C-659/15 *Pál Aranyosi and Robert Căldăraru v Generalstaatsanwaltschaft Bremen* [2016] EU:C:2016:198. 40
Case C-526/14 *Kotnik v Drzavni zbor Republike Slovenije* [2016] EU:C:2016:570. ....92, 96 97, 187
Case C-444/15 *Associazione Italia Nostra Onlus v Comune di Venezia and Others* [2016] EU:C:2016:665. 72
Case C-524/14 P *Commission v Hansestadt Lübeck* [2016] EU:C: 2016:971. 205
Case C-427/16 *CHEZ v Yordan Kotsev* [2017] EU:C:2017:890. 106
Case C-547/16 *Gasorba and Others v Repsol Comercial* [2017] EU:C:2017:891. 227

Case C-179/16 *F Hoffmann-La Roche and Others v Autorità Garante della Concorrenza e del Mercato* [2018] EU:C:2018:25......................................101
Case C-16/16 P *Belgium v Commission* [2018] EU:C:2018:79. 225
Case C-64/16 *Associação Sindical dos Juízes Portugueses v Tribunal de Contas* [2018] EU:C:2018:117..201
Joined Cases C-596/16 and C-597/16 *Enzo Di Puma v Commissione Nazionale per le Società e la Borsa and Commissione Nazionale per le Società e la Borsa v Antonio Zecca* [2018] EU:C:2018:192.....................246
Case C-537/16 *Garlsson Real Estate and Others v Commissione Nazionale per le Società e la Borsa* [2018] EU:C:2018:193. 246
Case C-524/15 *Criminal proceedings against Luca Menci* [2018] EU:C:2018:197. 246
Case C-216/118 *Criminal proceedings against LM* [2018] EU:C:2018:586. 40
Joined Cases C-54/17 and C-55/17 *Autorità Garante della Concorrenza e del Mercato (AGCM) v Wind Tre and Vodafone Italia* [2018] EU:C:2018:710. 138
Opinion of Advocate General Wahl in Case C-617/17 *Powszechny Zaklad Ubezpieczen na Życie v Prezes Urzedu Ochrony Konkurencji I Knsumentòw* [2018] EU:C:2018:976. 246
Case C-378/17 *Minister for Justice and Equality and Commissioner of An Garda Síochána v Workplace Relations Commission* [2018] EU:C:2018:979. 145
Opinion of Advocate General 1/17 *CETA* [2019] EU:C:2019:72. 126
Case C-724/17 *Vantaan kaupunki v Skanska Industrial Solutions Oy* [2019] EU:C:2019:204...170
Case C-617/17 *Powszechny Zaklad Ubezpieczen na Życie v Prezes Urzedu Ochrony Konkurencji I Knsumentòw* [2019] EU:C:2019:283. 246
Case C-654/17 P *Bayerische Motoren Werke and Freistaat Sachsen v Commission* [2019] EU:C:2019:634. ....174–75, 187
Case C-308/19 *Consiliul Concurenţei v Whitelalnd Import Export SRL* [2021] EU:C:2021:47..41
Case C-307/18 *Generics UK v Competition and Markets Authority* [2020] EU:C:2020:52..103
Joined Cases C-245/19 and C-246/19 *État luxembourgeois v B and Others* [2020] EU:C:2020:795...202
Case C-857/19 *Slovak Telekom v Protimonopolný ùrad Slovenskej republiky* [2021] EU:C:2021:139...248
Case C-165/19 *Slovak Telecom v Commission* [2021] EU:C:2021:239....................53
Case C-565/19 P *Carvalho and Others v Parliament and Council* [2021] EU:C:2021:252. 72
Case C-896/19 *Repubblika v Il-Prim Ministru* [2021] EU:C:2021:311. 201
Case C-57/19 P *Commission v Tempus Energy and Tempus Energy Technology* [2021] EU:C:2021:663. 266

Case C-647/19 P *Ja Zum Nurburgring v Commission* [2021] EU:C:2021:666. 267
Case C-594/18 P *Austria v Commission* [2020] EU:C:2020:742. ....vii, 69, 80, 93, 190, 217, 254, 259–61, 265, 288
Case C-882/19 *Sumal SL v Mercedes Benz Trucks España SL* [2021] EU:C:2021:800. 170
Cases C-156/21 *Hungary v Parliament and Council* [2022] EU:C:2022:97. 270
Case C-157/21 *Poland v Parliament and Council* [2022] EU:C:2022:98. 270
Case C-117/20 *BPost SA v Autorité belge de la concurrence* [2022] EU:C:2022:202. ....63, 138, 246–47
Case C-151/20 *Bundeswettbewerbsbehörde v Nordzucker* [2022] EU:C:2022:203. 246
Case C-377/20 *Servizio Elettrico Nazionale and Others v Autorità Garante della Concorrenza e del Mercato and Others* [2022] EU:C:2022:379. 185
Opinion of Advocate General Rantos in Case C-252/21 *Meta Platforms Inc v Bundeskartellamt* [2022] EU:C:2022:704. ....vii, 137–38
Case C-470/20 *AS Veejaam and OÜ Espo v AS Elering* [2022] EU:C:2022:981. 189
Case C-815/21 *Amazon v Commission* [2023] ECLI:EU:C:2023:308. 243
Case C-209/21 P *Ryanair v Commission* (pending). 228
Case C-320/21 P *Ryanair v Commission* (pending). 228
Case C-48/22 P *Google Alphabet v Commission* (pending). 166, 168

National Cases

Federal Court of Justice, Decision of 23 June 2020, KVR 69/19. (DE) 48
Federal Court of Justice, Judgment of 18 May 2021, KVR 54/20, DE:BGH:2021:180521BKVR54.20.0. (DE) 141
High Court, Chancery Division, *Streetmap EU Ltd v Google* [2016] EWHC 253 (CH) (12 February 2016). (UK) 245
Competition Appeal Tribunal, *Rachel Kent v Apple Inc and Apple Distribution International Ltd* [2021] 1403/7/7/21. (UK) 245

TABLE OF COMMISSION DECISIONS AND DECISIONS OF NATIONAL COMPETITION AUTHORITIES

Commission Decisions

Commission Decision of 4 July 1984 relating to a proceeding under Article 85 of the EEC Treaty (Case IV/30.810 – Synthetic fibres) [1985] OJ L207/17. 100
Commission Decision of 29 April 1994 relating to a proceeding under Article 85 of the EC Treaty (Case IV/34.456 – Stichting Baksteen) [1994] OJ L131/15. 100
Commission Decision of 21 December 1994 relating to a proceeding pursuant to Article 85 of the EC Treaty and Article 53 of the EEA Agreement (Case IV/34.252 – Philips Osram) [1994] OJ L378/37. 162
Commission Decision of 24 January 1999 relating to a proceeding under Article 81 of the EC Treaty and Article 53 of the EEA Agreement (Case IV.F.1/36.718.CECED) [2000] OJ L187/47 177
Commission Decision of 16 October 2003 relating to a proceeding pursuant to Article 81 of the EC Treaty and Article 53 of the EEA Agreement (Cases COMP D3/35470 – ARA and COMP D3/35473 – ARGEV, ARO) [2004] OJ L24/59. 180
Commission Decision of 13 April 2011 relating to a proceeding under Article 101 of the Treaty on the Functioning of the European Union and Article 53 of the EEA Agreement (Case COMP/39579 – Consumer Detergents) [2011] OJ C193/14. 180
Commission Decision of 22 June 2011 relating to a proceeding under Article 102 of the Treaty on the Functioning of the European Union (Case COMP/39.525 – Telekomunikacja Polska) [2011] OJ C324/3. 247
Commission Decision of 3 October 2014, Non-opposition to a notified concentration (Case M.7217 – Facebook/WhatsApp) [2014] OJ C417/4. 48
Commission Decision (EU) 2015/658 of 8 October 2014 on the aid measure SA.34957 (2013/C) [2015] OJ L109/44. 288
Commission Decision (EU) of 21 August 2015 – Health contribution of tobacco industry businesses (2015/NN) [2015] OJ C277/24. 289

Commission Decision (EU) 2016/1848 of 4 July 2016 on the measure SA.40018 (2015/C) (ex 2015/NN) implemented by Hungary on the 2014 Amendment to the Hungarian food chain inspection fee C/2016/4056 OJ L282/63. 289
Commission Decision (EU) 2017/329 of 4 November 2016 on the measure SA.39235 (2015/C) (ex 2015/NN) implemented by Hungary on the taxation of advertisement turnover [2017] OJ L49/36. 289–90
Commission Decision (EU) 2017/2112 of 6 March 2017 on the measure/aid scheme/State aid SA.38454 (2015/C) [2017] OJ L317/45..........286
Commission Decision of 27 June 2017 relating to a proceeding under Article 102 of the Treaty on the Functioning of the European Union and Article 54 of the EEA Agreement (Case AT.39740 – Google Search (Shopping)) [2018] OJ C9/11....................47, 166, 168, 234, 251
Commission Decision of 27 September 2017 relating to a proceeding under Article 101 of the Treaty on the Functioning of the European Union and Article 53 of the EEA Agreement (Case AT.39824 Trucks) [2020] OJ C216/9. 181
Commission Decision of 24 January 2018 relating to a proceeding under Article 102 of the Treaty on the Functioning of the European Union and Article 54 of the EEA Agreement (Case AT.40220 – Qualcomm (Exclusivity Payments) [2018] OJ C269/25. 47
Commission Decision of 18 July 2018 relating to a proceeding under Article 102 of the Treaty on the Functioning of the European Union and Article 54 of the EEA Agreement (Case AT.40099 – Google Android) [2019] OJ C402/19....................47, 166, 168, 234
Commission Decision of 18 July 2019 relating to a proceeding under Article 102 of the Treaty on the Functioning of the European Union and Article 54 of the EEA Agreement (Case AT.40394 – Aspen) [2019] OJ C375/25....................47
Commission Decision of 6 February 2019 declaring a concentration to be incompatible with the internal market and the functioning of the EEA Agreement (Case M.8677 – Siemens/Alstom) [2019] OJ C/300/14....................147–48, 150
Commission Decision of 20 March 2019 relating to a proceeding under Article 102 of the Treaty on the Functioning of the European Union and Article 54 of the EEA Agreement (Case AT.40411 Google Search AdSense) [2020] OJ C369/6....................47, 166, 168, 234
Commission Decision of 17 December 2020 declaring a concentration to be compatible with the internal market and the EEA agreement (Case M.9660 Google/Fitbit) [2021] OJ C194/7. 165

Commission Decision of 8 July 2021 relating to a proceeding under Article 101 of the Treaty on the Functioning of the European Union and Article 53 of the EEA Agreement (Case AT.40178 Car Emissions) [2021] OJ C458/16. .... 163, 177
Commission Decision of 20 December 2022 relating to a proceeding under Article 102 of the Treaty on the Functioning of the European Union (TFEU) and Article 54 of EEA Agreement (Cases AT.40462 Amazon Marketplace and AT.40703 Amazon Buy Box) [2022] OJ C87/7. .... 47, 234, 242
Case AT.40437 Apple – App Store Practices (music streaming) (decision pending). 234
Case AT.40452 Apple – Mobile Payments – Apple Pay (decision pending). 234
Case AT.40652 Apple – App Store Practices (e-books/audiobooks) (decision pending). 234
Case AT.40670 Google – Adtech and Data-related practices (decision pending). 234, 244
Case AT.40684 Facebook Marketplace (decision pending). 234

Decisions of National Competition Authorities

German Competition Authority, Decision B1-72/12 of 9 July 2015 (Round timber in Baden Württemberg). 30
German Competition Authority, Decision B6-22/16 of 15 February 2019. .... 48, 136
Hungarian Competition Authority, Decision Vj-89/2003/58. 34
Hungarian Competition Authority, Decision Vj-199/2005/246. 34
Hungarian Competition Authority, Decision Vj-50/2009/226. 33
Hungarian Competition Authority, Decision Vj-69/2008/538. 34
Hungarian Competition Authority, Decision Vj-62/2012. 33–34
Hungarian Competition Authority, Decision Vj-67/2014/59. 33
Hungarian Competition Authority, Decision B/961/2018. 36
Italian Competition Authority, Decision No 27432/18. 137
French National Commission on Informatics and Liberty, Deliberation of the restricted committee No SAN-2021-023 of 31 December 2021. 137

TABLE OF LEGISLATION

EU Legislation

EEC Council Regulation No 17 First Regulation implementing Articles 85 and 86 of the Treaty [1962] OJ L13/204. 133

Regulation No 19/65/EEC of 2 March of the Council on application of Article 85 (3) of the Treaty to certain categories of agreements and concerted practices [1965] OJ L36/533. .... 133, 215

Council Regulation (EC) No 4064/89 of 21 December 1989 on the control of concentrations between undertakings [1989] OJ L395/1. 28

Council Regulation (EC) No 659/1999 of 22 March 1999 laying down detailed rules for the application of Article 93 of the EC Treaty [1999] OJ L83/1.... 256, 281

Regulation (EC) No 1049/2001 of the European Parliament and of the Council of 30 May 2001 regarding public access to European Parliament, Council and Commission documents [2001] OJ L145/43. .... 115, 129

Council Regulation (EC) No 1/2003 of 16 December 2002 on the implementation of the rules on competition laid down in Articles 81 and 82 of the Treaty [2003] OJ L01/1. .... 10, 27, 29, 35, 37, 42, 48, 52, 57, 59, 61–62, 64, 115, 118, 124, 127–28, 133–40, 142, 158, 160, 162–63, 165, 167, 169, 196, 198–203, 207–10, 216, 220, 226, 237, 243, 247–48, 250–51, 297, 301–02, 307

Council Regulation (EC) No 139/2004 of 20 January 2004 on the control of concentrations between undertakings (the EC Merger Regulation) [2004] OJ L24/1. .... 9–10, 27–28, 31, 42, 45, 47–48, 60, 64, 98–99, 128, 147, 149, 154–55, 160, 165, 167, 207–09

Commission Regulation (EC) No 773/2004 of 7 April 2004 relating to the conduct of proceedings by the Commission pursuant to Articles 81 and 82 of the EC Treaty [2004] OJ L123/18. .... 158, 167

Commission Regulation (EC) No 772/2004 of 27 April 2004 on the application of Article 81(3) of the Treaty to categories of technology transfer agreements [2004] OJ L123/11 (no longer in force). 128

Consolidated version of the Treaty on the Functioning of the European Union [2008] OJ C326/47. .... 200, 222, 288

Consolidated Version of the Treaty on European Union – Protocol (No 27) on the internal market and competition [2008] OJ C115/309. 146
Commission Regulation (EC) No 622/2008 of 30 June 2008 amending Regulation (EC) No 773/2004, as regards the conduct of settlement procedures in cartel cases [2008] OJ L171/3. 163
Commission Regulation (EU) No 330/2010 of 20 April 2010 on the application of Article 101(3) of the Treaty on the Functioning of the European Union to categories of vertical agreements and concerted practices [2010] OJ L102/1 (no longer in force). 128
Regulation (EU) No 1093/2010 of the European Parliament and of the Council of 24 November 2010 establishing a European Supervisory Authority [2010] OJ L331/12. 198
Regulation (EU) No 1094/2010 of the European Parliament and of the Council of 24 November 2010 establishing a European Supervisory Authority (European Insurance and Occupational Pensions Authority) [2010] OJ L331/48. 198
Regulation (EU) No 1095/2010 of the European Parliament and of the Council of 24 November 2010 establishing a European Supervisory Authority (European Securities and Markets Authority) [2010] OJ L331/84. 198
Council Regulation (EU) No 734/2013 of 22 July 2013 amending Regulation (EC) No 659/1999 laying down detailed rules for the application of Article 93 of the EC Treaty [2013] OJ L204/15. 165
Commission Regulation (EU) No 1407/2013 of 18 December 2013 on the application of Articles 107 and 108 of the Treaty on the Functioning of the European Union to de minimis aid [2013] OJ L352/1. 92
Directive (EU) 2014/104/EU of the European Parliament and of the Council of 26 November 2014 on certain rules governing actions for damages under national law for infringements of the competition law provisions of the Member States and of the European Union [2014] OJ L349/1. ....56, 169, 215–16, 245, 304
Commission Regulation (EU) No 316/2014 of 21 March 2014 on the application of Article 101(3) of the Treaty on the Functioning of the European Union to categories of technology transfer agreements [2014] OJ L93/17. 128
Commission Regulation (EU) No 651/2014 of 17 June 2014 declaring certain categories of aid compatible with the internal market in application of Articles 107 and 108 of the Treaty [2014] OJ L187/1. .... 92, 187
Council Regulation (EU) 2015/1589 of 13 July 2015 laying down detailed rules for the application of Article 108 of the Treaty on the Functioning of the European Union [2015] OJ L248/9. .... 9, 165, 206, 266, 270

Regulation (EU) 2018/1999 of the European Parliament and of the Council of 11 December 2018 on the Governance of the Energy Union and Climate Action [2018] OJ L328/1..257
Directive (EU) 2019/1 of the European Parliament and of the Council of 11 December 2018 to empower the competition authorities of the Member States to be more effective enforcers and to ensure the proper functioning of the internal market [2019] OJ L11/3. .... 30, 126, 134, 144, 195, 199–202, 209, 215–16, 235, 299
Regulation (EU) 2019/452 of the European Parliament and of the Council of 19 March 2019 establishing a framework of the screening of foreign direct investments into the Union (FDI Screening Regulation) [2019] OJ L79l/1. 148–49
Regulation (EU) 2019/943 of the European Parliament and of the Council of 5 June 2019 on the internal market for electricity [2019] OJ L158/54. 224
Directive (EU) 2019/944 of the European Parliament and of the Council of 5 June 2019 on common rules for the internal market for electricity and amending Directive 2012/27/EU [2019] OJ L158/125. 41
Regulation (EU) 2019/1150 of the European Parliament and of the Council of 20 June 2019 on promoting fairness and transparency for business users of online intermediation services [2019] OJ L186/57. ....235, 238–41
Regulation (EU) 2020/852 of the European Parliament and of the Council of 18 June 2020 on the establishment of a framework to facilitate sustainable investment and amending Regulation (EU) 2019/2088 [2020] OJ L198/13..78–79, 258, 265, 296, 306, 308
Regulation (EU) 2021/241 of the European Parliament and of the Council of 12 February 2021 establishing the Recovery and Resilience Facility [2021] OJ L57/17. ....78, 174, 273
Regulation (EU) 2021/1119 of the European Parliament and of the Council of 30 June 2021 establishing the framework for achieving climate neutrality and amending Regulations (EC) No 401/2009 and (EU) 2018/1999 ('European Climate Law') [2021] OJ L243/1............. 257, 265, 272, 305
Commission Regulation (EU) 2021/1237 of 23 July 2021 amending Regulation (EU) No 651/2014 declaring certain categories of aid compatible with the internal market in application of Articles 107 and 108 of the Treaty [2021] OJ L270/39...75
Regulation (EU) 2021/1767 of the European Parliament and of the Council of 6 October 2021 amending Regulation (EC) No 1367/2006 on the application of the provisions of the Aarhus Convention [2021] OJ L356/1. 267

Commission Regulation (EU) 2022/720 of 10 May 2022 on the application of Article 101(3) of the Treaty on the Functioning of the European Union to categories of vertical agreements and concerted practices [2022] OJ L134/4. .... 128, 142
Commission Delegated Regulation (EU) 2022/1214 amending Delegated Regulation (EU) 2021/2139 as regards economic activities in certain energy sectors and Delegated Regulation (EU) 2021/2178 as regards specific public disclosures for those economic activities [2022] OJ L188/1. 265
Regulation (EU) 2022/1925 of the European Parliament and of the Council of 14 September 2022 on contestable and fair markets in the digital sector and amending Directives (EU) 2019/1937 and (EU) 2020/1828 (Digital Markets Act) [2022] OJ L265/1. .... viii, 54, 58–64, 109, 138–39, 170, 173, 210, 233–38, 241, 246–47, 249, 252, 297–98, 305–06
Directive (EU) 2022/2464 of the European Parliament and of the Council of 14 December 2022 amending Regulation (EU) (EU) No 537/2014, Directive 2004/109/EC, Directive 2006/43/EC and Directive 2013/34/EU, as regards corporate sustainability reporting [2022] OJ L322/15. 79
Regulation (EU) 2022/2560 of the European Parliament and of the Council of 14 December 2022 on foreign subsidies distorting the internal market [2022] OJ L330/1. .... 14, 121, 123–25, 132, 149–50, 174, 195–96, 198, 203–06, 208–11, 297–98, 302, 304, 306–07

National Legislation

Cartel Act 2005 (as amended) (Bundesgesetz gegen Kartelle und andere Wettbewerbsbeschränkungen – Kartellgesetz 2005). (AT) 138
Federal Forestry Act of 2 Mai 1975 (as amended) (Bundeswaldgesetz). (DE) 30
Competition Act of 26 June 2013 (as amended) (Gesetz gegen Wettbewerbsbeschränkungen). (DE) 57, 138, 238
Act LVII of 1996 on the Prohibition of Unfair and Restrictive Market Practice (Competition Act). (HU) 34, 41
Act CLXXVI of 2012 (Agricultural Organisations Act). (HU) 33
Act CLXXXV of 2012 (Waste Disposal Act). (HU) 32–33

Government Decree No 322/2014. (HU) 32
Government Decree No 2/2023. (HU) 35
Government Regulation No 69/2016. (HU) 32
Government Decree No 229/2018. (HU) 35
The Competition (Amendment etc.) (EU Exit) Regulations 2019. (UK) 120
Subsidy Control Act 2022. (UK) 120

Introduction

CARLO MARIA COLOMBO, KATHRYN WRIGHT AND MARIOLINA ELIANTONIO[1]

I. Competition Law in Turbulent Times: Governance Transformations and Constitutional Challenges

European Union (EU) competition law – across the fields of antitrust, State aid and merger control – has played a fundamental role in the EU's economic constitution and the functioning of the internal market. The modernisation agenda[2] launched in the late 1990s heralded its latest significant transformation.[3] An enhanced economic effects-based approach, with a substantive emphasis on consumer welfare and market efficiencies, gradually took precedence over EU competition law's original core role in the creation of the single market, which in the meantime reached completion. From an institutional perspective, in response to the challenges posed by EU enlargement, decentralisation required consistent application of rules across the emerging multilevel enforcement system.[4] Despite the scale of

[1] Carlo Maria Colombo is Marie Skłodowska-Curie Fellow at Sciences Po, France, and Assistant Professor of Administrative Law at Maastricht University, the Netherlands, carlo.colombo@maastrichtuniversity.nl. Kathryn Wright is a Senior Lecturer in Law, University of York, kathryn.wright@york.ac.uk. Mariolina Eliantonio is a Professor in European and Comparative Administrative Law and Procedure, Maastricht University, m.eliantonio@maastrichtuniversity.nl. The authors are grateful to Kanerva Jalas and Sabine Kneepkens for their editorial assistance with this collection. Funded by the York-Maastricht Partnership and the European Union. Views and opinions expressed are however those of the author(s) only and do not necessarily reflect those of the European Union or the European Commission. Neither the European Union nor the European Commission can be held responsible for them.

[2] In the field of antitrust, see the Commission, 'White Paper on modernisation of the rules implementing Articles 85 and 86 of the EC Treaty', COM (1999) 27 final, Executive summary points 4, 8. In the field of State aid, the Commission adopted the State aid Modernization strategy in 2012. See Commission, 'Communication on State Aid Modernisation', COM (2012) 209 final.

[3] See M Monti, 'European Competition for the 21st Century' (2000) 24 *Fordham International Law Journal* 1602; DJ Gerber, 'Two Forms of Modernization in European Competition Law' (2008) 31 *Fordham International Law Journal* 1235; I Maher, 'Competition Law Modernization: an Evolutionary Tale?' in P Craig and G de Burca (eds), *The Evolution of EU Law* 2nd edn (Oxford, Oxford University Press, 2011).

[4] Claus-Dieter Ehlermann, a former Director General of DG IV, described the White Paper on modernisation in the field of antitrust as a 'legal and cultural revolution in proposing the fundamental reorganization of existing responsibilities between the Commission, national authorities and national courts': C-D Ehlermann, 'The Modernization of EC Antitrust Policy: A Legal and Cultural

reforms, the system has come out of this intense period remarkably well, although there has been no shortage of limitations and criticism.[5]

Current evolutions seem to mark yet another twist in EU competition law. At least since the 2008 banking meltdown and the following Eurocrisis, the field has found itself in the middle of turbulent times. Coming predominantly from outside, several simultaneous 'crises' – ranging from economic turmoil to climate emergency, digital disruptions and geopolitical and democratic threats – are introducing a new reality and causing challenges to the functioning of the EU's society, institutions and markets. In light of its fundamental role in the EU economic constitution, competition law has been called upon to play a major part in responding to this state of 'turbulence' or 'polycrisis'.[6] The current debate has been primarily characterised by a substantive focus on competition rules' and the underlying doctrines' fit with these crises. The involvement of issues transcending economic markets challenges economic logic and reignites vexed problems about the economic and non-economic objectives of competition law.[7] At the same time,

Revolution' (2000) 37 *Common Market Law Review* 537, 537. See also J Venit, 'Brave New World: The Modernization and Centralization of Enforcement under Articles 81 and 82 of the EC Treaty' (2003) 40 *Common Market Law Review* 545; W Wils, 'Ten Years of Regulation 1/2003 – A Retrospective' (2013) 4 *Journal of European Competition Law and Practice* 293; H Kassim and K Wright, 'Revisiting Modernisation: the European Commission, Policy Change and the Reform of EC Competition Policy' (2007) ESRC Centre for Competition Policy working paper 07-19; F Cengiz, 'Multi-Level Governance in Competition Policy: The European Competition Network' (2010) 35 *European Law Review* 661. For an analysis of the institutional implications of the State aid modernisation, see C Micheau, 'Evolution of State Aid Rules: Conceptions, Challenges, and Outcomes' in H Hofmann and C Micheau (eds), *State Aid Law of the European Union* (Oxford, Oxford University Press, 2016); C Quigley, 'The European Commission's Programme for State Aid Modernization' (2013) 1 *Maastricht Journal of European and Comparative Law* 35.

[5] Among the many, see more recently on the challenges to ensuring uniform administration of EU competition law in a decentralised enforcement regime, see O Brook, 'Struggling with Article 101(3) TFEU: Diverging Approaches of the Commission, EU Courts, And Five Competition Authorities' (2019) 56 *Common Market Law Review* 121. On the challenges of decentralised implementation of State aid law, see CM Colombo, 'State Aid Control in the Modernisation Era: Moving Towards a Differentiated Administrative Integration' (2019) 25 *European Law Journal* 292.

[6] Both terms are used in public administration and policy studies to describe the current complex situation the EU is confronted with. While mainstreamed lately by the historian Adam Tooze (see A Tooze, 'Chartbook #165: Polycrisis – Thinking on the Tightrope' *Chartbook*, 29 October 2022: adamtooze.substack.com/p/chartbook-165-polycrisis-thinking), in EU studies the term 'polycrisis' specifically encompasses repeated crises that generate a prolonged period of unease in the EU (see in this sense, among others, J Zeitlin, F Nicoli and B Laffan, 'Introduction: The European Union Beyond the Polycrisis? Integration and Politicization in an Age of Shifting Cleavages' (2019) 26 *Journal of European Public Policy* 963). The concept of 'turbulence', on the other hand, indicates the result of this state of 'polycrisis', which, due to the multilevel and widely distributed socio-economic system and the current intensification of political conflicts, leads to a highly unpredictable and variable period (see C Ansell, E Sørensen and J Torfing, 'Public Administration and Politics Meet Turbulence: The Search for Robust Governance Responses' (2023) 101 *Public Administration* 3). While recognising these nuances, for present purposes the two terms will be used interchangeably to describe the current state in which competition law operates in the EU.

[7] O Odudu, 'The Wider Concerns of Competition Law' (2010) 30 *Oxford Journal of Legal Studies* 599; C Townley, *Article 81 EC and Public Policy* (Oxford, Hart Publishing, 2009). On the more economic approach: J Drexl, W Kerber and R Podzsun (eds), *Competition Policy and the More Economic Approach: Foundations and Limitations* (Cheltenham, Edward Elgar Publishing, 2012); J Blockx, 'The Limits of the

a predominantly sectoral perspective shapes the scholarly analyses, which have so far focused on separate areas of competition law[8] and individual 'crises'.[9]

Yet, besides the substantive questions about the scope and objectives of competition rules, the transformations triggered in competition law by this repeated state of crisis also challenge the capability of the competition law system as an operative whole. Indeed, the turbulent conditions in which we live seem to stem from multiple interrelating developments that, in part because of the close social, economic and political interactions in current society, can easily cross over sectoral and political boundaries and generate new crises and conflicts that threaten existing rules. As such, these conditions test not only the substantive core of competition rules, but how these substantive rules feed into the institutional architecture needed to apply them, as well as their combined effect in structuring the solutions to the emerging crises also in their interaction with other areas of EU law. In its latest policy paper 'A Competition Policy Fit For New Challenges',[10] the Commission makes clear that one of its goals is to pursue a review of competition policy instruments with unprecedented scope and ambition, ensuring that all competition instruments remain fit for purpose and equipping itself with new tools aimed at addressing emerging challenges in the Single Market.

These developments prompt a set of related questions. The first one entails an investigation of how the governance of competition law, meant as an operative whole, is being transformed to tackle and adapt to this state of repeated crises. By governance, we mean the institutional eco-system of competition law, including the structures, processes and instruments used to coordinate actors' efforts to enforce competition law in the EU. As these repeated crises strain the roles and relationships among stakeholders, and the institutional processes through which EU competition law is implemented are inevitably affected, there is an urgent need to reconsider how the crisis-induced transformation of the EU continues to

"More Economic Approach" to Antitrust' (2019) 42 *World Competition* 475; G Monti, 'EU Competition Law from Rome to Lisbon: Social Market Economy' in C Heide-Jorgensen et al (eds), *Aims and Values in Competition Law* (Copenhagen, DJØF Publishing, 2013); A Witt, 'The Enforcement of Article 101 TFEU: What Has Happened to the Effects Analysis?' (2019) 55 *Common Market Law Review* 417.

[8] See for example, B Wardhaugh, *Competition Law in Crisis: The Antitrust Response to Economic Shocks* (Cambridge, Cambridge University Press, 2022).

[9] For a focus on single crises see for example on digitalisation: A Daly, *Private Power, Online Information Flows and EU Law* (Oxford, Hart Publishing, 2019); G Surblytė-Namavičienė, *Competition and Regulation in the Data Economy* (Cheltenham, Edward Elgar Publishing, 2020); B Lundqvist and MS Gal (eds), *Competition Law for the Digital Economy* (Cheltenham, Edward Elgar Publishing, 2019); on environmental protection: A Gerbrandy, *The Uneasy Relationship Between Sustainability and Competition Law* (Oxford, Hart Publishing, 2021); S Kingston, *Greening EU Competition Law and Policy* (Cambridge, Cambridge University Press, 2011); J Nowag, *Environmental Integration in Competition and Free-Movement Laws* (Oxford, Oxford University Press, 2017); and on economic and financial crises: W-G Ringe and P Huber (eds), *Legal Challenges in the Global Financial Crisis: Bail-outs, the Euro and Regulation* (Oxford, Hart Publishing 2015); J Broulík and K Cseres, *Competition Law and Economic Inequality* (Oxford, Hart Publishing, 2020).

[10] Commission, 'A Competition Policy Fit for New Challenges' (Communication) COM (2021) 713 final.

challenge the EU and its internal market. Previous governance discussions under the modernisation agenda, with their emphasis on decentralisation and networked governance, should be updated to reflect how this turbulent era is reshaping the area of competition law, highlighting continuities, changes and tensions.

The second question extends this investigation to exploring the relationship between these crises-induced governance transformations and the constitutional rationale and limits of EU competition law in the Treaties' framework. Besides discussing how competition law and its core rationale is evolving, it is vital to examine whether the resulting governance system fits the EU constitutional framework, which defines its substantive rationale and structural tenets in light of the Treaties.

These questions drive the various contributions to this book. Addressing these questions will probe competition law's capacity and legitimacy to contribute to the EU responses to govern these turbulent times.

This book, while revisiting the post-modernisation shifts against the backdrop of the recent multiple crises that are affecting the EU, examines the extent to which EU institutions can design and implement solutions fit for the governance challenges that the state of polycrisis presents to the EU and its internal market, while respecting the constitutional role and limits of the area, as resulting from the Treaties. To this end, it adopts an institutional perspective that examines changes in the main areas of competition law (merger control, antitrust and State aid law) meant as an operative whole – that is, the relationship among its components and with others within the framework of the Treaties, the factors affecting its functioning and the stresses and strains on and within it.[11] While far from providing an all-encompassing account of the evolving framework of EU competition law, the book's focus on some of the main governance transformations make a strong contribution to understanding how European and national institutions are approaching EU competition law enforcement in the context of repeated crises. Combining classical-doctrinal understanding of competition law with EU institutional law and enriching it with adjacent literatures (such as EU governance and EU compliance), this book sheds new light on the evolution of competition law and its institutional transformations in response to the present turbulent times.

This introductory chapter sets out and frames the analysis. It begins by outlining the general characteristics of the crises that are challenging the EU and its internal market, which require competition law to provide a response (Section II). This is a necessary starting point for understanding the extent to which these crises (should) prompt competition law to (re)think its normative and institutional tenets, and ascertain how far the proposed responses match the challenges raised. This chapter then sets out the constitutional limits and governance dynamics of competition law and how we would expect the new challenges to impact them (Section III). As competition law is called upon to answer crises whose exceptional

[11] DJ Gerber, 'The Transformation of European Community Competition Law?' (1994) 35 *Harvard International Law Journal* 98.

scope transcends economic markets, examining the constitutional building blocks and the potential of competition law is necessary. At the same time, being one of the many tools available to the EU institutions, this exploration is necessary to understand how competition law fits with other EU law policy areas. Finally, an explanation of the outline of the book and an overview of the different contributions closes this first chapter (Section IV).

II. Turbulence, Crises, and Competition Law

Many of the EU's constitutional moments have arisen out of necessity, in response to internal or external pressures. These critical moments or crises have in common that they often challenge the status quo, leading to potentially deep-seated impacts on the EU and its functioning.[12] Crises are hardly new to EU competition law either. Over time, crises – such as the energy crisis of the 1970s – have forcefully instigated changes in the way competition law has been enforced in the EU.[13] Substantially, Article 107(3)(b) TFEU offers the possibility of using State aid as an emergency power to 'remedy a serious disturbance in the economy of a Member State', while crises can be used as a public policy justification for suspending the application of competition rules.

Although crises have been a recurring feature in the EU's history and in the field of competition law as well, there is today a shared sense among policymakers[14] and scholars[15] that the period of crisis the EU is presently confronted with is somewhat different. Instead of single isolated critical moments, the EU is today faced with several repeated crises that affect multiple areas almost simultaneously. At the same time, in part because of our deeply interconnected and multilevel society, these crises interact in variable and inconsistent ways, in turn generating the risk of

[12] See, among others JHH Weiler, 'In the Face of Crisis: Input Legitimacy, Output Legitimacy and the Political Messianism of European Integration' (2012) 37 *Journal of European Integration* 825; L Papadopoulou, I Pernice and JHH Weiler (eds), *Legitimacy Issues of the European Union in the Face of Crisis – Dimitris Tsatsos in memoriam* (Baden-Baden, Nomos Publishing, 2017).

[13] See among others Gerber (n 11 above) 97; JJ Piernas López, *The Concept of State Aid Under EU Law: From Internal Market to Competition and Beyond* (Oxford, Oxford University Press, 2015).

[14] Former Commission President Juncker coined the term 'polycrisis' to talk about the critical moment experienced by the EU between the financial crisis and the sovereign debt crisis. See J Juncker, 'Speech by President Jean-Claude Juncker at the Annual General Meeting of the Hellenic Federation of Enterprises (SEV)' (Athens, 21 June 2016): https://ec.europa.eu/commission/presscorner/detail/en/SPEECH_16_2293. More recently, see also the 2021 State of the Union by Commission President von der Leyen. See U von der Leyen '2021 State of the Union Address by President von der Leyen' (Brussels, 15 September 2021): https://ec.europa.eu/commission/presscorner/detail/ov/SPEECH_21_4701.

[15] See, among the many, Zeitlin, Nicoli and Laffan (n 6 above); E Chiti, 'Managing the Ecological Transition of the EU: The European Green Deal as a Regulatory Process' (2022) 59 *Common Market Law Review* 19, 21–25; D Dinan, N Nugent and W Paterson, 'A Multi-Dimensional Crisis' in D Dinan, N Nugent and W Paterson (eds), *The European Union in Crisis* (Oxford, Hart Publishing, 2017) 1–15; M Rhinard, 'The Crisisification of Policy-Making in the European Union' (2019) 57 *Journal of Common Market Studies* 616.

political conflict and new crises. This has created an endemic condition of disruption that is challenging modern EU governance.[16] Drawing on policy studies, here we purposely use the terms 'turbulence' and 'polycrisis' to capture this period. Unlike other concepts used in the literature to describe it,[17] these terms allow us to encapsulate the period comprehensively (ie, as the result of the combined effect of various crises), as well as to convey the urgency and difficulty for the EU of devising solutions.

This period of turbulence or polycrisis is generally traced back to the 2008 global financial meltdown and the subsequent Eurocrisis, and spans across Brexit to the more recent COVID-19 and geo-political disturbances. Yet, in line with the book's aim to provide a comprehensive understanding of how this polycrisis is challenging EU competition law, we provide below four main types of crises, rather than discussing individual crises in isolation. These typologies, which will then be further addressed across the various chapters, have been selected based on their characteristics, effects and policy salience within the EU.

The first crisis can be broadly defined as democratic and encompasses the populist thrusts that are challenging the democratic values and economic functioning of the EU both from within – from Brexit to the more recent crisis of the rule of law in some Central and Eastern European countries – and from outside – including geopolitical pushes related to the emergence of opposing blocs of like-minded countries that threaten the EU's democratic and market structures. The second crisis is related to the effects of the climate emergency. As the consequences of climate change are increasingly frequent, severe and long-lasting, this emergency has generated the urgency to offset emissions from our economic activities. At the same time, it also prompts a rethinking of our social and economic model as ecologically constrained, in line with the broader ambitions of the European Green Deal.[18] The third crisis is related to the role assumed by digital disruptions in our society. Due to their market power, digital technologies have the potential to revolutionise the EU economy and accelerate the transformation of our economy. However, because of their scale and profound implications in almost all aspects of life, they also pose a threat to the EU's economic and democratic model. The fourth and final typology concerns economic crises, which include sudden shocks (like those created by the COVID-19 pandemic, which is the main focus in many chapters, but also 2008 banking crisis and the latest energy crisis) that spread rapidly across multiple sectors and policy areas and cause major disruptions in markets.

As discussed earlier, while seen in isolation these crises may feature specific characteristics and effects, their combined interaction is generating a period of

[16] Ansell, Sørensen and Torfing (n 6 above).

[17] Specifically, in the field of competition law, authors generally refer to societal challenges or public policy as terms more in line with the legal framework of the field. See, among others, A Gerbrandy, 'Rethinking Competition Law within the European Economic Constitution' (2019) 57 *Journal of Common Market Studies* 127.

[18] See Chiti (n 15 above).

turbulence that is affecting the overall capacity of the EU and its competition rules to govern them. This is clearly emerging in the EU Commission's latest policy program 'A Competition Policy Fit for New Challenges'.[19] Therein, the Commission recognises that, due to the interdependence of our systems, multiple crises are emerging, making its task of developing short-term recovery and long-term solutions daunting. At the same time, such complex interactions and combined effects seem to have influenced the framing and perception of these events by EU institutions. In line with general trends of 'crisisification' in the EU,[20] the focus on crises seems to have shaped a reflection over whether its toolbox, boundaries and role within the EU constitution are fit for purpose. Thus, unlike modernisation, in which changes were mainly incremental and in response to the internal evolution of the EU integration process,[21] this agenda seems to unveil a different way of acting by the Commission in which external events generate post-modernisation shifts that push competition law to evolve with crisis-oriented reactions.

Drawing from policy studies is also relevant to provide some key dimensions to discuss how the governance of EU competition law should be moving throughout such turbulent times. Specifically, a robust governance paradigm is predicated to navigate a period of turbulence.[22] By this, scholarship refers to the capacity of a governance system to carry on in the face of shifting and challenging conditions by upholding basic systemic values and developing capacities for continuous transformations.[23] Robustness represents therefore an instance of dynamic conservatism[24] through which a system responds to heightened periods of crises by going in new and innovative directions while at the same time adapting the existing forms of governance to preserve basic ambitions, functions and values. To allow this flexible adaptation, these robust responses should develop along three key dimensions.[25] First, because in turbulent times crises constantly change and create new problems, the structural dimension of a robust response points to the elements of the governance model needed to match the need for

[19] Commission, 'A Competition Policy Fit for New Challenges' (n 10 above).

[20] Rhinard (n 15 above).

[21] See I Maher, 'Competition Law Modernization: an Evolutionary Tale?' in P Craig and G de Burca (eds), *The Evolution of EU Law* 2nd edn (Oxford, Oxford University Press, 2011).

[22] See, among others, Ansell, Sørensen and Torfing (n 6 above); J Trondal, G Haslerud and N Kühn, 'The Robustness of National Agency Governance in Integrated Administrative Systems' (2021) 81 *Public Administration Review* 121. Unlike 'resilience' (see J Nowag, 'Resilience and Competition Law, in Times of Emergencies and Crises: Two Research Agendas' (2020) 8 *Journal of Antitrust Enforcement* 296), which refers to the ability of a system to bounce back to its previous state of equilibrium in the wake of disruption triggered by external events, the former adds the capacity of a system to also dynamically adapt to future goals. As such, it allows to best capture the present strategy of the Commission which combines both elements of 'bouncing back' and 'future proofing' for future challenges.

[23] Ansell, Sørensen and Torfing (n 6 above) 16.

[24] C Ansell, A Boin and M Farjoun, 'Dynamic Conservatism: How Institutions Change to Remain the Same' in MS Kraatz (ed), *Institutions and Ideals: Philip Selznick's Legacy for Organizational Studies* (Bingley, Emerald Publishing, 2015).

[25] Ansell, Sørensen and Torfing (n 6 above) 10–11.

continuous transformation and adaptation. Second, the temporal dimension highlights how short- and long-term responses must be combined to govern a state of turbulence. While the former needs reactive adaptability to the immediate shocks, the latter enables design for the future evolutions. Third, since turbulence is prone to generate the risk of political reaction and confrontation, its responses require both leadership capable of formulating transformative solutions, but also the involvement of all relevant and affected interests, as well as expert knowledge, to devise them. Placed within the constitutional limits and governance dynamics of EU competition law as they emerge from the EU Treaties and modernisation as the last major reform in the field, these key dimensions will serve to discuss the transformations developed by the Commission to enable competition law to navigate through this period of turbulence.

III. Competition Law, Constitutional Limits, and Governance Dynamics

A discussion of the constitutional limits and governance dynamics of EU competition law requires consideration of the basis of competition law as set out in the Treaties; the changes resulting from modernisation, which established the current governance framework; and how this governance framework is being challenged by the current state of polycrisis.

In terms of the substantive scope and boundaries of competition law, it is axiomatic that competition has always been connected to integration and the internal market, supporting the four freedoms. In the Treaties, the EU's objectives in Article 3(3) TEU make clear that '[T]he Union shall establish an internal market. It shall work for … a highly competitive social market economy',[26] and Articles 101, 102 and 107 TFEU prohibit certain behaviour as 'incompatible with the internal market'. As internal market rules do not exist in isolation, the competition provisions also come into contact with other relevant cross-cutting provisions, such as Article 11 TFEU requiring environmental protection and sustainable development requirements to be integrated into the definition and implementation of the Union's policies and activities.[27]

The EU's exclusive competence for establishing competition rules necessary for the functioning of the internal market, set out in Article 3(1)(b) TFEU, is relevant for the scope of responses to societal disruptions. In particular, regarding antitrust, as set out in the primary legal base of Article 103 TFEU the EU Commission must define, among other competences, the scope of Article 101 and

[26] See Monti (n 7) for a discussion.

[27] J Nowag, 'The Environmental Integration Obligation of Article 11 TFEU' in *Environmental Integration in Competition and Free Movement Laws* (n 9).

102 TFEU in branches of the economy, and determine the relationship between national laws and EU competition provisions.[28] Merger control was initially developed through the Court's case law on Article 102,[29] and the EU Merger Regulation (EUMR)[30] was partly adopted on the basis of the flexibility clause (Article 352 TFEU) on measures necessary to attain the EU's objectives where the Treaties have not provided necessary powers. In the area of State aid, pursuant to Article 108 TFEU, the Commission retains exclusive competence to decide whether national aid measures are compatible with the internal market, based on Article 107(2) and (3) TFEU. These two provisions give more or less discretion depending on the justification used to provide State aid provisions. On their side, Member States, as the main counterpart of the Commission, are requested to block provisions that fulfil the conditions under Article 107(1) TFEU until completion of a centralised assessment of their compatibility carried out by the Commission through a bilateral administrative procedure.[31]

Through their interpretation, the competition provisions have been able to accommodate changing societal contexts, such as through public policy justifications in Article 101(3), and public policy or public interest considerations in merger control and State aid. The adaptation to different contexts has also developed through soft law instruments, such as notices and guidelines, which are ubiquitous in competition law.[32] Soft law instruments have been used to signal how the Commission would use its discretion, and to give guidance to national authorities.

Anticipating the 2004 enlargement, modernisation, as the last major reform of governance across all areas of competition law, aimed to reorganise the Commission's stretched resources,[33] while also presenting an opportunity to implement a more effects-based economic approach to competition analysis.[34]

[28] Other tasks in Art 103 TFEU are to ensure compliance with Arts 101 and 102 TFEU and provide for fines; to lay down rules for the application of Art 101(3) TFEU ensuring effective supervision and to simplify administration, and to define the functions the Commission and the CJEU. For a discussion of competences see G Monti, 'Legislative and Executive Competences in Competition Law' in L Azoulai (ed), *The Question of Competence in the European Union* (Oxford, Oxford University Press, 2014).

[29] Case 6-72 *Europemballage Corporation and Continental Can Company v Commission* [1973] EU:C:1973:22.

[30] Council Regulation (EC) No 139/2004 on the control of concentrations between undertakings (Merger Regulation) [2004] OJ L24/1.

[31] The centralised control procedure on State aid is regulated by Council Regulation (EU) No 2015/1589 laying down detailed rules for application of Article 108 TFEU [2015] OJ L248/9.

[32] L Senden, *Soft Law in European Community Law* (Oxford, Hart Publishing, 2004) 112; F Snyder, 'The Effectiveness of European Community Law: Institutions, Processes, Tools and Techniques' (1993) 56 *Modern Law Review* 19, 32; O Ştefan, *Soft Law in Court: Competition Law, State Aid and the Court of Justice of the European Union* (Leiden, Kluwer Law International, 2013); O Ştefan, 'Hybridity Before the Court: A Hard Look at Soft Law in the EU Competition and State Aid Case Law' (2012) 37 *European Law Review* 49.

[33] n 1 and n 2 above.

[34] n 6 above. An example was the 'significant impediment to effective competition' test in merger control, which changed the emphasis from the earlier form-based focus on creation or strengthening of a dominant position: Art 2(2) and (3) Merger Regulation (n 30 above).

Enforcement in both antitrust and State aid underwent an extensive decentralisation process, although with different nuances across those fields. Meanwhile, in merger control, jurisdiction between the EU and Member State level was determined by turnover thresholds, aimed at curtailing national champions by vesting control of the most significant mergers with a Community dimension in the Commission,[35] but with a referral mechanism between national and EU levels.[36]

Regarding decentralisation, in the field of State aid,[37] while leaving the Commission's exclusive power of control on domestic provisions untouched, modernisation instigated a remarkable enhancement of national implementation tasks.[38] Expanding the scope of the general block exemption regulation (GBER), which allowed Member States to grant State aid subject only to a random ex post check by the Commission, domestic institutions has been de facto empowered to implement over 90 per cent of new aid measures directly. Centralised enforcement through the Commission's own procedure, instead, has been limited to those cases most liable to distort competition. By so doing, the reform has tried to achieve three aims, to address the Commission's chronic lack of resources, to strengthen the quality of its scrutiny on the most distortive measures and promoting faster decisions on growth-oriented measures.

In antitrust, decentralisation allowed competition authorities and courts in the Member States authority to apply Article 101(3) through ex post enforcement, meaning they could balance pro- and anti-competitive effects of practices, which previously had been the preserve of the Commission's ex ante notification system. This decentralisation raised the question of ensuring consistent enforcement of EU antitrust rules. Networked governance provided a solution through the European Competition Network comprising the Commission and NCAs, formed with a combination of hard and soft law, with juridified rules for consistent application, case allocation, exchange of information and mutual assistance.[39] The EU general principles of loyal cooperation and effectiveness are an underlying basis for the network.[40]

[35] Art 1 Merger Regulation (n 30 above).

[36] Art 22 Merger Regulation (n 30 above).

[37] Commission, 'Communication on State Aid Modernisation' COM (2012) 209 final. For an analysis, see C Micheau, 'Evolution of State Aid Rules: Conceptions, Challenges, and Outcomes', in Hofmann and Micheau (eds), *State Aid Law of the European Union* (n 4 above); Quigley (n 4 above).

[38] Colombo (n 5 above).

[39] Art 11 Council Regulation (EC) No 1/2003 on the implementation of the rules on competition laid down in Arts 81 and 82 [101 and 102] of the Treaty (Modernisation Regulation) [2003] OJ L1/1; Commission Notice on Cooperation Within the Network of Competition Authorities (Network Notice) [2004] OJ C101/43; I Maher, 'Competition Law: Convergence through Law and Networks' in P Craig and G de Burca (eds), *The Evolution of EU Law* 3rd edn (Oxford, Oxford University Press, 2021).

[40] Art 35 of the Modernisation Regulation, which requires Member States to designate competition authorities in such a way that the provisions of the Regulation are effectively complied with. Under Art 11(6) of the Regulation, ultimately the Commission is able to relieve an NCA of its competence in order to uphold effective enforcement.

Within the multilevel and complex system emerging in all areas of EU competition law as a result of modernisation, uniform application of rules has traditionally been seen as self-evidently desirable,[41] linked to effective application. To ensure this, coordination, cooperation and communication between EU and national institutions play a crucial role.[42] This 'super-glue' can be achieved through a mix of constitutional provisions and governance mechanisms. These links encourage a uniformity of approach. At the same time, a further benefit of such networks is policy learning,[43] which would militate in favour of managed divergence. Calls to uncouple the link between uniformity and effectiveness and, conversely, allow greater divergence and innovation to enhance effectiveness would be in line with differentiation debates in other areas of EU law and policy.[44]

In terms of governance, the drive for uniformity to date has been underpinned by the interaction and coordination of national institutions.[45] This has been achieved through the linked governance tenets of technocratic expertise and independence. This coordination, particularly through the European Competition Network, implies recognition of national counterparts' standards. Unlike antitrust, coordination in the areas of State aid and merger control, however, has followed a different path. Because of the high political stakes and constitutional limits imposed by the principle of national procedural autonomy, the rules are implemented by a large (in State aid) set of national bodies that follow their own organisational approaches to ensuring compliance. In response to the potential structural problems arising from such a system, the Commission has exerted its influence through a range of mechanisms and strategies (soft law, networking, partnerships, conditionalities), which have in turn helped to create an epistemic community that is critical to ensuring shared enforcement of standards within the EU.[46]

Clearly, in the current turbulent times, these aspects that define the substantive scope, mechanisms and enforcement system of EU competition law are being tested. As indicated, several crises (eg, digital disruptions or geopolitical tensions) that the EU has been facing lately disrupt the dynamics of the internal market, from within and outside. Others (such as the climate emergency) necessarily force

[41] C Townley and A Türk, 'The Constitutional Limits of EU Competition Law – United in Diversity' *The Antitrust Bulletin*, 3 June 2019: https://doi.org/10.1177/0003603X19844626.

[42] C Harlow and R Rawlings, *Process and Procedure in EU Administrative Law* (Oxford, Hart Publishing, 2014).

[43] F Vantaggiato, 'The Drivers of Regulatory Networking: Policy Learning Between Homophily and Convergence' (2019) 39 *Journal of Public Policy* 443; CF Sabel and J Zeitlin, 'Experimentalism in the EU: Common Ground and Persistent Differences' (2012) 6 *Regulation & Governance* 410.

[44] See for example, B Leruth, S Gänzle and J Trondal, *The Routledge Handbook of Differentiation in the European Union* (Abingdon, Routledge, 2022); D Fromage (ed), *(Re-)Defining Membership: Differentiation in and outside the European Union* (Oxford, Oxford University Press, 2023 forthcoming).

[45] I Maher and O Ştefan, 'Competition Law in Europe: The Challenge of a Network Constitution' in D Oliver, T Prosser and R Rawlings (eds), *The Regulatory State: Constitutional Implications* (Oxford, Oxford University Press, 2010).

[46] Colombo (n 5 above).

one to rethink whether and how the current functioning of markets is in line with future objectives. As such, questions re-emerge not only about the economic and non-economic objectives of competition law and its relationship to other areas of law, but also about the mechanisms by which their solutions can be devised in practice. More broadly, competition law is being questioned within the Commission's toolbox and constitutional framework, opening up wide-ranging issues of how instruments from other areas or following other logics can combine the primarily reactive nature of EU competition law enforcement to solve broader implications of certain disruptions. At the same time, as economic crises provoke sudden shocks in the internal market, competition law is usually identified as one of the European Commission's main response measures. In line with previous experiences, including the well-documented banking crises of 2008, the Commission is inevitably forced to identify which mechanisms should allow for quick interventions beyond the existing control procedures. Equally central in this context is how to prevent politics from generating long-term distortive effects in the internal market. Finally, the politicised nature of certain crises, which inevitably creates rifts between institutions and within European society, has put the role of the technocratic model and the bilateral system of competition law enforcement to the test. The use of nationally protected competences (such as industrial policy or Member States' right to determine their energy fuel mix) can lead member states to design solutions that are contrary to the spirit of competition rules, urging the Commission to device effective reactions. Similarly, the role of civil society, while long being left as marginal in competition law structure, can no longer be ignored in the context of crises with severe and long-standing impacts on society. These are some of the most pressing issues that the Commission is facing in the present turbulent times, and to which this book aims to contribute.

IV. Introducing the Chapters of the Book

Following this Introduction by the editors, the book comprises 13 chapters organised into three parts. These three parts broadly cover the core foci to examine the features and evolution of governance systems from a legal perspective:[47] powers and competences, actors and relationships and instruments and processes. Without aiming to be all-encompassing, each contribution serves as a case study to discuss how one or more of the mentioned types of crises are transforming EU competition law across its areas. In doing so, the ultimate ambition is to develop a comprehensive understanding of the constitutional and governance implications

[47] See for example, the prominent work of H Hofmann, GC Rowe and A Türk, *Specialized Administrative Law of the European Union: A Sectoral Review* 1st edn (Oxford, Oxford University Press, 2018) 3.

of the current evolutions of EU competition law, meant as an operative whole, in response to the turbulent times affecting EU society and economy.

In the first part on Powers and Aims, four chapters will critically discuss how the transformations of competition law to specific types of crises – populist, digital, environmental and economic – test and fit within the constitutional competences and limits enshrined in the EU Treaties. The opening piece by Katalin Cseres discusses how competition law, in light of its role within the EU Constitution in ensuring a free society and open markets, could serve to protect democracy in the EU. Using the exemplary case of Hungary, the author analyses how the formal and informal institutions to enforce competition law in the EU can be undermined by national 'illiberal' regimes. This allows her to develop a critical reflection on how the principles and instruments of EU law can and should respond to these attacks on EU democratic values perpetrated by rising populism. Pieter Van Cleynenbreugel then considers EU competition law's responses to the disruptive effects of digitalisation on our society. Focusing on a number of recent antitrust cases brought against online platforms, he shows how the digital economy raises a set of structural, behavioural and foundational challenges that may put pressure on the application of Articles 101 and 102 TFEU to digital actors. While envisaged solutions involve combining an ex ante regulatory framework with the traditional ex post enforcement of competition rules, these changes look prone to raise additional legal challenges. Aljcia Sikora-Kalėda's contribution continues this substantive exploration by focusing on the (in)ability of EU competition and State aid law to promote environmental sustainability. Although competition and environment policies should mutually interact and reinforce each other in the EU's constitutional framework, the ambition of environmental policy to recalibrate the EU's economic model, as emerging from the EU Green Deal, is not entirely supported by competition law as currently enforced. The author therefore discusses how and to what extent some key tools of the green transition, such as the EU taxonomy and the 'do no significant harm' principle, can be appropriate tools of environmental recalibration in competition and State aid law. In the final chapter of this part, Francisco Costa-Cabral approaches EU competition law's crisis management capacity. Focusing on the Temporary Frameworks for State aid and for assessing antitrust issues related to business cooperation developed during the COVID-19 pandemic, the author contends that, unlike mainstream interpretations, the Commission has not resorted to exceptional rules to deal with systemic crisis. Rather, the flexibility of EU competition rules allows it to frame crisis responses in a way that is normatively coherent with its goals, principles and techniques.

The second part on Actors and Dynamics moves the attention to the institutional dynamics and tensions turbulent times are generating in EU competition law. Kathryn Wright opens the enquiry by reflecting on how EU competition rules can be unilaterally extended to non-EU countries to counter tensions created by unfair trading conditions that the fragmentation of the present global trade system is exacerbating. Specifically, focusing on instances of technocratic cooperation between the EU Commission and third country regulators, she reflects on how the former exports key EU constitutional principles in EU competition law – such as equivalence, transparency and requirements for independent regulators – beyond the EU's boundaries to ensure the playing field with the internal market. Giorgio Monti then shifts the focus to the role of Member States in enforcing EU competition law rules in the face of the present turbulence. Discussing how the complex enforcement system resulting from asymmetric allocation of executive competences has opened up a conversation between the EU and Member States over the scope and direction of EU competition law, the author reveals some crucial multilevel dynamics and tensions that may affect the strategic direction of EU competition law in this complex time. In the following contribution, Fernando Pastor-Merchante continues the reflection discussing the role of companies in the crisis-induced transformations of EU competition law. By breaking down the participatory and accountability functions that companies can play in this context and gauging their effects, the author discusses how these functions are not only necessary to infuse legitimacy into the Commission's activities but are in fact increasingly being promoted by the Commission to deal with the current period of turbulence. Phedon Nicolaides closes this part with a reflection on how the EU courts are reviewing the Commission's decisions in the context of the digital and green transitions. Critically discussing some recent judgments in the fields of antitrust and State aid law, the author shows how the EU courts are supporting the Commission's approach to solving these 'big questions' of our time, yet maintaining the high standard of proof and duty to state reasons that the Commission must adhere to in making its decisions.

As a final set of contributions, the third part on Instruments and Procedures takes a closer look at the evolution of various procedural tools used to enforce EU competition law in the face of present crises. The first chapter, by Filipe Brito Bastos, reflects on how the administrative procedures and instruments to enforce EU competition law are evolving in the face of political and economic headwinds in the EU. Focusing on the procedural design of two new instruments (the ECN+ Directive and the Foreign Subsidies Regulation), the author shows how the Commission is deliberately reusing established legislative techniques in EU administrative law, rather than creating new ones, and demonstrates how this procedural stability can benefit competition law enforcement against new crises. Oana Stefan then moves the analysis to a key governance tool in the field of EU competition law, namely soft law. The author notes that the Commission's strategy in the areas of antitrust and State aid to counter the effects of COVID-19 involved extensive use of soft guidance as an emergency tool. While their flexibility is praised for allowing greater experimentation and timeliness in responding to the crisis, the author argues that such an extensive use of soft law can be detrimental to respect for fundamental constitutional principles, and to achieve other competition and State aid policy objectives. The following contribution by Maria Ioannidou highlights the implications of the multilevel enforcement system of competition law to tackle the challenges of digitisation in Europe. Using their legal competences, EU and Member State competition enforcers have put in place a range of tools to counter big tech companies, effectively resulting in a complex multilevel system. The author uncovers various governance and constitutional limitations that result and suggests the proposal of a 'responsive' remodelling of competition law as a solution. Carlo Maria Colombo and Matteo Bonelli follow up by analysing the impact of the green transition on the administrative enforcement of EU State aid law. They discuss how some of the key elements in realising the ambitions of the EU Green Deal – the principle of environmental integration, access to justice and the imperative to meet decarbonisation targets – are being used to reshape State aid control. This allows the authors to highlight how these transformations are strengthening the authority and effectiveness of environmental rules but can also lead to uncertainties and emerging challenges. Finally, Nicole Lindstrom addresses the relationship between democratic backsliding and the long-standing issue of compliance with EU State aid law. Focusing on how Hungary, as a country where democratic values are at risk, implements rules in a highly politicised area such as State aid law, the author identifies various instances of 'creative compliance'. Through this practice, governments use their institutional capacity to formally comply with EU rules, yet de facto promoting the interests of domestic companies and industries. This brings the author to reflect on how the present democratic crisis could undermine the uniform application and credibility of EU internal market rules.

PART I

Powers and Aims of EU Competition Law

1

EU Competition Law and Democracy in the Shadow of Rule of Law Backsliding

KATALIN J CSERES*

I. Introduction

Competition is a vital component not only of functioning market economies but also of democratic legal and political systems. In Europe, one of the key questions so prominently advanced by the Ordoliberal School was how democratic repercussions of concentrated economic and political power should be addressed. Scholars in this school proposed a constitutional framework in which competition law plays a central role in safeguarding a pluralistic competitive process and maintaining a democratic society. The role of competition as a fundamental institution of a legal system has since remained a salient concept. It influenced the drafters of the Treaty of Rome, and its central role in creating democratic political systems was restated in the 1993 Copenhagen accession criteria of the European Union (EU).

By taking a historical and constitutional law perspective, this chapter argues that competition law has emerged in Europe as a key component of public policy-building and developed as a quasi-constitutional foundation of liberal democracy. Over the past seven decades, EU competition law has become a powerful institution to defend markets across Europe, to safeguard European undertakings' freedom of economic activity and to support consumers' choice. Crucially, this fundamental role of competition law has been transplanted into all EU Member States as a component of their economic policies. Today, however, the authority of EU competition law is being critically challenged by national economic policies that question neoliberal ideas of free trade and market competition, as well as by

* Associate Professor of Law, Amsterdam Centre for European Law and Governance, University of Amsterdam, k.j.cseres@uva.nl.

the backsliding of certain Member States on their commitment to the rule of law and democracy in the EU.

The central question in this chapter is therefore whether and how EU competition law as a legal and policy instrument can and should shape responses to the challenges of rising political populism and growing political and corporate concentration. How does the current constitutional crisis in some Member States impact the overall enforcement of EU competition law? And how can EU constitutional principles uphold an effective competition enforcement system?

In order to answer these questions, Section II of this chapter conceptualises competition law as a core element of a democratic legal and political system that strives to maximise its citizens' welfare. It then moves on to explore the fundamental role of competition law in governing the relationship between markets and democracy in the European integration project. Section III analyses the way this fundamental relationship has been transplanted into the EU Member States. Section IV follows this process of Europeanisation through enlargement and modernisation in 2004 and explores the challenges that the new enforcement framework of EU competition law has entailed from 2004 on. Section V discusses selected cases in Hungary that illustrate how formal and informal institutions of EU and national competition law have been undermined in ensuring effective competition and market oversight. In that light, Section VI analyses the central institutional premise of EU competition law: the role of the Commission and national competition authorities in protecting competition and citizens' economic rights and the implications when their roles are set aside and undermined by national measures. This section finishes by analysing how core constitutional principles must be upheld to ensure effective enforcement of EU competition law. The chapter closes with conclusions.

II. The Constitutional Value of EU Competition Law

A. Competition as a Fundamental Component of Democracy

Competition is a precious good which is an active ingredient of both functioning market economies and democratic legal and political systems. At the constitutional level, competition defines the boundaries of public power,[1] and by dispersing economic power it ensures the integrity and impartiality of political institutions, as it makes interest capture less likely. Thriving competition imposes checks and balances on private as well as on public market power and guarantees an inviolable sphere of private activity.[2] The democratic value of competition goes beyond

[1] T Prosser, *The Limits of Competition Law* (Oxford, Oxford University Press, 2005).

[2] E Deutscher and M Stavros, 'Exploring the Ordoliberal Paradigm: The Competition-Democracy Nexus' (2016) 11 *Competition Law Review* 181, 188; F Böhm, 'Democracy and Economic Power in

its expected positive economic effects; it is competition as a process that satisfies aggregate preferences in society and promotes citizens' welfare.[3] Competition law safeguards the competitive process in the interest of all market players and curbs overarching economic power that threatens the basic idea of a democratic society: safeguarding autonomy and freedom of choice for equally empowered citizens who exchange their commodities in free markets.[4]

Hence, economic rights to participate in markets on equal terms can be associated with rights to freedoms and economic opportunities as laid down in political rights language in national constitutions. This conceptualisation rests on the idea that the economic order is understood as the counterpart of the democratic order in which the former guarantees consumer sovereignty and the latter ensures participatory rights of citizens. The idea that competitive markets promote consumer sovereignty is traced back to William Harold Hutt's 1936 book.[5] Hutt's core argument for consumer sovereignty centres on its role in promoting political and social stability: 'The consumer is sovereign when, in his role of citizen, he has not delegated to political institutions for authoritarian use the power which he can exercise socially through his power to demand (or refrain from demanding)'.[6] Hutt paid little attention to the achievement of market efficiency but addressed issues concerning the exercise of power in a free society as these concerned sovereignty.[7] In Hutt's definition of consumer sovereignty, consumers are also citizens whose autonomous decision-making is safeguarded by competitive markets. In light of this definition, I propose to use the term citizen welfare as an analytical lens to examine the relationship between democracy and competition law and enforcement. The term was originally coined by Firat Cengiz in her work on collective worker action and competition law.[8] Following Cengiz's argument, citizen welfare takes into account that, in complex modern societies, individuals have multiple overlapping social, economic and political roles and identities.[9] Under a citizen welfare standard, competition authorities and courts should be able to look at how a specific behaviour in question affects citizens as a holistic group, rather than focusing on the interests of the narrow category of consumers along the lines of the consumer welfare test in a given market. The citizen welfare standard resonates with the view that preservation of economic freedom through competition rules is a precondition for democracy, as it safeguards against political and regulatory

Cartel and Monopoly in Modern Law [1961]' in DA Crane and H Hovenkamp (eds), *The Making of Competition Policy: Legal and Economic Sources* (Oxford, Oxford University Press, 2013) 273.

[3] A Ayal, 'The Market for Bigness: Economic Power and Competition Agencies' Duty To Curtail It' (2013) *Journal of Antitrust Enforcement* 221, 231.

[4] ibid 231.

[5] WH Hutt, *Economists and the Public: A Study of Competition and Opinion* (Michigan, Jonathan Cape, 1936) 257.

[6] WH Hutt, 'The Concept of Consumers' Sovereignty' (1940) 50 *The Economic Journal* 66.

[7] J Persky, 'Retrospectives: Consumer Sovereignty' (1993) 7 *Journal of Economic Perspectives* 183.

[8] F Cengiz, 'The Conflict Between Market Competition and Worker Solidary: Moving from Consumer to a Citizen Welfare Standard in Competition Law' (2021) 41 *Legal Studies* 73.

[9] ibid 76–77.

capture.[10] It also resonates with legal and political theory on how markets can contribute to democratic societies.[11] Thus, markets are said to multiply possibilities for meaningful economic participation by offering a plurality of options and safeguarding the freedom of self-determination (consumer sovereignty).[12] For example, competition law is particularly relevant in safeguarding the governance of strategically important sectors in society, such as utilities (energy, telecoms, waste)[13] and media markets,[14] or in counteracting corruption by controlling bid-rigging.[15] The citizen welfare lens is well reflected in the historical roots of competition law in Europe,[16] and in US antitrust laws.[17]

B. Competition Law as the Constitutional Charter of EU Law

The fundamental role of competition law in governing the relationship between markets and democracy has been a core part of the EU integration project from its early days. Constitutionalised at the EU level, it developed into the central pillar of the integration project.[18] Even though competition law in the EU (and globally) has mainly been interpreted along economic rationales, its historical roots clearly show that it was drafted to promote democracy and understood as a fundamental constitutional value.[19] In Europe, the ideology that competition law has a potential role in promoting democracy originated from the Ordoliberals who influenced

[10] Ayal, 'The Market for Bigness' (n 3 above); Deutscher and Stavros, 'Exploring the Ordoliberal Paradigm' (n 2 above).

[11] G Tagiuri, 'Can Supranational Law Enhance Democracy? EU Economic Law as a Market-Democratizing Project' (2021) 32 *European Journal of International Law* 57.

[12] ibid; H Dagan and H Heller, *The Choice Theory of Contracts* (Cambridge, Cambridge University Press, 2017) Introduction.

[13] L Hancher and CH Jones, *EU Energy Law Volume II: EU Competition Law and Energy Markets* (Deventer, Claeys and Casteels, 2019).

[14] K Bania, 'The Role of Media Pluralism in the Enforcement of EU Competition Law' (*PhD Thesis, European University Institute, 2015*).

[15] A Sanchez-Graell, *Public Procurement and EU Competition Rules* (Oxford, Hart Publishing, 2011).

[16] F Maier-Rigaud, 'On the Normative Foundations of Competition Law – Efficiency, Political Freedom and the Freedom to Compete' in D Zimmer (ed), *The Goals of Competition Law* (Cheltenham, Edward Elgar, 2012) 152; L Pace and K Seidel, 'The Drafting and the Role of Regulation 17: A Hard-Fought Compromise' in K Patel and H Schweitzer (eds), *The Historical Foundations of EU Competition Law* (Oxford, Oxford University Press, 2013) 66.

[17] The targeting of economic power was a strong point in favour of intervention in the early days of United States antitrust. The promotion and preservation of democracy was one of the goals of the drafters of state and federal antitrust law: SW Waller, 'Antitrust and Democracy' (2019) 46 *Florida State University Law Review* 807.

[18] M Ioannidis, 'Europe's New Transformations: How the EU Economic Constitution Changed During the Eurozone Crisis' (2016) 53 *Common Market Law Review* 1237; C Joerges, 'The European Economic Constitution and Its Transformation Through the Financial Crisis' (2015) 47 *ZenTra Working Paper in Transnational Studies* 1; C Joerges, 'Europe's Economic Constitution in Crisis and the Emergence of a New Constitutional Constellation' (2014) 15 *German Law Journal* 985.

[19] Maier-Rigaud, 'On the Normative Foundations of Competition Law' (n 16 above) 166. Pace and Seidel, 'The Drafting and the Role of Regulation 17' (n 16 above).

European competition law and its enforcement framework.[20] Emerging from the bitter historical lessons of how uncontrolled concentration of economic power can undermine the social and political preconditions of democracy, Ordoliberals warned of the dual danger of accumulated economic power undermining both the economy and democracy.[21] Their concern with economic power emanated from the risk that such power transgresses to the political sphere.[22] In their view, by being incorporated in a constitutional economic order, competition had an instrumental value, as it would allow only democratically legitimised economic and political power in society and would in turn entail good economic outcomes.[23] Importantly, the process of competition had to be protected from intervention by both the state, which could be tempted to instrumentalise it, and private economic power, which could manipulate it for its own benefit. When states regulated the process of competition they had to do so in a 'neutral' way and thus this mechanism required quasi-constitutional rules.[24]

These Ordoliberal ideas influenced the development of the German[25] and the European[26] competition law systems. In both, specific features of Ordoliberal thinking, such as the focus on individual rights and the rule of law, provided an apt basis for the structure and strengths of law, as well as enforcement institutions.

The Ordoliberal positions were particularly well suited to the project of EU integration, as they could justify the primacy of EU law and combine it with an 'economic constitutional' content. The theory of an economic constitution advocated a framework order which was to guarantee economic freedoms but, at the same time, to control them legally through the competition law system.[27] This law-based order committed to the rule of law and economic freedoms helped the Community to acquire legitimacy in the foundational period of the EU[28]

[20] Maier-Rigaud, 'On the Normative Foundations of Competition Law' (n 16 above) 137.

[21] ibid.

[22] ibid 139, 163.

[23] ibid 140–41. L Miksch, 'Wettbewerb als Aufgabe Grundsätze einer Wettbewerbsordnung' (1949) 62 *Weltwirtschaftliches Archiv* 48.

[24] L Zingales, 'Towards a Political Theory of the Firm' (2017) 31 *Journal of Economic Perspectives* 113.

[25] Eucken and Böhm of the Freiburg School of Economics had a formative influence on the development of post-war competition law regulation in Germany. They advocated the idea that freedom of action had to be protected not just from state intervention but also from self-destructive commercial forces. Therefore, the state was required to impose a regulatory framework. Moreover, Ludwig Erhard, who was minister of Economic affairs between 1949–63 and chancellor between 1963–66 advocated a strong competition regime as a cornerstone of the democratic order. Erhard considered a strong competition policy as embodying political and economic liberalism because its purpose was to defend citizens against an authoritarian threat coming from more powerful actors. A Künzler and L Warlouzet, 'National Traditions of Competition Law: A Belated Europeanisation through Convergence?' in Patel and Schweitzer, *The Historical Foundations of EU Competition Law* (n 16 above); F van Waarden and M Drahos, 'Courts and (Epistemic) Communities in the Convergence of Competition Policies' (2002) 9 *Journal of European Public Policy* 913; L Erhard, *Prosperity Through Competition* (New York, Praeger, 1958).

[26] Patel and Schweitzer, *The Historical Foundations of EU Competition Law* (n 16 above) Introduction.

[27] CH Joerges, 'The Law in the Process of Constitutionalising Europe' (*EUI Working Paper 04/2002*).

[28] Patel and Schweitzer, *The Historical Foundations of EU Competition Law* (n 16 above) 1–2. Joerges, 'The Law in the Process of Constitutionalising Europe' (n 27 above).

and contributed to its 'constitutional' character.[29] In this process of supranational constitution building, competition law took centre stage.[30] Consequently, in the Ordoliberal view, protection of the competitive process must be seen in fact as an implementation of Article 2 of the Treaty on the European Union (TEU), which lists, among others, the EU values of democracy, equality, rule of law and respect for human rights. These values form an 'untouchable core' of EU law.[31] When states join the EU, they commit to the EU's economic and legal order, which as a 'constitutional charter' explicitly includes the system of undistorted competition. Accordingly, by joining, Member States commit to the values of EU law as laid down in Article 2 TEU as well as a mutual promise that in the enforcement of competition law, they recognize and respect the EU's values and objectives. However, unlike the Article 2 TEU values, which are constrained by the EU's limited competences to legislate and enforce, EU competition law is an exclusive competence of the EU with powerful tools and a track record of enforcement. Compliance with Article 2 TEU is fundamental for the EU's functioning, as this forms the basis of Member States' mutual trust of each other's compliance with EU law, including competition law. This mutual trust applies in particular to promoting the EU's values and respecting European fundamental rights, but it also conveys an assurance that each other's governments – and judiciaries – will apply EU law fairly and evenly. In its Sped-Pro judgment, discussed below, the General Court recently confirmed that compliance with the fundamental values of Article 2 TEU applies to the enforcement mechanisms of Articles 101 and 102 of the Treaty on the Functioning of the European Union (TFEU).[32] This judgment is an important reminder of the fundamental connection between democracy and competition law.

III. Competition Law and Policy Gaining Ground in the EU and its Member States

A. Europeanisation of National Competition Laws as an Instrument for Strengthening Democracy

Despite the robust foundation at the EU level, it was not until the 1980s that national legislators and policymakers recognised the need for a solid competition

[29] Patel and Schweitzer, *The Historical Foundations of EU Competition Law* (n 16 above) 10.

[30] Joerges, 'The Law in the Process of Constitutionalising Europe' (n 27 above).

[31] N Lavranos, 'Revisiting Article 307 EC: The Untouchable Core of Fundamental European Constitutional Law Values and Principles' in F Fontanelli, G Martinico, and P Carrozza (eds), *Shaping Rule of Law through Dialogue: International and Supranational Experiences* (Groningen, Europa Law Publishing, 2009).

[32] Case T-791/19 *Sped Pro v Commission* [2022] EU:T:2022:67, para 85.

law system.[33] Beyond the widespread tendency to take more effective action against distortions of competition, most EU Member States not only drafted or modified their competition laws but also established an institutional setting with a high degree of independence and transparency.[34] International competition increased with the emergence of neoliberal policies in Western Europe and the globalisation process. Accompanied by the emergence of international networks of experts in competition policy, this process progressively strengthened competition policies across Europe.[35] The growing importance of these developments, and the convergence of experiences of national legislators, resulted in a gradual 'Europeanisation'.[36] National legislators began to turn their attention to European competition law, and convergence emerged with adoption of the legal principle of safeguarding competition as a focus of national economic policy, combined with the reformulation of statutory assessment criteria. Moreover, in many Member States the institutions for assessment of anticompetitive practices became more influential and independent.[37] With this favourable ideological and political context as backdrop, the rise of powerful EU competition policy took place starting in the 1980s. Neoliberalism, coupled with a personal leadership at Directorate General IV responsible for competition at the EU Commission, qualified majority decision-making after the Single European Act of 1986, and the support of the supranational Court of Justice affirmed the Commission's powers and the role of competition law.[38]

By the late 1990s, successful market integration and the process of EU constitutionalisation combined with solid supranational enforcement mechanisms led to a strong legal and policy field. This was coupled with increasing Europeanisation of competition norms at the Member State level. Competition law became a 'common core' of the EU and its Member States.[39] Unlike the Article 2 TEU values, which draw on the shared legal and constitutional traditions of the Member States,[40]

[33] Künzler and Warlouzet, 'National Traditions of Competition Law' (n 25 above) 119–20.

[34] ibid 117.

[35] Drahos and Van Waarden showed that the most important channel for the influence of EU competition law on national competition law in the Member States was an expert community and the development of competition case law. The decisional practice of the EU Commission and case law of the Courts have created foundational principles and set legal limits to national laws. This epistemic community functioned as a channel of information exchange, learning, imitation, and for the explicit transfer of legal concepts and arguments, thus contributing to convergence: van Waarden and Drahos, 'Courts and (Epistemic) Communities' (n 25 above).

[36] Europeanisation is understood as 'the reorientation or reshaping of politics in the domestic arena in ways that reflect policies, practices or preferences advanced through the EU system of governance': I Bache and A Jordan, 'Europeanisation and Domestic Change' in I Bache and A Jordan (eds), *The Europeanisation of British Politics* (London, Palgrave Macmillan, 2006) 30.

[37] Künzler and Warlouzet, 'National Traditions of Competition Law' (n 25 above) 112.

[38] L Warlouzet 'The Rise of European Competition Policy, 1950–1991: A Cross-Disciplinary Survey of a Contested Policy Sphere' (*EUI Working Paper RSCAS 2010/80*, 2010) 17.

[39] M Drahos, *Convergence of Competition Laws and Policies in the European Community: Germany, Austria, and Netherlands* (Hague, Kluwer, 2002).

[40] KL Scheppele, D Kochenov and B Grabowska-Moroz, 'EU Values Are Law, after All: Enforcing EU Values through Systemic Infringement Actions by the European Commission and the Member States of the European Union' (2020) 39 *Yearbook of European Law* 3, 20.

competition law was centrally established and developed with far-reaching powers unmatched in any other EU policy area.[41] By pursuing market integration as a public policy goal, EU competition law has acted as a vehicle for the proliferation of democracy and the rule of law.[42]

B. The Copenhagen Criteria and Enlargement to CEECs: Restating the Link between Democracy and Competition Law

An explicit restatement of competition law as a building block of market economies and democratic societies was formulated in the governance mechanism of the accession process for the Central and Eastern European countries (CEECs) from the late 1990s to the 2004 enlargement. The legal and institutional framework of EU accession and the legal basis for aligning domestic competition laws with that of the EU were laid down in bilateral agreements between the EU and the candidate CEECs.[43] These agreements and the associated White Paper[44] contained the legal and economic conditions of accession, such as establishment of a functioning market economy, adherence to the various political, economic and monetary aims of the EU, as well as the capacity to cope with competitive pressure and market forces within the EU. These so-called 'Copenhagen criteria'[45] played a key role in both the CEECs' accession and in their economic transformation and democratisation. Europeanisation of the competition rules interacted with market, constitutional and institutional reforms and was considered to enhance both the overall economic wellbeing and the political stability of the candidate countries.[46] Accession to the EU thus exercised significant

[41] Warlouzet (n 38 above) 1.

[42] SM Ramirez Perez and S van de Scheur, 'The Evolution of the Law on Articles 85 and 86 [Articles 101 and 102 TFEU]: Ordoliberalism and its Keynesian Challenge' in Patel and Schweitzer (eds), *The Historical Foundations of EU Competition Law* (n 16 above).

[43] The Europe Agreements were concluded with Hungary and Poland in December 1991, with Romania, Bulgaria, the Czech Republic and Slovakia in February 1995, with Estonia, Latvia and Lithuania in February 1998 and Slovenia in February 1999: KJ Cseres, 'Accession to the EU's Competition Law Regime: A Law and Governance Approach' (2014) 7 *Yearbook of Antitrust and Regulatory Studies* 31.

[44] Commission, 'Preparation of the associated countries of Central and Eastern Europe for integration into the Internal Market of the Union' (White Paper) COM(1995) 163 final.

[45] The Copenhagen criteria were established by the Copenhagen European Council in 1993 and strengthened by the Madrid European Council in 1995. The Copenhagen criteria are now reflected in Art 2 TEU which also represents the most important condition to be fulfilled before joining the EU, as hinted at in Art 49 TEU.

[46] F Schimmelfennig and U Sedelmeier, 'Governance by Conditionality: EU Rule Transfer to the Candidate Countries of Central and Eastern Europe' (2011) 11 *Journal of European Public Policy* 661. Transposition of the competition and state aid *acquis*, effective enforcement of these rules and strengthening of the administrative capacity through well-functioning competition authorities were among the obligations of the candidate countries: Cseres, 'Accession to the EU's Competition Law Regime' (n 43 above).

influence in shaping the competition law regimes in the CEECs that joined the EU in 2004, 2007 and 2013.[47]

The CEECs' accession period has widely been seen as a massive process of Europeanisation that was effective because these countries' strong desire to 'return to Europe' accorded the EU unprecedented power to influence their development.[48] Their adoption of EU rules was governed by strong EU conditionality,[49] which acted as a crucial incentive for political transformation. Hence, the Copenhagen criteria were a first explicit declaration of the intimate relationship between democracy and EU competition law and the latter's central role in acquiring EU membership. However, there are good reasons to revisit Europeanisation in the CEECs. Certain areas of the 'enlargement acquis', such as democracy, rule of law and administrative capacity, were part of the EU's accession conditionality but are not, or only to a limited extent, part of the EU acquis and thus cannot be legally enforced in the new Member States.[50]

Following accession, the competition law provisions of the bilateral agreements and EU conditionality were replaced by the EU's internal governance model: Regulation 1/2003 for Articles 101 and 102 TFEU and Regulation 139/2004 for merger control.[51]

C. Merger Control

Before moving to discuss the period after 2004, a brief note is warranted about the role of merger control in Europe. Merger control monitors concentrations in markets and assesses the magnifying or reducing economic power of the merging firms. At the same time, merger control has political and social consequences for citizens. It is a legal instrument that can decentralise economic power and enable economic opportunities for firms by encouraging a democratic political order. Concentrated economic power can reinforce the political

[47] F Cafaggi and others, 'The Europeanisation of Private Law in Central and Eastern Europe Countries (CEECs): Preliminary Findings and Research Agenda' (*EUI Working Paper 15/2010*).

[48] M Matlak, F Schimmelfennig and T Woźniakowski, (eds), *Europeanization Revisited: Central and Eastern Europe in the European Union* (Florence, European University Institute, 2018).

[49] Schimmelfennig defines conditionality as a direct mechanism of Europeanization. F Schimmelfennig, 'EU External Governance and Europeanization Beyond the EU' in D Levi-Faur (ed), *The Oxford Handbook of Governance* (Oxford, Oxford University Press 2012).

[50] Matlak, Schimmelfennig and Woźniakowski, *Europeanization Revisited* (n 48 above).

[51] Cseres, 'Accession to the EU's Competition Law Regime' (n 43 above); KJ Cseres and A Outhuisje, 'A Parallel Enforcement and Accountability: The Case of EU Competition Law' in M Scholten and M Luchtman (eds), *Law Enforcement by EU Authorities: Implications for Political and Judicial Accountability* (Cheltenham, Edward Elgar, 2017); KJ Cseres, 'Competition Law Enforcement Beyond the Nation-State: A Model for Transnational Enforcement Mechanisms?' in HW Micklitz and UA Weschler (eds), *The Transformation of Enforcement: European Economic Law in a Global Perspective* (Oxford, Hart Publishing, 2016).

power of capital and directly impact citizens' economic as well as non-economic interests, such as fundamental rights related to media pluralism or access to reliable information.[52]

While in the post-Second World War period many states considered mergers to be strategically important to safeguard their industries as a protective device against resource distribution to foreign firms, in 1989 various political and economic factors enabled the adoption and implementation of EU legislation on ex ante control of mergers. Merger regulation is today the principal instrument by which competition authorities control the structure of an industry.[53] As the EU treaties contained no rules on merger control, the rules were laid down first in Regulation 4064/89 and later in Regulation 139/2004.[54] Originally the EU Merger Regulation (EUMR) had the objective to control corporate reorganisations so that they did not result in lasting damage to competition in the internal market and to permit effective monitoring of all concentrations by considering their effects on the structure of competition in the EU.[55] Today a concentration is prohibited if it significantly impedes effective competition in the common market or in a substantial part of it.[56] The monitoring of mergers is shared between the Commission and the Member States by reference to quantitative criteria.[57] However, not all Member States have a merger control regime. The Commission has central and exclusive competence over mergers with a Community dimension, but Member States apply their national competition laws to mergers that do not meet that threshold.[58] Conversely, the Commission has no competence under the EUMR where the concentration does not have a Community dimension. However, the allocation of jurisdiction is subject to some corrective mechanisms and exceptions.[59] Hence, Member States still retain

[52] C Banasiński and M Rojszczak, 'The Role of Competition Authorities in Protecting Freedom of Speech: The PKN Orlen/Polska Press Case' (2021) 18 *European Competition Journal* 424.

[53] G Monti, *EC Competition Law* (Cambridge, Cambridge University Press, 2007) 246.

[54] On the fierce and long debate on EU merger control see L Warlouzet, 'The Centralization of EU Competition Policy: Historical Institutionalist Dynamics from Cartel Monitoring to Merger Control (1956–91)' (2016) 54 *Journal of Common Market Studies* 725.

[55] Council Regulation (EEC) No 4064/89 of 21 December 1989 on the control of concentrations between undertakings [1989] OJ L395/1, Recitals 5 and 6; Council Regulation (EC) No 139/2004 of 20 January 2004 on the control of concentrations between undertakings [2004] OJ L24/1 (Merger Control Regulation).

[56] Merger Control Regulation (n 55 above) Art 2.

[57] Criteria are based on both the worldwide and Community aggregate turnover thresholds of the merging parties. ibid Art 1(2).

[58] The so-called 'exclusivity principle'. Merger Control Regulation (n 55 above) Art 21; M Harker, 'Cross-Border Mergers in the EU: The Commission v the Member States' (2007) 3 *European Competition Journal* 503.

[59] The so-called two-third rule in Art 1(2)(3). Referrals from and to the Member States Arts 9 and 22. Art 21(4) of the EUMR stipulates the exception to the Commission's exclusive competence over these mergers. The provision allows Member States to intervene in merger proceedings that have been authorised by the Commission. As such, the legal framework of the EUMR currently only allows for negative state intervention. Á Sipiczki, 'Protecting Against Protectionism – The Case of Merger Control' (*Master Thesis, University of Amsterdam 2020*).

broad powers to authorise national champions and provide populist support to public interest national law provisions.[60]

IV. Post-Modernisation Challenges: Effective Enforcement of EU Competition Law in a Decentralised System

Regulation 1/2003 established a decentralised enforcement framework and delegated an active role for national actors to enforce Articles 101 and 102 TFEU. Regulation 1/2003 created a system of parallel competences between the Commission, the national competition authorities (NCA) and national courts, and obliged the national enforcers to apply EU and national competition laws simultaneously.[61] This enforcement system relies on a mix of substantive EU provisions and national procedural laws and institutional designs.[62] Hence, the challenge concerning the enforcement of Articles 101 and 102 TFEU is that it relies on the effective administrative enforcement of the treaty rules by national administrative authorities and procedures embedded in diverse political and institutional settings.[63] Some have praised the success of the decentralised enforcement system in developing a shared sense of competition policy and culture among the Member States, particularly through the European Competition Network (ECN).[64] However, decentralised enforcement has also been criticised regarding outward pulls from the Member States towards their national legal systems[65] and centripetal pushes from the Commission towards more centralisation.[66]

[60] A Jones and J Davies, 'Merger Control and the Public Interest: Balancing EU and National Law in the Protectionist Debate' (2014) 10 *European Competition Journal* 453.

[61] Council Regulation (EC) No 1/2003 of 16 December 2002 on the implementation of the rules on competition laid down in Articles 81 and 82 of the Treaty [2002] OJ L01/1, Art 3.

[62] KJ Cseres, 'Rule of Law Challenges and the Enforcement of EU Competition Law, A Case-Study of Hungary and Its Implications for EU Law' (2019) 14 *Competition Law Review* 319–39.

[63] O Brook and KJ Cseres, 'Member States' Interest in the Enforcement of EU Competition Law' in M Varju (ed), *Between Compliance and Particularism: Member State Interests and European Union Law* (New York, Springer, 2019); Cseres and Outhuisje, *Law and Enforcement by EU Authorities* (n 51 above).

[64] W Wils, 'Ten Years of Regulation 1/2003 – A Retrospective' (2013) 4 *Journal of European Competition Law and Practice* 293; H Kassim and K Wright, 'The European Competition Network: a European Regulatory Network with a Difference' (*European Consortium for Political Research, 2010*).

[65] Cseres, 'Rule of Law Challenges' (n 62 above) 319–39. Brook and Cseres, *Between Compliance and Particularism* (n 63 above). Sipiczki, 'Protecting Against Protectionism' (n 59 above). M Borgers, 'Putting the "Trust" in Antitrust: The Impact of the Rule of Law Crisis on Trust between National Competition Authorities Under Regulation 1/2003' (*Master Thesis, Amsterdam Centre for European Law and Governance 2021*).

[66] S Wilks, 'Agency Escape: Decentralization or Dominance of the European Commission in the Modernization of Competition Policy?' (2005) 18 *Governance* 431. G Monti, 'Independence, Interdependence and Legitimacy: the EU Commission, National Competition Authorities, and the European Competition Network' (*EUI Working Paper Law 01/2014*).

The motive for decentralisation reflected a political objective of bringing 'the decision-making process closer to citizens' by allowing consumers to address national enforcers.[67] Thus, decentralisation was seen as an important component to provide stronger and more democratic political support to the EU competition policy.[68] However, there were concerns that bringing decision-making closer to citizens carried the inherent risk that Member States would implement their own national interests within the EU legal and governance framework. It was feared that decentralisation would enable national governments to influence the outcome of enforcement, creating a risk of re-nationalising EU competition law.[69]

The shortcomings of the multilevel enforcement system were to some extent remedied by the European Competition Network Plus (ECN+) Directive,[70] which aims to empower NCAs to be more effective enforcers of competition law by laying down minimum harmonisation rules for NCAs' powers of investigation, decision-making (notably fining) and enforcement. Article 4 of the ECN+ Directive sets minimum safeguards for NCAs' independence and requires accountability to governments and parliaments.

The influence of Member States has been demonstrated, for instance, in the enforcement of Article 101 TFEU by the adoption of national procedural measures limiting the enforcement of Article 101, or by the application of the substantive provisions of the article in ways that have brought its enforcement in line with national interest.[71] For example, Member States can adopt substantive legislation that explicitly limits EU competition rules, such as Germany's national Federal Forests Act, which was amended to exclude agreements between the federal states and other forest owners fixing prices and restricting sales (by-object restrictions of competition) from the scope of national competition law, and effectively also from the scope of EU competition law by setting a presumption that they are justified under Article 101(3) TFEU.[72] Moreover, not all NCAs have an independent status as administrative authorities. Although some NCAs are institutionally, financially

[67] Commission, 'White Paper on Modernisation of the Rules Implementing Articles 85 and 86 of the EC Treaty' COM(1999) 101 final 9–10.

[68] ibid 10, 21.

[69] German Monopolies Commission, *Cartel Policy Change in the European Union? On the European Commission's White Paper of 28th April 1999*, 1st edn (Baden-Baden, Nomos Verlagsgesellschaft, 2000); B Baden and I Maher, 'Networking Competition Authorities in the European Union: Diversity and Change' in CD Ehlermann and I Anatasiu (eds), *European Competition Law Annual 2002: Constructing the EU Network of Competition Authorities* (Oxford, Hart Publishing, 2002) 204. These concerns were addressed by the Commission in various soft law documents as well as by promoting a 'more economics-based approach' and reframing Art 101(3) as an objective tool to support economic assessment so that the possibility for national enforcers to apply Art 101 TFEU would remain limited. Commission, 'Notice on cooperation within the Network of Competition Authorities' (Notice) [2004] OJ C101/3; Brook and Cseres, *Between Compliance and Particularism* (n 63 above).

[70] Directive (EU) 2019/1 of the European Parliament and of the Council of 11 December 2018 to empower the competition authorities of the Member States to be more effective enforcers and to ensure the proper functioning of the internal market [2019] OJ L11/3.

[71] Brook and Cseres, *Between Compliance and Particularism* (n 63 above).

[72] Federal Forestry Act of 2 Mai 1975 (as amended) (*Bundeswaldgesetz*), Section 46 (2); German Competition Authority, Decision B1-72/12 of 9 July 2015 (Round timber in Baden Württemberg).

and politically independent of their governments, others are considerably less so.[73] The provisions of the ECN+ Directive remain limited, for example, concerning de facto independence and accountability, not addressing the broader constitutional context of competition law enforcement.[74]

Concerning merger control the challenges have been similar, though not identical, due to the different allocation of competences between Member States and the Commission. The challenges of globalisation and the 2008 economic crisis motivated growing intervention by public authorities in the economy and raised questions regarding the role of competition policy.[75] After the adoption of the EU Merger Regulation, Member States gradually adopted and reformed their merger laws. These reforms pursued three objectives: to put independent agencies in charge of merger control enforcement, to make procedures predictable and transparent, and to adopt competition-based review criteria. Still, the new rules have not completely eliminated political influence.[76]

As Member States tried to recover from the financial and economic crisis, popular backlash against foreign control of key national businesses grew and a clash manifested between proponents of open market economies and those of protectionism.[77] A central concern remained how could EU law balance the EU law goals of undistorted competition against sensitive national interests expressed in protectionist measures.[78]

V. Under-Enforcement of Competition Law in Hungary

This section discusses selected cases from Hungary to illustrate how a national government can systematically undermine the values and institutions of the rule of law.[79] As checks and balances disappear, so too does rule of law control over the enforcement of competition law. The cases concern various regulatory measures enacted by the Hungarian government to exempt economic activities in often strategically important sectors of the economy from the pressures of competition.[80]

[73] M Guidi, 'Delegation and Varieties of Capitalism: Explaining the Independence of National Competition Agencies in the European Union' (2014) 12 *Comparative European Politics* 343. KJ Cseres, 'The Implementation of the ECN+ Directive in Hungary and Lessons Beyond' (2019) 12 *Yearbook of Antitrust and Regulatory Studies* 55.

[74] Cseres, 'Rule of Law Challenges' (n 62 above).

[75] D Geradin and I Girgenson, 'Industrial Policy and European Merger Control – A Reassessment' (*Tilburg University Discussion Papers 53/2011*).

[76] ibid.

[77] Jones and Davies, 'Merger Control and the Public Interest' (n 60 above).

[78] ibid 446.

[79] European Parliament resolution of 12 September 2018 on a proposal calling on the Council to determine, pursuant to Article 7(1) TEU, the existence of a clear risk of a serious breach by Hungary of the values on which the Union is founded [2018] OJ C433/66.

[80] State intervention and increasing state ownership further reduced competition and increased state control over strategic sectors and resources including finance and banking, land and water

Politicising the competitive process to support national economic interests has been a widespread practice of the Hungarian government since winning the elections in 2010.[81] A transformation of the constitutional system in the ensuing years resulted in economic regulation in which the accumulation of political power led to accumulation of economic power in the hands of a few.[82] The rate and scope of constitutional re-engineering of Hungary's economic governance systematically undermined key legal rules and independent institutions of the functioning Hungarian market economy.[83]

A. Public Procurement and Cartels

A fundamental concern relates to cartels, specifically legislation exempting certain transactions from review under the competition rules. Here, two high-profile cases merit discussion: the renationalisation of the waste management market and the so-called 'Watermelon cartel'.

The restructuring of the Hungarian waste management market took place under the supervision of the National Waste Management Agency,[84] which was responsible for managing the system of public contracts concluded with economic operators for waste management services.[85] The tender for renationalisation of the national waste management market was won by a specific group of Hungarian undertakings in 2013, but the government excluded the incumbents, largely foreign-owned undertakings, by restricting the issuance of operating licences to undertakings that were controlled by the state or local councils.[86] The Hungarian

management. M Varju and M Papp, 'The Crisis, Economic Patriotism in Central Europe and EU Law' in L Antoniolli, L Bonatti and C Ruzza (eds), *Highs and Lows of European Integration: Sixty Years After the Treaty of Rome* (New York, Springer, 2018).

[81] M Papp and M Varjú, 'The Crisis, National Particularism and EU Law: What Can We Learn from the Hungarian Case?' (2016) 53 *Common Market Law Review* 1647 and Cseres, 'Rule of Law Challenges' (n 62 above).

[82] G Gyori, *Hungarian Politics in 2021* (Budapest, Policy Solutions, 2022) Chapter 4.

[83] As the OECD recently acknowledged, 'the pro-competitive regulatory framework is little used. The competition authority is not sufficiently active in sectors with high risk of collusion, with few market studies and decisions.'

[84] The autonomous agency was shut down by Government Decree No 322/2014 and its functions were transferred to the National Environmental Authority. In April 2016, the National Waste Management Coordination and Asset Management Corporation was established to collect the fees, manage assets and debts, and to coordinate information on waste management public services provided by local government or by the State (Government Regulation No 69/2016). Papp and Varjú, 'The Crisis, National Particularism and EU Law' (n 81 above).

[85] The Hungarian waste market is regulated by Act CLXXXV of 2012 (Waste Disposal Act) on waste. It is a market with strong public service obligations and is characterised by increasing State- and other public ownership in certain segments. The Act implemented the EU Waste Framework Directive (Directive 2008/98/EC) and other EU legislation on waste with significant delay. The infringement procedure against Hungary was ultimately order in case C-310/12 *Commission v Hungary* [2013] EU:C:2013:556.

[86] Act CLXXXV of 2012 (Waste Disposal Act), Art 81. Papp and Varjú, 'The Crisis, National Particularism and EU Law' (n 81 above) 1661.

competition authority (GVH) suspected that the group of Hungarian undertakings had coordinated the actual bids, thus bid-rigging the public procurement procedures. When the GVH started its investigation, the Hungarian Parliament changed the relevant legislation on the financial grounding of the central budget to exclude the applicability of the competition rules concerning illegal conduct in public procurement procedures conducted in the years 2012–13. The legislation and exemption were instrumental in the authority's decision to close the investigation in 2015 due to the absence of 'public interest' in continuing.[87]

Another case – one which was harshly criticised – is that of the Watermelon cartel, in which legislation was introduced exempting allegedly anticompetitive practices from the enforcement of competition rules.[88] In 2012, the GVH initiated a competition supervision procedure against a number of Hungarian melon producers, the Hungarian Melon Association and the inter-branch organisation for fruits and vegetables. The issue concerned an alleged restrictive agreement on a 'fair' minimum price that would be charged from July 2012 for watermelons produced in Hungary and that would restrict the distribution of imported watermelons. The alleged agreement was initiated by the Ministry for Rural Development, which wanted to secure a fair standard of income for farmers through the action.[89] After the GVH started its investigation, the Hungarian Parliament adopted an amendment to the Act on Inter-branch Organisations[90] stating that subject to the approval of the Minister for Agriculture and Rural Development, an otherwise restrictive agreement in the agricultural sector could be exempted from the prohibition in Hungarian competition law. In addition, the amendment stated that the GVH must (a) suspend imposing a fine for anticompetitive practices in violation of Article 11 of the Competition Act or Article 101 TFEU conducted in respect of agricultural products and (b) call the involved parties to act in compliance with the applicable laws.

The amendment had substantial consequences. While the GVH had vigorously enforced competition rules, and most notably the cartel provision in the agricultural sector, before 2012,[91] it terminated its proceedings in the case after the

[87] Decision of the Hungarian Competition Authority, Vj-67/2014/59.

[88] Decision of the Hungarian Competition Authority, Vj-62/2012.

[89] Press Release, 'Termination order was issues – the end of the watermelon saga': www.gvh.hu/en/press_room/press_releases/archive/press_releases2013/8198_en_termination_order_was_issued__the_end_of_the_watermelon_saga.

[90] Act CLXXVI of 2012 (Agricultural Organisations Act) on inter-branch organisations and on certain issues of the regulation of agricultural markets adopted on November 19, which amended Act CLXXXV of 2012 (Waste Disposal Act). Art 18/A(1) provided that: 'The infringement of Section 11 of the Competition Act cannot be established in case of agricultural products if the distortion, restriction or prevention of competition resulting from an agreement according to Section 11 of the Competition Act does not exceed what is necessary for an economically justified, fair income, provided that the actors of the market affected by the agreement are not debarred from benefiting from such income and that Art 101 TFEU was not applied.'

[91] The GVH also closed its investigation in the *Sugar cartel* case in which it suspected that sugar producers had regularly coordinated their market behaviour with respect to prices, divided their industrial and retail purchasers and shared information related to the quantities sold. Hungarian Competition Authority, Decision Vj-50/2009/226, para 132.

minister found that the conditions for the exception were met.[92] Previously, price-fixing and market-sharing decisions of agricultural associations were among the most frequent type of cartel cases.[93] While a 2012 ECN study on the food sector showed that in the period 2004–11 the GVH was one of the eight most active enforcers among the Member States,[94] according to a 2018 Commission study, Hungary investigated only a single case in the agricultural sector in the period of 2012–17.[95]

Despite strong criticism of the exemption from academia,[96] international organisations[97] and the GVH,[98] the European Commission did not question the exemption itself. Focused only on the provisions that precluded the GVH from imposing fines where trade between Member States is affected, the Commission merely issued a reasoned opinion requesting Hungary to ensure effective enforcement of competition law.[99] Threatened by a possible infringement procedure against Hungary, the Hungarian Competition Act was changed in 2015, clarifying that the GVH may impose sanctions, including fines, when the agreement infringes EU competition law.[100] The Commission accordingly closed the case in 2015 without further action.

B. Merger Control: Public Interest Exemption

Debates about the conflict between achieving efficiency considerations and public interest policy objectives through competition have intensified in recent years as governments have more frequently intervened in markets of significant national

[92] Hungarian Competition Authority, Decision Vj-62/2012, paras 13–15, 42–46 and 56–57.

[93] Hungarian Competition Authority, Decision Vj-199/2005/246; Hungarian Competition Authority, Decision Vj-69/2008/538; Hungarian Competition Authority, Decision Vj-89/2003/58.

[94] European Competition Network, 'Report on competition law enforcement and market monitoring activities by European competition authorities in the food sector' (2012): www.ec.europa.eu/competition/ecn/food_report_en.pdf.

[95] Commission, 'Accompanying the document Report from the Commission to the European Parliament and the Council the application of the Union competition rules to the agricultural sector' (Staff Working Document) SWD(2018) 450 final, 33.

[96] B Csépai, 'The Ceasefire is Over' (2015) 36 *European Competition Law Review* 404; T Toth, 'The Fall of Agricultural Cartel Enforcement in Hungary' (*Competition Law Research Centre 17/2013*).

[97] Á Pina, 'Enhancing Competition and the Business Environment in Hungary' (*OECD Economics Department Working Papers 1123/2014*).

[98] Hungarian Competition Authority, Decision Vj-62/2012, paras 70–72, GVH, 'The GVH suggests enforceable ethical rules to the agricultural sector' (2009).

[99] In this opinion the Commission emphasised that since 2004 the Commission and the national competition authorities share parallel competences for the enforcement of EU competition law. They cooperate in the European Competition Network to exchange information and inform each other of proposed decisions to ensure an effective and consistent application of EU competition rules. Commission, 'April infringements package: main decisions' (Memo) COM(2014).

[100] Act LVII of 1996 on the Prohibition of Unfair and Restrictive Market Practice (Competition Act), Art 93/A. (5) paras (1)–(4) shall only apply to a case, if the necessity of the application of Art 101 of the TFEU does not arise. The necessity of the application of Art 101 of the TFEU shall be established by

importance using a variety of tools, including arranged mergers and foreign investment rules.[101] A 2016 Report of the Organisation for Economic Co-operation and Development (OECD) shows that merger exemptions on public interest grounds were common in other OECD countries, too, but they were implemented only after a full merger review by competition authorities and based on clear and explicit public interest grounds.[102]

In 2013, a new provision, Article 24/A, was introduced in the Hungarian Competition Act. The provision states that the Hungarian government 'may, in the public interest, in particular to preserve jobs and to assure the security of supply, declare a concentration of undertakings to be of strategic importance at the national level'. For these types of concentrations, no GVH authorisation is required. Moreover, the decision can be taken in a government regulation without proper reasoning and is not subject to judicial review. Since 2013, the government has approved 40 merger cases, in the energy, finance, telecommunications, IT and transport sectors, without the competition authority having authorised them on the basis of their impact on competition. For comparison, in Germany, since the ministerial authorisation procedure was inserted in the German competition law in 1970, there have been 23 applications for ministerial approval, of which only nine were granted.[103]

The risk such exceptions pose becomes especially tangible in two cases in Hungary: a 2018 merger case related to media pluralism and a 2023 telecommunications case concerning the acquisition of Vodafone Hungary by telecommunications company 4iG and the Hungarian State.[104] In the first case, the government issued Decree 229/2018,[105] creating a media conglomerate said to be of 'national strategic importance in the public interest', and it called for a merger affecting hundreds

the Hungarian Competition Authority in its competition supervision proceeding pursuant to Art 3(1) of Council Regulation (EC) No 1/2003 (n 61 above), before making the final resolution. GVH, 'Annual Report' (2015).

[101] OECD, 'Public interest considerations in merger control' DAF/COMP/WP3(2016)3 (2016) 14.

[102] In many jurisdictions (FR, GER, IT, NL, UK) the government (usually the minister of the economy) has the power to intervene in merger control. Such intervention is often ex post as it follows the competition authority's own assessment and is based on public interest clauses which allow the competition authorities' decision to be overruled. OECD, 'Public interest considerations in merger control' (n 101 above).

[103] OECD, 'Public interest considerations' (n 101 above) 15.

[104] At the beginning of 2023, the Hungarian government in its Government Decree No 2/2023 declared the acquisition of Vodafone Hungary by 4iG and by the Hungarian State as being of national strategic interest and exempted it from national merger control. Assessments showed that in the past the Hungarian government had already declared a number of telecom mergers of 'national strategic importance', which enabled 4iG to effortlessly acquire two big telecommunication companies in 2021–22 without fearing any control of compliance with the applicable competition rules. These completed mergers already resulted in very concentrated markets. See on this TGL Profs, 'TGL Profs urge DG Competition to review acquisition of Vodafone Hungary': www.thegoodlobby.eu/2022/12/19/the-good-lobby-profs-urge-dg-competition-to-review-planned-acquisition-of-vodafone-hungary-by-4ig-and-the-state/.

[105] Government Decree No 229/2018.

of broadcasters, online and print publications to be exempt from competition rules.[106] The merger comprised a foundation to which ten companies donated their media outlets, resulting in control and operation of nearly 480 publications by a publisher known for loyalty to the Hungarian prime minister. The foundation could be viewed as a massive concentration of advertising and readership, which up until then was not allowed to be formed. The exemption of the merger of the media companies from competition rules produced a large-scale concentration of political power, aggravating the already shrinking space for media pluralism in the country.[107]

A link has frequently been made between the unprecedented level of state capture of Hungary's media ecosystem and the general elections of 2022 and is argued to have contributed to another landslide victory of the Fidesz party.[108] State capture of the media is also a reoccurring theme of the rule of law reports issued by the European Commission, including the latest of 2022.[109]

Empirical evidence suggests that protectionist state intervention in merger control is not efficient in the long run and often has considerable welfare-reducing effects. There are thus significant political and economic reasons why state intervention in merger control should be minimised and should only be used where it genuinely aims at the protection of narrowly defined public interests.[110]

VI. The Relevance of Competition Authorities: Defending Citizens' Welfare

A. The Role of Competition Authorities

The Commission and the NCAs, as 'public enforcers', have a central and fundamental role in guaranteeing effective enforcement of competition law across the EU, which is why the curtailing of the competition authority's competence in Hungary is so significant. They are the 'driving institutional motor behind effective implementation of competition policy'[111] and form essential pillars for

[106] Hungarian Competition Authority, Decision B/961/2018.

[107] E Brogi and others, 'Assessing Certain Recent Developments in the Hungarian Media Market Through the Prism of the Media Pluralism Monitor' (*Centre for Media Pluralism and Media Freedom 01/2019*).

[108] International Press Institute, 'Mission Report: Media Freedom in Hungary Ahead of 2022 Election' (Vienna, 2022).

[109] The country chapters of the Commission's rule of law report are available at: https://commission.europa.eu/publications/2022-rule-law-report-communication-and-country-chapters_en.

[110] Sipiczki, 'Protecting Against Protectionism' (n 59 above) 12.

[111] I Maher, 'The Institutional Structure of Competition Law' in M Dowdle, J Gillespie and I Maher (eds), *Asian Capitalism and the Regulation of Competition: Towards a Regulatory Geography of Global Competition Law* (Cambridge, Cambridge University Press, 2013) 61.

'proper enforcement'[112] of the EU competition rules. Competition authorities are technocratic expert organisations that are 'required to separate politics from administration',[113] and they must be legally and functionally separated from market parties and from the legislative and executive powers. Their independence has traditionally been justified by the technical complexity of the regulated markets and thus the need for expert decision-making.[114]

In Europe, the blueprint for effective enforcement and institutional design was laid down by the Ordoliberals, and first implemented in the German competition law system in the 1950s. As part of their philosophy of competition and democracy, as discussed above, the Ordoliberals envisioned a specific procedural and institutional framework for enforcing substantive competition rules. The monopoly office would be a highly independent and autonomous entity with sole responsibility for enforcement. It was not to form part of the state bureaucracy, in order to prevent political influence.[115] Its actions and decisions would be subject to review by regular courts for their conformity with an economic constitution guaranteeing yet legally controlling market freedoms. This model left no room for the executive in the sense of government.[116] The independent monopoly office was regarded as a *sine qua non* of the modern *Rechtsstaat*, as essential as a highest court.[117] The Ordoliberals envisioned a quasi-judicial office that was solely guided by the application of judicial methods to authoritative texts. Accordingly, the monopoly office had to be a strong institution with significant enforcement authority and having sufficient resources to operate quickly and decisively, to attract and maintain well-qualified personnel and to effectively demand compliance.[118]

The Ordoliberal vision of a competition authority was principally implemented in Germany when it designed its own *Bundeskartellamt*, which enjoys a high level of independence from the ministerial bureaucracy. The role of the Bundeskartellamt in the German economy and legal and political system is well illustrated in Gerber's argument that, '[T]he GWB was not just another law, and the Bundeskartellamt was not just another administrative office. Together, they symbolized rejection of a failed regime and belief in a democratic alternative.'[119] Crucially, the independence and autonomy of the Bundeskartellamt originates from its internal organisation and procedures, which protect it from any political

[112] Council Regulation (EC) No 1/2003 (n 61 above) Recital 6.

[113] DA Crane, *The Institutional Structure of Antitrust Enforcement* (Oxford, Oxford University Press, 2011).

[114] Maher, 'The Institutional Structure of Competition Law' (n 111 above).

[115] The ordoliberals' conviction that the office had to be autonomous was related to their experience during the Weimar period when the capacity of cartels and large corporations to eviscerate attempts at control by putting political pressure on the executive branch.

[116] D Gerber, *Law and Competition in Twentieth Century Europe: Protecting Prometheus* (Oxford, Oxford University Press, 2001) 254.

[117] ibid.

[118] It thus needed career specialists with a high level of economic and legal training, and they had to be largely protected from outside political or pecuniary influences.

[119] Gerber, *Law and Competition in Twentieth Century Europe* (n 116 above) 282.

influence. Its decisions are taken by so-called 'decision sections' whose procedures largely follow a judicial model. Decisions are taken on the basis of juridical principles and procedures and must be carefully justified in writing by reference to the GWB and existing case law. This leaves little to no room for administrative discretion. The juridical nature of the Bundeskartellamt is reflected in its special status, as it is placed outside the regular administrative hierarchy with the statute making its decisions reviewable by the regular courts.[120]

When the enforcement of EU competition law was negotiated in 1961, Germany was the only Member State in which competition law had played a key role in the development of the national legal and economic order. Therefore, the German experience was particularly influential in the formulation of Regulation 17/62, and Germany's normative model of a centralised, independent, quasi-judicial competition authority significantly influenced the EU model.[121] The fact that competition became a powerful component of European integration and the development of the internal market was due to the institutional and procedural setting enshrined in Regulation 17/62. In the European Commission, DG IV (now DG Competition) stood out among the DGs because of its autonomy, judicial functions and the direct influence it could exert on the economy in the common market.[122] This institutional structure closely resembled Ordoliberalism, in that it revolved around the concept of a 'strong state' in which the task of government was to provide, protect and reliably enforce non-discriminatory general rules of the game for economic and social interaction without intervening in the process or becoming a player itself. The economic constitution is aimed not merely at preventing the accumulation of private economic power but also at prohibiting political interventions by any measures meddling with market mechanisms.[123] Over the past six decades, the strength of EU competition law has primarily been the result of this highly centralised and independent institutional decision-making as established in 1962, as well as the extensive enforcement powers of the Commission. It has guaranteed uniformity and coherence, provided legal certainty for firms and proved valuable for developing experience, expertise and authority in a sensitive

[120] ibid 282, 286, 287.

[121] According to Seidel and Pace, Germany's judicial approach and confinement to competition-related assessment criteria served as a strong and comprehensive dogma from its very beginning. Furthermore, the persistence and success of the Bundeskartellamt with respect to the enforcement of these policies meant that German officials could rely both on a refined theoretical doctrine, and on a growing body of experience as compared to its neighbours. Pace and Seidel, *The Historical Foundations of EU Competition Law* (n 16 above) 66.

[122] Seidel and Pace, *The Historical Foundations of EU Competition Law* (n 16 above) 66. Competition in the Common Market. Speech by H von der Groeben, Member of the Commission of the European Economic Community, during the debate on the draft regulation pursuant to Arts 85 and 86 of the EEC Treaty in the European Parliament (Strasbourg, 19 October 1961).

[123] K Horn, 'Ordoliberalism: Neither Exclusively German Nor an Oddity. A Review Essay of Malte Dold's and Tim Krieger's Ordoliberalism and European Economic Policy: Between Realpolitik and Economic Utopia' (2021) 35 *The Review of Austrian Economics* 547.

supranational setting.[124] The defining characteristic of DG Competition reflects a strong German influence and Ordoliberal view of competition law as part of an economic constitution guaranteeing market freedoms and the importance of *Rechtsstaat* values over *ad hoc* political decision-making.[125]

B. Testing Constitutional Principles in Effective Competition Law Enforcement

Competition law is often seen as a distinctive area of law, as it depends on economic theory to define most of its substantive content and it is functional in nature.[126] While both these characteristics put it at some distance from traditional conceptions of the rule of law, rule of law remains key to guard against arbitrary use of government power and to safeguard individual rights including in competition law cases. Hence, its instrumental nature does not preclude it from a rule of law scrutiny that seems indispensable regarding the challenges in the decentralised enforcement of Articles 101 and 102 and merger control as analysed above.

With decentralisation, the institutional design and autonomy of all the NCAs became crucial for enforcement of Articles 101 and 102 TFEU, as EU law enforcement came to rely on members states' procedures and administrative capacity. Despite the diversity of Member States' institutional settings as based on the principle of procedural and institutional autonomy,[127] the NCAs remain subject to a number of fundamental obligations under EU law. First is their obligation of cooperation with the Commission and other NCAs, founded 'on equality, respect, and solidarity and especially on the idea that Member States accept that their enforcement systems differ but nonetheless mutually recognize the standards of each other's system as a basis for cooperation'.[128] The decentralised system rests on the implicit safeguarding of mutual trust and sincere cooperation,[129] in which all trust each other in making use of their investigative and fining powers in order to deter uncompetitive conduct.[130]

[124] C Harlow and R Rawlings, *Process and Procedure in EU Administration* (Oxford, Hart Publishing, 2014) 199.

[125] ibid.

[126] Maher, *Asian Capitalism and the Regulation of Competition* (n 111 above) 424.

[127] Case 33/76 *Rewe-Zentral AG v Landwirtschaftskammer für das Saarland* [1976] EC:C:1976:188, para 5.

[128] Joint statement of the Council and the Commission on the functioning of the Network of competition authorities, https://competition-policy.ec.europa.eu/system/files/2021-07/joint_statement_en.pdf, Point 7.

[129] The decentralised enforcement framework relies heavily on the principle of 'sincere cooperation' laid down in Art 4(3) TEU and imposed on national courts and governments acting as agents of EU law.

[130] Opinion 2/13 of the Court of Justice of the European Union [2014] EU:C:2014:2454, paras 167–68.

This principle, as mentioned above, has now been confirmed by the General Court in its Sped-Pro judgment.[131] Herein, the court addressed rule of law issues to be considered when assessing whether a national competition authority is capable of effectively enforcing competition law and adequately safeguarding a complainant's rights.

Referring to its own case law developed in the area of the European Arrest Warrant (EAW),[132] the General Court found that, just as in the area of freedom, security and justice, the cooperation between the Commission, the competition authorities of the Member States and the national courts for the purposes of applying Articles 101 and 102 TFEU is based on the principles of mutual recognition, mutual trust and loyal cooperation.[133] According to these principles, each of these authorities and courts must presume that, save in exceptional circumstances,[134] all the others respect Union law and, more particularly, the fundamental rights recognised by that law.[135] Meanwhile, the Commission must take account of the additional condition of rule of law backsliding concerns when deciding to reject complaints and allocating cases.[136] Hence, the General Court's judgment marks an important milestone in the interpretation of these principles in EU competition law. It shows that the lack of independence of NCAs, analogous with the lack of judicial independence of authorities issuing the EAW, can justify the suspension of cooperation between Member States.

This is even more so considering the fact that the European Commission and NCAs have 'court-like' functions[137] as they protect the legal position of undertakings as well as citizens' rights to economic activity and free choice in markets.[138]

[131] Case T-791/19 *Sped Pro v Commission* (n 32 above).

[132] To recall, the mutual recognition and execution of EAWs was always based on 'the high degree of trust and solidarity between the Member States' that national authorities would dutifully execute EU law. More simply put, the act of accession to the EU constitutes an act of recognition and acceptance of the values of the EU, and in equal measure a promise that these values will be respected whenever EU law is enforced. Case C-216/118 *Criminal proceedings against LM* [2018] EU:C:2018:586.

[133] Case T-791/19 *Sped Pro v Commission* (n 32 above) paras 81–88.

[134] Exceptional circumstances doctrine is a two-step test that has been developed by the CJEU in the specific context of the EAW. The CJEU introduced this fundamental rights exception in Aranyosi and Căldăraru (Joined Cases C-404/15 and C-659/15 *Pál Aranyosi and Robert Căldăraru v Generalstaatsanwaltschaft Bremen* 2016] EU:C:2016:198). The rebuttal of the presumption of mutual trust serves to refuse execution of the EAW on the basis of possible fundamental rights violations in the issuing State. Therefore, the 'exceptional circumstances doctrine' and 'fundamental rights exception' in the EAW can be used interchangeably, as the law stands at present.

[135] Case T-791/19 *Sped Pro v Commission* (n 32 above) para 88.

[136] The Court concludes that respect for the principles of the rule of law is a relevant factor that the Commission had to take into account in determining the most appropriate competition authority to investigate a complaint and before rejecting a complaint for lack of an EU interest, to ensure that the national authorities are in a position adequately to safeguard the complainant's rights, para 92.

[137] K Wright, 'The "Judicial", the "Administrative" and Consistent Application After the Decentralisation of EC Antitrust Enforcement' (2009) European Union Studies Association Eleventh Biennial International Conference; I Maher, 'Juridification, Codification and Sanction in UK Competition Law' (2000) 63 *Modern Law Review* 544.

[138] In Germany this originated from the private law orientation of competition law that viewed competition law as a matter of rights and individual freedoms. Gerber, *Law and Competition in Twentieth Century Europe* (n 116 above) 286.

As such, effective enforcement of competition law not only is crucial for safeguarding undistorted competition within the internal market, but also forms part of effective judicial protection as laid down in Article 19 of the Charter of Fundamental Rights (CFR), relevant to both defendants and victims in the competition context.[139]

Furthermore, the Member States must use their sovereign powers to maximise the effectiveness of Articles 101 and 102 TFEU enforcement.[140] The principle of effectiveness, which is a central element of Regulation 1/2003 and Directive 2019/01, requires that Member States do not render the implementation of EU law impossible or excessively difficult. Moreover, they must ensure that the rules they establish or apply do not jeopardise the effective application of Articles 101 TFEU and 102 TFEU.[141] The principle of effectiveness also forms a legal basis to adopt independence requirements in EU law concerning competition and other regulatory authorities, as can be seen in the ECN+ Directive.[142] Accordingly, competition authorities' power to challenge conduct deemed hostile to competition, particularly when that conduct is by politically powerful actors, is an essential measure of their political standing. Consequently, even if competition authorities' formal independence is guaranteed,[143] Member States should be barred from adopting legislative or other measures that *de facto* eliminate the independence of its NCA, as the above Hungarian cases show.[144]

The courts have on various occasions emphasised the obligations Member States have on the basis of the principle of effectiveness, which 'demands the availability of sufficiently robust national enforcement structures so that Member States can discharge their overarching obligation to secure the meaningful application of EU law within the domestic system' (emphasis added).[145] Additionally, in the Schenker case, the General Court considered the circumstances in which an NCA can decline to impose fines for the violation of Article 101 TFEU.[146]

[139] Charter of Fundamental Rights of the European Union [2000] OJ C364/1, Art 19. N Dunne, 'Convergence in Competition Fining Practices in the EU' (2016) 53 *Common Market Law Review* 453.

[140] Case C-429/07 *Inspecteur van de Beslatingdeinst v X BV* [2009] EU:C:2009:359, paras 21. See also paras 34–39 on the link between effective enforcement and loyal cooperation. M Sousa Ferro, 'Institutional Design of National Competition Authorities: EU Requirements' (*University of Lisbon Law School 01/2017*).

[141] Case C-453/99 *Courage Ltd v Bernard Crehan* [2001] EU:C:2001:465, para 29; Case C-308/19 *Consiliul Concurenței v Whitelalnd Import Export SRL* [2021] EU:C:2021:47, para 46; Case C-360/09 *Pfleiderer AG v Bunderkartellamt* [2011] EU:C:2011:389, para 24.

[142] M Sousa Ferro, 'Institutional Design' (n 140 above) 118. Directive (EU) 2019/944 of the European Parliament and of the Council of 5 June 2019 on common rules for the internal market for electricity and amending Directive 2012/27/EU [2019] OJ L158/125, Recital 80.

[143] Act LVII of 1996 on the Prohibition of Unfair and Restrictive Market Practice (Competition Act), Arts 33, 35, 38. Cseres, 'Rule of Law Challenges' (n 62 above).

[144] See for a detailed discussion on how de facto independence has been undermined in Hungary, Cseres, 'Rule of Law Challenges' (n 62 above).

[145] Dunne, 'Convergence in Competition' (n 139 above). The authorities designated under Art 35(1) of Regulation No 1/2003 (n 61 above) must ensure that those Treaty articles are applied effectively in the general interest: C-439/08 *Vlaamse federatie van verenigingen van Brood- en Banketbakkers, Ijsbereiders en Chocoladebewerkers (VEBIC) v Belgium* [2010] EU:C:2010:739, para 56.

[146] Case C-681/11 *Schenker and others v Bundeswettbewerbsbehörde* [2013] EU:C:2013:404, paras 46–47, 49.

Therefore, effective enforcement principally relates to the deterrent effect that national sanctioning systems have on the conduct of market operators.[147] Undertakings should be deterred from engaging in anticompetitive conduct fearing prosecution and the obligation to pay a fine.[148] Such a deterrent effect is absent in a situation in which Articles 101 and 102 TFEU are systematically under-enforced. The interdependent nature of decentralised enforcement means that even where most NCAs engage in effective enforcement, the failure of some to apply Articles 101 and 102 TFEU undermines the system.[149]

The general deficiencies as analysed above in the selected Hungarian cases form a clear risk to the fundamental rights of market players, who are prevented from exercising their right to economic activity and equal access on the Hungarian market.[150] Such a systemic failure of an NCA to enforce Regulation 1/2003, given the risk this poses to the system of enforcement, should therefore be sufficient to suspend cooperation under Regulation 1/2003. Practically, such a suspension would mean that the other NCAs would no longer mutually recognise the concerned national system as able to effectively enforce Articles 101 and 102 TFEU, with the consequence that cases would be reallocated from such an NCA to other NCAs to ensure that Article 101 and 102 TFEU are enforced.[151] Moreover, on the basis of Article 11 (6) of Regulation 1/2003, the Commission can intervene if there is a serious risk of incoherence by relieving the national competition authority of its competence to act. It has, however, so far not made use of this possibility.

The same principles, however, may warrant a separate note with regard to merger control, in which no parallel application of the merger rules and no cooperation takes place among the NCAs and the Commission. This raises the crucial question of what is effective merger enforcement across the EU. More specifically, we might ask whether the systematic failure of a Member State to review mergers according to its competition rules qualifies as a distortion of competition in the common market and jeopardises the overall enforcement of competition law in the EU.

Even though the principle of effectiveness is not a central element of Regulation 139/2004 as it is in Regulation 1/2003, and even though public interest exceptions to the control of mergers are widely accepted across the EU and beyond, a disproportionately frequent and broadly construed application that eliminates competition-based scrutiny in each case is contradictory to the principle of loyal cooperation under Article 4(3) TEU. It also raises questions as to

[147] C Veljanovski, 'A Statistical Analysis of UK Antitrust Enforcement' (2014) 10 *Journal of Competition Law and Economics* 711.
[148] ibid.
[149] ibid.
[150] Case T-791/19 *Sped Pro v Commission* (n 32 above), paras 85–86.
[151] Borgers, 'Putting the "Trust" in Antitrust' (n 65 above).

the Member State's commitment to the EU values and to EU objectives such as undistorted competition in the internal market. Moreover, it risks directly harming citizens' welfare in strategically important sectors of the economy that, due to the frequent use of merger exceptions, are left to become more concentrated and less focused on citizens' economic interests.

VII. Conclusions

The protection of open and competitive markets is a fundamental economic right of citizens in all jurisdictions with a solid competition law system. Consumer welfare, as the generally accepted goal of competition law, only captures the economic dimension of such a fundamental right. Shifting the focus of enforcement to citizen welfare, this chapter argued, serves to deepen and broaden the policy goal of competition law enforcement. It is reminiscent of how markets contribute to democratic societies by guaranteeing meaningful economic participation for firms and safeguarding the plurality of options for citizens.

This chapter traced the fundamental connection between democracy and competition law in EU law as laid down by the Ordoliberal school. It then went on to analyse how this connection has been implemented by German legislators and later by officials drafting the EU treaties and their procedural framework. More importantly, this foundational link has not just remained in the supranational legal order, but has been transplanted into all the EU Member States through the process of EU integration. In fact, it is not merely a constituent of EU integration and the EU legal order, but also forms a value commonly shared by all Member States. Like the EU constitutional principles and the EU values laid down in Article 2 TEU, the EU competition rules seek to control excessive and arbitrary use of power. While the constitutional rules focus on monitoring public power, competition rules can keep private (or public) economic power in check. In this sense, competition law complements the protection provided by constitutional law to the effective protection of citizens' fundamental rights by making sure citizens (economically) benefit from the functioning of open and competitive markets. This fundamental complementarity was more recently confirmed in the Sped-Pro judgment which determined that, like national courts, NCAs must be independent in order to effectively protect individuals' rights. This judgment is especially important in light of the fact that while competition law forms an exclusive competence of the EU with far-reaching enforcement powers, its constitutional power can be threatened and undermined by Member States' systematic attacks on the rule of law and democracy. It confirms the constitutional relevance of NCAs, which have court-like functions and as such are key actors in upholding individual citizens' and undertakings' economic rights.

The Sped-Pro judgment verifies that when an NCA systematically fails to enforce or under-forces the rules laid down to protect the value of competition, as in the cases from Hungary referenced in this chapter, such a legal system endangers the functioning of markets and the protection of undertakings and citizens at the national and EU level. The current EU legal system has the tools to remedy such crisis situations, but solutions need to be sought and applied broadly across subdisciplines of EU law and across various Commission DGs. This compound analytical lens was once the foundation of EU integration and the EU's legal order. The history of EU integration has presented few more important moments than the present when this compound lens needs to be convincingly and urgently applied.

2

Digital Technology Disruptions and Competition Law: A Stress Test for the Existing Governance and Enforcement Frameworks?

PIETER VAN CLEYNENBREUGEL*

I. Introduction

Digital technologies have significantly disrupted the ways in which goods and services are offered and human communication takes place.[1] Digitalisation has resulted in new economic actors and transactions offering traditional and new goods and services via online means, amassing personal data along the way. Those activities are often – but certainly not exclusively – offered by so-called online platforms. Online platforms extend from search engines (such as Google) over e-commerce platforms (including Amazon) to social networks (with Facebook as the best-known example) and include both large multinational undertakings and smaller, local actors.[2]

Like any other economic actor qualifying as an 'undertaking',[3] those digital services providers have to respect European Union (EU) competition rules. It is not surprising, therefore, that Articles 101 and 102 of the Treaty on the Functioning of the European Union (TFEU) as well as the Merger Control Regulation 139/2004

* Professor of Law, Faculty of Law, Political Science and Criminology, University of Liège. Pieter.VanCleynenbreugel@uliege.be.

[1] See J van Dijk, T Poell and M de Waal, *The Platform Society – Public Values in an Interconnected World* (Oxford, Oxford University Press, 2018) 240.

[2] For an attempt at capturing the variety of platforms, see P Van Cleynenbreugel, *Plateformes en ligne et droit de l'Union européenne – un cadre juridique aux multiples visages* (Brussels, Bruylant, 2020) 30–37.

[3] Case C-41/90 *Klaus Höfner and Fritz Elser v Macrotron GmbH* [1991] EU:C:1991:161, para 21: 'the concept of an undertaking encompasses every entity engaged in an economic activity, regardless of the legal status of the entity and the way in which it is financed'.

have been applied to digital economy players as well.[4] At the same time, digital technologies create new markets and change competitive dynamics in existing ones. Important digital players such as Amazon or Facebook have indeed branched out into new markets and entered into direct competition with businesses making use of their intermediation services. As a result, questions have been raised as to whether the constitutional and governance arrangements in place suffice to address the disruptions caused by it.[5]

Against that background, the purpose of this chapter is to highlight the challenges digital disruption brings to the enforcement dynamics currently underlying EU competition law. To do so, the chapter charts the ongoing enforcement activities (Section II) prior to identifying three challenges digital disruptions bring for competition law enforcement (Section III). It subsequently outlines the initiatives taken to address those challenges and sketches their impact on the existing governance framework underlying Articles 101 and 102 TFEU (Section IV).

II. Competition Law and the Digital Economy: Business as Usual?

The rapid rise of digital players and their alleged dominance in certain markets challenges the established legal and governance frameworks underlying EU competition law. At first sight, it would be tempting to argue that the application of EU competition law and its governance framework to the digital economy seems to cause little or no problems. Making use of its well-known powers, the European Commission has not hesitated to impose heavy fines on online market players in ways similar to more traditional economic sectors. In doing so, the Commission generally relied on the well-known interpretations of legal concepts enshrined in Articles 101 and 102 TFEU. As those notions allow for a large degree of flexibility in their interpretation and application, the Commission believes its provisions can be tailored easily to fit the digital economy as well.[6]

By way of example, Google has been subject to EU competition enforcement on multiple occasions. The Commission imposed no fewer than three fines for abusing a dominant position. In 2017, Google was fined €2.42 billion because it deliberately favoured its own online buying service in the search results, to the

[4] For an overview of tendencies taking place in different EU Member States, see N Petit and P Van Cleynenbreugel, 'General Report Topic 3: EU Competition Law and the Digital Economy' in D Mandrescu (ed), *EU Competition Law and the Digital Economy: Protecting Free and Fair Competition in an Age of Technological (R)evolution – The XXIX FIDE Congress in The Hague, 2020 Congress Publications, Vol 3* (The Hague, Eleven International Publishers, 2020).

[5] For a US perspective, see LM Khan, 'Amazon's Antitrust Paradox' (2017) 126 *Yale Law Journal* 710 and LM Khan, 'The Separation of Platforms and Commerce' (2018) 119 *Columbia Law Review* 973.

[6] For that perspective, see also T Kramler, 'Institutional Report Topic 3: EU Competition Law and the Digital Economy' in Mandrescu (ed), *EU Competition Law and the Digital Economy* (n 4 above).

detriment of other online shopping platforms (Google Shopping).[7] In 2018, Google was fined €4.34 billion for obliging the Android operating system and the internet browser Chrome to manufacturers of smartphones, to the detriment of other browsers and operating systems (Google Android).[8] Finally, in 2019, Google was fined €1.49 billion for abusing its dominant position in negotiating exclusivity requirements in publicity contracts with advertisers wishing to promote their product online via the Google search engine (Google AdSense).[9] Google appealed these decisions to the General Court of the European Union.[10] In that context, the General Court largely upheld the Google Shopping decision and the fine imposed in that context.[11] The decision in Google Android was also largely upheld, although the fine was reduced to €4.125 billion.[12] An additional investigation is pending with regard to Google's alleged violation of EU competition law in restricting access to user data for advertising purposes.[13] Amazon has also been the subject of an investigation by the European Commission, which resulted in a commitment that Amazon would discontinue its practice of using non-public data of third-party sellers to compete with those very same sellers.[14] In all cases, the European Commission made use of its powers to enforce Articles 101 and 102 and applied its well-known substantive law frameworks to the activities of those undertakings. Similarly, producers of digital technologies were fined in this way. By way of example, Qualcomm has been imposed € 997 million and € 242 million fines, each time for abusing a dominant economic position in the market for chips used in the production of smartphones.[15] In the field of merger control, Regulation 139/2004

[7] Commission Decision of 27 June 2017 relating to proceedings under Article 102 of the Treaty on the Functioning of the European Union and Article 54 of the Agreement on the European Economic Area (Case AT.39740 – Google Search (Shopping)) [2018] OJ C9/11.

[8] Commission Decision of 18 July 2018 relating to a proceeding under Article 102 of the Treaty on the Functioning of the European Union and Article 54 of the EEA Agreement (Case AT.40099 – Google Android) [2019] OJ C402/19.

[9] Commission Decision of 20 March 2019 relating to a proceeding under Article 102 of the Treaty on the Functioning of the European Union and Article 54 of the EEA Agreement (Case AT.40411 Google Search AdSense) [2020] OJ C369/6.

[10] Case T-612/17 *Google v Commission* (*Google Shopping*) [2021] EU:T:2021:763; Case T-604/18 *Google v Commission* (*Google Android*) [2022] EU:T:2022:541; Case T-334/19 *Google and Alphabet v Commission* (pending).

[11] For an overview, see J Persch, 'Google Shopping: The General Court Takes its Position', *Kluwer Competition Law Blog*, 15 November 2021: https://competitionlawblog.kluwercompetitionlaw.com/2021/11/15/google-shopping-the-general court takes-its-position/

[12] ibid.

[13] Press Release, 'Antitrust: Commission opens investigation into possible anticompetitive conduct by Google in the online advertising technology sector': www.ec.europa.eu/commission/presscorner/detail/en/ip_21_3143.

[14] Commission Decision of 20 December 2022 relating to a proceeding under Article 102 of the Treaty on the Functioning of the European Union (TFEU) and Article 54 of EEA Agreement (Cases AT.40462 Amazon Marketplace and AT.40703 Amazon Buy Box) [2022] OJ C87/7.

[15] Commission Decision of 24 January 2018 relating to a proceeding under Article 102 of the Treaty on the Functioning of the European Union and Article 54 of the EEA Agreement (Case AT.40220 – Qualcomm (Exclusivity Payments) [2018] OJ C269/25 and Commission Decision of 18 July 2019 relating to a proceeding under Article 102 of the Treaty on the Functioning of the European Union and Article 54 of the EEA Agreement (Case AT.40394 – Aspen) [2019] OJ C375/25.

grants the European Commission the power to review concentrations (including mergers) between undertakings having a Community dimension.[16] Making use of these powers, the Commission fined Facebook for providing misleading information following the investigation into Facebook's acquisition of control of WhatsApp.[17] At the same time, however, concentrations, such as Facebook and Instagram, have not been scrutinised by the Commission, as the thresholds for the concentration to be having a 'Community dimension' were not met in those instances.

It is well-known that, since the entry into force of Regulation 1/2003, national competition authorities are also obliged to apply Articles 101 and 102 TFEU when a case presents an effect on inter-state trade.[18] EU competition law can be applied in parallel with national competition laws, as long as national law does not prohibit what is allowed under EU competition law.[19] In the same way, Regulation 1/2003 does not prohibit Member States from maintaining stricter prohibitions on certain types of unilateral conduct. National authorities have applied those norms to digital economy players. By way of example, the German competition authority – the Bundeskartellamt – backed by the German Federal Court of Justice – the Bundesgerichtshof – obliged Facebook to stop acquiring, combining and using personal data in certain ways because this would constitute an abuse of a dominant position under German competition law.[20] In the same way, the French Autorité de la concurrence imposed a fine on Google for disrespecting an order inviting Google to negotiate copyright payments with newspapers having their articles displayed on Google News. The case is still being analysed on the merits. In that context, it is likely that the Autorité establishes an abuse of dominance by Google in this respect, potentially imposing a very significant fine as a result.[21] This incomplete snapshot of enforcement decisions, fines and investigations show that the Commission – as well as national competition authorities – are at least applying the established legal frameworks on anticompetitive practices to digital economy players. It would therefore be tempting to argue that the unreserved application of existing competition law provisions is sufficiently able to deal with digital economy players.

[16] Council Regulation (EC) No 139/2004 of 20 January 2004 on the control of concentrations between undertakings (the EC Merger Control Regulation) [2004] OJ L24/1.

[17] Commission Decision of 3 October 2014, Non-opposition to a notified concentration (Case M.7217 Facebook/WhatsApp) [2014] OJ C417/4.

[18] Council Regulation (EC) No 1/2003 of 16 December 2002 on the implementation of the rules on competition laid down in Articles 81 and 82 of the Treaty [2002] OJ L01/1, Art 3(1).

[19] ibid Art 3(2).

[20] Federal Court of Justice, Decision of 23 June 2020, KVR 69/19 and German Competition Authority, Decision B6-22/16 of 15 February 2019.

[21] See Press Release, 'Rémunération des droits voisins: l'Autorité sanctionne Google à hauteur de 500 millions d'euros pour le non-respect de plusieurs injonctions': www.autoritedelaconcurrence.fr/fr/article/remuneration-des-droits-voisins-lautorite-sanctionne-google-hauteur-de-500-millions-deuros.

III. Three Challenges for EU Competition Law and Governance

Despite continuous enforcement practice, it has been also acknowledged that digitalisation brings particular challenges for the application of substantive EU competition law. More particularly, the digital economy can be said to raise three challenges: a structural (Section A), a behavioural (Section B) and a foundational one (Section C).

A. Structural Challenges

Within the digital economy, online platforms of various kinds (search engines, social networks, e-commerce platforms) essentially act as intermediaries between providers and recipients of other services. The intermediary role they play results in different market structures in place than the ones traditionally supposed present in competition law. As a result, the actual definition of markets and the importance of market shares that traditionally accompany EU competition law investigations may no longer be fully up to date. On the one hand, online intermediaries contribute to making it easier for different groups of platform users (sellers and buyers or advertisers and prospective buyers) to get in touch with each other. That intermediation activity is therefore referred to by economists as a two- or multi-sided market. In such a market structure, different groups of users are dependent on each other.[22] As a result, there are significant direct or indirect network effects, which are summarised by the Dutch competition authority as follows:

> [a]n indirect network effect means that a platform is more attractive to users on the one hand (consumers) the more users on the other side are (providers) of the platform. … A direct network effect means that the platform is more attractive as more users are on the same side, as with a social network. Network effects create a distinct competitive dynamic: platforms can quickly become major market players due to the exponential growth of the number of users. Platforms try to attract a critical mass of users as quickly as possible in order to drive network effects'.[23]

The two or more sides of markets can be important for the way in which the market is defined for the application of competition law. For the purposes of competition law, a market has been and still is defined traditionally by a simple model based on relatively stable and plentiful supply and demand on a single market.[24]

[22] M Rysman, 'The Economics of Two-Sided Markets' (2009) 25 *Journal of Economic Perspectives* 125; see also JC Rochet and J Tirole, 'Two-Sided Markets: A Progress Report' (2006) 35 *The RAND Journal of Economics* 645.

[23] Autoriteit Consument en Markt, *Grote platforms, grote problemen? Een beschouwing van online platforms vanuit mededingingsperspectief* (the Hague, ACM, 2016).

[24] That idea clearly underlines point 12 of the Commission Notice on the definition of relevant market for the purposes of Community competition law (Notice) [1997] OJ C372/5. That notice is in

In that framework, an online platform should be active in at least two markets by offering services to different categories of users in order to produce meaningful intermediation activities. The presence of network effects nevertheless means that online platforms are eager to attract as many users of a category as possible. Due to certain functionalities, a platform can very quickly succeed in winning over a lot of users. At the same time, developing a new and better platform can quickly make users switch to that better alternative.[25] As a result, the competitive dynamics of online platforms are different than in a traditional market. Different players do not compete with each other *in* a given market, but rather *for* a given market.[26]

On the other hand, since platforms tend to create their own 'niche' markets linking different categories of users, a platform company that has a high market share today is not necessarily always a dominant market player. After all, that market share can decrease sharply very quickly when a new, better market is created. The existence of stronger competition for a new, better market may therefore lead to consider market shares as less important and to look at other elements that influence the structure of a particular market. However, the classical way of determining market dominance still strongly relies on market shares as a parameter. Those classic parameters would no longer always automatically be relevant in the context of the digital economy. In EU competition law, market definition relies on a Commission soft law instrument of 1997, which still premises markets predominantly on one-dimensional supply and demand markets.[27] In that understanding, the importance of market shares to measure dominance is often assumed. However, the digital economy would be less market-share dependent because of its two-sided nature. The fact that competition occurs more often for, rather than in, a market does not automatically mean that there are no longer practices aimed at preventing the emergence of such new, better markets. For the time being, however, there is still uncertainty about which factors cause such impediments. It is certain that certain market behaviour can lead to the tilting of a market towards a dominant player (so-called 'market tipping').[28] This tilt is not necessarily the result of anticompetitive behaviour, but it cannot be ruled out that such behaviour may contribute to this. Current legal norms prohibiting abuse are mainly aimed at excluding certain companies from a certain clearly defined

the process of being updated – the 2022 successor notice is likely to take other market structures more explicitly into account, see Press Release, 'Competition: Commission publishes findings of evaluation of Market Definition Notice': www.ec.europa.eu/commission/presscorner/detail/en/IP_21_3585 for background.

[25] See J van Reenen, 'Increasing differences between firms: market power and the macroeconomy' (*LSE Centre for Economic Performance Discussion Papers 1576/2018*) 3.

[26] L Filistrucchi, D Geradin, E van Damme and P Affeldt, 'Market Definition in Two-Sided Markets: Theory and Practice' (2014) 10 *Journal of Competition Law and Economics* 293.

[27] Commission Notice on the definition of relevant market for the purposes of Community competition law (Notice) [1997] OJ C379/5.

[28] T Hossain and J Morgan, 'When Do Markets Tip? A Cognitive Hierarchy Approach' (2013) 32 *Marketing Science* 431.

market. Those standards are limited to curbing practices aimed at preventing the emergence of a new, better market. From that point of view, a more comprehensive legal framework capable of prohibiting newer forms of market abuse and precluding such a tilt in favour of a particular player may prove useful or even necessary. Absent legislative or soft law clarifications, the fact that the substantive rules pay little attention to those issues also result in competition authorities risking being less prone to interpret existing rules in a different, digital-tailored manner.

B. Behavioural Challenges

Digital disruptions also create 'behavioural' challenges for competition law and governance. Digital markets witness types of behaviour that are typical to a market environment in which more competition for the market takes place. For digital players, the renewed competitive dynamics that online platforms bring implies that companies would be more prone to carry out 'market-killing' transactions, which escape the attention of competition law and, in particular, the supervision of proposed concentrations.[29] It cannot be ruled out that an established online platform will acquire a smaller, but possibly more efficient platform in order to safeguard its own (becoming dominant) market position. When such an acquisition takes place at an early stage, the market share of the acquired platform is still very small. Due to that limited market share, such a transaction either does not have to be notified to the European Commission or national competition authorities, or it can be quickly concluded that this transaction does not pose any competition problems in the market on which both platforms are active. The acquisition of Instagram and WhatsApp by Facebook are considered an example of such potentially 'killer acquisitions'.[30] Indeed, such an acquisition could potentially have the effect of delaying or eliminating the creation of a better, new market to which platform users could switch. The risk of such 'killer acquisitions' is inherent in an environment in which competition increasingly takes place for, instead of on, a market. It is therefore not surprising that the danger of such killer practices, present in the pharmaceutical sector,[31] has also been raised in the context of the digital economy. The existing legal framework offers few possibilities to prohibit such acquisitions.[32] After all, the moment a larger platform acquires a

[29] C Cunningham, F Ederer and S Ma, 'Killer Acquisitions' (2021) 129 *Journal of Political Economy* 649.

[30] Those accusations have not directly resulted in infringement decisions taken against those undertakings, see S Stolton, 'Facebook accused of copy, acquire and kill tactics in the US antitrust hearing' *EURACTIV*, 30 July 2020: www.euractiv.com/section/digital/news/facebook-accused-of-copy-acquire-and-kill-tactics-in-us-antitrust-hearing/.

[31] See in particular Cunningham, Ederer and Ma, 'Killer Acquisitions' (n 29 above).

[32] M Bourreau and A de Streel, 'Big Tech Acquisitions: Competition and Innovation Effects and EU Merger Control' (*CERRE Issue Paper February 2020*).

smaller player, it is not yet certain that the smaller player will ever create a new, better market to the detriment of the currently large platform. Since competition authorities cannot find evidence to that effect, they have little choice but to authorise the acquisition, both at EU and Member States' levels. Because it is yet unclear when an acquisition will have such killer status, introducing stricter rules or bans in that regard remains controversial. Nevertheless, the challenge raised here again risks having an impact on the way in which competition law is governed within the European Union. To the extent that some Member States wish to modify their national competition laws to address the issue, the risk of divergence between different national laws is likely to increase. Such diversity is tolerated by Regulation 1/2003 in the regulation of unilateral conduct,[33] but may be detrimental to legal certainty and the coherent application of competition rules across the EU internal market.

C. Foundational Challenges

In addition to the previous challenges, a more foundational challenge inherent to digital markets may have a direct impact on the application of traditional competition law rules. In contrast with other sectors of the economy, competition between digital players is less centred on charging the lowest price to consumers in the short term. They rather operate in an environment where they are less dependent on prices charged for products.[34] In addition to the specificity of the markets in which online platforms operate, it is also established that those platforms collect and monitor a great deal of personal data from the various users of their services. Those data are used to influence the market behaviour of the users concerned. Because platforms have a lot of data and that data also largely explains their market power, the question has arisen whether keeping such an amount of personal data should also entail additional responsibilities under competition law.[35]

In that context, two fundamental questions emerge. On the one hand, the question arises to what extent platforms should have a special responsibility to grant other companies access to (part of) the data that they control themselves. To the extent that those data are a so-called essential facility for the development of a new product, Article 102 TFEU can in exceptional cases consider refusing access to them as an abuse of a dominant position.[36] The question therefore arises when and in what circumstances such access should be generalised beyond the

[33] Council Regulation 1/2003 (n 18 above) Art 3(2).

[34] J Newman, 'Antitrust in Zero-Price Markets: Foundations' (2015) 164 *University of Pennsylvania Law Review* 149.

[35] I Graef, *EU Competition law, Data Protection and Online Platforms: Data as Essential Facility* (Tilburg, Kluwer Law International, 2016) 422.

[36] Case C-7/97 *Bronner v Mediaprint Zeitungs* [1998] EU:C:1998:569.

scope of dominance as currently defined in EU competition law.[37] To do so at EU-wide level, new national and/or EU regulations would seem to be necessary. On the other hand, the concentration of data also facilitates the manipulation of that data through techniques of artificial intelligence. Fuelled by data, a computer program can automatically make decisions and even coordinate behaviours with other market actors. There is therefore a warning in legal doctrine about the risk of so-called algorithmic restrictions on competition (algorithmic collusion).[38] In the current state of the law, an explicit or implicit concurrence of wills is required to be able to speak of a restrictive competition practice under Article 101 TFEU.[39] Artificial intelligence techniques could, however, make it possible for computer programs to coordinate behaviour without human intervention. Such conduct may fall outside the scope of Article 101 TFEU.[40] Although the possibility of fully computerised behavioural coordination is still futuristic,[41] there is also a risk here that competition law will not be fully able to stop high-tech anticompetitive behaviour. Digitalisation contributes to those evolutions and thus also challenges the legal framework in this respect. The use of data and technologies thus raises important questions regarding the ways in which competition law would have to be upgraded or complemented by additional instruments of regulation.

IV. Stress Test for the Commission's Governance and Enforcement Frameworks?

All in all, the challenges mentioned in the previous section (market definition issues, new types of anticompetitive behaviour for instead of on markets and lack of rules on how to use data in a competitive manner) are not fundamentally new to competition law. The issue of market definition has been controversial in other dynamic market contexts as well.[42] In the same way, sectors characterised by some kind of natural monopoly have known competition for, instead of on, markets. To ensure that competition on markets took place, additional and

[37] Case C-165/19 *Slovak Telecom v Commission* [2021] EU:C:2021:239 offers a framework for analysis in that regard.

[38] See A Ezrachi and M Stucke, *Virtual Competition: The Promise and Perils of the Algorithm-Driven Economy* (Cambridge, Harvard University Press, 2016) 368.

[39] Joined Cases C-2/01 and C-3/01 *BAI and Commission v Bayer AG* [2004] EU:C:2004:2, para 97.

[40] A Heinemann and A Gebicka, 'Can Computers Form Cartels? About the Need for European Institutions to Revise the Concertation Doctrine in the Information Age' (2016) 7 *Journal of European Competition Law and Practice* 431.

[41] A Ittoo, A Gautier and P Van Cleynenbreugel, 'AI Algorithms, Price Discrimination and Collusion: A Technological, Economic and Legal Perspective' (2020) 50 *European Journal of Law and Economics* 405.

[42] See VHSE Robertson, *Competition Law's Innovation Factor – The Relevant Market in Dynamic Contexts in the EU and the US* (Oxford, Hart Publishing, 2020) 384.

complementary instruments of regulation have been envisaged in those domains in the past as well.[43] The use of data and access to them granted to competitors have already met its match with essential facilities calls in the context of technologies protected by intellectual property.[44] In those circumstances too, competition law and its interpretation have proven sufficiently strong to accommodate for certain changes in the interpretation and application of EU competition law. Nothing would seem to impede the Commission either refining its rules or adopting new soft law instruments (such as on the definition of digital markets or abuses in the digital field[45]), without having to fundamentally modify the governance framework in place.

What makes digital disruptions in a certain way 'special', is the impact digital actors have on the lives of individuals across different Member States and the loss of traditionally State-centred control and oversight their activities bring about. Given the multitude of individuals directly involved and the risks associated with online behaviour, Member States' governments and parliaments feel a certain pressure to act and to intervene ex ante in the organisation of digital activities. That is done on the one hand to meet popular demand by respective interest groups but also, on the other hand, to avoid future anticompetitive behaviour emerging and becoming too big to control at that stage. Those calls for action put pressure on the division of competences between the European Commission and the Member States. Member States would like to take action but can only do so in a limited manner. Yet within the confines of their mandate, they can go in important different directions. In the same way, confronted with a similar pressure, the European Commission may want to impose additional rules, but would risk duplicating the work of national authorities. As a result, a patchwork of rules may emerge, against the spirit of the governance framework put in place over the last two decades.

The challenges caused by digitalisation have indeed spurred debates on whether or not competition law and its governance framework are sufficiently fit to address them. Since digital actors can become dominant very rapidly and competition law lacks the tools to intervene whenever a dominant position is still in the process of being established absent a merger, calls for regulation complementing competition law have been made. At the EU level in particular, the European Commission proposed a so-called 'Digital Markets Act' (DMA), which, if adopted, would directly complement existing competition rules. That new legal framework, set up in 2022 raises fresh questions that, if unanswered, risk fundamentally changing the governance dynamics underlying EU competition law's decentralised enforcement system in the contexts of Articles 101 and 102 TFEU.

[43] For an overview, see P Nihoul, *Les télécommunications en Europe: concurrence ou organisation de marché* (Louvain-le-Neuve, Presses universitaires de Louvain, 2005) 600.

[44] Case C-418/01 *IMS health v NDC Health* [2004] EU:C:2004:257.

[45] A process currently ongoing, see Press Release, 'Competition' (n 24 above).

A. A Variety of Calls for Actions and Legislative Modifications

Outside of the European Union, the University of Chicago Booth Business School's Stigler Committee on Digital Platforms in 2019 presented a report[46] and policy brief.[47] Both documents indicated that the application of traditional antitrust rules alone needs to be strengthened, yet also embedded in a broader platform-focused regulatory framework. Antitrust rules alone would not be sufficient to tackle the emergence of new powerful markets and players in the digital economy. The Australian Competition and Consumer Commission also published a July 2019 Report,[48] containing a number of recommendations along the lines of the Stigler Centre's Report. According to the Australian Competition and Consumer Commission, in order to address the challenges presented by digital markets, regulatory changes need to be made within competition law, yet above all by strengthening other fields of regulation such as privacy and media laws. Codes of conduct would be required from digital markets' players in order to demonstrate their awareness of and compliance with those rules.[49]

In the United Kingdom, a digital competition expert panel drafted a report[50] – the Furman report – that suggested solutions mainly outside the realm of competition law. The major recommendation of this Report has been to 'establish and resource a pro-competition digital markets unit, tasked with securing competition, innovation, and beneficial outcomes for consumers and businesses'. That unit, the Report continues, 'should work with industry and stakeholders to establish a digital platform code of conduct, based on a set of core principles. The code would apply to conduct by digital platforms that have been designated as having a strategic market status'.[51] Another important recommendation concluded that

> Merger assessment in digital markets needs a reset. The [Competition and Markets Authority] should take more frequent and firmer action to challenge mergers that could be detrimental to consumer welfare through reducing future levels of innovation and competition, supported by changes to legislation where necessary.[52]

[46] Stigler Center, 'Stigler Committee on Digital Platforms Final Report' (September 2019): www.chicagobooth.edu/research/stigler/news-and-media/committee-on-digital-platforms-final-report.

[47] ibid.

[48] Australian Competition and Consumer Commission, 'Digital Platforms Inquiry Final Report' (June 2019): www.accc.gov.au/system/files/Digital%20platforms%20inquiry%20-%20final%20report.pdf.

[49] ibid 254.

[50] Digital Competition Excerpt Panel, 'Unlocking digital competition' (the Furman Report) (March 2019):https://assets.publishing.service.gov.uk/government/uploads/system/uploads/attachment_data/file/785547/unlocking_digital_competition_furman_review_web.pdf.

[51] ibid 9.

[52] ibid 12.

The UK government has vowed to move forward in this direction,[53] which resulted in the UK Competition and Markets Authority (CMA) commencing a market study, of which an interim report was published in December 2019.[54] In 2021, the Digital Markets Unit commenced shadow operations, anticipating its full entry into force upon adoption of the digital markets regulatory framework in the near future.[55]

Within the EU, the German Monopolies Commission was among the first in Europe to address the competition law challenges for the digital economy in a 2015 Report,[56] which was followed by the 9th Amendment to the German Competition Act in 2017.[57] The Report and Amendment have been followed by the setting up of a Competition Law 4.0 Commission at the German federal level. That Commission published a 2019 Report on 'A new competition law framework for the digital economy'.[58] The Report set out how German and EU competition law could be modified so as to be made fit for the digital economy. Following its analysis, the Report formulates specific recommendations, varying from a modification of the Commission's market definition notice over cross-market (interoperability) principles to the adoption of a Regulation obliging dominant platforms to adopt codes of conduct.[59] The recommendations in this Report are inspired by the Furman Report, yet focus more on substantive competition law or policy modifications. From that point of view, the Report also particularly calls for more clarity on how merger control rules will be applied to digital economy concentrations.[60] On top of that, however, the Commission also called for a better streamlining of antitrust and other policy fields. In that regard, it recommends that the newly elected European Commission establish a

[53] See C Caffara, 'The UK's Other Big Experiment: Regulating Online Platforms?', *Voxeu Blog Review*, 6 January 2020: https://cepr.org/voxeu/blogs-and-reviews/uks-other-big-experiment-regulating-online-platforms.

[54] Competition and Markets Authority, 'Online Platforms and Digital Advertising' (December 2019): https://assets.publishing.service.gov.uk/media/5dfa0580ed915d0933009761/Interim_report.pdf.

[55] See in that regard, Press Release, 'New watchdog to boost online competition launches': www.gov.uk/government/news/new-watchdog-to-boost-online-competition-launches--3.

[56] See for the English version of the Report, Monopolkommission, 'Competition policy: the challenge of digital markets' (September 2015): www.monopolkommission.de/images/PDF/SG/s68_fulltext_eng.pdf.

[57] The amendment transposed Directive 2014/104/EU on private damages actions, yet also added some clarifications as to the criteria to be considered when defining markets in the digital sphere. The English translation of the amended Act can be found at: www.bundeskartellamt.de/SharedDocs/Publikation/EN/Others/GWB.pdf?__blob=publicationFile&v=6.

[58] The Report has been translated into English and is available at: Commission 'Competition Law 4.0', 'A new competition framework for the digital economy' (2019): www.bmwk.de/Redaktion/EN/Publikationen/Wirtschaft/a-new-competition-framework-for-the-digital-economy.pdf?__blob=publicationFile&v=3.

[59] ibid 6–7.

[60] ibid 7.

Digital Markets Board with the General Secretariat which should be responsible for permanent coordination and harmonisation of the various policy areas in the interest of an overarching and coherent European digital policy. In addition, the Report

> advocates the temporary establishment of a Digital Markets Transformation Agency at EU level in order to improve the networking of the supervisory structures. It should be tasked with collecting and processing information about market developments and technical developments, coordinating with a corresponding network of Member State institutions.[61]

The agency should support the competent authorities at EU level and the EU Digital Markets Board.[62]

In partial response to that report, the German legislator introduced a 10th amendment to its Competition Act (Gesetz gegen Wettbewerbeschränkungen or GWB) on 18 January 2021.[63] That amendment sought to make German competition law ready to tackle the three challenges raised by digitalisation. Section 19a of that Act makes it possible

> to intervene at an early stage in cases where competition is threatened by certain large digital companies. As a preventive measure the [German Competition Authority (Bundeskartellamt) can prohibit certain types of conduct by companies which, due to their strategic position and their resources, are of paramount significance for competition across markets. Such conduct includes eg the self-preferencing of a group's own services or impeding third companies from entering the market by processing data relevant for competition.[64]

In doing so, the Bundeskartellamt can impose remedies and require digital undertakings to behave in certain ways. Additionally, mergers that do not meet normal notification thresholds now have to be notified to the Bundeskartellsamt.[65] Regulation 1/2003 allows Member States to impose stricter requirements on unilateral behaviour than the ones contained in Article 102 TFEU, making the German amendment in principle compatible with the spirit of Article 3(2) of Regulation 1/2003. Initiatives such as the German one could therefore perfectly be replicated in other Member States as well. So far, however, other Member States have taken more of a 'wait and see' attitude in this regard.[66]

[61] ibid 5.

[62] ibid 7, 20–21.

[63] Competition Act of 26 June 2013 (as amended) (*Gesetz gegen Wettbewerbsbeschränkungen*).

[64] GWB, 'Amendment of the German Act against Restraints of Competition' (2021): www.bundeskartellamt.de/SharedDocs/Meldung/EN/Pressemitteilungen/2021/19_01_2021_GWB%20Novelle.html.

[65] *Gesetz gegen Wettebewerbeschränkungen*, Section 39a.

[66] As follows from the reports analysed in N Petit and P Van Cleynenbreugel, *EU Competition Law and the Digital Economy* (n 4 above) 32–33.

B. The Digital Markets Act (DMA): Stress-Testing EU Competition Law Enforcement?

At the EU level, the 2019 Special Advisers Report entitled 'Competition policy for the digital era'[67] seemed to have more faith in competition law as a tool to tackle the rise of online platforms as strong market players. According to the Report, the existing legal framework in place would be sufficient to govern digital markets for now, provided that the analytical tools, methodologies and theories of harm are modified better to fit market realities in order better to identify and constrain abuses of market power.[68] One of the ways to do so, according to the Report, is to reverse the burden of proof in relation to dominant digital economy players. Rather than asking the authorities to prove the anticompetitive nature of those players' behaviour, the Report proposes to allocate the burden to prove the pro-competitive effects of their behaviour. If implemented, this change would mean that absent proof of pro-competitive effects, the behaviour concerned would be considered anticompetitive and therefore prohibited, without this conclusion having to be substantiated by the European Commission.[69] Such reversal would directly have an impact on the Commission's enforcement mandate. At present, that mandate can be justified by the need for the Commission to be able to find facts. Reversing the burden of proof could no longer justify significant inspection and enforcement powers the Commission and some national competition authorities currently enjoy. The Report additionally reflects on imposing data interoperability as a remedy and on better streamlining competition law with other regulatory regimes. At the same time, the Report also contemplates that

> a regulatory regime may be needed in the longer run. In particular, competition law enforcement may be overburdened to deal with the implementation and oversight of interoperability mandates imposed on dominant players. However, [it does] not envision a new type of 'public utility regulation' to emerge for the digital economy. The risks associated with such a regime – rigidity, lack of flexibility, and risk of capture – are too high.[70]

However, despite the Report's conclusions, the European Commission in 2020 also proposed the foundations for a New Competition Tool (NCT). The tool was either to be focused on the finding of dominance or on a fresh analysis of market structures and could be limited to a specific sector or could be of cross-sector (horizontal) application.[71] Given its regulatory component, it would be based

[67] Commission, 'Competition policy for the digital era' (Special Advisers Report) (2019): https://ec.europa.eu/competition/publications/reports/kd0419345enn.pdf.
[68] ibid 15.
[69] ibid 51.
[70] Commission, Special Advisers Report (n 67 above) 131.
[71] See Commission, 'Single Market – new complementary tool to strengthen competition enforcement' (2020): www.ec.europa.eu/info/law/better-regulation/have-your-say/initiatives/12416-Single-Market-new-complementary-tool-to-str engthen-competition-enforcement_en.

partly on Article 114 TFEU, highlighting its impact beyond the scope of competition law. In the end, the choice was made to envisage an NCT only in the realm of digital markets, which resulted in the proposal for the DMA Regulation on 15 December 2020.[72] That proposal gave rise to the adoption of Regulation 2022/1925 in October 2022.[73] Although the DMA adds a layer of centralised supranational regulation, it also undermines to a certain extent the governance framework set up by Regulation 1/2003. That question will therefore undoubtedly require additional attention in future DMA operations.

i. The DMA's Regulatory Setup

The DMA applies only to undertakings having gatekeeper status.[74] The designation of an undertaking as a gatekeeper will be the prerogative of the European Commission following a market investigation. In order to qualify as such, substantive and quantitative criteria are proposed.[75]

The DMA subsequently outlines in considerable detail the behaviour that cannot be engaged in by gatekeepers. It first of all lists prohibitions applicable to all gatekeepers. Those prohibitions are directly inspired by types of behaviour of which businesses such as Google, Facebook and Amazon have been accused and for which EU competition law provisions had been mobilised.[76] By way of example, data drawn from core and non-core services cannot be combined, business users must be allowed to offer their services on different platforms, to promote their services through the platform and to have access to the aggregated data their activities generate, to name but a few requirements.[77]

In addition, the Regulation contains a list of obligations that can be specified and detailed further in each specific case by the European Commission. Among those obligations figure the requirements for gatekeepers to refrain inter alia from requiring businesses to use their supplementary services, rank their own services over similar services offered by business users and from making interoperability

[72] Proposal for a Regulation of the European Parliament and of the Council on contestable and fair markets in the digital sector (DMA Proposal) COM(2020) 842 final.

[73] Regulation (EU) 2022/1925 of the European Parliament and of the Council of 14 September 2022 on contestable and fair markets in the digital sector and amending Directives (EU) 2019/1937 and (EU) 2020/1828 (DMA) [2022] OJ L265/1. See also M Ioannidou, 'Unpacking Multilevel Elements in Digital Markets: Informing Effective Enforcement and Remedial Design in EU Competition Law', Ch 11 in this volume.

[74] DMA (n 73 above) Art 1(6). According to Art 1(3), the Regulation does not apply to electronic communications network markets and non-interpersonal communication services offered on such markets.

[75] DMA (n 73 above) Arts 1–4; see D Geradin, 'What is a digital gatekeeper? Which platforms should be captured by the EC proposal for a Digital Markets Act?' (*Tilburg Law and Economics Center 18/2021*).

[76] See for that argument, C Caffarra and F Scott Morton, 'The European Commission Digital Markets Act: a Translation' (2021): www.cepr.org/voxeu/columns/european-commission-digital-markets-act-translation.

[77] DMA (n 73 above) Art 5.

between different platform services providers impossible.[78] Again, that list is directly inspired by current business practices engaged in by Google, Facebook and others. Service providers have to organise an independent audit confirming their compliance with those obligations vis-à-vis their consumers.[79] The European Commission could, by means of a delegated Regulation, modify or update those obligations and requirements.[80] To the extent that those gatekeepers do not comply with those requirements,[81] the Commission can impose sanctions or remedies on them.

The Commission also has to be informed of any concentrations (mergers, acquisitions, creation of joint ventures) gatekeepers plan to engage in with another core online platform services provider or any other business providing any kind of information society services, even when such a transaction would not have a 'Community dimension' under Merger Control Regulation 139/2004.[82] Failure to respect regulatory obligations can result in a non-compliance decision and accompanying sanctions adopted by the College of Commissioners. The procedure outlined in the DMA essentially resembles the one applicable in Article 101 and 102 enforcement procedures.[83]

A non-compliance decision requires the gatekeeper to cease and desist the non-compliance within an appropriate deadline and to provide explanations on how it plans to comply with the decision. That decision can be accompanied by a fine of up to 10 per cent of the global turnover in the previous financial year of the core online platform service provider concerned. Periodic penalty payments of up to 5 per cent of the average daily turnover in the previous year can also be imposed in order to ensure swifter compliance with the decisions taken.[84] Those sanctions are essentially inspired by the framework the Commission applies in relation to Articles 101 and 102 TFEU.

Additionally, the Commission would be able to go so far as to break up existing undertakings in cases of systemic non-compliance by ordering so-called structural remedies. Systematic non-compliance refers to a situation in which the Commission has issued at least three non-compliance or fining decisions against a gatekeeper in relation to any of its core platform services within a period of five years prior to the adoption of the decision opening a market investigation.[85]

[78] ibid Art 6(5).

[79] ibid Art 15.

[80] ibid Art 12.

[81] ibid Art 8. Temporary suspensions or non-applications of requirements are possible in exceptional circumstances, see Arts 9–10 DMA.

[82] ibid Art 14(1). See for that dimension, Council Regulation (EC) No 139/2004 (n 16 above) Art 1(2).

[83] As argued also by P Van Cleynenbreugel, 'Digital Markets Act: Beware of Procedural Fairness and Judicial Review Booby-Traps!', *European Law Blog*, 24 June 2021: https://europeanlawblog.eu/2021/06/24/digital-markets-act-beware-of-procedural-fairness-and-judicial-review-booby-traps/.

[84] DMA (n 73 above) Arts 29–31.

[85] ibid Recital 75.

Commission decisions will be preceded by a right of access to the file and the right to be heard.[86] Once adopted, they would be reviewable acts before the Court of Justice of the European Union (CJEU) in accordance with Article 263 TFEU. The DMA additionally confirms that, in accordance with Article 261 TFEU, the CJEU has unlimited jurisdiction to review decisions by which the Commission has imposed fines or periodic penalty payments. It may cancel, reduce or increase the fine or periodic penalty payment imposed.[87]

ii. A Stress Test for EU Competition Law and its Governance?

The supranational regulatory framework set up by the DMA has been marketed as an instrument complementary to and different from the existing EU competition law enforcement framework. At the same time, however, little attention has been paid to the envisaged interactions between (national) competition law enforcement and the Commission's DMA powers.

For its part, the DMA contains important building blocks for a truly supranational ex ante market regulation framework. Without having to prove the existence of a dominant position or of restrictive anticompetitive harm, the European Commission would be able to prohibit types of behaviour considered to be or leading to anticompetitive practices when a provider is considered a gatekeeper. Although the DMA would pursue a laudable cause, its approach is prone to criticism. The obligations it imposes have been inspired by ongoing or closed competition law investigations and market practices that have shown to be problematic in the past. However, it cannot be excluded that in a rapidly evolving market environment, other practices will soon become more problematic. Legitimate questions can therefore be raised about the future-proof nature of those obligations.[88] Gatekeeper status is evaluated and reviewed every two years. It can nevertheless be questioned whether this review mechanism would be sufficiently flexible.[89] The Regulation also does contain the possibility for the Commission to modify the gatekeeper designation methodologies and regulatory obligations by means of delegated acts.[90] That instrument allows for flexible modifications but raises questions as to whether those choices can effectively be held to account.[91]

In addition, the competition law enforcement framework, which is governed by Regulation 1/2003, obliges national competition authorities to apply Articles 101 and 102 TFEU – if necessary, in parallel with their national competition

[86] ibid Art 34.

[87] ibid Art 45.

[88] Caffarra and Scott Morton, 'The Digital Markets Act' (n 76 above).

[89] A de Streel and others, 'The European Proposal for a Digital Markets Act: A First Assessment' (*CERRE Report 2021*) 27.

[90] DMA (n 73 above) Art 12.

[91] See in that regard among others, M Chamon, 'Limits to Delegation Under Article 290 TFEU: The Specificity and Essentiality Requirements Put to the Test' (2021) 25 *Maastricht Journal of European and Comparative Law* 231.

laws – whenever market behaviour affects interstate trade, remains in place. In that context, Regulation 1/2003 determines that national authorities cannot prohibit what is not prohibited under EU law, with the exception of certain kinds of unilateral behaviour. As the German example shows, nothing would impede Member States restricting such unilateral behaviour in a more ex ante way than traditional competition law rules generally do. Within that framework, structural or behavioural remedies could be imposed on undertakings once it has been determined they have engaged in unlawful behaviour.[92] Although Regulation 1/2003 does not state so explicitly, those remedies could theoretically consist in breaking up dominant undertakings or obliging those undertakings to make good any harm inflicted.[93]

As such, the remedial framework in place in EU competition law strongly resembles the remedies the DMA allows for. The major difference is nevertheless the fact that a certain kind of anticompetitive and therefore illegal behaviour needs to have taken place prior to allowing a remedy to be imposed. In the DMA framework, persistent failure to comply with ex ante regulatory standards is in itself illegal (absent any specific indication as to its anticompetitive nature) and may result in sanctions.

An additional important distinction between both frameworks concerns the involvement of national authorities. Within the framework set up in competition law, national competition authorities retain competences to apply national competition laws. The European Competition Network (ECN) ensures that enforcement remains somewhat coordinated and ensures the informal discussion of case allocation decisions. The original proposal contained no similar references to national competition authorities. Regulation 2022/1925 nevertheless explicitly highlights the role of the ECN as a means for information exchange and cooperation with regard to gatekeepers as well.[94] Despite the introduction of similar cooperation and coordination measures, the fact remains that, under the regime set up by Regulation 1/2003, national competition law may still target unilateral behaviour by undertakings, resulting in similar ex ante obligations as part and parcel of national competition law regimes. The DMA leaves those rules unaffected.[95]

A potential practical problem that remains in this regard concerns ne bis in idem. It is well-known that the same person cannot be tried and/or punished twice for the same offence. This principle, which has been enshrined explicitly in

[92] Council Regulation 1/2003 (n 18 above) Art 7(1). That provision confirms that the Commission may impose on undertakings any behavioural or structural remedies which are proportionate to the infringement committed and necessary to bring the infringement effectively to an end. However, structural remedies can only be imposed either where there is no equally effective behavioural remedy or where any equally effective behavioural remedy would be more burdensome for the undertaking concerned than the structural remedy.

[93] On EU competition law remedies, see C Ritter, 'How Far Can the Commission Go When Imposing Remedies for Antitrust Infringements?' (2016) 7 *Journal of European Competition Law & Practice* 587.

[94] DMA (n 73 above) Arts 37–39.

[95] ibid Art 1(6)(b).

Article 50 of the EU Charter of Fundamental Rights (CFR), has nevertheless been interpreted not to exclude complementary and distinct enforcement proceedings, particularly in the context of regulatory and competition law enforcement procedures.[96] In such a scenario, two sets of rules would need to protect two different objectives of general interest and contain coordination mechanisms in order to avoid that excessive sanctions are imposed.[97] The DMA has most directly taken this case law into account. Per its recitals, it aims to protect a different legal interest from that protected by competition law rules and it should apply without prejudice to their application.[98] In addition, to avoid overlaps and conflicts, the Commission and national authorities should work 'in close cooperation and coordinate their enforcement actions to ensure coherent, effective and complementary enforcement of available legal instruments applied to gatekeepers'.[99] It is clear that, through less formal network governance mechanisms, the Commission hopes to guarantee that EU and national enforcement complement, rather than overlap with, each other. Questions can nevertheless be raised as to whether DMA and national competition law procedures would serve sufficiently distinct general interest objectives to be considered complementary in nature.[100] The exact extent to which two different types of enforcement are truly complementary remains to be seen. One could imagine the hypothetical situation where the German Bundeskartellamt uses its new powers to impose sanctions on a digital market player, prior to the European Commission applying the DMA in that context. It can be asked whether those sanctions are really of a different nature and complementary, rather than overlapping. It is likely that in such a situation, the CJEU will have to determine the bis in idem nature of both procedures. To the extent that this is the case, the Commission would not be able to proceed with its procedure or, alternatively, that the German initiatives would be considered contrary to the DMA, resulting in Germany having to repair the situation and potentially being held liable for breach of EU law. In either of those situations, the at first sight complementary role of national and DMA enforcement practices risks directly to give rise to frictions and stress in the existing EU competition law enforcement system. At present, it is therefore not entirely clear whether both competition law and DMA enforcement can co-exist as peacefully as the European Commission and the DMA recitals seem to maintain. It indeed remains to be seen how the DMA and national competition law enforcement will play out in practice. In that context, it seems almost inevitable that the Court will have to intervene – when asked to do so – to resolve those issues.

[96] Case C-117/20 *BPost SA v Autorité belge de la concurrence* [2022] EU:C:2022:202, paras 41–49.

[97] P van Cleynenbreugel, '*BPost* and *Nordzucker*: Searching for the Essence of ne bis in idem in EU Law' (2022) 18 *European Constitutional Law Review* 367.

[98] DMA (n 73 above) Recital 11.

[99] ibid Art 37.

[100] That question is assessed on a case-by-case basis, see CJEU, Case C-117/20 *BPost SA v Autorité belge de la concurrence* (n 96 above), paras 50–54.

V. Conclusions

This chapter identified the key challenges underlying the application of EU competition law in the digital economy. Although competition authorities have applied Articles 101 and 102 TFEU as well as Regulation 139/2004 to digital markets, that application is not without structural, behavioural and foundational challenges. In response to those challenges, calls for complementary regulation have been made successfully. As a result, German competition law has granted the Bundeskartellamt more enforcement tools against digital undertakings. In the same way, the European Commission is in the process of setting up a complementary ex ante supranational regulatory framework by virtue of its DMA.

The chapter argued that digital technology disruptions may put stress on the EU competition law governance framework and the relatively clear division of competences underlying it as set up principally by Regulation 1/2003 in four ways. First, digital disruptions have resulted in tailored substantive competition in some Member States such as Germany. The adoption of such rules, although tolerated by Regulation 1/2003, risks endangering the coherent and legally certain application of EU competition law originally envisaged by that very same Regulation. Second, digital technologies have generated problems in terms of proving anti-competitive conduct. For that reason, the proposal to reverse the burden of proof in competition law investigations has been made. Should that proposal become law, it would fundamentally alter one of the foundations upon which competition law enforcement powers have been based. At this stage, it remains to be seen whether those proposals will ever materialise. Third, the adoption of complementary supranational regulation by means of the DMA brings about coherence and legal certainty challenges within EU law as well. Although the Commission goes beyond the ambit of traditional competition law with its DMA and considers the latter to be complementary to the former, there remains a clear potential overlap between the two. It will have to be determined in practice how both regimes will interact in practice and whether this will give rise to sector-specific competition law governance frameworks. That is all the more the case should similar additional regulations be envisaged in other sectors as well. Fourth, the parallel extension of national competition authorities' powers in tackling unilateral behaviour and the Commission's DMA powers are also likely to bring about fresh governance questions about how the division of tasks implicitly underlying EU competition law enforcement is to be refined in the digital context. The boundaries between EU regulation and (national) competition law enforcement and the role of EU law general principles such as ne bis in idem in that context will have to be to be further stress-tested in the case law of the Court of Justice. Although that is not necessarily problematic, it shows that the complementary nature of digital regulation and competition law remains to be fine-tuned in practice.

3

A Clash of Titans: EU Competition and State Aid Law and the Impact of the European Green Deal

ALICJA SIKORA*

I. Introduction

> Regulatory measures should be taken when competition law cannot achieve the results that are needed, or when the results of using competition law would be too uncertain or would take too long to obtain. If competition can achieve the desired results, then it should be allowed to do so.[1]

The purpose of this chapter is to highlight selected constitutional aspects pertaining to the mutual interaction between the European Union's (EU) competition policies and its environmental policies, in particular, following adoption of the European Green Deal (EGD),[2] which is meant to be a core instrument for recalibrating the EU's economic model. Against the background of the economic genesis of European integration[3] and the 'constitutional absorption' of environmental protection in the EU's legal order,[4] the chapter explores current challenges surrounding various scenarios of complementarity and tension arising between,

* Senior Lecturer, Faculty of Law, Jagiellonian University; Legal Adviser to the Council of the European Union and the European Council, alicja.1.sikora@uj.edu.pl. All views expressed are those of the author, not of the Council or the Council of the European Union.

[1] This chapter is dedicated to the late John Temple Lang, a friend. In 2006, in his article 'Some Background to Sven Norberg Negotiations' in M Johansson, N Wahl and U Bertnitz (eds), *A European for all Seasons. Liber Amicorum in Honour of Sven Norberg* (Brussels, Bruylant, 2006), John Temple Lang concluded *en hommage* with Samuel Johnson's tribute to Oliver Goldsmith '*Tetigit nihil quod non adornavit*'. John Temple Lang equally touched nothing which he did not adorn. Quotation by J Temple Lang, 'Competition Law and Regulation Law from an EC Perspective' (1999) 23 *Fordham Journal of International Law* 116, 117.

[2] Commission, 'The European Green Deal' (Communication) COM(2019) 640 final.

[3] P Demaret, 'The Treaty Framework' in D O'Keeffe and P Twomey (eds), *Legal Issues of the Maastricht Treaty* (Chichester, Wiley Chancery, 1994).

[4] A Sikora, *Constitutionalisation of Environmental Protection in EU Law* (Zutphen, Europa Law Publishing, 2020).

on the one hand, EU competition and state aid law, which is perceived as a sanctuary of the EU's economic model, and on the other hand, environmental considerations, which constitute the inevitable course of development of the EU's constitutional dimension. Indeed, while EU competition law instruments certainly have the potential to support the EU's objective of sustainability and evolution towards climate neutrality by 2050, the present analysis questions the extent that EU competition and state aid law and policy are open to the inclusion of environmental and sustainability goals, in particular insofar as their systemic model is at stake.

The remainder of this chapter is organised as follows. Section II introduces selected aspects of EU competition and state aid law that fall within the reach of environmental considerations. Section III focuses on the EGD as a novel regulatory approach which is also relevant from the constitutional perspective, including the perspective of civic rights and environmental democracy. This section discusses how the EGD has thus far affected competition and state aid law, albeit without triggering major shifts in the existing instruments. In the absence of systemic solutions, reliance on green transition tools, such as the EU taxonomy and the 'do no significant harm' principle, emblematic of other areas of EU economic law, might constitute adequate instruments of environmental recalibration in the area of competition and state aid law. This is the subject of Section IV. Section V concludes the analysis, calling for a prudent reassessment of the relationship between the EU's economic genetic code and its evolving environmental constitutional dimension.

II. EU Competition and State Aid Law within the Reach of Environmental Considerations

From the outset, the EU legal order has been grounded in the economic rationale of the internal market. One of the perennial questions to be asked when assessing the evolution of the EU legal order is what a treaty is trying to achieve[5] beyond the internal market. Such a question implies reading the objectives of the Union in a historical perspective while capturing them through the lenses of the economic, political and legal challenges of a given momentum, such momentum being nowadays the global threat of climate change. While the Treaty of Rome sought to create the common market, a major boost for this economic union being the creation of the single market as of 1993,[6] it has become gradually apparent that major tensions driving the evolution of EU law oscillate between an economic and a

[5] M Demetriou and A Higgins, 'Free Movement and the Environment: Seeing the Wood for the Trees' in M Hoskins and W Robinson (eds), *A True European Essays for Judge David Edward* (Oxford, Hart Publishing, 2004).

[6] D Bailey, 'Competition Law and Policy in the EU' in D Bailey and LE John (eds), *European Union Law of Competition* 8th edn, (Oxford, Oxford University Press, 2019).

socio-environmental dimension.[7] Following the Lisbon Treaty, under Article 3(3) of the Treaty on European Union (TEU), the Union is to both establish an internal market and work for the sustainable development of Europe based on balanced economic growth and notably high-level protection and improvement of the quality of the environment. The Union is equally determined to combat social exclusion and discrimination, to promote economic and social cohesion, and to foster solidarity among the Member States. Unavoidable tensions and conflicts between these various objectives reveal natural steps of legal evolution, in particular, in the context of an autonomous legal order of such scope, ambition and complexity as EU law. The central question therefore is not how to avoid clashes and tensions, but how to resolve them.[8] This conclusion equally applies to the inevitable tensions between competition law and other public interest considerations.

While the objectives of the Union as set out in Article 3(3) TEU have equal status,[9] environmental pre-eminence has nevertheless occasionally been voiced in the context of balancing freedoms within the single market, including by reference to Article 11 of the Treaty on the Functioning of the European Union (TFEU).[10] It is, however, common knowledge that the positive environmental integration duty, as upgraded by the Maastricht Treaty,[11] although considered initially as 'unique amongst other policies' and liable to herald environmental prioritisation over other areas of the Union's law and policy,[12] has not led to an environmental revolution within the EU legal order. Rather, as rightly noted by some commentators,[13] 'proliferation of integration duties'[14] has weakened the concept as such, excluding for many years any attempt to consider environmental protection as being given 'unique and distinctive legal status in the scheme of the Treaty'.[15] Whereas in many fields of EU law, integration of environmental requirements has meaningfully reshaped the EU regulatory framework,[16] one of the most telling illustrations being public procurement, the principle of integration under Article 11 TFEU has

[7] Demetriou and Higgins, 'Free Movement and the Environment' (n 5 above).

[8] A Keessen, A Freriks and M van Rijswick, 'The Clash of the Titans: The Relation Between the European Water and Medicines Legislation' (2010) 47 *Common Market Law Review* 1429.

[9] M Klamert, 'Article 3 TEU' in M Kellerbauer, M Klamert and J Tomkin (eds), *The EU Treaties and the Charter of Fundamental Rights* (Oxford, Oxford University Press, 2019).

[10] See Opinion of Advocate General Bot in case C-204/12 *Essent Belgium v Vlaamse Reguleringsinstantie voor de Elektriciteit* [2013] EU:C:2013:294, paras 95–96.

[11] M Hession and R Macrory, 'Maastricht and the Environmental Policy of the Community. Legal Issues of a New Environment Policy' in D O'Keeffe and P Twomey (eds), *Legal Issues of the Maastricht Treaty* (Chichester, Wiley Chancery, 1994).

[12] DH Scheuing, 'Umweltschutz auf der Grundlage der Einheitlichen Akte' (1989) 2 *Europarecht* 152, quoted after S Bar and R Kramer, 'European Environmental Policy after Amsterdam' (1998) 10 *Journal of Environmental Law* 315.

[13] R Macrory, 'The Amsterdam Treaty: An Environmental Perspective' in D O'Keeffe and P Twomey (eds), *Legal Issues of the Maastricht Treaty* (Chichester, Wiley Chancery, 1994). JH Jans, 'Stop the Integration Principle?' (2011) 33 *Fordham International Law Journal* 1533.

[14] Macrory, 'The Amsterdam Treaty' (n 13 above).

[15] ibid.

[16] N Dhondt, *Integration of the Environmental Protection into Other EU Policies. Theory and Practice* (Groningen, Europa Law Publishing, 2003).

not reached an overarching constitutional status, neither has it been successfully relied upon as a yardstick of legality of internal market measures before the EU courts.[17]

Against this background, EU competition and state aid law and policies, as such, are rightly considered as not being 'special'.[18] EU competition and state aid law have been within the reach of environmental considerations for a long time. Phenomena of greening EU competition and state aid law have been largely addressed in EU legal doctrine,[19] debated at the institutional level[20] and reflected in the practice of the European Commission, with the notable exception of Article 102 TFEU (whose parameters and 'their interrelation with environmental protection factors' have constituted relatively 'uncharted territory' for many years).[21] Integration of environmental and social goals into the economic disciplines has inevitably taken place. In state aid law, a notable example is the progress of the environmental state aid guidelines under Article 107(3) TFEU. In the area of antitrust, this is illustrated by the assessment of 'sustainability agreements' against Article 101(3) TFEU, although marked by a certain lack of coherence between the practice of the European Commission, the case law of the EU courts and the decisions of the national authorities.[22] Furthermore, reliance on general principles of EU law, in particular where the proportionality assessment is conducted, is considered as having potential to enhance the relevance of environmental considerations in the area of Articles 101 and 102 TFEU.[23] By the same token, authors suggest reliance on purely environmental principles, such as 'the polluter pays', to be activated in the assessment of anticompetitive behaviour, notably under Article 101(3) TFEU.[24] Finally, proposals for a new, green competition law have been formulated by some EU law scholars.[25]

[17] The possible enforceability of the principle of integration might be clarified in the context of the still-pending mobility package cases. See Transport Ministers of nine Member States, 'Member States take action before EU Court against First Mobility Package', *EURACTIV*, 28 October 2020: www.euractiv.com/section/economy-jobs/opinion/member-states-take-action-before-eu-court-against-first-mobility-package/.

[18] S Kingston, 'Integrating Environmental Protection and EU Competition Law: Why Competition Isn't Special' (2012) 16 *European Law Journal* 780.

[19] S Kingston, *Greening the EU Competition Law and Policy* (Cambridge, Cambridge University Press, 2011); J Nowag, *Environmental Integration in Competition and Free-Movement Laws* (Oxford, Oxford University Press, 2016).

[20] Council and European Parliament Resolution on Environmental Agreements of 17 July 1997 [1997] OJ C286/254; Council Resolution of 7 October 1997 on Environmental Agreements [1997] OJ C321/6.

[21] Kingston, *Greening the EU Competition Law* (n 19 above) 294.

[22] O Brook, 'Struggling with Article 101(3) TFEU: Diverging Approaches of the Commission, EU Courts and Five Competition Authorities' (2019) 56 *Common Market Law Review* 121.

[23] M Hjärtström and J Nowag, 'General Principles of EU Law in EU Antitrust; for the General Role of Environmental Requirements' in KS Ziegler, PJ Neuvonen and V Moreno-Lax, *Research Handbook on General Principles of EU Law* (Cheltenham, Edward Elgar Publishing, 2022).

[24] M Dolmans, 'Sustainable Competition Policy and the "Polluter Pays" Principle' in S Holmes, D Middelschulte and M Snoep (eds), *Competition Law, Climate Change and Environmental Sustainability* (Paris, Concurrences, 2021).

[25] G Monti, 'Four Options for a Greener Competition Law' (2020) 11 *Journal of European Competition Law and Practise* 124.

Notwithstanding the step-by-step nature of environmental integration, competition and state aid law has kept its distance at the systemic level as a self-contained, treaty-shaped regime. Whilst it is true that discussion on assessing the impact of non-economic policy factors in the competition field is not new,[26] an orthodox approach driven by purely economic factors rationale,[27] particularly tangible in the field of Article 102 TFEU,[28] has been continuously advocated. Likewise, even in the field of EU state aid policy, where environmental protection and sustainability considerations have been welcome and successfully applied for the purpose of the green transition, the judgment of 22 September 2020 in the case *Austria v Commission* (hereinafter *Hinkley Point*)[29] does not make the environmental objectives and principles bite enough in the context of the state aid compatibility assessment. It is true that the court recalled that state aid which contravenes provisions or general principles of EU law cannot be declared compatible with the internal market.[30] The court thus specified in the *Hinkley Point* judgment that since Article 107(3)(c) TFEU applies to state aid in the nuclear energy sector covered by the Euratom Treaty, state aid for an economic activity falling within that sector and shown upon examination to contravene EU environmental rules cannot be declared compatible with the internal market.[31] Some commentators find that in *Hinkley Point* the court empowered the Commission 'to effectively decide on breaches of EU law in general while relying on the procedure provided for state aid', thereby undermining an institutional balance in relation to Article 258 TFEU in particular.[32] Others suggest a more moderate appraisal of the consequences of this ruling.[33]

From a systemic point of view, there are however notable points of tangency between EU competition and environmental policies. Such tangency both illustrates the constitutive nature of economic and environmental policies for the EU internal market and expounds potential difficulties in their reciprocal permeability.

[26] C Townley, *Article 81 and Public Policy* (Oxford, Oxford Hart Publishing, 2009); Monti, 'Four Options' (n 25 above).

[27] L Peeperkorn, 'European Union' in S Holmes, D Middelschulte and M Snoep (eds), *Competition Law, Climate Change and Environmental Sustainability* (Paris, Concurrences, 2021).

[28] MC Iacovides and C Vrettos, 'Falling Through the Cracks No More? Article 102 TFEU and Sustainability: The Relation Between Dominance, Environmental Degradation, and Social Injustice' (2022) 10 *Journal of Antitrust Enforcement* 32; V Mauboussin, 'Environmental Defences as a Shield from Article 102 TFEU' (2022) 30 *Concurrences* 33.

[29] Case C-594/18 P *Austria v Commission* [2020] EU:C:2020:742. See P Nicolaides, 'The Response of EU Courts to Society's Digital and Green Challenges in the Field of Competition and State aid', Ch 8 in this volume, and CM Colombo and M Bonelli, 'Governing the Green Transition Through State Aid Control', Ch 12 in this volume.

[30] Case C-390/06 *Nuova Agricast Srl v Ministero delle Attivita Produttive* [2008] EU:C:2008:224, paras 50–51.

[31] Case C-594/18 P *Austria v Commission* (n 29 above) paras 44–45.

[32] O Stefan, 'General Principles in EU State Aid Law' in KS Ziegler and others (eds), *Research Handbook on General Principles of EU Law* (Cheltenham, Edward Elgar Publishing, 2022).

[33] L Hancher and A Bouchagiar, 'Hinkley Point C: Trimming the SAM, While Extending the Reach of Wider EU Law Infringements?' (2021) 20 *European State Aid Law Quarterly* 529.

In its classic understanding, EU competition law consists of 'legal rules that are intended to protect the process of competition, so that goods are sold at competitive prices and the consumers have a choice as to goods and services they wish to purchase'.[34] The objective of EU competition law, albeit not without controversies in the legal doctrine, is traditionally encapsulated as enhancement of consumer welfare.[35] As suggested in the literature, where environmental protection and competition coincide and, thus, where 'conflicts between market and environment could be resolved' is 'by the build-up of market power' and 'fair share' of the benefits given to the consumers in order to compensate for the anticompetitive effects of an agreement under Article 101 TFEU.[36] In this context, it is worth noting that EU competition law itself contains an internal balancing component, aiming at reconciling 'public policy interests' and economic interests.[37] Thus, greening EU competition and state aid law and policy in a traditional sense based on the principle of integration under Article 11 TFEU implies another level of reconciliation and (re)consideration of multiple, horizontal consequences and policy choices. As noted however in the legal doctrine, what distinguishes EU competition law from other legal systems worldwide is 'the single market imperative', with Articles 101 and 102 TFEU relied upon to prevent any action meant to compartmentalise the single market.[38] While the economics of market power and the high accord given to environmental protection express distinct objectives in the meaning of the treaty, they share awareness that 'resources in the world are limited, but demand for them is not'.[39] Indeed, as confirmed in case law, EU competition law is driven by market integration considerations.[40] From this angle, both EU competition law and environmental protection objectives contribute to the single market consolidation, albeit in different ways. Competition focuses on open and fair markets and economic growth, but is limited to dealing with anticompetitive behaviour.[41] Thus, the primary effect of competition law is 'to enhance the competitive environment in product markets by constraining the illegal exercise of market power'.[42] Assessing compatibility of state aid implies in particular 'separating good from

[34] Bailey, 'Competition Law and Policy in the EU' (n 6 above).

[35] Kingston, *Greening the EU Competition Law* (n 19 above) 9 and references to the legal doctrine.

[36] MP Schinkel and L Treuren, 'Green Antitrust: Friendly Fire in the Fight Against Climate Change', *Competition Policy International*, 22 December 2020: www.competitionpolicyinternational.com/green-antitrust-friendly-fire-in-the-fight-against-climate-change/.

[37] O Brook, 'Priority Setting as A Double-Edged Sword: How Modernization Strengthened the Role of Public Policy' (2020) 16 *Journal of Competition Law and Economics* 435, 444.

[38] R Whish, 'EU Competition Policy and the Single Market Imperative' in F Amtenbrink and others (eds), *The Internal Market and the Future of European Integration, Essays in Honour of Laurence W Gormley* (Cambridge, Cambridge University Press, 2019).

[39] V Korah, *EC Competition Law and Practice* (Oxford, Hart Publishing, 2004) 9.

[40] Case 56/64 *Consten and Grundig v Commission* [1966] EU:C:1966:41, para 340.

[41] A Zac, 'Competition Law and Economic Inequality: A Comparative Analysis of the US Model of Law' (2022) 25 *Journal of International Economic Law* 484, 485.

[42] Temple Lang, 'Competition Law and Regulation Law' (n 1 above).

bad aid' from the point of view of the internal market balance.[43] Environmental protection, for its part, permeates the whole of the EU's regulatory framework with non-economic building blocks, gradually modifying the Union's economic rationale and its growth strategy. Going beyond regulatory measures, sustainability and environmental protection considerations equally trigger tangible behavioural change among market participants and thus affect the way in which the modern consolidation of the internal market takes place.

III. The Union's Turning Point: The EGD and 'Environmental Pressure' within the EU Legal Order

While discussing the relationship between the economy and the environment in a world conscious of the global threat of climate change, one could recall the Stern Review's definition of climate change as 'the greatest market failure the world has ever seen'.[44] Mapping the mutual relationship between the consequences of the EGD and the EU's competition and state aid model entails a new chapter, enabling environmental benefits to be admitted into the analysis pertaining to the economic realm. Such an analysis must build on an awareness of the scale of the challenge to be discussed. On the one hand, the EGD's ambition equates with its all-economy scope and momentum, coupled with the global climate change emergency. On the other hand, EU competition rules, which unlike other treaty provisions, have remained by and large unchanged since the conclusion of the founding treaties,[45] are of systemic and constitutional relevance for the Union's legal order.[46] Their relationship may be considered the Titanomachy between two constitutional dimensions of EU law: one growing, overwhelming and irreversible, and the other a landmark, existing since the beginning and symbolising a model of the Union's economic integration.

The EGD is indeed a different animal, a novelty. Encapsulating a real soft law (r)evolution,[47] this policy of the European Commission is not primarily about striking a right balance between colliding objectives amid constitutional conversations. Rather,

[43] A Nowak-Salles, 'Minimisation of the Expected Cost of Error in EU State Aid Enforcement' (*PhD Thesis, European University Institute, 2020*) 359–69.

[44] N Stern, *The Economics of Climate Change: The Stern Review* (Cambridge, Cambridge University Press 2007) 27.

[45] JL Buendia Sierra, 'Writing Straight with Crooked Lines: Competition Policy and Services of General Economic Interest in the Treaty of Lisbon' in A Biondi, S Ripley and P Eeckhout (eds), *EU Law after Lisbon* (Oxford, Oxford University Press, 2012).

[46] L Flynn, 'Competition Policy and Public Services in EC Law after the Maastricht and Amsterdam Treaties' in D O'Keeffe and P Twomey (eds), *Legal Issues of the Amsterdam Treaty* (London, Bloomsbury Publishing, 1999).

[47] A Sikora, 'European Green Deal – Legal and Financial Challenges of the Climate Change' (2021) 21 *ERA Forum* 681; more broadly, see I Maher, 'Revisiting Soft Law: Governance, Regulation and

given the overwhelming, uncontested global threat of climate change, it presupposes an environmentally oriented qualitative and quantitative reconsideration of the Union's economic rationale. It responds therefore in a holistic way to the uncontested scientific evidence according to which 'climate change is a serious global threat, and it demands an urgent global response'.[48] Indisputably, the EGD expresses an environmental and sustainability policy credo of the Union of unprecedented scope. Yet, the EGD is a signal enabling a change, not a change in itself. Whereas the EGD has already triggered a massive legislative reform, the question of coherence and multidimensional consequences of its follow-up for the internal market remain to be seen.[49]

The EGD has also contributed to constitutional change at the level of the Union. In recent years, the overarching concept of high-level environmental protection and improvement of the quality of the environment, as enshrined in Article 3(3) TEU, Article 191(2) TFEU and Article 37 of the Charter of Fundamental Rights (CFR), has been construed and elevated to a transversal concept with a constitutional dimension.[50] Furthermore, following the rise of economic, political and legal consciousness of climate change, environmental protection has become a component of a specific 'constitutional consensus'[51] at the level of the EU Member States, and a meaningful factor of the EU 'environmental democracy', a novel element of the ecological EU citizenship.[52] Environmental protection and climate protection are thus nowadays discussed in the Union from the angle of climate justice, fundamental rights[53] and an intergenerational perspective of the common good.[54] A new reading of the EU treaties may reveal that the Union, as a community of states and citizens, has entered a new phase of its evolution wherein environmentally driven choices amount to 'extraordinary moments of intense constitutional deliberation and participation'.[55] The constitutional dimension of environmental

Networks' in M Eliantonio, E Korkea-aho and O Stefan (eds), *EU Soft Law in the Member States* (Oxford, Hart Publishing, 2021).

[48] Stern, *The Stern Review* (n 44 above).

[49] E Chiti, 'Managing the Ecological Transition of the EU: The European Green Deal as a Regulatory Process' (2022) 59 *Common Market Law Review* 19.

[50] D Missonne, 'The Court of Justice of the European Union and the High Level of Environmental Protection: Transforming a Policy Objective into a Concept Amenable to Judicial Review' in C Voigt (eds), *International Judicial Practice on the Environment* (Cambridge, Cambridge University Press, 2019). See Case C-444/15 *Associazione Italia Nostra Onlus v Comune di Venezia and Others*, Opinion of Advocate General Kokott [2016] EU:C:2016:665, paras 24–25.

[51] R O'Gorman, 'The Case of Enshrining a Right to Environment Within EU Law' (2013) 19 *European Public Law* 583; more specifically about the consolidation of the EU constitutional heritage, V Constantinesco, 'A la recherché du 'Patrimoine constitutionnel européen' in B Bertrand, F Picos, and S Roland (eds), *Identité du droit de l'Union européenne* (Brussels, Bruylant, 2015).

[52] Sikora, 'Constitutionalisation of Environmental Protection in EU Law' (n 4 above) 62–68. See also, European Citizen's Initiatives of environmental dimension: www.europa.eu/citizens-initiative/_en.

[53] Case T-330/18 *Carvalho and Others v Parliament and Council* [2019] EU:T:2019:324 and Case C-565/19 *P Carvalho and Others v Parliament and Council* [2021] EU:C:2021:252.

[54] U von der Leyen, 'State of the Union' (Strasbourg, 14 September 2022).

[55] MW McConnell, 'The Forgotten Constitutional Moment, Constitutional Commentary' (1994) 11 *Constitutional Commentary* 115.

protection in EU law equates with a reinterpretation of the economic objectives of the Union and transformation of the Union's primary economic law tools, such as competition and state aid law.

Despite its vocation and ambition, the EGD does not address the core of EU economic law as established by the treaties, but focuses on legislative changes.[56] Not a single reference to the specific competition policy instruments can be found in the EGD, with the notable exception of state aid, regarding a further review of the state aid guidelines[57] and the Important Projects of Common European Interest (IPCEI), as recently illustrated by the IPCEI Hy2Use Commission decision.[58] This despite the fact that enabling decarbonisation, a circular economy and sustainability embraces all EU policies. Thus, unsurprisingly, as noted in the legal doctrine, the EGD does not trigger a revolution in the EU competition and state aid systemic model.[59]

Notwithstanding the lack of explicit focus on the EU's established model of economic integration, 'spillover effects' of the EGD should not be neglected, in particular through the lens of its innovative, transversal regulatory approach. Indeed, the EGD has already generated notable measures in the competition and state aid areas. In the area of competition law addressing the behaviour of economic operators, under Articles 101 and 102 TFEU, this is exemplified by the potential for embracing non-economic concerns within Article 101(3) TFEU. In the area of state aid law aiming at Member States' policy choices, a particular emphasis is placed on the large scope of derogatory measures under Article 107(3) TFEU. In this regard, the EGD's novelty resides in a new interpretation of the Union's interest embracing climate change and its economic consequences. Given the systemic relevance of EU competition and state aid law for the internal market and for the Union's economy, the green transformation tools of EU competition law should therefore follow tailored solutions allowing preservation of these two dimensions of competitiveness under EU law.

[56] The flagship EU Green Deal Fit for 55 legislative package equally did not pertain to the competition law. Fit'55 is focusing on regulatory measures within 'the EU's climate, energy, land use, transport and taxation policies fit for reducing net greenhouse gas emissions by at least 55% by 2030, compared to 1990 levels': Council, 'Fit for 55': www.consilium.europa.eu/en/policies/green-deal/fit-for-55-the-eu-plan-for-a-green-transition/.

[57] See Roadmap, Annex to the Commission's Communication Review of the relevant State aid guidelines, including the environment and energy State aid guidelines: Commission, 'The European Green Deal' (n 2 above).

[58] Press Release, 'State Aid: Commission approves up to 5.2 billion of public support by thirteen Member States for the second Important Project of Common European Interest in the hydrogen value chain': www.ec.europa.eu/commission/presscorner/detail/en/ip 22 5676.

[59] Chiti, 'Managing the Ecological Transition of the EU' (n 50). See Commission, 'Communication from the Commission Criteria for the analysis of the compatibility with the internal market of State aid to promote the execution of important projects of common European interest 2021/C 528/02' (Communication) [2021] OJ C528/10.

Regarding specific measures adopted in the context of the EGD, in September 2020 a general debate was launched by Executive Vice-President of the European Commission Margrethe Vestager, 'on how the competition rules work with green policies – and how they could support those policies even better'.[60] While a notable competition policy brief of September 2021[61] constituted an attempt to illustrate the ways in which EU competition law might support the green transition, a number of sectoral, industry-tailored consultations were launched in parallel by the Commission. In the field of antitrust, the revision of the guidelines on horizontal cooperation agreements is the most telling example. The new guidelines,[62] inter alia, 'aim to make it easier for undertakings to cooperate in ways which are economically desirable and thereby, for example, contribute to the green and digital transitions and to fostering the resilience of the internal market'.[63] In light of the Commission's commitment to fulfil the EGD's objectives, these guidelines 'provide guidance on how the most common horizontal cooperation agreements will be assessed under Article 101 when they pursue sustainability objectives'.[64] This is but an example of a wider approach that proves sustainability is indeed a concept 'relevant to all areas of competition law'.[65] Sustainability in the area of EU competition law has been largely addressed in the legal doctrine which conveys an economic rationale permeated with environmental and social ideas.[66] While Article 101 TFEU already encompasses sustainability in practice,[67] new concepts are emerging in the field of Article 102 TFEU, in particular regarding objective justification.[68] That being said, as rightly argued in EU law doctrine, 'EU competition law has a sustainability gap, particularly when it comes to enforcing Article 102 TFEU as a "sword" to prohibit dominant undertakings' unsustainable conduct'.[69]

[60] See Speech by Executive M Vestager at the Renew Webinar (22 September 2020) and keynote speech by M Vestager at the 25th IBA Competition Conference, delivered by I Bernaerts, Director, Directorate-General for Competition (10 September 2021). For further information about the Competition policy's contribution see Commission, 'Competition policy's contribution': https://competition-policy.ec.europa.eu/consumers/green-gazette/competition-policy_en.

[61] European Commission, Directorate-General for Competition, Competition policy brief. 2021-01, September 2021, European Commission, 2021, https://data.europa.eu/doi/10.2763/962262.

[62] Commission, 'Guidelines on the applicability of Article 101 of the Treaty on the Functioning of the European Union to horizontal cooperation agreements' (Communication) [2022] OJ C164/01.

[63] ibid point 1.

[64] ibid point 3.

[65] S Holmes, 'Sustainability and Competition Policy: An Overview of EU and National Case Law' (2022) *Concurrences* No 104072.

[66] Nowag, *Environmental Integration* (n 19 above). See also E van den Brink and J Ellison, 'Article 101(3) TFEU: the Roadmap for Sustainable Cooperation' in S Holmes, D Middelschulte and M Snoep (eds), *Competition Law, Climate Change and Environmental Sustainability* (Paris, Concurrences, 2021).

[67] Commission, 'Guidelines on the applicability of Article 101' (n 62 above).

[68] CH Thomas, 'Exploring the Sustainability of Article 102' in S Holmes, D Middelschulte and M Snoep (eds), *Competition Law, Climate Change and Environmental Sustainability* (Paris, Concurrences, 2021).

[69] MC Iacovides and C Vrettos, 'Falling Through the Cracks No More? Article 102 TFEU and Sustainability: The Relation Between Dominance, Environmental Degradation, and Social Injustice' (2022) 10 *Journal of Antitrust Enforcement* 32.

Likewise, the potential of state aid tools in promoting environmental sustainability is convincingly argued in the scholarship.[70] The field of state aid was meant to be the flagship of the green transition.[71] In particular, the Commission considers state aid measures, which are subject to the notification requirement under Article 107(3)(c) TFEU, as a tool enabling the Member States to accomplish the EGD's objectives 'efficiently and with minimum distortions of competition'.[72] The single market is thus viewed as inherently environmentally oriented, with decarbonisation of the energy sector being a top priority. In the most recent Guidelines on State Aid for Climate, Environmental Protection and Energy (CEEAG),[73] the scope of measures is broadened, in particular to address technological developments such as hydrogen infrastructure and to support new areas, such as biodiversity. In parallel, the Commission requires Member States to ensure that state aid measures respect EU environmental law requirements. According to the CEEAG, prior to the notification of an aid measure, other than in duly justified exceptional circumstances, Member States must consult publicly on the competition impacts and proportionality of the measure to be notified.[74] The green transition is also reflected in the currently ongoing General Block Exemption Regulation (GBER)[75] reform, which exempts national authorities from the Article 108 TFEU notification obligation.[76] In particular, the GBER revision:

> aims to widen the scope of the GBER to cover aid for investments in new technologies such as hydrogen and carbon capture, storage or usage, which are essential to address strategic dependencies. The scope of the GBER will be extended to areas that are key to achieve the objectives of the European Green Deal, for example resource efficiency and biodiversity.[77]

On 9 March 2023, the Commission has endorsed the GBER amendment,[78] which is meant to support the EU's digital and green transitions, making it easier for

[70] N Robins, A Burger and L Puglisi Oxera, 'The Role of State Aid in Promoting Environmental Sustainability' in S Holmes, D Middelschulte and M Snoep (eds), *Competition Law, Climate Change and Environmental Sustainability* (Paris, Concurrences, 2021).

[71] Commission, 'A Competition Policy Fit for New Challenges' (Communication) COM(2021) 713 final.

[72] Press Corner, 'Guidelines on State aid for climate, environmental protection and energy 2022': www.ec.europa.eu/commission/presscorner/detail/en/qanda_22_566.

[73] Commission, 'Guidelines on State aid for Climate, Environmental Protection and Energy 2022' (Communication) [2022] OJ C80/01.

[74] ibid Point 4.1.3.4, which applies from 1 July 2023.

[75] Commission Regulation (EU) 2021/1237 of 23 July 2021 amending Regulation (EU) No 651/2014 declaring certain categories of aid compatible with the internal market in application of Articles 107 and 108 of the Treaty [2021] OJ L270/39.

[76] Commission, 'Targeted review of the General Block Exemption Regulation (State Aid): Revised Rules for State Aid Promoting the Green and Digital Transition': https://competition-policy.ec.europa.eu/public-consultations/2021-gber_en.

[77] Directorate for Financial and Enterprise Affairs, Competition Committee 'Annual Report on Competition Policy Developments in the European Union' DAF/COMP/AR(2022)39.

[78] https://competition-policy.ec.europa.eu/state-aid/legislation/regulations_en. As indicated on the DG Competition website, the formal adoption of the Regulation will take place once the translation of the text into all official languages is finalised.

Member States to grant aid without prior notification. In particular, this facilitation focuses on the areas of environmental protection, energy and training as well as implementation of certain ICPEI-related projects.[79]

However, the question could be raised as to whether broadening the respective scopes of the CEEAG and GBER contributes effectively to the green transformation while warranting measures against greenwashing within EU competition law. Likewise, novel technology-oriented measures, as illustrated by the concept of a European Hydrogen Bank (EHB),[80] require careful assessment as regards calibration between EU state aid, energy and environmental policies. Finally, in December 2022, the Commission adopted new state aid rules in the field of agriculture, forestry, fishery and aquaculture, and it is notable that these were aligned with the EGD.[81]

In parallel, sustainability-tailored evolution of the competition model is steadily taking place at the national level, where the objectives of the EGD are being echoed by national competition authorities (NCAs).[82] Recent examples include the French NCA, which announced further integration of sustainability goals into its decision-making process.[83] Likewise, Austria[84] and the Netherlands[85] have included sustainability in antitrust law and guidelines since 2021.[86] The Greek NCA, too, has expressed the need to address a possible conflict between sustainable development and competition law.[87] The Netherlands Authority for Consumers and Markets (ACM) and the Hellenic Competition Commission (HCC) jointly commissioned a study focused on benefits relating to environmental sustainability.[88] The German

[79] Communication to the Commission of 09.03.2023, C(2023) 1712 final and Annex to this Communication, available at https://competition-policy.ec.europa.eu/document/9a1802e1-cedc-4f87-a1f6-d6759e4d4660_en.

[80] Speech by U von der Leyen, '2022 State of the Union Address by President von der Leyen' (Strasbourg, 14 September 2022).

[81] Press Release, 'State Aid: Commission Adopts New Rules for Agriculture, Forestry and Fishery and Aquaculture Sectors' (2022): www.ec.europa.eu/commission/presscorner/detail/en/IP_22_7670.

[82] Holmes, 'Sustainability and Competition Policy' (n 65 above).

[83] See Press Release, 'Après une activité très soutenue en 2020, l'Autorité de la concurrence annonce ses priorités pour 2021, qui seront centrées sur l'économie numérique': www.autoritedelaconcurrence.fr/fr/communiques-de-presse/apres-une-activite-tres-soutenue-en-2020-lautorite-de-la-concurrence-annonce.

[84] M Gassler, 'New Draft Sustainability Guidelines for the New Austrian Sustainability', *Kluwer Competition Law Blog*, 2 June 2022: https://competitionlawblog.kluwercompetitionlaw.com/2022/06/02/new-draft-sustainability-guidelines-for-the-new-austrian-sustainability-exemption/.

[85] Authority for Consumers and Markets, 'Guidelines on sustainability agreements are ready for further European coordination': www.acm.nl/en/publications/guidelines-sustainability-agreements-are-ready-further-european-coordination.

[86] R Inderst and S Thomas, 'Sustainability Goals and Competition Law Between Harmony and Restrictions' *SAFE Finance Blog*, 11 February 2022: www.safe-frankfurt.de/news-latest/safe-finance-blog/details/sustainability-goals-and-competition-law-between-harmony-and-restrictions.html.

[87] See Hellenic Competition Commission, 'Draft Staff Discussion Paper on Sustainability Issues and Competition Law' (2020): www.epant.gr/files/2020/Staff_Discussion_paper.pdf.

[88] R Inderst, E Sartzetakis and A Xepapadeas, 'Technical Report on Sustainability and Competition' (2020): www.epant.gr/en/enimerosi/publications/research-publications/item/1284-technical-report-on-sustainability-and- competition.html.

Agenda 2025, meant to outline a reform of antitrust law, relies on a concept of 'sustainable competition as a cornerstone of the social-ecological market economy'.[89] Among the core aspects of the recently published reform of the German antitrust law, which embodies the German Sustainable Development Strategy 2021,[90] sustainability and economic transformation are coupled with a call for digitalisation, innovation and social justice.[91] The EGD has also been reflected in outings of the UK and the Nordic competition authorities.[92] In this context, calls for a uniform approach have been heard within the European Competition Network.[93] These demonstrate the extent that a horizontal and holistic reflection at the EU level is needed, in order to remedy disparate measures taken at various levels by Member States' NCAs and national courts, alongside private sustainability initiatives.[94]

IV. Enabling Transformation Through Novel Instruments

Whereas the preceding analysis demonstrates that the impact of the EGD in the field of EU competition law is evolving, it is worth noting that the EGD and surrounding policy initiatives mainly rely on the idea that competition instruments are meant *to contribute* to the effectiveness of the EU climate neutrality goals.[95] This concept relies on a classic understanding of the role of EU competition policy, which '[s]ince the creation of the European Union … has contributed to preserving and fostering the Union's economic prosperity'.[96] The Commission focuses equally on an overall picture encompassing all competition instruments (mergers, antitrust and state aid control).[97] However, little has been explored at the institutional level in order to discuss the need for a genuine internal transformation of EU competition and state aid law. Ultimately, since the ambition underlying

[89] Bundesministerium fur Wirtschaft und Klimaschutz, 'The competition policy agenda of the Federal Ministry for Economic Affairs and Climate Action up to 2023' (21 February 2022); D'Kart, 'Competition Policy Agenda of the BMWK Until 2025', *D'Kart Antitrust Blog*, 21 February 2022: www.d-kart.de/en/blog/2022/02/21/die-wettbewerbspolitische-agenda-der-bundesregierung/.

[90] German Federal Government, 'German Sustainable Development Strategy, Update 2021' (2021): www.bundesregierung.de/resource/blob/974430/1940716/1c63c8739d10011eb116fda1aecb61ca/german-sustainable-development-strategy-en-data.pdf?download=1.

[91] D'Kart, 'Spotlight Off: A Review and Outlook on Agenda 2025', *D'Kart Antitrust Blog*, 27 September 2022: www.d-kart.de/en/blog/2022/09/27/spotlight-aus-ein-ruckblick-und-ausblick-zur-agenda-2025/.

[92] G Gürkaynak, K Uçar and H Demirkan, 'Sustainability Factors in Merger Control Assessments: Do Ambitious Efforts Fall Short of Expectations?' (2021) *Concurrences* No 103263.

[93] D'Kart, 'Agenda 2025: Eine Kleine Gruppe Nachdenklicher Verbraucher Kann Die Welt Verändern?', *D'Kart Antitrust Blog*, 2 August 2022: www.d-kart.de/en/blog/2022/08/02/agenda-2025-eine-kleine-gruppe-nachdenklicher-verbraucher-kann-die-welt-veraendern/.

[94] G Monti and J Mulder, 'Escaping the Clutches of EU Competition Law: Pathways to Assess Private Sustainability Initiatives' (2017) 42 *European Law Review* 635.

[95] See Commission Competition Policy Brief issued on 10 September 2021 which explores 'how EU competition rules can complement environmental and climate policies more effectively'; see Directorate-General of Competition, 'Competition Policy Brief' (2021).

[96] Commission, 'A Competition Policy Fit for New Challenges' (n 71 above).

[97] ibid point I.

the EGD is to reshape the economic model of the Union, the way EU competition and state aid law operates needs to be reconsidered.

In the absence of explicit systemic change, a number of concepts existing in other areas of EU law may be relied upon to enable gradual internal transformation of EU competition and state aid law. Among the most recent ideas to be scrutinised are the EU taxonomy[98] and 'do no significant harm' principle.[99] These could contribute to the transformation process, while avoiding a clash of titans. More importantly, given their economic and technical suitability, these and similar concepts could play a fundamental role in this respect while at the same time preventing greenwashing.

The Taxonomy Regulation aims at defining a classification system (taxonomy) of what amounts to an 'economically sustainable' activity, thus providing economic operators with a common pattern. Stemming from the financial sector, the concept of a taxonomy has progressively achieved an overarching status and use, as illustrated by the EU cohesion funds, including the post-COVID economic recovery instruments,[100] and novel EU financial instruments.[101] Although highly controversial in political terms, especially in the context of assessment of fossil fuels, the taxonomy is one of the most innovative legal tools of the green transition.[102] In the competition area, the taxonomy is considered an adequate instrument for the purpose of assessing sustainability agreements under Article 101 TFEU.[103]

It is worth noting that the 2011 Commission guidelines[104] do not contain a separate chapter on 'environmental agreements' as was the case in the previous guidelines.[105] Whereas mostly dealt with in the standardisation chapter, according to the Commission, 'depending on the competition issues "environmental agreements" give rise to, they are to be assessed under the relevant chapter of these guidelines'.[106] This approach illustrates the extent that environmental and sustainability related aspects permeate the concept of competitiveness within the internal market. In particular, where environmental standards fulfil, a priori, the criteria of Article 101(3) TFEU, the same rationale could be applied to

[98] Regulation (EU) 2020/852 of the European Parliament and of the Council of 18 June 2020 on the establishment of a framework to facilitate sustainable investment and amending Regulation (EU) 2019/2088 [2020] OJ L198/13 (Taxonomy Regulation).

[99] Commission, 'The European Green Deal' (n 2 above).

[100] Regulation (EU) 2021/241 of the European Parliament and of the Council of 12 February 2021 establishing the Recovery and Resilience Facility [2021] OJ L57/17.

[101] Commission, 'NextGenerationEU Green Bonds': www.ec.europa.eu/info/strategy/eu-budget/eu-borrower-investor-relations/nextgenerationeu-green-bonds_en.

[102] Press Release, 'Taxonomy: MEPs object to Commission's plan to include gas and nuclear activities':www.europarl.europa.eu/news/en/press-room/20220613IPR32812/taxonomy-meps-object-to-commission-s-plan-to-include-gas-and-nuclear-activities.

[103] D Wouters, 'Sustainability Agreements vs Greenwashing under Article 101 TFEU'. *Kluwer Competition Law Blog*, 3 June 2021: https://competitionlawblog.kluwercompetitionlaw.com/2021/06/03/sustainability-agreements-vs-greenwashing-under-article-101-tfeu/.

[104] Commission, 'Guidelines on the applicability of Article 101' (n 62 above).

[105] ibid, see footnote 14.

[106] ibid.

economically sustainable activities in the meaning of the Taxonomy Regulation. More importantly, the Taxonomy Regulation, in its Recital 11, contains an attempt at defining greenwashing as 'the practice of gaining an unfair competitive advantage by marketing a financial product as environmentally friendly, when in fact basic environmental standards have not been met'.[107] Given its simplicity and potentially transversal applicability, such an approach could be relied upon in particular within the framework of Article 101(3) TFEU. Furthermore, in the context of state aid compatibility assessment under Article 107(3)(c) TFEU, 'economically sustainable' activities could enhance the concept of facilitating development of certain economic areas. Finally, the taxonomy, together with recent corporate sustainability EU law instruments,[108] substantially contribute to reducing asymmetric information, thus fighting market inequalities.

A parallel concept which stems directly from the EGD communication is the so-called 'principle' of 'do no significant harm'. Its legal status has as yet remained far from clear, in particular as compared to the existing legal concepts enshrined in the treaties, such as high-level environmental protection and the specific environmental principles under Article 191 TFEU. Nevertheless, 'do no significant harm' has gradually been expounded in the context of the EU cohesion policy. At its current stage of development, the concept builds on the Taxonomy Regulation.[109] As such, it has become a yardstick for assessment of national recovery plans under the Recovery and Resilience Facility (RRF) Regulation, according to which no measure included in a recovery and resilience plan should lead to significant harm to environmental objectives within the meaning of Article 17 of the Taxonomy Regulation. While the Commission's technical guidance on the 'do no significant harm' principle is limited to setting out its application in the context of the RRF,[110] the principle nonetheless encapsulates a new concept which, given further legal consolidation, could be applied, notably, in the context of a state aid compatibility review. In particular, it is liable to contribute to the interpretation of the common interest under Article 107(3)(c) TFEU, wherein not harming the environment could be seen as a value underlying economic development of the Union. Relying on significant harm avoidance within the compatibility assessment of state aid measures could trigger a novel, environmental dimension of Article 107 TFEU,

[107] Regulation (EU) 2020/852 of the European Parliament and of the Council of 18 June 2020 on the establishment of a framework to facilitate sustainable investment and amending Regulation (EU) 2019/2088 [2020] OJ L198/13 (Taxonomy Regulation), recital 11.

[108] Directive (EU) 2022/2464 of the European Parliament and of the Council of 14 December 2022 amending Regulation (EU) No 537/2014, Directive 2005/109/EC, Directive 2006/43/EC and Directive 2013/34/EU, as regards corporate sustainability reporting [2022] OJ L322/15. See also, recent developments in relation to the corporate sustainability due diligence: Press Release, 'Council adopts position on due diligence rules for large companies': www.consilium.europa.eu/en/press/press-releases/2022/12/01/council-adopts-position-on-due-diligence-rules-for-large-companies/.

[109] Art 17 of the Taxonomy Regulation defines what constitutes 'significant harm' for the six environmental objectives covered by this regulation.

[110] Commission, 'Technical guidance on the application of "do no significant harm" under the Recovery and Resilience Facility Regulation 2021/C 58/01' (Notice) [2021] OJ C58/01.

completing recent judicial developments in the *Hinkley Point* ruling. Thus, when the Commission checks whether state aid for an economic activity meets the first condition laid down in Article 107(3)(c) TFEU, whereby the aid must be intended to facilitate development of certain economic areas:

> [The Commission] must ... check that that activity does not infringe rules of EU law on the environment. If it finds an infringement of those rules, it is obliged to declare the aid incompatible with the internal market without any other form of examination.[111]

One could question a priori the practicalities and effectiveness of such an 'environmental compliance' assessment to be conducted by the Commission under Article 107(3) TFEU. In this context, 'do no significant harm' could be relied upon by the Commission to check that a given measure does not infringe EU environmental rules. As regards the second condition of Article 107(3)(c) TFEU, under which the aid must not adversely affect trading conditions to an extent contrary to the common interest, this condition, according to the Court of Justice, 'entails weighing up the positive effects of the planned aid for the development of the activities that that aid is intended to support and the negative effects that the aid may have on the internal market'.[112] However, since the court has upheld a narrow interpretation of the internal market, the Commission is not under an obligation to take into account the negative effects of the examined measure on sectors other than trade and competition.[113] Reliance on the 'do no significant harm' concept could potentially widen this interpretation and enable contributing to environmental protection within the internal market as a whole.

V. Conclusions

To conclude, the classic model of EU competition and state aid law is on the cusp of the most important and inevitable challenge since its inception. The heralding of climate neutrality and environmental recalibration of the Union's economy is still tremendously daunting, bearing in mind the 'big idea' at the heart of the founding treaties and the heretofore oscillation between predominantly economic and socio-environmental visions of the 'ever closer union'.[114] Even though the EGD is not a competition-tailored instrument, it implies a new, transformational approach in EU competition law. As the analysis in this chapter has demonstrated, this transformational approach is to some extent already taking place, both at the EU level and at the level of national competition law. This gradual evolution

[111] ibid, para 100.
[112] *Hinkley Point* (n 30) para 101.
[113] A Sikora, 'Applicability of the EU State Aid and Environmental Rules in the Nuclear Energy Sector: Case C-594/18 P *Republic of Austria v Commission* ("Hinkley Point")' (2020) 19 *European State Aid Law Quarterly* 515.
[114] Flynn, 'Competition Policy and Public Services' (n 46 above) 186.

visibly affects all areas of EU competition and state aid law. Nonetheless, in order to address the expectations and horizontal ambitions inherent in the EGD, this evolution must be complemented by a cross-cutting and comprehensive reflection as to the necessity of genuine recalibration at the EU constitutional level. If climate neutrality is meant to be achieved and not remain a political slogan, it may require both a novel reading of the objectives of the treaty and transformation of the constitutional framework of the Union, including a reassessment of the relationship between the internal market identity and environmental considerations.

4

From Crisis Cartels to COVID-19 State Aid and Cooperation: The Non-Exceptionality of Crisis Management by EU Competition Law

FRANCISCO COSTA-CABRAL*

I. Introduction

As the COVID-19 CRISIS unfolded, the European Commission (Commission) started labelling its enforcement of European Union (EU) competition law as exceptional. A Temporary Framework for State Aid was issued for the 'current exceptional circumstances'[1] describing multiple types of aid dealing with the crisis that Member States could grant under Article 107.[2] Over 1.5 trillion euros was authorised by the Commission in 2020, leaving the aid granted during the financial crisis far behind,[3] and more followed until the framework's scheduled end in June 2022.[4] A Temporary Framework for Cooperation was also issued in 'underlying exceptional circumstances', detailing how undertakings cooperating to address

* Tilburg Law and Economics Center (TILEC) Fellow, F.Costa-Cabral@tilburg.edu. I thank the editors and Carla Farinhas for the comments, and Or Brook and Oke Odudu for the discussions on this topic.

[1] Commission, 'Temporary Framework for State aid measures to support the economy in the current COVID-19 outbreak' (Communication) [2020] OJ C 91I, as amended. References are to the consolidated version: https://competition-policy.ec.europa.eu/system/files/2021-11/TF_consolidated_version_amended_18_nov_2021_en_2.pdf, para 39.

[2] All references are to the Treaty on the Functioning of the EU (TFEU) unless otherwise indicated.

[3] See n 4 of the Temporary Framework for State Aid (above n 1), and I Agnolucci, 'Will COVID-19 Make or Break EU State Aid Control? An Analysis of Commission Decisions Authorising Pandemic State Aid Measures' (2022) 13 *Journal of European Competition Law and Practice* 3.

[4] For a list of approved aid, see Commission, 'Coronavirus Outbreak – List of Member State Measures Approved under Articles 107(2)b, 107(3)b and 107(3)c TFEU and under the State Aid Temporary Framework' (2023): https://competition-policy.ec.europa.eu/system/files/2023-02/State_aid_decisions_TF_and_107_2b_107_3b_107_3c.pdf.

product shortages could avoid being sanctioned under Article 101.[5] Before this framework, the Commission had joined a European Competition Network (ECN) statement of non-intervention against cooperation to ensure 'supply and fair distribution of scarce products'.[6] The framework was withdrawn in October 2022 but was yet another escalation from the financial crisis, when the Commission signalled that rules continued to apply as normal.[7] These two temporary frameworks were soft law,[8] based on the Commission's discretion to interpret and apply competition rules. Nonetheless, they created a generalised sense that a set of exceptional rules allowed aid and cooperation that would normally be prohibited.[9]

These rules were contrasted with 'normal' enforcement in a crisis, namely sector crises and difficulties by individual undertakings. Before the 'modernisation' of the Commission's enforcement,[10] industries with excess production due to technological lag and falling demand could enter into agreements to reduce overcapacity – so-called 'crisis cartels' – eligible for an exemption under Article 101(3) due to benefits of sector reorganisation and workforce management.[11] However, with modernisation's emphasis on consumer welfare, the Commission guidance started requiring efficiencies benefiting consumers for such an Article 101(3) exemption.[12] Hence, during the financial crisis, the understanding was that crisis cartels were no longer allowed.[13] Crises were better left to the market to solve by rewarding innovation and removing inefficient producers, a principle

[5] Commission, 'Temporary Framework for assessing antitrust issues related to business cooperation in response to situations of urgency stemming from the current COVID-19 outbreak' (Communication) [2020] OJ C116l para 21, and Commission, 'Withdrawal of Temporary Framework for assessing antitrust issues related to business cooperation in response to situations of urgency stemming from the current COVID-19 outbreak' (Communication) [2022] OJ C381/3.

[6] European Competition Network, 'Antitrust: Joint Statement by the European Competition Network (ECN) on Application of Competition Law During the Corona Crisis (2020): www.ec.europa.eu/competition/ecn/202003_joint-statement_ecn_corona-crisis.pdf.

[7] N Kroes, 'Competition Policy and the Crisis – The Commission's Approach and Beyond' (2010) 55 *Antitrust Bulletin* 715.

[8] On the EU law-wide reaction to COVID-19 through soft law, see M Eliantonio, E Korkea-Aho and S Vaughan, 'COVID-19 and Soft Law: Is Soft Law Pandemic-Proof?' (2021) 12 *European Journal of Risk Regulation* 1.

[9] The Temporary Framework for State Aid has been qualified from 'generous' to 'unprecedented relaxation'. See in this sense A Bouchagiar, 'State Aid in the Context of the COVID-19 Outbreak, Including the Temporary Framework 2020' in L Hancher, T Ottervanger and PJ Slot (eds), *EU State Aids* (Edinburgh, Sweet and Maxwell, 2021) and Agnolucci, 'Will COVID-19 Make or Break' (n 3 above). At the same time, the Temporary Framework for Cooperation was considered to tolerate 'more cooperation than usual' in G Monti, 'Business Cooperation in Times of Emergency: The Role of Competition Law', *Competition Policy International*, 10 May 2020: competitionpolicyinternational.com/business-cooperation-in-times-of-emergency-the-role-of-competition-law/.

[10] Amongst many, F Costa-Cabral, 'Future-Mapping the Three Dimensions of EU Competition Law: Legislative Proposals and COVID-19 Framework' (2020) 7 *Journal of International and Comparative Law* 308.

[11] B Wardaugh, 'Crisis Cartels: Non-Economic Values, the Public Interest and Institutional Considerations' (2014) 10 *European Competition Journal* 311, 313–17.

[12] Commission, 'Guidelines on the application of Article 101(3) TFEU (formerly Article 81(3) of the Treaty)' (Notice) [2004] OJ C101/97 (Article 101(3) Guidelines) 33.

[13] See Kroes, 'Competition Policy and the Crisis' (n 7 above).

that limits aid for undertakings in difficulty under modernisation's Rescue and Restructuring Guidelines (RR Guidelines).[14] The temporary frameworks, therefore, attempted to preserve this normal enforcement from their exceptionality: the Temporary Framework for Cooperation stated that the crisis could not be used as a cover for anti-competitive behaviour,[15] while the Temporary Framework for State Aid in principle only applies to undertakings that were not in difficulty before COVID-19.[16]

Exceptionality seems the clearest when rules were suspended during the COVID-19 crisis. Notably, Article 101(1) was suspended for certain agricultural products under the Commission's competences for managing the Common Agricultural Policy (CAP).[17] In the United Kingdom (UK), several orders were issued temporarily excluding competition rules based on public interest,[18] covering situations (in particular, preventing shortages in the groceries sector) that in the EU could fall under the Temporary Framework for Cooperation. This led to a debate on which would be preferable in a crisis – discretionary guidance or formal exclusion – comparing the precision of guidance against the legal certainty of an exclusion.[19] Temporary frameworks and suspension were thus considered equivalent in dealing with behaviour otherwise prohibited.[20] A practical suspension of State aid rules was also mooted as a result of the Temporary Framework for State Aid,[21] if not as a whole, at least regarding their function of securing the integrity of the internal market, as aid granted was skewed largely to Member States with more financial resources.[22]

[14] Commission, 'Guidelines on State aid for rescuing and restructuring non-financial undertakings in difficulty' (Communication) [2014] OJ C249/1, 6. This stance also derives from *Beef Industry Development Society LtD (BIDS)* finding that sector agreements were restrictive by the object under Art 101(1), as will be discussed, Case C-209/07 *Competition Authority v Beef Industry Development Society Ltd and Barry Brothers Meats Ltd* [2008] EU:C:2008:643.

[15] Commission, 'Temporary Framework for assessing antitrust issues' (n 5 above) 6.

[16] For an overview, Bouchagiar, 'State Aid in the Context of the COVID-19' (n 9 above).

[17] Art 4 TFEU and Press Release, 'Coronavirus: Commission adopts package of measures to further support the agri-food sector': www.ec.europa.eu/commission/presscorner/detail/en/IP_20_788.

[18] Department for Business, Energy and Industrial Strategy, 'Competition law exclusion orders relating to coronavirus (COVID-19)' (Guidance) (2022): www.gov.uk/guidance/competition-law-exclusion-orders-relating-to-coronavirus-covid-19.

[19] Monti, 'Business Cooperation in Times of Emergency' (n 9 above) 5, and O Odudu, 'Feeding the Nation in Times of Crisis: The Relaxation of Competition Law in the United Kingdom' (2020) 19 *Competition Law Journal* 68.

[20] Odudu, 'Feeding the Nation in Times of Crisis' (n 19 above) 69–70.

[21] A Biondi, 'Governing the Interregnum: State Aid Rules and the COVID-19 Crisis' (2020) 4 *Market and Competition Law Review* 17.

[22] See Agnolucci, 'Will COVID-19 Make or Break' (n 3 above), Bouchagiar, 'State Aid in the Context of the COVID-19' (n 9 above), D Ferri, 'The Role of EU State Aid Law as a "Risk Management Tool" in the COVID-19 Crisis' (2021) 12 *European Journal of Risk Regulation* 195, and AL de Pablo and JS Buendia 'A Moment of Truth for the EU. A Proposal for a State Aid Solidarity Fund' (2020) 11 *Journal of European Competition Law and Practice* 1. Agnolucci's work provides an empirical survey of Member State distribution, while de Pablo and Buendia propose that part of aid granted be allocated to a solidarity fund.

This chapter will argue, contrary to the generalised view, that enforcement under COVID-19 did not apply a set of exceptional competition rules. As will be detailed, the Temporary Framework for State Aid resorted to justifications defined and used previously, from more limited natural disasters and other serious disturbances, as well as the economic development that also justifies aid for undertakings in difficulty. It will be discussed how the Temporary Framework for Cooperation, despite not being based on Article 101(3) as other Commission guidance, still used a public policy justification as elaborated by the case law of the Court of Justice of the European Union (CJEU) (the Court, unless specifically the General Court). In addition, the prohibitions of State aid and anticompetitive collusion continued to operate and even attributed a higher priority to COVID-19 related cases. It can therefore be concluded that crisis management is an in-built feature of regular enforcement. The notion that competition rules normally leave crises to be resolved by the market presupposes a legal categorisation of normal and exceptional crises that, as will be demonstrated, does not exist. Any crisis, from sector crises to COVID-19, may be part of the legal and economic context relevant for a variety of competition rules. Crisis management is the cumulative effect of all those rules, allowing EU competition law to frame and tackle crises normatively coherent with its goals, principles and techniques.[23]

The exceptionality announced by the Commission therefore relates to the exercise of its own enforcement discretion. Due to the economic approach of modernisation, the Commission is keen to underplay how competition rules allow State aid and anticompetitive behaviour to be justified (simply) in the public interest. The Commission's discretion in defining and applying those justifications is not unfettered, as will be described, and is especially limited by the proportionality principle. Nevertheless, proportionality is a more lenient test than the balance of economic effects applied by other guidance.[24] Exceptionality is thus a device to exaggerate the Commission's discretion in crisis management and preserve its economic approach elsewhere. This all speaks against suspending competition rules based on public interest, allowed in the UK, as a misunderstanding that such interest can already be taken into account.[25] Suspension is exceptional precisely because it evades crisis management – which prioritises crisis-related infringements – and is only appropriate to sectors already heavily regulated like the CAP. Otherwise, justification and prioritisation under the Commission's discretion have

[23] Ferri, 'The Role of EU State Aid Law' (n 22 above) refers to State aid law as a 'risk management tool' and the Commission as a '*de facto* crisis-management authority' as part of a risk-based analysis (complementary to the substantive one here).

[24] Commission, 'Guidelines on State aid for rescuing and restructuring non-financial undertakings in difficulty' (n 14 above) para 38(f) and Commission, 'Guidelines on the application of Article 101(3) TFEU' (n 12 above) para 43.

[25] UK law is in principle consistent with EU rules pre-Brexit, Competition Act [1998] Section 60. Evading the proportionality test may lead to gains in legal certainty but as will be discussed, the exercise of discretion regarding public policy is also significantly insulated from legal challenges.

proven the resilience of crisis management by competition law,[26] dispensing with the legislative intervention seen in other areas of EU law.

This chapter will analyse the rules on State aid and anticompetitive behaviour. Although the temporary frameworks for COVID-19 have now expired (after multiple extensions), the war in Ukraine has led to a further temporary framework for State aid – already amended and extended – and another ECN joint statement for temporary cooperation to address shortages and comply with sanctions.[27] Successive extensions and new frameworks are normalising this (supposedly exceptional) kind of crisis management. The chapter's emphasis will be placed on their integration with substantive rules, not on procedural arrangements to speed up enforcement or provide legal certainty. The second section will briefly consider the absence of a legal concept of crisis and classify crises based on legal and economic context. The third section discusses State aid, focusing on the several justifications under Temporary Framework for State Aid, and the fourth anti-competitive behaviour, from general rules to the failing-firm defence, Article 101(3), and public interest justification. The last section will summarily conclude on the traditional notion of crisis in EU law and the success of crisis management.

II. Types of Crises

EU competition law has not needed a definition of crisis in order to manage them. COVID-19 has been grouped with the financial, immigration and climate change crises as a 'multidimensional crisis' from 2008 to the present.[28] Nevertheless, multiple crises were also playing out before the financial crisis. In June 2008, the conclusions of the European Council expressed a familiar concern for a 'surge in oil and gas prices and their social and economic consequences' and promoted 'competition in energy markets' as well as 'alternative technologies, inter alia, electric cars'.[29] Shortly afterwards, in September 2008, an extraordinary European Council met to address Russia's military action in Georgia.[30] When the 'international economic and financial crisis' became the main concern of the conclusions of October 2008, they still did not neglect climate change and energy security, including Russia and relations with Eastern neighbours.[31] Former President of the

[26] J Nowag, 'Resilience and Competition Law, in Times of Emergencies and Crises: Two Research Agendas' (2020) 8 *Journal of Antitrust Enforcement* 296.

[27] Commission, 'Temporary Crisis Framework for State Aid measures to support the economy following the aggression against Ukraine by Russia' (Communication) [2022] OJ C 131I/1.

[28] E Chiti, 'Managing the Ecological Transition of the EU: the European Green Deal as a Regulatory Process' (2022) 59 *Common Market Law Review* 19.

[29] Council, 'Brussels European Council 19/20 June 2008 Presidency Conclusions' (2008) 11018/1/08 Rev 1, paras 27 and 39.

[30] Council, 'Extraordinary European Council, Brussels 1 September 2008 Presidency Conclusions' (2008) 12594/2/08 Rev 2.

[31] Council, 'Brussels European Council 15 and 16 October 2008 Presidency Conclusions' (2008) 14368/08.

Commission, Juncker coined the term 'polycrisis' from the cascading effects of the financial and sovereign debt crises,[32] but arguably polycrisis has been with the EU for longer.[33] Competition law in particular has been dealing with sector crises since the Coal and Steel Community and the European Economic Community.[34] What is notable is that, throughout polycrisis, crises are identified politically without entailing a legal definition.

There are few references to crisis in the Treaties and none specifically for competition.[35] An operative legal concept of 'crisis' is thus lacking. This is not to say that crises and their consequences cannot be identified, only that they are filtered through other concepts. The ones more closely associated with crisis are in the justification of State aid under Article 107, namely aid to 'make good the damage caused by natural disasters or exceptional occurrences' in (2)(b) and 'remedy serious disturbance in the economy of a Member State' in (3)(b). Aid 'to facilitate the development of certain economic activities or of certain economic areas' (in short, 'economic development') in (3)(c) may also be deployed in a crisis, but is used much more generally. Rules on anticompetitive behaviour also apply generally and thereby cover crisis situations, namely their examples of prohibited behaviour: Article 101(1) refers to collusion to 'directly or indirectly fix purchase or selling prices or any other trading condition' in (a) and 'limit or control production' in (b), which are the basis for prohibiting crisis cartels, while Article 102 mentions the abuse of 'directly or indirectly imposing unfair purchase or selling prices or other unfair trading conditions' in (a), which has been associated with 'price gouging' in a crisis.[36] Crisis cartels may be exempted by Article 101(3), as mentioned already, under the broader justification of 'improving the production or distribution of goods' or 'promoting technical or economic progress'.

The application of competition rules therefore depends on their operative concepts being met in the context of a crisis. This puts the Commission in a key position insofar as it defines those concepts in its guidance. By dividing the guidance between general guidelines and temporary frameworks, the Commission has fuelled the interpretation that crises are subject to exceptional rules as set out in the introduction. This further implies that there are two types of crises: 'exceptional circumstances' like the financial crisis and COVID-19, which would lead

[32] J Juncker, 'Speech by President Jean-Clause Juncker at the Annual General Meeting of the Hellenic Federation of Enterprises (SEV)' (Athens, 21 June 2016): https://ec.europa.eu/commission/presscorner/detail/en/SPEECH_16_2293.

[33] Some have used polycrisis for the consequences of a globalised capitalist economy, see A Tooze, 'Chartbook #165: Polycrisis – thinking on the tightrope' *Chartbook*, 29 October 2022: adamtooze.substack.com/p/chartbook-165-polycrisis-thinking.

[34] E Mestmäcker, 'The Applicability of the ECSC-Cartel Prohibition (Article 65) during a "Manifest Crisis"' (1984) 82 *Michigan Law Review* 1399 and I Kokkoris, 'Should Crisis Cartels Exist Amid Crises?' (2010) 55 *The Antitrust Bulletin* 727.

[35] The term 'crises management' is only used for the Common Foreign and Security Policy in Arts 38 and 43 of the Treaty on EU (TEU), and the single reference to crisis in the TFEU is Art 144 for temporary measures in adopting the Euro.

[36] A Jones, 'Cartels in the Time of COVID-19' (2020) 8 *Journal of Antitrust Enforcement* 287.

to those exceptional rules, and all other crises, which would be effectively ignored by being resolved under 'normal' rules. That interpretation is misconstrued. The financial crisis and COVID-19 were obviously particular, but they did not lead to a distinctive concept of crisis based on exceptionality. This was recognised by the European Council on the eve of the financial crisis:

> In the current exceptional circumstances, European rules must continue to be implemented in a way that meets the need for speedy and flexible action. The European Council supports the Commission's implementation, in this spirit, of the rules on competition policy, particularly State aids, while continuing to apply the principles of the single market and the system of State aids.[37]

By emphasising continuity through exceptional circumstances, the European Council did not qualify the financial crisis as a crisis allowing a derogation from normal rules. On the contrary, it safeguarded the application of those rules by calling for procedural adaptations. The conclusions of March 2022 show a hardening of this position for COVID-19, calling for 'strictly implementing and enforcing the Single Market rules and ensuring that all companies comply with EU harmonised standards and competition rules'.[38] As such, crisis management is not the product of a concept of crisis based on exceptional circumstances but the consequence of extending rules that already apply outside of a crisis context. For those purposes, the remainder of this section will explore a simple categorisation of crises based on their legal and economic context.

Crises have been primarily categorised based on economic differences, notably between the crises prompting temporary frameworks and those behind crisis cartels. On one level, there are differences of scope: the first affects the whole of a Member State's economy, even the EU, sometimes being qualified as 'systemic crises', while the others are limited to certain sectors, and are also referred to as 'sector crises'. It will be seen that systemic crises open the way for aid addressing a general economic downturn, and that sector crises are relevant both for aid remedying direct damage and exempting industry-wide cooperation. Economic scope can be further tightened to individual undertaking(s) in a crisis, which can also receive aid or allowances for cooperation. Crises have alternatively been differentiated on their effect on supply and demand: temporary frameworks would deal with undersupply, such as shortages of credit or medical equipment, while crisis cartels would involve oversupply, as industries deal with overcapacity and fall in demand.[39] Finally, crises are differentiated on their periodicity: systemic crises would be exceptional 'one-off' events, and therefore deserving of temporary frameworks, while sector or individual crises would split between the 'cyclical'

[37] Council, Presidency Conclusions 14368/08 (n 31 above).

[38] European Council, 'European Council Meeting (24 and 25 March 2022) – Conclusions' (2022) EUCO 1/22, para 21.

[39] MP Schinkel and A d'Ailly, 'Corona Crisis Cartels: Sense and Sensibility' (*Amsterdam Law School Legal Studies Research Paper No 31/2020*) 3.

adjustments to growth and recession and the 'structural' inability to conduct that adjustment, determining their exemption under Article 101(3).[40]

Crises can also be normatively categorised according to the goal pursued: efficiency, various public interests and mixed. Enforcing competition rules allows markets to function efficiently in a crisis, as emphasised by Vice-President Vestager, the Commissioner for competition.[41] That is why some were wary of cooperation to deal with shortages during COVID-19: the market could theoretically adjust by ramping up production.[42] Moreover, sector or individual crises can be seen as a by-product or an opportunity for innovation. This has led the Commission, as will be discussed, to (only) justify crisis cartels based on the structural inability to reduce overcapacity and operate efficiently. Aid for COVID-19 has also been connected with efficiency, as it helps undertakings that would otherwise be viable.[43] Vestager has nonetheless added that Temporary Framework for State Aid was due to 'fairness', a competing reason for helping viable undertakings – contrary to the financial crisis, there is no 'moral hazard' of aid coming to the rescue of those responsible for the crisis[44] – which also explains the exceptions of aid to undertakings already in difficulty referred below. This view of mutually supporting efficiency and fairness pursues a mixed normative goal and has become typical of the Commission's recent enforcement.[45] Under the economic approach of modernisation, public interest is usually (only) considered as a justification. Thus, State aid is authorised in the public interest, such as the aid to safeguarding employment and protecting public health also in the temporary framework. This goal is more disputed for the rules applying to undertakings, as will be discussed when the Temporary Framework for Cooperation is attributed a public health justification.

III. State Aid

Although the 'exceptional occurrences' and 'serious disturbance in the economy' in Article 107(2)(b) and (3)(b) are more easily associated with crises, the main rule of crisis management is the prohibition of State aid in (1): this means that all transfers of State resources to undertakings in response to a crisis must be notified and checked for their effects on competition. Considering the ubiquity of that

[40] Directorate for Financial and Enterprise Affairs, Competition Committee, 'Crisis Cartels, Contribution from the European Union' DAF/COMP/GF/WD(2011)20, 5–6.

[41] M Vestager, 'Keynote speech at the European Competition day 2022 in Prague, "Fairness and Competition Policy"' (Prague, 10 October 2022): www.ec.europa.eu/commission/presscorner/detail/en/SPEECH_22_6067.

[42] Schinkel and d'Ailly, 'Corona Crisis Cartels' (n 39 above) 4.

[43] Commission, 'Temporary Framework for State Aid' (n 1 above) 8.

[44] F Costa-Cabral and others, 'EU Competition Law and COVID-19' (*TILEC Discussion Paper No 007/2020*) 6.

[45] For a discussion of Vestager speeches, see N Dunne, 'Fairness and the Challenge of Making Markets Work Better' (2020) 84 *Modern Law Review* 230.

response, Article 107(1) alone is enough to demonstrate that crises follow the same rules and that their management is an integral part of enforcement. The remainder of this section will analyse how a crisis context is taken into consideration in justifying aid. It will be confirmed that there is no legal concept of crisis imposing the authorisation or prohibition of the aid but that, depending on the circumstances and Commission discretion, a particular justification may or not apply. This aligns crises with other situations: aid for exceptional occurrences follows the conditions of commonplace natural disasters, aid for serious economic disturbance demands objectives of common interest like other kinds of aids, and crises participate in the general availability of aid for economic development. As will be shown, the type of damage – not the crisis – is the defining criterion for assigning different justifications. Aid for COVID-19 did benefit from procedural adjustments in guidance and evaluation that allowed it to reach a higher order of magnitude. Nevertheless, when the temporary framework proposed to 'use the full flexibility foreseen under State aid rules to tackle this unprecedented situation',[46] it meant flexibility within the rules and not the freedom to change them. This section will first examine this in relation to the case law (III.A), then for the Commission guidance by focusing on the Temporary Framework for State Aid (III.B) and finally compare it with the RR Guidelines (III.C).

A. Case Law Principles

Aid for natural disasters, exceptional occurrences, and all the grounds in Article 107(2) is stated to 'be compatible with the internal market'.[47] This compatibility is tempered by the case law finding that, as an exception to the prohibition in (1), those grounds must be interpreted narrowly.[48] Aid to remedy an exceptional occurrence like COVID-19[49] follows the conditions set for Article 107(2)(b) – which means the same conditions for both exceptional occurrences and natural disasters. Indeed, because of the CAP, the leading case law is dedicated to natural disasters which are a fairly common occurrence in agriculture such as bad weather and animal disease.[50] The narrow interpretation instead requires a 'direct link' between the aid and the damage caused as well as such damage being assessed

[46] M Vestager, 'Statement by Executive Vice-President Margrethe Vestager on a draft proposal for a State aid Temporary Framework to support the economy in the context of the COVID-19 outbreak' (Brussels, 17 March 2020): https://ec.europa.eu/commission/presscorner/detail/en/STATEMENT_20_479.

[47] Case 730/79 *Philip Morris Holland BV v Commission* [1980] EU:C:1980:209, para 17.

[48] Joined Cases C-346/03 and 529/03 *Atzenis v Regione autonoma della Sardegna* [2006] EU:C:2006:130, para 79.

[49] Case T-259/20 *Ryanair v Commission* [2021] EU:T:2021:92, para 26.

[50] Accepted as natural disasters even though aid was ultimately rejected because of only a general connection with them, Joined Cases C-346/03 and 529/03 *Atzenis v Regione autonoma della Sardegna* (n 48 above) paras 81–82.

as precisely as possible (ie, prohibiting overcompensation).[51] *A contrario*, aid addressing the occurrence or disaster generally or exceeding the damage is not accepted.[52] As such, the management of systemic crisis is (in this regard) similar to sector or even individual crises: what matters is direct damage as indicated by the legal and economic context.

One of the main features of the case law is the latitude given to the Commission under the justifications of Article 107(3) where, contrary to just seen for Article 107(2), aid 'may be considered to be compatible'. A 'wide discretion' is recognised to the Commission in assessing that compatibility due to the 'complex economic and social assessments' involved.[53] The Commission may limit this discretion by adopting and publishing rules of conduct,[54] such as its guidance including temporary frameworks for crises. However, regarding the serious disturbance in a Member State economy under Article 107(3)(b), the Member State may claim exceptional circumstances, not for the purpose of applying a temporary framework, but to deviate from it and apply the Treaty justification directly.[55] When Greece sought that direct application during the financial crisis, the Court was not satisfied with proof of a serious disturbance as showing exceptional circumstances (the sector concerned already being covered by the temporary framework).[56] This confirms that a crisis from a serious disturbance is not in and of itself an exceptional circumstance.

An issue left open by the case law is the role of objectives of common interest for aid to a serious disturbance under Article 107(3)(b) as well as to develop certain economic areas in (c). Economic development has been the preferred justification for the Commission to control State aid[57] because of the room it allows to its already wide discretion: it is a catch-all for aid that is not expressly justified under other provisions and the compatibility test of 'not adversely affect[ing] trading conditions to an extent contrary to the common interest' is relatively open. Commission guidance has thus required that such aid pursue an 'objective of common interest', understood (in the economic approach of modernisation) as

[51] Joined Cases C-346/03 and 529/03 *Atzenis v Regione autonoma della Sardegna* (n 48 above) para 79 and Case T-259/20 *Ryanair v Commission* (n 49 above) para 24.

[52] See Joined Cases C-346/03 and 529/03 *Atzenis v Regione autonoma della Sardegna* (n 48 above) and Case T-259/20 *Ryanair v Commission* (n 49 above) para 25.

[53] Case C-431/14 P *Greece v Commission* [2016] EU:C:2016:145, para 68.

[54] Which it cannot depart from without breaching the principles of equal treatment and legitimate expectations, ibid para 69.

[55] Case C-431/14 P *Greece v Commission* (n 53 above) 70–72 and Case C-526/14 *Kotnik v Drzavni zbor Republike Slovenije* [2016] EU:C:2016:570, para 41.

[56] Case C-431/14 P *Greece v Commission* (n 53 above) paras 73–75.

[57] Notably Commission Regulation 651/2014 declaring certain categories of aid compatible with the internal market in application of Articles 107 and 108 of the Treaty [2014] OJ L187/1, 1 (General Block Exemption Regulation) and Commission Regulation 1407/2013 on the application of Articles 107 and 108 of the Treaty on the Functioning of the European Union to de minimis aid [2013] OJ L352/1 (De Minimis Regulation).

either equity or efficiency objectives.[58] For example, the RR Guidelines define an objective of common interest as aiming to 'prevent social hardship' or 'address market failure'.[59] However, the Court threw the guidance in disarray by finding in *Hinkley Point* that Article 107(3)(c) does not demand such an objective of common interest.[60] Article 107(3)(c) would only require balancing the economic development envisaged with the negative effects on competition.[61] Although the Commission enjoys a wide margin of discretion in this balancing, it must not improperly reduce the scope of Article 107(3)(c).[62] In *obiter dictum*, *Hinkley Point* stated that Article 107(3)(c) differs from (b) in relation to an objective of common interest.[63] Such an objective has not been expressly checked before, so the Court seems to read it in Article 107(3)(b) itself (which refers to a project of European interest together with the serious disturbance).

B. Commission Guidance

The Commission guidance considers crises implicitly, through general instruments that also apply in a crisis context, and explicitly, through dedicated instruments like temporary frameworks. The Temporary Framework for State Aid thus stated that aid in response to COVID-19 may fall within Block Exemption Regulations or, for undertakings that have their difficulties aggravated, be notified under the RR Guidelines.[64] This confirms that these general instruments are also part of crisis management, not only for a systemic crisis like COVID-19 but also for less conspicuous ones that also fall within their scope. A single crisis can thus trigger several justifications depending on context. For COVID-19, the temporary framework categorised aid according to the damage caused: direct damage fell under 107(2)(b), indirect damage under (3)(b) and aggravating difficulties under (3)(c).

[58] Understood, in the economic approach of modernisation, as either equity or efficiency objectives, Commission, 'Common principles for an economic assessment of the compatibility of state aid under Article 87.3': www.ec.europa.eu/competition/state_aid/reform/economic_assessment_en.pdf (a draft communication).

[59] Commission, 'Guidelines on State aid for rescuing and restructuring (n 14 above) 43. Examples given are high unemployment, essential service disruption, systemic importance, service of general economic interest (SGEI) disruption, credit failures, and knowledge loss, Commission, 'Guidelines on State aid for rescuing and restructuring (n 14 above) 44.

[60] Case C-594/18 *Austria v Commission (Hinkley Point)* [2020] EU:C:2020:742, para 20. See also CM Colombo and M Bonelli, 'Governing the Green Transition Through State Aid Control', Ch 12 in this volume and P Nicolaides, 'The Response of EU Courts to Society's Digital and Green Challenges in the Field of Competition and State Aid', Ch 8 in this volume.

[61] *Hinkley Point*, ibid para 101.

[62] ibid paras 21 and 24.

[63] Case C 594/18 *Austria v Commission* (n 60 above) para 20. The General Court has followed by indicating that a balancing with negative effects is unnecessary under Art 107(3)(b), Case T-259/20 *Ryanair v Commission* (n 49 above) paras 67–69.

[64] Commission, 'Temporary Framework for State Aid' (n 1 above) 13–14.

The case law demands direct and specified damage for an exceptional occurrence under (2)(b), which the temporary framework applied to measures forcing the cessation of certain activities – even if the undertaking was already in difficulties, as such difficulties were necessarily unrelated to specific COVID-19 damage.[65] This meant indirect damage from general measures such as social distancing and mask-wearing, as well as from a generalised fall in demand, came under (3)(b).

Most of the Temporary Framework for State Aid was therefore dedicated to aid for a serious disturbance under 107(3)(b), referring to the economic downturn caused by COVID-19 – namely the lack of liquidity of undertakings which endangered their viability.[66] Conditions were set for several types of aid: limited amounts of aid; loan guarantees and subsidised interest rates; credit incentives for banks; and deferrals of taxes and social contributions and subsidies to avoid lay-offs.[67] In addition, Member States were allowed to participate in the recapitalisation of undertakings – arguably the most significant kind of aid since reinforcing undertakings' solvency is highly distortive of competition.[68] The temporary framework therefore subjected recapitalisation to extensive conditions relating to inter alia the undertakings' difficulties, objectives of common interest (which as mentioned are admitted for Article 107(3)(b) in *Hinkley Point*), and competitive guarantees such as prohibiting the use of aid in commercial expansion, acquisitions, advertising the aid and cross-subsidisation.[69] Financial benefits like dividend payments, share buy-backs and management bonuses were prohibited.[70] The remaining aid in the framework was for economic development under 107(3)(c), namely to incentivise public health activities, invest in a sustainable recovery, and provide solvency support.[71] Per *Hinkley Point*, the framework does not refer an objective of common interest (which is nonetheless apparent in the purpose of the aid)[72] and simply balanced their effects.

Contrary to the arguments referred to in the introduction, the Temporary Framework for State Aid did not introduce exceptional rules to facilitate aid. Previous to the temporary framework, there were doubts about whether the narrow interpretation of Article 107(2)(b) would unduly limit Member States' response to COVID-19.[73] Expanding the notion of direct damage would be the logical step to allow more aid, since such aid would be automatically compatible. The framework nevertheless stuck with the existing approach, emphasising the prohibition of overcompensation while channelling aid for conditional approval

[65] ibid 15–15 ter.

[66] ibid 18.

[67] See the corresponding sections in Bouchagiar, 'State Aid in the Context of the COVID-19' (n 9 above) 28–057, 28–082, 28–111 and 28–116.

[68] ibid sections 28–122 and 28–128.

[69] Commission, 'Temporary Framework for State Aid' (n 1 above) 49.

[70] ibid 77–78.

[71] ibid 34–39 and 88–102.

[72] Bouchagiar, 'State Aid in the Context of the COVID-19' (n 9 above) 28–103.

[73] Costa-Cabral and others, 'EU Competition Law and COVID-19' (n 44 above) 5–6.

under Article 107(3) by providing much more detailed guidance for that purpose. This confirmed that the proportionality of the aid would be ensured regardless of being based on Article 107(2) or (3).[74] It may nevertheless be questioned whether this also involved a restrictive interpretation of (3)(b) according to the Commission practice stated in the framework.[75] Such interpretation is reasoned on (3) also being an exception to the prohibition of (1), and has even been confirmed by the General Court.[76] However, it is doubtful (and yet unconfirmed by the Court) that this restriction is needed absent the stated compatibility of (2) and given the Commission's discretion under (3). A restrictive interpretation was certainly not on display when *Hinkley Point* railed against reducing the scope of Article 107(3)(c). In any event, it flies in the face of the framework favouring aid under Article 107(3).

The conclusion that the same rules applied for COVID-19 may appear hard to square with the unprecedented amount of aid. This could be due to the added guidance and speedy evaluation procedure, State aid law being mainly procedural.[77] Nevertheless, the counterfactual of no temporary framework is unavailable, and it is hard to believe that Member States would refrain from using justifications already quite well-defined for direct and indirect crisis damage. The shorter evaluation cuts both ways in allowing and prohibiting aid, since competitive distortions can also be addressed in their infancy. The only certainty is that both authorised and distortive aid were considered an enforcement priority. Another question is whether the framework substantially enhanced the justifications available to Member States.[78] Even assuming that soft law de facto sets these conditions, it implies that they are more favourable to aid than previous (or no) guidance. However, the framework did tighten conditions where the risk of distortion is greater, subjecting recapitalisation to an objective of common interest (when, as commented for *Hinkley Point*, this objective is assumed from the justification) as well as imposing commercial and management limitations.[79] An alternative explanation for the amount of aid may be that their context expanded, not the justifications.[80] It is true that aid has been disproportionately granted by some Member States, but this distortion is a consequence of the rules as they always were: aid is controlled for its justification, not Member State track-record. The framework also attempted to limit internal market distortions by precluding the aid to be conditional on relocation.[81] While

[74] ibid 6.

[75] Commission, 'Temporary Framework for State Aid' (n 1 above) 17.

[76] Joined Cases T-132/96 and T-143/96 *Freistaat Sachsen v Volkswagen* [1999] EU:T:1999:326, para 167.

[77] Biondi, 'Governing the Interregnum' (n 21 above) 23.

[78] Ferri, 'The Role of EU State Aid Law' (n 22 above) 178.

[79] Conditioning aid to non-competitive factors was already discussed during the financial crisis, Costa-Cabral and others, 'EU Competition Law and COVID-19' (n 44 above) 7.

[80] The most criticised aid was for undertakings already in difficulty under the RR Guidelines, not the temporary framework. See Ferri, 'The Role of EU State Aid Law' (n 22 above) 188.

[81] Commission, 'Temporary Framework for State Aid' (n 1 above) 16.

it could have done more under the Commission's wide discretion, discussion on what exactly that would be[82] shows that it is such change that would be exceptional.

C. Resolution by the Market

The remaining possibility of an exceptional application of competition rules is the argument that crises are in general left to the market to resolve. Since that is not manifestly the case for COVID-19, the argument goes that the reaction to 'exceptional' systemic crises is fundamentally different from 'normal' sector crises. For that purpose, the argument can rely on the unquestionable role of safeguarding competitive markets that the prohibition of State aid plays in crisis management. For example, aid for agricultural disasters under Article 107(2)(b) has been contrasted with 'difficulties relating to a crisis in the market concerned' which, as the Commission and Court agreed, were 'the expression of the market forces which must be faced by any business'.[83] The tests of compatibility of aid under the justifications of Article 107(3) also play out against a market counterfactual. As *Kotnik* stated:

> Such aid must be necessary for the attainment of the objectives specified in that provision, in the sense that, without it, market forces alone would not succeed in getting the recipient undertakings to adopt conduct likely to assist attainment of those objectives.[84]

The argument that aid for systemic crises is exceptional nevertheless turns on the RR Guidelines. The guidelines do not mention crisis explicitly[85] but the undertakings in difficulty to which they apply fit sector or individual crises due to being overtaken by 'more efficient and technologically advanced' competitors.[86] The guidelines take an assumedly market-driven approach to such difficulties, namely that inefficient undertakings should in principle exit the market so that their assets are reapplied to more productive uses.[87] Aid to those undertakings is considered 'among the most distortive' since it interferes with this market resolution.[88] Insolvency proceedings would be a better remedy than aid, which therefore should only be available after undertakings have 'exhausted all market options'.[89] Even the prospect of aid might create a 'moral hazard' by leading undertakings to unsustainable practices or distorting their financial value.[90] As such, the argument

[82] See n 22 above.
[83] Joined Cases C-346/03 and 529/03 *Atzenis v Regione autonoma della Sardegna* (n 49 above) 80.
[84] Case C-526/14 *Kotnik v Drzavni zbor Republike Slovenije* (n 55 above) 49.
[85] Beyond a passing reference to the financial crisis (to exclude its application to financial undertakings), Commission, 'Guidelines on State aid for rescuing and restructuring (n 14 above) 17.
[86] ibid 6.
[87] Commission, 'Guidelines on State aid for rescuing and restructuring (n 14 above).
[88] ibid.
[89] ibid 8–9.
[90] ibid.

would conclude, the reason why the Temporary Framework for State Aid did not apply to undertakings in difficulty would be to preserve this treatment of crises and not allow them to benefit from exceptional aid.

However, the argument does not hold because safeguarding competitive markets is compatible with aid for objectives unachievable by market forces alone – the rationale for State aid control which is just as valid for crisis management. On a simple level, each of the above statements can be contextualised. A narrow interpretation of Article 107(2)(b) says nothing about justifying the same aid under (3). *Kotnik* expresses the principle of proportionality, whereby aid will not be justifiable if it is unnecessary to achieve its objectives. Despite the reservations of the RR Guidelines, aid is still granted to undertakings in difficulty, and this has been made even easier by *Hinkley Point*. On a more complex level, a categorisation of crises is just as incapable of capturing market resolution as it is of determining legal treatment. The Temporary Framework for State Aid nominally addresses a systemic crisis but applies to sectors and undertakings in crisis, be it sectors suffering from direct damage or undertakings requiring liquidity.[91] There is no hard border between the framework and not being in difficulty before COVID-19, as the requirement is waived on a number of situations[92] and pre-existing difficulties can be aggravated by direct and indirect damage.[93] This shows the contextual openness of the rules: a sector crisis that could possibly be worked out by market forces can have other policy implications, the same way those objectives are balanced against market effects. That is why crisis management cannot be reduced to exceptional temporary frameworks, as it extends and feeds from the whole of the system of State aid control.

IV. Anticompetitive Behaviour

As with State aid, crisis management by rules on anticompetitive behaviour is concerned both with preserving competitive markets and allowing certain justifications. It was noted in the introduction that Articles 101 and 102 refer to fixing prices, limiting production and unfair conditions. In a crisis, these practices can cover price increases taking advantage of market power[94] and collectively apportioning quotas to deal with shifts in demand. Crises can also lead to market

[91] Otherwise the aid might not be selective – as understood by the temporary framework highlighting social support that would escape State aid control, Commission, Temporary Framework for State Aid (n 1 above) 42.

[92] From micro and small enterprises to preserving employment, Bouchagiar, 'State Aid in the Context of the COVID-19' (n 9 above) 28–31.

[93] Direct damage falling under the temporary framework and indirect damage under the RR Guidelines.

[94] The notion of 'situational monopolies' has been advanced by applying a temporal dimension to market definition, Costa-Cabral and others, 'EU Competition Law and COVID-19' (n 44 above) 11. However, substitutability already presupposes the timespan to meaningfully constrain price-setting.

concentration due to changes in market conditions or companies' valuation, and therefore merger control also plays a role in preventing price increases or coordinated action resulting from that concentration.[95] Despite crises being very much present in undertakings' motivations for engaging in these kinds of behaviour, they are managed implicitly by broader prohibitions of anti-competitive behaviour and by justifications such as benefits to consumers in Article 101(3) and the 'failing firm' defence in mergers. Crisis management becomes explicit when an efficiency or public policy justification is based on a crisis context. This section will therefore start by examining how Articles 101 and 102 and merger control apply in a crisis (IV.A), and then analyse in more detail the justifications in crisis cartels (IV.B) and the Temporary Framework for Cooperation (IV.C).

A. General Rules

Price increases in a crisis can be tackled by the prohibitions of cartels in Article 101 and of excessive prices in Article 102. Collusion between competitors to price-fix is commonly characterised as a cartel.[96] In turn, excessive prices are understood as an excessive difference between cost and price which results in an unfair price.[97] These practices are especially profitable in a crisis due to increased demand or losses. As such, the Temporary Framework for Cooperation warned there would be no tolerance of 'taking advantage' of COVID-19 for 'exploiting customers and consumers (eg, by charging prices above normal competitive levels) or limiting production to the ultimate prejudice of consumers (eg, by obstructing attempts to scale up production to face shortages of supply)'.[98] No adaptation of the rules was mentioned, and neither did it seem necessary. There had been doubts whether price hikes were better left for national 'price gouging' laws protecting consumers without the technical apparatus of competition law cases.[99] Another concern was the historic reluctance of the Commission to pursue cases of excessive prices.[100]

Thus, the temporary framework (only) refers to 'dominant positions conferred by the particular circumstances of this crisis', Commission, Temporary Framework for assessing antitrust issues (n 5 above) 20.

[95] Council Regulation 139/2004 on the control of concentrations between undertakings [2004] OJ L24/1 (Merger Regulation) and Guidelines on the assessment of horizontal mergers under the Council Regulation on the control of concentrations between undertakings [2004] OJ C31/5 (Horizontal Merger Guidelines) 22.

[96] Case C-67/13 P *CB v Commission* [2014] EU:C:2014:2204, para 51. Being a restriction by object, that is to say harmful to competition by its very nature, cartels dispense the proof of negative effects but a restriction by effect remains equally available.

[97] Case 27/76 *United Brands v Commission* [1978] EU:C:1978:22, paras 250 and 252.

[98] Commission, 'Temporary Framework for assessing antitrust issues' (n 5 above) 20.

[99] Costa-Cabral and others, 'EU Competition Law and COVID-19' (n 44 above) 8.

[100] Commission, 'Guidance on the Commission's enforcement priorities in applying [Article 102 TFEU] to abusive exclusionary conduct by dominant undertakings' (Communication) [2009] OJ C45/7, 7.

Competition authorities did end up pursuing a number of such cases,[101] confirming that unfairness is easier to find when prices change during a crisis (rather than an ongoing margin rewarding investment).

Although merger control also contributes to preventing price increases in a crisis, it includes a concept with an even closer affinity to crises: the failing firm defence. As seen for the RR Guidelines, the exit of less efficient undertakings would return their assets to the market for more productive use.[102] However, the acquisition of these assets by a competitor may trigger merger control[103] and be considered a significant impediment to effective competition,[104] preventing the crisis from being efficiently solved by the market. The Horizontal Merger Guidelines thus admit a so-called failing firm defence if the alternative to the merger is the exit of the undertaking together with its assets.[105] The guidelines attribute this to 'exceptional circumstances'[106] but again there is no exceptional rule, only an implicit context of sector or individual crisis, considering that the failing firm defence applies the same counterfactual analysis that determines whether any merger has negative effects[107] together with a proportionality test to the benefits of redeploying the assets. Indeed, the Commission resisted calls to relax the failing firm defence during the financial crisis,[108] and there have been no claims of an exceptional merger policy for COVID-19 beyond the temporary extension of deadlines.[109]

The view of the Commission guidance is that the general rules on anticompetitive behaviour are orientated by consumer welfare.[110] This is the product of the economic approach of modernisation which, as developed below, dismissed public interest in interpreting competition rules. Such interest is specifically legislated for in merger control, with Member States being able to block a merger based on their public interest.[111] This possibility is available in a crisis but overall it is very rarely applied (although it was used to secure energy supply in the event of a possible crisis).[112] As will be seen next, whether consumer welfare or public interest are represented in crisis cartels and the Temporary Framework for Cooperation is a matter of debate. The social benefits of crisis cartels were side-lined by

[101] B Kianzad, 'Excessive Pricing During COVID-19 Crisis in EU: An Empirical Inquiry' (*Concurrences No 1-2021*).

[102] See Commission, 'Guidelines on State aid for rescuing and restructuring' (n 14 above) 8–9.

[103] Either in itself or by gaining control of the exiting undertaking, Merger Regulation (n 25 above) Art 3(1).

[104] ibid Art 2(3).

[105] Horizontal Merger Guidelines Regulation (n 95 above) 90.

[106] ibid 12.

[107] ibid 9 and 89.

[108] Costa-Cabral and others, 'EU Competition Law and COVID-19' (n 44 above) 17–18.

[109] Commission, 'Mergers Practical Information': https://competition-policy.ec.europa.eu/mergers/practical information_en.

[110] Costa-Cabral, 'Future-Mapping the Three Dimensions of EU Competition Law' (n 10 above) 323–24.

[111] Merger Regulation (n 25 above) Art 21(4).

[112] A Jones and J Davies, 'Merger Control and the Public Interest: Balancing EU and National Law in the Protectionist Debate' (2014) 10 *European Competition Journal* 453.

modernisation, but a guarded possibility remains of consumer benefits under Article 101(3). In contrast, the conditions of the temporary framework follow the proportionality test of a public policy justification under Article 101(1). Hence, it should be clear from the outset, both crisis cartels and the temporary framework are just part of the general rules of Article 101, and not an exceptional regime.

B. Crisis Cartels

Crisis cartels, as the name indicates, are the most common association between competition law and crises. The term came to designate a series of cases where, after initial European integration and globalisation led to sector crises of overcapacity and lower demand, industry-wide arrangements to coordinate production were considered to fall under Article 101.[113] The designation 'crisis cartels' hints at harmful cartel-like behaviour, but the fact that these agreements have not always been sanctioned as such acknowledges that a crisis context may set them apart – indeed, the designation is a misnomer since it has applied to both sanctioned and exempted agreements. In any event, crisis cartels are considered a restriction by object under Article 101(1) requiring a justification in order to be allowed. The Commission discussed a block exemption regulation in the 1970s for agreements aimed at balancing excess capacity with declining demand.[114] Reportedly, such a regulation was rejected out of fear of opening the floodgates to cartelisation and modifying the criteria of Article 101(3).[115] As explained next, aiming to reduce overcapacity is not in itself a guarantee of clearing Article 101(3) but is not barred from satisfying its conditions either.

The Commission clarified how crisis cartels could be exempted under Article 101(3) through its decisional practice. Setting quotas, closing off Member State markets and fixing prices failed to be exempted.[116] Non-applicability decisions based on Article 101(3) eventually arrived in *Synthetic Fibres*, involving the largest European manufacturers, and *Stichting Baksteen*, for the brick industry in the Netherlands.[117] They allowed coordinated reductions of capacity that did not operate by production quotas (such as closing plants), which counted as improvements in production – in particular the social aspect of coordinating the redundancy or retaining of workers.[118] Consumers were also found to benefit from better products

[113] For a survey, see Kokkoris, 'Should Crisis Cartels Exist' (n 34 above).
[114] ibid 733.
[115] ibid 734.
[116] ibid 735–36.
[117] Commission Decision of 4 July 1984 relating to a proceeding under Article 85 of the EEC Treaty (Case IV/30.810 – Synthetic fibres) [1985] OJ L207/17 and Commission Decision of 29 April 1994 relating to a proceeding under Article 85 of the EC Treaty (Case IV/34.456 – Stichting Baksteen) [1994] OJ L131/15. The Commission also exempted mutual acquisitions in the petrochemicals sector under the same principles, Kokkoris, 'Should Crisis Cartels Exist' (n 34 above) 747, 753, 744, and 746.
[118] See Wardaugh, 'Crisis Cartels' (n 11 above).

in the long run, counting as a fair share of the benefits, and residual competition remained from the parties and external producers, not completely excluding competition.[119] At the same time, cartels that dealt with quotas or price claiming a crisis justification obtained at most a (non-mandatory) reduction of the fine.[120] Indeed, the crisis cartels allowed were notified to the Commission under the pre-modernisation procedure mandatory for any exemption, thus being understood as fulfilling the conditions of Article 101(3) rather than crisis-specific rules.[121]

This all changed with modernisation: not only did the Commission stop issuing exemptions (for any agreement) but its guidance also put crisis cartels practice in doubt. Notably, Article 101(3) Guidelines limited the benefits that could be taken into account to efficiencies.[122] Although crisis cartels were attributed long-term benefits to consumers, the abstract account in the decisions is not on par with the guidelines' standard for demonstrating efficiencies and pass-on to consumers.[123] It has been advanced that this economic approach was intended to constrain national competition authorities' power to also apply Article 101(3), after modernisation ended the mandatory notification to the Commission, lest they subordinate competition to their Member State's industrial policy.[124] This would apply particularly to the failing industries of crisis cartels. At the same time, the guidelines also vowed to examine practices according to effects on consumer welfare instead of formal categories,[125] opening the way to reconsider the prohibition of crisis cartels under Article 101(1).

The consequences of modernisation were tested in *Beef Industry Development Society LtD (BIDS)*, a preliminary reference over the qualification as a restriction by object of an industry agreement to reduce capacity.[126] The parties argued (in line with the Commission guidance) that there were no negative effects on consumer welfare.[127] Crisis cartels would thus differ from true cartels, where such effects were 'obvious' since the output restriction still comfortably met demand.[128] The Court however applied its definition of restrictions by object as harmful by their very nature to normal competition.[129] This dismissed a legitimate objective to address

[119] Kokkoris, 'Should Crisis Cartels Exist' (n 34 above) 744 and 747–48.

[120] ibid 751–52.

[121] Ibid 737.

[122] Commission, 'Guidelines on the application of Article 101(3) TFEU' (n 12 above) 50 and 85.

[123] Wardaugh, 'Crisis Cartels' (n 11 above) 323.

[124] O Brook, 'Priority Setting as A Double-Edged Sword: How Modernization Strengthened the Role of Public Policy' (2020) 16 *Journal of Competition Law & Economics* 435.

[125] Commission, 'Guidelines on the application of Article 101(3) TFEU' (n 12 above) 21–22; see Costa-Cabral, 'Future-Mapping the Three Dimensions of EU Competition Law' (n 10 above) 311.

[126] Case C-209/07 *Competition Authority v Beef Industry Development Society Ltd and Barry Brothers Meats Ltd* (n 14 above) 13–14.

[127] ibid 19.

[128] Case C-209/07 *Competition Authority v Beef Industry Development Society Ltd and Barry Brothers Meats Ltd* (n 14 above) paras 22 and 25. This suggested consumers would not be affected, dismissing a restriction by effect, hence the discussion over object.

[129] ibid 17, now settled case law, Case C-179/16 *F Hoffmann-La Roche and Others v Autorità Garante della Concorrenza e del Mercato* [2018] EU:C:2018:25, para 78.

the crisis[130] and concentrated on the objective to affect market structure.[131] From that perspective, an agreement to reduce overcapacity and encourage exit would conflict with the principle that 'each economic operator must determine independently the policy which it intends to adopt'.[132] In particular, it would save the parties from 'intensifying their commercial rivalry or resorting to concentrations'.[133] Such an agreement would therefore by these circumstances alone constitute a restriction by object.[134] After the judgment, the Commission read it as arrangements to limit capacity being 'hardcore restrictions' unlikely to be exempted under the Article 101(3) Guidelines.[135] However, *BIDS* only showed that crisis cartels restricted competition by object, not that they cannot be justified – a possibility left open by the Court.[136]

The Commission eventually accepted that Article 101(3) could apply to crisis cartels when an exemption was sought before the national court of *BIDS*. At a time when the financial crisis was ongoing (March 2010), the Commission submitted an *amicus curiae* brief with a positive view.[137] The brief accepts the efficiencies of removing less efficient producers (when an uncontrolled reduction could harm more efficient ones) and increased output per producer.[138] Cyclical recession would be solved by exit of inefficient competitors unless the crisis were structural, defined as sustained reductions of capacity utilisation and operating losses without prospect of medium-term improvement.[139] This was backed up by an economic theory of 'war of attrition', whereby undertakings would not heed market signals in the expectation of using capacity when others leave the market.[140] The national court ended up not ruling on an exemption, but the brief reads as an *ex post* tailoring of the crisis cartels to the economics of modernisation.

The Commission nevertheless hardened its position in a contribution to the OECD forum on crisis cartels (January 2011). Overcapacity is further connected with (desirable) technological change and (undesirable) overinvestment – with a notable reference to State aid and political concerns over employment[141] directly putting into question exemptions based on social benefits. A failing firm defence

[130] Case C-209/07 *Competition Authority v Beef Industry Development Society Ltd and Barry Brothers Meats Ltd* (n 14 above) para 21.

[131] ibid para 31.

[132] ibid para 34.

[133] ibid paras 34–35.

[134] The Court also found that the means to attain this objective were restrictive by object, Case C-209/07 (n 14 above) paras 37–38.

[135] Commission, 'Antitrust: Commission welcomes Court ruling in Irish beef case' (2008) MEMO/08/728.

[136] Case C-209/07 *Competition Authority v Beef Industry Development Society Ltd and Barry Brothers Meats Ltd* (n 14 above) para 21.

[137] Commission, 'Amicus curiae observations – Antitrust': https://competition-policy.ec.europa.eu/antitrust/national-courts/amicus-curiae-observations_en.

[138] ibid 20 and 24.

[139] ibid 33 and 35.

[140] Commission, 'Amicus curiae observations' (n 137 above) 36.

[141] OECD, 'Crisis Cartels' DAF/COMP/GF(2011)11 (Paris, 2011) Commission Contribution 6.

and specialisation agreements are also added as least restrictive alternatives for sector reorganisation[142] even though they do not seem so: the redeployment of productive assets under a failing firm defence would fail to reduce overcapacity, while specialisation at (the necessary) industry-level would likely exceed the market share to qualify for a block exemption.[143] The contribution concludes that, were the market not to correct excess capacity by itself, the coordination would still not result in price reductions for consumers unless there were 'important learning economies'.[144] Failing to satisfy the condition of passing-on benefits to consumers, the contribution thus declares an Article 101(3) exemption 'very unlikely'.[145]

Despite this, the legality of crisis cartels remains a possibility. The absence of further exemptions does not mean their off-hand dismissal, only that – coherently with post-modernisation exercise of the Commission's discretion – when Article 101(3) conditions appear to be fulfilled the case is not pursued to a final decision.[146] It is not excluded that this may deviate from the interpretation in the brief and contribution. The case law has also changed in the interim, presently holding that pro-competitive effects might raise doubts over an agreement's harmful nature and thereby dismiss a restriction by object under Article 101(1).[147] This would allow advancing pro-competitive effects of sector rationalisation without stumbling on pass-on to consumers. Nonetheless, the restriction by object in *BIDS* was confirmed just before pro-competition effects were integrated in the case law.[148] The Commission's oscillation on the efficiency of crisis cartels also shows it cannot be fully relied on. Social benefits end up providing a more stable justification, since it is uncontested that crisis cartels achieve them. No such claim was made in *BIDS*, which explains leaving a legitimate objective based on economic benefits for Article 101(3) when, as seen next, public policy has been accepted under (1). It is therefore also possible that crisis cartels have continued to be allowed by not pursuing them for public policy reasons.[149]

C. Temporary Framework for Cooperation from COVID-19

The Temporary Framework for Cooperation was set up differently from crisis cartels. As already outlined, it substantively allowed agreements addressing

[142] ibid 43 and 45.

[143] ibid 48.

[144] ibid 58. The brief had already stated that cutting fixed costs by removing overcapacity was less likely to reduce the variable (marginal) costs that determine the final price, but this was left case-by-case without the innovation condition of the contribution, Commission, 'Amicus curiae observations' (n 137 above) 41–42.

[145] Commission Contribution (n 141 above) 62.

[146] Brook, 'Priority Setting as A Double-Edged Sword' (n 124 above) 440.

[147] Case C-307/18 *Generics UK v Competition and Markets Authority* [2020] EU:C:2020:52, para 103.

[148] Case C-67/13 P *CB v Commission* (n 96 above) 83–85.

[149] Notably by accepting commitments, Brook, 'Priority Setting as A Double-Edged Sword' (n 124 above) 473.

the shortage of products – notably but not limited to medicines and medical equipment – as well as their procedural notification to the Commission to obtain a comfort letter.[150] It also reminded that modernisation established a system of self-assessment based on 'consolidated' guidance,[151] which has since led the Commission to refrain from issuing non-applicability decisions and even informal guidance letters.[152] The framework describes itself as facilitating that self-assessment, but its very existence shows that the guidance was not consolidated after all. The focus on supply shortages appeared to differentiate it from crisis cartels but, when describing the COVID-19 crisis, it also mentioned oversupply from the 'abrupt decline in consumer demand'.[153] This could lead to coordinated pauses in production very similar to crisis cartels, as in the CAP markets where competition rules were suspended.[154] The framework's alignment with the guidance nevertheless weighs towards a deliberate refusal to engage with crisis cartels.

The key issue of the Temporary Framework for Cooperation is the legal basis for allowing agreements that may infringe competition rules. The notification procedure, even if no longer mandated after modernisation, still falls within the Commission's discretion and does not appear to have affected enforcement substantially.[155] Before the temporary framework, the ECN stated they would not intervene against temporary measures to avoid shortages as 'such measures are unlikely to be problematic', as they would either 'not amount to a restriction of competition under Article 101' or 'generate efficiencies that would most likely outweigh any such restriction'.[156] The comparison with the two situations identified in the temporary framework is relevant. Only exchanges of information through a central entity to identify and predict shortages would 'not raise antitrust concerns'.[157] In contrast, output and distribution coordination by exchange of commercially sensitive information were considered 'in normal circumstances problematic under EU competition rules'.[158] If these remained problematic in the exceptional circumstances of COVID-19, they would still 'not give rise to an enforcement priority' as long as they were 'designed and objectively necessary to

[150] Commission, 'Temporary Framework for assessing antitrust issues' (n 5 above) 18.
[151] ibid 6.
[152] Monti, 'Business Cooperation in Times of Emergency' (n 9 above) 4.
[153] Commission, 'Temporary Framework for assessing antitrust issues' (n 5 above) 2.
[154] See, Press Release, 'Coronavirus' (n 17 above).
[155] Only two comfort letters were published (with no apparent deviation from the temporary framework), www.ec.europa.eu/competition/antitrust/medicines_for_europe_comfort_letter.pdf and Directorate-General for Competition, 'Comfort letter: cooperation at a Matchmaking Event – Towards COVID-19 vaccines upscale production' COMP/E-1/GV/BV/nb (2021/034137).
[156] See European Competition Network, 'Antitrust: Joint Statement' (n 6 above).
[157] As long as the information did not flow back to competitors, Commission, 'Temporary Framework for assessing antitrust issues' (n 5 above) 12–13. The reasoning is not made explicit, with only a general reference to the Horizontal Guidelines, but it seems premised on the absence of collusion (due to competitors not being privy to information) and foreclosure (by only circulating information and not managing output).
[158] Commission, 'Temporary Framework for assessing antitrust issues' (n 5 above) 15.

actually increase output in the most efficient way'; 'temporary in nature'; and 'not exceeding what is strictly necessary'.[159] The framework added that encouragement or coordination by a public authority would be taken into account for both not raising concerns and not being a priority.[160]

The Temporary Framework for Cooperation unnecessarily obfuscated this exercise of discretion. As any other guidance, it binds the Commission within its discretion and cannot go against the case law. But whereas general guidance is framed with reference to Article 101 conditions, the temporary framework painted itself as a pure exercise of discretion by not referring to the case law. It is within the Commission's wide discretion to refrain from pursuing an infringement in the Union interest,[161] but that is associated with managing resources and (low) importance.[162] The framework did the opposite by stating that undertakings taking advantage of the crisis to breach competition rules would be closely monitored, which – in line with the high stakes described – sets these cases as an enforcement priority. 'Taking advantage' applies as much to raising prices as to coordinating production and distribution which, as *BIDS* demonstrated, may be restrictive by object even if pursuing a legitimate objective – and could also increase prices in the context of COVID-19.[163] The risk of being pursued as cartels is why, as stated in the introduction, this coordination requires the assurance of guidance or rule suspension.[164] Were the investigation of such infringements both prioritised in their description and deprioritised in their enforcement, the framework's statement of reasons and internal coherence would be open to judicial challenge. It would further set a dangerous precedent of Commission guidance instructing parties on how to infringe competition rules, as highlighted by those that argued against a relaxation of rules during COVID-19.[165]

The Temporary Framework for Cooperation should therefore be read as deprioritising agreements that, despite involving a high-priority restriction, were also likely to be justified. This would align the temporary framework with the general guidance as well as the practice of not issuing form non-infringement decisions when a justification is likely. The question is the justification at work. The ECN referred to Article 101(3), but the framework did not. The conditions of increasing

[159] ibid.

[160] ibid. An 'imperative request from public authorities' is also mentioned, but this would preclude an infringement in the first place.

[161] Case C-119/97 P *Ufex and Others v Commission* [1999] EU:C:1999:116, paras 88–89.

[162] Case T-712/14 *CEAHR v Commission* [2017] EU:T:2017:748, para 36.

[163] Schinkel and d'Ailly, 'Corona Crisis Cartels' (n 39 above) 7.

[164] It is therefore unlikely that the restriction is ambiguous, otherwise undertakings could rely on the current practice of not pursuing effects-only cases due to the resources required for their analysis. *Contra*, Monti has suggested that problematic agreements would have 'sizeable pro-competitive effects', the framework dismissing a restriction by object and formalising the lower priority of effects, Monti, 'Business Cooperation in Times of Emergency' (n 9 above) 3. Regardless of the ambiguity of the restriction, the framework arguably also attributes priority to negative effects on essential products in the crisis.

[165] Schinkel and d'Ailly, 'Corona Crisis Cartels' (n 39 above) 13.

output 'in the most efficient manner' and 'not exceeding what is strictly necessary' could perhaps be read as efficiencies and proportionality under the Article 101(3) Guidelines. However, it must be kept in mind that the purpose of modernisation was to promote economic analysis, and so the guidelines demand that efficiencies be specified, quantified and balanced against negative effects.[166] For the temporary framework to apply Article 101(3) consistently, efficiencies would have to be expressly mentioned ('most efficient' might still be inefficient in relation to cost) and undertakings would be required to substantiate both efficiencies and pass-on to consumers. Even accounting for indications rather than hard evidence, it cannot be assumed that a restriction increasing output would automatically benefit consumers – in principle competition is the best way to respond to increased demand.[167] As the Commission's objections to crisis cartels show, failing to safeguard pass-on to consumers excludes Article 101(3).[168]

Under the Temporary Framework for Cooperation, legality only depended on the agreements being proportional to the objective of increasing output. This is how the conditions of the temporary framework should be read, as they all relate to a proportionality test: namely, the steps of appropriateness ('efficient manner'), necessity ('objective necessity'), and proportionality *stricto sensu* or balance of interests ('not going beyond the necessary').[169] Proportionality is also why the arrangements must be 'temporary', since extending them beyond the COVID-19 crisis is manifestly unnecessary. In turn, proportionality is associated with a 'legitimate objective' escaping the prohibition of Article 101(1), a justification which has applied to professional and sports associations since *Wouters*.[170] This case law has covered regulatory activity and is thus considered to reflect objectives of public interest.[171] The Commission guidance has so far ignored *Wouters* as part of the economic approach of modernisation, as it has done for the pre-modernisation case law opening Article 101(3) to benefits other than consumer welfare.[172] The Commission cannot disavow the case law, but it also has discretion on what is covered by the guidance. Regardless, *Wouters* is a route for public

[166] Commission, 'Guidelines on the application of Article 101(3) TFEU' (n 12 above) 51–55.

[167] Schinkel and d'Ailly, 'Corona Crisis Cartels' (n 39 above) 4.

[168] Costa-Cabral, 'Future-Mapping the Three Dimensions of EU Competition Law' (n 10 above) 323.

[169] W Sauter, 'Proportionality in EU Law: A Balancing Act?' (2013) 15 *Cambridge Yearbook of European Legal Studies* 448.

[170] Case C-309/99 *Wouters v Algemene Raad van de Nederlandse Orde van Advocaten* [2002] EU:C:2002:98 97. The legitimate objective and the proportionality test were made explicit after Case C-519/04 P *Meca-Medina and Majcen v Commission* [2006] EU:C:2006:492, paras 42 and 45.

[171] Brook, 'Priority Setting as A Double-Edged Sword' (n 124 above) 11. Those objectives have included the independence and qualification of professions and the integrity of sporting competitions. Regulatory powers may be given to private bodies to be exercised in the public interest but lack the public authority or last-resort intervention by the State to be considered public action outside Art 101, Case C-427/16 *CHEZ v Yordan Kotsev* [2017] EU:C:2017:890, paras 45–49.

[172] Brook, 'Priority Setting as A Double-Edged Sword' (n 124 above) 12.

interest to be taken into account under Article 101 without demanding benefits to consumers.

By applying a public interest justification subject to proportionality, the Temporary Framework for Cooperation could be considered the first guidance on *Wouters*. Were efficiency the concern of the temporary framework, existing guidance would suffice.[173] By prioritising the output of medicines and medical products over efficiency, the temporary framework showed a concern for public health.[174] This would align it with the public interest justification in *Wouters* – it arguably outranks the interests accepted by that case law. Arrangements appropriate to their objective and a tolerance for inefficiency are the hallmarks of *Wouters*.[175] The temporary framework also considered public encouragement or coordination which, in light of the case law dismissing it for finding a restriction,[176] can only be squared with a public policy justification.[177] Indeed, the involvement of public authorities would overcome a possible limitation of *Wouters* to private entities endowed with regulatory functions – which does not hold in any event, since it is neither a condition of the case law nor does it reflect that industry-wide agreements have the same effect as private regulation (as crisis cartels demonstrate). The two comfort letters granted under the temporary framework confirm this analysis:[178] they refer to benefits for patients or public health, not to consumers, and while the first did come from an association of undertakings, the second originated in contracts for an event. As such, rather than relaxing the rules for cooperation, the temporary framework merely provided guidance on decade-long case law.

V. Conclusions

Crises have a traditional meaning in EU law: exposing the insufficiencies of an evolving system and prompting new bouts of integration. Jean Monnet famously predicted that the EU would be shaped by crisis. Thus, while dealing with a financial crisis, the European Council was also concerned with the European Pact on

[173] Costa-Cabral, 'Future-Mapping the Three Dimensions of EU Competition Law' (n 10 above) 326.

[174] Public health has already been considered for anti-competitive behaviour, Dunne, 'Fairness and the Challenge' (n 15 above) 18. Other shortages to which the temporary framework could have applied might also have had a public interest (such as preventing hoarding or social anxiety).

[175] Indeed, there is a parallel with privileging the health of athletes rather than their economic activity by allowing the prohibition and sanctioning of doping in *Meca-Medina:* Case C-519/04 P (n 170 above).

[176] Case C-198/01 *CIF v Autorità Garante della Concorrenza e del Mercato* [2003] EU:C:2003:430, para 56.

[177] Dunne, 'Fairness and the Challenge' (n 15 above) 8.

[178] See Commission, 'Temporary Framework for assessing antitrust issues' (n 5 above) 15.

Immigration and Asylum and the second Irish referendum on the Lisbon Treaty. This is the EU law dimension of polycrisis. What is remarkable is that the legislative and constitutional change across EU law has had little impact on competition law. This chapter has shown that COVID-19, and crisis more generally, does not lead to exceptional rules. Normal rules are simply applied to the crisis context: competitive markets continue to be safeguarded, State aid is authorised for the justifications that emerge, coordination is allowed for efficiency or public interest. This resilience can be attributed to three factors: the consensus on the importance of competition for the internal market,[179] the flexibility of broad prohibitions and justifications, and the discretion afforded to the Commission in guidance and prioritisation – as stated at the outset, crisis management remains coherent with competition law's goals, principles, and techniques.

This chapter considered a shift from the legislative intervention typical of EU crisis to the administrative action seen for COVID-19. This raises questions of legitimacy and transparency. Avoiding legislation limits the input of the Council and European Parliament, but the conclusions of the European Council show the Commission is not acting freely in issues of such political importance. Indeed, this is more direction than competition policy is usually subject to. In addition, multiple revisions of instruments like the Temporary Framework for State Aid provide an opportunity for dialogue with Member States and the European Parliament. It is nevertheless apparent that the Commission is comfortable with the reinforcement of its technocratic legitimacy. Some have added crisis to the reasons for changing the modernisation practice of resolving cases through discretion instead of non-infringement decisions,[180] but a rapidly evolving situation and greater public interest probably recommends this speed and flexibility – arguably the European Council directed so.[181] The effectiveness of enforcement was not however analysed in this chapter, only the substance of the rules. In that regard, it was seen that the Temporary Framework for Cooperation went too far in ignoring the case law on public interest justification to describe itself solely as the product of discretion.

The resilience of competition law has two facets. On one side, it is a success of the economic governance of the EU that competition policy can be relied upon in polycrisis. On the other, when competition law is affected in the sense of an EU crisis it is for reasons that would hardly register elsewhere. The most significant legislative intervention, modernisation, was arguably (only) a reaction to a crisis of the Commission's economic analysis due to the formalism adopted for

[179] A crisis of EU competition law was therefore averted by not drawing any legal consequence from the Treaty of Lisbon moving the reference to competition from the provision on the objectives of the internal market to Protocol 27.

[180] Monti, 'Business Cooperation in Times of Emergency' (n 9 above) 8.

[181] See Council, 'Presidency Conclusions 14368/08' (n 31 above).

notified agreements and the annulment of several merger decisions.[182] It is possible that the distortion in the amount of aid granted by Member States during the COVID-19 crisis will lead to a comparable substantive change in State aid control. More importantly, the current climate change and environmental crises might show competition law finally being affected by polycrisis, as it is being integrated in the European Green Deal. It nevertheless remains to be seen whether sustainability will be accommodated in the crisis management described in this chapter or will uncover a more fundamental contradiction with the enforcement of competition rules.

[182] Costa-Cabral, 'Future-Mapping the Three Dimensions of EU Competition Law' (n 10 above) 308. As argued there, the recent regulation of the technological sector could arguably be as significant as modernisation, but whether it reacts to an 'enforcement gap' able to constitute a crisis is doubtful. See also Regulation 2022/1925 of the European Parliament and of the Council on contestable and fair markets in the digital sector (Digital Markets Act) [2002] OJ L 265/1.

PART II

Actors and Dynamics in EU Competition Law

5

Levelling the Playing Field: EU Regulatory Extension Through Technocratic Cooperation

KATHRYN WRIGHT*

I. Introduction

The European Union's (EU) external regulatory power has recently been tested by Brexit, the burgeoning economic power of China and an undermined multilateral trade system. A key issue facing the EU is how to manage regulatory divergence and maintain its competitiveness in the absence of globally harmonised standards. The European Commission's recent Trade Policy Review (TPR) renews focus on extending the EU's regulatory impact beyond its borders: through international regulatory cooperation, and 'levelling the playing field' through implementation of trade agreements and tackling competitive distortions caused by third State intervention.[1] These level playing field measures aim to shield EU firms from unfair external competition due to lower standards elsewhere outside the EU. The Commission's philosophy is 'open strategic autonomy', striking a balance between rules-based cooperation based on global and bilateral engagement, and developing unilateral tools to deploy against unfair trading conditions on the EU internal market.[2]

In the EU's external trade relations, competition can be understood in the sense of competition law and enforcement (antitrust, mergers and State aid/subsidies),

* Senior Lecturer in Law, University of York, kathryn.wright@york.ac.uk. With thanks to my co-editors, Nicolas Rennuy, and the participants of 'The Evolving Governance of EU Competition Law in Times of Disruptions: a Constitutional Perspective' conference, particularly Giorgio Monti for comments on an early version.

[1] Commission, 'Trade Policy Review – An Open, Sustainable and Assertive Trade policy' (Communication) COM(2021) 66 final, Section 3.2, 11.

[2] Commission, 'Trade Policy Review' (n 1 above) Sections 2.1, 2.4; Proposal for a Regulation of the European Parliament and of the Council on foreign subsidies distorting the internal market COM(2021) 223 final, explanatory memorandum, 1.

and in a wider sense as regulatory competition or competitiveness between jurisdictions. The EU utilises a range of instruments to manage its relationships with third countries. Such instruments span legally binding rules and softer commitments through best practice and guidelines. While some of these instruments encompass substantive competition rules, it is administrative cooperation and inter-agency agreement that are the backbone of the EU's relationships with third countries regarding competition, often as a substitute for harmonisation.[3] In addition, non-regression clauses on standards in Free Trade Agreements (FTAs) such as those with Canada, South Korea, Japan and Ukraine and, in the case of the UK, the Trade and Cooperation Agreement's (TCA) level playing field provisions, operate at the nexus of trade and competition, covering a number of policy areas, such as environmental and labour standards, to manage regulatory competition. Once provisions are included in FTAs, their implementation is a further question. Overarching dispute settlement mechanisms in trade agreements are blunt tools for managing the relationship between States. Softer cooperation mechanisms between regulators can play a significant role 'on the ground'.

This chapter makes two principal contributions. First, it brings together the literature from law and political science on EU external governance, regulatory networks and epistemic communities, and integration without EU membership. This literature demonstrates the significance of technocratic cooperation with third country regulators to manage divergence in various sectors. Second, going further, the chapter explores how the EU co-opts third country regulators in competition policy, arguing that it lays the foundation for technocratic cooperation through exporting in trade instruments EU constitutional principles such as equivalence, transparency, and requirements for independent regulators. More specifically, in some areas it looks to mirror internal and external provisions on cooperation.

These principles are fundamental to EU competition law and regulation. In the absence of substantive harmonisation, the EU principle of mutual recognition operates by assuming that Member States' regulatory standards are equivalent.[4] The principle of equivalence, twinned with the principle of effectiveness, also arises in institutional settings. In areas of domestic enforcement of EU law, the relevant procedural and institutional conditions are left to the Member State, as long as claims based on EU law are not treated less favourably than national law claims (equivalence) or render the enforcement of EU rights by individuals practically impossible or excessively difficult (effectiveness).[5] Each Member State

[3] See for example A Papadopoulos, *The International Dimension of Competition Law and Policy* (Cambridge, Cambridge University Press, 2010) ch 3.

[4] Case 120/78 *Rewe-Zentral AG v Bundesmonopolverwaltung für Branntwein* (Cassis de Dijon) [1979] EU:C:1979:42, para 14: 'There is … no valid reason why, provided that [goods] have been lawfully produced and marketed in one of the Member States, [they] should not be introduced into any other Member State'.

[5] Case 33/76 *Rewe-Zentral AG v Landwirtschaftskammer für das Saarland* [1976] EU:C:1976:188, para 5; Joined cases C-279/96, C-281/96 and C-281/96 *Ansaldo Energia SpA v Amministrazione delle Finanze dello Stato* [1998] EU:C:1998:403, para 27.

may designate the courts or authorities having jurisdiction over claims based in EU law.[6] Independent national authorities are promoted in various areas of EU regulation,[7] and are at the heart of enforcement of EU competition law, linked to effective and consistent enforcement.[8] Transparency is a central value of EU law.[9] In the regulatory context, transparency is one of the good governance principles underpinning the EU Better Regulation agenda,[10] and invoked in the TPR both in terms of EU internal legitimacy in the conduct of trade negotiations and improving the external multilateral trade framework.[11]

The chapter proceeds by outlining the modes by which the EU extends its regulatory influence, before focusing on technocratic cooperation. The relevant literature on EU external governance, regulatory networks and (administrative) integration without membership is explored in section II. Section III frames level playing field provisions as means for recognising equivalence. Section IV assesses how the EU promotes independent and effective third country authorities as counterparts, and section V discusses transparency tools as precursors to cooperation and mutual monitoring. A final section concludes.

II. Modes for EU Regulatory Extension and the Role of Technocratic Institutions

The EU's relationship with third countries tests its influence on States themselves, regulators and firms. Regulatory extension can occur through different modes,[12] which are not necessarily mutually exclusive: via the 'Brussels effect',[13]

[6] *Rewe-Zentral*, ibid para 5.

[7] See for example S De Somer, 'The Powers of National Regulatory Authorities as Agents of EU Law' (2018) 18 *European Research Area Forum* 581; B Rangoni and M Thatcher, 'National De-delegation in Multi-Level Settings: Independent Regulatory Agencies in Europe' (2023) 36 *Governance* 8.

[8] See eg Council Regulation (EC) No 1/2003 of 16 December 2002 on the implementation of the rules on competition laid down in Articles 81 and 82 of the Treaty [2002] OJ L01/1, 1–25, Art 35(1): '1. The Member States shall designate the competition authority or authorities responsible for the application of Articles [101] and [102] of the Treaty in such a way that the provisions of this regulation are effectively complied with.'

[9] For example, Arts 11(2) and (3) TEU, Art 42 EU Charter on Fundamental Rights, Regulation (EC) No 1049/2001 of the European Parliament and of the Council of 30 May 2001 regarding public access to European Parliament, Council and Commission documents [2001] OJ L145/43, 43, Joined Cases C-39/05 P and C-52/05 P *Sweden and Maurizio Turco v Council* [2008] EU:C:2008:374; see A Alemanno, 'Unpacking the Principle of Openness in EU Law: Transparency, Participation and Democracy' (2014) 39 *European Law Review* 72.

[10] Commission, 'Better Regulation Guidelines' (Commission Staff Working Document) SWD(2021) 305 final.

[11] Commission, 'Trade Policy Review' (n 1 above) 7, 8, 12, 21–22.

[12] S Lavenex, 'The Power of Functionalist Extension: How EU Rules Travel' (2014) 21 *Journal of European Public Policy* 885.

[13] A Bradford, 'The Brussels Effect' (2015) 107 *Northwestern University Law Review* 1; A Bradford, *The Brussels Effect: How the European Union Rules the World* (Oxford, Oxford University Press, 2020).

through legislation or intergovernmental agreements, and/or through technocratic cooperation.

First, the Brussels effect emphasises the roles of the market and the incentivised conduct of firms. It concerns the behaviour of multinational market actors in complying with EU rules and norms – even in their non-EU market activities, contributing to the diffusion of EU rules and norms beyond the territory of the EU. According to Bradford, the EU has capacity for unilateral regulatory globalisation by virtue of its market power, regulatory capacity, preference for strict rules, focus on inelastic targets and non-divisibility of standards. Third country governments adopt EU rules because they, or their firms and regulators, wish to avoid the costs from being unable to access the Single Market.[14]

Differences in product standards between jurisdictions lead to increased costs and uncertainty for businesses since different production lines for sale in different countries are inefficient. A de facto 'Brussels effect' operates when firms and market actors required to produce goods to EU standards for the EU market rationally decide to comply with those same standards for their other geographic markets. This incentive to over-comply with EU rules is reflected in Bradford's condition of 'non-divisibility of standards', whether economic, technical or legal. In terms of economic standards, it is less financially costly for producers to comply with one standard rather than several. Regarding technical standards, firms may be unable to produce goods with different specifications for different markets.

This compliance incentive is linked to Bradford's third type of non-divisibility of standards: legal non-divisibility, developed by Scott.[15] Going beyond de facto incentives, firm-level territorial extension requires third country companies to comply with EU law even when they are not producing goods for the EU market, for example through standardisation requirements. Country-level territorial extension operates to make EU market access conditional upon the content of third country law, giving rise to the de jure Brussels effect. The de jure effect occurs when a third country incorporates EU standards into its domestic legislation.[16] This incorporation may occur at the behest of firms lobbying for similar standards in their domestic markets so as not to put themselves at a disadvantage with domestic competitors.[17]

[14] ibid; Lavenex, 'The Power of Functionalist Extension' (n 12 above) 887; D Bach and A Newman, 'The European Regulatory State and Global Public Policy: Micro-Institutions, Macro-Influence' (2007) 14 *Journal of European Public Policy* 827; C Damro, 'Market Power Europe' (2012) 19 *Journal of European Public Policy* 682.

[15] Bradford, 'The Brussels Effect', 17–19; J Scott, 'The Global Reach of EU Law' in M Cremona and J Scott (eds), *EU Law Beyond Borders: The Extraterritorial Reach of EU Law* (Oxford, Oxford University Press, 2019) 32–33.

[16] Scott, 'The Global Reach of EU Law' (n 15 above) 31.

[17] A Bradford, 'Exporting Standards: The Externalization of the EU's Regulatory Power Via Markets' (2015) 42 *International Review of Law and Economics* 158, 167.

Therefore, both political and technocratic institutions remain central to the diffusion of EU standards.[18] The second mode for regulatory extension – the foreign policy approach between the EU and third States – includes trade agreements, legislation extending regulatory commitments to third-country market players and regulators,[19] or conditionality requirements for EU accession countries,[20] typically formulated through the classical EU institutions of the Commission and Council. This mode is characterised by some element of rule-based discipline (with implementation and enforcement) through public institutions.[21] The overarching governance structures of the EU-UK TCA and some FTAs exemplify this. These instruments include the European Economic Area (EEA) agreement, agreements with candidate and neighbouring countries,[22] dedicated competition cooperation agreements and memoranda of understanding[23] and competition provisions in other bilateral agreements,[24] in addition to participation in multilateral fora (such as the International Competition Network (ICN), the Organisation for Economic Co-operation and Development (OECD), the United Nations Conference on Trade and Development (UNCTAD) and the World Trade Organization (WTO)).[25] Cooperation modes within bilateral instruments include discussions of expected policy developments and dialogue on approaches to particular competition issues,[26] technical cooperation[27] and mutual assistance in enforcement in

[18] Lavenex, 'The Power of Functionalist Extension' (n 12 above) 893.

[19] Scott, 'Extraterritoriality and Territorial Extension in EU Law' (2014) 62 *American Journal of Comparative Law* 87; Lavenex, 'The Power of Functionalist Extension' (n 12 above); Scott, 'The Global Reach of EU Law' (n 15 above).

[20] Conditionality as a threat of sanctions or the promise of rewards in exchange for compliance with a certain demand: F Schimmelfennig and U Sedelmeier, 'Governance by Conditionality: EU Rule Transfer to the Candidate Countries of Central and Eastern Europe' (2004) 11 *Journal of European Public Policy* 661. Here, approximation with the EU acquis is dependent on the third country's incentives as an associate or candidate country.

[21] K Armstrong, 'Regulatory Autonomy after EU Membership: Alignment, Divergence and the Discipline of Law' (2020) 45 *European Law Review* 207.

[22] Such as Stabilisation and Association Agreements with candidate and Western Balkans countries. Commission, 'Bilateral Agreements with Candidate Countries and Western Balkan Countries': https://competition-policy.ec.europa.eu/international/legislation/candidate-countries-and-western-balkan-countries_en.

[23] Commission, 'Bilateral relations on competition issues': https://competition-policy.ec.europa.eu/bilateral-relations_en; Commission, 'Dedicated competition cooperation agreements': https://competition-policy.ec.europa.eu/international/legislation/dedicated-competition-cooperation-agreements_en; Commission, 'Memoranda of understanding': https://competition-policy.ec.europa.eu/international/legislation/memoranda-understanding_en.

[24] For a discussion see V Demedts, 'Which Future for Competition in the Global Trade System: Competition Chapters in FTAs' (2015) 49 *Journal of World Trade* 407.

[25] Commission, 'Multilateral texts': competition-policy.ec.europa.eu/international/legislation/multilateral-texts_en.

[26] For example the Memorandum of Understanding on a dialogue concerning the EU State aid control regime and China's Fair Competition Review System.

[27] For example with India, Japan, South Korea and the ASEAN country authorities through the Competition Cooperation EU-Asia Partnership (2018–2022) – see Directorate-General for Competition, 'Management Plan 2021' Ref.Ares(2021)847979, 20.

individual cases,[28] sharing information and capacity building. Some instruments are concluded with the States themselves through FTAs, whereas others involve direct cooperation with third country authorities.

This leads us to the third mode for regulatory extension, and the focus of this chapter: cooperation between agencies. Rules may be developed not only through intergovernmental rule-making and primary legislation, but at a sectoral level between regulators and in some cases with stakeholders themselves.[29] This latter type of institutional interaction through technocratic cooperation also includes enforcement between sectoral regulatory agencies. This mode emphasises the importance of networks and epistemic communities. An epistemic community denotes a network of experts, across different countries, in a particular policy area who share a set of norms and authoritative claims to knowledge.[30] Networks imply sharing or production of that knowledge among communities of, inter alia, regulatory authorities:[31] 'within these networks, EU influence works not on the basis of rule imposition but through more subtle mechanisms of learning and socialisation'.[32] In this way, third country regulators are co-opted through functionalist extension of EU law and policy in a particular sector or policy area.[33]

Within EU competition law in the narrower sense, even before the framework of Regulation 1/2003[34] which led to increased decentralisation of enforcement and cooperation in antitrust through the European Competition Network

[28] For example exchange of information and enforcement cooperation in Art 259 (and Art 260 on consultations) Ukraine Deep and Comprehensive Trade Area (DCFTA): Association Agreement between the European Union and its Member States, of the one part, and Ukraine, of the other part [2014] OJ L161/3; exchange of evidence under second generation agreements eg with Switzerland (2014), negotiations with Canada ongoing: Directorate-General for Competition, 'Management Plan 2021' (n 27 above) 17. A more far-reaching example is the Mexico administrative agreement on cooperation (2018), through positive comity (requests to initiate enforcement action and obligations to consider a request and inform the other side of the outcome) and negative comity (in the avoidance of conflicts) to recognise the other side's interests: Administrative Arrangement on Cooperation in the Field of Competition Law and Enforcement between on the one side the Directorate-General for Competition of the European Commission and, on the other side the Federal Economic Competition Commission of Mexico: https://competition-policy.ec.europa.eu/system/files/2021-06/Mexico-EU_memorandum-of-understanding_2018_en.pdf.

[29] See A Héritier, 'New Modes of Governance in Europe: Policy Making without Legislating?' (2002) 81 *Institut fur Höhere Studien* 24, on 'policy-making without legislating' through transgovernmental committees and regulatory agencies.

[30] PM Haas, 'Epistemic Communities and International Policy Coordination' (1992) 46 *International Organization* 1.

[31] M Egeberg, *Multilevel Union Administration: The Transformation of Executive Politics in Europe* (London, Palgrave Macmillan, 2006); D Coen and M Thatcher, 'Network Governance and Multi-Level Delegation: European Networks of Regulatory Agencies' (2008) 28 *Journal of Public Policy* 49; I Maher, 'Competition Law in the International Domain: Networks as a New Form of Governance' (2002) 29 *Journal of Law and Society* 129.

[32] Lavenex, 'The Power of Functionalist Extension' (n 12 above) 890.

[33] ibid 887, 890.

[34] Council Regulation (EC) No 1/2003 of 16 December 2002 on the implementation of the rules on competition laid down in Articles 81 and 82 of the Treaty [2002] OJ L01/1.

(ECN), an epistemic community of competition officials – together with the input of the European Commission and the Court of Justice of the European Union (CJEU) – was 'a channel for the exchange of information, ideas, solutions and arguments between the systems and levels of law'.[35] Such socialisation led to the convergence of national competition policies.[36] This networked approach extends beyond the EU, through other networks involving third country authorities such as the OECD, the Nordic network, and horizontal relations between Member State and third country competition authorities.

The role of regulators and administrative institutions is significant in the trajectory of trade relationships and competition. The presence of independent regulatory bodies and 'regulatory clashes between jurisdictions creates a demand for cross-national initiatives to "solve" these clashes, whether through formal or informal means'.[37] Transnational executive bodies are therefore open for mutual influence in regulatory co-ordination.[38] While trade agreements may include provisions setting a framework for cooperation, regulatory differentiation also follows sector-specific functionalist dynamics that are only loosely linked to these overarching foreign policy agreements.[39] Of particular relevance to the UK's position as a former Member State, institutional path dependencies are significant in extending governance modes beyond the EU's territory, and political structures lack the ability to fully steer them.[40]

In the particular case of the UK post-Brexit, mechanisms of European integration still have an effect even without membership given the interdependence of the EU and UK markets, and institutional interactions matter. As Trondal and Kühn observe drawing from the position of Norway, administrative officials are tightly interwoven into and influenced by EU institutions, largely as a result of 'increased institutionalisation of the European multilevel administrative system in which national agencies have acquired a larger position as access points for EU agencies'.[41] Their longitudinal data on the domestic context showed that officials had become more integrated into the EU's multilevel administration over time, and that '(administrative) integration beyond membership is promoted and nudged by

[35] F van Waarden and M Drahos, 'Courts and (Epistemic) Communities in the Convergence of Competition Policies' (2002) 9 *Journal of European Public Policy* 913, 933.

[36] ibid.

[37] H Farrell and AL Newman, 'Domestic Institutions beyond the Nation-State: Charting the New Interdependence Approach' (2014) 66 *World Politics* 331, 345.

[38] S Lavenex, 'The External Face of Differentiated Integration: Third Country Participation in EU Sectoral Bodies' (2015) 22 *Journal of European Public Policy* 836, 839.

[39] ibid, giving the examples of the European Economic Area (EEA), the European Neighbourhood Policy, and the bilateral agreements with Switzerland.

[40] S Lavenex, D Lehmkuhl and N Wichmann, 'Modes of External Governance: a Cross-National and Cross-Sectoral Comparison' (2009) 16 *Journal of European Public Policy* 813, 813.

[41] J Trondal and N Kühn, 'Governing a Post-Brexit Europe and the Case of Norway: Integration Without Membership in an Affiliated State' in S Gänzle, B Leruth and J Trondal (eds), *Differentiated Integration and Disintegration in a Post-Brexit Era* (Abingdon, Routledge, 2019).

favourable organizational conditions at the domestic level'.[42] Thus, they expect the UK to experience 'silent EEA-isation'.[43] While the UK does not have Norway-style alignment or extension of the EU acquis as a 'quasi-member' through the EEA, it starts from a position of even greater integration as a former full EU Member State. EU law is already embedded through the UK's domestic legislation and administrative institutions.[44] Moreover, withdrawal from the EU affects the UK's future domestic regulatory architecture, either by designating existing authorities or establishing new ones to perform previously EU competences.

Network analysis based on quantitative and qualitative data shows that the UK Competition and Markets Authority (CMA) was an active and prominent member of the ECN.[45] The TCA provides that the European Commission, Member State and UK competition authorities should 'endeavour to cooperate and coordinate, with respect to their enforcement activities concerning the same or related conduct or transactions, where doing so is possible and appropriate'[46] and may exchange information as permitted by each party's law.[47] There is explicit reference to a separate subsequent cooperation agreement between the Commission, Member State and UK authorities, 'which may include conditions for the exchange and use of confidential information'.[48] Similarly, the TCA provisions on subsidies/State aid allow for a cooperation framework between the respective independent authorities, which the UK was required to establish on leaving the EU.[49] (The UK has set up a Subsidy Control Unit within its designated authority, the CMA.[50]) Here the parties 'encourage their respective independent authorities or bodies to cooperate with each other on issues of common interest within their respective functions'.[51] In practice there is some evidence of ad hoc cooperation in antitrust and merger investigations between the UK CMA and the European Commission's Directorate

[42] ibid 165, 241.

[43] S Gänzle, B Leruth and J Trondal, 'Whither Differentiated (Dis)Integration in a "Post-Brexit Era"'? in S Gänzle, B Leruth and J Trondal (eds), *Differentiated Integration and Disintegration in a Post-Brexit Era* (Abingdon, Routledge, 2019).

[44] There were no immediate changes to the substance of UK competition law, incorporated through retained EU law. The Retained EU Law (Revocation and Reform) Act 2023 makes provision for revoking, replacing or updating it. New EU decisions or rulings are no longer binding on the UK, but national courts and authorities should act with a view to ensuring there is no inconsistency with pre-31 December 2020 EU law: see s 60A(2) UK Competition Act 1998 inserted by the Competition (Amendment etc.) (EU Exit) Regulations 2019.

[45] F Vantaggiato, H Kassim and K Wright, 'Internal Network Structures as Opportunity Structures: Control and Effectiveness in the European Competition Network' (2021) 28 *Journal of European Public Policy* 571.

[46] Trade and Cooperation Agreement between the European Union and the European Atomic Energy Community, of the one part, and the United Kingdom of Great Britain and Northern Ireland, of the other part [2021] OJ L149/10 (TCA), Art 361(2) TCA.

[47] ibid Art 361(3).

[48] TCA, Art 361(4); Press Release, 'Regulating After EU Exit': www.nao.org.uk/press-release/regulating-after-eu-exit/, paras 3.15, 3.16, 3.22.

[49] TCA, Art 371(1).

[50] Operational from autumn 2022, established by the UK Subsidy Control Act 2022.

[51] TCA, Art 371(2).

General for Competition (DG COMP), and with a small number of Member State authorities on a bilateral basis.[52]

Having considered how regulatory cooperation may be employed to manage divergence, the following sections explore how trade instruments encompass EU constitutional principles – equivalence, independence and transparency – to lay the foundation for interactions with third country authorities.

III. Level Playing Field and Equivalence

In the wider sense of regulatory competition, the EU has increased its focus on third country subsidies and standards in various policy areas, as reflected in the Foreign Subsidies Regulation (FSR)[53] alongside bilateral provisions in FTAs. In the context of FTAs, the role of regulatory authorities is important not only in implementing regulatory commitments, but also in assessing any divergence for the purposes of the level playing field provisions. Level playing field provisions provide a 'floor' for recognising third country standards as equivalent. These provisions in external trade agreements are inspired by the EU principle of mutual recognition, albeit with a much more limited acknowledgement of equivalent standards.[54]

A. Free Trade Agreements

As a starting point, some agreements explicitly recognise the regulatory autonomy of the parties, such as the EU-Japan Economic Partnership Agreement (2019)[55]

[52] According to the CMA annual plan 2022–23 through alternative networks to the ECN on policy such as the OECD, ICN and UNCTAD. The CMA and DG COMP coordinated dawn raids for the first time post-Brexit in April 2022 end of life vehicle recycling investigations; there were also three parallel cases on dominance in digital technology, eg, Press Release, 'Antitrust: Commission opens investigation into possible anticompetitive conduct by Google and Meta, in online display advertising': www.ec.europa.eu/commission/presscorner/detail/en/ip_22_1703, March 2022 – agreement between Google and Meta.

[53] Regulation (EU) 2022/2560 of the European Parliament and of the Council of 14 December 2022 on foreign subsidies distorting the internal market (FSR) [2022] OJ L330/1.

[54] For a discussion of different types of mutual recognition see K Nicolaidis and G Schaffer, 'Transnational Mutual Recognition Regimes: Governance without Global Government' (2006) 68 *Michigan Review of International Law* 267; A Correia de Brito, C Kauffmann and J Pelkmans, 'The Contribution of Mutual Recognition to International Regulatory Cooperation' (*OECD Regulatory Policy Working Papers No 2/2006*); K Wright and D Webb, 'Future Trade with the EU: Mutual Recognition' (*House of Commons Library briefing paper 8384/2018*).

[55] Agreement between the European Union and Japan for an Economic Partnership [2022] OJ L330/3 27 (consolidated 1.2.2022), Art 16.2(1): '1. Recognising the right of each Party to determine its sustainable development policies and priorities, to establish its own levels of domestic environmental and labour protection, and to adopt or modify accordingly its relevant laws and regulations, consistently with its commitments to the internationally recognised standards and international agreements to which the Party is party'...

and the UK-EU Trade and Cooperation Agreement (2020).[56] The purpose of the level playing field is 'not to harmonise the standards of the Parties'.[57] However, non-regression commitments and convergence to international standards set minimum standards. Such non-regression commitments aim to avoid a 'race to the bottom'. They set the prevailing standards at the time of the conclusion of the agreement as the existing baseline and aim to avoid new distortions of competition which would result from such weakened standards. Parties should not encourage trade and investment by weakening or reducing levels of protection.[58]

Non-regression commitments are limited in the sense that they do not include a requirement to 'ratchet up' levels of protection in future. Some provisions, such as in the EU-Japan agreement and the EU-UK TCA, go further than non-regression to include references to maintaining and improving respective high standards.[59] These are relatively soft commitments, since they do not require the other party to match if one party raises its standards domestically.[60] Although the parties shall 'strive' to increase their respective levels of protection,[61] if standards are raised, in the TCA there is no evolution clause to raise the benchmark from that at the end of the transition period (as the EU had originally included in its negotiating position).

In labour and social and environmental and climate chapters, disputes are to be dealt with exclusively through the level playing field panel of experts for non-regression areas as laid out in Articles 408–410, rather than the horizontal dispute resolution procedure[62] (although they are subject to arbitration tribunals

[56] TCA, Art 356(1) on the right to regulate, precautionary approach, and scientific and technical information, Art 387 (1) on labour and social standards; TCA, Art 391 on environmental standards) with similar wording: 'The Parties affirm the right of each Party to set its policies and priorities in the areas covered by this Chapter, to determine the … level of protection it deems appropriate and to adopt or modify its law and policies in a manner consistent with each Party's international commitments, including those under this Chapter.'

[57] TCA, Art 355(4) Title XI: Level Playing Field for Open and Fair Competition and Sustainable Development.

[58] Eg, TCA, Arts 387(2) and 391(2); Comprehensive Economic and Trade Agreement (CETA) between Canada, of the one part, and the European Union and its Member States, of the other part [2017] OJ L11/23, Art 24.5(1) on 'weakening or reducing' environmental law; Free Trade Agreement between the European Union and its Member States, of the one part, and the Republic of Korea, of the other part [2011] OJ L127/1, Art 13.7(2) regarding environmental and labour protections; EU-Japan Agreement Art 16.2.(2) on 'relaxing or lowering' standards in respect of labour or environmental laws and regulations.

[59] Art 16.2(1) EU-Japan agreement, Art 355(4) TCA Title XI: Level Playing Field for Open and Fair Competition and Sustainable Development.

[60] M Bronckers and G Gruni, 'Retooling the Sustainability Standards in EU Free Trade Agreements' (2021) 24 *Journal of International Economic Law* 25; E Lydgate, 'Non-regression Clauses: Sufficient to Maintain the UK-EU Future Relationship on Environmental Standards and Regulation'? (*University of Sussex Working Paper 2018:* https://sro.sussex.ac.uk/id/eprint/81765/3/Non-regression%20clauses.pdf). An even stronger mechanism of 'dynamic alignment' was proposed by the EU, and rejected by the UK, at one point in the TCA negotiations.

[61] TCA, Arts 387(4) and Art 391(5).

[62] ibid Arts 389(2), Art 396(2) and Art 407(2).

for rebalancing measures, together with the subsidies chapter).[63] The inclusion of panels of experts shows a further role for epistemic communities.

The TCA provisions can be compared and contrasted with examples in the EU's other agreements with third countries, for example South Korea, Canada, Japan and Singapore.

These provisions often use international standards as benchmarks.[64] For example, in the EU-Japan Agreement, the right of the parties to determine their own policies and priorities and to adopt or modify laws or regulations is tempered by 'consisten[cy] with [their] commitments to the internationally recognised standards and international agreements'[65] to which they are party. These international standards are viewed as neutral benchmarks, though they may be based on EU standards uploaded to the international level.

As reflected in the EU's 'open strategic autonomy' of its Trade Policy Review, cooperative mechanisms need to be underpinned by enforcement and safeguarding measures. A strong example is to be found in the EU-UK TCA. If a subsidy causes or seriously risks causing a 'significant negative effect on trade or investment between the Parties',[66] proportionate remedial measures may be imposed to remedy that effect or risk. The other party may request an arbitral tribunal.[67] If the arbitral tribunal finds the remedial measure inconsistent or disproportionate, it must cease or be adjusted, otherwise the other party may apply compensation measures through suspension of obligations in any area of the TCA.[68]

There are also prohibitions on failing to effectively enforce those laws and regulations in a way which would encourage trade or investment.[69] These implementation and enforcement obligations, ultimately backed up by dispute settlement procedures, underline the role of third country regulators since they embed obligations in the domestic setting.

B. Foreign Subsidies Regulation

The recently adopted Foreign Subsidies Regulation further extends the level playing field beyond the EU.[70] It aims to close the regulatory gap whereby Member States are subject to State aid rules, but third country subsidies to firms operating within

[63] ibid Art 411.
[64] TCA, Arts 387(1) and 391(1), Title XI Chapter 8 on sustainable development TCA, Art 384 TCA on tax using OECD standards.
[65] EU-Japan agreement Art 16.2(1).
[66] TCA Art 374(1).
[67] ibid Art 374(9) in accordance with Art 739.
[68] ibid Arts 374(12) and 761.
[69] ibid Arts 387(2), and 391(2); EU-Japan Agreement Art 16.2(2), CETA Art 24.5(3), EU-South Korea Agreement Art 13.7(1). See the 2021 Report of the Ad Hoc Panel of Experts Constituted Under Art 13.15 of the EU-Korea Free Trade Agreement 7, *International Labor Rights Case Law*, 243–56.
[70] n 53.

the internal market do not face equivalent scrutiny. The Regulation's approach involves first uncovering such subsidies,[71] with criteria and procedures for assessing their potential distortive effect on the internal market, before applying tools to remedy those distortions. The Regulation centres on two ex ante notification procedures – in the context of concentrations and public procurement respectively – and an ex officio market investigation tool. Businesses operating on the EU market and benefiting from foreign subsidies, above certain thresholds, are required to notify the subsidies to the Commission, which has sole enforcement power. The market investigation tool echoes the powers in Regulation 1/2003[72] Article 17, and the possibility of ex post enforcement through the existing EU competition rules (which may involve Member State competition authorities alongside the Commission) remains open.

The Commission envisages that the Foreign Subsidies Regulation 'may prompt third countries to increase efforts to seek multilateral solutions as well as to reassess the use of subsidies in their investment policies'.[73] In this way the Commission views third country authorities as agents to address those domestic subsidies. In its legislative proposal, the Commission asserted the rationale that 'jurisdictions that have in place … subsidy control systems are expected to be better placed to identify and address subsidies that distort the EU internal market'.[74] This view underlines the importance of regulators as counterparts. While third country regulators are not directly engaged in enforcement, which is the preserve of the Commission, the Commission may engage them with information requests or in consultations throughout a notification procedure or investigation. The provisions on information requests from third country authorities to an extent mirror EU internal exchange with Member State competition authorities. Whereas under Article 13(5) 'At the request of the Commission, Member States shall provide it with all necessary information to carry out the duties assigned to it by this Regulation',[75] under Article 13(6) 'The Commission may also request a third country concerned to provide all necessary information'.[76] 'Third country' could be interpreted here as the entity granting the subsidy or benefit, or as a regulatory authority. Clearly no duty for a third country entity to provide information can be imposed, but inferences will be drawn from the available facts, and inaccurate or misleading

[71] The definition of a subsidy is a financial contribution, provided directly or indirectly by a third country, conferring a benefit which is limited to one or more undertakings or industries: FSR (n 53 above) Art 3.

[72] n 34. See F Brito Bastos, 'Repurposing Administrative Procedures to Meet Novel Challenges in EU Competition Law', Ch 9 in this volume.

[73] Proposal for a Regulation of the European Parliament and of the Council on foreign subsidies distorting the internal market COM(2021) 223 final, legislative financial statement.

[74] ibid.

[75] See F Brito Bastos, 'Repurposing Administrative Procedures to Meet Novel Challenges in EU Competition Law' (n 72 above) in this volume regarding cooperation between the Commission and national competition authorities in the Foreign Subsidies Regulation.

[76] See also preliminary review in the FSR (n 53 above) Art 10.

statements discounted.[77] Regarding market investigations, the Commission may also request the third country concerned to supply information.[78]

In terms of a wider dialogue, the Regulation specifically provides for the Commission to 'engage in a dialogue with the third country concerned, to explore options aimed at obtaining the cessation or modification of such subsidies with a view to eliminating their distortive effects on the internal market'[79] in instances where 'the Commission suspects the existence of repeated distortive foreign subsidies, or where several enforcement actions under this Regulation identify distortive foreign subsidies granted by the same third country'.[80] Although not in the main provisions, recital 60 raises the possibility of using consultation mechanisms in existing bilateral agreements which cover distortive subsidies to facilitate this dialogue.[81] As implied by the Commission's proposal,[82] relations with third country regulators allow for more direct and timely resolution than the blunt, high-level, instruments of rebalancing measures and arbitration in FTAs mentioned earlier.

Engaging third country authorities regarding implementation once a decision is made is not explicitly addressed, as the remedy or fines would be implemented on operations within the EU. Though it does not amount to input before a formal decision is made, under Article 40(1) of the Regulation, a third country can express its view on the Commission's published summary decision.

Finally, in its amendments the European Parliament raised the issue of equivalent systems of subsidy control. It encouraged the Commission to consider in its assessment of a distortion whether the third country has a system of subsidy control and review at least equivalent to the EU system, with the inference that it would make subsidies granted by that third country less likely to distort the EU market.[83] This proposal was not directly adopted in the final text, but in an annexed statement[84] the Commission commits to clarifying within 12 months the application of Article 4(1) on the existence of a distortion caused by a foreign subsidy, the application of the Article 6 balancing test weighing negative effects

[77] ibid Art 16.
[78] ibid Art 36(1).
[79] ibid Art 37(1).
[80] ibid.
[81] The European Parliament's (EP) amendments, not ultimately adopted, sought to amplify the EU's influence by 'raising the matter in any relevant international forum or through cooperation with any other third country affected by the same systemic distortive subsidies, or with any interested third country': Recital 43a and Art 34a of the EP text: Parliament, 'Texts adopted, Distortive foreign subsidies I' P9_TA(2022) 143. Recital 69 of the adopted text does make clear that the Regulation 'should complement the Union effort to improve multilateral rules on addressing distortive subsidies', for example through the WTO.
[82] Proposal for a Regulation (n 73 above) Legislative financial statement, para 1.5.4.
[83] Arts 3(1)(c), 3(2a) and Recital 14 in EP position: Parliament, 'Distortive foreign subsidies' (n 81 above).
[84] Commission, 'Statement of the European Commission on clarifications as regards the application of Regulation 2022/2560 pursuant to Article 46 thereof 2022/C491/04' [2022] OJ C491/8, 8.

of a subsidy against the positive effects of the subsidised activity on the internal market, and the Article 27(1) assessment of a distortion in a public procurement procedure, which may include this criterion. This potential consideration of equivalence echoes the approach in some FTAs and underlines the role of third country authorities as enforcers.

IV. Independent and Effective Authorities as Counterparts for Enforcement

Effective dialogue depends on counterparts. Given that the EU principle of mutual trust is not applicable in relations between the EU and a non-Member State,[85] requiring effective and/or independent authorities is a way of building common ground and a basis for recognition. Setting these requirements serves a further important purpose in the context of competition: to ensure that an international competition culture, as a norm championed by the European Commission and shared by the epistemic community, is promoted, and protected. These requirements seek to empower independent authorities both internally (within the EU) and externally vis-à-vis governments.[86] In the same way that ECN procedural and institutional rules aim to empower technocratic independent authorities in the respective Member States, provisions of FTAs and competition cooperation agreements aim at giving leverage to regulators in third countries. In turn, those authorities are networked.

Notably, the terminology of a 'level playing field' is also used in the EU internal context, to be achieved by formal guarantees on independence, adequate resources and minimum enforcement and fining powers in the application of Articles 101 and 102 TFEU and parallel national competition law.[87] Some competition chapters in trade agreements with third countries aim to mirror the EU internal regime. The establishment of 'well-functioning operationally independent competition authorities that build up a solid enforcement record' is also one of the European Commission's policy objectives in neighbouring candidate countries.[88]

[85] Opinion of Advocate General 1/17 CETA [2019] EU:C:2019:72, para 129.

[86] On independent authorities see for example S de Somer, 'The Powers of National Regulatory Authorities' (n 7 above), F Gilardi and M Maggetti, 'The Independence of Regulatory Authorities' in D Levi-Faur (ed), *Handbook of Regulation* (Cheltenham, Edward Elgar, 2010); M Thatcher, 'Regulation after Delegation: Independent Regulatory Agencies in Europe' (2002) 9 *Journal of European Public Policy* 954.

[87] Directive (EU) 2019/1 of the European Parliament and of the Council of 11 December 2018 to empower the competition authorities of the Member States to be more effective enforcers and to ensure the proper functioning of the internal market [2019] OJ L11/3 (ECN+ Directive), Recital 8.

[88] Directorate-General for Competition, 'Management Plan 2021' (n 27 above) 20.

The TCA and the Ukraine Deep and Comprehensive Free Trade Area (DCFTA) through the Association Agreement[89] set requirements for an 'independent' – beyond an 'effective' – competition authority. In the TCA there are requirements to maintain a competition regime with independent authorities and an enforcement system.[90] For example, Article 360 TCA states that '[e]ach Party shall take appropriate measures to enforce its competition law in its territory [and] shall maintain an operationally independent authority or authorities competent for the effective enforcement of its competition law'. While no further specific institutional requirements are laid down, Article 360(3) requires that 'Each Party shall apply its competition law in a transparent and non-discriminatory manner, respecting the principles of procedural fairness, including the rights of defence of the economic actors concerned, irrespective of their nationality or ownership status'. Similar principles appear in the Ukraine Association Agreement, where the parties recognise the importance of applying their respective competition laws in a transparent, timely and non-discriminatory manner, respecting the principles of procedural fairness and rights of defence.[91] In particular, and echoing Member State obligations in the EU Charter of Fundamental Rights (CFR),[92] there are specific rules on rights of defence before a competition authority imposes a sanction or remedy against any natural or legal person and after provisional conclusions are communicated,[93] and during judicial review proceedings.[94]

To an extent these rules again mirror the internal EU regime of the European Competition Network, such as Article 35 of Regulation 1/2003[95] with its focus on designation of authorities to ensure effective application of EU competition law, and the subsequent European Competition Network Plus (ECN+) Directive[96] regarding specific institutional features and powers. One of the objectives of that Directive was to address the lack of independence of some Member State authorities.[97] Article 360(3) TCA echoes the safeguards in the ECN+ Directive

[89] Association Agreement between the European Union and its Member States, of the one part, and Ukraine, of the other part [2014] OJ L161/3.

[90] TCA, Arts 359 and 360.

[91] Ukraine Association Agreement, Art 255(3).

[92] Charter of Fundamental Rights of the European Union [2000] OJ C364/01, Art 47. European Convention for the Protection of Human Rights and Fundamental Freedoms, as amended by Protocols Nos 11 and 14 [1950] (ECHR), Art 6; G Gentile, 'Two Strings to One Bow? Article 47 of the EU Charter of Fundamental Rights in the EU Competition Case Law: Between Procedural and Substantive Fairness' (2020) 4 *Market and Competition Law Review* 169.

[93] Ukraine Association Agreement (n 89 above) Art 255(3) (a).

[94] ibid Art 255(3)(b).

[95] n 8 above.

[96] Directorate-General for Competition, 'Management Plan 2021' (n 27 above). For further consideration of the ECN+ Directive, see F Brito Bastos, 'Repurposing Administrative Procedures to Meet Novel Challenges in EU Competition Law', Ch 9 in this volume.

[97] ECN+ Directive (n 87 above) Art 4 and Recitals 3 and 5. Operational independence is especially to be achieved in terms of rules on appointment and dismissal of competition authority boards (Arts 4(3), 4(4), Recital 17) and protection from external pressure in decision-making and priority setting (Arts 4(2), 4(5), Recital 17).

concerning fundamental rights, particularly rights of defence.[98] The TCA does not go as far as the specific institutional requirements as expressed in the Directive on resources, dismissal, etc. However, in the Ukraine Association Agreement, Article 255(2) requires the parties not only to maintain authorities responsible for the effective enforcement of competition law, but also that those authorities be 'appropriately equipped'. This echoes the provisions on resourcing in Article 5 of the ECN+ Directive.

The requirement for an 'an operationally independent authority … entrusted with the powers necessary' relates to State aid, whereas the competition (ie, antitrust and merger) rules should be 'effectively' enforced.[99] This difference may be because the existing competition authority was already established and explicitly named in the agreement, whereas a State aid authority was still to be set up within three years of the agreement, to include powers to authorise state aid schemes and individual aid grants.[100] Ukraine is also required to approximate its substantive competition law and enforcement practices to those of the EU.[101] This explicitly includes specific legislation: Regulation 1/2003 on the implementation of Articles 101 and 102 of the Treaty on the Functioning of the European Union (TFEU) regarding concerted practices and agreements between firms and abuse of dominant position,[102] the EU Merger Regulation 139/2004[103] and the block exemption regulations on vertical agreements[104] and technology transfer.[105] While not explicitly using the language of a 'level playing field',

> the Parties recognise the importance of free and undistorted competition in their trade relations … [and] acknowledge that anti-competitive business practices and transactions have the potential to distort the proper functioning of markets and generally undermine the benefits of trade liberalisation.[106]

[98] ECN+ Directive (n 87 above) Art 3.

[99] Ukraine Association Agreement (n 89 above) Arts 267(1) and 255(2).

[100] ibid Art 267(1).

[101] ibid Art 256.

[102] n 34 above.

[103] Council Regulation (EC) No 139/2004 of 20 January 2004 on the control of concentrations between undertakings [2004] OJ L24/1.

[104] Commission Regulation (EU) No 330/2010 of 20 April 2010 on the application of Article 101(3) TFEU to categories of vertical agreements and concerted practices [2010] OJ L102/1, superseded by Commission Regulation (EU) 2022/720 of 10 May 2022 on the application of Article 101(3) of the Treaty on the Functioning of the European Union to categories of vertical agreements and concerted practices [2022] OJ L134/4.

[105] Commission Regulation (EC) No 772/2004 of 27 April 2004 on the application of Article 81(3) of the Treaty to categories of technology transfer agreements [2004] OJ L123/11, superseded by Commission Regulation (EU) No 316/2014 of 21 March 2014 on the application of Article 101(3) of the Treaty on the Functioning of the European Union to categories of technology transfer agreements [2014] OJ L93/17.

[106] Ukraine Association Agreement (n 89 above) Art 254.

The ECN+ Directive provides for public periodic reports on activities and resources (to a governmental or parliamentary body).[107] Such transparency tools are also evident in the TCA and other FTAs as peer review mechanisms.

V. Transparency Tools as Peer Review

The designation of authorities, whether 'independent' or 'effective', is a precursor to administrative cooperation. Awareness of each side's regulatory framework is a precondition towards managing divergence. Transparency is a central value of EU law, particularly applied to EU decision-making processes and public access to documents.[108] In the regulatory context, transparency is one of the good governance principles underpinning the EU Better Regulation agenda,[109] and invoked in the TPR both in terms of EU internal legitimacy in the conduct of trade negotiations and improving the external multilateral trade framework.[110] In WTO law, lack of transparency of national regulations is additionally recognised as a barrier to trade.[111] This regulatory transparency is a first step in cooperation, in addition to providing opportunities for mutual monitoring.[112] As noted above, relations with third country regulators allow for more direct and timely problem-solving than blunt, high-level dispute settlement mechanisms. Most FTAs include transparency obligations and consultations, often in chapters on good regulatory practice and regulatory cooperation, as preliminary tools to manage divergence and means to address distortive subsidies. These measures include sharing new legislative initiatives and transparency in the grant of subsidies through reporting requirements. Some provide for the publication of authorities' guidelines to market actors, increasing transparency in implementation. For example, the EU–Singapore[113] and EU–South Korea FTAs provide for regular reports on subsidies including

[107] ECN+ Directive (n 87 above) Art 5(4).

[108] For example, Arts 11(2) and (3) TEU, Art 42 Charter of Fundamental Rights (n 92 above), Regulation (EC) No 1049/2001 of the European Parliament and of the Council of 30 May 2001 regarding public access to European Parliament, Council and Commission documents [2001] OJ L145/43, Joined Cases C-39/05 P and C-52/05 P *Sweden and Maurizio Turco v Council* (n 9 above), A Alemanno, 'Unpacking the Principle of Openness in EU Law' (n 9 above).

[109] Commission, 'Better Regulation Guidelines' (n 10 above).

[110] Commission, 'Trade Policy Review' (n 1 above) 7, 8, 12, 21–22.

[111] See GATT Art X requiring members to notify the WTO Secretariat of new or modified rules, to publish rules promptly and before applying them, and not to apply national trade laws and regulations unfairly or arbitrarily; P Ala'I, 'From the Periphery to the Centre? The Evolving WTO Jurisprudence on Transparency and Good Governance' (2008) 11 *Journal of International Economic Law* 779.

[112] For example, OECD, 'Guiding Principles for Regulatory Quality and Performance' (2005): www.oecd.org/fr/reformereg/34976533.pdf. L Biuković, 'Transparency Norms, The World Trade System and Free Trade Agreements: The Case of CETA' (2012) 39 *Legal Issues of Economic Integration* 93.

[113] Free Trade Agreement between the European Union and the Republic of Singapore [2019] OJ L296/3, Art 11.9(1).

their legal basis or objective, form, amount and, where possible, recipients. The EU–South Korea FTA is more wide-ranging in that it covers any sector rather than only trade in goods and service (unlike the Singapore FTA), the report should be annual, it includes sectoral distribution of aid and there is an option to request and exchange further information on specific individual cases, subject to professional and business secrecy.[114] In both agreements the information is deemed provided if it is exchanged directly between the parties or made available on a public website.[115]

The Ukraine agreement also includes provisions on transparency specifically regarding State aid.[116] These provisions can be seen as a precursor to the notification system found in the Foreign Subsidies Regulation. In the Ukraine agreement, given the broader trade relationship established between the parties, these requirements operate on a general basis – for example, ensuring that financial relations between public authorities and public undertakings are transparent,[117] annually notifying the other party of the total amount, types and the sectoral distribution of state aid which may affect trade between the Parties, or making it available on a public website[118] – rather than a case-specific basis. However, upon request 'the other party shall provide further information on any state aid scheme and particular individual cases of state aid' affecting trade between the EU and Ukraine.[119]

In addition, the Ukraine agreement encompasses transparency in implementation and enforcement of competition laws and legislation, which in practice also requires Ukraine to set up guidelines 'explaining the principles to be used in the setting of any pecuniary sanctions imposed for infringements of the competition laws'[120] and 'explaining the principles used in the assessment of horizontal mergers'.[121]

In the EU–UK TCA there are wider obligations across regulatory fields. While there is no overarching provision to notify policy and legislative changes on each side which would allow review of alignment or divergence over time, under the transparency Title Article 335(1) states that 'each Party shall ensure that its laws, regulations, procedures and administrative rulings of general application are promptly published'. The good regulatory practices Title contains a general requirement for information on planned 'major' (as understood by each party) regulatory measures to be released at least once a year, and for those measures

[114] Free Trade Agreement (Korea) (n 58 above) Art 11.12.
[115] Free Trade Agreement (Singapore) (n 113 above) Art 11.9(2); Free Trade Agreement (Korea) (n 58 above) Art 11.12(2).
[116] Ukraine Association Agreement (n 89 above) Art 263.
[117] ibid Art 263(3).
[118] ibid Art 263(1).
[119] ibid Art 263(2).
[120] ibid Art 255(5).
[121] ibid Art 255(6).

to include public consultation on drafts and impact assessments.[122] A publicly available register of regulatory measures in force is also required.[123]

Transparency obligations can be seen as more limited enforcement mechanisms. Nevertheless, in the absence of substantive harmonisation the mutual monitoring potential of transparency measures through softer peer review and benchmarking can enhance policy convergence.[124] The European Commission itself places transparency alongside dispute settlement mechanisms, where approximation with the EU acquis or prohibition of particular types of subsidies has not been agreed.[125]

VI. Conclusion

Level playing field measures seek to shield EU firms from unfair external competition due to lower standards elsewhere outside the EU. Competition can be understood in the sense of competition law and enforcement (antitrust, mergers and State aid/subsidies), and in a wider sense as regulatory competition or competitiveness between jurisdictions in the context of trade. The EU's relationship with third countries tests its influence on States themselves, regulators and firms. This chapter focused on the role of technocratic cooperation in extending the EU's regulatory impact beyond its borders, in particular showing how EU constitutional principles are exported.

In terms of the distribution of competences, exclusive competence for competition rule-making and the conclusion of trade agreements under the common commercial policy rests at the EU level. This allows EU to lay the foundation for this cooperation and to co-opt third country regulators by incorporating and exporting constitutional principles and elements recognised in EU law: equivalence, independence and transparency. In particular, in some areas it looks to mirror internal and external provisions on cooperation. Rules set out by legislators in intergovernmental trade agreements need to be implemented by executive institutions. In some cases, the parameters for cooperation are set out in such trade instruments, whereas in others cooperation agreements are made between agencies themselves in sector-specific policy communities.

Level playing field provisions provide a 'floor' for recognising third country standards as equivalent. Commitments are frequently linked to convergence with

[122] ibid Art 345.
[123] ibid Art 349.
[124] Eg, OECD, 'Country reviews of competition policy frameworks': www.oecd.org/competition/countryreviewsofcompetitionpolicyframeworks.htm.
[125] Directorate-General for Competition: 'more limited enforcement mechanisms like transparency, consultations and a dispute settlement system': Commission, 'Facing the challenges of globalisation': competition-policy.ec.europa.eu/international_en.

international standards (often in practice, based on EU standards), including a duty to review adherence and explain any divergences from those standards. These substantive provisions involve regulators across policy areas. Furthermore, prohibitions on failing to effectively enforce laws and regulations in a way which would encourage trade or investment embed obligations in the domestic setting and affect the domestic regulatory architecture (as shown by the creation of the Subsidy Control Unit in the UK). Requiring effective and/or independent authorities is a way of establishing counterparts and a basis for recognition, often through networks as softer influencing mechanisms. These relationships with counterparts have the aim of promoting and protecting an international competition culture as championed by the European Commission and the epistemic community. Transparency tools, for example requirements to notify new regulations, are precursors to cooperation. Transparency also allows for peer accountability and mutual monitoring as enforcement mechanisms. The role of regulatory authorities is important not only in implementing regulatory commitments, but also in assessing and managing divergence.

This export of EU constitutional principles through links with third country regulators allow for more direct and timely resolution than the blunt, high-level, instruments of rebalancing and enforcement mechanisms such as those in bilateral FTAs and the Foreign Subsidies Regulation. However, the possibility to use those overarching governance arrangements acts as a 'safety net', explicitly aiming to constrain or disincentivise regulatory competitiveness with the internal market. This exemplifies the EU's efforts to balance global engagement and unilateral tools to protect against unfair trading conditions on the internal market, reflected in the 'open strategic autonomy' approach of its Trade Policy Review.[126]

[126] Commission, 'Trade Policy Review' (n 1 above) 5 at 2.1.

6

Shaping the EU's Competition Law and Policy: Space for Multiple Actors?

GIORGIO MONTI*

I. Introduction

Competition policy is the first supranational policy of the European Union (EU).[1] Unique among Treaty competences, the Commission was empowered to act against anticompetitive conduct by undertakings and to issue block exemption regulations.[2] By the 1990s the leadership of Commissioners Sutherland and Brittan established a robust antitrust enforcement system.[3] With the so-called modernisation project in the early 2000s the Commission decentralised enforcement.[4] It took the view that the culture of competition had by then been understood by Member States and that national competition authorities (NCAs) could be entrusted with the enforcement of EU competition law.[5] The relationship between Member States and NCAs on the one side and the Commission on the other is generally unproblematic and constitutionally well-designed.

* Professor of Competition Law, Tilburg Law School, G.Monti@tilburguniversity.edu.

[1] L McGowan and S Wilks, 'The First Supranational Policy in the European Union: Competition Policy' (1995) 28 *European Journal of Political Research* 141.

[2] EEC Council Regulation No 17 First Regulation implementing Articles 85 and 86 of the Treaty [1962] OJ L13/204 and Regulation No 19/65/EEC of 2 March of the Council on application of Article 85 (3) of the Treaty to certain categories of agreements and concerted practices [1965] OJ L36/533.

[3] M Cini and L McGowan, *Competition Policy in the European Union* 2nd edn (Basingstoke, Palgrave Macmillan, 2008).

[4] Council Regulation (EC) No 1/2003 of 16 December 2002 on the implementation of the rules on competition laid down in Articles 81 and 82 of the Treaty [2003] OJ L01/1. In parallel to this institutional reform the Commission also embarked on a process of rethinking the substantive rules by the use of economics to aid it in determining which conduct infringes competition law. On the synergies between the procedural and substantive reforms, see DJ Gerber, 'Two Forms of Modernization in European Competition Law' (2007) 31 *Fordham International Law Journal* 1235.

[5] Commission, 'White Paper on Modernisation of the Rules Implementing Articles 85 and 86 of the EC Treaty' COM(1999) 101 final. See CD Ehlermann, 'The Modernization of EC Antitrust Policy, A Legal and Cultural Revolution' (2000) 37 *Common Market Law Review* 537.

EU competition law enforcement by NCAs reveals that they are largely willing participants in a concerted effort to optimise enforcement.[6] Member States are generally happy to have independent competition agencies enforcing the law: their agreement to the European Competition Network Plus (ECN+) Directive, which serves to strengthen and harmonise the powers of NCAs, is evidence of this.[7] Some illiberal regimes are challenging the operation of NCAs, but this development is not covered here.[8] Instead, the chapter analyses the extent to which the system leaves space for policy divergence in the development of competition law and the merits of affording this space: does it make EU competition policy more capable to address societal challenges? In particular, we discuss how far Member States and NCAs can adopt divergent policies or pressure the EU to adapt its stance on matters pertaining to competition policy. Contemporary debates surrounding the role of industrial policy, the challenges faced with the regulation of big tech firms and the debates on environmental sustainability serve to illustrate this discussion. It reveals that there is an ongoing conversation between the EU and Member States over the scope and direction of EU competition policy.

In section II the focus is on the relationship between the Commission and the application of national competition law by NCAs in what may be described as the allocation of executive competences. We discuss two aspects of this. In section II.A we consider the relationship between EU and national competition law: is the fact that NCAs may at times apply stricter national competition law a threat to the unity of competition policy in the EU? In section II.B we study the emphasis placed on ensuring that NCAs apply EU competition law in a uniform manner. Should we allow NCAs to explore different solutions to shared competition problems?

In section III the focus is on the relationship between the European Union and Member States in matters of EU antitrust policy. In section III.A we suggest that this has largely been harmonious. However, there are two tensions. The first, discussed in section III.B, is that because industrial policy remains a national competence,[9] Member States may resort to anticompetitive regulation. Nevertheless, Article 120 of the Treaty on the Functioning of European Union (TFEU) requires Member States to pursue their economic policies 'with a view to contributing to the achievement of the objectives of the Union'. This includes 'the principle of an open market economy with free competition, favouring an

[6] Commission, 'Ten Years of Antitrust Enforcement under Regulation 1/2003: Achievements and Future Perspectives' COM(2014) 453 final.

[7] Directive (EU) 2019/1 of the European Parliament and of the Council of 11 December 2018 to empower the competition authorities of the Member States to be more effective enforcers and to ensure the proper functioning of the internal market [2019] OJ L11/3.

[8] See KJ Cseres, 'EU Competition Law and Democracy in the Shadow of Rule of Law Backsliding', Ch 1 in this volume and M Bernatt, *Populism and Antitrust: The Illiberal Influence of Populist Government on the Competition Law System* (Cambridge, Cambridge University Press, 2022).

[9] The EU only has a supporting competence (Art 6(b) TFEU), by which it may only co-ordinate and complement national policy.

efficient allocation of resources'. In this setup, while EU Law could be developed to challenge national economic policies further when these harm the achievement of the internal market, the Commission has been careful not to antagonise Member States too much. The effect of this is that the achievement of competition in the internal market is more limited than the EU's constitutional architecture would allow one to expect. The second tension, discussed in section III.C, is that Member States are at times concerned that the application of EU competition law runs against their preferred industrial policy strategy. A challenge for the EU is how to respond to this, in particular with the present Commission's Industrial Strategy, which seems to advocate a more interventionist EU industrial policy.[10] Might we see a different competition policy emerge at EU level, based on demands from Member States and the Commission's own policy reorientation?

II. The Commission and National Competition Authorities

A. The Legal Framework Empowering NCAs: Minimum Harmonisation

The Commission's original proposal for what became Regulation 1/2003 was that when an NCA considered conduct which infringes Articles 101 or 102 TFEU then the NCA would apply EU competition law exclusively.[11] National competition law would apply only if conduct did not affect trade between Member States. The intention behind this was to secure maximum harmonisation of EU Law. However, this proved controversial because some jurisdictions had stricter national competition laws (in particular rules about the abuse of economic dependence).[12] The compromise that was reached provides that NCAs shall apply Articles 101 and 102 TFEU in parallel with corresponding provisions of national competition law. This envisages three scenarios:

When applying Article 101 TFEU and the corresponding national law provisions, the latter cannot be interpreted in a manner stricter than that provided for under Article 101 TFEU.[13] In other words, if an agreement does not infringe Article 101 TFEU it cannot be held that the agreement infringes national competition law governing restrictive practices.

[10] Commission, 'A New Industrial Strategy for Europe' COM(2020) 102 final. This has been updated to, inter alia, relax state aid rules: 'A Green Deal Industrial Plan for the Net-Zero Age' COM(2023) 623 final. See Editorial Comments, 'Paying for the EU's Industrial Policy' (2023) 60 *Common Market Law Review* 617.

[11] Proposal for a Council Regulation on the implementation of the rules on competition laid down in Articles 81 and 82 of the Treaty and amending Regulations, COM(2000) 582 final, Art 3.

[12] G Monti, *EC Competition Law* (Cambridge, Cambridge University Press, 2007) 406–08.

[13] Regulation 1/2003 (n 5 above) Art 3(1).

When applying Article 102 TFEU, however, Member States are free to apply 'on their territory stricter national laws which prohibit or sanction unilateral conduct engaged in by undertakings'.[14]

Finally, Member States and NCAs remain free to apply 'provisions of national law that predominantly pursue an objective different from that pursued by [Articles 101 and 102 TFEU]'.[15]

When it comes to the relationship between the Commission and NCAs, the rules above provide for convergence between the application of national and EU competition law. The policy underpinning this is that 'harmonised rules contribute to ensuring that businesses operating across the EU benefit from a level playing field, which in turn can contribute to the proper functioning of and to enhancing the European Single Market'.[16] This is supplemented by the possibility for NCAs to consult the Commission when it applies EU competition law.[17]

An ongoing dispute gives us the opportunity to discuss the residual scope of national competition law. In 2019 the German NCA issued a decision applying German competition law by which it found that Facebook's data collection constituted an abuse of dominance because the terms of service allowed Facebook to collect user data from non-Facebook services and integrate this with data obtained from Facebook. It concluded that this constituted an exploitative abuse which harmed users and also served to cement Facebook's dominance, foreclosing rivals. The NCA applied Section 19(1) of the German Act Against Restrictions of Competition, which is worded analogously to Article 102 TFEU. It justified not applying EU Law because the German courts had recognised a principle whereby to determine an abuse of dominance, it is possible to take into account fundamental rights and secondary legislation, in this case the General Data Protection Regulation (GDPR). The NCA took the view that this principle did not inform the interpretation of Article 102 TFEU, so there was no duty to apply EU Law.[18] In other words, this case falls within the second scenario identified above: the application of stricter national competition law to unilateral conduct.

However, it has been argued, convincingly, that the conduct in question probably falls within the scope of Article 102 TFEU and therefore this is a setting where national and EU competition law must be applied in parallel by the NCA.[19]

[14] ibid Art 3(2).

[15] ibid Art 3(3).

[16] Commission, 'Evaluation of the Vertical Block Exemption Regulation' (Staff Working Document) SWD(2020) 172 final, 59. See also Regulation 1/2003 (n 5 above) Recital 8.

[17] Regulation 1/2003 (n 5 above) Art 11.

[18] German Competition Authority, Decision B6-22/16 of 15 February 2019.

[19] W Wils, 'The Obligation for the Competition Authorities of the EU Member States to Apply EU Antitrust Law and the Facebook Decision of the Bundeskartellamt' (2019) 3 *Concurrences* 58. One approach is to argue that the collection of off-Facebook data is not necessary for the delivery of the service, on analogy with Case 127/73 *BRT v SABAM* [1974] EU:C:1974:25.

What are the legal consequences of an NCA failing to comply with this obligation in Article 3? Some authors have taken the draconian view that this infringement means that the decision is void and unenforceable.[20] This might be justified if an NCA elects to apply only national law with a view to either apply a stricter standard or to find a way of authorising conduct which would be prohibited if one applied Article 101 or 102 TFEU. The legislative history behind Regulation 1/2003 suggests that such an approach would frustrate the purpose of decentralisation and such a legal consequence would be justifiable in those settings. However in the present case, the application of Article 102 TFEU would have led to a finding of abuse as well, so the German NCA's decision may be technically contrary to Article 3, but there are no adverse economic consequences of this.

Facebook (now Meta) appealed against the decision of the German NCA challenging the application of competition law to its conduct. This litigation has raised an issue which was not foreseen in Article 3: what is the relationship between national competition law and other rules of EU Law? On the facts, it was noted conduct challenged by the NCA is argued to be contrary to the GDPR: considering that the competent body to apply these norms is the Irish Data Protection Commission, is it lawful for the German NCA to apply competition law based on its interpretation of the GDPR? Furthermore, given that the Irish regulator appeared to be investigating the facts at hand, is this an infringement of the duty of loyal cooperation enshrined in Article 4(3) TFEU?[21] Formally, the answer appears to be that nothing prevents the German NCA from applying national competition law, in particular because in so doing it safeguards a set of interests that are different from those that are protected by the GDPR. Moreover, one of the reasons for the German NCA having taken this action is the slow pace at which the Irish regulator is proceeding. For the same reason, other Member States have also moved against the data collection practices of other platforms based in Ireland using consumer law or privacy legislation.[22] Furthermore, the decision of the NCA does not prevent the Irish regulator from taking action and nothing prevents it from reaching a different decision from that of the competition authority. The Court's judgment confirms the view taken above: a national competition authority may, when determining if there has been an abuse of dominance, consider whether the dominant undertaking has infringed the GDPR because to do otherwise 'would be liable to undermine the effectiveness of competition law within the European Union'.[23] The Court did not discuss the relationship between national competition law and EU law because by that time it was agreed that the conduct also infringed Article 102 TFEU.[24]

[20] J Faull and A Nikpay, *The EU Law of Competition* 3rd edn (Oxford, Oxford University Press, 2014) 107.

[21] Case C-252/21 *Meta Platforms Inc v Bundeskartellamt* [2022] EU:C:2023:537.

[22] Italian Competition Authority, Decision No 27432/18; French National Commission on Informatics and Liberty, Deliberation of the restricted committee No SAN-2021-023 of 31 December 2021 concerning Google LLC and Google Ireland Ltd, applying privacy law.

[23] Case C-252/21 *Meta Platforms Inc v Bundeskartellamt* (n 23 above) para 51.

[24] Case C-252/21 *Meta* (n 23 above) para 36.

The applicants in *Facebook* are rightly asking whether there can be other general legal principles that prevent a party from being entangled in multiple, possibly conflicting obligations. On the one hand, the EU legislator can prescribe a hierarchy in secondary legislation,[25] but this becomes impossible when there are overlaps between EU Laws and national laws which pursue different objectives.[26] Article 4(3) TEU imposes a duty of sincere cooperation, but so far this only applies to instances where national laws have anticompetitive effects, and then only in limited circumstances.[27] The Court required cooperation among regulators.[28] For example, they should exchange information, or determine which will act first. This, however, is an approach that could work only ex ante – that is, by facilitating the creation of a supranational fora for regulators to meet and discuss matters of shared concern, which may facilitate the identification of overlapping concerns. However, even if there are no principles limiting an NCA's choice to apply national competition law, is this evidence of a gap in the distribution of competences? As we suggest in section II.B below, there may be good reasons for allowing single NCAs to apply competition rules that diverge from the EU ones, provided this experience is used wisely.

Finally, it is worth noting that while at the time of writing Regulation 1/2003 Member States had few antitrust rules that were stricter than EU law, this is changing. In the realm of digital markets some jurisdictions (eg, Germany and Austria) are reforming national competition laws to address competition harms caused by digital giants.[29] This creates a scenario where dominant players may face multiple regulatory oversight: by NCAs applying the new rules, by the Commission or other NCAs applying Article 102 TFEU and in the future by the Commission applying the Digital Markets Act (DMA), a bespoke ex ante framework to address big tech firms.[30] The DMA foresees this overlap and manages the relationship between the enforcement of the DMA and the enforcement of EU and national competition law by NCAs in the following way.

[25] Eg, Joined Cases C-54/17 and C-55/17 *Autorità Garante della Concorrenza e del Mercato (AGCM) v Wind Tre and Vodafone Italia* [2018] EU:C:2018:710.

[26] This is a diagonal conflict, see C Schmid 'Diagonal Competence Conflicts between European Competition Law and National Regulation – A Conflict of Laws Reconstruction of the Dispute on Book Price Fixing' (2000) 8 *European Review of Private Law* 155.

[27] The joint application of Arts 4(3) TEU and 101 TFEU for example is triggered when the state supports an anticompetitive agreement.

[28] Case C-252/21 *Meta* (n 23 above) paras 52–63. In Case C-117/20 *Bpost SA v Autorité belge de la concurrence* [2022] EU:C:2022:202, in the context of the parallel application of competition law and sector regulation, the Court also requires co-ordination.

[29] The eleventh and twelfth amendments to the Competition Act of 26 June 2013 (as amended) (*Gesetz gegen Wettbewerbsbeschränkungen*), Cartel Act 2005 (as amended) (*Bundesgesetz gegen Kartelle und andere Wettbewerbsbeschränkungen – Kartellgesetz* 2005), Art 4a, adjusting the definition of dominance for the platform economy. See OECD, 'News Media and Digital Platforms – Note by Austria' DAF/COMP/WD(2021)54.

[30] Regulation (EU) 2022/1925 of the European Parliament and of the Council of 14 September 2022 on contestable and fair markets in the digital sector and amending Directives (EU) 2019/1937 and (EU) 2020/1828 (DMA) [2022] OJ L265/1.

First, NCAs may not issue 'decisions which run counter to a decision adopted by the Commission under this Regulation'.[31] Second, a co-ordination mechanism is established whereby once an NCA starts an investigation regarding a gatekeeper whose conduct falls to be regulated by the Commission under the DMA then the NCA is expected to keep the Commission appraised of its investigation including submitting draft decisions. The Commission may stop the NCA's efforts however by starting its own proceedings under the DMA.[32] This approach, which mirrors the cooperation procedures in the application of EU competition law by NCAs found in Regulation 1/2003, secures the primacy of the DMA in regulating gatekeepers but it leaves space for NCAs to apply stricter national competition rules to these undertakings. For the purposes of this chapter, the key point to note is that the EU has limited powers to completely control the application of stricter national competition law and the challenge is how far the Commission's collaboration with NCAs will suffice to persuade NCAs to take the view that EU-level enforcement is sufficient to address competition concerns. On the other hand, as we argue in the next subsection, some divergences may not be harmful for the development of competition law.

B. Decentralisation: Opportunities for Harmonisation, Experimentation, or Intellectual Leadership?

Early research on Regulation 1/2003 showed that decentralisation came with control.[33] NCAs must keep in close contact with the Commission throughout the lifetime of a case when they apply Articles 101 and 102 TFEU: the Commission may comment and advise NCAs and it may even withdraw a case unilaterally from an NCA.[34] This nuclear button (withdrawal) is there to prevent NCAs from taking decisions that would deviate from those that the Commission would consider to be a proper application of EU competition law. These provisions are those that led commentators to suggest that the project turned NCAs into agencies doing the Commission's work under the Commission's supervision, releasing much needed resources to allow the Commission to prioritise enforcement.[35]

[31] DMA (n 31 above) Art 1(7).
[32] ibid Art 38.
[33] S Wilks, 'Agency Escape: Decentralization or Dominance of the European Commission in the Modernization of Competition Policy?' (2005) 18 *Governance* 431; G Monti, 'Independence, Interdependence and Legitimacy: The EU Commission, National Competition Authorities, and the European Competition Network' (*EUI Department of Law Research Paper No 01/2014*).
[34] Regulation 1/2003 (n 5 above) Art 11(6).
[35] Wilks, 'Agency Escape' (n 34 above).

However, the drive to harmonise and control NCAs may not always be achieved successfully. One power that NCAs lack is that of issuing non-infringement decisions.[36] Instead, NCAs who consider that a practice that they have investigated does not harm competition, should simply stop the procedure. According to one study, abandoned cases are a fairly large proportion of the NCA's business and there is a concern that abandoning cases allows the NCA to hide from the Commission certain kinds of decisions to which the Commission may take exception.[37] Another study finds that some NCAs appear to determine that practices have no effect on trade between states (in spite of the very broad formulation of the effects test) and thus apply solely national competition law.[38] It remains unclear how far these tactics undermine harmonised enforcement but they reveal an absence of control when the NCA under-reports its activities.

In parallel to Regulation 1/2003 the EU Council agreed (politically) to institute a network comprising the NCAs and the Commission, the so-called European Competition Network (ECN).[39] Formally the ECN is a site for sharing information about ongoing cases and for re-assigning cases across jurisdictions. However lacking any precise legal mandate, its members have turned it into a policy-making body. This function is manifested in two ways.

First, its principal policy-making task has been to strengthen national procedures. These had not been harmonised by Regulation 1/2003, but the ECN generated a number of papers explaining what procedures make competition law work effectively. This appeared to be a strategy to influence national governments in upgrading the powers of NCAs. Subsequently, the Commission launched the ECN+ project which led to a Directive that requires all NCAs to be conferred powers of inspection and enforcement that are on par with those of the Commission. This project was the result of a coincidence of wills: the Commission saw the absence of procedural harmonisation as a major gap in Regulation 1/2003 and many NCAs wished for greater powers. Many of the powers provided in the Directive correspond to the findings in the ECN discussions.[40]

[36] Case C-375/09 *Prezes Urzędu Ochrony Konkurencji i Konsumentów v Tele2 Polska sp. z o.o., devenue Netia SA* [2011] EU:C:2011:270.

[37] A Svetlicinii, M Bernatt and M Botta, 'The Dark Matter in EU Competition Law: Non-Infringement Decisions in the New EU Member States Before and After Tele2 Polska' (2018) 43 *European Law Review* 424.

[38] M Bernatt, M Botta and A Svetlicinii, 'The Assessment of the Effect on Trade by the National Competition Authorities of the "New" Member States: Another Legal Partition of the Internal Market?' (2015) 52 *Common Market Law Review* 1247.

[39] Contrary to what some say, this creature is political – it is not the result of a legislative instrument establishing an EU institution. See Joint Statement of the Council and the Commission on the Functioning of the Network of Competition Authorities (2002, 15435/02 ADD 1).

[40] G Monti, 'The Proposed Directive to Empower National Competition Authorities: Too Much, Too Little or Just Right?' (2017) 3 *Competition Law and Policy Debate* 40.

Second, it appears the ECN is also a site to discuss and understand how other agencies address shared problems.[41] This ranges from technical matters (eg, how to secure electronic evidence) to more general discussions about the optimal approach to certain kinds of restrictive practices. In this context it is a learning platform where agencies feel relatively free to speak openly about a range of competition concerns. It is difficult to evaluate how these conversations impact enforcement, but there is a tension between the openness of the ECN as a platform for discussion and the Commission's approach to shaping EU competition policy. We can see this by considering two strands of enforcement: vertical restraints and environmental sustainability agreements.

The regulation of distribution agreements has been an enforcement priority for NCAs: in the period 2010 to 2020 NCAs have started 392 cases, which led to 257 infringement decisions.[42] During the review of the system one of the recurring concerns was the divergent interpretations given by NCAs, not only with agreements where there is limited case-law (eg, platform bans, dual pricing and price parity clauses), but also in the application of rules where the law is more certain (eg, resale price maintenance).[43] The Commission also observed that existing methods for securing harmonised enforcement are not sufficient.[44] In this review process, the Commission considered this divergence as problematic because of the legal uncertainty this generates and NCAs are reported as seeking further clarification from the Commission.

An alternative approach to the diverse results obtained by NCAs might have been considered: one could examine the diverging approaches as a resource for learning which regulatory approach is superior. There has been one episode where this approach surfaced, and this relates to the regulation of agreements between hotels and on-line travel agents. The latter insisted on price parity clauses so that a hotel would not advertise a hotel online at different prices in different online platforms or on its own website. Most competition authorities in the EU took the view that 'wide' price parity clauses restrict competition (these clauses prevent a hotel from offering better terms on any other platform), but in Germany the NCA took the view that in addition, 'narrow' price parity clauses (which allow hotels to offer better terms to other platforms but prevent the hotel from offering better terms on its website) are also restrictive of competition.[45] This provided an excellent natural experiment to determine which of the two approaches is superior in terms of welfare.[46] While a study was produced early

[41] See also FP Vantaggiato, H Kassim and K Wright, 'Internal Network Structures as Opportunity Structures: Control and Effectiveness in the European Competition Network' (2020) 28 *Journal of European Public Policy* 571.

[42] Commission, 'Evaluation of the Vertical Block Exemption Regulation' (n 17 above) 47.

[43] ibid 61.

[44] ibid 59.

[45] This approach was supported by the court, see Federal Court of Justice, Judgment of 18 May 2021, KVR 54/20, DE:BGH:2021:180521BKVR54.20.0.

[46] S Ennis, M Ivaldi and V Lagos, 'Price Parity Clauses for Hotel Room Booking: Empirical Evidence from Regulatory Change (*Toulouse School of Economics Working Papers No 1106/2022*).

on by the Commission, this was inconclusive.[47] A more recent study of a selection of Member States, some of which has passed laws banning online travel agents from imposing wide and narrow price parity clauses also led to mixed findings about the extent to which the presence or absence of price parity clauses affected the price of rooms.[48] In the new Vertical Block Exemption Regulation the Commission harmonised the competition rules by providing that a wide price parity clause in an agreement does not benefit from the exemption.[49] This means that parties may use narrow price parity clauses but an NCA may find that they too have an anticompetitive effect and prohibit them.[50] This outcome puts a premium on harmonisation and gives hardly any scope for an approach which encourages divergence among NCAs as a mechanism for learning what the superior approach is. It may be argued that this policy is mandated by Regulation 1/2003 which requires close cooperation between NCAs and the Commission. Even before this Regulation, the European Court of Justice (ECJ) had already held that the Commission 'is responsible for defining and implementing the orientation of Community competition policy'.[51]

However, the debate on environmental sustainability agreements indicates that some NCAs are not always willing to accept their role as executors of the Commission's enforcement policy. The Dutch NCA has been prominent in exploring pathways to exempt agreements which restrict competition on the one hand by seeking to achieve sustainability objectives on the other. Early on this policy line was not welcomed by the Commission who took the view that this approach would be out of line with its interpretation of EU competition law. Strongly worded letters were sent to the Dutch from Directorate-general for Competition (DG COMP) expressing concerns at divergent interpretations of competition law.[52] However, more recently, the von der Leyen Commission has prioritised the Green Deal and now the Commission is itself considering whether and how sustainability considerations should be part of EU competition law.[53] Nevertheless the Dutch NCA's approach to assessing sustainability agreements demonstrates a greater willingness to allow cooperation among competitors than the

[47] Report on the monitoring exercise carried out in the online hotel booking sector by EU competition authorities in 2016 (2016): www.ec.europa.eu/competition/ecn/hotel_monitoring_report_en.pdf.

[48] Commission, 'Market study on the distribution of hotel accommodation in the EU COMP/2020/OP/002 Final Report' (2022): https://competition-policy.ec.europa.eu/system/files/2023-01/kd0722783enn_hotel_accomodation_market_study.pdf.

[49] Commission Regulation (EU) 2022/720 on the application of Article 101(3) of the Treaty on the Functioning of the European Union to categories of vertical agreements and concerted practices [2022] OJ L134/4, Art 5(1)(d).

[50] Commission, 'Guidelines on vertical restraints' COM(2022) 3006 final, paras 369–71.

[51] Case C-344/98 *Masterfoods Ltd v HB Ice Cream Ltds* [2000] EU:C:2000:249, para 46.

[52] G Monti and J Mulder, 'Escaping the Clutches of EU Competition Law: Pathways to Assess Private Sustainability Initiatives' (2017) 42 *European Law Review* 635.

[53] Commission, Directorate-General for Competition, 'Competition policy brief 1/2021 in Support of Europe's Green Ambition': https://op.europa.eu/en/publication-detail/-/publication/63c4944f-1698-11ec-b4fe-01aa75ed71a1.

Commission.[54] At the same time the visionary head of the Hellenic Competition Commission has also led its NCA to publish a major reflection on the interaction between sustainability and competition.[55] This then led the Greek and Dutch NCA to support a study to assist in the analysis of these types of agreement.[56] While enforcement experience is limited, this episode reflects the possibility that NCAs can serve as catalysts for reform of EU competition policy. While this role is not foreseen in the legal framework, it seems important to take advantage of the knowledge gathered by NCAs for the development of EU competition policy and recognise their capacity for intellectual leadership, together with the Commission.[57]

In sum, the harmonisation narrative, which places the Commission in control of the development of competition policy, is well grounded in the legal texts. However, the system is open to other configurations which give NCAs a greater role in shaping EU competition policy.[58] First, experimentalist governance is not prevented, and this could allow NCAs to explore different enforcement options to allow for a determination of superior policy, but evidence of this occurring is scant.[59] Second, NCAs can have an effect on the Commission's consideration of new policy initiatives, as illustrated by NCAs pioneering new approaches to regulating environmental sustainability agreements. Obviously, there is a trade-off: allowing for divergences in the enforcement of competition policy can allow one to identify superior policies but reduces legal certainty. However, in instances where the application of competition law confronts new societal challenges, affording space for NCAs some role in influencing policy is a valuable means to identify new approaches which will make competition policy more robust in the long term.

III. The Commission and the Member States

A. Convergence

Even before the Commission's modernisation drive, many Member States voluntarily amended their national competition rules and aligned them to Articles 101

[54] Authority for Consumers and Markets, 'Second draft version: Guidelines on Sustainability Agreements – Opportunities within competition law' (2021): www.acm.nl/en/publications/second-draft-version-guidelines-sustainability-agreements-opportunities-within-competition-law.

[55] Hellenic Competition Commission, 'Staff Discussion Paper on Sustainability Issues and Competition Law' (2020): www.epant.gr/files/2020/Staff_Discussion_paper.pdf.

[56] R Inderst, S Eftichios and X Anastasios, 'Technical Report on Sustainability and Competition' (2021): www.epant.gr/en/enimerosi/publications/research-publications/item/1284-technical-report-on-sustainability-and-competition.html.

[57] Y Svetiev, *Experimentalist Competition Law and the Regulation of Markets* (Oxford, Bloomsbury, 2020) 42.

[58] For further discussion see C Townley, *A Framework for European Competition Law: Co-ordinated Diversity* (Oxford, Hart Publishing, 2018).

[59] B Rangoni and G Monti, 'Competition Policy in Action: Regulating Tech Markets with Hierarchy and Experimentalism' (2021) 60 *Journal of Common Market Studies* 1106. And see generally, Svetiev, *Experimentalist Competition Law* (n 58 above).

and 102 TFEU. Some have explained this development by reference to industry lobbying: firms preferred a system where rules were aligned, while others have explained this by reference to the emergence of a shared competition culture.[60] After modernisation, the ECJ intervened to further align national rules with a spate of judgments that placed limits on the powers of NCAs in the name of securing the uniform application of EU Law. In *VEBIC*, the ECJ held that the institutional design in Belgium, by which the NCA was not able to defend its decision on appeal, was contrary to EU Law because this was 'likely to compromise the exercise of the specific obligation on national competition authorities under the regulation to ensure the effective application of Articles 101 and 102 TFEU'.[61] In *Schenker*, the ECJ held that a national leniency programme must not 'undermine the requirement of effective and uniform application of Article 101 TFEU'.[62] Judgments such as these cement the harmonisation policy pursued by the Commission. This kind of negative integration is well-known in EU law, and it has the potential to challenge every aspect of national competition law: are NCAs sufficiently funded to ensure the application of EU competition law? Are the fining rules sufficient to achieve deterrence?

In addition to judicial developments, the Commission has used the financial crisis and the mechanisms to oversee the development of national economic policy as tools to require amendments to the operation of national competition authorities. Irish and Cypriot competition laws were amended on the basis of a Memorandum of Understanding to confer greater powers to the NCA,[63] Spanish competition law was amended as a result of evaluations carried out via the European Semester by which the Commission expressed concerns about the independence of the NCA.[64]

Ultimately, these piecemeal steps to adjust national competition laws culminated in the ECN+ Directive.[65] This serves to harmonise the powers of NCAs, largely mirroring the powers that the Commission enjoys. The Directive also mandates the independence of NCAs and sets out criteria to secure this. It also requires Member States to ensure that NCAs have sufficient resources to discharge

[60] H Buch-Hansen and A Wigger, 'Revisiting 50 years of Market-Making: The Neoliberal Transformation of European Competition Policy' (2010) 17 *Review of International Political Economy* 20. H Vedder, 'Spontaneous Harmonisation of National (Competition) Laws in the Wake of the Modernisation of EC Competition Law' (2004) 11 *Competition Law Review* 5.

[61] Case C-439/08 *Vlaamse federatie van verenigingen van Brood- en Banketbakkers, Ijsbereiders en Chocoladebewerkers (VEBIC) v Belgium* [2010] EU:C:2010:739, para 58.

[62] Case C-681/11 *Schenker and Others v Bundeswettbewerbsbehörde* [2013] EU:C:2013:404, para 47.

[63] Commission, Directorate-General for Economic and Financial Affairs, 'Economic Adjustment Programme for Ireland Autumn 2013 Review' (Occasional Papers, 2013): https://ec.europa.eu/economy_finance/publications/occasional_paper/2013/pdf/ocp167_en.pdf; Commission, Directorate-General for Economic and Financial Affairs, 'The Economic Adjustment Programme for Cyprus' (Occasional papers, 2013): https://op.europa.eu/en/publication-detail/-/publication/9abde1cb-a369-4900-a4eb-d024cd8e5e02.

[64] Commission, 'Assessment of the 2013 national reform programme and stability programme for Spain' (Staff Working Document) SWD(2013) 359 final, 30–33.

[65] Directive (EU) 2019/1 (n 8 above).

its tasks. It remains to be seen how well this Directive is implemented but Member States on the whole have demonstrated a commitment to effective competition enforcement, but with some gaps as we discuss below.

B. The Advocacy Gap

Who is in charge of monitoring anticompetitive state action? In theory this is a job for the Member States first and for the Commission as a last resort. The ECJ has noted how Member States who have granted special or exclusive rights to undertakings must keep such grants under review and amend national laws when the state's action has anticompetitive effects.[66] The ECJ has also held that national courts must disapply national laws that are incompatible with EU competition law.[67] This is part of a more general obligation national courts and national bodies have to disapply national laws that are incompatible with EU Law.[68] Putting these two approaches together, Member States appear to have an onerous burden to open markets to competition. However there are few incentives for legislators to carry out such systemic reviews, not least because much anticompetitive state action protects the rents of certain groups and injecting competition is politically risky.

This explains why the Commission utilised the window of opportunity offered by the financial crisis to require Member States who received financial support to take measures to open up a range of economic sectors to competition and to review the anticompetitive effects of national legislation. In this context, the Memorandum of Understanding between the Commission and Greece is particularly significant because in addition to requiring the systematic review of national laws following the OECD's competition toolkit, there is also a requirement to create 12 additional posts at the advocacy unit of the Hellenic Competition Commission.[69] Furthermore, a number of Member States have empowered their NCAs to serve a variety of advocacy functions, from advising the government on draft legislation to challenging some national regulations in court when this harms competition.[70]

[66] This is from a spate of cases in 1990–92 which signalled the commencement of a public turn in competition enforcement: ie, a greater focus on anticompetitive state action. N Reich, 'The November Revolution of the Court of Justice: Keck, Meng and Audi Revisited' (1994) 31 *Common Market Law Review* 459.

[67] Case C-198/01 *CIF v Autorità Garante della Concorrenza e del Mercato* [2003] EU:C:2003:430.

[68] Case C-378/17 *Minister for Justice and Equality, Commissioner of An Garda Síochána v Workplace Relations Commission* [2018] EU:C:2018:979. The case-law goes back to Case 106/77 *Amministrazione delle Finanze dello Stato v Simmenthal* [1978] EU:C:1978:49.

[69] Memorandum of Understanding between the European Commission (acting on behalf of the European Stability Mechanism), the Hellenic Republic and the Bank of Greece (2015): https://ec.europa.eu/economy_finance/eu_borrower/mou/2012-03-01-greece-mou_en.pdf, 25.

[70] Notable examples of jurisdictions with this power are Spain and Italy. For Spain, see Law 3/2013 of 4 June 2013 creating the National Markets and Competition Commission (Comisión Nacional de los

From this perspective, it is unfortunate that during the discussion about the ECN+ Directive the Commission did not consider granting NCAs stronger advocacy powers so as to embed this across the EU. It means that national policies contradicting the EU's competition policy are not regulated systematically.

C. The Direction of EU Competition Policy

When it comes to the application of Articles 101 and 102 TFEU the Commission has not encountered significant pushback from the Member States. This might be due to careful case selection and a strategy of imposing relatively low fines in the initial period. Moreover, during the economic crises of the 1970s and 1980s the Commission was accommodating in allowing crisis cartels to assist in industry restructuring.[71] State aid law was not enforced strictly until the EU exited this crisis. The Commission was also cautious when challenging state monopolies where liberalisation occurred gradually to allow states to make the necessary adjustments.[72] It thus came as somewhat of a surprise when during the latest reforms of the EU Treaties the then French President questioned the primacy given to competition policy in the Treaty.[73] Originally the European Community (EC) Treaty provided that one of the objectives of the Community included 'a system ensuring that competition in the internal market is not distorted'.[74] However, in the Treaty on European Union the reference to competition was dropped from the foundational articles: Article 3 TEU simply provides that the Union 'shall establish an internal market'. A Protocol attached to the TEU provides that the reference to the internal market in Article 3 TEU 'includes a system ensuring that competition is not distorted'.[75] Politically the French were able to sell this as a victory because competition policy would not be pursued for its own sake.[76] However, legally the change had no noticeable impact: the ECJ saw no difference and has referred to the Protocol as one of the justifications for

Mercados y la Competencia), Art 5: www.boe.es/eli/es/l/2013/06/04/3. In its Strategic Plan 2021–2026 the Spanish NCA confirms the importance of improving regulation to make markets work better.

[71] See eg, G Amato, *Antitrust and the Bounds of Power: the dilemma of liberal democracy in the history of the market* (Oxford, Hart Publishing, 1997) 58–64.

[72] D Geradin, 'Twenty Years of Liberalization of Network Industries in the European Union: Where Do We Go Now?' (*Tilburg Law and Economics Center No 24/2006*).

[73] For discussion see G Monti, 'EU Competition Law from Rome to Lisbon: Social Market Economy' in C Heide-Jorgensen and others (eds), *Aims and Values in Competition Law* (Copenhagen, DJØF Publishing, 2013).

[74] Consolidated Version of the Treaty Establishing the European Community [1997] OJ C340/173, Art 3(1)(g).

[75] Consolidated Version of the Treaty on European Union – Protocol (No 27) on the internal market and competition [2008] OJ C115/309.

[76] B Van Rompuy, 'The Impact of the Lisbon Treaty on EU Competition Law: A Review of Recent Case Law of the EU Courts', *Competition Policy International*, 13 December 2011: www.competitionpolicyinternational.com/the-impact-of-the-lisbon-treaty-on-eu-competition-law-a-review-of-recent-case-law-of-the-eu-courts/-.

expanding the interpretation of competition rules.[77] If anything the economic turmoil caused by the financial crisis first and the pandemic more recently have seen a stricter application of competition law. During the financial crisis the Commissioner for competition made it clear that the earlier policy facilitating crisis cartels would not be followed.[78] The pandemic brought a more conciliatory approach, with the Commission announcing that it would tolerate some limited forms of cooperation but requiring clear evidence that this was necessary in the economic climate.[79] Member States did not object to this tougher line.[80]

However, Member States were less willing to confer the Commission powers to review mergers and they have been reluctant to extend the scope of application of the EU Merger Regulation (EUMR).[81] Regular attempts by the Commission to lower the notification thresholds for mergers have largely been unsuccessful. The result of this is that the part of antitrust law which is mostly linked to industrial policy remains in the hands of Member States who remain free to use merger control to pursue national policies.[82] It has been argued that while the Commission could challenge the authorisation of anticompetitive mergers by Member States, that this is not always possible.[83]

There is therefore a possible dissonance between national and EU control of mergers. This materialised in the aftermath of the *Siemens/Alstom* merger decision. The Commission blocked a merger that would have harmed competition in the EU but which the parties claimed was necessary to establish a global champion in the market for high-speed rail.[84] This has led to a number of governments (France and Germany followed by Italy and Poland) putting forward recommendations

[77] Case C-52/09 *Konkurrensverket v TeliaSonera Sverige AB* [2011] EU:C:2011:83, paras 20–22.

[78] D Chalmers, G Davies and G Monti, *European Union Law: Text and Materials* 4th edn (Cambridge, Cambridge University Press, 2019) 878–79.

[79] G Monti, 'Business Cooperation in Times of Emergency: The Role of Competition Law', *Competition Policy International*, 10 May 2020: www.competitionpolicyinternational.com/business-cooperation-in-times-of-emergency-the-role-of-competition-law/. Two cases have been reviewed favourably by the Commission and no other notifications seem to have been made.

[80] The story is of course different when it comes to state aid: for both crises the Commission facilitated state support.

[81] '[T]here are a number of transactions with significant cross-border effects which would appear to remain outside the scope of the EC Merger Regulation.' Commission, 'Report on the functioning of Regulation No 139/2004' COM(2009) 281 final, para 13. However thresholds were not lowered as a result of this finding.

[82] A Scott, 'National Champions and the Two-Thirds Rule in EC Merger Control' (*CCP Working Paper 06 6/2006*) discusses one merger which fell outside the scope of the EUMR, and which might have been authorized taking into consideration national policies. The Commission has insisted that there should be substantive convergence in merger control, observing 'notable points of divergence are national laws that still allow a government to overrule an NCA's competition-based decision and authorise an anti-competitive merger on the basis of other public-interest considerations.' Commission, 'White Paper Towards more effective EU merger control' COM(2014) 449 final, para 19.

[83] A Jones and J Davies, 'Merger Control and the Public Interest: Balancing EU and National Law in the Protectionist Debate' (2014) 10 *European Competition Journal* 153.

[84] Commission Decision of 6 February 2019 declaring a concentration to be incompatible with the internal market and the functioning of the EEA Agreement (Case M.8677 – Siemens/Alstom) [2019] OJ C/300/14.

to amend merger control so as to facilitate the emergence of EU champions.[85] The suggestions that have been made range from the technocratic (eg, changing the approach to assessing markets by taking greater account of global competitive effects in the long run) to the transformative (eg, that for some mergers there should be an additional industrial policy assessment so that the Commission can carry out an informed trade-off between competition interests and other policies).[86] This would align the EU system to certain national merger rules where the government can overrule a decision of the NCA when there are more salient public policy considerations that should be taken into account.[87] However, other Member States (the Czech Republic, Estonia, Finland, Ireland, Latvia, Lithuania and the Netherlands) have taken a stance against such changes to competition policy.[88]

The review of the EUMR is forthcoming and it remains to be seen how far the Commission will take these considerations into account. At the time of writing, the Union has responded to the political fallout of the *Siemens/Alstom* merger decision with two initiatives.[89] The first is the Foreign Direct Investment (FDI) Screening Regulation, which provides that Member States may maintain or establish mechanisms that test any proposed foreign direct investment which leads to a foreign investor acquiring or taking control over a company.[90] The Member States should be able to intervene and block this if such acquisition or control would result in a threat to their security or public order. While the protection of these interests is the competence of the Member State, the Regulation foresees using this procedure to facilitate an EU-wide consideration of transactions which may be harmful to the EU's interest. This is achieved by mandating a procedure for this screening which allows other Member States and the Commission to have a say in how any FDI may impact on public interests.[91] In the aftermath of the pandemic the Commission followed this up with a communication urging Member States to be watchful of FDI that might have an adverse impact on the healthcare and

[85] German Minister for Economic Affairs and Energy, 'Manifesto for a European industrial policy fit for the 21st century' (2019): www.gouvernement.fr/sites/default/files/locale/piece-jointe/2019/02/1043_-_a_franco-german_manifesto_for_a_european_industrial_policy_fit_for_the_21st_century.pdf.

[86] B Deffains, O d'Ormesson and T Perroud, 'Competition Policy and Industrial Policy: For a reform of European Law' (2020) *Robert Schuman Foundation.*

[87] Jones and Davies, 'Merger Control and the Public Interest' (n 84 above).

[88] S Stolton, 'Commission resists competition reform plans until 2021', *Euractiv*, 11 March 2020: www.euractiv.com/section/digital/news/commission-resists-competition-reform-plans-until-2021/.

[89] A third, less visible, initiative was a review of the Commission's market definition notice through which a discussion can be had as to whether the Commission's approach to the geographical scope of markets should be adjusted to take into consideration the long term development of global competition.

[90] Another reading is offered by SW Schill, 'The European Union's Foreign Direct Investment Screening Paradox: Tightening Inward Investment Control to Further External Investment Liberalization' (2019) 46 *Legal Issues of Economic Integration* 105, who argues that the Regulation is leverage whose ultimate objective is to secure better access to foreign markets.

[91] Regulation (EU) 2019/452 of the European Parliament and of the Council of 19 March 2019 establishing a framework for the screening of foreign direct investments into the Union (FDI Screening Regulation) [2019] OJ L79l/01, Arts 6–8.

related industries, lest foreigners take away vital resources.[92] Of particular note for the purposes of this chapter is that this Communication insists that Member States keep an eye out for FDIs that may have an adverse impact for the Union as a whole. As we discussed in section II above, the approach that the EU has taken to the decentralised enforcement of competition law is to apply the country of destination principle, by which each NCA is competent to review the effects that anticompetitive conduct has on its territory. It is somewhat surprising then that for the purposes of FDI the exhortation is for Member States to take the EU position into account.

The second initiative was a White Paper where it expressed concern that non-EU firms buying up EU undertakings with the assistance of subsidies should be regulated:

> the subsidy may allow the subsidised acquirer to pay a higher price to acquire the asset than it would otherwise have paid and can thus distort the valuation of EU assets. Foreign subsidies therefore may lead to excessive purchase prices (outbidding) and at the same time prevent non-subsidised acquirers from achieving efficiency gains or accessing key technologies.[93]

This is now addressed by the Foreign Subsidies Regulation.[94] The Regulation will empower the Commission to intervene in two situations. First, mergers where the acquired firm or one of the parties has an EU turnover of at least €500 million and the transaction involves a foreign financial contribution of at least €50 million have to be notified by the parties to the Commission. Second, the Commission has the discretion to intervene in any other merger and request a notification if it suspects that there is a foreign subsidy that may distort competition. This means that some mergers will require a double notification (under the Merger Regulation and the Foreign Subsidies Regulation). At a substantive level, the proposal is that mergers where the acquirer was funded by a foreign state would be tested to see if the merger may distort the internal market.[95] Indicators to determine this may include the size of the funding, the concentration of the market and whether the takeover is in technology markets. Some of these criteria are linked to competition law considerations, others instead seem to reflect the importance of protecting EU industries. In this respect this Regulation builds on the FDI screening Regulation and attempts to secure some competence for the Commission to review certain forms of FDI in the EU's interest.

[92] Commission, 'Guidance to the Member States concerning foreign direct investment and free movement of capital from third countries, and the protection of Europe's strategic assets, ahead of the application of Regulation' (Communication) (EU) 2019/452 (n 92 above).

[93] Commission, 'White Paper on levelling the playing field as regards foreign subsidies' COM(2020) 253 final, 7.

[94] Regulation (EU) 2022/2560 of the European Parliament and of the Council of 14 December 2022 on foreign subsidies distorting the internal market [2022] OJ L330/1; see F Brito Bastos, 'Repurposing Administrative Procedures to Meet Novel Challenges in EU Competition Law', Ch 9 in this volume.

[95] Regulation (EU) 2022/2560, ibid Arts 4 and 5 and Chapter 3.

In sum, the Commission seized the *Siemens/Alstom* merger controversy to push an industrial policy agenda, but in a direction different from that sought by Member States. Rather than creating space for a more accommodating policy for mergers creating EU champions, it pushed for reforms that would tackle mergers by foreign firms as a means of safeguarding EU industries.

IV. Conclusions

The shaping of a uniform competition policy for the EU has largely been a success built upon the Commission's leadership in shaping policy and the EU's choices to strengthen NCAs while creating a policy space (the European Competition Network) where there is close cooperation between the Commission and the NCAs. However, in this chapter, we have shown that there are some aspects of EU competition policy that are not fully harmonised and that NCAs and Member States are challenging the EU's primacy over the shape and scope of EU competition policy.

First, this happens when Member States wish to reduce the scope of application of EU competition policy in order to protect national interests. For instance, states guard the retained powers to apply national merger laws jealously. The EU has powers to counter protectionist application of merger rules, but it may not always be politically expedient to do this. As we have seen, the Commission treads carefully when applying competition law in sectors or times where national interests are at stake. This may also explain why advocacy powers were not harmonised with the ECN+ Directive. The pursuit of harmonisation, therefore, is guided by political sensitivity. From a constitutional perspective this is puzzling: since Article 120 TFEU requires that national policies are to be guided by 'the principle of an open market with free competition' it would seem that national policies that depart from this principle should be pursued actively by the EU. Potentially, a bigger challenge might be facing the EU with the review of the EUMR. Will Member States who have taken a view that competition considerations should make way for industrial policy succeed in carving out some exceptions in the EUMR? So far the Commission has deflected this by initiating other industrial policy measures like the Foreign Subsidies Regulation that are consistent with the primacy of competition policy, but this might not be enough. However, from a constitutional perspective, any bending to Member State preferences for a strategic merger regime that allows anticompetitive mergers in the name of EU champions would call into question the primacy of EU competition policy.[96] This explains why the EU is resisting pressures to relax its emphasis on strict competition law enforcement and parrying Member State challenges by identifying other legal instruments that support an industrial policy based on competitive markets.

[96] But see K Tuori, *European Constitutionalism* (Cambridge, Cambridge University Press, 2015) ch 5, for a thoughtful reflection on the primacy of competition policy.

Second, the chapter suggests that harmonisation may not always be the superior policy option even if there is agreement among the Commission and Member States on the pursuit of competition policy. Instead, allowing NCAs to apply stricter national rules or providing different interpretations of EU competition law could facilitate modes of governance which would strengthen enforcement. As indicated, this approach could be particularly fruitful in developing the EU's competition policy with respect to agreements aiming to achieve environmental sustainability, in the regulation of e-commerce, and in the regulation of big tech firms. Two approaches were suggested. The first is that NCAs could experiment with different interpretations of EU competition law or NCAs that have been empowered to apply national laws that are stricter than the rules provided for by EU law should be encouraged to explore the extent to which these may afford more effective regulation of digital markets. The effects of applying divergent rules could then be assessed ex post to identify what approach works best. This kind of experimentalist governance has shown promise in other policy fields.[97] The second is that some NCAs could provide a catalyst for the review of EU policy: policy initiatives should not be the exclusive preserve of the Commission. While close cooperation between NCAs and the Commission is necessary to operationalise both suggested approaches, the claim here is that by allowing some divergence and examining the outcomes and merits of different approaches to regulating markets, one can identify superior means to apply EU competition law.

[97] CF Sabel and J Zeitlin, *Experimentalist Governance in the European Union: Towards a New Architecture* (Oxford, Oxford University Press, 2010).

7

The Role of Companies in the Strategic Turn of EU Competition Law

FERNANDO PASTOR-MERCHANTE*

I. Introduction

The purpose of this chapter is to reflect upon the role of companies in the transformational change that competition law and policy is currently going through in the European Union (EU). The main causes of the disruption are well known. The EU's commitment to tackling global warming and climate change, as expressed in the European Green Deal, affects EU competition law and policy.[1] The weight that environmental considerations should have in antitrust and merger control remains controversial,[2] but the movement towards a greener EU competition policy has gained track over the last few years.[3] The objective of transforming the EU economy to make it more sustainable goes hand in hand with the objective of adapting it to the new digital reality.[4] The ramifications of the so-called digital transition are also felt in the area of competition law, if only because of the need to rethink how some of its most basic tenets apply in

* Associate Professor of Administrative Law, IE University Law School and IE/Pérez-Llorca Chair of Commercial Law, Fernando.Pastor@ie.edu. Research reported in this chapter was partially funded by the Spanish *Agencia Estatal de Investigación* (AEI) – 10.13039/501100011033 Grant No. PID2020-115834RA-C33.

[1] Commission, 'The European Green Deal' (Communication) COM(2019) 640 final.

[2] MP Schinkel and L Treuren, 'Green Antitrust: (More) Friendly Fire in the Fight Against Climate Change' (*Amsterdam Law School Research Paper No 72/2020*).

[3] See, eg, G Monti, 'Four Options for a Greener Competition Law' (2020) 11 *Journal of European Competition Law and Practice* 124; K Majcher and V Robertson, 'The Twin Transition to a Green and Digital Economy: The Role for EU Competition Law' (*Graz Law Working Paper No 05/2022*). See also OECD, 'Environmental considerations in competition enforcement, OECD Competition Committee Discussion Paper': www.oecd.org/daf/competition/environmental-considerations in competition-enforcement.htm.

[4] Commission, 'Shaping Europe's Digital Future' (Communication) COM(2020) 67 final; Commission, 'Digital Compass: The European Way for the Digital Decade' (Communication) COM(2021) 118 final.

the digital sphere.[5] Finally, as a result of the recent COVID-19 and Ukrainian crises, the EU has embraced the goal of improving the resilience of its industry.[6] In sum, the challenge is to ensure that EU competition policy remains 'fit for purpose' while contributing to the transition towards a 'green, digital and resilient single market'.[7] Because of the structural and long-term implications of this challenge, it is apposite to refer to this transformative moment as the 'strategic' turn in EU competition law.

Companies cannot be alien to these developments because they are the 'subjects' of EU competition law.[8] Companies are, in practice, the main addressees of the prohibitions of anticompetitive agreements and abuse of dominant position of Articles 101 and 102 of the Treaty on the Functioning of the European Union (TFEU). They are also the main target of the EU Merger Control Regulation.[9] As the standard beneficiaries of State aid measures, companies are also central to this branch of EU competition law, even if its rules target Member States rather than private undertakings. Consequently, the involvement of companies in the strategic turn of EU competition law is of paramount importance if the changes 'are to work and be accepted'.[10] In other words, their involvement is necessary in order to preserve the effectiveness of EU competition law and policy, but also from the perspective of the legitimacy of the transformation process. Indeed, the EU legal order places great value upon the principles of openness and participation, which are now enshrined in Article 11 of the Treaty on European Union (TEU). Thus, if EU competition law and policy is to transform itself, companies should necessarily partake in the process.

In order to analyse their actual and potential contribution to the process, the chapter maps out the different avenues through which companies can bring their input to the strategic reshaping of the Commission's competition policy. The chapter considers their role in the definition of this policy through the administrative rule-making and soft-law initiatives of the Commission, as well as in the actual enforcement of EU competition law and policy. The participatory opportunities enjoyed by companies in the enforcement of EU competition law are a function of the position that they occupy within the procedures launched by the Commission, which is why the chapter addresses separately the roles

[5] J Cremer, Y Montjoye and H Schweitzer, 'Competition Policy for the Digital Era: Final Report' (2019): www.ec.europa.eu/competition/publications/reports/kd0419345enn.pdf.

[6] Commission, 'A New Industrial Strategy for Europe' (Communication) COM(2021) 102 final.

[7] Commission, 'A Competition Policy Fit for New Challenges' (Communication) COM(2021) 713 final.

[8] W Wouters, 'The Undertaking as Subject of EC Competition Law and the Imputation of Infringements to Natural or Legal persons' (2000) 25 *European Law Review* 99, 100, who discusses the differences between the concepts of 'undertaking' and 'company' – a relevant discussion that I overlook here. See also C Townley, 'The Concept of an "Undertaking": The Boundaries of the Corporation – A Discussion of Agency, Employees and Subsidiaries' in G Amato and CD Ehlermann (eds), *EC Competition Law: A Critical Assessment* (Oxford, Hart Publishing, 2007).

[9] Council Regulation (EC) No 139/2004 of 20 January 2004 on the control of concentrations between undertakings (EC Merger Regulation) [2004] OJ L24/01.

[10] Commission, 'The European Green Deal' (n 1 above) 2.

of investigated and third-party companies. Needless to say, the institutional specificities of the three areas of EU competition law also condition the role that companies can play under each of them. The analysis pays close attention to those specificities throughout the chapter. Finally, the chapter only touches upon the role of companies in the judicial review of competition law decisions tangentially since the topic is addressed more squarely in the next chapter.[11]

II. The Role of Companies in the Definition of EU Competition Policy Through Administrative Rule-Making Procedures

As is well known, the foundational provisions of EU competition law have primary law status, because they are codified in Articles 101 to 109 TFEU. It is on the basis of these provisions that the EU legislator has fleshed out the substantive and institutional rules that govern the three areas of EU competition law. However, EU primary and secondary law leave the Commission a wide margin of discretion in the definition of its policy in all three areas.[12] This is something that the Commission does through its enforcement endeavours, but also through an intense administrative rule-making activity. Administrative rule-making is here understood in its broader sense, as a phenomenon that encompasses the definition of competition policy through the legislative initiatives of the Commission, through its regulatory acts, and through its communications, guidelines and other soft-law instruments.[13]

Soft-law instruments are particularly important in that regard, because they play a crucial role in the definition of EU competition policy. In the area of antitrust, the Commission's dense web of soft-law instruments performs a key steering function within the European Competition Network.[14] Similarly, soft-law plays an important role in the control of concentrations, making up for the absence of substantive guidelines in the Merger Control Regulation.[15] Soft-law has also been key in the juridification of the State aid discipline and in the emergence of an actual EU State aid policy.[16] Moreover, soft-law has a significant role to play

[11] See P Nicolaides, 'The Response of EU Courts to Society's Digital & Green Challenges in the Field of Competition and State aid', Ch 8 in this volume.

[12] H Hofmann, 'Negotiated and Non-negotiated Administrative Rule-making: The Example of Competition Policy' (2006) 43 *Common Market Law Review* 153.

[13] J Mendes, 'Executive Rule-making: Procedures in Between Constitutional Principles and Constitutional Entrenchment' in C Harlow, P Leino and G Cananea (eds), *Research Handbook on EU Administrative Law* (Cheltenham, Edward Elgar, 2017) 371 and 377.

[14] O Stefan, *Soft Law in Court: Competition, State Aid and the Court of Justice of the European Union* (Alphen aan den Rijn, Wolters Kluwer, 2013) 26.

[15] Hofmann, 'Negotiated and Non-negotiated Administrative Rule-making' (n 12 above) 154.

[16] M Cini, 'The Soft Law Approach: Commission Rule-making in the EU's State Aid Regime' (2001) 8 *Journal of European Public Policy* 192; M Blauberger, 'Of "Good" and "Bad" Subsidies: European State aid Control through Soft and Hard Law' (2009) 32 *West European Politics* 719.

in the specific context of the strategic turn of EU law, since the Commission has made (and is likely to continue making) extensive use of this type of instrument in order to steer the transition towards a green, digital and resilient single market. Indeed, the Commission announced its commitment to this objective and its new strategic priorities in communications such as the European Green Deal,[17] the 2030 Digital Compass[18] and the New Industrial Strategy for Europe.[19] Finally, the Commission has laid out the implications of the green and digital transitions for EU competition law and policy in its communication on 'A competition policy fit for new challenges', where it also announced a revision of antitrust, merger control and State aid guidelines in light of its new strategic priorities.[20]

As is well known, EU primary law does not confer upon companies the right to participate in the Commission's rule-making procedures. The reference judgment in that regard remains *Atlanta*, where the Court held that the Treaty does not recognise any 'right to be heard prior to the adoption of a legislative act',[21] a holding that is generally understood to apply to legislative and non-legislative acts alike.[22] However, the *Atlanta* doctrine has not impeded the development of a widespread consultation practice in the context of the rule-making initiatives of the Commission, fuelled by the better regulation agenda launched more than 20 years ago by the White Paper on Governance.[23] One of the main objectives of the better regulation agenda is to improve the quality of EU legislation and public consultations plays an important role in that context, as a means of gathering evidence to inform the policymaking of the Commission[24] and of promoting 'trust in the European Union'.[25] Stakeholder participation normally takes place along a three-phase consultation process, which allows the Commission to receive feedback on its initiatives.[26] From the perspective of companies, public consultations are an opportunity to voice their concerns and to bring their input to the policy-making initiatives of the Commission.

Companies have been able to do that in the context of the general consultations launched by the Commission on the impact that the green and digital transition could have in the area of competition law. For example, following the publication of the European Green Deal, the Commission launched a public consultation on how competition policy could contribute to achieving the objectives set in

[17] Commission, 'The European Green Deal' (n 1 above).
[18] Commission, 'A New Industrial Strategy for Europe (n 6 above).
[19] Commission, 'Digital Compass' (n 4 above).
[20] Commission, 'A Competition Policy Fit for New Challenges' (n 7 above).
[21] Case C-104/97 P *Atlanta AG and others v Commission* [1999] EU:C:1999:498, para 35.
[22] Mendes, 'Executive Rule-making' (n 13 above) 386; L Senden and T Brink, *Checks and Balances of Soft EU Rule-Making* (Brussels, Parliament Policy Department, 2012) 31.
[23] Commission, 'European Governance – A White Paper' (White Paper) COM(2001) 428 final.
[24] Commission, 'Better Regulation Guidelines' (Staff Working Document) SWD(2017) 350 final, 13.
[25] Commission, 'Better regulation: Joining forces to make better laws' (Communication) COM(2021) 219 final, 4.
[26] Commission, 'Better Regulation toolbox – November 2021 edition': https://commission.europa.eu/system/files/2023-02/br_toolbox-nov_2021_en.pdf, 438.

that plan.[27] The call contained questions covering the three areas of competition law and the Commission gathered submissions by many stakeholders, including numerous companies.[28] The Commission also launched a public consultation on the 2030 Digital Compass, seeking input in order to operationalise the vision presented in that communication. Of the 101 submissions received, 60 per cent were submitted on behalf of companies or business associations.[29] More to the point, there was a parallel consultation process for the Digital Services Act package and the New Competition Tool, with the objective of gathering feedback on the competition law problems raised by large, digital gatekeeper platforms and on the need to set up a new complementary tool to strengthen competition enforcement in digital markets. Again, more than 60 per cent of the submissions received were submitted on behalf of companies or business associations.[30] Granted, these figures only reflect the relative amount of submissions made by companies in the public consultations carried out by the Commission in the field of EU competition law (rather than the actual impact of those submissions upon the Commission's competition policy). Still, they show that companies can and do routinely avail themselves of this opportunity to voice their interests in the shaping of EU competition policy.

As announced in the communication on 'A competition policy fit for new challenges', the Commission is currently engaged in an ambitious revision of its soft-law armoury in light of the new strategic priorities. This is yet another opportunity for companies to try to influence the strategic reshaping of the Commission's competition policy. For example, in the field of antitrust the Commission recently concluded a public consultation on the revision of the Horizontal Guidelines in order to adapt them to the green and digital transitions.[31] Similarly, the Commission launched a public consultation on the Notice on the definition of relevant market, which is relevant in antitrust and merger control.[32] The main goal of the process was to adapt the notice to the challenges

[27] Commission, Directorate-General for Competition, Competition policy brief 2021-01, September 2021, https://data.europa.eu/doi/10.2763/962262.

[28] Speech by M Vestager, 'Competition Policy in Support of the Green Deal' (IBA Competition Conference, 10 September 2021).

[29] Commission, 'Summary Report on the targeted consultation on the 2030 Digital Compass: the European way for the Digital Decade' (2021).

[30] Commission, 'Summary Report on the open public consultation on the Digital Services Act Package': https://digital-strategy.ec.europa.eu/en/library/summary-report-open-public-consultation-digital-services-act-package and Commission, 'The new complementary tool to strengthen competition enforcement': www.ec.europa.eu/info/law/better-regulation/have-your-say/initiatives/12416-Single-Market-new-complementary-tool-to-strengthen-competition -enforcement_en.

[31] Commission, 'Public consultation on the draft revised Horizontal Block Exemption Regulations and Horizontal Guidelines (2022): https://competition-policy.ec.europa.eu/public-consultations/2022-hbers_en.

[32] Commission, 'Evaluation of the Commission Notice on the definition of relevant market for the purposes of Community competition law of 9 December 1997' (Staff Working Document) SWD(2021) 199 final.

raised by digital markets.[33] Many State aid guidelines have undergone similar consultation processes, including the Climate, Energy and Environmental Aid Guidelines[34] and the Regional Aid Guidelines.[35]

Soft-law instruments are not the only ones subject to public consultations, which is why some of the recent legislative and regulatory initiatives of the Commission in the field of EU competition policy have also been subject to this process. At the time of writing, there is an open call for evidence on the evaluation of EU antitrust rules (namely, Regulation 1/2003[36] and its implementing Regulation 773/2004[37]). The goal is to assess the antitrust legal framework in light of the experience gained over 20 years of application and to identify gaps or opportunities generated by the most important changes occurring throughout that period, with specific reference to the digitalisation of the global economy.[38] Earlier this year, the Commission conducted a public consultation on the revision of the State aid General Block Exemption Regulation in light of the European Green Deal and Industrial and Digital Strategies.[39]

The participation of companies in administrative rule-making procedures is not exempt from difficulties. The leverage that individual companies may exert through this channel is probably minimal because the process is conceived as an information-gathering device with little procedural guarantees in their favour. Moreover, consultation processes in the adoption of soft-law instruments are known to be unsystematic.[40] This is in no small part due to the tendency to dispense with them in times of crisis, as illustrated by the lack of transparency regarding the consultation processes undergone by the State aid and antitrust temporary frameworks and by their successive updates approved in the course of the recent COVID-19 crisis.[41] Still, stakeholder consultations are an important information-aggregating tool that allows administrative authorities to gather feedback on their proposals from affected stakeholders. This is particularly important

[33] Commission, 'Support study accompanying the evaluation of the Commission Notice on the definition of relevant market for the purposes of Community competition law' (2021): https://competition-policy.ec.europa.eu/system/files/2021-06/kd0221712enn_market_definition_notice_2021_1.pdf.

[34] Commission, 'Public consultation on the revised Climate, Energy and Environmental Aid Guidelines (CEEAG)': https://competition-policy.ec.europa.eu/public-consultations/2021-ceeag_en.

[35] Commission, 'Review of the Regional Aid Guidelines (RAG) 2014–2020': https://competition-policy.ec.europa.eu/public-consultations/2020-rag_en.

[36] Council Regulation (EC) No 1/2003 of 16 December 2002 on the implementation of the rules on competition laid down in Articles 81 and 82 of the Treaty [2003] OJ L01/1.

[37] Commission Regulation (EC) No 773/2004 of 7 April 2004 relating to the conduct of proceedings by the Commission pursuant to Articles 81 and 82 of the EC Treaty [2004] OJ L123/18.

[38] Call for evidence on the evaluation of EU antitrust procedural rules (2022): https://ec.europa.eu/info/law/better-regulation/have-your-say/initiatives/13431-EU-antitrust-procedural-rules-evaluation_en.

[39] Commission, 'Public consultation of the draft revised Horizontal Block Exemption Regulations and Horizontal Guidelines': https://competition-policy.ec.europa.eu/public-consultations/2022-hbers_en.

[40] M Eliantonio and O Stefan, 'The Elusive Legitimacy of EU Soft Law: An Analysis of Consultation and Participation in the Process of Adopting COVID-19 Soft Law in the EU' (2021) 12 *European Journal of Risk Regulation* 159, 165.

[41] ibid 172.

when they venture into uncharted waters, which is the direction in which the strategic turn of EU competition law seems to be leading the Commission. This may explain the numerous consultation processes launched in connection to the green and digital transitions and, more generally, the eagerness of the Commission to gather stakeholder input in this context. Thus, their limitations notwithstanding, stakeholder consultations are the first tool that companies have at their disposal to try to influence the strategic reshaping of EU competition policy

III. The Position of Investigated Companies in the Enforcement of EU Competition Law

A. The Position of Companies in the Enforcement of EU State Aid Law

Administrative rule-making plays a key role in the definition of EU competition policy. However, EU competition policy is also defined through the enforcement endeavours of the Commission. The role of companies in that regard depends to a great extent on whether they are the target of the Commission's investigations and procedures (investigated companies) or not (third-party companies). This section focuses on the former, while the next one focuses on the latter. Before going any further, though, it is necessary to make a few preliminary observations regarding the peculiar position of companies in the area of State aid.

Companies can have high stakes in the enforcement of State aid rules, especially when they are the actual or potential beneficiaries of State aid: for example, when the main issue at stake in a procedure is whether they are entitled to receiving some form of state financial support or, even more so, whether they should return the subsidy or financial advantage that they have already received.[42] And yet, no matter how high their stakes, companies are never the formal target of State aid procedures. This is because one of the distinctive features of the discipline is that the addressees of State aid rules and procedures are Member States, rather than companies or other private stakeholders. Far from being a mere formality, this proposition has far-reaching implications. The main one is the 'bilateral' character of the system of State aid control: the idea that the administration of the rules on State aid unfolds as an exclusive dialogue between the Commission and the affected Member State.[43] The upshot is that the only actors protected by the rights

[42] F Rivery, S Thibault-Liger and J Derenne, 'Procedure' in J Derenne and M Merola (eds), *Economic Analysis of State Aid Rules. Contributions and Limits* (Berlin, Lexxion, 2007) 190.

[43] Opinion of Advocate General Mengozzi in Case C-487/06 P *British Aggregates Association v Commission* [2008] EU:C:2008:419, para 74.

of the defence in the area of State aid are Member States themselves.[44] The other side of the coin is that companies always have the status of third party and hence limited information and participatory rights.[45]

The status of private parties in State aid procedures is a contentious issue, especially with regard to beneficiary companies. Their peripheral role is premised on the assumption that their interest is aligned with the interest of the granting Member State, which makes it unnecessary to give them voice. However, the assumption does not always hold true, if only because the financial impact of negative and recovery decisions falls exclusively upon the shoulders of those companies. This is the reason why the position of beneficiary companies within State aid procedures is very controversial.[46] In any event, their position cannot be compared to the position of investigated companies in the two other areas of EU competition law (antitrust and merger control), which is why the peculiar position of beneficiary companies in State aid proceedings will not be considered any further in this section.

B. The Special Position of Notifying Companies in Merger Control Procedures

The peripheral role assigned to beneficiary companies in State aid proceedings stands in stark contrast with the central role played by investigated companies in the two other areas of EU competition law. This is not to say that the position of investigated companies in EU antitrust and merger control procedures is identical. There are some important institutional differences between both areas, especially since the decentralisation of EU antitrust enforcement operated through Regulation 1/2003. Prior to the reform, the Commission had a monopoly over the application of the exemptions laid down by current Article 101(3) TFEU. Things changed dramatically after the reform, because national competition authorities and national courts acquired the ability to apply that provision in full. From an institutional and procedural perspective, this set EU antitrust and merger control apart along two different dimensions.

The first dimension concerns the allocation of powers between the Commission and national authorities. The system of EU merger control is heavily centralised, since the Commission has exclusive jurisdiction over concentrations of EU dimension, as defined in Article 1(2) of the Merger Control Regulation. Indeed, the thresholds that define the EU dimension of concentrations operate as a jurisdictional demarcation line between the powers of the Commission and national

[44] Joined Cases C-74/00 and 75/00 *Falck SpA and Acciaierie di Bolzano SpA v Commission* [2002] EU:C:2002:524, para 81.

[45] Case C-276/03 P *Scott v Commission* [2005] EU:C:2005:590, para 34.

[46] See eg, L Hancher, 'The Administrative Procedure. The Privileged Dialogue' in H Hofmann and C Micheau (eds), *State Aid Law of the European Union* (Oxford, Oxford University Press, 2016).

competition authorities, which project themselves upon different operations in accordance with the 'one-stop shop principle'.[47] On the contrary, the current system of EU antitrust enforcement is truly decentralised, in the sense that the Commission and national competition authorities share the task of ensuring compliance with EU antitrust rules and of taking action against companies that violate its provisions. The focus of this chapter is on the enforcement of EU competition law by the Commission itself. However, the interaction between companies and national competition authorities is also relevant – and the analysis conducted here could certainly be extended to that context.

The second dimension has to do with the timing of the Commission's intervention in antitrust and merger control procedures. The system of EU merger control is based on the notification of concentrations and on the need to obtain the greenlight of the Commission prior to their conclusion. On the contrary, the system of EU antitrust enforcement no longer relies on notifications and on the Commission's ex ante supervision. The contrast between the ex ante design of the system of EU merger control and the ex post design of the system of EU antitrust enforcement obviously affects the position of investigated companies under their respective provisions.

Indeed, the involvement of notifying companies in merger control procedures is more intense than the involvement of investigated companies in antitrust, if only because the merger control procedure is designed as a dialogue between the Commission and notifying parties. Although the Commission welcomes preliminary informal contacts, the most important element in that dialogue is the information provided by the parties in their notification forms. Notification forms can be very detailed, so much so that they can be thought of more as a 'report' than as 'just a form'.[48] This is important, because it means that notifying companies can use them to channel their 'submissions regarding the relevant market, the competitive context of the notified operation, and the effects of that operation'[49] – and, in this manner, try to frame the subsequent analysis of the Commission.

From the perspective of the strategic turn in EU competition law, this means that companies have a key role to play in the green and digital reshaping of EU merger control. Albeit in passing, the Commission acknowledged this fact in the communication on 'A competition policy fit for new challenges', where it noted that the environmental considerations can only be taken into account in merger control procedures 'to the extent that they are put forward by the parties'.[50] The seminal *Philips-Osram* case offers a good illustration thereof, since the green

[47] See, eg, M Kekelekis, *The EC Merger Control Regulation: Rights of Defence. A Critical Analysis of DG COMP Practice and Community Courts' Jurisprudence* (Alphen aan den Rijn, Kluwer Law International, 2006) 29.

[48] LO Blanco (ed), *EU Competition Procedure* 3rd edn (Oxford, Oxford University Press, 2013) 743.

[49] ibid.

[50] Commission, 'A Competition Policy Fit for New Challenges' (n 7 above) 11.

synergies that the Commission considered in clearing the temporary joint venture proposed by both companies were put forward by the parties.[51] Of course, this is not to say that the Commission is bound by the parties' submissions. However, if merger control is to go through a green and digital transition, notifying companies have a key role to play in producing the evidence and shaping the theories of harm that fuel the transition.

C. The Rights of the Defence and the Transactionalisation of EU Competition Law

There are thus fundamental differences between the positions occupied by notifying or investigated companies in the areas of EU antitrust and merger control. Yet there are also certain elements that blur these differences – or, at least, the implications that they have from the perspective of the leverage that companies can exert over the outcome of administrative procedures in both areas.

The first such element is the information and participatory rights that companies derive from the rights of the defence. Indeed, notifying companies (in the case of merger control) and investigated companies (in the case of antitrust) are protected by the bundle of rights that EU administrative law groups under the generic reference to the rights of the defence.[52] As is well known, the ultimate purpose of these rights is to ensure that private parties can participate in administrative procedures in a meaningful way or, to put it differently, that they can have 'an effective influence on the outcome of the decision'.[53]

The second element that blurs the differences between the position of companies in merger control and antitrust is the so-called 'transactionalisation' of EU competition law, which refers to the multiplication of negotiated or cooperative elements within the procedures for the enforcement of this area of EU law.[54] This is yet another consequence of the reform operated by Regulation 1/2003, one of whose novelties was the introduction of the possibility to close antitrust investigations through the so-called commitment decisions foreseen in Article 9 of that regulation. Commitment decisions allow the Commission to close an investigation without fines, when it considers that the remedies voluntarily offered by investigated companies are appropriate to address the competitive concerns that

[51] See eg, Commission Decision of 21 December 1994 relating to a proceeding pursuant to Article 85 of the EC Treaty and Article 53 of the EEA Agreement (Case IV/34.252 – Philips Osram) [1994] OJ L378/37.

[52] See eg, Case C-413/06 P *Bertelsmann AG and others v Commission* [2008] EU:C:2008:392, para 62 (merger control) and Case C-204/00 P *Aalborg Portland and others v Commission* [2004] EU:C:2004:6, para 66 (antitrust).

[53] EB de La Serre, 'Procedural Justice in the European Community Case-Law Concerning the Rights of the Defense: Essentialist and Instrumental Trends' (2006) 12 *European Public Law* 225, 233.

[54] D Geradin and E Mattioli, 'The Transactionalisation of EU Competition Law: A Positive Development?' (2017) 8 *Journal of European Competition Law and Practice* 634.

justified the launching of the investigation in the first place. These decisions may offer certain advantages in novel cases, such as those that drive the strategic turn of EU competition law. On the one hand, because of their negotiated genesis, the remedies imposed in commitment decisions may be more effective in addressing novel and often complex problems, for which the Commission has little experience. On the other hand, commitment decisions are better aligned with the principle of legitimate expectations, insofar as they allow companies to escape fines and the risk of follow-on litigation for practices whose anticompetitive effects may not have been clear beforehand. Of course, commitment decisions are not exempt from difficulties, both from the perspective of investigated companies (because of the risk that they accept remedies that the Commission would not be able to impose unilaterally) and from the perspective of the discipline (because this practice reduces administrative and judicial precedents, which may interfere with its evolution).[55]

Although commitment decisions are not available in hardcore cartel cases, there is also some room for cooperation between the Commission and companies in this type of case. Indeed, companies may also acknowledge their liability and make 'settlement' submissions in the course of cartel investigations.[56] Unlike decisions adopted under Article 9, settlement decisions declare the existence of an infringement, for which they impose a fine. However, companies may obtain a reduction of up to 10 per cent in the amount of the fine. This is precisely how the Commission put an end to its investigation into the car emissions cartel, which is a standard reference in the green antitrust context.[57] In that case, the Commission found that Daimler, BMW and Volkswagen had colluded in breach of Article 101 TFEU, by agreeing to stick to minimum standards imposed by EU environmental legislation rather than developing more ambitious nitrogen oxide cleaning technologies. The case is a good illustration of the potential advantages of cooperation in cases raising novel issues, since this was the first prosecution launched against a cartel on the sole basis of the limitations imposed upon potential technical development (rather than upon price, quality or market partitioning).

[55] See, eg, M Wathelet, 'Commitment Decisions and the Paucity of Precedent' (2015) 6 *Journal of European Competition Law and Practice* 553; A Gautier and N Petit, 'Optimal Enforcement of Competition Policy: the Commitments Procedure Under Uncertainty' (2018) 45 *European Journal of Law and Economics* 195; N Dunne, 'A "Tunney Act for Europe"? Settlement and the Re-Judicialisation of European Commission Enforcement' (2020) 11 *Journal of European Competition Law and Practice* 423.

[56] Commission Regulation (EC) No 622/2008 of 30 June 2008 amending Regulation (EC) No 773/2004, as regards the conduct of settlement procedures in cartel cases [2008] OJ L171/3; Commission, 'Commission Notice on the conduct of settlement procedures in view of the adoption of Decisions pursuant to Article 7 and Article 23 of Council Regulation (EC) No 1/2003 in cartel cases' [2008] OJ C167/1.

[57] Commission Decision of 8 July 2021 relating to a proceeding under Article 101 of the Treaty on the Functioning of the European Union and Article 53 of the EEA Agreement (Case AT.40178 Car Emissions) [2021] OJ C458/16.

The discussion of the cooperative elements present in the enforcement of EU antitrust law cannot conclude without a reference to the possibility for companies to seek informal guidance from the Commission when they have doubts as to the compatibility with the EU antitrust rules of a certain agreement or practice.[58] The possibility to request so-called 'guidance letters' can be of particular relevance when circumstances change, and companies and regulators face new problems and challenges. This is the reason why the Commission encouraged companies to make use of this possibility in the context of the COVID-19 crisis, expressing its willingness

> to provide such guidance and comfort to undertakings or associations of undertakings in order to facilitate initiatives that need to be swiftly implemented in order to effectively tackle the COVID-19 outbreak, notably where there may still be uncertainty about whether such initiatives are compatible with EU competition law.[59]

For the same reasons, Commissioner for Competition Vestager recently expressed the willingness of the Commission to provide companies with guidance in the context of the novel problems raised by the so-called green transition.[60]

IV. The Role of Companies as Third Parties in the Enforcement of EU Competition Law

A. The Instrumental Value of Third-Party Companies in the Enforcement of EU Competition Law

As the main addressees of antitrust and merger control provisions, companies often occupy the position of investigated parties in the enforcement of EU competition law. However, companies may occupy other positions. The purpose of this section is to reflect upon the role that companies play when they act as third parties. In antitrust and merger control, this is the position of all companies acting in any capacity other than as notifying or investigated companies. In State aid, for the reasons explained earlier, this is the position of all companies without exception.

In principle, the procedural position of third-party companies is weaker, because their involvement in the enforcement of EU competition law is primarily conceived in instrumental terms: as an opportunity for the Commission to gather additional evidence, rather than as an opportunity for third-party companies to defend their interests. In other words, third-party companies are first and

[58] Commission, 'Notice on informal guidance relating to novel questions concerning Articles 81 and 82 of the EC Treaty that arise in individual cases' (guidance letters) [2004] OJ C101/78.

[59] Commission, 'Temporary Framework for assessing antitrust issues related to business cooperation in response to situations of urgency stemming from the current COVID-19 outbreak 2020/C' 116 I/02 (Communication) [2020] OJ C116I/7.

[60] Speech by M Vestager, 'Competition Policy in Support of the Green Deal' (IBA Competition Conference, 10 September 2021).

foremost a source of information for the Commission, whose investigatory powers include requests for information, interviews, and inspections (Articles 18–20 of Regulation 1/2003 and Articles 11–13 of the EU Merger Control Regulation). Although these tools can serve to obtain additional information from investigated parties, they are often also used to incorporate into the administrative record evidence gathered from third-party companies.[61]

As far as State aid investigations are concerned, Member States remain the main source of information for the Commission. However, the latest reforms of the procedural legislation applicable in that field have strengthened the information-gathering powers of the Commission vis-à-vis companies.[62] As a result, the Commission is now empowered to request market information from companies in standard State aid procedures (Article 7 Procedural Regulation (PR)), as well as in the context of its cross-border investigations into specific sectors or aid instruments (Article 25(1) PR). These new powers are subject to certain limitations, but they qualify the bilateral character of State aid procedures, since they amount to a recognition that the information provided by Member States is often insufficient to assess the full range of implications of this type of measure.[63]

The fact that third-party companies are primarily seen as a source of information for the Commission does not mean that they are completely deprived of agency. The most interesting area on this front is probably State aid law, because the right of third parties to take an active role in the enforcement of its provisions is enshrined in the treaty itself. Indeed, Article 108(2) TFEU recognises the right of 'concerned' third parties to submit comments in the second phase of State aid procedure. Albeit not enshrined in primary law, third-party companies may also participate in antitrust and merger control procedures. Their status has been developed through secondary legislation. In the case of antitrust, Article 27(3) of Regulation 1/2003 provides that third parties may request to be heard and that the Commission shall grant those applications when they 'show a sufficient interest'. Article 18 of the Merger Control Regulation affords third-party companies with similar rights in merger control procedures.

Granted, the leverage that companies may exert in their capacity as third parties cannot be compared to the power of influence of notifying and investigated companies, since their information and participation rights are more limited. However, these rights give them the possibility to shape the content of the administrative file. This may be more important than it seems, especially in subsequent litigation, given the importance attached to the duty of care (also known as the

[61] See eg, Commission Decision of 17 December 2020 declaring a concentration to be compatible with the internal market and the EEA agreement (Case M.9660 Google/Fitbit) [2021] OJ C194/7, paras 20–24.

[62] Council Regulation (EU) No 734/2013 of 22 July 2013 amending Regulation (EC) No 659/1999 laying down detailed rules for the application of Article 93 of the EC Treaty [2013] OJ 204/15, repealed by Council Regulation (EU) 2015/1589 of 13 July 2015 laying down detailed rules for the application of Article 108 of the Treaty on the Functioning of the European Union [2015] OJ L248/9.

[63] Hofmann and Micheau, *State Aid Law of the European Union* (n 46 above) 366–67.

duty of diligent and impartial examination) and to the reasons-giving requirement in the judicial review of competition decisions. Both standards basically assess the rationality of Commission's decisions in light of the information compiled in the administrative file,[64] which is why they somewhat make up for the limited involvement of third parties in administrative procedures.[65] Thus, despite its limitations, the right to participate in antitrust, merger control and State aid procedures is one of the avenues that third-party companies have at their disposal to try to shape EU competition policy.

This avenue may be particularly relevant in times of change, as a tool that allows companies to exert some influence over the outcome of disruptive cases that can define the course of EU competition law and policy. This is probably the reason why recent digital antitrust cases, such as the parallel proceedings launched against Google for abuse of dominant position, mobilised numerous third-party companies. Besides submitting written comments, some of these companies were granted the opportunity to meet with the Commission (and Google actually took issue with this fact, complaining that the Commission had allegedly failed to provide it with adequate access to the minutes of those meetings, a plea dismissed by the Commission).[66]

The structure of the State aid procedure, which is closed to the input of third parties during the first phase, means that in some cases it is not feasible for third-party companies to participate in the administrative procedure. When that happens, lodging an action of annulment against clearing decisions adopted at the end of the preliminary phase may be the only option for them. A good illustration thereof is Ryanair's multifront battle against State aid schemes for the airline sector approved during the COVID-19 pandemic. In the case of Germany's State aid in favour of Condor, France's State aid in favour of KLM and Portugal's State aid in favour of TAP, Ryanair did not participate in the administrative examination of these measures, which had been duly notified by the Member States. However, it subsequently challenged the decisions of the Commission not to take objections and the General Court annulled them.[67] Although the decisions were annulled

[64] F Pastor-Merchante, 'Por qué lo llaman procedimiento cuando quieren decir expediente? Sobre las funciones dogmáticas del expediente administrativo' (2021) 4 *Teoría y Método. Revista de Derecho Público* 153, 169.

[65] L Azoulai, 'Les garanties procedurales en droit communautaire: recherches sur la procédure et le bon gouvernment' (*PhD Thesis, European University Institute, 2000*) 237.

[66] Commission Decision of 27 June 2017 relating to a proceeding under Article 102 of the Treaty on the Functioning of the European Union and Article 54 of the EEA Agreement (Case AT.39740 – Google Search (Shopping)) [2018] OJ C9/11, para 118 ff, which was upheld for the most part in Case T-612/17 *Google v Commission* (*Google Shopping*) [2021] EU:T:2021:763. Appeal pending in Case C-48/22 P *Google Alphabet v Commission* (pending); Commission Decision of 18 July 2018 relating to a proceeding under Article 102 of the Treaty on the Functioning of the European Union and Article 54 of the EEA Agreement (Case AT.40099 – Google Android) [2019] OJ C402/19, para 52 ff; Commission Decision of 20 March 2019 relating to a proceeding under Article 102 of the Treaty on the Functioning of the European Union and Article 54 of the EEA Agreement (Case AT.40411 Google Search AdSense) [2020] OJ C369/6, para 62 ff.

[67] Case T-665/20 *Ryanair v Commission (Condor)* [2021] EU:T:2021:344; Case T-643/20 *Ryanair v Commission (KLM; Covid-19)* [2021] EU:T:2021:286; Case T-465/20 *Ryanair v Commission (TAP; Covid-19)* [2021] EU:T:2021:284.

on insufficient reasoning grounds, the ultimate purpose of Ryanair's action was to force the Commission to go through the second phase of the procedure and to gather comments from itself and other third parties if it were to approve the contested State aid schemes.

B. The Role of Companies as Complainants

Third-party companies may play an even more active role in the enforcement of EU competition law when they lodge complaints with the Commission. Both Regulation 1/2003 and the State aid procedural regulation allow interested third parties to lodge complaints, as a means of bringing to the Commission's attention infringements that could otherwise go unnoticed (Article 7(2) of Regulation 1/2003 and Article 24(2) PR). The procedure for handling complaints is roughly equivalent in both areas, given the Commission's obligation to allow third parties to provide additional information when their submissions are deemed to be incomplete (Article 7 of Commission Regulation 773/2004 and Article 24 PR), although antitrust legislation foresees a closer involvement of complainants in the procedure (Article 6 of Commission Regulation 773/2004). The EU Merger Control Regulation does not foresee any role for complaints in that area, although the European judicature has made it clear that the Commission is also bound to examine complaints related to concentrations of EU dimension.[68]

One of the most significant considerations to assess the leverage that companies can exert through complaints is the degree of 'enforcement discretion' – if any – enjoyed by administrative authorities (ie, the ability not to act on certain complaints). In the areas of antitrust and merger control, it is settled case law that the Commission is not obliged to take a position on the merits of complaints. The other side of the coin is that the Commission is entitled to develop and implement its own enforcement agenda and to refrain from investigating complaints that fail to meet that agenda. Of course, the enforcement discretion of the Commission is not unfettered because the famous *Automec II* judgment requires the Commission to examine complaints carefully and to provide complainants with a reasoned explanation whenever it closes the file without a fully-fledged investigation of their allegations[69] The same limitations apply in merger control.[70]

The status of complainants in State aid cases is less clear. The reference case is *Athinaïki Techniki*, where the Court essentially imported to the realm of State aid the procedure for the handling of complaints foreseen in antitrust.[71] The problem is that the *Athinaïki Techniki* judgment did not clarify whether that decision had to address the merits of the complaint or whether it could be an *Automec II*-type

[68] Case C-170/02 P *Schlüsselverlag J S Moser and Others v Commission* [2003] EU:C:2003:501, para 27.
[69] Case T-24/90 *Automec Srl v Commission* [1992] EU:T:1992:97, para 75 and 79. See also Case C-282/95 P *Guérin automobiles v Commission* [1997] EU:C:1997:159.
[70] Case C-170/02 P *Schlüsselverlag J S Moser and Others v Commission* (n 68 above) para 27.
[71] Case C-521/06 P *Athinaïki Techniki AE v Commission* [2008] EU:C:2008:422, para 39.

of decision: namely, a decision laying out the reasons why the allegations made in the complaint would not be investigated. To complicate things even further, the State aid procedural regulation underwent an important reform after the *Athinaïki Techniki* judgment. The reform raised the admissibility bar of State aid complaints, since it introduced stricter standing and formal requirements, as well as the possibility to register as mere market information insufficiently substantiated complaints. However, the reform basically codified the *Athinaïki Techniki* procedure without clarifying the issue, which remains unclear.[72]

The point to note is that the Commission's ability to set priorities and to carry out a selective enforcement strategy is itself a tool that can be used to further certain policies, for example to prioritise investigations having sustainability implications.[73] From this perspective, complainants can be an ally in the strategic turn of EU competition law, when they push the Commission to investigate cases that are relevant from the perspective of its new strategic priorities. For example, some of the best known digital cases decided by the Commission over the last few years had their origin in complaints lodged by third-party companies, including the three famous sanctions imposed on Google for abuse of dominant position in connection to its comparison shopping service,[74] the tying of its search app in the Android store[75] and its search advertising services.[76] At the same time, though, complainants can be an obstacle when they deviate from those objectives, which is where the enforcement discretion of the Commission can come into play.

C. The Role of Third-party Companies in the Enforcement of EU Competition Law before National Competition Authorities and Courts

The discussion so far has focused on the role that third-party companies play in the enforcement of EU competition law by the Commission itself, be it as informants

[72] See, eg, F Pastor-Merchante, 'The Status of Complainants in State Aid Cases: A Look Back into the Athinaïki Techniki Saga' in C Buts and JL Buendia Sierra (eds), *Milestones in State Aid Case Law* 2nd edn (Berlin, Lexxion, 2022) 219– 21; A Sanchez-Graells, 'Digging Itself out of the Hole? A Critical Assessment of the European Commission's Attempt to Revitalize State Aid Enforcement After the Crisis' (2016) 4 *Journal of Antitrust Enforcement* 157; HP Nehl, '2013 Reform of EU State Aid Procedures: How to Exacerbate the Imbalance between Efficiency and Individual Protection' (2014) 13 *European State Aid Law Quarterly* 235, 241; Hofmann and Micheau, *State Aid Law of the European Union* (n 46 above) 361.

[73] OECD, 'Environmental Considerations in Competition Enforcement' (Competition Committee Discussion Paper, 2021) 44.

[74] Commission Decision (n 66 above) in Case AT.39740 Google Search (Shopping), which was upheld for the most part in Case T-612/17 *Google and Alphabet v Commission* [2021] EU:T:2021:763. Appeal pending in Case C-48/22 P.

[75] Commission Decision (n 66 above) in Case AT.40099 (Google Android).

[76] Commission Decision (n 66 above) in Case AT.40411 (Google Search AdSense).

or as complainants. The analysis would not be complete without a reference to the possibility for these companies to resort to national competition authorities or to national courts in order to push for the enforcement of EU competition law against other market players.

One of the consequences of the decentralisation of EU antitrust law operated by Regulation 1/2003 was the empowerment of national competition authorities to enforce EU antitrust law in full. This is relevant from the perspective of our inquiry, for it means that national competition authorities are an alternative forum where third-party companies may lodge complaints against alleged violations of EU antitrust law committed by other undertakings.[77] The corollary is that national competition authorities may also have a role to play in the strategic reshaping of the discipline. The French Competition Authority's investigation into Google's ad tech business offers a good illustration thereof, since the trigger was a complaint lodged by various local publishers.[78] The case resulted in a decision imposing a multi-million fine on Google for breach of Article 102 TFEU and of the corresponding French provisions on abuse of dominant position. The point to note is that the case confronted the French Competition Authority with novel issues pertaining to the application of Article 102 TFEU in the digital context – and that the fine and the commitments that it rendered binding had an impact upon Google's general ad tech strategy in the EU, and not only in France.

The decentralisation of EU antitrust law also transformed the role of national courts in the enforcement of its provisions. Not in vain, one of the goals of the reforms introduced by Regulation 1/2003 was the promotion of private enforcement before national courts as a means of strengthening the effectiveness of the discipline.[79] The idea was that 'companies and individuals should increasingly feel encouraged to make use of private action before national courts in order to defend the subjective rights conferred on them by the EC competition rules'.[80] The importance attached to private enforcement by the EU institutions has not waned over the last two decades, as shown by the adoption and entry into force of the Antitrust Damages Directive, which explicitly enshrines the right to full compensation of antitrust victims.[81] Through its case law, the Court of Justice of

[77] 'Commission Notice on the handling of complaints by the Commission under Articles 81 and 82 of the EC Treaty' (Notice) [2004] OJ C101/05, paras 19–25.

[78] See, eg, T Höppner, M Volmar and P Westerhoff, 'The French Competition Authority Fines a Big Tech Company €220 Million for Abuse of a Dominant Position Through Self-Preferencing in the Ad Tech Industry' (2021) *Concurrences* No 102324.

[79] Commission, 'White Paper on the Modernisation of the Rules Implementing Articles 85 and 86 of the EC Treaty' (White Paper) COM(1999) 101 final, paras 25, 36–39 and 46.

[80] Speech by Commissioner M Monti, 'Effective Private Enforcement of EC Competition Law' (Sixth EU Competition Law and Policy Workshop, 1–2 June 2001) 2.

[81] Directive 2014/104/EU of the European Parliament and of the Council of 26 November 2014 on certain rules governing actions for damages under national law for infringements of the competition law provisions of the Member States and of the European Union Text with EEA relevance [2014] OJ L349/1, Art 3.

the European Union has also contributed to the promotion of private enforcement: for example, holding that under certain conditions, parent companies may be held liable for the antitrust violations committed by their subsidiaries[82] and, conversely, that there are circumstances where subsidiary companies may have to respond for their parent companies' anticompetitive actions.[83]

The trucks cartel saga is a good example of a case with environmental implications where the Commission's infringement decisions gave rise to a considerable volume of national litigation, as a result of the actions for damages brought by the purchasers of the trucks produced by the cartelised firms.[84] Granted, the potential impact of this type of follow-on litigation upon the strategic reshaping of EU antitrust law is limited, because it relies on the determinations made by the Commission or by national competition authorities in their prior infringement decisions. Thus, the most significant changes or novelties – if any – are likely to be found in those decisions. Of course, companies can also bring antitrust suits from scratch, without grounding their actions on any prior infringement decision. However, stand-alone litigation is probably less attractive in general (because of the uncertainty generated by the absence of a prior infringement decision to back up the applicants' claims) and in particular in novel cases (because national courts may be less willing than the Commission or than national competition authorities to entertain new theories of harm).[85] In any event, it is certainly a possibility and there are actually some precedents in the digital context: for example, the action taken by Nekdoktor against the cooperation agreement between Google and the German Federal Ministry of Health.[86]

Private litigation before national courts is also an option for third-party companies in the field of State aid. Indeed, the direct effect of the standstill clause of Article 108(3) TFEU empowers third-party companies to apply for the suspension and recovery of unlawful State aid measures, as well as for the compensation of damages suffered as a result of their implementation.[87] Since the adoption of the first Notice on cooperation,[88] the promotion of private enforcement has had pride of place in the Commission's State aid agenda.[89] As a result of these efforts, the volume of national litigation in the area of State aid

[82] Case C-724/17 *Vantaan kaupunki v Skanska Industrial Solutions Oy* [2019] EU:C:2019:204.

[83] Case C-882/19 *Sumal SL v Mercedes Benz Trucks España SL* [2021] EU:C:2021:800.

[84] See, eg, F Marcos, 'Truck Cartel Damages Claims: Thousand and Odd Judgments Issued by Spanish Appeal Courts' (*Working Paper Zeitschrift für Europäisches Privatrecht No 1/2023*).

[85] R Podszun, 'Private Enforcement and Gatekeeper Regulation: Strengthening the Rights of Private Parties in the Digital Markets Act' (2022) 13 *Journal of European Competition Law and Practice* 254, 255.

[86] ibid.

[87] Study on the enforcement of State aid rules and decisions by national courts (Luxembourg, Publication Office of the European Union, 2019) 60.

[88] Commission, 'Notice on cooperation between national courts and the Commission in the State aid field' (Notice) [1995] OJ C312/8.

[89] Commission, 'State Aid Action Plan – Less and better targeted state aid: a roadmap for state aid reform 2005–2009' (Consultation Document) COM (2005) 107 final.

has increased.[90] However, it is important to note that national litigation before national courts can only have limited impact upon the making and evolution of EU State aid policy. This is because the main issue at stake in this type of case is the procedural regularity of contested State aid measures (ie, whether they were implemented in violation of the standstill clause), rather than their substantive compatibility (ie, whether they may be lawfully implemented under the public interest exemptions of Articles 107(2) and (3) TFEU). The fact that the Commission retains a monopoly over those provisions necessarily limits the significance that private litigation triggered by third-party companies can have upon the strategic transition of EU State aid policy.

V. Conclusion

The starting point of this chapter was the observation that, if EU competition law is to transform itself, companies should have a say in the process. Without their involvement, the process risks putting the effectiveness of the discipline in peril. Moreover, as the main subjects of EU competition law, the involvement of companies is also necessary to shore up the legitimacy of any process of transformational change, if only because of the constitutional value placed on the principles of openness and stakeholder participation by EU constitutional and administrative law.

It is against this background that the chapter has mapped out the different channels through which companies can bring their input to the strategic reshaping of the Commission's competition policy. The analysis has shown that the first avenue through which companies can bring their input to the transition is through the consultation processes to which the Commission routinely subjects its legislative, regulatory and soft-law initiatives. Of course, EU competition policy is also defined through the enforcement endeavours of the Commission, in the context of which companies also have an important role to play, either as the target of those procedures or as third parties. Although their degree of involvement is different in both scenarios, they have certain tools to voice their concerns and to try to shape the outcome of EU competition procedures, a possibility of particular relevance in the kind of novel or disruptive cases that can redefine the course of EU competition policy.

More importantly, the chapter has also shown that the involvement of companies in the strategic turn of EU competition law is not a mere possibility, but rather an actual reality. It is in the context of the rule-making initiatives of the Commission where this is most obvious, given the numerous consultation

[90] See, eg, F Pastor-Merchante and G Monti, 'The Functions of National Courts in the Private Enforcement of State Aid Law' in PL Parcu, G Monti and M Botta (eds), *EU State Aid Law: Emerging Trends at the National and EU Level* (Cheltenham, Edward Elgar, 2020).

processes that we have recently witnessed in connection to the impact of the green and digital transitions in the area of EU competition law. Indeed, the Commission seems eager to gather the input of companies in the framework of its strategic revision of EU competition policy, which is probably due to the fact that it is venturing into uncharted waters. The chapter has also highlighted the important role played by investigated and third-party companies in some of the cases that are generally considered to be most relevant from the perspective of the strategic turn in EU competition law. These cases show that companies can also be a valuable source of information for the Commission in its attempts to align the enforcement of EU competition law with the objective of achieving a green, digital and resilient internal market.

8

The Response of EU Courts to Society's Digital and Green Challenges in the Field of Competition and State Aid

PHEDON NICOLAIDES*

I. Introduction

The European Court of Justice has played a prominent role in the process of integration in the European Union (EU), especially in interpreting rules that have a general application such as the competition provisions of the Treaty on the Functioning of the European Union (TFEU).[1] Although the letter of these provisions has hardly changed since the establishment of the European Economic Community in 1958, their interpretation and application have evolved significantly in response to market, technological and policy developments.[2]

During the past decade or so, competition law has been confronted with three major challenges: (1) The digitisation of the economy and the emergence of dominant players in internet-based commerce and digital platforms;[3] (2) three waves of crises (the financial crisis of 2008–15, the health crisis of 2020–21 and the ongoing war in Ukraine); and (3) the transition to a greener

* Professor at the University of Maastricht and the University of Nicosia, phedon.nicolaides@maastrichtuniversity.nl. I am grateful to comments and suggestions I received from the editors on a previous draft.

[1] For excellent reviews of the role of the Court of Justice see K Alter, *The European Court's Political Power* (Oxford, Oxford University Press, 2009); M Dawson, B De Witte and E Muir (eds), *Judicial Activism at the European Court of Justice* (Cheltenham, Elgar Publishing, 2013); L Vilhena de Freitas, 'The Judicial Activism of the European Court of Justice' in LP Coutinho, M La Torre and S Smith (eds), *Judicial Activism* (New York, Springer, 2015).

[2] See chapters 1 and 2 on the evolution of EU competition policy in R Whish and D Bailey, *Competition Law* 10th edn (Oxford, Oxford University Press, 2021).

[3] See the recitals of Regulation (EU) 2022/1925 of the European Parliament and of the Council of 14 September 2022 on contestable and fair markets in the digital sector and amending Directives (EU) 2019/1937 and (EU) 2020/1828 (Digital Markets Act) [2022] OJ L265/1.

economy.[4] One may also mention the challenge posed by foreign subsidies which, however, in relative terms is of a smaller magnitude as it affects only some sectors of the European economy, while the perceived 'source' of the problem is the policies of only a handful of third countries.[5]

The emergence of dominant players operating platforms through which much internet-based commerce is conducted has been the focus of antitrust rules (ie, Articles 101 and 102 TFEU). The EU and Member States have reacted to the successive crises and have sought to expedite the transition to a more digital and greener economy with new rules and subsidies. The new rules have introduced stricter standards, both financial and environmental, established common supervisors and created new funds both at the national level and European level, such as the Recovery and Resilience Fund.[6] The European Commission has had to adopt, sometimes at very short notice, new state aid guidelines – the so-called Temporary Frameworks – to steer public subsidies towards less distortive actions and maintain a level playing field among Member States.[7]

In practice, EU courts interpret Union competition rules in two contexts: in appeals against Commission decisions and in references for preliminary rulings. Given that in the field of competition it is the Commission that adopts antitrust and state aid exemption regulations and guidelines, shares the task with national authorities of enforcing the prohibitions of Articles 101(1), 102 and 107(1) and exercises the exclusive right of authorising state aid, this chapter focuses on the interaction between EU courts and the Commission, as the Commission adjusts the relevant rules to facilitate the digital and green transition.[8]

EU courts have on the whole been accommodative of the Commission's initiatives and shifting enforcement priorities. They have maintained, especially in the field of state aid, that the Commission enjoys wide discretion in assessing complex matters such as when determining whether, for example, a business practice is abusive or whether an aid measure is compatible with the internal market.[9] Nevertheless, as will be seen in the review of the evolving interpretation

[4] See Commission, 'The European Green Deal' (Communication) COM(2019)640 final; Commission, 'Shaping Europe's Digital Future' (2020).

[5] See Regulation (EU) 2022/2560 of the European Parliament and of the Council of 14 December 2022 on foreign subsidies distorting the internal market [2022] OJ L330/1.

[6] See Regulation (EU) 2021/241 of the European Parliament and of the Council of 12 February 2021 establishing the Recovery and Resilience Facility [2021] OJ L57/17. See also the dedicated website on the RRF and the explanation of how it supports the different aspects of the digital and green transition and facilitates economic recovery: Commission, 'The Recovery and Resilience Facility': https://commission.europa.eu/business-economy-euro/economic-recovery/recovery-and-resilience-facility_en.

[7] The Temporary Frameworks can be accessed at: Commission, 'State aid rules and coronavirus': https://competition-policy.ec.europa.eu/state-aid/coronavirus_en, and Commission, 'Temporary Crisis and Transition Framework': https://competition-policy.ec.europa.eu/state-aid/ukraine_en.

[8] Whish and Bailey, *Competition Law* (n 2 above) ch 2.

[9] See for example, cases C-441/07 P *Commission v Alrosa Company* [2010] EU:C:2010:377, para 67: 'By so doing, the General Court put forward its own assessment of complex economic circumstances and thus substituted its own assessment for that of the Commission, thereby encroaching on the discretion enjoyed by the Commission instead of reviewing the lawfulness of its assessment'; and C-654/17

of Articles 101, 102 and 107 TFEU in response to the digital and green transition, EU courts have not lowered the high standards of proof that the Commission must meet, nor have they relaxed the Commission's duty to duly reason its decisions.

As will be shown later on, the overall conclusion of this review is that EU courts are unlikely to interpret competition rules in a way that hinders the digital and green transition. But at the same time, they will expect the Commission to base its decisions on credible theories and rigorous analysis.

This chapter is structured as follows. The application of Article 101 TFEU and the exemption of cooperation between undertakings are analysed in conjunction with the transition to a greener economy. The application of Article 102 is analysed in conjunction with the prevention of obstacles to the transition to a more digital economy. Lastly, the application of Article 107 TFEU is analysed in conjunction with the incentives given to undertakings to make investments both in digital and greener technologies. The next section summarises the enforcement of competition rules in view of the challenges posed by the digital and green transition. The last section pulls together the overall conclusions.

II. An Overview of the Evolving Enforcement Priorities

In November 2021, the Commission published a Communication entitled 'A competition policy fit for new challenges'.[10] It referred to the crises buffeting the EU and argued that 'all this calls for strong and effective competition policy and enforcement, to give the European economy the agility to mount the recovery path and meet its twin green and digital ambitions in a sustainable, socially and territorially inclusive manner'.[11] In other words, strong enforcement of competition policy was not an obstacle to the recovery and to the green and digital transition. Rather, it facilitated the achievement of those ambitions.[12]

P *Bayerische Motoren Werke and Freistaat Sachsen v Commission* [2019] EU:C:2019:634, paras 79–80: 'The assessment of the compatibility of aid measures with the internal market, under Article 107(3) TFEU, comes within the exclusive competence of the Commission … In this regard, the Commission enjoys wide discretion, the exercise of which involves complex economic and social assessments'.

[10] Commission, 'A competition policy fit for new challenges' (Communication) COM(2021) 713 final.

[11] ibid 2.

[12] For a detailed analysis of the competition challenges posed by digital platforms and the collection of consumer data see J Crémer, Y de Montjoye and H Schweitzer, *Competition Policy for the Digital Era* (Luxembourg, Publications Office of the European Union, 2019). For a more detailed explanation of how competition policy can facilitate the green transition see Directorate-General for Competition, 'Competition Policy in Support of Europe's Green Ambition' (2021): https://op.europa.eu/en/publication-detail/-/publication/63c4944f-1698-11ec-b4fe-01aa75ed71a1. For a review of recent literature examining the arguments, mostly, in favour and against the suitability of competition law

The Communication explained that, for that purpose, the Commission launched a review of competition policy and that it sought 'to equip itself with new instruments aimed at tackling emerging challenges in the Single Market, such as digital gatekeepers or the distortive effects of foreign subsidies'.[13]

First, as the recovery from the shock of the COVID-19 pandemic gained strength, the Commission announced the gradual phasing out of the state aid Temporary Framework.[14] Then, the Commission identified 'competition policy's contribution' to the green and digital transition. With respect to supporting the EU's environmental sustainability, the Communication cited the following: (1) ensuring strong and competitive markets that send the right price signals;[15] (2) adaptation of the state aid guidelines and in particular those on climate, environmental protection and energy savings to enable well-targeted public subsidies and level playing field among Member States;[16] and (3) amendment of the antitrust guidelines to enable companies to cooperate to pursue genuinely green initiatives jointly, while preventing 'greenwashing' that would harm consumers.[17]

With respect to supporting the EU's digital transition, the Communication, first, recalled the unexpected positive impact of the pandemic which induced literally overnight remote working and led to an exponential increase in internet commerce. Then the following actions were identified: (1) facilitating public support to fill the 'digital investment gap' through revision of state aid guidelines (eg, the guidelines on state aid for broadband networks, the guidelines on R&D, etc);[18] (2) keeping the market power of dominant platforms in check;[19] and (3) competition rules to reflect the specificities of digital markets.[20] The last two actions are reviewed in more detail in the following section together with the facilitation of cooperation of companies on green initiatives.

to support environmental policy see: MC Comba, 'EU Competition Law and Sustainability: The Need for an Approach Focused on the Objectives of Sustainability Agreements' (*Erasmus Law Review No 2/2022*); A Gerbrandy, 'Solving a Sustainability-Deficit in European Competition Law' (2017) 40 *World Competition* 539; J Malinauskaite, 'Competition Law and Sustainability: EU and National Perspectives' (2022) 13 *Journal of Competition Law and Practice* 336; G Monti, 'Four Options for a Greener Competition Law' (2020) 11 *Journal of European Competition Law and Practice* 124; G Monti and J Mulder, 'Escaping the Clutches of EU Competition Law: Pathways to Assess Private Sustainability Initiatives' (2017) 42 *European Law Review* 635; J Nowag, *Environmental Integration in Competition and Free-Movement Laws* (Oxford, Oxford University Press, 2016); J Nowag, 'Competition Law's Sustainability Gap? Tools for an Examination and a Brief Overview' (*Lund University Legal Research Paper Series No 3/2019*).

[13] Commission, 'A competition policy' (n 10 above) 3.
[14] ibid 3–5.
[15] ibid 8.
[16] ibid 8–10.
[17] ibid 11.
[18] ibid 12–13.
[19] ibid 13–14.
[20] ibid 15.

III. Articles 101 and 102 TFEU and the Digital and Green Transitions

It is instructive to start this section on the evolution of antitrust law with a more detailed analysis of the recently identified actions with respect to cooperation between companies on green initiatives, the operation of digital platforms and the Commission's perceived specificities of digital markets.

A. Facilitating the Green Transition: Sustainability Agreements between Undertakings

Article 101(1) TFEU prohibits agreements and concerted practices between undertakings which distort competition.[21] In July 2021, the Commission imposed a fine of EUR 875 million on five carmakers for colluding to slow down the deployment of technologies with potential to reduce car pollution. Therefore, competition policy can contribute to environmental protection through vigorous enforcement of the rules that preserve competition on the market.[22]

However, Article 101(3) TFEU allows, under certain conditions, agreements or cooperation between undertakings that generate benefits for consumers without eliminating competition. The conditions laid down in Article 101(3) TFEU are 'technologically neutral' or 'policy neutral' in the sense that they do not prioritise or exclude any particular technology or policy. Therefore, in principle, cooperation between two or more undertakings on green initiatives, such as more stringent environmental standards, can benefit from the exemption of Article 101(3) TFEU.

Indeed, as early as 1999, the Commission approved an agreement between domestic appliance producers to phase out energy inefficient washing machines (the *CECED* case).[23] The Commission found the agreement to conform with the conditions of Article 101(3) TFEU.

It is rather obvious that agreements that can bring about significant environmental improvements must include most products placed on the market. It follows that if such agreements contain any restrictive clauses or generate restrictive effects, they are unlikely to fall outside the scope of Article 101(1) TFEU for being *de minimis* in nature or for not affecting trade between Member States.[24]

[21] An excellent analysis of the case law on Arts 101(1), 101(3), 102 and 107 TFEU is provided in Whish and Bailey, *Competition Law* (n 2 above).

[22] See Commission Decision of 8 July 2021 relating to a proceeding under Article 101 of the Treaty on the Functioning of the European Union and Article 53 of the EEA Agreement (Case AT.40178 Car Emissions) [2021] OJ C458/16.

[23] See Commission Decision of 24 January 1999 relating to a proceeding under Article 81 of the EC Treaty and Article 53 of the EEA Agreement (Case IV.F.1/36.718.CECED) [2000] OJ L187/47.

[24] See Commission, 'Guidelines on the effect on trade concept contained in Articles 81 and 82 of the Treaty' (Notice) [2004] OJ C101/81 and Commission, 'Notice on agreements of minor importance

In principle, nothing prevents the Commission from taking into account the positive effects of any nature generated by an agreement. After all, EU courts have acknowledged that the Commission enjoys a wide discretion in the enforcement of competition law.[25] Competition law does not present an obstacle to undertakings that wish to cooperate to produce environmentally friendly products or practices or more energy-efficient products. However, so far, the Commission has not approved an agreement that generated environmental benefits for society at large without any 'private' benefits for the participating undertakings in terms of, for example, reduction of costs, increased productivity, accelerated research, wider reach, and so on. Nor have EU courts dealt with such an agreement. After all, if undertakings are not forced by law to alter their production practices, why would they incur costs to generate benefits which they cannot translate into more profits?

A more difficult case for exemption under Article 101(3) TFEU is when an agreement leads to efficiencies that benefit consumers but also create negative environmental externalities for society at large. For example, two or more undertakings build a mega factory with large economies of scale that causes pollution. This is a situation where we have what may be called 'environmentally harmful efficiencies'. Then the question is whether the Commission may take into account the negative environmental externalities created by the agreement. A similar case would be when the agreement causes substantial distortion of competition, but at the same time reduces environmental pollution. This is a situation where we have what may be called 'environmentally friendly distortions'. Then the question is whether the Commission may take into account the positive environmental effects to offset the distortion of competition.

The assessment of either situation entails some kind of weighing of diverse effects that goes beyond the traditional balancing of the positive effects from cooperation against the negative effects it has on competition.[26] The negative or positive environmental externalities materialise outside the standard competition effects or the interaction among cooperating undertakings or between cooperating undertakings and their competitors. Such an approach has not yet been tested before EU courts. Although Article 101(3) TFEU requires that consumers do obtain a 'fair share' of the benefits from cooperation, it says nothing about other benefits such as reduction of carbon emissions that may be only an indirect consequence of cooperation to place a new product or service on the market. And are 'consumers' in the meaning of Article 101(3) TFEU the same as 'citizens' or 'persons' in the meaning of environmental policy objectives?[27]

which do not appreciably restrict competition under Article 101(1) of the Treaty on the Functioning of the European Union' (Communication) [2014] OJ C291/1.

[25] See, for example, Case T-76/14 *Morningstar v Commission* [2016] EU:T:2016:481.

[26] Some commentators have lent their support to this approach. See, for example, M Dolmans, 'Sustainable Competition Policy' (2020) 6 *Competition Law and Policy Debate* 3.

[27] It is interesting to note that the new Commission Guidelines on horizontal cooperation agreements state the following: 'For example, drivers purchasing less polluting fuel are also citizens who

Furthermore, while Article 101(3) TFEU prohibits unnecessary restrictions and elimination of competition, it is silent on whether harmful effects beyond competition may be taken into account.[28]

Therefore, with respect to the interpretation of Article 101(3) TFEU there are two related problems: the nature of the effects that may be taken into account and the weighing of such effects.

Aside from the legal problem of the interpretation of Article 101(3) TFEU, there is also the practical problem of how external benefits or harm may be measured. Commission practice and the case law on Article 101(3) TFEU do not indicate that there is a threshold for the 'fair share' of the benefits that should go to consumers.[29] In fact, despite the fact that the case law refers to the 'balancing' of benefits and costs of restrictive agreements and concerted practices, it does not actually require that the positive effects quantifiably outweigh the negative effects.[30] In practice, the Commission has to establish that an agreement contributes to technical or economic progress, that some of the benefits can eventually be obtained by consumers, that the agreement contains no unnecessary restrictions and that it does not eliminate competition. From past Commission practice and current case law on Article 101(3) TFEU, it is far from clear what weight or significance the Commission may attach to external environmental effects, even assuming that it would be legally possible for the Commission to do so. And, it must be borne in mind that the burden of proof falls on the undertakings that seek exemption for their cooperation under Article 101(3) TFEU.[31] Should undertakings be trusted with the quantification of social benefits? Are they competent to measure effects that, by definition, are external to them? Regardless of who measures external benefits or costs, their identification and quantification are difficult tasks.[32]

would benefit from cleaner air, if less polluting fuel is used. To the extent that a substantial overlap of consumers (the drivers in this example) and the beneficiaries (citizens) can be established, the sustainability benefits from cleaner air are in principle relevant for the assessment and can be taken into account if they are significant enough to compensate consumers in the relevant market for the harm suffered.' It does not explain, however, what is 'substantial overlap'. Commission, 'Guidelines on the applicability of Article 101 of the Treaty on the Functioning of the European Union to horizontal co-operation agreement' (Communication) [2022] OJ C164/1.

[28] On the differences and inconsistencies in the interpretation of Art 101(3) TFEU between EU courts, the Commission and national competition authorities see O Brook, 'Struggling with Article 101(3) TFEU: Diverging Approaches of the Commission, EU Courts, and Five Competition Authorities' (2019) 56 *Common Market Law Review* 121.

[29] Case C-238/05 *Asnef-Equifax, Servicios de Informatción sobre Solvencia y Crédito, SL v Asociacion de Usuarios de Servicios Bancarios (Ausbanc)*[2006] EU:C:2006:734, para 72.

[30] Case T-65/98 *Van den Bergh Foods Ltd v Commission* [2003] EU:T:2003:281, para 107; Case T-112/99 *Métropole télévision (M6) v Commission* [2001] EU:T:2001:215, para 74; Case T-328/03 *O2 v Commission* [2006] EU:T:2006:116, para 69.

[31] See, for example, Case C-501/06 P *GlaxoSmithKline Services v Commission* [2009] EU:C:2009:610.

[32] For an analysis of the complexity of the tasks see R Inderst and S Thomas, 'Integrating Benefits from Sustainability into the Competitive Assessment – How Can We Measure Them?' (2021) 12 *Journal of European Competition Law and Practice* 705. See also Nowag, 'Competition Law's Sustainability Gap?' (n 12 above).

However, in one of the earliest cases that concerned external environmental benefits – the *CECED* case mentioned above – not only did the Commission specify the external benefits but was also able to quantify and include them in the balancing exercise. It made a distinction between collective (ie, social) and individual benefits and found that

> on the basis of reasonable assumptions, the benefits to society brought about by the *CECED* agreement appear to be more than seven times greater than the increased purchase costs of more energy-efficient washing machines. Such environmental results for society would adequately allow consumers a fair share of the benefits even if no benefits accrued to individual purchasers of machines.[33]

Four years later, in decision 2004/208, the Commission found that collaboration in the collection and recycling of packaging waste would result in significant economies of scale and scope and would facilitate implementation of environmental legislation. However, it made no distinction between 'collective' or 'individual' benefits or external social benefits or costs.[34]

In 2011, the Commission rejected the claims of detergent manufacturers that their 'environmental initiative' which was supposedly 'designed to promote more sustainable consumption of laundry detergents' justified its restrictive effects. In this case the Commission found no benefits for consumers.[35]

Therefore, although there is supporting evidence it is rather difficult to generalise with much certainty from the *CECED* case how external environmental effects can be treated under competition law because there have not been other similar Commission decisions. It appears that external benefits enjoyed by citizens instead of consumers can indeed be taken into account.

The case law on such issues is equally scant. There are only a few judgments that have considered claims of environmental benefits by collaborating undertakings. All of these judgments have endorsed Commission decisions. For example, in a judgment concerning the 'green point' system in Germany on the collection of waste packaging, the General Court endorsed the Commission decision which had found that the agreement in question could be exempted under Article 101(3) TFEU on condition that certain contractual obligations were of limited time duration.[36]

In the *Altstoff Recycling* case, the General Court upheld the decision of the Commission by which cooperation in the collection and recycling of waste

[33] Commission Decision (CECED) (n 23 above) para 56.

[34] Commission Decision of 16 October 2003 relating to a proceeding pursuant to Article 81 of the EC Treaty and Article 53 of the EEA Agreement (Cases COMP D3/35470 – ARA and COMP D3/35473 – ARGEV, ARO) [2004] OJ L24/59.

[35] See Commission Decision of 13 April 2011 relating to a proceeding under Article 101 of the Treaty on the Functioning of the European Union and Article 53 of the EEA Agreement (Case COMP/39579 – Consumer Detergents) [2011] OJ C193/14.

[36] Case T-289/01 *Der Grüne Punkt – Duales System Deutschland v Commission* [2007] EU:T:2007:155, endorsed by the Court of Justice in C-385/07 P *Der Grüne Punkt – Duales System Deutschland v Commission* [2009] EU:C:2009:456.

was approved on condition that certain exclusivity clauses in contracts were removed.[37] The claims of the applicant that duplication of collection and recycling operations would have a detrimental environmental effect were rejected both by the Commission and by the General Court. Neither the Commission nor the Court accepted that the exclusivity clauses were necessary for the effective collection and recycling of waste.

More recently, the General Court upheld the decision of the Commission in case AT.39824 concerning an agreement between a truck manufacturer and distributors. Among other things, the Commission fined Scania for colluding to raise the prices of trucks and more specifically to fix the timing and passing on of costs related to compliance of trucks with higher environmental standards.[38] Meeting higher standards did not justify collusion, nor was price fixing necessary for the achievement of the higher standards. The General Court endorsed the findings of the Commission and dismissed the appeal.[39]

The judgments cited above, by confirming the findings of the Commission, indirectly recognise that the benefits that fall within the scope of Article 101(3) TFEU do not have to be the direct economic benefits to consumers but may also cover broader societal and qualitative benefits linked to environmental protection. However, as has already been observed by others, EU courts are not consistent in their treatment of Article 101(3) TFEU.[40] For example, the General Court has also stated explicitly the following:

> (418) It should be borne in mind, in that respect, that, in order to meet that first requirement [of Article 101(3) TFEU], an agreement must contribute to improving the production or distribution of goods or to promoting technical or economic progress. That contribution is not identified with all the advantages which the undertakings participating in the agreement derive from it as regards their activities, but with appreciable objective advantages, of such a kind as to offset the resulting disadvantages for competition.

It also considered in the same ruling that '(422) the efficiency gains referred to in Article 101(3) TFEU consist in the production of pro-competitive effects on the market, and thus in objective advantages, and not just subjective benefits for the parties such as an increase of their profits'.[41]

By linking cooperation benefits to pro-competition advantages, the General Court seems to exclude benefits accruing to society at large such as those from reduction of environmental harm. Nonetheless, EU courts have not yet given us an explicit statement to that effect. Therefore, much depends on how the

[37] Case T-419/03 *Altstoff Recycling Austria v Commission* [2011] EU:T:2011:102.

[38] See Commission Decision of 27 September 2017 relating to a proceeding under Article 101 of the Treaty on the Functioning of the European Union and Article 53 of the EEA Agreement (Case AT.39824 Trucks) [2020] OJ C216/9.

[39] Case T-799/17 *Scania and Others v Commission* [2022] EU:T:2022:48.

[40] Brook, 'Struggling with Article 101(3) TFEU' (n 28 above).

[41] Case T-705/14 *Unichem Laboratories v Commission* [2018] EU:T:2018:915.

Commission will treat societal benefits from cooperation between undertakings. The Commission has already indicated how it will treat 'sustainability agreements' in section 9 of its new Guidelines on Horizontal Agreements that are applied as of 1 January 2023.[42]

Chapter 9.4 of the Guidelines stresses that in order to benefit from the exemption in Article 101(3), sustainability agreements must '(577) contribute to objective efficiencies … encompassing not only reductions in production and distribution costs but also increases in product variety and quality, improvements in production or distribution processes, and increases in innovation'. However, the Guidelines go on to provide examples of efficiencies: '(588) Sustainability agreements can produce efficiencies, such as the use of cleaner production or distribution technologies, less pollution, improved conditions of production and distribution, more resilient infrastructure or supply chains, better quality products, etc.'

Normally, the concept of efficiency denotes reduction in costs for the same output or increase in output for the same cost. It is evident, therefore, that the Commission uses a broad definition of efficiencies that also encompasses reduction of pollution or other forms of environmental harm.

The consumers who must receive a fair share of the claimed benefits are the

> (588) direct or indirect users of the products covered by the agreement. Consumers receive a fair share of the benefits when the benefits deriving from the agreement outweigh the harm caused by the same agreement, so that the overall effect on consumers in the relevant market is at least neutral. Therefore, sustainability benefits that ensue from the agreements have to be related to the consumers of the products covered by those agreements.

The Guidelines conclude that cooperating undertakings

> (606) should be able to: (a) describe clearly the claimed benefits and provide evidence that they have already occurred or are likely to occur; (b) define clearly the beneficiaries; (c) demonstrate that the consumers in the relevant market substantially overlap with the beneficiaries or are part of them; and (d) demonstrate what part of the collective benefits occurring or likely to occur outside the relevant market accrue to the consumers of the product in the relevant market.

In conclusion, there is very little case law on environmental issues or sustainability agreements and Article 101(1) TFEU, only a handful of cases on the application of Article 101(3) and even fewer cases on its application to agreements which have a positive impact on the environment. One may wonder why so few cases have been brought to the attention of the CJEU. Perhaps cooperation on more environmentally friendly products generates broad benefits that do not outweigh the costs borne by companies themselves. Or such cooperation needs to involve the majority of producers in order to be effective. Or, before

[42] Commission, 'Guidelines on the applicability of Article 101' (n 27 above).

the Commission adopted the new horizontal Guidelines, it was difficult for cooperating undertakings to prove the significance of benefits to society at large and how they could be taken into account. Under these conditions, it is rather difficult to predict how EU courts would interpret Article 101(3) in relation to sustainability agreements.

However, a rather safe conclusion can be drawn from the above analysis. Because the assessment of the compatibility of sustainability agreements with Article 101 will be more complex, EU courts are likely to defer to the Commission's analysis, especially given the Commission's acknowledged wide margin of discretion.

But, as will be shown in the next section, if the case law on Article 102 TFEU is of any guidance, EU courts do not allow the Commission to use its discretion arbitrarily. In cases concerning the enforcement of Article 102, EU courts have consistently demanded that the Commission articulates a credible theory of how corporate practices may distort competition and harm consumers.[43] They are likely to demand the same standard or quality of analysis in the case of assessment of environmental harm or benefits from cooperation agreements.

B. Facilitating the Digital Transition: Preventing Abuse of Dominance

By contrast to the facilitation of the green transition, which is about permitting agreements that generate environmental benefits, the facilitation of the digital transition is about preventing dominant companies from abusing their market power and creating barriers to the entry of competitors that thwart the growth of online commerce and the adoption of new technologies.[44]

The Commission Communication of November 2021 on the new challenges of competition policy devotes chapter 3.2 to the role of competition policy in supporting the digital transition.[45] It refers, first, to the state aid rules on investment in digital infrastructure such as broadband networks and then turns its attention to digital platforms with market power. This is exactly the area where EU courts have been quite active recently.

[43] For example, in case T-235/18 *Qualcomm v Commission* [2022] EU:T:2022:358, the General Court annulled the Commission decision at issue because there were inconsistencies between the Commission's 'theory of harm' and the conclusions drawn by the Commission. Similarly, see Case T-814/17 *Lietuvos geležinkeliai v Commission* [2020] EU:T:2020:545.

[44] Although this chapter focuses on the relationship between Art 102 TFEU and the digital transition because of recent case law, the reader should not infer that the green transition does not raise any issues with respect to Art 102. For a review of such issues and, in particular, the possibility of 'objective justification' of abusive practices – which are analysed in this chapter too – for the pursuit of environmental protection see, for example, V Mauboussin, 'Environmental Defences as a Shield from Article 102 TFEU' (*No 3/2022 Concurrences No 107124*). However, he notes that so far there has been no discussion of objective justification on the grounds of protecting the environment.

[45] Commission, 'A competition policy' (n 10 above).

So far, EU courts have been reluctant to endorse wholeheartedly Commission action against dominant digital undertakings (eg, Microsoft, Google, Intel). In fact, EU courts have not shied away from questioning the rigour of Commission analysis and its theory of harm. Table 1 below provides a list of recent hi-tech cases and their outcome. Most Commission decisions were found to contain errors even when decisions were largely upheld. Decisions were annulled where the Commission's 'theory of harm' was considered to be incomplete (eg, T-286/09 RENV concerning royalty rebates by Intel). That is, the practice in question could also be consistent with non-abusive behaviour. Where decisions were based on incorrect calculations or unexplained data, EU courts would not annul them as long as the main conclusions of the Commission could still be supported by other calculations and data.

Table 1 Cases of alleged abuse of dominant market position by undertakings producing or operating digital technologies

Undertaking	Case and subject-matter	Outcome
Google	T-612/17: Prioritisation of own products on digital shopping platform	Substance of Commission decision mostly upheld
	T-604/18: Tying with Android system	Substance of Commission decision mostly upheld
Intel	T-286/09: Loyalty rebates	Commission decision upheld
	C-413/14 P: Loyalty rebates	Judgment of General Court set aside
	T-286/09 RENV: Loyalty rebates	Substance of Commission decision mostly annulled
Microsoft	T-201/04: Tied media player	Substance of Commission decision upheld
	T-167/08: Operating system interoperability	Substance of Commission decision upheld
Qualcomm	T-371/17: Request for information	Commission decision upheld
	C-466/19 P: Request for information	Judgment of General Court upheld
	T-235/18: Payments to buyer of chips to buy exclusively from Qualcomm	Commission decision annulled

However, EU courts have also rejected all arguments put forth by defendants to justify abusive behaviour. According to the database of the Court of Justice, in the 16-year period between January 2007 and December 2022, there were 92 judgments concerning abuse of dominance. Some of the defendant undertakings in those 92 cases claimed that there were objective reasons that justified the abusive practices. None of those claims was successful even though EU courts have accepted, in principle, that an otherwise abusive practice may be objectively justified. As expressed by the Court of Justice,

> where a competition authority shows that a practice of an undertaking in a dominant position is capable of impairing effective and undistorted competition in the internal market, it remains possible for that undertaking, in order to prevent that practice from being regarded as abuse of a dominant position, to show that that practice is or was justified objectively, either by certain circumstances of the case, which must, inter alia, be external to the undertaking concerned …, or, having regard to the objective ultimately pursued by Article 102 TFEU, by the interests of consumers.[46]

Since 'competition on the merits' (ie, competing without engaging in abusive practices) means lower price, higher quality or wider choice,

> the dominant undertaking can provide justification for conduct that is liable to be caught by the prohibition laid down in Article 102 TFEU by showing that the exclusionary effect capable of being produced by its conduct was counterbalanced or even outweighed by advantages in terms of efficiency that also benefit consumers.[47]

It follows that, in the context of this chapter, a dominant undertaking must show that its abusive practice is justified by making its digital products or services more widely available to consumers or that it generates other benefits for consumers. However, it is difficult to imagine how typical abusive practices such as price discrimination, loyalty discounts, tied sales or exclusionary conduct can lead to increased supply, more online transactions or better quality. It is even more difficult to construct a theory that can demonstrate that a dominant undertaking would have an incentive to engage in practices that weaken competition and at the same time generate benefits for consumers. That is a tall order.

In conclusion, until a dominant undertaking succeeds in proving that the digital (and also the green transition) can be facilitated by exploitative or exclusionary conduct, EU courts will remain deeply sceptical of such claims. This scepticism will not only be sustained by the hitherto absence of any compelling empirical evidence, but also by the theoretical implausibility of abusive conduct generating benefits. At the same time, EU courts will also persist in demanding that the Commission relies on credible theories of harm and applies them consistently.[48] Both of these likely outcomes suggest that EU courts will continue to interpret strictly Article 102 TFEU accepting neither exaggerated claims of benefits for consumers, nor unsubstantiated theories of harm to consumers.

[46] Case C-377/20 *Servizio Elettrico Nazionale and others v Autorità Garante della Concorrenza e del Mercato and Others* [2022] EU:C:2022:379, para 84.

[47] ibid para 86.

[48] See Case T-235/18 *Qualcomm v Commission* (n 43 above) paras 420, 421 and 509.

IV. Article 107: State Aid to Incentivise Undertakings to Invest in Digital and Green Technologies

Antitrust rules seek to prevent undertakings from distorting competition and harming consumers. By contrast, the purpose of state aid is to induce undertakings to do something they would not otherwise do under normal market conditions. Therefore, state aid is the tool by which public authorities incentivise undertakings to act in a way that generates benefits for society.

However, it must be clarified at the outset that state aid is not the only available policy instrument and may not even be the most appropriate instrument for incentivising the green or digital transition. Member States may also use regulation or taxation. For example, to address the potential market failure of lack of coordination in the switch from analogue to digital broadcasting, most Member States relied on regulations that set a date for a coordinated switch. More recently, certain obligations imposed on distributors of electricity to purchase more expensive green electricity have been found to be free of state aid as the extra costs of such obligations are not funded through state resources.[49]

Naturally, taxation is the main instrument that public authorities use to penalise harmful activities and internalise the negative external costs they cause. The General Court held, in the *British Aggregates* case, that Member States are free to levy taxes to protect the environment.[50] However, on appeal, the Court of Justice annulled the judgment of the General Court on the grounds that the objective of the measure was irrelevant with respect to its classification or not as state aid.[51] As expressed by the General Court in a later case,

> it would be to disregard Article 107(1) TFEU to hold that Member States are free, in balancing the various interests involved, to set their priorities as regards the protection of the environment and, as a result, to determine which goods or services they decide to subject to an environmental levy, with the result that the fact that such a levy does not apply to all similar activities which have a comparable impact on the environment would not mean that such activities which are not subject to the levy benefit from a selective advantage.[52]

The main legal basis for the exemption of state aid intended to protect the environment is Article 107(3)(c) which allows aid for the 'development of certain economic activities'. For aid that is intended to support digital technologies there are two legal bases: Article 107(3)(c) and also Article 107(3)(b) which allows aid for 'important projects of common European interest'.

At this point it is worth explaining that there is no rule in state aid law that obliges Member States to grant state aid or that entitles undertakings to demand

[49] Case C-379/98 *PreussenElektra v Schhleswag AG* [2001] EU:C:2001:160.
[50] Case T-210/02 *British Aggregates v Commission* [2006] EU:T:2006:253, para 115.
[51] Case C-487/06 P *British Aggregates Association v Commission* [2008] EU:C:2008:757, para 86.
[52] Case T-251/11 *Austria v Commission* [2014] EU:T:2014:1060, para 118.

aid, even if their competitors in other Member States receive aid. The decision whether to grant aid falls entirely within the discretion of Member States. Therefore, Member States are free to determine whether to grant aid and for which purpose.

The Commission may not use the powers granted to it by Article 108 TFEU to force Member States to grant aid even if it is necessary to correct market failure by internalising external costs or even if it would, in general, make society better off. The Commission may only assess the compatibility of proposed aid with the internal market. Indeed, the assessment of the compatibility of state aid under Article 107(3) falls within the exclusive competence of the Commission.[53] In this regard, the Commission enjoys wide discretion.[54]

In order to guide Member States to notify state aid that it would be in a position to find it compatible with the internal market, the Commission has issued guidelines. These guidelines are binding on the Commission in the sense that the Commission may not deviate from them.[55] In addition, the guidelines themselves must conform with general principles of EU law and the interpretation of the Court of Justice.[56]

For the support of digital technologies, the Commission has published guidelines on (1) 'important projects of common European interest', (2) 'research and innovation' and (3) 'broadband networks'. For the support of environmental protection and the green transition, the Commission has published guidelines on (1) 'climate, environmental protection and energy efficiency' and (2) 'trading of emission allowances for greenhouse gases'.[57]

In addition, the Commission has adopted several block exemption regulations, of which the currently applicable is Regulation 651/2014 also known as the General Block Exemption Regulation.[58] The Regulation exempts, among other things, state aid for research and innovation (Articles 25–30), environmental protection, energy efficiency and green energy (Articles 36–49) and broadband networks and digital connectivity (Articles 52–52c).

No Member State has succeeded to challenge before EU courts any of the Commission guidelines or a block exemption regulation and no judgment has ever questioned the objective, structure or contents of these guidelines or

[53] Case T-263/15 *Gmina Miasto Gdynia v Commission (RENV)* [2021] EU:T:2021:927, para 207; Case C-654/17 P *Bayerische Motoren Werke and Freistaat Sachsen v Commission* (n 9 above) para 79.

[54] Case T-778/17 *Autostrada Wielkopolska v Commission* [2019] EU:T:2019:756, para 179; C-654/17 P *Bayerische Motoren Werke and Freistaat Sachsen v Commission* (n 9 above) para 80.

[55] In Case T-304/08 *Smurfit Kappa v Commission* [2012] EU:T:2012:351.

[56] Case C-75/05 P *Germany v Kronofrance and Commission* [2008] EU:C:2008:482, para 65; Case C-526/14 *Kotnik v Drzavni zbor Republike Slovenije* [2016] EU:C:2016:570, para 39; C-654/17 P *Bayerische Motoren Werke and Freistaat Sachsen v Commission* (n 9 above) para 81.

[57] All the guidelines can be accessed at: Commission, 'State Aid Legislation': https://competition-policy.ec.europa.eu/state-aid/legislation_en.

[58] Commission Regulation (EU) No 651/2014 of 17 June 2014 declaring certain categories of aid compatible with the internal market in application of Articles 107 and 108 of the Treaty [2014] OJ L187/1 (General Block Exemption Regulation).

regulations. In fact, in the context of acknowledging the wide discretion of the Commission in determining the compatibility of state aid with the internal market, EU courts have also held that the Commission may adjust its guidelines and rules to reflect developments in the internal market.[59] Given that the concept of state aid is 'objective', the Commission is not even bound by its own past decisions.[60] This is because each case has to be examined on its own merits.[61]

It is in this context of the exclusive competence of the Commission and its wide discretion to determine the compatibility of state aid that the case law on the digital and green transition has to be examined.

There is no case law as of yet on important projects of common European interest in the field of new technologies. In the case of state aid to support the expansion of broadband networks, the few judgments by the General Court have all endorsed Commission decisions.[62]

By contrast, in the field of environmental aid, there is a substantial volume of case law. The rules on environmental protection, energy efficiency and green energy are more accommodative and, at the same time, stricter than other state aid rules. They are more accommodative of national policies because they allow both investment aid and aid to cover operating expenses.[63] At the same time, the rules are also stricter in the sense that investment aid is allowed only for the extra costs of investing in environmentally cleaner or more efficient technology or equipment, rather than for the full amount of the investment.

The General Block Exemption Regulation has a special chapter on state aid for the support of environmental protection, energy savings and the generation of energy from renewable sources. The current guidelines on climate, environmental and energy aid came into force in early 2022.[64] They are substantially wider in scope than the previous ones that expired in 2021. For example, they contain a brand new chapter on prevention of climate change. In this respect, they now permit Member States to provide incentives for investments that reduce CO_2 emissions, something that was not possible under the previous guidelines. The Commission has also inserted in the guidelines new rules to address explicitly actions such as the deployment of recharging or refuelling infrastructure (ie, for electric or hydrogen cars), support for the transition to a circular economy, rehabilitation of natural habitats and ecosystems, protection or restoration

[59] Case C-110/03 *Belgium v Commission* [2005] EU:C:2005:223, para 73.

[60] Case T-396/08 *Freistaat Sachsen v Commission* [2010] EU:T:2010:297, para 54; Case T-363/19 *UK v Commission* [2022] EU:T:2022:349, para 213.

[61] Case T-251/11 *Austria v Commission* (n 52 above) para 215.

[62] See judgments in cases T-226/09 *British Telecommunications v Commission* [2013] EU:T:2013:466; Case T-362/10 *Vtesse Networks v Commission* [2014] EU:T:2014:928; Case T-79/10 *Colt Télécommunications France v Commission* [2013] EU:T:2013:463; Case T-462/13 *Comunidad Autónoma del País Vasco v Commission* [2015] EU:T:2015:902.

[63] Case C-409/00 *Spain v Commission* [2003] EU:C:2003:92, paras 97–99.

[64] Commission, 'Guidelines on State aid for climate, environmental protection and energy 2022' [2022] OJ C80/1.

of biodiversity and implementation of nature-based solutions for climate change adaptation and mitigation.

Therefore, it is fair to conclude that the Commission has adjusted and widened the relevant guidelines so as to make it both easier and legally safer for Member States to implement more expansive policies to protect the environment, curb atmospheric emissions, improve resource sustainability and accelerate the switch to renewable sources of energy.[65]

However, the environmental objective of an aid measure or the need for state intervention cannot by itself remove that aid measure from the scope of prohibition of Article 107(1) TFEU. Therefore, the fact that an aid measure seeks to facilitate the green transition can only be taken into account at the level of the assessment of its compatibility with the internal market. In other words, this is a task reserved exclusively for the Commission.[66]

For state aid to be compatible with the internal market it must comply both with certain general principles defined in the case law and the provisions of Commission guidelines. The principles defined in the case law are that state aid must be appropriate for the objective it seeks to achieve, necessary and proportionate.[67] In essence, Commission regulations and guidelines elaborate those general principles and explain their application in different sectors of the economy. EU courts have never upheld actions by Member States against Commission regulations and guidelines.[68] In this respect, they have not limited the type or form of aid that the Commission may consider compatible with the internal market.[69]

However, with respect to the possible negative effects of state aid on the environment, the Court of Justice and the General Court have recently held that the Commission may not authorise state aid which contravenes any principle of EU law, including environmental rules. In this connection, a criticism that has been levelled against the Commission is that it is not strict enough in its assessment of aided projects that indirectly harm the environment.[70] For example, transporting the increased output to a new factory that benefits from investment

[65] For a critical assessment of the environmental and energy guidelines and the environmental and energy provisions in the GBER, see J Maillo, 'Energy And State Aid Control, Balancing Environmental Protection, Competitiveness and Competition: A Critical Assessment of the GBER and the EEAG' (2017) 16 *European State Aid Law Quarterly* 4; V Musardo, 'Green Deal and Incentive Effect: What Is Truly Environmental Aid?' (2021) 20 *European State Aid Law Quarterly* 217; S Verschuur and C Sbrolli, 'The European Green Deal and State Aid: The Guidelines on State Aid for Environmental Protection and Energy Towards the Future' (2020) 19 *European State Aid Law Quarterly* 284.

[66] Case C-470/20 *AS Veejaam and OÜ Espo v AS Elering* [2022] EU:C:2022:981, para 29.

[67] Case T-417/16 *Achemos Grupė v Commission* [2019] EU:T:2019:597, para 68 and case law cited therein.

[68] For a critical review of the case law see L Hancher, 'Milestone or Tombstone? Climate Change and State Aid Procedures – Tempus Fugit?' (2022) 21 *European State Aid Law Quarterly* 72.

[69] Case C-75/05 P *Germany v Kronofrance and Commission* (n 56 above) para 65.

[70] See chapter 3 of Client Earth, 'A State Aid Framework for a Green Recovery: Mainstreaming climate protection in EU State aid law' (2020): www.clientearth.org/media/c45naoms/2020-09-30-a-state-aid-framework-for-a-green-recovery-coll-en.pdf.

aid may contribute to more road congestion. In this connection, EU courts have been reluctant to impose an obligation on the Commission to prohibit any aid that may have an indirect harmful impact on the environment.[71] They have only ruled that the Commission must prohibit aid measures whose objective is 'inextricably' linked to a contravention of EU environmental law, not just any aid measure that may have an indirect negative effect.

More specifically, in the landmark judgment of December 2014, in case *Castelnou Energia v European Commission*, the General Court ruled that the Commission is obliged to prohibit aid which is 'inextricably linked' to an infringement of EU law.[72] This was confirmed by the Court of Justice in case *Austria v European Commission* of September 2020 concerning the nuclear power station Hinkley Point C in the UK.[73] However, both the Court of Justice, in *Hinkley Point C*, and the General Court in another similar case brought by Austria against the Commission,[74] also stressed that Member States have the right to choose their energy mix (both cases concerned nuclear energy) and that the Commission could take into account possible negative environmental impact of state aid only if it affected trade and distorted competition in the internal market.

Therefore, the unavoidable conclusion is that, as the case law stands today, the Commission must prohibit state aid whose objectives are inextricably linked to a contravention of EU environmental law. However, it may not prohibit state aid whose effects harm the environment if such effects do not constitute an impediment to free movement in the internal market.

The question that arises is what 'inextricable' link means. EU courts, in the case cited above, also referred to 'indissoluble' link. Unfortunately, they have not provided any further detail. The Commission in a recent decision authorising state aid for the construction of charging points for electric vehicles in Germany examined possible breaches of EU law and concluded that

> there is nothing to suggest that a breach of Union law, including of public procurement rules, would relate to an aspect that is so inextricably linked to the object of the aid that it is impossible to evaluate them separately … In particular, there is no indication that a breach of Union law has altered the object, the beneficiary or the amount of the aid or that it has produced additional distortions of competition and trade on the relevant market.[75]

This interpretation suggests that the Commission can use its state aid powers to address a violation of EU environmental law when that violation is connected

[71] Case T-57/11 *Castelnou Energia SL v Commission* [2014] EU:T:2014:1021; Case C-594/18 P *Austria v Commission* (Hinkley Point C) [2020] EU:C:2020:742; Case T-101/18 *Austria v Commission* (Paks II) [2022] EU:T:2022:728. See CM Colombo and M Bonelli, 'Governing the Green Transition Through State Aid Control', Ch 12 in this volume.

[72] Case T-57/11 *Castelnou Energia SL v Commission* (n 71 above) paras 182–85.

[73] Case C-594/18 P *Austria v Commission* (n 71 above).

[74] Case T-101/18 *Austria v Commission* (Paks II) (n 71 above).

[75] Commission, 'State Aid SA.104749 (2022/N) – Germany Aid scheme for High Power Charging infrastructure for electric vehicles in Germany' COM(2022) 9395 final.

to the aim of the aid, its amount and its beneficiaries or creates unnecessary impediments to intra-EU trade.

In conclusion, EU courts have endorsed Commission decisions finding environmental aid to be compatible with the internal market. Since they have never annulled any Commission regulation or guidelines, it is unlikely that they will strike down decisions based on the 2022 guidelines on state aid for climate, environmental protection and energy which are wider in scope and allow for larger amounts of aid than the guidelines they replaced.

At the same time, however, EU courts have not imposed any additional obligation on the Commission, despite requests by Member States such as Austria and Luxembourg, to prohibit state aid that may have an indirect harmful effect on the environment. The Commission, of course, is free to use the infringement procedure in Article 258 TFEU to challenge any public measure it considers to infringe EU environmental law. But it may not use its exclusive state aid powers to prohibit public measures that harm the environment without being illegal.

V. Conclusions

This chapter has explored how the enforcement of EU competition rules and their interpretation by EU courts have evolved in response to technological and environmental challenges facing European society. There is no evidence that EU courts and the Commission consider that competition policy can be an obstacle to the digital and green transition. On the contrary, the strict enforcement of competition rules is seen as a facilitator of that transition.

Antitrust rules do allow cooperation between companies to develop higher environmental standards, more environmentally friendly products and more technologically advanced products and services. New Commission guidelines on cooperation between companies also cover sustainability agreements. However, they also seek to prevent 'greenwashing' and the creation of barriers to competition by dominant companies.

State aid rules have been recently revised to explicitly allow more diverse measures that can support investments in new technologies, environmentally friendly technologies and products and energy savings.

However, there is uncertainty with respect to the following three questions. First, can cooperating undertakings rely on the exemption of Article 101(3) TFEU, if the cooperation generates benefits for society as a whole and not for the direct consumers of the product that is the subject of the cooperation? It seems that they can, if consumers obtain some benefits. The extent of such benefits has not yet been tested in the case law.

Second, can dominant undertakings in digital markets justify otherwise abusive practices, if such practices can be shown to be necessary for the achievement of significant efficiencies? It is theoretically possible that they can, but so far, they have not succeeded in proving that.

Third, can the Commission prohibit aid measures that may indirectly harm the environment without infringing EU law? It is likely that it can, but only if it shows that the harm is linked to distortion of competition in the internal market.

EU courts may soon be called to clarify these issues. The review of the case law in this chapter suggests that EU courts are unlikely to find that benefits from improved environmental or digital performance fall outside the scope of the various exemptions allowed by competition rules. At the same time, however, they are very likely to continue to demand that the Commission bases its analysis on credible theories that can explain observed corporate behaviour. Undertakings that claim that their practices generate benefits for consumers and society will also be expected to provide proof in the form of robust and consistent empirical evidence. EU courts are unlikely to prohibit cooperation between undertakings, corporate practices or public funding of investments that generate technological improvements and protect the environment, respectively, as long as benefits for society outweigh the costs from the distortion of competition.

In essence, EU case law is likely to evolve in step with the EU's policy priorities as long as exceptions from the fundamental principle of undistorted competition are based on robust reasoning and supported by consistent evidence. However, it must be borne in mind that, while competition policy can indeed facilitate the digital and green transition and has an important role to play on the one hand, in preventing anti-competitive practices and, on the other, in incentivising extra investments, it is not always the most appropriate instrument for supporting that transition. Its enforcement in the digital and green sectors is still evolving, given that the case law has not yet dealt with all of the issues that have arisen so far.

PART III

Instruments and Procedures in a Multilevel Competition Law Landscape

9

Repurposing Administrative Procedures to Meet Novel Challenges in EU Competition Law

FILIPE BRITO BASTOS*

I. Novel Challenges and Familiar Choices

The chapter considers two recent legislative developments in EU competition law – the European Competition Network Plus (ECN+) Directive and the Foreign Subsidies Regulation.[1] The two instruments address two crucial political and economic challenges. The ECN+ Directive aims to ensure competition law enforcement in the EU internal market, which is undergoing rapid digital transformation. By contrast, the new Foreign Subsidies Regulation represents a decisive step to tackle exposure to foreign subsidies which currently threatens the level playing field of undertakings operating in the EU internal market – thus ensuring the EU's policy of 'open strategic autonomy'.[2]

The chapter argues that, despite the relative novelty of the economic and political issues in question, the design of administrative procedures in the two instruments resorts to what is, in fact, a well-established legislative technique in EU administrative law. The technique consists in repurposing pre-existing types of administrative procedures and powers to pursue new policy objectives. European administration is constantly shaped by the need to adjust to shifting political and economic realities. Not always do such shifts require revolutionary innovation on the procedural or institutional level. Indeed, there may be some

* Assistant Professor of Public Law, NOVA School of Law; researcher at CEDIS (*Centro de I&D de Direito e Sociedade*), filipe.bastos@novalaw.unl.pt.

[1] Directive (EU) 2019/1 of the European Parliament and of the Council of 11 December 2018 to empower the competition authorities of the Member States to be more effective enforcers and to ensure the proper functioning of the internal market [2019] OJ L11/3 and Regulation (EU) 2022/2560 of the European Parliament and of the Council on foreign subsidies distorting the internal market [2022] OJ L330/1 (Regulation on Foreign Subsidies).

[2] On the concept, see Commission, 'An Open, Sustainable and Assertive Trade Policy' (Communication) COM(2021) 66 final.

virtue in ensuring some continuity with procedural regimes which are already familiar to the practitioners who will work in the field.

It was against the background of competition law that the most important concepts and principles of European administrative law emerged,[3] in the case law as well as in its founding doctrinal texts.[4] It is now against the background of competition law that the EU legislator shows what innovative combinations can be made within the full range of pre-existing procedural models from a variety of policy areas in order to address new economic and political challenges. Building on the decentralised approach to antitrust law enforcement initiated by Regulation 1/2003, the ECN+ Directive provides national competition authorities (NCAs) with a uniform and broad set of decision-making powers which replicate those that the Commission already deploys in antitrust enforcement. It further introduces a cooperation technique that has proven successful in other policy areas, namely the mutual recognition of national administrative decisions. In contrast, the Proposed Regulation on Foreign Subsidies heavily centralises decision-making power in the Commission. It also repurposes and combines pre-existing procedural models drawn from state aid review, antitrust law and merger control.

The argument will proceed as follows. Section II briefly conceptualises two basic issues of procedural design in European administrative law. The first concerns the reasons to allocate power to national or Union administration; the second concerns how its exercise is structured by the Union legislator – often by an approach of repurposing procedural models already used in other EU policy sectors. Sections III and IV analyse the procedural regimes of the ECN+ Directive and the Foreign Subsidies Regulation in that light. Section V summarises the chapter's findings. It further submits that, by reusing familiar procedural models, the Union legislator may achieve a desirable aim of safeguarding legal certainty and stability at a time of quick-paced economic and political change.

II. Allocation of Powers and Procedural Models

The intensity of cooperation and degree of involvement of national and Union bodies will depend upon what can be described as a legislative judgement of

[3] Just to offer an example, it was from competition law that the key rulings which introduced the right to be heard in Union law emerged. See C-58/64 *Consten and Grundig v Commission* [1966] EU:C:1966:41; Case 17/74 *Transocean Marine Paint v Commission* [1974] EU:C:1974:106 and Case 85/76 *Hoffmann-La Roche & Co Ag v Commission* [1979] EU:C:1979:36. In the literature, see V Korah, 'The Rights of the Defence in Administrative Proceedings under Community Law' (1980) 33 *Current Legal Problems* 73.

[4] EU competition law provided the most important backdrop to the development of foundational writings on EU administrative law. See J Schwarze, *Europäisches Verwaltungsrecht* Vol I, 1st edn (Baden-Baden, Nomos, 1992).

comparative institutional analysis.[5] Comparative institutional analysis involves recognising that 'different institutions are good at making different kinds of decisions [so that] when allocating the authority to decide it is crucial that we take these relative strengths and weaknesses into account'.[6]

When compared to Union administration, national administration has much better knowledge of domestic economic and bureaucratic realities which may affect implementation of EU policies. It also often enjoys far greater human and material resources. The Union administration, by contrast, is much better placed to promote the exchange of national authorities' combined information and expertise; to grasp the needs and obstacles to the European public interest; and to decide without interference from parochial political pressures. Crucially, and unlike national authorities, whose powers are typically confined within national territorial jurisdictions,[7] the Union administration may take decisions valid throughout the EU.[8] All these traits make Union administration especially well-placed to ensure uniform and independent enforcement of EU law.

How power should be allocated between national and Union administration is an essential issue of procedural design. Yet other questions are equally important – those which pertain to the kinds of decisions that may be taken and the sequence of procedural stages and measures which must be taken in that process. In the absence of a general code of administrative procedure, or even of a legal basis for it to be enacted, the administrative implementation of Union law has remained rather fragmentary and highly sector specific. Some factors, however, do contribute to a degree of consistency. One is the development of general principles of administrative procedure such as procedural rights.[9] Another is that the Union legislator has tended to resort to repurposing of existing procedural models, ie, of types of decision-making powers and procedural designs.[10]

Such repurposing occasionally occurs simultaneously in multiple, interrelated policy sectors – the powers and decision-making processes of the three European Supervisory Agencies (ESAs), established on the same day, provide a

[5] For an overview of comparative institutional analysis, see N Komesar, *Imperfect Alternatives: Choosing Institutions in Law, Economics, and Public Policy* (Chicago, University of Chicago Press, 1997) 3.

[6] J Zglinski, *Europe's Passive Virtues: Deference to National Authorities in EU Free Movement Law* (Oxford, Oxford University Press, 2020) 162.

[7] Case C-230/14 *Weltimmo SRO v Nemzeti Adatvédelmi és Inofrmációszabadság Hatóság* [2015] EU:C:2015:639, para 56.

[8] M Scholten, 'Mind the Trend! Enforcement of EU Law Has Been Moving to "Brussels"' (2017) 24 *Journal of European Public Policy* 1348, 1354.

[9] In the CJEU's own words, eg in the Case T-429/18 *BFR and SHP Comercio e Industria de Alimentos v Commission* [2020] EU:T:2020:322, para 93: 'respect for the rights of the defence is, in all proceedings initiated against a person … a fundamental principle of EU law which must be guaranteed *even in the absence of any rules governing the proceedings in question*' (emphasis added).

[10] D de Pretis, 'Procedimenti amministrativi nazionali e procedimenti amministrativi europei' in G Falcon (ed), *Il procedimento amministrativo nei diritti europei e nel diritto comunitario* (Padua, CEDAM, 2008).

case in point.[11] However, it is usually the case that pre-existing procedures used in one policy sector reappear later in a distinct policy sector. The best example is perhaps the circulation of practically identical rules on decision-making powers and procedures in areas linked to the regulation of public health risks.[12] The current procedural regime for release of genetically modified organisms (GMOs) into the environment illustrates it well. The legislative process explicitly recognised the value of instituting an administrative procedure where the Union administration would intervene to settle potentially dysfunctional disagreements between national regulators, 'as in the case of Community legislation dealing with marketing authorisation for foods, pharmaceuticals and feed'.[13]

As will be shown below, the ECN+ Directive and the Foreign Subsidies Regulation illustrate how questions of allocation of powers and procedural design remain topical in EU administrative and competition law. Both instruments reflect a concern to allocate power to the administration that is better placed to decide and to mitigate the disadvantages resulting from its respective institutional setup. Both instruments rely on the technique of repurposing pre-existing procedural regimes.

III. In the Image of the Commission: NCAs and the ECN+ Directive

Traditionally, EU antitrust law used to be enforced in a highly centralised fashion. As the system was based on notifications to the Commission, the latter tended to be overburdened with cases. Regulation 1/2003 was adopted to address this problem. More authorities became competent to apply EU competition law rules whenever they applied national law to agreements affecting interstate trade. NCAs were also required to enforce competition law in a cooperative manner within the framework of the European Competition Network (ECN).[14]

[11] See in particular Art 8 of all three Regulations, which list practically identical tasks and powers to be exercised by the European Banking Authority (Regulation (EU) No 1093/2010 of the European Parliament and of the Council of 24 November 2010 establishing a European Supervisory Authority [2010] OJ L331/12 (European Banking Authority)), by the European Insurance and Occupational Pensions Authority (Regulation (EU) No 1094/2010 of the European Parliament and of the Council of 24 November 2010 establishing a European Supervisory Authority [2010] OJ L331/48 (European Insurance and Occupational Pensions Authority)), and by the European Markets and Securities Authority (Regulation (EU) No 1095/2010 of the European Parliament and of the Council of 24 November 2010 [2010] OJ L331/84).

[12] L De Lucia, 'Conflict and cooperation within European composite administration (Between Philia and Eris)' (2012) 5 *Review of European Administrative Law* 43, 49.

[13] Proposal for a European Parliament and Council Directive amending Directive 90/220/EEC on the deliberate release into the environment of genetically modified organisms COM(1998) 85 final, 3.

[14] For an overview of the institutional structure and legal issues raised within the ECN, see D Reichelt, 'To What Extent Does the Cooperation Within the European Competition Network Protect the Rights of Undertakings?' (2005) 42 *Common Market Law Review* 745.

And yet, discrepancies remained between the enforcement tools that national laws placed at the disposal of NCAs. The Directive's impact assessment noted, for instance, that some lacked the power to inspect the homes of persons associated with investigated undertakings; the power to access laptops, mobile phones and servers; or the power to investigate data stored in cloud servers located in different countries. As many as 22 NCAs lacked the power to collect fines from undertakings situated in other Member States if said undertakings had no presence within the NCA's territorial jurisdiction.[15] Lastly, even though, under Regulation 1/2003, an NCA could already request other NCAs to conduct investigations on its behalf, inconsistencies in enforcement powers hindered effective inspections or information-gathering from undertakings in the jurisdiction of requested NCAs.[16]

Crucially, the Directive's recitals, as well as the Explanatory Memorandum to the Commission's original legislative proposal, reflect a concern that the absence of harmonised powers could undermine the development of economic sectors of increasing importance and with strong cross-border dimensions.[17] Effective enforcement of EU competition rules is deemed essential to create 'an open, competitive and innovative internal market … in important sectors of the economy, in particular, the energy, telecoms, digital and transport sectors'.[18]

Even though, as even before Regulation 1/2003, the Commission is in principle the institution best placed to solve cross-jurisdictional enforcement issues, the lack of uniformity in NCAs' powers was addressed by reforming the decentralised ECN system. Directive 2019/1 draws on the success proven by that system in generating a common competition law enforcement culture and reciprocal trust among NCAs. Through Directive 2019/1, the role of NCAs was consolidated; their uneven powers standardised; their reciprocal cooperation enhanced. The Directive therefore pushed further the institutional choice already made in 2003 to enlist NCAs in the exercise of competition law enforcement tasks that had hitherto belonged to the Commission. It finally gave NCAs the means they required in order to secure the 'uniform all-European competition culture' which had to a significant extent justified the creation of the ECN itself,[19] and which, by encouraging NCAs to rely on each other, improves the consistency and effectiveness of competition law enforcement. In short, the ECN+ Directive mitigates the comparative institutional disadvantages of NCAs in respect of

[15] See the Commission, 'Impact Assessment Accompanying the Document Proposal for a Directive of the European Parliament and of the Council to empower the competition authorities of the Member States to be more effective enforcers and to ensure the proper functioning of the internal market' Part 1/2 (Staff Working Document) SWD(2017) 114 final, 18.

[16] See Commission, 'Impact Assessment' (n 15 above) at 15 and 17.

[17] Cf Directive (EU) 2019/1 (n 1 above) Recitals (7) and (30).

[18] See Commission, 'Impact Assessment' (n 15 above) 2.

[19] See C Potocnik-Manzouri, 'The ECN+ Directive: An Example of Decentralised Cooperation to Enforce Competition Law' (2021) 6 *European Papers* 987, 988; Commission, 'Notice on cooperation within the Network of Competition Authorities' (Notice) [2004] OJ C101/43.

the Commission – that is, their hitherto uneven, jurisdictionally limited, and often ineffective powers. It does so by equipping NCAs with a substantial set of common enforcement tools which are intended to secure the ECN's ability to address the EU internal market's present and future challenges.

However, the toolkit of powers that NCAs enjoy under Directive 2019/1 is not entirely novel. In fact, it illustrates well how the Union legislator often turns to pre-existing, tried-and-tested models of administrative decision-making when designing or reforming administrative governance in distinct policy areas. What is peculiar in the ECN+ reform is that most instances of such replication or adaptation of prior decision-making models tend to occur in a horizontal fashion, in the sense of taking the design of administrative procedures used in one policy area and reintroducing it in another (eg, taking the design of procedures for the regulation of medicines and reintroducing them in the regulation of genetically modified organisms). The ECN+ Directive, by contrast, represents a vertical transplant of decision-making models. The new powers of NCAs mirror the powers long exercised by the Commission under Regulation 1/2003.[20]

Indeed, the ECN+ Directive aims at 'aligning the competences of NCAs with those of the Commission',[21] or, as an author puts it, at granting NCAs 'Commission-like powers'.[22] Similarly, others have noticed that the ECN+ Directive's requirements to ensure NCAs' independence – one other major objective of the reform – are modelled on the independent status of the Commission itself.[23] The reform therefore transforms the role of NCAs as enforcers of EU competition law. When Regulation 1/2003 instituted the ECN, it vested NCAs with the task of enforcing the same rules as the Commission. The ECN+ Directive, in addition, requires NCAs to fulfil that task by exercising essentially the same powers as the Commission, and by deciding as independently as the Commission – by acting like the Commission, as it were.[24]

It is striking how the Directive's provisions replicate – at points even word for word – the equivalent provisions on the Commission's powers under Regulation 1/2003.[25] Member States are required, inter alia, to ensure that NCAs have, like

[20] Cf G Monti, 'Strengthening National Competition Authorities' (2018) 13 *The Competition Law Review* 103; F Rizzuto, 'The ECN Plus Directive: Empowering National Competition Authorities to Be More Effective Enforcers of EU Competition Law' (2019) 3 *European Competition and Regulatory Law Review* 80, 98.

[21] Potocnik-Manzouri, 'The ECN+ Directive' (n 19 above) 994.

[22] Rizzuto, 'The ECN Plus Directive' (n 20 above) 99.

[23] W Wils, 'The European Commission's 'ECN+': Proposal for a Directive to Empower the Competition Authorities of the Member States to be More Effective Enforcers' (2017) 4 *Concurrences* 60, 70 ff. Cf Arts 4(2) and (3) of Directive (EU) 2019/1 (n 1 above). See also Treaty on the Functioning of the European Union [2008] OJ C326/47 (TFEU) Arts 245 and 247.

[24] Indeed, as an author puts it, 'NCAs can finally behave fully like European agencies': N Dzino and C Rusu, 'The Real Challenge of Boosting the EU Competition Law Enforcement Powers of NCAs: In Need of a Reframed Formula?' (2018) 13 *The Competition Law Review* 30, 55.

[25] Cf Arts 20, 21 and 18 of Council Regulation (EC) No 1/2003 of 16 December 2002 on the implementation of the rules on competition laid down in Articles 81 and 82 of the Treaty [2002] OJ L01/1.

the Commission, sufficient powers to inspect the business premises of undertakings without prior announcement. This includes the power 'to examine books and other records related to the business irrespective of the medium on which they are stored', which extends to electronic messages.[26] The exercise of such a power must be subject to prior judicial authorisation, if required by national law. NCAs – again, subject to judicial authorisation – must also have the power to conduct unannounced inspections in 'any premises, land or means of transport … including the homes of directors, managers, and other members of staff of undertakings or associations of undertakings'.[27] NCAs must also be empowered to request information from investigated undertakings.[28]

A unified set of powers fosters legal certainty, as NCAs in need of assistance can anticipate the course of action that other NCAs will be empowered to take. In turn, such fosters mutual trust between NCAs, as every NCA may expect its counterparts to have the ability to handle cross-jurisdictional cases effectively. Mutual trust between NCAs informs the entire ECN reform.[29] Much as the existence of shared values and principles between the Member States justifies their trust in one another,[30] so does the ECN+ 'common ground' of shared legal standards, which all NCAs must observe and presume all other NCAs to observe as well, justify mutual trust in competition law enforcement.

However, the ECN+ does not only promote, but in fact presupposes mutual trust between NCAs. This is well reflected in two instances where the Directive re-employs pre-existing techniques of administrative governance found in policy areas which are in fact unrelated to competition law.

The first concerns the introduction of horizontal composite procedures. Article 24 of the ECN+ Directive, complementing Article 22(1) of Regulation 1/2003, enables NCAs to address requests for information to other NCAs. The latter will then be required to adopt fact-finding measures in respect of undertakings located within their own territorial jurisdiction. Recent rulings of the CJEU concerning judicial review of practically identical administrative procedures, in the field of taxation, will provide useful guidance in the future to determine which

In fact, in some regards, the ECN+ Directive even gives NCAs powers that are even greater than those exercised by the Commission under that Regulation. See also N Dzino and C Rusu, 'Public Enforcement of EU Antitrust Law: A Circle of Trust?' (2019) 12 *Review of European Administrative Law* 127, 145.

[26] See Directive (EU) 2019/1 (n 1 above) Art 6 and Recital (32).

[27] ibid Art 7.

[28] ibid Art 8.

[29] Dzino and Rusu, 'The Real Challenge' (n 24 above).

[30] M Kozak, 'Mutual Trust as a Backbone of EU Antitrust Law' (2020) 4 *Market and Competition Law Review* 127, 138. See also Case C-896/19 *Repubblika v Il-Prim Ministru* [2021] EU:C:2021:311, para 62. Though primarily developed in cases relating to the Area of Freedom, Security and Justice (AFSJ), the principle of mutual recognition has only recently been fleshed out by the CJEU as a general constitutional principle of EU law. See Case C-64/16 *Associação Sindical dos Juízes Portugueses v Tribunal de Contas* [2018] EU:C:2018:117, para 30. For an overview of the principle of mutual trust in the AFSJ, see F Maiani and A Migliorini, 'One Principle to Rule Them All? Anatomy of Mutual Trust in the Law of the Area of Freedom, Security and Justice' (2020) 57 *Common Market Law Review* 7.

jurisdiction – that of the requesting or of the requested Member State – is competent to ensure judicial review.[31]

The second instance concerns the use of the technique of administrative decisions subject to mutual recognition.[32] Indeed, to achieve the aim of strengthening existing mechanisms of mutual assistance among NCAs under Article 22 of Regulation 1/2003, the ECN+ Directive provides that an applicant NCA may request another NCA for a fine or periodic penalty to be enforced in the requested authority's territory.[33] The introduction of mutual recognition in the ECN+ context is not a purely technical or a practical choice. Mutual recognition is certainly useful to pursue the policy objective of effective enforcement. Yet the very fact that it is seen to constitute a viable enforcement tool already presupposes a state of affairs where national authorities can realistically be expected to exercise their own powers to the benefit of one another and, in turn, expect other authorities to do the same for them. Mutual recognition, in short, presupposes mutual trust.[34]

Through the combination of decentralised enforcement and the strengthening of such enforcement with powers modelled upon those of the Commission, NCAs are entrusted with the task of acting in the Commission's stead. One simple example, particularly important in the digital sector, is the fact that NCAs will be empowered, just like the Commission, to examine an inspected undertaking's records, irrespective of the medium – including digital – on which they are stored.

The administrative governance of the ECN after Directive 2019/1 continues to recognise the disadvantage of centralising enforcement in the Commission, which would overburden its limited resources, and to exploit the relative advantages of decentralising enforcement to NCAs given their expertise, proximity to local realities and habits of reciprocal cooperation. Yet the Directive also prevents the risks that decentralisation can raise for uniform implementation. All NCAs are granted an identical set of effective, Commission-like powers, as well as the means to trust and rely on one another sufficiently to act in unison when needed.

[31] See L Arroyo Jiménez, 'Effective Judicial Protection and Mutual Recognition in the European Administrative Space' (2021) 22 *German Law Journal* 344; P Mazzotti and M Eliantonio, 'Transnational Judicial Review in Horizontal Composite Procedures: Berlioz, Donnellan, and the Constitutional Law of the Union' (2020) 5 *European Papers* 41. In the case law, see Joined Cases C-245/19 and C-246/19 *État Luxembourgeois v B and Others* [2020] EU:C:2020:795.

[32] On this category of mutual recognition of administrative decisions, see L De Lucia, 'From Mutual Recognition to EU Authorization: A Decline of Transnational Administrative Acts?' (2016) 8 *Italian Journal of Public Law* 90.

[33] Directive (EU) 2019/1 (n 1 above) Recitals (68–69) and Art 26.

[34] See for instance C Janssens, *The Principle of Mutual Recognition in EU Law* (Oxford, Oxford University Press, 2013) 28. Similarly, see S Dorigo, M Eliantonio and R Lanceiro, 'The Principle of Mutual Recognition in European Administrative Law: Still Alive and Kicking?' (2020) 13 *Review of European Administrative Law* 183, 184. Earlier examples in CJEU case law of mutual recognition and mutual trust in the internal market included, eg, Case 25/88 *Criminal proceedings against Esther Renée Bouchara, née Wurmser, and Norlaine SA* [1989] EU:C:1989:187, para 18, and Case C-5/94 *The Queen v Ministry of Agriculture, Fisheries and Food, ex parte Hedley Lomas (Ireland)* [1996] EU:C:1996:205, para 19.

IV. Foreign Subsidies, Strategic Autonomy and Centralised Power

The Foreign Subsidies Regulation institutes a regime to prevent the distortion of the internal market due to subsidies given to undertakings by third states. From the lens of administrative procedure, that regime appears to stand in total contradiction with the ECN+ Directive's approach to consolidate the decentralised enforcement system in antitrust. Indeed, just two years after ECN+ Directive was adopted, the Foreign Subsidies Regulation envisages a centralised model of administrative enforcement. National administrative authorities appear to barely play any role at all. The Commission, in turn, will exercise extensive powers which include ordering undertakings to repay subsidies they have received and can be as invasive as effectively vetoing award decisions in potentially any national public procurement procedure. How to explain the apparently sudden turn from enhanced decentralised enforcement in antitrust to highly centralised enforcement in the new domain of foreign subsidies control?

It is not that the Commission did not consider alternative models. This becomes apparent if one considers the White Paper that preceded the Regulation's Proposal ('the Proposal'), published in the spring of 2020. In the White Paper, a shared model of enforcement was suggested which would have involved both the Commission and specific national supervision authorities, with the latter investigating subsidies in their own countries.[35] Indeed, the White Paper even explicitly mentions Regulation 1/2003 – the legal basis for the decentralised ECN system – as a possible model to follow, at least in regard to some kinds of foreign subsidies.[36] The final choice is unlikely to have been unanimous, as the results of the public consultation conducted in regard to the White Paper show that the Member States were divided as to whether enforcement should be shared between the Commission and national supervision authorities.[37]

Three factors may explain the choice for centralisation which would not apply in the context of the ECN. First, as the Impact Assessment Report accompanying the Proposal stated, 'exclusive Commission enforcement power would mirror the system of enforcement for … state aid rules'.[38] Such rules aim to prevent distortive effects in the internal market which can be indistinguishable from those of foreign subsidies. Second, the Regulation's recitals themselves hold that 'the Commission should be the sole authority competent to apply [the] Regulation' because of the need for consistent enforcement of anti-subsidy

[35] Commission, 'White Paper on Levelling the Playing Field as Regards Foreign Subsidies' (White Paper) COM(2020) 253 final, 21–22.

[36] ibid 32.

[37] Commission, 'Impact Assessment Accompanying the Proposal for a Regulation of the European Parliament and of the Council on foreign subsidies distorting the internal market' (Staff Working Document) SWD(2021) 99 final, 48.

[38] See Commission, 'Impact Assessment' (n 15 above) 44.

rules.[39] Third, and crucially, the EU's response to the distortion of competition caused by foreign subsidies in the internal market is of immediate significance for the EU's strategic outlook regarding the world at large. Addressing such distortion, as the Proposal's Explanatory Memorandum stated, is about a broader doctrine of 'open strategic autonomy' that the EU is pursuing in its relations with the rest of the world.

The notion of 'open strategic autonomy' draws on the motto of 'strategic autonomy' already in vogue for many years in the context of the EU's Common Foreign and Security Policy. It appears to have been rediscovered and broadened in industrial and trade policy as well. In a Communication adopted in 2021, titled, 'Trade Policy Review – An Open, Sustainable and Assertive Trade Policy',[40] the Commission takes 'open strategic autonomy' to refer to a cluster of interrelated components. Open strategic autonomy includes, among others,

> 'The EU's ability to make its own choices and shape the world around it through leadership and engagement, reflecting its strategic interests and values';
>
> 'The EU's fundamental belief that addressing today's challenges requires more rather than less global cooperation';
>
> '[The principle] that the EU continues to reap the benefits of international opportunities, while assertively defending its interests, protecting the EU's economy from unfair trade practices and ensuring a level playing field';
>
> 'Assertiveness and rules-based cooperation to showcase the EU's preference for international cooperation and dialogue, but also its readiness to combat unfair practices and use autonomous tools to pursue its interests where needed'.

The object of the Foreign Subsidies Regulation chiefly concerns the two latter components. Recognising that 'many foreign subsidies would be problematic if they were granted by Member States and assessed under EU State aid rules', the Proposal also acknowledged a need to prevent 'state-sponsored trading practices with a view to building up dominance'.[41] There must be a balance between keeping the EU open to foreign investment, on the one hand, and the strategic interest of protecting the internal market against third state economic practices that undermine competition and place European businesses at disadvantage. Such a balance concerns nothing less than how the EU chooses to position itself in the world economy and its relations with other major economic powers, the most pressing question being the relation with China.[42] This makes decisions on foreign subsidies a specifically European general interest of the kind that

[39] See Regulation on Foreign Subsidies (n 1 above) Recital (8).

[40] Commission, Trade Policy Review (n 2 above) 4 ff.

[41] Proposal for a Regulation of the European Parliament and of the Council on foreign subsidies distorting the internal market COM(2021) 223 final, 4–5.

[42] Similarly, J Kühling, T Weck and P Reinhold, 'Third Country State Aid Regulation: The European Debate on Foreign Subsidies' (2021) 2022 *Asian Yearbook of International Economic Law* 149.

should rest in the hands of the Commission under Article 17(1) of the Treaty on European Union.[43] Indeed, returning to the framework of comparative institutional analysis, the Commission is undeniably better placed than any individual national authority to decide on issues that may pose a threat to the EU's strategic interests and to the internal market as a whole.

Concerning its scope of application, the Regulation applies to 'subsidies granted to an undertaking engaging in an economic activity in the internal market'. Economic activity includes participation in public procurement or the acquisition of control or merger with an undertaking established in the EU.[44] Foreign subsidies are defined in Article 3 as financial contributions which confer a benefit to an undertaking engaging in an economic activity in the internal market, which benefits specific undertakings or industries. 'Financial contribution' is defined in very broad terms and includes the provision of goods or services, the transfer of funds or liabilities, fiscal incentives, grants or loans. The specific meaning of foreign financial contribution is that it is provided by a third country's government or governmental authorities or public or private entities whose actions can be attributed to that third country.[45] Lastly, the foreign subsidy must have an effect of distorting the internal market. All these criteria make the notion of foreign subsidy in the Proposed Regulation remarkably similar to the CJEU's interpretation of State aid. Classification of a measure as State aid

> requires all the following conditions to be fulfilled. First, there must be an intervention by the State or through State resources. Second, the intervention must be liable to affect trade between Member States. Third, it must confer a selective advantage on the recipient. Fourth, it must distort or threaten to distort competition.[46]

The existence of a foreign subsidy with potentially distortive effects in the internal market suffices for the Commission to deploy the general instrument of ex officio review.[47] In contrast, the notification procedures for concentrations and public procurement must be followed whenever a foreign subsidy exceeds the Regulation's thresholds in terms of the amounts of received financial contributions or how recently such contributions were made.[48]

While there are some procedural differences between them, the three instruments provided for in the Foreign Subsidies Regulation – the general mechanism of ex officio review of foreign subsidies and the two specific mechanisms for merger control and public procurement – are governed by a set of shared procedural rules. Those are the 'common procedural provisions' set out in Chapter 5 as

[43] The provision reads: 'The Commission shall promote the general interest of the Union and take appropriate initiatives to that end'.
[44] Art 1(2).
[45] Art 3(2)(a).
[46] Case C 524/14 P *Commission v Hansestadt Lübeck* [2016] EU:C:2016:971, para 40.
[47] Art 9.
[48] See Arts 20(3), 21, 27, 28(1), 29(1).

well as a significant extent of the procedural regime of the ex officio review mechanism, which the Regulation renders applicable to the merger control and public procurement mechanisms.[49]

While the subject-matter of the Foreign Subsidies Regulation is entirely novel, many of its procedural aspects will be familiar both to competition law and to European administrative law specialists. It represents yet another instance of how pre-existing procedural models from other domains of Union law are repurposed. Indeed, from a procedural perspective, the Foreign Subsidies Regulation crafts a procedural framework for foreign subsidies by combining aspects of the regimes of state aid review, merger control and antitrust. The likeness with those regimes appears to respond to concerns raised during public consultations that the Regulation should be consistent with other instruments relevant for EU competition law.[50] Given the abundant case law on those instruments, awareness of the procedural similarities may be helpful in interpreting rules on foreign subsidies control.

A. Structure and Conduct of the Administrative Procedure

The general review instrument is initiated ex officio by the Commission, as prescribed in Article 9. The source of inspiration for the provision is unmistakably Article 12(1) of the State aid Procedural Regulation.[51] This is appropriate given the substantially similar effects of state aid and foreign subsidies. There is however a key difference. Whereas, under the State Aid Procedural Regulation, the Commission is required to examine complaints made by interested parties, under the Regulation it enjoys a degree of discretion – it 'may' examine information 'from any source'.[52]

In contrast, the concentrations and the public procurement instruments are notification based. It is the concerned undertaking itself, if it has benefitted from a foreign financial contribution, which is obliged to notify the Commission in the context of concentrations and the national contracting authority or entity in the context of public procurement.[53] In either case, the Commission is required to initiate the preliminary review stage.[54] Interestingly, once a notification is submitted, the specific procedure for public procurement becomes a composite

[49] Art 25(1) and 30(1), Arts 10, 11(1), 11(3), 11(4), 13, 14, 15, 16, 18 apply to *all* three instruments.

[50] See 'Summary of the responses to the public consultation on the White Paper on levelling the playing field as regards foreign subsidies': www.ec.europa.eu/competition/international/overview/WP_foreign_subsidies2020_summary_public_consultation.pdf.

[51] Council Regulation (EU) 2015/1589 of 13 July 2015 laying down detailed rules for the application of Article 108 of the Treaty on the Functioning of the European Union [2015] OJ L248/9 (State aid Procedural Regulation).

[52] Art 9(1).

[53] Arts 21 and 29.

[54] Arts 24, 25(2), implicitly, and Art 30(2).

administrative procedure.[55] The national contracting authority or entity acts as an intermediary between the undertaking and the Commission. It is required to forward the notification to the Commission, which must then initiate a preliminary review and ultimately take the decision as to whether there was a financial contribution which is compatible with the internal market.[56]

The administrative procedure followed at the level of the Commission, however, is essentially identical in cases of ex officio review or notifications in concentrations and public procurement. The Commission follows a two-stage administrative procedure, consisting of a preliminary review stage and an in depth investigation stage, clearly drawing on procedures in state aid review (preliminary versus formal investigations) as well as merger control (phase I versus phase II investigations).[57]

Much as the preliminary examination stage in the state aid review procedure, the aim of the preliminary review stage under the Proposed Regulation is to form a prima facie view as to whether there is sufficient evidence of a foreign financial contribution with distortive effects in the internal market.[58] At the conclusion of the preliminary review stage, if it finds sufficient indications that an undertaking has been granted a foreign subsidy that distorts the internal market, the Commission will take a decision to initiate an in depth investigation.[59] The in depth investigation stage is similar to the 'formal investigation' stage in state aid review – where the Commission may be in doubt as to whether a national measure constitutes state aid or whether it is compatible with the internal market.

At the conclusion of the administrative procedure, the Commission may adopt decisions which will vary according to its own assessment of each case and according to the instrument against foreign subsidies that has been triggered. Many of the possible decision types have clear parallels in the Merger Control Regulation as well as Regulation 1/2003, in regard to anti-competitive agreements or abuse of dominant position.

The Commission clearly enjoys very broad discretionary powers in the decisions it may take.[60] The Proposed Regulation gives the Commission an ample margin of assessment in determining whether a subsidy distorts the internal market; as to what redressive measures it will impose and what commitments it

[55] For a summary of different aspects involved in the notion of composite administrative procedure, see F Brito Bastos, 'An Administrative Crack in the EU's Rule of Law: Composite Decision-making and Nonjusticiable National Law' (2020) 16 *European Constitutional Law Review* 63, 66; M Eliantonio, 'Judicial Review in an Integrated Administration: The Case of 'Composite Procedures' (2014) 7 *Review of European Administrative* Law 65.

[56] Art 29.

[57] Council Regulation (EC) No 139/2004 of 20 January 2004 on the control of concentrations between undertakings [2004] OJ L24/1, (Merger Control Regulation) Arts 6(1)(c) and 8(3).

[58] See Recital (30).

[59] Art 10(3). See Art 38(1) for the limitation periods to initiate an investigation.

[60] For an overview of the concept of administrative discretion under EU law, see M Wendel, *Verwaltungsermessen als Mehrebenenproblem* (Tübingen, Jus Publicum, 2019) 45 ff, and the contributions in J Mendes (ed), *EU Executive Discretion and the Limits of Law* (Oxford, Oxford University Press, 2019).

will accept; and as to whether a foreign subsidy's potential positive effects on the development of an economic activity (eg, by not discouraging foreign investment) outweigh its negative effects in terms of distorting the internal market.[61]

The Commission may conclude the administrative procedure with decisions imposing redressive measures or commitments. The former are imposed on the undertakings concerned and are modelled on decisions existing in State aid review – for example, the repayment of aid by an undertaking.[62] Commitments are offered by the undertakings concerned and made binding by a Commission decision if deemed appropriate and sufficient to remedy a distortion. Here, the source of inspiration for the Proposed Regulation appears to be the commitments decisions under Article 9 of Regulation 1/2003 and Article 6(2) and 8(2) of the Merger Control Regulation. The substance of possible redressive measures and commitments is listed in Article 6 – for instance, undertakings may commit (or be required to) reduce capacity or market presence, dissolve a concentration, repay the foreign subsidy or refrain from certain investments.

In concentrations and public procurement alike, the Commission may, in case of a foreign subsidy with distortive effects, conclude the in-depth investigation stage with three categories of measures. The Commission may take a no objection decision, a decision accepting and formalising undertakings' commitments, or a decision prohibiting a concentration or award of a contract.[63]

B. Issues Relevant Throughout and after the Conclusion of the Administrative Procedure

The exact sequence of stages that must be followed in the three administrative procedures is not the only regard in which the Foreign Subsidies Regulation resembles pre-existing legal regimes. It also provides for a set of tools that may be applied irrespectively of any particular procedural stage or indeed after the conclusion of the decision-making process. Those tools clearly draw on tried-and-tested procedural law provisions in antitrust and state aid law, even the wording of those provisions is, at points, practically replicated in the Foreign Subsidies Regulation.

Such repurposing is obvious in several Articles. First, in Article 12, which endows the Commission with a broad margin of discretion to adopt interim measures whenever necessary to prevent irreparable harm to competition in the internal market.[64] Second, in the broad range of investigation measures that the Commission may take, such as requests for information from undertakings,

[61] Arts 3–7.
[62] Proposal for a Regulation (n 41 above).
[63] See Arts 25(3) and 31(2).
[64] Council Regulation (EC) No 1/2003 (n 25 above), Art 8 and Recital (24); State Aid Procedural Regulation, Arts 12–13.

the taking of statements[65] or inspections.[66] The extensive case law and literature on the limits of inspections in antitrust – like requirements of proportionality and respect for fundamental rights[67] – are certain to inform the enforcement of the foreign subsidies regime. However, one important difference is that such inspections are restricted to business premises and cannot be carried out in the homes of undertakings' directors and managers as well.[68] A third aspect where the influence of antitrust and State aid procedural law is visible concerns Article 18. The provision authorises the Commission to revoke prior decisions which relied on an incorrect or incomplete factual basis.[69]

There are also issues which the Foreign Subsidies Regulation governs in an entirely different manner from existing administrative procedures in State aid. Article 42 enshrines undertakings' 'rights of the defence' – even though, in fact, it merely alludes to one such right, the right to be heard.[70] The right to be heard will have to be observed before the Commission decides to initiate in-depth investigations or to impose redressive measures, commitments, fines, compulsory penalties, prohibitions of concentrations under Article 25(3) or of the award of a contract under Article 31(2). Despite the fact that foreign subsidies have a competition distorting impact that is substantially identical to State aid, undertakings subsidised by third states appear to benefit from a higher degree of procedural protection than undertakings subsidised by Member States currently enjoy under similar circumstances. Indeed, the CJEU considers the latter as a procedure initiated only in respect of the Member State granting aid – which enjoys the right to be heard[71] –and not in respect of the beneficiary – which is, at best, a mere 'source of information' without any right to be heard before a decision is taken which will require the recovery of aid.[72] As a result, it appears that

[65] Arts 13–14, and 17.

[66] See Arts 14–15. See State Aid Procedural Regulation, Art 5 and Council Regulation (EC) No 1/2003 (n 25 above), Arts 17–21. In regard to inspections in business premises, see Merger Control Regulation (n 57 above) Art 13.

[67] Case T-325/16 *České dráhy v Commission* [2018] EU:T:2018:368; Case T-402/13 *Orange v Commission* [2014] EU:T:2014:991. See also M de Bellis, 'Multi-level Administration, Inspections and Fundamental Rights: Is Judicial Protection Full and Effective?' (2021) 22 *German Law Journal* 416.

[68] See Council Regulation (EC) No 1/2003 (n 25 above) Art 21 and Directive (EU) 2019/1 (n 1 above) Art 7.

[69] See Merger Control Regulation (n 57 above) Arts 6(3) and 11 and the State aid Procedure Regulation, respectively

[70] The procedural protection of undertakings should not be harmed by the textual absence in Art 42 of other good administration rights enshrined in Art 41 of the Charter of Fundamental rights, such as the right of access to the case file or the Commission's duties of impartiality and care. As the CJEU's case law unequivocally states, all rights of the defence need to be observed even if no legal provisions exist that enshrine them. See, for many, Case C-418/11 *Texdata Software v Landesgericht Innsbruck* [2013] EU:C:2013:588, para 83.

[71] Joined Cases C-74/00 and C-75/00 *Falck SpA and Acciaierie di Bolzano SpA v Commission* [2002] EU:C:2002:524, para. 81.

[72] See Cases C-276/03 P *Scott v Commission* [2005] EU:C:2005:590, paras 33–34 and T-468/08 *Tisza Erömü v Commission* [2014] EU:T:2014:235, para 206. For a critical view, see A Bartosch, 'Procedural Rights Denied for Too Long: Is Legal Conservativism Finally Heading for Its "Götterdämmerung"?' (2011) 10 *European State Aid Law Quarterly* 579, 579.

undertakings subsidised by third states will enjoy a robust level of procedural protection that is more comparable to antitrust enforcement cases.[73]

V. Procedural Stability in an Age of Great Change

The internal market is undoubtedly one the crowning achievements of European integration. To remain so, it must be adaptive to changing economic, social and political circumstances. Swift digital transformation and increasing exposure to the strategic interests of third states are two of the defining challenges that the internal market faces in our time. Effectively addressing such challenges requires an appropriate administrative framework. The administrative framework envisaged by the two instruments considered in this chapter, the ECN+ Directive and the Foreign Subsidies Regulation, reflects an overarching aim of preventing changing circumstances from compromising the integrity of the internal market.

The two instruments illustrate how legislative choices on the allocation of powers between national and Union administration may go in different directions. Locating the level of administration that is better situated to decide, in light of its own institutional characteristics, is an essential question when choosing to decentralise enforcement – as in the case of the ECN+ – or to centralise enforcement – as in the domain of foreign subsidies.

Political considerations certainly play a role in making such choices, as the prospect of further empowering the Union administration has always been a sensitive issue. Yet the stark differences between the enhanced decentralised system of the ECN+ Directive and the highly centralised system of the Foreign Subsidies Regulation show that the Commission does consider centralisation of power a viable option depending on the policy goals it wishes to see pursued. One needs to look no further than the Digital Services Act and the Digital Markets Act to understand how far proposals for heavily centralised enforcement may go. Moreover, empowering NCAs in one area of competition law, while empowering the Commission in another, may perhaps even be telling of the direction in which the Commission is refocusing its resources as promoter of the 'general interest of the Union'. The Commission today does not only preserve the historical achievements of effective antitrust enforcement – a task at which NCAs have proven so successful that they will now take up its mantle in a heavily digitalised internal market. The Commission is now also ready to assume the new challenge of defending the internal market against external threats as a question of strategic autonomy in a globalised world economy.

Despite reflecting opposite approaches as to how enforcement powers should be divided between the Union and the Member States, the ECN+ Directive

[73] Council Regulation (EC) No 1/2003 (n 25 above) Art 27.

and the Foreign Subsidies Regulation follow the same basic approach to the design of administrative procedure. Both illustrate the technique of repurposing existing procedural models to new policy areas. The enforcement of rules on foreign subsidies draws heavily on State aid and, to an extent, antitrust law; the ECN+ Directive, by contrast, constitutes a rather unique example of vertical repurposing – that is, of endowing national administration with procedures and powers that had previously been created for the Commission.

The ECN+ Directive and the Foreign Subsidies Regulation showcase the current stage of maturity of European administrative law. It is a sign of its resilience that, when searching for an adequate distribution of administrative power and the appropriate procedures to regulate its exercise, the Union legislator needs to look no further than to past experiences to find at least a useful starting point.

Procedural repurposing may be useful to promote equal treatment before the law between market actors which operate in substantially similar circumstances. The two instruments ensure equal treatment between beneficiaries of third states' subsidies and beneficiaries of Member States' subsidies, in the case of the Foreign Subsidies Regulation; and between undertakings operating in different Member States, but under the exact same competition rules, in the case of the ECN+ Directive.

However, repurposing existing procedures may also have a unique value in an age of so much technological, economic and geopolitical disruption. Such repurposing may provide some stability and legal certainty in an unstable and uncertain context of enforcement. The context where the ECN is called upon to act is one where competition needs to be ensured in a new and ever-changing digital environment. The context where the Commission is called upon to act is also one where the EU's strategic autonomy needs to be protected from new economic threats. Both challenges will have a profound impact on the EU's administrative and competition law for many years to come.

10

Soft Law in EU Competition and State Aid: An Imperfect Solution to Grand Regulatory Challenges

OANA ŞTEFAN*

I. Introduction

European Union (EU) soft law consists of rules of conduct that have no legally binding force but may have legal and practical effects.[1] These are the recommendations and opinions mentioned in Article 288(5) of the Treaty on the Functioning of the European Union (TFEU), but also the notices, communications, letters, frameworks, codes of conduct, guidelines and so on issued by the EU institutions. Such instruments are flexible, in that they do not follow regular decision-making patterns, procedures and especially timelines. This makes soft law ideal to deal with societal challenges, from tackling the consequences of crises such as the financial crisis, the pandemic, the climate crisis or the war in Ukraine, to navigating disruptions such as the rapid expansion of the digital economy.

It is unsurprising therefore that much of the soft law issued in competition and State aid attempts to answer to such challenges. After all, these sectors have been regulated by a mix of soft and hard law since their inception. Initially, soft law was issued to simply cover regulatory gaps in these areas of exclusive competence, where the hard law of Articles 101, 102 and 107 TFEU has been the only hard law that the Commission could rely on for years in its enforcement activities. The aim of soft law switched soon enough from purely explaining the hard law to experimenting with and orienting various policy choices. This illustrates that EU

* Reader in Law, King's College London, oana.stefan@kcl.ac.uk. Many thanks to the editors for comments on a previous version – and generally many fruitful discussions in the past years. All errors should be pretty well obfuscated now. Websites accessed 22 January 2023 or thereabouts.

[1] F Snyder, 'The Effectiveness of European Community Law: Institutions, Processes, Tools and Techniques' (1993) 56 *The Modern Law Review* 19, 32.

soft and hard law have fuzzy boundaries,[2] and they hardly ever exist in isolation from each other. Given this hybrid regulatory landscape, it is established now that academic inquiry should focus on the relationship between soft(er) and hard(er) sources of law.[3]

This chapter illustrates how, together with hard law, soft law has had an important role in expanding the goals of competition and State aid to tackle the big societal challenges of the day. In its second section, by engaging with previous historical accounts of competition[4] and State aid,[5] the chapter will show that soft law has always been sensitive to the changes in policy choices which in turn have been oriented by societal issues. This happens at both the quantitative level (ie, higher or lower proportions of soft law in the policy mix) and the qualitative level (ie, the content of soft law). At the quantitative level, non-binding emergency instruments have been promptly and copiously issued to deal with the effects of various crises, such as the financial crisis, the pandemic or the war in Ukraine. At the qualitative level, we see updates of instruments with an emphasis on environmental protection or social rights.

Following these empirical observations, section III goes on to assess clashes between soft law and principles of the EU constitutional legal order. The flexibility of soft law, an advantage in regulating societal challenges, also means that soft law suffers from a legitimacy deficit. This is highly problematic if we consider that some of these instruments are dealing with salient issues for society at large, such as worker's rights in the sharing economy, or protecting the environment during a climate crisis. The prevalence of soft law in recent crisis situations (such as the COVID-19 pandemic, or the war in Ukraine) meant that even less legitimacy could be preserved, as not even usual consultation procedures could be followed. Being non-binding, soft law is potentially risk-free, allowing for regulatory experiments on issues such as the application of competition rules to novel situations arising from the digital economy. However, the non-binding character of soft law instruments defeats the purpose of bringing clarity for those regulated, as transparency and openness of administrative action are suffering. Finally, crisis instruments might have had a wider impact than tackling the crisis itself, thus challenging important goals of competition and State aid policy. It emerges that wider reflections are needed as to the links and potential clashes between emergency soft law and other policy instruments, and of course, as to whether emergency soft law is really necessary to deal with certain crises.

[2] F Terpan, 'Soft Law in the EU – The Changing Nature of EU Law' (2015) 21 *European Law Journal* 68.

[3] DM Trubek, P Cottrell and M Nance, '"Soft Law", "Hard Law" and the EU Integration' in G de Búrca and J Scott (eds), *Law and New Governance in the EU and the US* (Oxford, Hart Publishing 2006).

[4] I Maher, 'Regulation and Modes of Governance in EC Competition Law: What's New in Enforcement?' (2008) 31 *Fordham International Law Journal* 1713.

[5] M Blauberger, 'Of "Good" and "Bad" Subsidies: European State Aid Control through Soft and Hard Law' (2009) 32 *West European Politics* 719.

II. The Evolution of EU Competition and State Aid Law: A Story of Hybridity

A. Hybrid Regulation as an Answer to Regulatory Challenges in Competition and State Aid

In a classical evolutionary account of competition policy, Gerber identified three phases up to 1994: 15 years of learning for the Commission, when the system was established with the support of the Court; the consolidation of the system under strict court control, dating from the oil crisis to the Single European Act; and a shift of power from the courts to the Commission, coupled with a focus on regulating governmental intervention in the market.[6] In 2011, Maher notes a fourth phase: the modernisation of antitrust, a phase of decentralised enforcement, characterised by an increasingly economic approach to competition law analysis and by a reliance on self-regulation by firms, as opposed to detailed scrutiny by the European Commission.[7] Ten years later, she finds that a potential fifth stage of transformation is emerging, with the implementation of the latest Directives on European Competition Network Plus (ECN+) and damages.[8]

These phases have all seen important changes in the regulatory mix in competition, fuelled by shifts in the regulatory objectives. Treaty articles were further implemented by hard law provisions since the beginning, when regulations were issued.[9] The number of soft law increased over the years in competition, with peak times in the 1990s (after the Single Market programme) and in the 2000s, following decentralisation.[10] In the 1990s the substantive focus was on unified, fair, and open markets, which raised the challenge that competition law was straying away from its real economic purpose. The soft law issued in the years 2000 responded to this challenge, with an economic-based approach to enforcement introduced through Commission guidance.[11] The Commission was also accumulating a significant

[6] DJ Gerber, 'The Transformation of European Community Competition Law?' (1994) 35 *Harvard International Law Journal* 97.

[7] I Maher, 'Competition Law Modernization: an Evolutionary Tale?' in P Craig and G de Burca (eds), *The Evolution of EU Law* 2nd edn (Oxford, Oxford University Press, 2011).

[8] Directive (EU) 2019/1 of the European Parliament and of the Council of 11 December 2018 to empower the competition authorities of the Member States to be more effective enforcers and to ensure the proper functioning of the internal market [2019] OJ L11/3 and Directive (EU) 2014/104/EU of the European Parliament and of the Council of 26 November 2014 on certain rules governing actions for damages under national law for infringements of the competition law provisions of the Member States and of the European Union [2014] OJ L349/1. On this, see I Maher, 'Competition Law: Convergence Through Law and Networks' in P Craig and G de Burca (eds), *The Evolution of EU Law* 2nd edn (Oxford, Oxford University Press, 2021).

[9] Regulation No 19/65/EEC of 2 March of the Council on application of Article 85 (3) of the Treaty to certain categories of agreements and concerted practices [1965] OJ 36/533.

[10] P Ibáñez and A Kalintiri, 'The Evolution of EU Antitrust Policy: 1966–2017' (2020) 83 *The Modern Law Review* 321, 362.

[11] Maher, 'Competition Law Modernization' (n 7 above) 830.

backlog and attempted to solve the matter by issuing individual soft law, comfort letters, instead of formal decisions, and by issuing general soft law[12] delegating enforcement downstream to the national level. When such initiatives failed,[13] hard law was added to the regulatory mix and decentralisation of competition law was done through Regulation 1/2003.[14] A monumental constitutional challenge, this effectively transformed enforcement of competition law into a shared competence,[15] further generating the need for more soft law.[16] Soft law thus became the core of the enforcement business,[17] a swift tool to manage diversity of national approaches and to clarify the law for economic operators.[18] Diversity in the application of competition law was also managed through network governance, with the European Competition Network ensuring coordination between the authorities. The light touch in regulating the European Competition Network (ECN) meant divergences with regards to procedures and sanctions, which again posed a threat to the coherence and soundness of the law.[19] This called hard law back in, through the introduction of the Damages Directive and the ECN+ Directive.[20]

In State aid, the law has been both resilient and adaptable to societal challenges, growing in sophistication in times of liberalisation, enlargement or economic crisis.[21] Soft law was for a long time the only regulatory instrument apart from the Treaty provisions. The embryonic enforcement practice of the Commission in the 60s and 70s evolved into the first sectoral guidance in the 70s and 80s, and towards a systematisation of common objectives from the mid-80s following the White Paper on the completion of the Internal market.[22] Much of the soft law issued in State aid dealt with the application of Article 107(3): aid which may be declared, at the Commission's discretion, compatible with the internal market. The initial approach towards regulation was industry-specific and soft law instruments

[12] Commission, 'Notice on cooperation between national courts and the Commission in applying Arts 85 and 86 EEC' (Notice) [1993] OJ C39/6; Commission, 'Notice on coordination with national authorities' (Notice) [2004] OJ C101/03.

[13] Maher, 'Competition Law Modernization' (n 7 above) 832.

[14] Council Regulation (EC) No 1/2003 of 16 December 2002 on the implementation of the rules on competition laid down in Articles 81 and 82 of the Treaty [2003] OJ L01/1.

[15] C Townley and A Türk, 'The Constitutional Limits of EU Competition Law – United in Diversity' (2019) 64 *The Antitrust Bulletin* 235.

[16] See on this N Petit and MP Rato, 'From Hard to Soft Enforcement of EC Competition Law – A Bestiary of "Sunshine" Enforcement Instruments' in C Gheur and N Petit (eds), *Alternative Enforcement Techniques in EC Competition Law: Settlements, Commitments and Other Novel Instruments* (Paris and Brussels, Bruylant, 2009); and also D Lehmkuhl, 'On Government, Governance and Judicial Review: The Case of European Competition Policy' (2008) 28 *Journal of Public Policy* 139, 147.

[17] Maher, 'Regulation and Modes of Governance' (n 4 above) 1740.

[18] Lehmkuhl, 'On Government, Governance and Judicial Review' (n 16 above) 147.

[19] Maher, 'Competition Law Modernization' (n 7 above) 733.

[20] See Directive (EU) 2019/1 and Directive (EU) 2014/104/EU (n 9 above).

[21] A Biondi and E Righini, 'An Evolutionary Theory of State Aid Control' in D Chalmers and A Arnull (eds), *The Oxford Handbook of EU Law* (Oxford, Oxford University Press, 2015).

[22] Commission, 'Completing the Internal Market: White Paper from the Commission to the European Council' COM(1985) 310 final.

were issued in coal and steel,[23] motor vehicles[24] and fisheries.[25] The end of the 1990s were marked by a turn to hard law, with the Commission being delegated the power to issue block exemption regulations. The literature interpreted these developments as a shift in the soft-hard legal continuum towards harder rules,[26] showing, once again, that soft law is far from static, and it can transform over time.

In order to achieve greater reductions in the level of aid, a shift towards horizontal objectives of Community interest (education, research, employment and regional development) is noted in State aid policy at the beginning of the Millennium, through the 2005 State Aid Action Plan (SAAP).[27] This led to a reform of soft law as well, and a significant fall in the overall level of state aid from 2007.[28] The modernisation of State aid (SAM) started in 2012[29] following the financial crisis, to foster sustainable, smart and inclusive growth in a competitive internal market, focusing on ex ante scrutiny of cases with the biggest impact on the internal market, whilst strengthening the Member States' (MS) cooperation in state aid enforcement and streamlining the rules and providing for faster decisions.[30] Both soft and hard law have been revamped, with most of the revisions occurring after 2014. State aid guidelines and frameworks were made consistent with common principles for the assessment of compatibility and eliminated the disparities in treatment that existed under different soft law instruments. The importance and the sophistication in the assessment of these principles was endorsed by the Court in *Hinkley Point*, a case confirming that a measure to aid the nuclear energy sector was proportionate given its positive effect on the security of supply.[31] Since 2020, much of this soft law is being changed, against the backdrop of seismic events, such as the COVID-19 pandemic and the war in Ukraine. New revisions of guidelines, such as the Rescue and Restructuring and the Environmental guidelines,[32] are occurring at the same time as State aid deals with the pandemic, showing how

[23] Letter to the Member States of 20 April 1977 SG (77) A/5039.

[24] Commission, 'Community Framework on State Aid to the Motor Vehicle Industry' (Communication) [1989] OJ C123/03.

[25] Commission, 'Commission Communication concerning State involvement in the promotion of agricultural and fisheries products' (Communication) [1986] OJ C272/3.

[26] M Aldestam, 'Soft Law in the State Aid Policy Area' in U Mörth (ed), *Soft Law in Governance and Regulation: An Interdisciplinary Analysis* (Cheltenham, Edward Elgar, 2004).

[27] Commission, 'State Aid Action Plan, Less and better targeted state aid: a roadmap for state aid reform 2005–2006' (Consultation Document) COM(2005) 107 final.

[28] C Quigley, *European State Aid Law and Policy* (Oxford, Hart Publishing, 2009) 179–81.

[29] Commission, 'EU State Aid Modernisation' (Communication) COM(2012) 209 final.

[30] ibid para 8.

[31] Judgment in Case C-594/18 P *Austria v Commission* [2020] EU:C:2020:742, para 77. See A Sikora-Kaléda, 'A Clash of Titans: EU Competition and State Aid Law and the Impact of the European Green Deal', Ch 3 in this volume, P Nicolaides, 'The Response of EU Courts to Society's Digital and Green Challenges in the Field of Competition and State aid', Ch 8 in this volume, and CM Colombo and M Bonelli, 'Governing the Green Transition Through State Aid Control', Ch 12 in this volume.

[32] Commission, 'Guidelines on State aid for rescuing and restructuring non-financial undertakings in difficulty' (Communication) [2014] OJ C249/01 and Commission, 'Guidelines on State aid for climate, environmental protection and energy' (Communication) [2022] OJ C80/01.

both this crisis and other societal challenges such as the rise of the digital and the environmental crisis are currently spurring massive transformations of the field.

What emerges from this picture is that all phases of policy development in competition and State aid were characterised by hybrid regulation. The changing approach in policy was accompanied either by a switch in the soft-hard law configurations, or by a change in the regulatory goals pursued by the soft law instruments. The following subsections will show an emerging trend in contemporary soft law adopted to deal with major societal challenges, both in competition and in State aid.

B. Hybrid Regulation as an Answer to the Major Challenges in Competition Law

It is safe to say that, at least since the millennium, soft law was issued either to reinforce the economic approach towards competition law or to deal with procedural challenges stemming from decentralisation. In the area of Articles 101 and 102 of the TFEU, Commission guidance for a long-time showed reluctance in promoting more than economic efficiency. This corresponds perhaps with the general narrative that competition law should be about consumer welfare and maximising economic efficiency. To cite from the Guidance on Article 101(3), the types of efficiencies listed in that article 'are broad categories which are intended to cover all objective economic efficiencies'.[33] Indeed, the Commission guidance on the application of Article 101 (3) is 'littered'[34] with references to economic benefits, albeit alongside a 'timid' reference that 'goals pursued by other Treaty provisions can be taken into account to the extent that they can be subsumed under the four conditions of Art 101 (3)'.[35]

Yet, most recent soft law shows a qualitative shift towards more non-economic goals, responding to current challenges such as the environmental crisis and the societal problems connected to the rise of digital platforms. This matches perhaps the finding that nowadays enforcement has focused on certain industries, going hand-in-hand with EU-policy initiatives, including the digital single market.[36]

With regards to the current environmental challenges, this back-and-forth from economics to wider societal and policy goals can be illustrated by the history of the Horizontal Cooperation Guidelines,[37] whose revisions have been including

[33] Commission, 'Guidelines on the application of Article 81(3)' (Communication) [2004] OJ C101/97, para 59.

[34] J Buhart and D Henry, 'Think Green Before You Apply: EU Competition Law and Climate-Change Abatement' (2021) 44 *World Competition* 147, 156 and ff.

[35] Commission, 'Guidelines on the application of Article 81(3)' (n 33 above).

[36] Ibáñez and Kalintiri, 'The Evolution of EU Antitrust Policy' (n 10 above) 368.

[37] Commission, 'Guidelines on the applicability of Article 101 of the Treaty on the Functioning of the European Union to horizontal cooperation agreements' (Communication) [2011] OJ C11/01.

and deleting references to the environment and sustainability as assessment criteria. The 2001 version of the Guidelines included a full section on 'environmental agreements' concluded in order 'to achieve pollution abatement'.[38] The focus was still on economic benefits, but the Commission was ready to take 'a positive stance on the use of environmental agreements as a policy instrument to achieve the goals enshrined … in the Treaty'.[39] Interestingly, the 2011 Revision of the Notice scraps this section completely; even if the Commission insisted that the assessment of environmental agreements was not downgraded as a result, but on the contrary, was better streamlined under the other relevant headings of the Notice.[40] The most recent revision of the Notice contains a chapter on sustainability agreements. Sustainability is here understood not only in relation to environmental protection (as in the 2001 Notice), but also in relation to economic and social development, by reference to the 2030 United Nations (UN) Agenda for Sustainable Development.[41]

The Revision of the Notice happens in a context where NCAs have already adopted a sustainability perspective in their own guidance documents or practice. This is the case of the Dutch Competition Authority which updated its Guidelines on sustainability agreements, an initiative dating back to 2014.[42] Similarly, in the post-Brexit UK, the Competition and Markets Authority has advocated for more clarity to help businesses understand how sustainability considerations are taken into account in competition law.[43] This goes to show that EU soft law is hardly ever static, and the various updates in European guidance happen in the context of wider overhauls of soft laws within the Members or the neighbouring States.

With regards to the digital market, one challenge which is currently tackled (also) through soft law is the difficult situation of individuals employed by platforms facilitating various services. The Commission Guidelines on the application of Union competition law to collective agreements regarding the working conditions of solo self-employed persons,[44] holds that Article 101 TFEU does not apply to collective agreements regarding the working conditions of solo self-employed people who are in a situation comparable to workers. This would help counteract the practice of some firms to give a self-employed status to people working

[38] Commission, 'Guidelines on the applicability of Article 81 of the EC Treaty to horizontal cooperation agreements' (Notice) [2001] OJ C3/02, Section 7.

[39] ibid para 192.

[40] Commission, 'Competition: Commission adopts revised competition rules on horizontal co-operation agreements' (Memo) MEMO/10/676.

[41] Commission, 'Approval of the content of a draft for a Communication from the Commission – Guidelines on the applicability of Article 101 of the Treaty on the Functioning of the EU to horizontal co-operation agreements (Draft Communication)' [2022] OJ C164/01, para 543.

[42] Authority for Consumers and Markets, 'Second draft version: Guidelines on Sustainability Agreements – Opportunities within competition law' (2021): www.acm.nl/en/publications/second-draft-version-guidelines-sustainability-agreements-opportunities-within-competition-law.

[43] Press Release, 'CMA publishes environmental sustainability advice to government': www.gov.uk/government/news/cma-publishes-environmental-sustainability-advice-to-government.

[44] Commission, 'Guidelines on the application of Union competition law to collective agreements regarding the working conditions of solo self-employed persons 2022/C 374/02' (Communication) [2022] OJ C374/02.

for them, which would mean, under the Treaty competition provisions, that such individuals could not enter into agreements with their peers, hence losing bargaining power regarding their conditions of work. The Guidelines are part of broader soft[45] and hard law initiatives[46] to deal with the uneasy interaction between labour law and current realities of the digital economy, again underlining hybridity of regulation.

The recent revival of informal individual guidance is another soft law route through which antitrust enforcement could be used to tackle big new societal challenges. Prior to decentralisation, individual guidance in the form of 'comfort letters' was copiously used to ease the Commission backlog in authorising agreements. Regulation 1/2003 allowed informal guidance in the context of decentralisation,[47] yet, a 2004 Notice limited excessively the circumstances under which the Commission could provide such guidance, which meant that the practice was discontinued.[48] In 2020, an Antitrust COVID Temporary Framework expressly provided for the possibility for the Commission to assess business cooperation projects linked to the situation of urgency,[49] which led to a revival of comfort letters/individual guidance after the pandemic. The 2004 Notice was thus renewed in 2022,[50] setting out two circumstances under which informal guidance can be provided. First there should be a novel or unresolved question, which means that the assessment of an agreement or practice poses a question where there is no sufficient clarity in the existing Union framework. Second, there should be a Union interest in providing the guidance.

These two conditions create the optimal premises for comfort letters to be used to deal with matters raised by current challenges posed by the evolution of our societies, such as digitalisation or greening the economy, as declared by

[45] Commission, 'Better working conditions for a stronger social Europe: harnessing the full benefits of digitalisation for the future of work' (Communication) COM(2021) 761 final.

[46] Proposal for a Directive of the European Parliament and the Council on improving working conditions in platform work COM(2021) 762 final.

[47] Council Regulation (EC) No 1/2003 (n 14 above) Recital 38.

[48] Press Release, 'Competition: Commission adopts a more flexible antitrust Informal Guidance Notice; withdraws Antitrust COVID Temporary Framework': www.ec.europa.eu/commission/presscorner/detail/en/ip_22_5887. Commission, 'Commission Notice on informal guidance relating to novel questions concerning Articles 81 and 82 of the EC Treaty that arise in individual cases (guidance letters)' [2004] OJ C101/78.

[49] Commission, 'Communication from the Commission Temporary Framework for assessing antitrust issues related to business cooperation in response to situations of urgency stemming from the current COVID-19 outbreak 2929/C 116 l/02' [2020] OJ C116l/7. Two letters were issued in this regard: 'Comfort letter: coordination in the pharmaceutical industry to increase production and to improve supply of urgently needed critical hospital medicines to treat COVID-19 patients' (COMP/OG – D(2020/044003)) and Commission, 'Comfort letter: cooperation at a Matchmaking Event – Towards COVID19 vaccines upscale production' (COMP/E-1/GV/BV/nb (2021/034137)).

[50] Commission, 'Notice on informal guidance relating to novel questions concerning Articles 81 and 82 of the EC Treaty that arise in individual cases (guidance letters)' [2004] OJ C101/78 revised as Commission, 'Notice on informal guidance relating to novel or unresolved questions concerning Articles 101 and 102 of the Treaty on the Functioning of the EU that arise in individual cases (guidance letters)' [2022] OJ C381/07.

the Director-General.[51] One of the indicators for an 'interest' in providing the guidance is the relevance of the agreement or practice for the achievement of the Commission's priorities. A practical confirmation is that the Commission has issued informal guidance to GAIA-X, an organisation having as a declared purpose to provide the next generation of data infrastructure.[52] Another indicator of the 'interest' criterion is the extent to which the agreement or practice could correspond to a more widely spread usage in the Union. This implies that there is a will to signal the approach that the Commission would take for similar future behaviours, with the 2022 Notice alluding that these comfort letters could be used as interpretative instruments beyond the respective case. Thus, whether a problem is 'novel' needs to be assessed in relation not only to the case law of the Court of Justice of the European Union (CJEU), and general soft law, but also prior individual guidance. Provision is made in the Notice that such informal guidance will be published on the website of the Commission, with an obvious transparency goal. Ultimately, this practice enables the Commission to regulate by simply publishing information online.

C. Hybrid Regulation as an Answer to the Major Challenges in State Aid

The financial crisis, and now the COVID-19 pandemic and the Ukraine war, determined the entrenchment of emergency soft law in State aid, triggering not only challenges as to transparency and legal effects, but also questioning fundamental principles of the internal market. During the financial crisis, MS rushed to the rescue of their banks, risking subsidy races across Europe and severe distortions of competition. By September 2009, some three trillion Euro of state guarantees were provided to European banks under schemes approved by the European Commission, in addition to over 300 billion Euro in capital injections from MS governments.[53] The measures taken comprise a communication from 2008 laying down the rules applicable to state aid measures in the context of the financial crisis,[54] a communication on measures for the recapitalisation of financial institutions,[55] several communications relating to support measures in favour of

[51] A Boyce, 'Climate cooperation should get 'comfort' from EU antitrust officials', *Mlex*, 14 September 2020: https://mlexmarketinsight.com/news/insight/climate-cooperation-should-get-comfort-from-eu-antitrust-officials-guersent-says.

[52] Commission, 'Feedback on the membership criteria and internal working rules of GAIA-X COMP/C.6/SS/RI/vvd.

[53] Commission, 'Tackling the financial crisis': www.ec.europa.eu/competition/recovery/financial_sector.html.

[54] Commission, 'The application of State aid rules to measures taken in relation to financial institutions in the context of the current global financial crisis' (Communication) [2008] OJ C270/8

[55] Commission, 'The recapitalisation of financial institutions in the current financial crisis: limitation of aid to the minimum necessary and safeguards against undue distortions of competition' (Communication) [2009] OJ C10/02.

banks in the context of the financial crisis,[56] and so on. Most importantly, in striving to support the real economy, the Commission loosened, for a limited amount of time, the rules applicable to horizontal aid, facilitating speedy access to credit by businesses through the adoption of Temporary Frameworks (TF).[57]

A vast array of national aid measures[58] have been approved by the Commission to counteract the negative effects of various pandemic lockdowns on the economy of the MS. This was done under the exceptional rules issued by the European Commission, first through a Communication on a coordinated economic response to the COVID-19 Outbreak,[59] and then by a targeted Coronavirus TF.[60] The European Commission also adopted a Temporary Crisis Framework for State aid[61] in the context of Russia's invasion of Ukraine, meant to mitigate the economic impact of the war and EU sanctions by supporting severely affected businesses. The Ukraine TF contains provisions aimed at compensating companies for additional costs incurred due to the high energy prices but goes beyond this goal and provides support measures to businesses otherwise affected by the crisis, such as agriculture and the food industry, cut off from important sources of supply. As with the previous TFs, the Ukraine TF was issued under the Commission's discretionary power to approve State aid 'to remedy a serious disturbance to the economy of a MS'.[62] Most recently, the Commission prolonged the Ukraine TF and extended it to a Temporary Crisis and *Transition* Framework (emphasis added).[63] The latter also pursues environmental goals, specifically addressing support measures in sectors which are key for the transition to a net-zero economy, in line with the Green Deal Industrial Plan.

[56] Commission, 'Communication from the Commission on the treatment of impaired assets in the community banking sector' (Communication) [2009] OJ C72/01; Commission, 'Communication from the Commission on the application, after 1 January 2011, of State aid rules to support measures in favour of banks in the context of the financial crisis (Banking Communication)' (Communication) [2010] OJ C329/7; Commission, 'Communication from the Commission on the application, from 1 January 2012, of State aid rules to support measures in favour of banks in the context of the financial crisis' (Communication) [2011] OJ C356/7.

[57] Commission, 'Temporary framework for State aid measures to support access to finance in the current financial and economic crisis' [2009] OJ C83/1; Commission, 'Temporary Union framework for State aid measures to support access to finance in the current financial and economic crisis (Communication) [2011] OJ C6/5 – now expired.

[58] A comprehensive list is available: Commission, 'The State Aid Temporary Framework': https://competition-policy.ec.europa.eu/state-aid/coronavirus/temporary-framework_en.

[59] Commission, 'Coordinated economic response to the COVID-19 Outbreak' COM(2020) 112 final, point 5 and annex 3.

[60] Commission, 'Temporary Framework for State aid measures to support the economy in the current COVID-19 outbreak' (Communication) [2020] OJ C91I/1.

[61] Commission, 'Temporary crisis framework for state aid measures to support the economy following the aggression against Ukraine by Russia' (Communication) [2022] OJ C131I/01.

[62] Consolidated Version of the Treaty on the Functioning of the European Union (TFEU) [2012] OJ C326/47, Art 107 (3) (b).

[63] Communication from the Commission Temporary Crisis and Transition Framework for State Aid measures to support the economy following the aggression against Ukraine by Russia [2023] OJ C 101/ 3.

Soft law is not the only answer to grand problems of our societies in State aid. The recent discussions around research, development and innovation confirm that hybridity is still relied on to deal with the challenges of the digital world. The Research, Development and Innovation (RDI) framework[64] has been very recently updated to respond to such challenges. At the same time, the Commission has proposed hard, and put forward soft, law in the form of a 'European Chips Act', to reinforce Europe's technological competitiveness in international trade, by pooling together investments from the Union and the MS in the field of semiconductor technology.[65]

This brief account shows that shifts towards harder or softer regulation in competition and State aid correspond, as expected, with major turns in policy approaches. In both sectors, major shifts in the regulatory mix are determined by concerns to increase effectiveness in the application of the rules. At the substance level, we note that in competition law the turn to soft law has been dictated by changes in approach from a completion of the internal market goal towards more modern and economic orientations, and most recently tend to include wider societal goals. Conversely, reforms of the soft law in State aid are spurred mostly by grand societal changes, as well as crises. One important takeaway needs to be drawn from the above: soft law is not a static instrument, its flexibility being its most praised characteristic, and allowing it to change, improve, or even translate into hard law is an answer to external challenges or simply the evolution of the legal framework. The next section turns to challenges raised using soft law in tackling wider societal problems in State aid and competition.

III. Evaluation

The usefulness of soft law is obvious: its speedy adoption processes allow a swift response in a fast-changing landscape, dictated by the rapid evolutions of trade and economics. Competition and State aid are areas of exclusive EU competence, where the European Commission enjoys wide discretion. Explaining this discretion through guidance is vital for transparency, and ultimately increases legal certainty. Such principles are often put forward as rationale in the preambles of various soft law instruments. In turn, Courts rely on these principles to extract even binding legal effects of soft law for the enacting institution.[66] Yet, competition and State aid soft law is not immune to the general rule of law concerns: the lack of legitimacy safeguards of these instruments and their potential for overstepping

[64] Press Release, 'State aid: Commission adopts revised State aid Framework for research development and innovation': www.ec.europa.eu/commission/presscorner/detail/en/ip_22_6233.

[65] Press Corner, 'European Chips Act – Questions and Answers': www.ec.europa.eu/commission/presscorner/detail/en/qanda_22_730.

[66] O Ştefan, *Soft Law in Court. Competition Law, State Aid and the Court of Justice of the EU* (Alphen aan den Rijn, Kluwer, 2013).

competence boundaries, as well as the uncertainty surrounding their effects in the multi-level governance system of the EU. Finally, the entrenchment of emergency soft law in State aid raises significant issues regarding the potential of these instruments to undermine EU integration goals.

A. Legitimacy of EU Soft Law

Given its lack of legally binding force, soft law is not constrained by the list of competences provided for in the TFEU, and the general basis used for issuing such instruments is Article 17 TEU, providing in its first paragraph sweepingly that 'The Commission shall promote the general interest of the Union and take appropriate initiatives to that end'. Whilst this might be less of an issue for areas of exclusive competence, some problems can still arise in practice. For instance, State aid environmental guidance was used to regulate the security of electricity supply, falling within an area of energy, a shared competence. Indeed, capacity mechanisms – or financing measures meant to ensure the security of supply to avoid blackouts – have been regulated through State aid guidelines[67] before the adoption of a dedicated hard law instrument within the recent Clean Energy Package.[68] Further, the Notice on the Notion of Aid,[69] sits uncomfortably with the principle that the discretion of the Commission is limited under Article 107(1) TFEU. Traditionally, the Commission has issued an important number of soft law instruments with the objective of informing its stakeholders of the way in which it intended to exercise its discretion under Article 107(3) TFEU. However, it is surprising to see the Commission publishing such a detailed instrument dealing with Article 107(1) TFEU criteria – an area where it has only limited discretion to exert or explain.[70]

It is worrying that there are no clear procedures or rules for soft law-making, especially since soft law is now tackling social issues, such as the precarious condition of workers in the sharing economy.[71] Flexibility is undoubtedly praised in times of emergency, such as the pandemic, or more generally when a swift action is necessary to adapt to changing market circumstances. Yet, flexibility also means that the legitimate decision-making channels are not used, with a big absence from the EU soft law landscape: the European Parliament.[72] Soft law in competition and

[67] Commission, 'Guidelines on State aid for environmental protection and energy 2014–2020' (Communication) [2014] OJ C200/01.

[68] Regulation (EU) 2019/943 of the European Parliament and of the Council of 5 June 2019 on the internal market for electricity [2019] OJ L158/54.

[69] Commission, 'Commission Notice on the notion of state aid as referred to in Article 107(1) of the Treaty on the Functioning of the European Union' (Notice) [2016] OJ C262/1.

[70] A Biondi and O Ştefan, 'The Notice on the Notion of State Aid: Every Light Has Its Shadow' in B Nascimbene (ed), *The Modernisation of EU State Aid Control: Evolution and Perspectives of the EU Rules on State Aids and Services of General Economic Interest* (New York, Springer, 2018).

[71] Thanks to Carlo Colombo for this point.

[72] Parliament, 'Institutional and legal implications of the use of "soft law" instruments' (resolution) 2007/2028(INI), at 1.

State aid is generally issued by the European Commission and published online and in the C series of the Official Journal, although publication is not compulsory for soft law.[73]

One should not imagine that soft law is produced out of thin air. It emerges, most of the time, from complex and lengthy consultations with the stakeholders. There are usually several rounds of consultations, as well as targeted discussions with various stakeholders, or negotiations with MS, all published online on the website of the Directorate-General (DG) of competition.[74] All in all, competition and State aid soft law-making appears to be much more transparent than in other sectors.[75] Yet, such processes are not a panacea in relation to ensuring legitimacy: in the absence of a clear recognition of participatory rights, expressly in the text of the Treaty or through the European Court of Justice (ECJ) case law, the Commission remains free to organise these consultations and take them into consideration as it sees fit. Furthermore, with the rise of Temporary Frameworks, consultations are stripped to a minimum and rendered opaque, presumably in the interest of urgency.[76] The Coronavirus TF is a perfect example, with amendments being brought at an incredibly fast pace (six times in less than two years), following consultations with MS only, vaguely mentioned in various press releases.[77] The Ukraine TF is following a similar path, although a slightly more participative consultation process was engaged for its recent update into a Temporary Crisis and Transition Framework.[78] This is the third time that extraordinary State aid emergency soft law is adopted through procedures that depart from the established public consultation routes. Whilst it is perhaps to be expected that in case of emergency it is difficult to comply with burdensome procedural requirements, the worry is that this modus operandi will become entrenched, creating a category of emergency soft law, published with even lower legitimacy standards than regular soft law.

What is more, soft law cannot be subject to direct judicial review.[79] Even if the Court accepted such judicial review, one may wonder how far its scrutiny could go. Indeed, the Commission enjoys vast discretion in the area of Article 107 (3)

[73] TFEU (n 62 above) Art 297.

[74] See for an example Press release, 'State Aid: Commission endorses the new Guidelines on State aid for Climate. Environmental protection and Energy': www.ec.europa.eu/commission/presscorner/detail/en/ip_21_6982.

[75] A contrario, J Scott, 'In Legal Limbo: Post-legislative Guidance as a Challenge for European Administrative Law' (2011) 48 *Common Market Law Review* 329, 336.

[76] A Biondi, 'Governing the Interregnum: State Aid Rules and the COVID-19 Crisis' (*King's College London Law School Research Paper No 48/2020*).

[77] M Eliantonio and O Ştefan, 'The Elusive Legitimacy of EU Soft Law: An Analysis of Consultation and Participation in the Process of Adopting COVID-19 Soft Law in the EU' (2021) 12 *European Journal of Risk Regulation* 159.

[78] Survey and targeted consultation as per the Press Release of 9 March 2023 available here: https://ec.europa.eu/commission/presscorner/detail/en/ip_23_1563.

[79] Judgment in Case C-16/16 P *Belgium v Commission* [2018] EU:C:2018:79.

TFEU, and the Court's review is limited to checking if rules of procedure and the duty to state reasons were respected, and that there is no manifest error in assessing facts, or error of law and no misuse of powers.[80] The accountability of soft law thus cannot rest on courts, but on alternative channels such as permanent (and transparent) dialogue with the stakeholders.

B. Uncertain Legal Effects

In the absence of legally binding force, it is unclear what legal effects soft law can produce. The recently issued guidelines on the collective agreements concluded by the self-employed clearly state that they 'do not create any social rights or obligations' and neither do they affect the distribution of competences between the EU and the MS.[81] Non-binding effects might create further uncertainty which ultimately is detrimental to workers' rights.[82] Whilst the guidelines apply to *all* self-employed persons, the Commission has also proposed a Directive to deal with the specific situation of digital platforms.[83] Such a hardening of the legal framework would be probably more conducive to legal certainty, as it would leave less scope for variation in the application at the national levels.

The revival of individual guidance in competition law also raises concerns. Comfort letters were already criticised pre-decentralisation from the point of view of legal certainty or transparency:[84] in most cases, these were only published in short form.[85] Yet, practitioners welcome the reintroduction of such letters, given that the Commission has never followed up on the possibility to provide informal guidance under Regulation 1/2003.[86] Their effects are still far from clear. As per the 2022 Notice on individual guidance, applicants remain responsible to carry out their own self-assessment of the applicability of Articles 101 and 102 TFEU, regardless of the letter they received. Such letters do not prejudge the assessment by the Court of Justice, and the Commission is not entirely bound by such letters either. In case of general guidance, the Commission would be allowed to depart from its own soft law, if they provide arguments that are compliant with

[80] Case C-333/07 *Régie Networks v Direction de contrôle discal Rhône-Aples bourgogne* [2008] EU:C:2008:764.

[81] Commission, 'Guidelines on the applicability of Article 101' (n 41 above) Preamble, para 10.

[82] N Countouris, C Stefano and I Lianos, 'The EU, Competition Law and Workers' Rights' (*Centre for Law, Economics and Society, Research Paper No 2/2021*).

[83] Proposal for a Directive on improving the working conditions in platform work: Commission, 'Commission proposals to improve the working conditions of people working through digital labour platforms': https://ec.europa.eu/social/main.jsp?langId=en&catId=89&furtherNews=yes&newsId=10120#navItem-relatedDocuments.

[84] H Cosma and R Whish, 'Soft Law in the Field of EU Competition Policy' (2003) 14 *European Business Law Review* 25, 43–44.

[85] F Montag, 'The Case for a Reform of Regulation 17/62: Problems and Possible Solutions from a Practitioner's Point of View' (1998) 22 *Fordham International Law Journal* 827.

[86] J Buhart and D Henry, 'COVID-20: The Comfort Letter Is Dead. Long Live the Comfort Letter?' (2020) 43 *World Competition* 305.

legal certainty and legitimate expectations.[87] There might be a difference between general and individual guidance: the Commission can subsequently examine the agreements or the practice that were subject to an individual letter, and they are only bound to *take the letter into account*, and even this subject to a long list of caveats.[88] However, applicants who relied on the letter in good faith cannot, in principle, have fines imposed on them.[89]

The 2022 Notice also provides that letters do not bind MS' authorities and Courts, who could take them into consideration 'as they see fit'.[90] This is reminiscent of older case law, such as *Guerlain* and *Lancome* where comfort letters were considered mere factors 'which the national courts may take into account'.[91] Theoretically, if a national authority decides to pursue investigations regarding an activity covered by individual guidance, they are free to do so. National authorities do not seem to be constrained, in the case of individual guidance, by any duty to state reasons or by the respect of principles such as sincere cooperation, uniformity, and effectiveness of EU law – as it happens for instance when they would investigate cases which were subject to commitment decisions.[92]

All in all, governing through soft law in multi-level settings such as the EU can at the same time provide clarity for national regulators, but also increase fragmentation of the law because of uncertain legal status.[93] EU competition soft law is used by the NCAs and Courts, even though sometimes certain decisions or judgments specifically mention that authorities and judges do not feel bound by such instruments.[94] The attitude of authorities towards a certain piece of EU soft law can vary in time, as shown by the initial reluctance[95] to rely on the Guidance Paper on Article 102 TFEU[96] which is now more frequently mentioned at the national level.[97] Soft law is incorporated in the legal orders of the MS through

[87] Joined Cases C-189/02 P, C-202/02 P, C-205/02 P to C-208/02 P and C-213/02 P *Dansk Rørindustri and Others v Commission* [2005] EU:C:2005:408, para 211.

[88] Commission, 'Commission Notice on informal guidance' (n 50 above) para 25.

[89] ibid.

[90] ibid para 27.

[91] Joined Cases 253/78 and 1 to 3/79 *Procureur de la République v Giry and Guerlain* [1980] EU:C:1980:188, para 13; Judgment in Case 99/79 *SA Lancôme v Etos and Albert Heijn* [1980] EU:C:1980:193, para 11.

[92] Case C-547/16 *Gasorba and others v Repsol Comercial* [2017] EU:C:2017:891, paras 28–29.

[93] I Maher, 'Functional and Normative Delegation to Non-Majoritarian Institutions: The Case of the European Competition Network' (2009) 7 *Comparative European Politics* 414, 425.

[94] O Ştefan and others, 'EU Competition and State Aid Soft Law in the Member States: Finland, France, Germany, Italy, the Netherlands, Slovenia and the UK' (2020) *King's College London Law School Research Paper* 24.

[95] Z Georgieva, 'The Judicial Reception of Competition Soft Law in the Netherlands and the UK' (2016) 12 *European Competition Journal* 54.

[96] Commission, 'Guidance on the Commission's enforcement priorities in applying Article 82 of the EC Treaty to abusive exclusionary conduct by dominant undertakings' (Communication) [2009] OJ C45/7.

[97] M Dobbs and O Ştefan, 'EU Soft Law in the UK on the Eve of Brexit: (Not) Much Ado About Nothing?' in M Eliantonio, E Korkea-aho and O Stefan (eds), *EU Soft Law in the Member States: Theoretical Findings and Empirical Evidence* (Oxford, Hart Publishing, 2021).

various means, from brief references on national authorities' websites to national soft law or even national hard law.[98] Yet, such fragmentation is not *always* a negative outcome. Take the revision of the *de minimis* notice[99] which was prompted by the refusal of the French Autorité de la Concurrence to apply it, and the follow-up preliminary reference at the CJEU.[100] It appears thus that the dialogue between the various levels of governance can change soft law instruments, potentially improving them. This can even ultimately strengthen the legitimacy of soft law, given that it adapts to stakeholders' views.

C. Putting in Abeyance Established EU Law Principles

Pandemic regulation shows another danger of EU soft law, as entrenched emergency soft law can put in abeyance established EU law principles. In State aid, the EU has issued two frameworks to deal with the effects of two overlapping crises: the COVID-19 pandemic and the Ukraine war. These frameworks have effectively allowed MS to help their economies through subsidies, thus pausing the prohibition provided for in Article 107 TFEU. Whilst it is too soon to offer a full evaluation of the effects that these frameworks had on the internal market, one thing is certain: they both have a huge potential to distort the level playing field between the MS. France and Germany are the absolute leaders of pandemic State aid spending between March and December 2020,[101] as they account for almost 80 per cent of the state aid notified under the COVID TF.[102] Many of the schemes approved on the basis of the TF are currently challenged in Court, with serious allegations being brought regarding breaches of the non-discrimination principle, a cornerstone of EU law. Although the General Court declared several schemes that favoured companies on the basis of their links to the national economies compatible with the State aid rules,[103] the literature found such an approach problematic, as it fails to consider other more objective criteria for granting aid, such

[98] O Ştefan, 'Soft Law and the Promise of Transparency in the Member States' in M Eliantonio, E Korkea-aho and O Stefan (eds), *EU Soft Law in the Member States: Theoretical Findings and Empirical Evidence* (Oxford, Hart Publishing, 2021).

[99] Commission, 'Notice on agreements of minor importance which do not appreciably restrict competition under Article 101(1) of the Treaty on the Functioning of the EU' (Communication) [2014] OJ C291/1.

[100] Case C-226/11 *Expedia Inc v Autorité de la concurrence and Others* [2012] EU:C:2012:795.

[101] I Agnolucci, 'Will COVID-19 Make or Break EU State Aid Control? An Analysis of Commission Decisions Authorising Pandemic State Aid Measures' (2021) 13 *Journal of European Competition Law and Practice* 3.

[102] Remarks by Executive Vice-President Vestager on the proposal for a State aid Temporary Crisis and Transition Framework, 1 February 2023, available at https://ec.europa.eu/commission/presscorner/detail/en/speech_23_527.

[103] Case T-379/20 *Ryanair v Commission* [2021] EU:T:2021:195, para 87 and T-238/20 *Ryanair v Commission* [2021] EU:T:2021:91. Appeals before the CJEU in pending cases C-320/21 P and C-209/21 P.

as the actual contribution of companies to the economy, or indeed, the degree of damage suffered by extraordinary circumstances such as the pandemic.[104] Thus, the Framework attacks the very rationale of State aid control in Europe, creating a danger for subsidy races and internal market distortions.

Often fraught with contradictions, crisis soft law can clash with regulatory goals in other fields. Some of the most important sustainability goals of modern State aid policy have been put on hold by the Commission in its efforts to deal with the pandemic.[105] The green and digital agendas were not appropriately pursued by the Commission pandemic State aid policy.[106] This is not offset by some MS pushing green agendas in sectors such as transport during the pandemic.[107] This illustrates that emergency soft law should be carefully tuned to pre-existing or planned hard and soft law. The second amendment of the COVID TF stated it 'complements rather than replaces existing possibilities under EU State aid rules for MS to provide support'[108] according to the Risk Finance Guidelines[109] or the (then upcoming) Climate, Energy and Environmental Aid Guidelines (CEEAG).[110]

These interlinkages between various policy instruments have been exploited by the Commission in tackling the energy crisis even in the wake of the Ukraine crisis and the corresponding TF. The REPowerEU Communication[111] already mentioned that the new Emissions Trading System (ETS) State aid guidelines might also tackle the conundrum between security of supply, greening, and competition. Similarly, the Commission has announced it will prioritise its assessment of the notifications for the first Important Projects of Common European Interest on hydrogen.[112] Since energy market design is not an instant matter, the EU has been grappling with this issue for years, designing three energy packages, a Clean Energy for All Europeans 'package', as well as a Green Deal. Out of the measures suggested in the Commission Toolbox on Energy Prices.[113] State aid appears to be a quick fix,

[104] P Nicolaides, 'The Limits of "Proportionate" Discrimination' (2021) 20 *European State Aid Law Quarterly*, 384.

[105] Agnolucci, 'Will COVID-19 Make or Break EU State Aid Control?' (n 102 above).

[106] J van Hove, 'Impact of state aid on competition and competitiveness during the COVID-19 pandemic: an early assessment', Study for the Committee on Economic and Monetary Affairs, Policy Department for Economic, Scientific and Quality of Life Policies, European Parliament (Luxembourg, 2020).

[107] S Truxal, 'State Aid and Air Transport in the Shadow of COVID-19' (2020) 45 *Air and Space Law* 61, 81.

[108] Commission, 'Amendment to the Temporary Framework for State aid measures to support the economy in the current COVID-19 outbreak' (Communication) [2020] OJ C164/3, recital 14.

[109] Commission, 'Guidelines on State aid to promote risk finance investments' (Communication) [2014] OJ C19/4.

[110] Commission. 'Guidelines on State aid for climate, environmental protection and energy' (n 32 above).

[111] Commission, 'REPowerEU: Joint European Action for more affordable, secure and sustainable energy' (Communication) COM(2022) 108 final.

[112] Commission, 'Joint European Action' (n 111 above) Section 2.1.3.

[113] Commission, 'Tackling rising energy prices: a toolbox for action and support' (Communication) COM(2021) 660 final.

part of a bigger framework. The goal is to achieve short-term measures to help the consumers, whilst at the same time creating a long-term vision for the electricity market. The only worry might be that the quick fix might undermine long-term goals.

Whilst it is a matter of fact that economic sanctions can backfire on the EU's internal market, the question is whether it was necessary to adopt *general* rules to deal with State aid granted by the MS to address such collateral damage. The Ukraine TF rightly states that aid cannot be granted to undertakings under sanctions adopted by the EU.[114] Apart from the obvious scenario where aid cannot be granted to entities specifically named on the sanction list, aid cannot be granted to undertakings *controlled* by such entities, raising the question of what the threshold of 'control' is. Furthermore, aid cannot be granted to 'undertakings active in *industries targeted by sanctions* adopted by the EU, insofar as the aid *would undermine the objectives of the relevant sanctions*'.[115] Yet, this would imply in and of itself that a case-by-case analysis will be necessary in such scenarios, defeating the purpose of soft law measures aimed at providing transparent, reasonably general criteria for the assessment of aid. Such case-by-case analysis is likely to be complex, given the evolving, sophisticated character of economic sanctions: just two weeks after the TF, multiple other packages were adopted, including energy bans and the exclusion of Russian businesses from accessing European public procurement or EU money.

The above concerns show that temporary frameworks need to be used with caution. The question is what qualifies as an emergency, and what is the necessary urgency threshold that needs to be employed for consultations with the MS to be carried outside of the public domain. Different degrees of urgency can be noticed already between the Coronavirus TF and the Ukraine TF. In the case of the former, the unprecedented health crisis and lockdown measures called for intervention to keep jobs and salvage entire economic sectors. In the case of the latter, we notice that already in October 2021 the Commission advised that the state aid tool could be used in order to deal with the extraordinary increase in energy prices.[116] The seriousness of the crisis in Ukraine and the overspill on European markets cannot be contested, but one may wonder whether, in the future, a drought in the South of Europe would not also trigger the issuing of a Temporary Framework on the basis of Article 107 (3) (b) effectively putting in abeyance established rules and practices. Most worryingly, the trend to prolong these Temporary Frameworks potentially *ad infinitum* is confirmed by the recent recasting of the Ukraine TF into a Temporary Crisis and Transition Framework. We see here how security goals, combined with (nobler) environmental goals serve as a justification for using soft law to put on hold the hard law of the Treaty.

[114] Para 33 Ukraine TF (n 61 above).
[115] Para 52(c) Ukraine TF (n 61 above). Emphasis added.
[116] Commission, 'A toolbox for action and support' (n 113 above).

IV. Conclusion

The various combinations between hard and soft norms in the competition landscape match various challenges raised at the level of procedures, namely the decentralisation and its aftermaths. At the qualitative level we see that competition soft law is becoming increasingly a tool to promote environmental and social protection goals, or, in the case of individual guidance, any 'novel' issues. In State aid, soft law has been issued since the very beginning to orient the discretion of the European Commission in approving measures fulfilling a whole host of non-economic goals. This has allowed for whole policy sectors, such as energy, to be regulated initially through State aid guidance. A tendency to include more objective economic assessments is clear in the various modernisation packages, yet we see that following the Coronavirus pandemic and the Ukraine war, State aid rules have been effectively put in abeyance, with consequences that are yet to be witnessed.

Whilst it is difficult to contest the usefulness of these tools, which have been an established part of the regulatory landscape in these sectors for over half a century, their drawbacks need also to be considered. The relatively more transparent and more streamlined consultation procedures for competition and State aid soft law cannot necessarily make up for regulating, through such instruments, areas of shared competence such as environment or energy. The uncertain legal effects that soft law can produce in the multi-level EU context make individual guidance an awkward solution for clarifying 'novel' issues in antitrust. Finally, emergency soft law, issued following cursory consultations and challenging fundamental integration principles needs to be used with parsimony and care. Soft law is however not static and needs to be always considered in relationship with its regulatory environment. As such, it has either the potential to translate into hard law, if necessary, or to be changed because of the interactions with the stakeholders or as a result of its application in concrete cases. To improve soft law and to counteract its negative consequences one should start by focusing on these processes.

11

Unpacking Multilevel Elements in Digital Markets: Informing Effective Enforcement and Remedial Design in EU Competition Law

MARIA IOANNIDOU*

I. Introduction

The past three years have witnessed an unprecedented proliferation of discussions and policy reports about the adequacy of competition law rules and competition law enforcement to address the challenges in digital markets.[1] At European Union (EU) level, these discussions have culminated in the adoption of the Digital Market Act (DMA),[2] on regulating ex ante the conduct of digital gatekeepers,

* Senior Lecturer in Competition Law, Queen Mary University of London; former Commissioner-Rapporteur, Member of the Board, Hellenic Competition Commission, m.ioannidou@qmul.ac.uk.
I would like to thank Carlo Colombo, Mariolina Eliantonio, Kathryn Wright as well as the participants at the conference 'The Evolving Governance of EU Competition Law in Time of Disruptions: a Constitutional Perspective' (19 November 2020) for comments on earlier drafts. The views expressed herein, and any errors are the author's own. In accordance with the ASCOLA declaration of ethics, I have nothing to disclose.

[1] See, for example, Digital Competition Excerpt Panel, 'Unlocking Digital Competition: Report from the Digital Competition Expert Panel' (2019): www.gov.uk/government/publications/unlocking-digital-competition-report-of-the-digital-competition-expert-panel; Stigler Center, 'Committee for the Study of Digital Platforms: Report by the Market Structure and Antitrust Subcommittee' (2019): https://research.chicagobooth.edu/-/media/research/stigler/pdfs/market-structure---report-as-of-15-may-2019.pdf; J Crémer, Y de Montjoye and H Schweitzer, Competition Policy for the digital era: Final report (2019): https://ec.europa.eu/competition/publications/reports/kd0419345enn.pdf; Committee on the Judiciary (Subcommittee on Antitrust, Commercial and Administrative Law), 'Investigation of Competition in Digital Markets' (Majority Staff Report and Recommendations) (2020): www.govinfo.gov/content/pkg/CPRT-117HPRT47832/pdf/CPRT-117HPRT47832.pdf. Brazil, Russia, India, China and South Africa, Competition Law and Policy Centre, 'Digital Era Competition: a BRICS view' (2019): www.publications.hse.ru/mirror/pubs/share/direct/321442173.pdf.

[2] See Regulation (EU) 2022/1925 of the European Parliament and of the Council of 14 September 2022 on contestable and fair markets in the digital sector and amending Directives (EU) 2019/1937 and (EU) 2020/1828 (Digital Markets Act) [2022] OJ L265/1.

that is powerful digital platforms acting as gateways for business and end users alike.[3] These rules complement existing enforcement efforts. The Commission has concluded three cases against Google resulting in high fines[4] and two cases against Amazon resolved with commitments.[5] It has ongoing investigations into Google's adtech business,[6] Apple[7] and Facebook.[8] At the same time, many Member States have introduced or are in the process of introducing new rules to address the conduct of powerful platforms and many National Competition Authorities (NCAs) have launched enforcement action under domestic and EU competition law provisions.

At the legislative stage, NCAs and national regulators are particularly active and have proposed various changes in addition to (or beyond) the Commission proposals, which seek to capture conduct by digital gatekeepers. These proposals, even when they concern changes to competition law (as an ex post tool), have an ex ante regulatory undertone and create a variable legislative geometry between various Member States and the EU. *With respect to enforcement*, enforcement efforts by competition authorities at national and EU level result in parallel cases running against the same companies – often for similar, if not identical, conduct.[9]

This chapter will highlight in particular those multilevel elements and their respective impact on EU competition law enforcement governance in a bid to propose improvements in the enforcement apparatus and remedial design. Remedial design in digital markets is more complex than in more 'traditional' market settings, since it may call for proactive remedies such as the redesign of a product or changing certain core business models.[10] In addition to this complexity due to the nature and timing of intervention within competition law enforcement,[11] various regulatory initiatives at Member State and EU level render remedial design

[3] Gatekeepers are suppliers of core platform services (Art 2(2) DMA) that meet certain criteria (Art 3(1) DMA) and size-based thresholds (Art 3(2) DMA).

[4] Commission Decision of 27 June 2017 relating to the proceedings under Article 102 of the Treaty on the Functioning of the European Union and Article 54 of the Agreement on the European Economic Area COM(2017) 4444 final (Google Search (Shopping)); Commission Decision of 18 July 2018 relating to a proceeding under Article 102 of the Treaty on the Functioning of the European Union (the Treaty) and Article 54 of the EEA Agreement Com(2018) 4761 final (Google Android); Commission Decision of 20 March 2019 relating to a proceeding under Article 102 of the Treaty on the Functioning of the European Union and Article 54 of the EEA Agreement (Case AT.40411 Google Search AdSense) [2020] OJ C369/6.

[5] Commission Decision of 20 December 2022 relating to a proceeding under Article 102 of the Treaty on the Functioning of the European Union (TFEU) and Article 54 of EEA Agreement (Cases AT.40462 Amazon Marketplace and AT.40703 Amazon Buy Box) [2022] OJ C87/7.

[6] Case AT.40670 Google – Adtech and Data-related practices.

[7] Case AT.40437 Apple – App Store Practices (music streaming); Case AT.40652 Apple – App Store Practices (e-books/audiobooks); Case AT.40452 Apple – Mobile Payments – Apple Pay.

[8] Case AT.40684 Facebook Marketplace.

[9] For case law examples see section II.B.ii below.

[10] See PI Colomo, 'The Role and Limits of Competition Law in Digital Markets: On the Reports and the Reforms Proposed' (2021) 29 *Zeitschrift für Europäisches Privatrecht* 8.

[11] See P Van Cleynenbruegel, 'Digital Technology Disruptions and Competition Law: a Stress Test for the Existing Governance and Enforcement Frameworks?', Ch 2 in this volume.

even more complicated. First, this chapter begins by discussing these emerging *multilevel elements* and highlights the *governance* and *constitutional challenges* they pose. Constitutional challenges include the impact of such multilevel elements on the *distribution of competences in EU competition law enforcement* as well as *general principles of EU law*, in particular the principle of sincere cooperation, legal certainty and ne bis in idem. Then, and in light of these developments, the chapter puts forward the normative argument calling for better cooperation mechanisms and more flexibility in remedial design rather than resorting to prescriptive rules.

II. Unpacking the Multilevel Elements

Section II discusses first legislative developments at EU and Member States level (multilevel legislative efforts) (section II.A). At EU level, it presents different regulatory instruments complementing EU competition law, in particular the Digital Markets Act (DMA)[12] and the Platform-to-Business (P2B) regulation.[13] Second, section II covers multilevel enforcement and, in particular, instances where competition law provisions and regulation may be applicable against the same conduct as well as instances where NCAs and the Commission have invoked competition law against the same digital gatekeepers, sometimes also involving similar conduct. It also discusses the emerging increase in private enforcement (section II.B). The aim of the discussion is to highlight the governance challenges that the herein identified multilevel elements pose for competition law enforcement. Such governance challenges impact and test EU constitutional principles (section II.C).

A. Multilevel Legislative Efforts

Several national competition laws have already been amended or are in the process of being amended (in Belgium, Bulgaria, Austria, Romania, Lithuania, Iceland, Germany and Greece).[14] This proliferation of rules, to some extent, risks the fragmentation of the EU legal framework and points to the need for coordination or possibly orchestrated harmonisation.[15] In order to highlight this point, section II.A first discusses the DMA and the P2B Regulation and then the amendment of the German competition law as an example from the Member States' perspective.

[12] See Regulation (EU) 2022/1925 (DMA) (n 2 above).

[13] Regulation (EU) 2019/1150 of the European Parliament and of the Council of 20 June 2019 on promoting fairness and transparency for business users of online intermediation services [2019] OJ L186/57 (P2B Regulation).

[14] 'Summary of the contributions of the National Competition Authorities to the impact assessment of the new competition tool' (2020). www.ec.europa.eu/competition/consultations/2020_new_comp_tool/summary_contributions_NCAs_responses. pdf, 11.

[15] Commission, 'Impact Assessment Report accompanying the Proposal for a Digital Markets Act' (Staff Working Document) SWD(2020) 363 final, 108 ff.

i. Digital Markets Act

By pointing to 'the continuum between competition law and the DMA', the NCAs have welcomed this new regulation, which built on the Commission's and NCAs' enforcement activities in the digital sector in the last 20 years.[16] The NCAs view the DMA as an additional ex ante regulatory tool complementing the deterrent effect of competition law enforcement, both by public authorities and private parties.[17] The DMA aims at ensuring contestability and fairness in markets, where gatekeepers are active, whereas it explicitly distinguishes its objectives from the protection of undistorted competition.[18] In as much as the DMA's protective scope is different to EU competition law as well as national competition laws, the DMA proclaims that it is without prejudice to their application.[19] Yet, their relationship would need to be better specified,[20] since it risks the invocation of two sets of rules (the ex ante regulatory DMA and ex post competition law provisions) against similar conduct.[21]

In terms of enforcement, the Commission has sole enforcement responsibility for the DMA,[22] since only the Commission can designate gatekeepers, clarify their respective obligations, monitor their compliance and impose sanctions and even behavioural and structural remedies in case of systemic non-compliance. However, designating the Commission as the sole enforcement authority for the DMA does not avoid the risk of fragmentation, since NCAs can still apply EU and national competition law against gatekeepers. Such NCAs' enforcement precedes the DMA and may as well follow its adoption, thereby highlighting the need for coordinated enforcement.

In order to alleviate the risk of fragmentation and bolster coordination, the DMA explicitly requires that the Commission and national authorities cooperate closely and coordinate their enforcement actions to achieve 'a coherent, effective and complementary enforcement of available legal instruments'.[23] The DMA makes

[16] European Competition Network, 'Joint paper of the heads of the national competition authorities of the European Union: How national competition agencies can strengthen the DMA' (2021), para 14.

[17] ibid para 12.

[18] DMA (n 2 above) Recitals 5, 10 and 11.

[19] DMA (n 2 above) Art 1(6). The draft DMA (Commission proposal) mentioned explicitly that '[t]he current proposal minimises the detrimental structural effects of unfair practices ex ante, without limiting the ability to intervene ex post under EU and national competition rules', 4. See DMA (n 2 above).

[20] In this context, see the common position paper published by Germany, France and the Netherlands on 27 May 2021 calling for a clearer specification of the relation of the DMA to European competition law and a strengthening of Member States' role in DMA's enforcement, amongst others. See 'Strengthening the Digital Markets Act and Its Enforcement: www.bmwk.de/Redaktion/DE/Downloads/M-O/non-paper-friends-of-an-effective-digital-markets-act.pdf?__blob=publicationFile&v=4. See also P Akman, 'Regulating Competition in Digital Platform Markets: A Critical Assessment of the Framework and Approach of the EU Digital Markets Act' (2022) 47 *European Law Review* 85.

[21] For a discussion see G Monti, 'The Digital Markets Act – Institutional Design and Suggestions for Improvement' (*Tilburg Law and Economics Center 04/2021*) 14–15.

[22] DMA (n 2 above) Recital 91.

[23] DMA (n 2 above) Art 37.

specific provisions for the cooperation and coordination between the Commission and NCAs through the European Competition Network (ECN).[24] NCAs have an obligation to inform the Commission when they intend to launch an investigation on gatekeepers under EU competition law and such information may be made available to other NCAs.[25] In addition, where a NCA is contemplating to impose obligations on gatekeepers based on national competition laws (including national competition rules that prohibit other forms of unilateral conduct insofar as they are applicable to undertakings other than gatekeepers or impose additional obligations on gatekeepers) it shall, no later than 30 days before its adoption, share the draft measure with the Commission explaining the reasons for the measure. Such information may be communicated to other NCAs as well.[26] NCAs, if so allowed by national law, may – on their own initiative – conduct an investigation into a case of possible non-compliance with gatekeepers' obligations on their territory. However, NCAs cannot impose any sanctions under the DMA. They can only inform the Commission, which may then open its own investigation and thereby relieve the NCA of its competences.[27] The DMA also provides for cooperation between the Commission and national courts.[28] In a similar vein as when they apply EU competition law,[29] national courts shall not give a decision running counter to a decision adopted by the Commission under the DMA. In addition, they must also avoid issuing a decision which would conflict with a contemplated Commission decision and may assess whether it is necessary to stay their proceedings to that effect.[30]

With respect to the origin, nature and future evolution of the DMA, one cannot deny the close links with competition law enforcement, despite the ex ante nature of the DMA. Such links are also reflected in the proposed enforcement powers of the Commission in the DMA, since the Commission's enforcement (eg request of information, powers to take statements/interviews, powers to carry inspections), remedial and sanctioning powers (interim measures, commitments and fines)[31] resemble the enforcement toolbox in Regulation 1/2003.[32] As a corollary, such substantive rules and enforcement powers should be complemented by similar cooperation and coordination mechanism provided for in Regulation 1/2003.[33]

[24] ibid Art 38.
[25] ibid Art 38(2).
[26] ibid Art 38(3).
[27] ibid Art 38(7).
[28] ibid Art 39.
[29] See Council Regulation (EC) No 1/2003 of 16 December 2002 on the implementation of the rules on competition laid down in Articles 81 and 82 of the Treaty [2003] OJ L1/01, Art 16.
[30] DMA (n 2 above) Art 39 (5).
[31] ibid Chapter 5.
[32] Regulation 1/2003 (n 29 above). On June 30, 2022, the Commission has launched a public consultation on possible amendments to Regulation 1/2003. See Press Release, 'Antitrust: Commission seeks feedback on performance of EU antitrust enforcement framework' www.ec.europa.eu/commission/presscorner/detail/en/ip_22_4194.
[33] On the point that a similar ECN type cooperation framework should be set up for the application of the DMA see European Competition Network, 'Joint paper' (n 16 above) para 26.

This has been addressed to some extent in the DMA. Arguably, the centralised enforcement model may avoid fragmentation in the application of the new rules. However, in as much as there are observed overlaps in the prescribed obligations in the DMA and cases against Big Tech brought by the Commission and NCAs, the risk of fragmentation remains and may be exacerbated by the potential application of the DMA before national courts.

ii. P2B Regulation

P2B Regulation is applicable to online intermediation services and online search engines, introducing new rules to promote fairness and transparency for business users.[34] The DMA has also fairness as a driving consideration within a more limited personal scope of application. The P2B Regulation introduces the baseline of transparency and fairness rules applicable to all online platforms regardless of their size whereas the DMA is applicable to a limited number of very large platforms – gatekeepers. Despite though the similarity in their respective objectives and the complementarity of the rules, the enforcement approach is different. The P2B Regulation puts forward an essentially private enforcement system and different remedies. On the one hand, the DMA calls for public enforcement action by the Commission, while allowing private actions, and on the other the P2B regulation relies primarily on the actions of private parties.[35]

iii. 10th Amendment – German Competition Act

The new German rules took effect on 19 January 2021, and amongst others, target structural competition law problems to prevent market tipping and the leveraging of powerful platforms' market power into adjacent markets.[36] Section 19(a) aims to prevent powerful platforms from entrenching their position in other markets. Under this provision, the German NCA can designate undertakings with 'paramount significance for competition across markets' and provides for a list of factors for declaring such position. If an undertaking is found to have 'paramount significance for competition across markets', then section 19a (2) provides an indicative list of prohibited conducts which include self-preferencing, leveraging (particularly by means of data), envelopment, market tipping and constraining data portability.[37] Section 19a (2) prohibits such conduct without establishing an

[34] P2B Regulation (n 13 above).

[35] C Caufmann, 'New EU Rules on Business-to Consumer and Platform-to Business Relationships' (2019) 26 *Maastricht Journal of European and Comparative Law* 469.

[36] See T Weck, 'The New Abuse Rules in the German Competition Act – What's in it for the EU?', *Competition Policy International*, 14 April 2020: www.competitionpolicyinternational.com/the-new-abuse-rules-in-the-german-competition-act-whats-in-it-for-the-eu/. Competition Act of 26 June 2013 (as amended) (*Gesetz gegen Wettbewerbsbeschränkungen*).

[37] According to the President of the Bundeskartellamt, German Competition Act is broader than the DMA, since it provides only some examples yet leaving space for identifying new anticompetitive

exclusionary effect, and in that respect it is different to the application of Article 102 of the Treaty on the Functioning of the Union (TFEU), yet the undertaking bears the burden to put forward an objective justification. The Bundeskartellamt has already launched section 19a (1) proceedings against Google, Amazon, Facebook and Apple (GAFA).[38]

Regarding market tipping, a new section 20(3)(a) is added, which will be applied below the threshold of dominance and prohibit the creation of an 'unfair impediment' for competitors. Section 20 though has been traditionally a private enforcement instrument – with the first injunction already brought before the Berlin Regional Court.[39] Very important here is the time of intervention and the remedies adopted, as if competition authorities intervene too little too late, they run the risk that the market has already tipped. The amendments will also facilitate the granting of interim measures (section 32a) and the authority's powers to grant access to data.

B. Multilevel Enforcement Efforts

The proliferation of different regulatory instruments, some of which were discussed in section II.A above, in conjunction with the increased invocation of EU and national competition law provisions against Big Tech, results in a complex enforcement landscape. Section II.B threads out certain overlapping and parallel enforcement actions, which may raise governance and constitutional challenges.

i. Member States Level: Competition Law, P2B Regulation and Abuse of Economic Dependence

Competition law has been proven as a very powerful tool to address problematic conduct by powerful platforms. A good example here is the Amazon case in Germany. Even before its latest amendment discussed above, national competition law applied to practices now partially caught by the P2B Regulation. The German NCA has started an investigation into Amazon's retail business, which ended with Amazon's commitment to amend its business services agreement worldwide, ahead of the EU probe.[40] These amendments address various sellers' complaints

conduct. See J Espinoza and E Solomon, 'EU draft tech rules too 'narrow', says German competition head', *Financial Times*, 14 July 2021: www.ft.com/content/6cff1987-9263-4bc6-8d8d-6426ef303325.

[38] See section II.B.ii below.

[39] See P Offergeld, 'Bundeskartellamt in Action', *D'Kart Antitrust Blog*, 25 June 2021: www.d-kart.de/en/blog/2021/06/25/bundeskartellamt-in-action/

[40] Press Release, 'Bundeskartellamt obtains far-reaching improvements in the terms of business for sellers on Amazon's online marketplaces' (2019): www.bundeskartellamt.de/SharedDocs/Meldung/EN/Pressemitteilungen/2019/17_07_2019_Amazon.html. See also similar probe by the Austrian National Competition Authority. Press Release, 'BWB informs: Amazon modifies its terms and conditions' (2019): www.bwb.gv.at/en/news/detail/bwb-informs-amazon-modifies-its-terms-and-conditions-1.

about the unilateral exclusion of liability to Amazon's benefit. Amazon amended its liability provisions bringing them in conformity with European standards. Complaints also concerned the termination as well as blocking of sellers' accounts. Amazon committed to give 30 days' notice prior to termination of a seller's account and change its jurisdiction clause allowing, under certain conditions, the dispute to be brought before domestic courts, thus changing Luxembourg as the only court of jurisdiction. Further, Amazon changed its rules on returns and reimbursement. With respect to product information and the rights of use, sellers can now use material of higher quality or more specific product information and descriptions/images on other websites, thus the 'parity requirement' seized to apply. Also, with respect to product reviews and sellers' rating now Amazon's own 'Vine' rating programme, which previously was only available to suppliers of Amazon Retail, will be gradually made available to those marketplace sellers which own a brand name registered with Amazon.[41]

During the proceedings, the German NCA was in close contact with the Commission, and had also exchanged information on these proceedings with other competition authorities.[42] In particular, the Bundeskartellamt had intensive discussions with the Austrian and Luxembourgish NCAs since they were also investigating Amazon practices at the time.[43] The Austrian NCA closed its proceedings on the same day referring to the close cooperation with their German counterpart.[44] In this case the German NCA managed to secure commitments that applied globally, which shows that NCAs may rise as quasi global regulatory authorities.[45]

Apart from the P2B Regulation, practices by powerful platforms not directly caught by competition law, may fall under *the rules on abuse of economic dependence*. National competition laws in some Member States, such as Germany, France and more recently Belgium,[46] contain provisions prohibiting the abuse of economic dependence and indicate a revived appetite to invoke such provisions. The French NCA, for example, has invoked the respective national provisions after

[41] Press Release, 'Bundeskartellamt obtains far-reaching improvements' (n 40 above).

[42] ibid.

[43] ibid.

[44] Press Release, 'BWB informs' (n 40 above). See also S Heinz, 'Bundeskartellamt ends abuse probe after Amazon agrees to changing business terms for dealers', *Kluwer Competition Law* Blog, 30 July 2019: https://competitionlawblog.kluwercompetitionlaw.com/2019/07/30/bundeskartellamt-ends-abuse-probe-after-amazon-agrees-to-changing-business-terms-for-dealers/.

[45] See also the Google adtech case in France, D Katsifis, 'The Autorité de la concurrence hands out a €220 millions fine' (n 52 above).

[46] The respective prohibition in Belgium was published in the Official Gazette on 12 August and entered into force on 22 August 2020. See Belgian Competition Authority, 'Entry into force of abuses of economic dependence' (13 August 2020) (Press Release No 32/2020): www.belgiancompetition.be/sites/default/files/content/download/files/20200813_press_release_32_bca.pdf.

almost a decade, imposing a fine against Apple for abusing its economic power over its resellers amongst others.[47]

ii. Parallel Actions: Public Competition Law Enforcement

In anticipation of the DMA entering into force,[48] enforcement actions against GAFA keep mounting both at Member States and EU level with no signs of abating.[49] At the time of writing there is a number of completed cases as well as ongoing investigations against Google in the EU,[50] in Germany (under the newly amended German competition law),[51] in France[52] and Italy.[53] Amazon has seen its cases resolved with commitments in the EU,[54] and has been under scrutiny in Germany,[55] and Italy as well,[56] while Facebook is under investigation in the EU,[57]

[47] On abuse of economic dependence see D Mantzari, 'Power Imbalances in Online Marketplaces: At the Crossroads of Competition Law and Regulation' (*Center for Law, Economics and Society, University College London, Research Paper Series 4/2021*).

[48] See DMA (n 2 above).

[49] Digital giants face enforcement actions in multiple jurisdictions. For the purposes of this chapter the focus is on enforcement activity in the EU.

[50] See section I above.

[51] Press Release, 'Bundeskartellamt examines Google News Showcase': www.bundeskartellamt.de/SharedDocs/Meldung/EN/Pressemitteilungen/2021/04_06_2021_Google_Showcase.html; Press Release, 'Alphabet/Google subject to new abuse control applicable to large digital companies – Bundeskartellamt determines "paramount significance across markets"' (2022): www.bundeskartellamt.de/SharedDocs/Meldung/EN/Pressemitteilungen/2022/05_01_2022_Google_19a.html.

[52] Press Release, 'The Autorité de la concurrence hands out a €220 millions fine to Google for favouring its own services in the online advertising sector' (2021): www.autoritedelaconcurrence.fr/en/press-release/autorite-de-la-concurrence-hands-out-eu220-millions-fine-google-favouring-its-own.

[53] Press Release, 'A529–ICA: Google fined over 100 million for abuse of dominant position' (2021): www.en.agcm.it/en/media/press-releases/2021/5/A529; Press Release, 'A542–ICA: investigation opened against Google for an alleged abuse of dominant position in the Italian market for display advertising' (2020): https://en.agcm.it/en/media/press-releases/2020/10/A542.

[54] See section I above.

[55] Press Release, 'Amazon now subject to stricter regulations – Bundeskartellamt determines its paramount significance for competition across markets (Section 19a GWB)' (2022): www.bundeskartellamt.de/SharedDocs/Meldung/EN/Pressemitteilungen/2022/06_07_2022_Amazon.html; L Hornkohl, 'Brand Gating: German Competition Authority Once Again Launches An Investigation Into Amazon (and Apple)', *Kluwer Competition Law Blog*, 6 November 2020: https://competitionlawblog.kluwercompetitionlaw.com/2020/11/06/brand-gating-german-competition-authority-once-again-launches-an-investigation-into-amazon-and-apple/.

[56] Press Release, 'I842–ICA: investigation launched against Apple and Amazon for banning the sale of Apple- and Beats-branded products to retailers who do not join the official programme' (2020): https://en.agcm.it/en/media/press-releases/2020/7/I842; Press Release, 'A528–Amazon: avviata istruttoria su possibile abuso di posizione dominante in marketplace e-commerce e servizi di logistica' (2019): www.agcm.it/media/comunicati-stampa/2019/4/Amazon-avviata-istruttoria-su-possibile-abuso-di-posizione-dominante-in-marketplace-e-commerce-e-servizi-di-logistica.

[57] See section I above.

Germany[58] and France.[59] Apple is under scrutiny in the EU,[60] the Netherlands,[61] Germany[62] and Italy.[63]

Some of these cases against Big Tech look at similar practices, often simultaneously, which may create cooperation problems and lead to fragmentation, jeopardising legal certainty and the consistent application of EU competition law. A good example here is the EU Commission Amazon case and the parallel probe in Italy. On 17 July 2019, the European Commission opened its first investigation against Amazon focusing on Amazon's use of sensitive data from independent retailers, who sell their products on its marketplace.[64] The Commission has sent a Statement of Objection to Amazon with respect to this first investigation and opened a second investigation into Amazon's e-commerce practices looking at whether Amazon afforded preferential treatment to its retail offers and those of third party sellers that use Amazon's logistics and delivery services.[65] According to the Statement of Objections, the use of non-public marketplace seller data enables Amazon to substitute normal risks of competition and to leverage its dominant position in the market for the provision of marketplace services in France and Germany, which are the biggest markets for Amazon in the EU.[66] With respect to the second investigation, the Commission announced that it will cover the whole European Economic Area, except Italy, since the Italian NCA started to investigate

[58] Press Release, 'Bundeskartellamt examines linkage between Oculus and the Facebook network' (2021): www.bundeskartellamt.de/SharedDocs/Meldung/EN/Pressemitteilungen/2020/10_12_2020_Facebook_Oculus.html?nn=3591568; Press Release, 'New rules apply to Meta (formerly Facebook) – Bundeskartellamt determines its "paramount significance for competition across markets"' (2022): www.bundeskartellamt.de/SharedDocs/Meldung/EN/Pressemitteilungen/2022/04_05_2022_Facebook_19a.htm; Press Release, 'Bundeskartellamt prohibits Facebook from combining user data from different sources' (2019): www.bundeskartellamt.de/SharedDocs/Meldung/EN/Pressemitteilungen/2019/07_02_2019_Facebook.html.

[59] Press Release, 'Dans le cadre d'une instruction ouverte devant l'Autorité dans le secteur de la publicité en ligne, Facebook propose des engagements' (2021): www.autoritedelaconcurrence.fr/fr/communiques-de-presse/dans-le-cadre-dune-instruction-ouverte-devant-lautorite-dans-le-secteur-de-la.

[60] See section I above.

[61] Authority for Consumers and Markets, 'ACM launches investigation into abuse of dominance by Apple in its App Store' (2019): www.acm.nl/en/publications/acm-launches-investigation-abuse-dominance-apple-its-app-store; Authority for Consumers and Markets, 'ACM can continue its investigation into the Apple App Store' (2021): www.acm.nl/en/publications/acm-can-continue-its-investigation-apple-app-store.

[62] Press Release, 'Proceeding against Apple based on new rules for large digital companies (Section 19a(1) GWB) – Bundeskartellamt examines Apple's significance for competition across markets' (2021): www.bundeskartellamt.de/SharedDocs/Meldung/EN/Pressemitteilungen/2021/21_06_2021_Apple.html. Press Release, 'Bundeskartellamt reviews Apple's tracking rules for third-party apps' (2022): www.bundeskartellamt.de/SharedDocs/Meldung/EN/Pressemitteilungen/2022/14_06_2022_Apple.html?nn=3591568.

[63] In Italy and Germany for brand-gating agreements with Amazon. See Hornkohl, 'Brand Gating' (n 55 above) and Press Release, 'A528–Amazon' (n 56 above).

[64] Case AT. 40462 (n 6 above).

[65] Case AT.40703 (n 6 above).

[66] ibid.

partially similar concerns a year before in the Italian market. The Commission committed to continue the close cooperation with the Italian NCA throughout the investigation.[67] Both Commission cases have now been resolved with commitments.[68]

While the Commission investigation was ongoing, the Italian NCA imposed a record fine of 1.1 billion euros and behavioural remedies on Amazon for leveraging to favour its own logistics service – Fulfilment by Amazon (FBA) – to the detriment of rival logistics businesses.[69] Amazon has challenged the Commission decision to carve out Italy from its respective investigation, since according to the company, there is an overlap in the scope of the two investigations. The General Court (GC) dismissed the action as inadmissible, since the Commission decision to open an investigation was of a preliminary nature.[70] The GC concluded that the fact that the Commission excluded Italy from the scope of its investigation is a purely procedural consequence arising from the initiation of that investigation, does not affect Amazon's legal situation and does not transform the decision initiating proceedings into a challengeable act.[71] This is despite the fact that – as Amazon claims – first, the company had to defend itself before two different authorities and, second, the parallel proceedings risk leading to a divergent application of EU competition law and divergent penalties.[72] According to the GC, this risk would not flow from the decision to initiate proceedings but rather it would be a consequence of the final decisions.[73] The GC decision has now been upheld by the CJEU that noted that since the territorial scope of the Commission proceedings was different, then the protection against parallel proceedings under Article 11(6) of Regulation 1/2003 did not apply.[74]

Apart from the Amazon case, where the point of parallel probes was expressly raised, there are other examples of multilevel enforcement. Investigations into Google's adtech business in France, the EU and Italy also present a good example. On 8 June 2021, the French NCA has imposed a 220 million euro fine and rendered binding the commitments offered by Google for alleged abusive conduct

[67] ibid.

[68] See n 5 above.

[69] Press Release, 'A528 – Italian Competition Authority: Amazon fined over € 1,128 billion for abusing its dominant position' (2021): https://en.agcm.it/en/media/press-releases/2021/12/A528. At the time of writing, Amazon has offered commitments to address the identified competition concerns in the Commission investigation. Such commitments exclude Italy with respect to the Buy Box and Prime since the Italian NCA had already imposed remedies on Amazon in the Italian market. See Press Release, 'Antitrust: Commission seeks feedback on commitments offered by Amazon concerning marketplace seller data and access to Buy Box and Prime' (2022): www.ec.europa.eu/commission/presscorner/detail/el/IP_22_4522

[70] Case T-19/21 *Amazon v Commission* [2021] EU:T:2021:730.

[71] Case T-19/21 *Amazon v Commission* (n 70 above) para 34.

[72] ibid para 35.

[73] ibid para 36.

[74] Case C-815/21 *Amazon v Commission*, ECLI:EU:C:2023:308, para 34.

in the adtech industry.[75] The French NCA was the first to impose a fine on Google for favouring its own services in the online advertising sector to the detriment of competitors and publishers. Most importantly the French NCA in the first decision worldwide to look into Google's advertising algorithmic auction processes, secured commitments that will change the way its advertising service DoubleClick For Publishers (DFP) and its sales platform AdX function, with changes being made not only in France but worldwide.[76] The Italian NCA is also looking into Google's advertising practices and in particular into Google's potential discriminatory use of data for display advertising.[77] On 22 June 2021, the Commission has launched an investigation into Google's online display advertising business.[78] The Commission investigation looks into the apparent favouring of AdX by DV360 and/or Google Ads and the potential favouring of DV360 and/or Google Ads by AdX. The French NCA sanctioned similar practices. The Commission, similarly, to the Italian probe, will also examine whether Google's conduct with respect to the treatment of users' data available to Google's own advertising intermediation services and restrictions on access by third parties (advertisers, publishers and competing online display advertising intermediaries) for advertising purposes are abusive.

Apple is another case with probes running in parallel. The Dutch NCA has announced that its investigation into Apple App store practices can proceed in parallel with the EU probe with the two authorities maintaining regular discussions.[79] It has ordered Apple to adjust the unreasonable App Store conditions applicable to dating-app providers within two months, or else pay a periodic penalty of five million euros per week up to a maximum of 50 million euros.[80]

iii. *Multiple Actions: Private Enforcement*

Apart from public enforcement actions, there is a growing number of private actions against digital platforms. The public enforcement actions presented above may

[75] See Katsifis, 'The Autorité de la concurrence hands out a €220 millions fine' (n 52 above). On this case see D Katsifis, 'Google fined € 220 million by French Autorité de la concurrence for breaching competition law in ad tech offers commitments', *The Platform Law Blog*, 8 June 2021: https://theplatformlaw.blog/2021/06/08/google-fined-e-220-million-by-french-autorite-de-la-concurrence-for-breaching-competition-law-in-ad-tech-offers-commitments/.

[76] See M Gomri, 'Some Changes to Our Ad Technology', *Google in Europe*, 7 June 2021: https://blog.google/around-the-globe/google-europe/some-changes-our-ad-technology/.

[77] See above n 53.

[78] Case AT.40670 (n 6 above).

[79] See Authority for Consumers and Markets, 'ACM can continue its investigation into the Apple App Store' (2021): www.acm.nl/en/publications/acm-can-continue-its-investigation-apple-app-store.

[80] Authority for Consumers and Markets, 'ACM obliges Apple to adjust unreasonable conditions for its App Store' (2021): www.acm.nl/en/publications/acm-obliges-apple-adjust-unreasonable-conditions-its-app-store. Authority for Consumers and Markets, 'Apple changes unfair conditions, allows alternative payments methods in dating apps' (2022) www.acm.nl/en/publications/acm-apple-changes-unfair-conditions-allows-alternative-payments-methods-dating-apps.

also trigger follow-on damages actions.[81] Yet, it is true that private actions emerge in those jurisdictions that have a rather established culture of private competition litigation and a system that gives incentives to litigants to pursue such actions. The EU Google cases have prompted private litigation in the United Kingdom (UK),[82] Germany[83] and France.[84] Similarly, the Apple App store public enforcement cases have prompted collective actions in the UK with a case filed to the UKs Competition Appeal Tribunal. According to this case, Apple's 30 per cent commission fee on the App Store constitutes an abuse and should be compensated.[85]

C. Multilevel Elements and Constitutional Challenges

The multilevel elements discussed above may challenge the distribution of competences between the Commission and NCAs. The principle of sincere cooperation, legal certainty and ne bis in idem may aide in addressing cooperation and enforcement challenges, yet the multiplication of legislative and enforcement efforts point to their respective limits. The principle of loyalty/sincere cooperation enshrined in Article 4(3) of the Treaty of the European Union (TEU) concerns primarily the vertical relationship between the EU and Member States, though it also applies horizontally among Member States.[86] It constitutes an 'institutional' or 'structural' general principle shaping the 'institutional space' and 'deep structure' of the EU. Legal certainty and ne bis in idem derive from the rule of law and are linked to the protection of individuals.[87]

[81] On the binding effect of NCAs decisions see Directive 2014/104/EU of the European Parliament and of the Council and of the Council of 26 November 2014 on certain rules governing actions for damages under national law for infringements of the competition law provisions of the Member States and of the European Union [2014] OJ L349/01, Art 9.

[82] See, for example, High Court, Chancery Division, *Streetmap EU Ltd v Google* [2016] EWHC 253 (CH) (12 February 2016). See also actions by Foundem and Kelkoo. G Corfield, '£1bn lawsuit by Google Shopping rival staggers back to feet in London High Court' (2021): www.theregister.com/2021/06/23/google_kelkoo_high_court_1bn_lawsuit_order/.

[83] C Gluz, 'Idealo verklagt Google auf Schadensersatz wegen Missbrauchs seiner marktbeherrschenden Stellung' (2019): www.idealo.de/magazin/e-commerce/idealo-verklagt-google?cmpReload=true.

[84] In France see, for example, FY Chee, 'Google faces damages claim from French rival 1PlusV', *Reuters*, 28 June 2011.

[85] Competition Appeal Tribunal, *Rachel Kent v Apple Inc and Apple Distribution International Ltd* [2021] 1403/7/7/21. Notice of an application to commence collective proceedings under section 47B of the Competition Act 1998. On this case in the US see M Ioannidou, 'Apple v. Pepper: Rethinking Standing Rules in Private Antitrust Litigation' in N Charbit and S Gachot (eds), *Herbert Hovenkamp – The Dean of American Antitrust Law, Liber Amicorum* (Paris, Concurrences, 2021).

[86] M Claes, 'The Equality of the Member States' in K Ziegler, P Neuvonen and V Moreno-Lax (eds), *Research Handbook on General Principles in EU Law* (Cheltenham, Edward Elgar 2022).

[87] On the distinction see P Neuvonen and K Ziegler, 'General Principles in the EU Legal Order: Past, Present and Future Directions' in Ziegler, Neuvonen and Moreno-Lax (eds), *Research Handbook* (n 86 above). With further references to T Tridimas, *The General Principles of EU Law* 2nd edn (Oxford, Oxford University Press, 2007) 4–5; B de Witte, 'Institutional Principles: A Special Category of General Principles of EC Law' in U Bernitz and J Nergelius (eds), *General Principles of European Community Law* (Aphen aan den Rijn, Kluwer Law International, 2000); M Wimmer, 'The Dinghy's

Parallel investigations run the risk of inconsistent decisions and different remedial approaches. In addition, the adoption of the DMA as well as changes in national competition laws, such as the ones in Germany, aggravate such risk. The enforcement experience to date reveals that the Commission and NCAs make every effort to cooperate. Yet, in certain instances, such cooperation may not be enough. In *Amazon* the GC, even though the action was dismissed on procedural grounds, implicitly appears to accept that there may be a risk of fragmentation flowing from final decisions.[88]

Further, multilevel legislative and enforcement efforts may lead to a multiplication of sanctions, which can be limited by the principle of ne bis in idem, as enshrined in Article 50 of the Charter of Fundamental Rights of the European Union (CFR).[89] This principle essentially precludes to punish someone twice for the same conduct and essentially answers the question, '[h]ow many competition authorities in Europe [and/or regulatory authorities] may deal with one and the same [conduct] and impose penalties on the participating undertakings?'.[90] In competition law the Court of Justice of the European Union (CJEU) devised a three-fold test – as opposed to the general two-fold test.[91] In competition law cases, the ne bis in idem principle is applicable when the facts, the offender and the protected legal interest are the same.[92] More recently it clarified its case law in *BPost*[93] and *Nordzucker*.[94] The first case concerns the concurrent enforcement of competition law and regulation, whereas the second concerns the parallel enforcement of EU and national competition laws. Following these judgments, the CJEU limits the three conditions of the ne bis in idem test, to the same persons and set of facts, thereby bringing the examination of the principle in competition law enforcement in line with other areas of EU law.[95] However, the protected legal interest may be taken into account as a justification for a possible limitation of the fundamental right guaranteed by Article 50 CFR under Article 52(1) CFR.

Rudder: General Principles of European Union Law through the Lens of Proportionality' (2014) 20 *European Public Law* 331, 334.

[88] See text to n 70 above.

[89] Charter of Fundamental Rights of the European Union [2012] OJ C 326/391.

[90] Paraphrasing AG Kokott in Case C-17/10 *Toshiba Corporation and others v Úřad pro ochranu hospodářské soutěže* [2011] EU:C:2011:389, para 1.

[91] See Case C-524/15 *Criminal proceedings against Luca Menci* [2018] EU:C:2018:197; Case C-537/16 *Garlsson Real Estate and others v Commissione Nazionale per le Società e la Borsa (Consob)* [2018] EU:C:2018:193; Joined cases C-596/16 and C-597/16 *Enzo Di Puma v Commissione Nazionale per le Società e la Borsa (Consob) and Commissione Nazionale per le Società e la Borsa (Consob) v Antonio Zecca* [2018] EU:C:2018:192.

[92] Case C-17/10 *Toshiba Corporation and others v Úřad pro ochranu hospodářské soutěže* (n 90 above) para 97. Joined cases C-204/00 P, C-205/00 P, C-211/00 P, C-213/00 P, C-217/00 P and C-219/00 P *Aalborg Portland and Others v Commission* [2004] EU:C:2004:6, para 338. For a discussion of the relevant case law see Opinion of AG Wahl in Case C-617/17 *Powszechny Zaklad Ubezpieczen na Życie v Prezes Urzędu Ochrony Konkurencji i Konsumentów* [2018] EU:C:2018:976.

[93] Case C-117/20 *Bpost SA v Autorité belge de la concurrence* [2022] EU:C:2022:202.

[94] Case C-151/20 *Bundeswettbewerbsbehörde v Nordzucker* [2022] EU:C:2022:203.

[95] Case C-117/20 *Bpost SA v Autorité belge de la concurrence* (n 93 above) paras 28, 35. Case C-151/20 *Bundeswettbewerbsbehörde v Nordzucker* (n 94 above) para 40.

According to the CJEU in *BPost* 'a duplication of proceedings and penalties respects the *essence of Article 50 CFR*, provided that the national legislation … *provides only for the possibility of a duplication of proceedings and penalties under different legislation*'.[96] Such limitation is proportionate provided that the duplication does not represent an excessive burden for the implicated undertakings.[97] The protected legal interest is to be taken into account in the assessment of proportionality of the duplication.[98] With regard to the strict necessity of such duplication, it should be assessed whether clear and precise rules exist allowing the prediction of the acts or omissions that may be liable to be subject to a duplication of proceedings and penalties as well as the prediction of coordination between the different authorities. In addition, it should be evaluated whether the two sets of proceedings have been conducted in a sufficiently coordinated manner and within a proximate timeframe and whether the first penalty imposed was taken into account in the assessment of the second penalty.[99] Following the CJEU articulation in *BPost*, the imposition of a second penalty needs to account for the fact that the company has already been sanctioned under a different set of rules.[100]

In *Nordzucker* the Court had to assess whether the idem condition was met with respect to the geographical dimension of a given conduct. It held that the national court has to assess all relevant circumstances with respect whether the German NCA decision took account of the effect of the cartel on not only in the German market but also in the Austrian market.[101] If that is the case, the idem condition is met and the principle of ne bis in idem may be limited under Article 52 CFR, as long as the essence of the right is respected, and the limitation is proportionate. In this case, by invoking 3(2) Regulation 1/2003 prescribing that national law prohibiting anticompetitive agreements cannot prohibit conduct allowed under Article 101 TFEU, the Court found that Article 101 TFEU and the national equivalent pursue the same objective and therefore a duplication of proceedings is not justified.[102] Since it was not relevant for this case, the CJEU did not pronounce on the relationship between Article 102 TFEU and the national equivalent on abuse of dominance, an area where Member States can adopt stricter rules.[103] This scenario is relevant for the concurrent application of Article 102 TFEU and national competition law (including abuse of economic dependence).

[96] Case C-117/20 *Bpost SA v Autorité belge de la concurrence* (n 93 above) para 43. Emphasis added.
[97] ibid para 49.
[98] ibid.
[99] Case C-117/20 *Bpost SA v Autorité belge de la concurrence* (n 93 above) paras 51, 58.
[100] This was the Commission approach in Commission Decision of 22 June 2011 relating to a proceeding under Art 102 of the Treaty on the Functioning of the European Union (TFEU) (Case COMP/39.525 – Telekomunikacja Polska) [2011] OJ C324/3, paras 144–145. See DMA (n 2 above) Recital 86.
[101] Case C-117/20 *Bpost SA v Autorité belge de la concurrence* (n 93 above) para 44.
[102] ibid paras 54–57.
[103] This scenario was raised by the Opinion by AG Bobek in Case C-117/20 *Bpost SA v Autorité belge de la concurrence* (n 93 above), para 51.

III. Digital Markets: In Need of Remedial Flexibility

Given the various multilevel elements at play and the associated risks, as discussed in section II, the question is how best to navigate through these and construct effective remedies against possible competition law violations in digital markets without compromising the uniform and effective application of EU competition law. Such multilevel legislation and ensuing enforcement calls for increased cooperation between the various actors (NCAs, the Commission, courts and private parties) and more flexible enforcement and remedial approaches.

In this vein, section III argues that 'responsive' remodelling of competition law enforcement has the potential to address various enforcement challenges posed by multi-level legislation and enforcement and result in more effective remedial design, especially for complex remedies involving, for example, product redesign or altering T&Cs of digital gatekeepers.

A. EU Competition Law Enforcement: A Multilevel System

Within the decentralised enforcement system, the Commission has the central role, with the NCAs and national courts being simultaneously ascribed as full-time enforcers of EU competition law.[104] Regulation 1/2003 provides for *cooperation* between the Commission and NCAs within the European Competition Network (ECN), as well as the Commission and national courts.[105] Such cooperation should form the backbone of the decentralised enforcement of EU competition law in order to ensure compliance with the principles of legal certainty and uniformity in EU competition law enforcement in a system of parallel powers.[106] As discussed in section II above, parallel actions against the same companies have been observed. In this context, the CJEU has held that Article 11(6) Regulation 1/2003 should be interpreted in a way that, when the Commission initiates proceedings, NCAs are relieved from their competences to bring proceedings against the same company for the same practice in the same product and geographical market during the same time period.[107] Furthermore, the parallel application of competition rules cannot be at the expense of undertakings.[108] The GC dismissed Amazon's action

[104] See Regulation 1/2003 (n 29 above). See also Commission Notice on cooperation within the Network of Competition Authorities (Notice) [2004] OJ C101/43; Commission Notice on the handling of complaints by the Commission under Articles 81 and 82 of the EC Treaty (Notice) [2004] OJ C101/65; Commission Notice on the cooperation between the Commission and the Courts of the EU Member States in the Application of Articles 81 and 82 EC (Notice) [2004] OJ C101/54.

[105] On the NCAs-Commission cooperation, see Regulation 1/2003 (n 29 above) Arts 11–13. On the cooperation between the Commission and national courts see ibid Art 15.

[106] On the uniform application of EU competition law see Regulation 1/2003 (n 29 above) Recital 22 and Art 16.

[107] Case C-857/19 *Slovak Telekom a.s. v Protimonopolný úrad Slovenskej republiky* [2021] EU:C:2021:139, para 30.

[108] ibid para 32.

as inadmissible since it found that the Commission decision to initiate proceedings is not a challengeable act. However, the fact that the Italian NCA and the Commission have been investigating similar conduct, even if it does not concern the same geographic market, runs the risk of inconsistent decisions with respect to the substance of the infringement as well as the imposition of remedies.

B. Responsive Remodelling: The Theory

NCAs and the Commission within the respective ECN cooperation mechanisms should opt for more responsive enforcement mechanisms towards potential competition law infringements,[109] especially in the context of digital markets. Responsive enforcement is particularly suited in the context of digital markets, where possible violations present novel legal questions and where the emerging multilevel elements discussed in Section II may jeopardise legal certainty, uniformity and the effective enforcement of EU competition law. 'Responsive' remodelling of competition law enforcement transcribes the main tenets of responsive regulation and restorative justice,[110] namely the enforcement pyramid, tripartism and restorative processes and values in competition law enforcement mechanisms.[111] It instructs competition authorities, when investigating an alleged competition law infringement, to adopt a flexible approach, employ consensual processes, allow a wider participation of stakeholders and adopt remedies that correspond to the alleged infringement and the behaviour of the perpetrator.

Responsive remodelling resting on regulatory theories is an appropriate lens to rethink competition law enforcement especially in digital markets in light of the evolving quasi-regulatory competition law framework and the increased need of cooperation between the various actors (NCAs, the Commission, other regulators, civil society organisations and industry). In anticipation of the DMA entering into force, which will introduce additional layers of complexity in competition law enforcement creating a host of questions of interaction between competition law and the competent enforcement authorities, responsive remodelling can inform competition law enforcement and the construction of effective remedies in digital markets and point to more effective cooperation and building of networks between affected actors (tripartism) and the ensuing adoption of responsive remedies (enforcement pyramid incorporating restorative processes and values).

[109] See M Ioannidou, '"Responsive" Remodelling of Competition Law Enforcement' (2020) 40 *Oxford Journal of Legal Studies* 846.

[110] ibid.

[111] On constructing the theory of responsive regulation see I Ayres and J Braithwaite, *Responsive Regulation: Transcending the Deregulation Debate* (Oxford, Oxford University Press, 1992); on advancing responsive regulation in combination with restorative justice attributes see J Braithwaite, *Restorative Justice and Responsive Regulation* (Oxford, Oxford University Press, 2002).

The multilevel elements discussed above clearly call for a closer coordination of enforcement efforts and cooperation between the different actors; first, cooperation between administrative authorities (Commission, NCAs and regulators) and national courts and second increased participation and cooperation with affected stakeholders during public as well as private enforcement processes. Thus, the Commission and NCAs should strive to make a more diligent application of Article 11(4) Regulation 1/2003 with NCAs informing the Commission about on-going cases, maintaining regular discussions with the Commission which will culminate in the Commission commenting on the draft decisions. Such cooperation should be established early on in the investigations and definitely earlier than the 30 days' timeframe prescribed in Regulation 1/2003 before the adoption of a decision by the NCAs. During those deliberations, the Commission and NCAs can also discuss potential remedies. In addition, Article 11(4) Regulation 1/2003 deliberations can be potentially informally applied to cases where NCAs contemplate the adoption of decisions against unilateral conduct by invoking stricter national laws, even if NCAs have such competence under Article 3(2) Regulation 1/2003. In addition, NCAs should maintain regular cooperation with their counterparts when looking into practices by the same incumbents and the Commission should not shy away from invoking Article 11(6) Regulation 1/2003 in cases where centralised enforcement would advance the uniform application of EU competition law.[112] Finally, Article 15 Regulation 1/2003 on the cooperation between the Commission and national courts should be diligently applied, especially in private enforcement cases. According to Article 15(3), the NCAs and the Commission may submit observations before national courts. Such powers highlight the link between private and public enforcement and should be invoked in cases where the courts may adopt divergent approaches, which in light of the multilevel elements discussed in section II is indeed a real risk. Increased cooperation at an earlier stage will serve to highlight the investigated facts and whether they are the same as well as the protected legal interest, thereby alleviating ne bis in idem concerns.

Second, in the course of public enforcement – and in light of the complementary aims of public and private enforcement,[113] various actors should be more actively implicated in the process and inform remedial design towards restorative solutions both in terms of restorative market outcomes as well as restoration of the harm to affected parties. A wider participation of stakeholders, such as competitors, civil society organisations including consumer organisations, digital rights and data protection activists as well as data protection authorities, will enable a better understanding of possible competition law infringements in digital markets, the interplay with other fields of law and the construction of the ensuing sanctions

[112] See Directorate-General for Competition, 'Antitrust – Manual of Procedures' (2012): https://antitrustlair.files.wordpress.com/2012/03/antitrust-manuel-of-procedure-commission-march-2012.pdf, chapter 3, para 73.

[113] See Ioannidou (n 110).

and remedies.[114] Cooperation between NCAs and data protection authorities has begun to emerge[115] and in light of digital platforms business models relying on data accumulation and exploitation should be explored further.[116] Competition authorities should form networks with various regulators. At EU level, Article 11 Regulation 1/2003 can be extended to include not only NCAs but also other national regulatory authorities, if such cooperation and discussions have taken place at national level. The NCAs would still be the first port of call for the discussions within the ECN, but they should be encouraged to open up the discussion to other regulatory authorities as well.

Apart from cooperation with other regulators, the involvement of civil society stakeholders may contribute to the better framing of the competition law problems and theories of harm as well as the articulation of effective remedies. 'Responsive' remodelling suggests that sanctions or remedies adopted should correspond to the violation and allow, if possible, for the restoration of the harm to affected parties. During the Google Shopping investigation,[117] the Commission received many complaints and requests from firms and consumer organisations to be involved as third parties and sent a very high number of information requests.[118] This reality suggests that the views of various stakeholders with opposing interests were heard, although the remedy adopted to materialise equal treatment did not appease competitors and consumers.[119] Despite existing examples of stakeholders' participation, as the Google case shows, to date this participation takes place in an adversarial manner. 'Responsive' remodelling, on the contrary, instructs in favour of consensual solutions, which will enable a better understanding of possible competition law infringements in digital markets and the construction of the ensuing sanctions and remedies. It can also contribute to navigate through the multi-level legislative and enforcement elements and thereby tackle the risk of fragmentation in the application of EU competition law.

[114] Discussing the possibility to transplant remedies from data protection law to tackle exploitative abuses (eg excessive data accumulation and the imposition of unfair terms) see M Botta and K Wiedemann, 'Exploitative Conducts in Digital Markets: Time for a Discussion after the Facebook Decision' (2019) 10 *Journal of European Competition Law and Practice* 465. On competition law's potential to be applied against practices by dominant platforms directly exploiting consumers in digital markets – collectively termed as 'digital agoraphobia' – see M Ioannidou, '"Digital Agoraphobia": Exploitative Abuses in Digital Markets' in I Kokkoris and C Lemus (eds), *Research Handbook in Competition Enforcement* (Cheltenham, Edward Elgar, 2022)

[115] See Facebook case in Germany, Press Release, 'Bundeskartellamt examines linkage' (n 58 above).

[116] See, for example, C Caffarra and J Ryan, 'Why Privacy Experts Need a Place at the Antitrust Table', *Promarket*, 28 July 2021: www.promarket.org/2021/07/28/privacy-experts-antitrust-data-harms-digital-platforms/. See Press Release, 'ICO and CMA set out blueprint for cooperation in digital markets' (2021): www.gov.uk/government/news/ico-and-cma-set-out-blueprint-for-cooperation-in-digital-markets.

[117] Commission Decision of 27 June 2017 (n 4 above).

[118] ibid paras 38–105.

[119] See N Hirst, 'Vestager kicks off new chapter in Google Shopping probe', *Politico*, 16 February 2018: www.politico.eu/article/commission-probes-google-shoppings-antitrust-remedy-document/. T Hoppner, 'Google's (Non-) Compliance with the EU Shopping Decision – a study based upon empirical data of 25 comparison shopping services' (2020): www.hausfeld.com/uploads/documents/googles_(non)_compliance_with_google_search_(shopping).pdf.

IV. Conclusion

As the discussion in Section II has highlighted, the DMA complementing EU competition law enforcement will complicate further the already complex enforcement landscape against Big Tech, raising questions on the interplay between the proposed rules, EU competition law, other EU legislative initiatives, as well as the interplay between the proposed rules and national legislative initiatives, such as the amendments to the German Competition Act. Such multilevel legislation and enforcement naturally risk the effective and uniform application of EU competition law and raise many challenges with respect to competence distribution within the ECN and the application of the principle of ne bis in idem.

Responsive remodelling can bring some much needed order in the concurrent enforcement activity by both the Commission and NCAs. Such concurrent actions are based on EU competition law provisions, national competition laws – some, such as German competition law recently amended to assume a quasi ex ante nature – and provisions on abuse of economic dependence. This may create a risk of divergent approaches, thus jeopardising the uniform application of EU competition law, and calling for better cooperation and coordination mechanisms between the various actors. In addition, apart from public enforcement, there is the possibility of private damages actions before national courts, with private actions already emerging in some Member States adding yet another layer of complexity.

These elements of multilevel legislation and enforcement highlight the continuum between competition and regulation in digital markets. This continuum in terms of the aims pursued by substantive provisions (undistorted competition, fair and contestable markets) can be mirrored also in enforcement and as explained in Section III, responsive regulation can provide a normative lens in that regard pointing to a much needed remodelling of competition law enforcement at first instance. Responsive remodelling calls for better coordination and cooperation mechanisms between the various actors, as well as a holistic approach to enforcement where public and private enforcement mechanisms serve deterrence, induce compliance and bring redress to affected parties. Such a fused approach to enforcement requires an increased participation of affected stakeholders and civil society and the construction of remedies relevant to the alleged misconduct and the behaviour of the perpetrator. Finally, it calls for the construction of responsive remedies, both in terms of attaining competitive market conditions as well as 'responding' to the inflicted harm to private parties.

12

Governing the Green Transition Through State Aid Control

CARLO MARIA COLOMBO AND MATTEO BONELLI*

I. Introduction

After long being prefigured by scientists as a potential danger to our societies, environmental hazards have now become a clear emergency affecting our daily lives. Possibly more than previous crises, this global threat challenges virtually all domains of human activity and is thus forcing public authorities to redesign entire political agendas around it. In the European Union (EU) context, the European Green Deal (EGD), elaborated by the Commission in 2019, has the ambition of restructuring many fundamental EU policies with the objective of creating a 'competitive and resource-efficient economy in which … growth is decoupled from resource use'.[1]

Public subsidies are an important part of this plan. As a policy instrument, they act as 'carrots', incentivising recipients to pursue environmental or 'green' goals. The Commission has shown a clear awareness of the potential that subsidies represent in directly supporting the green transition with EU funds. In addition, the Commission has sought to channel national spending towards environmental objectives through its power to prohibit state aid deemed incompatible with the internal market.[2] This chapter focuses on this second direction of EU action and

* Carlo Maria Colombo is Marie Skłodowska-Curie Fellow at Sciences Po, France, and Assistant Professor of Administrative Law at Maastricht University, the Netherlands, carlo.colombo@maastrichtuniversity.nl. Matteo Bonelli is an Assistant Professor of European Law at Maastricht University, matteo.bonelli@maastrichtuniversity.nl. The authors would like to thank Catherine Derenne (ClientEarth), Phedon Nicolaides and Raymond Luja (Maastricht University), as well as the other editors of this book, for comments on earlier drafts. Any errors are the authors' own. Funded by the European Union. Views and opinions expressed are however those of the author(s) only and do not necessarily reflect those of the European Union or the European Commission. Neither the European Union nor the European Commission can be held responsible for them.

[1] Commission, 'Communication from the Commission, 'The European Green Deal' COM(2019) 640 final.

[2] ibid 13–14.

reflects on the ability of the EU state aid framework to advance the EGD's environmental goals.

Aligning state aid with the EGD is not without difficulties. For some time, the EU state aid framework has attempted to balance environmental concerns with its core mission of ensuring a level playing field in the internal market, yet not always with adequate emphasis on environmental goals.[3] With its focus on environmental goals and obligations, the EGD now requires major readaptations of state aid policy and governance. These, in turn, are bound to raise fundamental issues of EU law, including respect for the principle of conferral, institutional balance, horizontal policy integration and the protection of fundamental rights.

Combining constitutional and governance perspectives, this chapter reflects on the transformative force of the EGD on state aid. It answers two research questions: how is the state aid framework changing to promote the green transition in the EU, and what are the constitutional and governance implications of this process? The chapter, specifically, examines three legal elements necessary to deliver the EGD's ambitions: the environmental integration principle, access to justice, and the imperative to comply with decarbonisation goals. It explores how these are affecting several central features of the state aid legal framework, namely, the exercise of discretion by the Commission, public participation in state aid control and the attachment of conditions to state aid decisions. In doing so, this analysis aims to complement early reflections on the influence of the EGD on state aid law,[4] and it is also timely, since most state aid guidelines and regulations are presently being revised. Moreover, major decisions by the EU and international institutions have provided fundamental clarifications on the relationship between environmental protection and state aid policy.

The chapter is organised as follows. After this introduction, Section II discusses the main organisational and constitutional tenets of state aid and their evolution. Section III isolates some of the key legal elements for achieving the EGD goals, while Section IV then discusses their influence on the transformation of the state aid framework, as well as the emerging constitutional and governance implications of this process. The chapter argues that, to realise the EGD's green ambitions, state aid policy needs to integrate environmental considerations in state aid assessment, promote public access to justice and condition subsidies to green goals. Although several uncertainties remain for the Commission to address in practice, these

[3] See on the relationship between state aid and environmental protection J Nowag, *Environmental Integration in Competition and Free-Movement Laws* (Oxford, Oxford University Press, 2016); S Kingston, *Greening EU Competition Law and Policy* (Cambridge, Cambridge University Press, 2012).

[4] Among the manifold reflections on the field, see S Verschuur and C Sbrolli, 'The European Green Deal and State Aid: The Guidelines on State Aid for Environmental Protection and Energy towards the Future' (2020) 19 *European State Aid Law Quarterly* 284; S Lünenbürger, C Holtmann and J Delarue, 'Implementation of the Green Deal: Integrating Environmental Protection Requirements into the Design and Assessment of State Aid' (2020) 19 *European State Aid Law Quarterly* 418; S Kingston, 'State Aid and the European Green Deal: The Implications of Case C-594/18 P Austria v Commission' (2021) 46 *European Law Review* 365.

changes appear to be supported by the constitutional and institutional flexibility of the field and appear set to move state aid control to a complement of other environmental enforcement instruments, thus enhancing the authority and effectiveness of environmental rules across the EU.

II. State Aid Control: An Evolving Framework within an Unchanged Constitutional Setup

The EU Treaties' provisions on state aid follow the logic of negative integration and aim to limit Member States' ability to distort the internal market by subsidising undertakings selectively. Specifically, while Article 107(1) of the Treaty on the Functioning of European Union (TFEU) contains a general prohibition of any state intervention that meets certain criteria, the following provisions include a set of reasons that make (under Article 107(2) TFEU) or may make (under Article 107(3) TFEU) an aid exceptionally compatible with the internal market. Procedurally, these rules are enforced through a system of centralised administration in which the Commission alone is empowered to check state aid compatibility, subject to the EU courts' review.

Over time, this system has undergone several transformations, demonstrating resilience and adaptability.[5] Building on earlier studies,[6] some lines of development can be identified. From a substantive perspective, the interpretation of state aid law has evolved steadily. When the European Economic Community (EEC) was still in its infancy, state aid policy was strongly linked to the creation of a common market. Accordingly, the Commission's investigations focused on aid measures in sectors seen as important and liable to harm out-of-state undertakings. In the wake of the 1970s' oil crisis and the vast amount of aid granted in response to it, the rationale of state aid policy moved to reducing public funding to companies and improving the functioning of the internal market. To this end, the Commission tightened the concept of 'advantage' in the definition of state aid.[7] It also developed the 'compensatory justification principle', according to which state aid can be justified under Article 107(3)(c) TFEU only if it incentivises behaviour beyond the normal play of market forces.[8] During the same period, and even

[5] A Biondi and E Righini, 'An Evolutionary Theory of EU State Aid Control' in A Arnull and D Chalmers (eds), *The Oxford Handbook of European Law* (Oxford, Oxford University Press, 2015).

[6] See among the many JJ Piernas López, *The Concept of State Aid Under EU Law: From Internal Market to Competition and Beyond* (Oxford, Oxford University Press, 2015); C Micheau, 'Evolution of State Aid Rules: Conceptions, Challenges, and Outcomes' in H Hofmann and C Micheau (eds), *State Aid Law of the European Union* (Oxford, Oxford University Press, 2016).

[7] See D Grespan and S Santamato, 'Favouring Certain Undertakings or the Production of Certain Goods: Advantage' in W Mederer, N Pesaresi and others (eds), *EU Competition Law*, Volume IV, Book One (Leuven, Claeys & Casteels, 2016) 30.

[8] K Mortelmans, 'The Compensatory Justification Criterion in the Practice of the Commission in Decisions on State Aids' (1984) 21 *Common Market Law Review* 405.

more so after the 1985 White Paper on the completion of the internal market,[9] the Commission began to use rulemaking – in the form of soft law and, later, hard law such as 'block exemption' regulations – to codify the criteria for state aid deemed compatible. With the 2005 State Aid Action Plan (SAAP),[10] these criteria were more closely linked to the policy goals agreed upon by the European Council. In promoting the idea that national spending is justifiable if it is aimed at achieving EU objectives, the Commission has developed its own vision of 'good' state aid policy, thus generating positive integration that directly influences national aid policies.[11] At the same time, to improve the effectiveness of state aid policy and counter market failures, the role of economic analysis in state aid assessment has grown, aligning the field more closely with competition law.

From a procedural perspective, state aid control has undergone equally significant changes. While state aid enforcement was initially weak due to limited practice and the reluctance of Member States to notify relevant measures,[12] the growing number of aid measures in the 1970s led the Commission to more proactively enforce the notification requirement and recovery orders. However, it was not until 1999, after a 40-year effort, that procedural rules were codified in the form of a council regulation (hereafter the 'State Aid Procedural Regulation'[13]), thereby improving transparency and legal certainty of state aid examinations.[14]

With the state aid modernisation (SAM) of 2012,[15] the Commission further adapted this system to the changing times. With the aim of using limited public resources more efficiently, it updated most regulations and guidelines and issued a new communication to make the application of the notion of aid more intelligible.[16] New transparency requirements for the publication of information on state aid and its ex post evaluation were added as well, allowing the effectiveness of state aid to be measured in terms of achieving its objectives and its impact on the internal market. This has helped to further decentralise state aid control.[17]

[9] Commission, 'Completing the Internal Market: White Paper from the Commission to the European Council' COM(1985) 310 final.

[10] Commission, 'State aid action plan – Less and better targeted state aid: a roadmap for state aid reform 2005–2009' COM(2005) 107 final.

[11] M Blauberger, 'Of "Good" and "Bad" Subsidies: European State Aid Control through Soft and Hard Law' (2009) 32 *West European Politics* 719.

[12] See Piernas López, *The Concept of State Aid Under EU Law* (n 6 above) 46.

[13] Council Regulation (EC) No 659/1999 of 22 March 1999 laying down detailed rules for the application of Article 108 of the Treaty on the Functioning of the European Union [1999] OJ L83/1.

[14] A Sinnaeve and PJ Slot, 'The New Regulation on State Aid Procedures' (1999) 36 *Common Market Law Review* 1153.

[15] Commission, 'Communication from the Commission to the European Parliament, the Council, the European Economic and Social Committee and the Committee of the Regions, EU State Aid Modernisation (SAM)' COM(2012) 209 final.

[16] Commission, 'Notice on the Notion of State Aid as referred to in Article 107(1) of the Treaty on the Functioning of the European Union' (Notice) [2016] OJ C262/01. For a critical analysis, see among others P Nicolaides, 'A Critical Review of the Commission Notice on the Notion of State Aid' (2016) 23 *Maastricht Journal of European and Comparative Law* 842.

[17] CM Colombo, 'State Aid Control in the Modernisation Era: Moving Towards a Differentiated Administrative Integration?' (2019) 25 *European Law Journal* 292.

Repeated crises, too, have forced readjustments. In response to the 2008 banking crisis, the Commission used rulemaking to clarify in advance and in a timely manner the conditions for rescuing distressed banks and was quite flexible in approving most aid granted to banks.[18] The same approach was followed more recently, during the COVID-19 pandemic. Here, the Commission established in a set of non-binding guidelines a temporary framework for managing and mitigating the effects of the pandemic.[19] In this way, Member States were able to quickly help their economies while trying to minimise market distortions.

III. State Aid and the Green Deal: Horizontal Integration, Access to Justice and Compliance with the Decarbonisation Trajectory

The current environmental emergency represents a new challenge bound to reshape the EU and thus also state aid policy. Heralded as the EU's 'man on the moon moment',[20] the EGD is the EU's flagship initiative to address the environmental crisis. It expresses the sweeping ambition to reorient the EU's social and economic model towards a harmonious relationship between humans and the environment.[21]

To achieve this, the EGD relies on various types of measures. A first category is legislative acts aiming, indirectly or directly, to mitigate emissions. The chief example is the EU Climate Law of 2021,[22] which implements the Paris Agreement by setting the legally binding targets of reducing greenhouse gas (GHG) emissions by 55 per cent by 2030 and achieving climate neutrality by 2050. Herein, Member States are required to develop 'national climate and energy plans' and align their measures to said targets,[23] subject to the regulatory authority of and monitoring by the Commission. While questions of the enforceability and scope

[18] C Ahlborn and D Piccinin, 'The Great Recession and Other Mishaps: The Commission's Policy of Restructuring in a Time of Crisis' in E Szyszczak (ed), *Research Handbook on State Aid* (Cheltenham, Edward Elgar, 2011) 151.

[19] D Ferri, 'The Role of EU State Aid Law as a "Risk Management Tool" in the COVID-19 Crisis' (2021) 12 *European Journal of Risk Regulation* 176.

[20] U von der Leyen, 'Press remarks on the occasion of the adoption of the European Green Deal Communication' (Brussels, 11 December 2019) 1.

[21] For an in-depth analysis see E Chiti, 'Managing the Ecological Transition of the EU: The European Green Deal as a Regulatory Process' (2022) 59 *Common Market Law Review* 19; A Sikora-Kaléda, 'European Green Deal – Legal and Financial Challenges of the Climate Change' (2021) 21 *Journal of the Academy of the European Law* 681.

[22] Regulation (EU) 2021/1119 of the European Parliament and of the Council of 30 June 2021 establishing the framework for achieving climate neutrality and amending Regulations (EC) No 401/2009 and (EU) 2018/1999 [2021] OJ L243/1.

[23] The national energy and climate plans (NECPs) had been introduced by Art 3 Regulation (EU) 2018/1999 of the European Parliament and of the Council of 11 December 2018 on the Governance of the Energy Union and Climate Action [2018] OJ L328/1.

of the Commission's powers are still open,[24] the Climate Law is crucial. By complementing existing legislation setting similar targets, it establishes a trajectory that Member States must comply with towards climate neutrality, thereby potentially affecting any measure issued by them. A second category of instruments developed in the context of the EGD is documents and strategies, both cross-cutting and sectoral, to align existing policies with the EGD goals.[25] Finally, the EGD relies on a vast set of financial measures to incentivise and manage the costs of the green transition, including the NextGenerationEU (NGEU) plan and other EU, national and private investments,[26] as well as the Taxonomy Regulation, which classifies which investments are deemed environmentally sustainable.[27]

Clearly, the EGD represents a far-reaching and complex policy package. As Chiti observed,[28] besides having a forward-looking focus, it distinctively covers most of the EU's sectors, levels and geographic space in an attempt to mobilise all forces towards the common objectives of the green transition. The EGD is thus distinct and possibly more ambitious than responses to previous crises and might open a new phase of the EU integration process. In other words, it could have 'transformative force' for the Union and its society.[29]

This transformative character of the EGD raises fundamental constitutional and governance questions. While operating within an unchanged treaty framework, the EGD effectively forces a transformation of EU constitutional law and of its substantive policies. In particular, the objectives of the EGD – expressed in secondary legislation and policy documents – could conflict with other EU objectives established at the treaty level, such as promotion of the internal market and competition, or it may require that environmental objectives and principles in the treaties be made effective across the policy spectrum. For instance, to deliver the EGD's ambitions, it will be key understand whether and to what extent the 'mainstreaming' clauses of Article 11 TFEU and Article 37 of the Charter of Fundamental Rights can support horizontal integration of environmental rules and goals across the board and contribute to solving possible clashes with other objectives.[30] These constitutional questions also have major governance consequences, as they urge

[24] See for a critical overview, among others, M Peeters and D Misonne, 'The European Union and its Rule-Creating Force on the European Continent for Moving to Climate Neutrality by 2050 at the Latest' in L Reins and J Verschuuren (eds), *Research Handbook on Climate Change Mitigation Law* (Cheltenham, Edward Elgar, 2022) 69–70.

[25] See eg the European Industrial Strategy, Communication from the Commission to the European Parliament, the European Council, the Council, the European Economic and Social Committee and the Committee of the Regions, A New Industrial Strategy for Europe COM(2020) 102 final.

[26] For an overview of the NGEU package, see B De Witte, 'The European Covid-19 Recovery Plan: The Legal Engineering of an Economic Policy Shift' (2021) 58 *Common Market Law Review* 635.

[27] Regulation (EU) 2020/852 of the European Parliament and of the Council of 18 June 2020 on the establishment of a framework to facilitate sustainable investment and amending Regulation (EU) 2019/2088 [2020] OJ L198/13.

[28] See Chiti, 'Managing the Ecological Transition of the EU' (n 21 above) 26.

[29] ibid 19.

[30] On Art 11 TFEU, see B Sjåfjell, 'The Environmental Integration Principle: A Necessary Step Towards Policy Coherence for Sustainability' in F Ippolito, ME Bartoloni and M Condinanzi (eds), *The EU and the Proliferation of Integration Principles under the Lisbon Treaty* (Abingdon, Routledge, 2020).

the EU to set up processes and instruments to ensure that environmental obligations and goals are monitored and met.

These fundamental questions inevitably urge reflection on state aid as well. From a constitutional perspective, while retaining the area's core aim of limiting distortive effects of national subsidies in the internal market, the EU Treaties allow the Commission to take environmental considerations into account in state aid examinations.[31] These considerations have so far played a main role in compatibility assessments and a limited one in application of the notion of aid, especially in quantification of the economic advantage for Services of General Economic Interest (SGEI)[32] and evaluation of the selective nature of environmentally beneficial measures.[33] Clearly, how the horizontal integration of environmental objectives is to be promoted in the field of state aid becomes crucial in the context of the EGD. From a governance perspective, how state aid supports the EGD is central from at least two perspectives. First, as the Commission recently acknowledged,[34] the EGD's ambitions require that state aid control tools and processes be adequate to promote the green transition. Second, the EGD urges a reflection on the role of state aid enforcement in the broader set of EU institutions' policy instruments, since others, such as regulation and taxation, may be more suitable for environmental protection, as the Commission argued in a recent call for consultation.[35]

To contribute to this debate and address these sets of questions, three key legal components of the EGD are here singled out for analysis, with the aim of critically examining their implications for state aid. The first is the environmental integration principle. The EGD's emphasis on environmental protection in the transition to an ecologically based growth model requires attention to how environmental principles and obligations are integrated into state aid policy. As indicated, this integration process, or balancing, takes place primarily through the exercise of discretion under Article 107(3)(c) TFEU, which is the legal basis for most state aid. However, various issues related to this process are still open. In addition, the Court of Justice recently provided important clarifications on this balancing in *Hinkley Point*,[36] a case concerning Austria's appeal against a Commission compatibility

[31] See in this regard the analyses of Nowag, *Environmental Integration* (n 3 above) and Kingston, *Greening EU Competition Law* (n 3 above).

[32] See Kingston, *Greening EU Competition Law* (n 3 above) 384.

[33] See, among others, on the selective scope of justification of environmental taxation schemes based on their environmental objectives, Case C-487/06 P *British Aggregates v Commission* [2008] EU:C:2008:419.

[34] See the result of the latest Fitness check of State aid rules, available at Commission, '2012 State aid modernisation package, railways guidelines and short-term export credit insurance – fitness check': www.ec.europa.eu/info/law/better-regulation/have-your-say/initiatives/2044-2012-State-aid-modernisation-package-railways-guidelines-and-short-term-export-credit-insurance-fitness-check_en.

[35] See the Call for contributions 'Competition Policy supporting the Green Deal', available at: www.competition-policy.ec.europa.eu/system/files/2021-08/2021_green_deal_conf_call_for_contributions_en.pdf.

[36] Case C-594/18 P *Austria v Commission* [2020] EU:C:2020:742. See also A Sikora-Kaléda, 'A Clash of Titans: EU Competition and State Aid Law and the Impact of the European Green Deal', Ch 3 in this volume, P Nicolaides, 'The Response of EU Courts to Society's Digital and Green Challenges in the Field of Competition and State Aid', Ch 8 in this volume. For a case analysis, see Kingston, 'State

decision on a United Kingdom aid measure for a nuclear power plant, urging an examination of its implications in the context of the EGD.

The second involves access to justice. Recognition of access to justice for the public and for environmental NGOs represents an important means for bolstering environmental protection in the EU. Since state aid can support polluting practices, a broad right to challenge state aid decisions would allow third parties to contribute to preventing environmental risks deriving from these. With the EGD, the Commission has pledged to improve access to justice against decisions with environmental implications.[37] Yet, structural complexities in the state aid context have so far limited this evolution, thus generating questions about how to ensure broad access to justice in the field.

The third involves the imperative to comply with decarbonisation goals. With the indicated complex legal framework, the EGD aims to place EU and national measures on a time trajectory to move the continent towards climate neutrality. Since domestic subsidies can support activities that delay or undermine this effort, state aid decisions could help bring these in line with the future targets. To date, however, the structure of state aid control has relied primarily on ex ante and one-time assessments, with still limited room for ex post evaluations of the economic effects of aid measures.[38] Solutions are therefore needed to adapt the state aid framework to the temporal logic of the EGD, especially for those aid measures that favour activities which, while not prohibited, have negative environmental effects.

In sum, a focus on these key legal components of the EGD is necessary to appreciate its effects on state aid. The dilemma is to understand the extent that the increased role of environmental obligations and principles requires transformations of the state aid framework in place, as well as to grasp the constitutional and governance implications of this process. These two main questions drive the analysis below.

IV. The Evolution of State Aid Policy in the Green Transition

This section examines how the framework of state aid is evolving to deal with the growing importance given to environmental protection in the context of the

Aid and the European Green Deal' (n 4 above); P Nicolaides, 'Shedding Light into the 'Black Box' of State Aid: The Impact of Hinkley Point C on the Assessment of the Compatibility of State Aid' (2021) 20 *European State Aid Law Quarterly* 4; L Hancher, 'Euratom, State Aid and Environmental Protection: Hinkley Point Case C-594/18 P, Republic of Austria v Commission (Hinkley Point), Judgment of the Court of Justice (Grand Chamber) of 22 September 2020, EU:C:2020:742' (2021) 58 *Common Market Law Review* 1491.

[37] See Commission, 'The European Green Deal' (n 1 above) 23.

[38] See in this sense Kingston, 'State Aid and the European Green Deal' (n 4 above) 377. For the ex post evaluation of environmental aid, see H Friederiszick and others, 'Ex Post State Aid Evaluation in Environmental Aid' (2018) 17 *European State Aid Law Quarterly* 509.

EGD. To do so, it focuses on three elements of state aid governance, namely, the exercise of Commission discretion, public participation in state aid control, and the use of conditional state aid decisions. All of these elements are affected by the legal transformations identified above as required to deliver the EGD's ambitions. Furthermore, the governance and constitutional effects of these transformations are investigated.

A. Structuring Discretion when Environmental Considerations are at Stake

As noted above, Article 107(3)(c) TFEU grants the Commission wide discretion to assess when an aid measure's contribution to a public policy objective, such as environmental protection, outweighs its negative effects on the market and is therefore lawful. In light of the previous discussion, it may be asked how the Commission can use this balancing to ensure environmental protection in the context of the EGD.

A first issue concerns whether the Commission can use its discretion to influence the content of domestic support for environmental protection. As discussed, the EU executive has over time codified some common assessment principles for state aid compatibility, thereby aligning national aid policies with the EU's broader goals. In the Court of Justice's decision in the *Hinkley Point* case, this 'tactical' use of discretion seems at first sight curtailed. Based on a literal interpretation of Article 107(3)(c) TFEU, the Grand Chamber clarified that the compatibility of aid does not depend on its pursuing an objective of common interest.[39] Rather, the Commission must balance a positive condition – whether the aid may facilitate the development of certain economic activities – against a negative one – whether the aid does not have an adverse effect on trade contrary to the common interest.[40] Admittedly, *Hinkley Point* provides a welcome clarification of the constitutional limits from which the Commission's discretion cannot depart. Some authors go further, arguing that the judgment is also set to return the power to define the objectives of aid measures to national authorities, thus reducing the Commission's influence.[41]

This concern is legitimate. However, one wonders whether the Commission is truly willing to give up its role. In the 2022 Guidelines on State Aid for Climate, Environmental Protection and Energy (CEEAG), the Commission significantly expands the categories of activities that national authorities can directly support and requires Member States to still demonstrate how aid contributes to environmental protection and the Union's climate policy as part of the criteria of

[39] Case C-594/18 P *Austria v Commission* (n 36 above) para 20.
[40] ibid para 19.
[41] See Hancher, 'Euratom, State Aid and Environmental Protection' (n 36 above) 1516.

contributing to 'the development of economic activities' held in *Hinkley Point*.[42] As such, the post-*Hinkley Point* change has resulted in a reformulation rather than a full-scale rethinking of the Commission's position. The Commission, in fact, appears to still hold a 'stick' to steer national aid regimes towards the EGD's objectives, maintaining and possibly expanding the trend towards positive integration initiated with the 2005 SAAP. This choice seems appropriate to promote state support that fosters the green transition, in line with the EGD.

A second issue is how the Commission should treat EU environmental law non-compliance by way of state aid provisions. Although violations of EU law rules other than state aid are checked during state aid investigations, an open question concerns the nature and scope of this task. The uncertainty has been fuelled by the General Court, which has consistently held that the Commission's compliance check is to be performed only when EU law violations have an indissoluble link with the object of the aid so that 'any failure to comply with those provisions would necessarily affect [the] compatibility' of the state aid.[43] This interpretation was based on the earlier *Iannelli* judgment,[44] in which the Court of Justice ruled that, when an aspect of an aid measure essential to its object or operation infringes both competition rules and free movement of goods, only the Commission can verify compliance and make compatibility declarations. Over time, the Court has expanded this jurisprudence. Its initial aim was to safeguard the division of powers in the Treaties.[45] This then shifted to the protection of the autonomy of administrative procedures and remedies at the EU level, as well as of the institutional balance between the Commission and the Court of Justice,[46] as the latter is alone empowered to enforce environmental law infringements under Article 258 TFEU. Consequently, compliance checks with EU environmental law were excluded for state aid that did not directly pursue an environmental objective, because such violation did not adversely affect the establishment of the internal market.[47]

In *Hinkley Point*, the Court of Justice appears to have changed its orientation. After reaffirming, as in *Nuova Agricast*,[48] that state aid that conflicts with other treaty provisions cannot be declared compatible,[49] it clarified that such a

[42] See Section 3.1.1 of Commission, 'Communication from the Commission – Guidelines on State aid for climate, environmental protection and energy 2022' [2022] OJ C80/01.

[43] See Case T-57/11 *Castelnou Energía, SL v Commission* [2014] EU:T:2014:1021, para 189.

[44] Case 74/76 *Iannelli and Volpi v Meroni* [1977] EU:C:1977:51, para 14.

[45] A Biondi and P Eeckhout, 'State Aids and Barriers to Trade' in A Biondi, P Eeckhout and J Flynn (eds), *The Law of State Aid in the European Union* (Oxford, Oxford University Press, 2004) 103.

[46] L Hancher and A Bouchagiar, 'Hinkley Point C: Trimming the SAM, While Extending the Reach of Wider EU Law Infringements?' (2021) 20 *European State Aid Law Quarterly* 529, 539.

[47] See Case T-57/11 *Castelnou Energía SL v Commission* (n 43 above) paras 189–90. See P Nicolaides, 'The Response of EU Courts to Society's Digital and Green Challenges in the Field of Competition and State Aid', Ch 8 in this volume.

[48] Case C-390/06 *Nuova Agricast Srl v Ministero delle Attivitá Produttive* [2008] EU:C:2008:224, paras 50–51.

[49] ibid para 44.

check may relate to the subsidised economic activity (*in casu*, a nuclear power plant)[50] and emphasised that state aid for activities with harmful environmental effects must comply with Article 11 TFEU and Article 37 of the Charter, as well as EU secondary environmental law.[51] Then, leaving aside any references to the 'indissoluble link' requirement, it concluded that the Commission has a positive obligation to verify the conformity of the aid and subsidised activity with EU environmental law, based on the first condition of Article 107(3)(c) TFEU,[52] namely, that the aid facilitates the development of certain economic activities or areas, and to declare it incompatible if this is not the case.[53] As such, the ruling appears to have expanded the compliance checks beyond areas of EU law manifestly related to the object of the aid, clarifying that the Commission has an obligation to verify violations of EU environmental law, including secondary legislation. In all new guidelines, the Commission has sought to embrace this interpretation, requiring that both the aided activity and the aid be checked for compliance with relevant EU law.[54] Clearly, this still begs the question of the scope of such checks and what 'relevant' EU law truly means.

Recently, the General Court returned to the point in *Paks II*,[55] interestingly another Austrian claim against a compatibility decision on an aid measure for a nuclear power plant for failure to consider EU procurement rules in the construction contract. In an apparent revival of its earlier case law, the General Court ruled that when one aspect of the aid is suspected of infringing other provisions of EU law, the Commission is obliged to check its compatibility during the state aid investigation only if those aspects are so inextricably linked to the object of the aid that it is impossible to assess them separately.[56] Hence, since Austria did not show how the violation of EU procurement rules could produce an additional distortion of competition, such a conformity check was deemed unnecessary.[57] At the same time, the General Court made important clarifications in relation to *Hinkley Point*. It confirmed that the Commission has an obligation to verify any violation of EU law when this is created by the subsidised economic activity (ie, the production of nuclear energy), and since in *Hinkley Point* the contested violation concerned the object of the aid (ie, the development of a power plant), this justified the lack of reference to the indissoluble link.[58]

It is submitted here that *Hinkley Point*'s far-reaching interpretation is more in line with the EGD's environmental ambitions. By imposing environmental compliance

[50] ibid para 22.
[51] ibid paras 42–43.
[52] ibid para 45.
[53] ibid para 100.
[54] See Section 3.1.3 of Commission, 'Guidelines on State aid for climate' (n 42 above).
[55] Case T-101/18 *Austria v Commission* [2022] EU:T:2022:728.
[56] ibid para 25.
[57] ibid para 26.
[58] ibid paras 27–29.

checks in state aid control, it appears to rule out compatibility of state aid if any of its aspects have harmful environmental consequences, in line with Article 11 TFEU.[59] Furthermore, it appears set to promote greater centralisation of environmental enforcement in the hands of the Commission, as seen in other fields.[60] By contrast, the General Court's restrictive interpretation in *Paks II* seems to leave various questions open. First, the General Court's use of different wording to explain what is meant by economic activity (nuclear power) and the object of aid (development of the nuclear power plant) makes one wonder what the compatibility check of the former includes and if there are any differences with the latter. Past case law is not fully clear in this regard,[61] and it remains uncertain whether an activity ancillary to the subsidised economic activity (such as transportation services to a nuclear facility) can give rise to a breach that can be enforced via state aid control.

Second, when the EU law violation is on an aspect or condition of the aid that is inextricably linked with its object, *Paks II* requires the Commission to check compliance not per se, but as part of the compatibility assessment and in relation to its additional effects on the internal market. This suggests that such evaluation should fall under the second negative condition of Article 107(3)(c) TFEU. However, besides weakening the obligation to integrate environmental considerations into state aid control in case an infringement is not enforced, this interpretation leaves unresolved how the negative effects caused by EU law non-compliance should be compared with the positive effects of the aid in the Commission's discretionary assessment. More generally, it runs the risk of justifying Commission practices that, as recently pointed out in doctrine,[62] limit control as much as possible and fall short of the EGD's environmental ambitions.

A third question is whether, even when EU environmental law is respected, the Commission's compatibility assessment can lead to a banning or limiting of state support for polluting activities. This is a burning question, particularly regarding state support for fossil fuels. Albeit central in the current energy crisis, these energy sources are inconsistent with (present or future) emissions reduction targets, and support for them can also stand in the way of later adoption of low-carbon

[59] As advocated by S Kingston, *The Role of Environmental Protection in EC Competition Law and Policy* (Doctoral Thesis, Leiden, University of Leiden, 2009) 274.

[60] See R Bieber and F Maiani, 'Enhancing Centralized Enforcement of EU Law: Pandora's Toolbox?' (2014) 51 *Common Market Law Review* 1057, 1078.

[61] For instance, while in *Castelnou* (Case T-57/11 *Castelnou Energía SL v Commission* (n 43 above) paras 182–85) the object is equated to the purpose of the aid (in *casu*, to safeguard the security of the energy supply) and differs from the economic activity of energy production, in *Thermenhotel* (Case T-158/99 *Thermenhotel Stoiser Franz and Others v Commission* [2004] EU:T:2004:2, paras 158–59) the object of the aid is identified as a hotel project, which is also the supposed economic activity.

[62] See eg the analysis on recent Commission's decisions in C Ziegler, 'One Time, Last Time, or Why the CE Oltenia Lignite Restructuring Aid Approval Makes for an Accident, Not a Precedent' (2022) 21 *European State Aid Law Quarterly* 181, and C Ziegler, 'The Decommissioning of Lignite- and Coal-Fired Power Plants in the Commission's State Aid Practice and the European Green Deal' (2022) 21 *European State Aid Law Quarterly* 237.

alternatives (so-called 'carbon lock-in'). Yet, legal limits prevent EU institutions from banning their support directly.[63] First, in the delegated acts adopted pursuant to Article 10(2) of the Taxonomy Regulation, the Commission classifies these fossil fuels as 'transitional' activities.[64] Second, as held in *Hinkley Point*, Article 194(2) TFEU protects the national right to determine the local energy mix, and the Commission cannot interfere with those choices.[65] Given these limitations, it may be questioned whether the two-pronged compatibility assessment under Article 107(3)(c) TFEU may indirectly serve to limit or ban state support for these polluting activities. One way to accomplish this is to focus on their negative effects on competition. As argued elsewhere,[66] if the aid is structured such that the beneficiary is relieved from bearing the full burden of a price imposed on a form of pollution, the measure may be considered to improve the financial position of the recipient and thus distort competition. This consideration has been incorporated in the CEEAG,[67] and the onus is now on the Commission to clarify exactly when and how these negative externalities outweigh the positive effects of the aid. Another way is to check whether the positive effects of the aid in terms of increased environmental protection outweigh its negative consequences for the internal market. While not ruling out this possibility for subsidies to natural gas, the new CEEAG makes it clear that it will be difficult to prove that support for these has positive effects in terms of environmental protection, especially because such subsidies are prone to generating lock-in effects, thus obstructing the uptake of cleaner energy sources. One suggested way forward is to link the aid measure to national decarbonisation plans with binding targets and to commitments from the beneficiary to adopt alternative sources in the future.[68] However, these assessments involve prospective evaluations and require methodologies that can provide reasonable certainty about how aid measures can achieve the Union's environmental goals and avoid the risks of carbon lock-in. The methodologies presently available, however, are still uncertain, and the Commission may not yet have the expertise to apply them adequately in practice. In addition, there is a legal certainty issue: if a national decarbonisation plan is declared unlawful by a national court, there is a risk that state aid allowed based on the plan would later be declared illegal and need to be recovered.[69]

[63] See for analysis of the legal problems related to phasing out coal in the EU, A Boute, 'Phasing Out Coal Through Electricity Market Regulation' (2022) 59 *Common Market Law Review* 1007.

[64] See Commission Delegated Regulation (EU) 2022/1214 amending Delegated Regulation (EU) 2021/2139 as regards economic activities in certain energy sectors and Delegated Regulation (EU) 2021/2178 as regards specific public disclosures for those economic activities [2022] OJ L188/1.

[65] Case C-594/18 P *Austria v Commission* (n 36 above) paras 48–49.

[66] Kingston, 'State Aid and the European Green Deal' (n 4 above).

[67] See Section 3.3 of Commission, 'Guidelines on State aid for climate' (n 42 above).

[68] ibid.

[69] See in this regard G Monti, 'The European Climate Law: Making the Social Market Economy Fit for 55?' (2021) 58 *Common Market Law Review* 1321, 1327.

B. Opening Up State Aid Control to the Public

State aid control procedure – which consists of a preliminary stage to form a prima facie assessment and a formal examination stage whose opening is at the Commission's discretion – is designed as a bilateral dialogue between the Commission and the Member State concerned. This structure is in line with the jurisprudence of the Court of Justice, according to which the right of defence should be granted 'in all proceedings initiated against a person which are liable to culminate in a measure adversely affecting that person'.[70] As a result, only the Member State to which the Commission's decision is addressed enjoys full procedural rights.[71] In contrast, interested third parties can only ask the Commission to act against unlawful aid in the preliminary stage;[72] they cannot force the Commission to open a formal investigation,[73] and they have limited rights in this phase.[74]

This constricted procedural guarantee is amplified by a restricted degree of judicial protection for third parties.[75] Under Article 263(4) TFEU, third parties must prove that they are directly and individually concerned by the Commission's state aid decisions when they seek annulment of such before the EU courts. For individual aid recipients, these eligibility criteria have not posed problems in light of their distinct position. However, actions against the prohibition of a sectoral aid scheme are generally considered inadmissible if brought by a *potential* beneficiary affected by virtue of membership in the influenced sector.[76] Competitors face even greater limitations. When the Commission finds an aid measure to be prima facie compatible without initiating the formal examination stage, competitors wishing to obtain respect for the procedural safeguards they would have enjoyed at the formal stage must demonstrate that they are 'interested parties'

[70] Case 40/85 *Belgium v Commission* [1986] EU:C:1986:305, para 28.

[71] See Art 5–7–9 of the Council Regulation (EU) 2015/1589 of 13 July 2015 laying down detailed rules for the application of Article 108 of the Treaty on the Functioning of the European Union [2015] OJ L248/9, 9.

[72] See Art 12 of the Council Regulation (EU) 2015/1589 (n 71 above). On the interpretation of this provision see Case T-678/20 *Solar Electric and Others v Commission* [2021] EU:T:2021:780, paras 50–53.

[73] See in this regard the recent Case C-57/19 P *Commission v Tempus energy and Tempus Energy Technology* [2021] EU:C:2021:663. This case significantly limits the Commission's investigative tasks during the preliminary examination stage of state aid proceedings, as it allows the Commission to focus on the evidence and considerations presented before it. This greatly consolidates the preliminary stage as a bilateral procedure between the Commission and Member States.

[74] See Arts 24–25 Council Regulation (EU) 2015/1589 (n 71 above). The introduction of Art 25 has exacerbated this imbalance, as the Commission can now request information from market participants and conduct sector inquiries, with penalties for noncompliance. See HP Nehl, '2013 Reform of EU State Aid Procedures: How to Exacerbate the Imbalance between Efficiency and Individual Protection' (2014) 13 *European State Aid Law Quarterly* 235.

[75] HP Nehl, 'Direct Actions and Judicial Review before the Union Courts' in H Hofmann and C Micheau (eds), *State Aid Law of the European Union* (Oxford, Oxford University Press, 2014).

[76] Potential recipients of aid schemes do not in fact have the *right* to receive aid. See Case C-519/07 P *Commission v Koninklijke Friesland Campina NV* [2009] EU:C:2009:556, para 53.

within the meaning of Article 108(2) TFEU to have standing.[77] When the merit of the Commission's preliminary or final decision is instead at stake, they then need to provide pertinent reasons to show that their market position is substantially jeopardised by the contested aid decision, in line with the strict *Plaumann* test on individual concern.[78] Equally limited are the possibilities to challenge state aid decisions for applicants protecting general interests, such as environmental NGOs.[79] This disparity is further increased by the fact that private enforcement allows national courts to review whether a measure qualifies as state aid, but not the Commission's compatibility assessment on it.[80]

This approach has been criticised from a rule of law perspective in the EU.[81] Yet, it seems even more untenable for aid with environmental effects. As part of the proceduralisation turn of environmental law in the 1990s,[82] the EU signed the United Nations Economic Commission for Europe (UNECE) Convention on Access to Information, Public Participation in Decision-Making and Access to Justice in Environmental Matters of 25 June 1998 (the 'Aarhus Convention').[83] This international convention grants members of the public and environmental NGOs the right of access to administrative or judicial review to challenge acts or omissions that contravene domestic environmental rules (Article 9(3)), as well as the right to adequate and effective remedies (Article 9(4)). Yet, while state aid decisions can violate environmental law, the Aarhus Regulation transposing the convention in the EU legal order excludes the EU institutions from its scope, even after the latest reform.[84]

The recent *Hinkley Point* saga seems nevertheless to open new scenarios. In 2015, a group of NGOs filed a complaint to the Aarhus Convention Compliance Committee (ACCC) stating the EU's failure to comply with the rights granted by the Aarhus Convention.[85] Building on the ruling in the *Hinkley Point* case,

[77] Among others, see Case C-78/03 P *Commission v Aktionsgemeinschaft Recht und Eigentum* [2005] EU:C:2005:761, paras 35–36.

[78] Case 25/62 *Plaumann v Commission* [1963] EU:C:1963:17.

[79] Regarding locus standi of NGOs protecting public interests, this has been held to exist for an association defending the interest towards public enjoyment of a particular sport facility (a racetrack) in a case concerning the provision of state aid to the operator of such facility which instead sought profit maximisation (see Case C-647/19 P *Ja Zum Nurburgring v Commission* [2021] EU:C:2021:666, para 66). Given the lack of such close link in the case where the public interest involves a common resource such as the environment, it seems reasonable to assume that this case law excludes the standing of NGOs to act against environmental aid.

[80] Among others, Case 78/76 *Steinike und Weinlig v Germany* [1977] EU:C:1977:52, para 9.

[81] Nehl, '2013 Reform of EU State Aid Procedures' (n 74 above) 246.

[82] C Harlow and R Rawlings, *Process and Procedure in EU Administration* (Oxford, Hart Publishing, 2014) 301.

[83] UNECE Convention on Access to Information, Public Participation in Decision-making and Access to Justice in Environmental Matters (adopted in Aarhus on 25 June 1998, entered into force on 30 October 2001) [2161] UNTS 447.

[84] Regulation (EU) 2021/1767 of the European Parliament and of the Council of 6 October 2021 amending Regulation (EC) No 1367/2006 on the application of the provisions of the Aarhus Convention [2021] OJ L356/01.

[85] Communication ACCC/C/2015/128 European Union.

that state aid may contravene EU environmental law, the ACCC found that the Commission's decisions constitute 'acts under environmental law'. In addition, it held that the right of NGOs, as interested parties, to ask the Commission to start a formal investigative procedure does not provide access to an administrative or judicial procedure under Article 9(3) of the Aarhus Convention, as the Commission retains discretion to follow up on this request. Finally, it concluded that equally insufficient are the possibilities to initiate annulment proceedings under Article 263(4) TFEU, which are linked to the limited procedural safeguards.

As a result, environmental law, this time at the international level, seems to open the door for more safeguards for the public in state aid control. Although the ACCC findings have not been made binding,[86] the EU institutions are taking steps to adapt to them. First, the new CEEAG requires national authorities, for some categories of environmental aid, to organise public consultations to gather inputs on the negative impact of an aid measure on the market.[87] While intended primarily to promote competition and not innovative in absolute terms,[88] this step shows an awareness of the public's role in state aid investigations. Second, the Commission is working with stakeholders to implement the ACCC's conclusions.[89] Given that a reform of Article 263(4) TFEU is highly complex and unlikely, the Commission has proposed to create an internal review mechanism that, similarly to what the Aarhus Regulation provides for in other areas, allows environmental NGOs and the public to ask for a review of state aid decisions, as well as to make them addressees of the Commission's reply. Being in line with the right of access to an administrative or judicial procedure under Article 9(3) of the Aarhus Convention, this proposal seems in principle capable of promoting greater participation in the control procedure and removing obstacles to providing standing to environmental NGOs and members of the public in the EU courts against such decisions.

Procedural and practical issues do, however, remain. The Commission has proposed several options to introduce this reform. The first one – amending the Code of Best Practices on State Aid – looks practically expedient but legally inadequate. While aimed at guiding national authorities in the notification process,

[86] The ACCC's findings, if endorsed by Meeting of the Parties to the Aarhus Convention, gain the status of official interpretation of the Aarhus Convention, therefore binding upon the Contracting Parties and the Convention Bodies. Yet, the findings in this case have not yet been endorsed.

[87] See the procedural requirement for Aid for the reduction and removal of greenhouse gas (Section 4.1.3.4) and for Aid for the security of electricity supply (Section 4.8.4.4) set in Commission, 'Guidelines on State aid for climate' (n 42 above).

[88] For instance, Member States were required to carry out public consultations to define correctly the genuine public policy interests in the area of state aid to Services of General Economic Interest. See Commission, 'European Union framework for State aid in the form of public service compensation' (Communication) [2012] OJ C8/15.

[89] Commission Communication on the findings adopted by the Aarhus Convention Compliance Committee in case ACCC/C/2015/128 as regards State aid: Analysing the implications of the findings and assessing the options available.

the code contains a certain undertaking by the Commission to act in specific ways.[90] Hence, to the extent that it establishes internal rules, the code binds the Commission to follow these in practice and not to derogate from its legal bases, which includes the State Aid Procedural Regulation.[91] Yet, the latter in its current formulation precludes such possibility. The second option of removing the legal exclusion in the Aarhus Regulation, seems legally more sound, as it would align state aid with other areas of EU (environmental) law. Ideally, this proposal would be combined with a reform of the State Aid Procedural Regulation that would add the indicated internal review process and extend it to all state aid measures, since potentially any funded activity may harm the environment and be subject to emissions reduction and environmental obligations. However, since the procedure under Article 108(2) TFEU is laid down in a Council Regulation, this requires that Member States allow third parties to participate in the control procedure, something that cannot be taken for granted. Furthermore, this proposal would not allow third parties to participate in the control of most state aid provisions, since 95 per cent of aid measures are today implemented on the basis of the General Block Exemption Regulation (GBER),[92] which is not covered by the procedural regulation on state aid. It would also likely generate delays in the Commission's centralised control procedure.

C. Conditioning State Aid to Compliance with Green Commitments

The EU Climate Law and other related legislation in the context of the EGD require Member States to establish a longitudinal trajectory towards meeting EU emissions reduction targets. On the basis of the Court of Justice's decision in *Hinkley Point*, state aid must be made consistent with this pathway, as enshrined in EU secondary legislation. Yet, as indicated, public support for some fossil fuels, such as natural gas, generates challenges in this regard. Although support for these energy sources remains possible and is even bound to increase in the context of the energy crisis and in the interim towards the green transition, these sources do not meet the Union's long-term climate targets and can stand in the way of later adoption of greener alternatives. This raises the question of whether and how state aid control can be used as a tool to phase them out in line with EU law.

[90] H Hofmann, G Rowe and A Turk, *Administrative Law and Policy of the European Union* (Oxford, Oxford University Press, 2012) 563–64.

[91] Joined Cases C-189/02 P, C-202/02 P, C-205/02 P to C-208/02 P and C-213/02 P *Dansk Rørindustri and Others v Commission* [2005] EU:C:2004:415.

[92] According to the 2018 State Aid Scoreboard (Commission, 'Scoreboard': https://competition-policy.ec.europa.eu/state-aid/scoreboard_en), 'since 2015, more than 96% of new measures for which expenditure has been reported for the first time fell under the General Block Exemption Regulation', representing 'about 82% of all measures were block exempted in 2017' or, in terms of total spending per Member State, 'about 48% of their total spending'.

To this end, translating the conditionality logic developed in other areas of EU law to the field of state aid law seems a compelling course. Originally deployed in EU external relations,[93] conditionality-based instruments – that is, instruments that proffer benefits on the condition that the recipient engage in a certain behaviour – are now a common governance tool for EU internal matters.[94] In a wide range of policies, EU institutions impose conditions on benefits, financial or otherwise, for both Member States and individuals, with the function of enforcing EU law or promoting certain EU policy objectives.[95] The advantage of the conditionality logic lies in its flexibility. Conditional instruments can be used to impose a commitment before or after receiving a benefit. In addition, they can deal with the same policy area as the benefit, or a different one, as in the case of macroeconomic conditions linked to EU Structural and Investment Funds (ESI Funds).[96]

In the field of state aid, the logic of conditionality is not entirely new. Conditionality tools have been used to structure national compliance and administrative capacity to effectively execute state aid rules, most notably in the enlargement process and ESI Funds framework.[97] Furthermore, the procedural regulation for state aid control empowers the Commission to take conditional decisions that subject payment of state aid to commitments to protect the internal market,[98] such as by implementation of a restructuring plan or by assuring that no state support is disbursed to beneficiaries that have yet to repay illegal aid.

To ensure that future decarbonisation commitments are met, one might consider attaching commitments to aid measures that a supported fossil fuel will ultimately be phased out.[99] Unlike other types of conditions, these green conditionalities would lie at the crossroads of environmental and competition law, as they aim both to secure compliance with environmental obligations and to avoid externalities in the market in the form of carbon lock-in. Accordingly, they raise key constitutional and practical questions.

One of these is that, like conditionality tools in other areas of EU law,[100] it must be understood whether the Commission has the power to attach these green

[93] See eg E Fierro, *The EU's Approach to Human Rights Conditionality in Practice* (London, Nijhoff, 2003); L Bartels, *Human Rights Conditionality in the EU's International Agreements* (Oxford, Oxford University Press, 2005). In the context of the EU enlargement process see, among others, C Pinelli, 'Conditionality and Enlargement in Light of the EU Constitutional Developments' (2004) 10 *European Law Journal* 354.

[94] See generally V Viță, 'Revisiting the Dominant Discourse on Conditionality in the EU: The Case of EU Spending Conditionality' (2017) 19 *Cambridge Journal of European Legal Studies* 116.

[95] On the functions of conditionality see Bieber and Maiani, 'Enhancing Centralized Enforcement of EU Law' (n 60 above) 1073.

[96] See the discussion in Bieber and Maiani, 'Enhancing Centralized Enforcement of EU Law' (n 60 above) and Viță, 'Revisiting the Dominant Discourse on Conditionality in the EU' (n 94 above).

[97] See Colombo, 'State Aid Control in the Modernisation Era' (n 17 above) 309.

[98] Art 9 of the Council Regulation (EU) 2015/1589 (n 71 above).

[99] See Kingston 'State Aid and the European Green Deal' (n 4 above).

[100] See for example the debate on whether the EU had the competence to adopt the so-called 'Rule of Law Conditionality Regulation' resolved by the Court in Cases C-156/21 *Hungary v Parliament and Council* [2022] EU:C:2022:97 and C-157/21 *Poland v Parliament and Council* [2022] EU:C:2022:98.

'strings' to state aid. The answer seems to be in the affirmative. As explained, such green conditions relate to matters falling within the scope of EU competences, and *Hinkley Point* mandates the Commission to verify compliance of aid measures with EU environmental law. Furthermore, the horizontal integration of green conditions in other EU policies is supported by the mainstreaming obligations of Article 11 TEU and Article 39 of the Charter. Some instances of green conditions are starting to emerge in practice. For example, in the guidelines on state aid for activities under the Emissions Trading Scheme (ETS) – a market-based system to combat climate change that subjects the most polluting installations to a decreasing amount of tradable carbon allowances – the Commission allows Member States to compensate companies for a portion of the higher electricity prices resulting from the ETS compared to companies that moved production to jurisdictions with more lenient climate policies.[101] Yet, because of the carbon-intensive activities involved, it requires Member States to condition support on additional decarbonisation efforts, such as implementing recommendations of energy efficiency audits and monitoring their concrete implementation.[102] Similarly, in the new CEEAG, the Commission suggests that fossil fuel aid can be considered compatible if conditional on the recipient making binding commitments to phase in low-carbon technologies in line with national decarbonisation plans.[103] Finally, in the temporary framework of state aid in the context of COVID-19, the Commission made clear that compatible recapitalisation support should come with strings attached, albeit loose ones, consisting of a generic reporting on how funds have been used to meet EU and national green objectives, including the goal of climate neutrality.[104]

Another issue is whether attaching green conditions to state subsidies represents an appropriate decarbonisation tool. Particularly at the peak of the pandemic, a lively debate emerged about the opportunity of conditioning aid to societal goals.[105] Nevertheless, the temporary framework of state aid has introduced only light conditions, as detailed above. Considering *Hinkley Point*, however, the position seems less tenable. The Commission now has an obligation to check that any compatible aid complies with EU environmental law, which includes the EU Climate Law and other legislation setting similar targets. In this context, imposing green commitments seems necessary. In the absence of such conditions, it would

[101] Commission, 'Communication from the Commission Guidelines on certain State aid measures in the context of the system for greenhouse gas emission allowance trading post-2021 2020/C 317/04' [2020] OJ C317/5.

[102] ibid Section 5.

[103] See Section 3.3 of Commission, 'Guidelines on State aid for climate' (n 42 above).

[104] See page 35 of the informal consolidated version of the Communication from the Commission Temporary Framework for State aid measures to support the economy in the current COVID-19 outbreak, available at: https://competition-policy.ec.europa.eu/system/files/2021-11/TF_consolidated_version_amended_18_nov_2021_en_2.pdf.

[105] See for instance the stance against state aid conditionality of the Executive Vice-President Margrethe Vestager, available at www.energymonitor.ai/policy/green-deals/is-eu-competition-policy-killing-the-green-deal/.

be difficult to ensure that state support for carbon-intensive activities does not obstruct meeting binding targets and that lock-in effects can be avoided, thus calling into question the legality of the aid measures themselves. If any, the problem seems to lie in whether the EU is making adequate use of this conditionality logic.

A further open question is how the Commission can verify compliance with these green conditions. When conditional state aid decisions issued to protect the internal market are not respected, the Commission can initiate proceedings for misuse of aid or violation under Article 108(2) TFEU and impose recovery. Since environmental conditions become an integral part of the aid measure and ensure its legality, it seems reasonable to assume that the same consequences should follow a failure to comply with them. However, beyond the mentioned issues of the scientific expertise involved, this requires the Commission to monitor implementation to confirm it remains in line with the commitments made. Yet, the structure of state aid control is still mainly built around a one-time, ex ante examination. Although SAM has brought more attention to the ex post evaluation of state aid, this practice is still new and focused on the economic effects of some measures. If the Commission wants to ensure that these commitments are taken seriously, more attention will be needed to the expertise and capacity issues involved in their ex post evaluation.[106]

V. Concluding Reflections

Crises and transformations, both internal and external, have provided fertile ground for reforms of the EU. State aid is no stranger to this. Since its inception, the field has evolved in line with major EU developments, and its evolution has in turn contributed to achieving more integration and new policy objectives. Currently, the EGD's increased emphasis on environmental protection is generating additional challenges with regard to the state aid framework. In addition to urging that the control system be opened to the public, it calls for ways to better integrate environmental considerations into the assessment of state aid and to make state support effectively comply with green commitments. Many of these concerns are not new, yet the EGD offers a momentous opportunity to address them.

Overall, the constitutional framework of the Treaties has shown sufficient flexibility to allow the Commission to update the state aid framework in order to fulfil these green objectives. First, the weight of environmental factors in the compatibility assessment is increasing, although the case law is still relatively inconsistent on that point, and tools are being created to ensure that aid measures comply with environmental law. Second, the external pressure of international law – particularly the Aarhus Convention – is forcing an opening of the asymmetric, bilateral structure of state aid control to include the public. Third, the imperative to meet

[106] On the same line, see Monti, 'The European Climate Law' (n 69 above) 1336.

decarbonisation commitments is set to reinforce the role of ex post state aid evaluations, making green conditionalities an apt tool for aligning state subsidies with those commitments.

At the same time, this evolution testifies to two related implications. First, state aid control is moving closer to becoming an additional environmental check of national measures. By putting greater emphasis on environmental commitments and opening control to the public, the EU is set to strengthen centralisation of environmental rules enforcement and improve accountability of national policies for their environmental impact. In this sense, the Commission may be right in stating that other instruments are at the forefront of protecting the environment, in the sense that they aim directly at promoting green objectives. Yet, the aforementioned transformations and the EGD's ambitions make clear that state aid also has a role to play. Although this may increase workload and create management issues within the Commission, it seems an inevitable and welcome consequence in the context of the EGD.

Second, this process appears in line with a broader trend towards using money as an EU governance and integration tool, which we are also witnessing, most notably, in NGEU. As discussed earlier, in that context, EU funds are earmarked for specific green transition objectives. In other words, Member States are forced to use part of the money to promote environmental (but also digital) objectives if they want to have access to NGEU funding.[107] In the context of state aid, the approach is slightly different and more indirect, as of course here the funding comes directly from the Member States. But the strengthening of the environmental obligations in state aid control contributes to ensuring that the overall EGD objectives are respected and not undermined by national subsidies inconsistent with the common goals. The horizontal integration of environmental considerations in the state aid regime thus contributes to making sure that public spending, regardless of whether it comes from the EU or the national level, contributes to (or at the very least is not in conflict with) the ambitions of the green transition put forward by the EGD.

However, to determine whether and to what extent these effects will fully materialise, several outstanding issues need to be addressed. These specifically require that the right tools be chosen for controlling aid measures and for third parties to be involved in this process, as well as for developing the expertise and capacity to ensure that the Commission can measure the impact of environmental aid in state aid analysis. Since the process is still ongoing and many of the necessary transformations will likely take time, further research is needed to provide a definitive answer. So far, the Commission has taken on board some of the EGD's implications for state aid, but much still depends on future execution.

[107] On the NGEU package, see De Witte, 'The European Covid-19 Recovery Plan' (n 26 above). In particular, the Recovery and Resilience Regulation provides that at least 37 per cent of the funding available is made available for green transition projects: see Art 16(2)(b)(i) of Regulation 2021/241 establishing the Recovery and Resilience Facility.

13

Creative Compliance and the Politicisation of EU State Aid Implementation in Times of Crisis

NICOLE LINDSTROM*

I. Introduction

European state aid regulation has always been a highly political component of European competition policy, as it aims to control how Member State governments intervene in their economies to support domestic economic development.[1] State aid is becoming increasingly politicised in the context of repeated economic crises, the rise of China, geopolitical turmoil related to Russia's invasion of Ukraine and ongoing rule of law crises in EU Member States such as Hungary and Poland. Member state governments face intensifying domestic demands to protect and promote the interests of national firms and industries – and, by extension, the well-being of their citizens – against external pressures. The European Commission, meanwhile, tasked with monitoring and enforcing state aid rules, is more cognisant of the domestic pressures EU Member State governments face, and the growing scepticism about the legitimacy of supranational intervention in domestic political economic choices.[2] This raises the question: has increased politicisation of government intervention been accompanied by an increase in non-compliance with EU state aid rules? In other words, how does the changing nature of the relationship between the EU, Member States and economic actors in the evolving sphere of European competition policy, as examined in this book, shape the processes through which state aid rules are implemented at the domestic level?

* Senior Lecturer in Politics at the University of York, nicole.lindstrom@york.ac.uk

[1] H Kassim and B Lyons, 'The New Political Economy of EU State Aid Policy' (2012) 13 *Journal of Industry, Competition and Trade* 1.

[2] D Finke, 'At Loggerheads over State Aid: Why the Commission Rejects Aid and Governments Comply' (2020) 21 *European Union Politics* 474; D Finke, 'A Guardian in Need of Support: The Enforcement of EU State Aid Rules' (2020) 29 *Journal of European Public Policy* 629.

I argue that 'creative compliance' – or the practice of 'ingenious disobedience' in which a government follows the letter of the law but ignores its spirit – is more prevalent than outright non-compliance when EU rules conflict with domestic political agendas.[3] Creative compliance provides a useful tool for governments to evade traditional command-and-control instruments. For example, governments can issue direct subsidies to individual firms or sectors, calculating that if the Commission ultimately rules the aid to be competition-distorting, they have nevertheless achieved their initial goal. Creative compliance can also be utilised in alternative, soft law governance mechanisms. For instance, governments can classify direct subsidies to an individual firm or sector as meeting 'horizontal' aims to exempt the aid from ex ante Commission scrutiny. However, the extent to which Member State governments engage in creative compliance depends not only on the will to disobey European rules to aid certain domestic firms and industries; it also requires sufficient levels of administrative capacity to enable governments to manipulate rules skilfully to evade supranational control, while maintaining the appearance of rule-conforming behaviour.

Creative compliance offers important insights into the day-to-day implications of the politicisation of European state aid governance. It also provides a fresh approach to the study of EU compliance that goes beyond static formal indicators of compliance or non-compliance to explore dynamic processes of monitoring and enforcement.[4] This chapter first offers a conceptualisation of creative compliance, drawing on relevant academic literature. It then goes on to situate creative compliance within the changing legal and political context of European state aid policy. Thirdly, it examines three strategies of creative compliance – the 'exemption game', the 'Frankenstein strategy,' and 'two steps forward, one step back' – as applied to state aid regulation, using examples drawn from one Member State, Hungary. Hungary provides an ideal case to examine creative compliance given that its Prime Minister, Viktor Orbán, has, since coming to power in 2010, sought to pursue an 'illiberal' national political economic alternative to open competitive markets, enforced by the EU. Finally, this chapter concludes by suggesting that creative compliance is not, contrary to some pessimistic accounts, a sign of 'perpetual disintegration' where Member States simply ignore EU rules.[5] However, the practice of Member State strategising to evade meaningful enforcement risks diminishing the credibility of the Commission as an effective guardian of state aid rules in the context of increasing politicisation.

[3] M Moran, 'Review Article: Understanding the Regulatory State' (2002) 32 *British Journal of Political Science* 391, 400, quoted in A Batory, 'Defying the Commission: Creative Compliance and Respect for the Rule of Law in the EU' (2016) 94 *Public Administration* 685, 689.

[4] O Treib, 'Implementing and Complying with EU Governance Outputs' (2014) 9 *Living Reviews in European Governance* 1; E Thomann and F Sagar, 'Moving Beyond Legal Compliance: Innovative Approaches to EU Multilevel Implementation' (2017) 24 *Journal of European Public Policy* 1253.

[5] B Rosamond, 'Theorizing the EU in Crisis: Ce-Europeanisation as Disintegration' (2019) 9 *Global Discourse: An Interdisciplinary Journal of Current Affairs* 31.

II. Conceptualising 'Creative Compliance'

Batory argues 'creative compliance' can explain how the EU has often failed to effectively prevent Member State governments from violating basic rule of law principles.[6] She demonstrates how the Commission, lacking the necessary authority to force governments to reverse course on the violation of fundamental rights, turns to policy areas where it has the autonomy to use stronger enforcement tools, namely single market and competition rules. For example, if a government seeks to undermine freedom of the press or attempts to discriminate against a type of worker, the Commission can appeal to non-discrimination principles to argue that the government is engaging in prohibited anticompetitive behaviour. Batory shows how governments respond to such Commission pressure by making minor adjustments to comply with EU rules while still fulfilling their original illiberal objectives. While the Commission might ignore creative compliance for political or bureaucratic reasons, Batory argues that the lack of meaningful enforcement can ultimately contribute to legitimating such moves domestically while, at the same time, delegitimising the Commission's authority to uphold core EU principles.[7]

Extending the concept of creative compliance to core economic areas like European competition policy, where the Commission enjoys exclusive competence, the question arises: are governments ignoring the spirit of market-based competition rules while still conforming to the letter of EU law? Creative compliance is particularly relevant to understanding practical enforcement of European competition rules in a context where Member State governments are under pressure from a range of domestic actors, from industry groups to populist parties, to 'take back control' of economic decision-making. Scholars suggest that increased politicisation shapes the Commission's enforcement decisions, avoiding investigations in Member States where public trust in the Commission is low.[8] Creative compliance shifts our attention from the regulators to the regulated. It focuses on the active response of those subject to European laws. One response to unwanted Commission control is to lobby for changes in European competition rules at the European level. But creative compliance examines 'the *post hoc* manipulation of law to turn it – no matter what the intention of legislators or enforcers – to the service of their own interests and avoid unwanted control'.[9]

Creative compliance makes two main contributions to the existing literature on European competition rule enforcement. First, it offers a more two-dimensional account of European law in understanding EU rules as not only a means of controlling the actions of Member States, but also as a means of escaping control.

[6] Batory, 'Defying the Commission' (n 3 above) 689.

[7] ibid 696. See also RD Kelemen, 'The European Union's Authoritarian Equilibrium' (2020) 27 *Journal of European Public Policy* 481.

[8] Finke, 'A Guardian in Need of Support' (n 2 above) 629.

[9] D McBarnet and C Whelan, 'The Elusive Spirit of the Law: Formalism and the Struggle for Legal Control' (1991) 54 *The Modern Law Review* 848.

For instance, an irony of the Brexit slogan 'take back control' is the British government has been very adept at maintaining a strong record in formal compliance, while successfully avoiding meaningful compliance with EU rules it considered too costly to implement.[10] Second, a creative compliance framework opens the opaque black box of national administrations to assess how they aid their governments in implementing EU rules. Default accounts of non-compliance assume that a government otherwise inclined to implement EU rules is unable in practice due to weak administrative capacity.[11] On the flip side, governments registering high rates of compliance are assumed to have efficient national administrators capable of implementing EU rules timely and fully. A creative compliance approach suggests that 'compliance' is an active process that, in the hands of capable administrators, can achieve high rates of formal compliance while using expertise to escape meaningful Commission control so that a Member State government can achieve objectives that may conflict with underlying European free-market competition principles.

III. Creative Compliance and the Evolution of European State Aid Policy

Returning to our definition of creative compliance, it is useful to identify what constitutes the 'spirit' of state aid policy. Like other areas of competition policy, European state aid policy grants supranational agents – namely the Commission and the Court of Justice of the European Union (CJEU) – the authority to ensure that actors operating across the single market compete on a level playing field. Government interventions, such as direct subsidies, guaranteed loans or preferential tax arrangements to one firm or industry are considered market-distorting if they give recipient firms or industries an unfair advantage. A more fundamental principle underlying European state aid rules is that freer and more competitive markets improve overall efficiency, leading to superior goods and services at lower costs to consumers and, more indirectly, stronger economic growth. Following on from these basic principles, ignoring the spirit of state aid rules would entail embracing state intervention as an alternative to the market in allocating resources. Moreover, intervening to tilt the playing field to one Member State's advantage would contradict general EU constitutional principles of granting supranational authorities the authority to coordinate and enforce common regulatory rules

[10] L Warlouzet, 'Britain at the Centre of European Co-operation (1948–2016)' (2018) 56 *Journal of Common Market Studies* 955.

[11] M Blauberger, 'Of "Good" and "Bad" Subsidies: European State Aid Control through Soft and Hard Law' (2009) 32 *West European Politics* 719; M Cremona, 'State Aid Control: Substance and Procedure in the Europe Agreements and the Stabilisation and Association Agreements' (2003) 9 *European Law Journal* 265; CM Colombo, 'State Aid Control in the Modernisation Era: Moving Towards a Differentiated Administrative Integration' (2019) 25 *European Law Journal* 292.

applied equally to all Member States and economic actors operating within an integrated single market.

The closest that European state aid policy came to upholding these fundamental principles was in its so-called 'neoliberal' phase corresponding with the revitalisation of the single market in the 1980s and the passage of the Maastricht Treaty in 1993.[12] A gap existed in the previous post-war 'interventionist' phase between European state aid rules set out in the Treaties and their practical enforcement. Dirigiste governments – or, in other words, governments that play a strong role in directing the economy – were reluctant to cede practical control of strategically and politically important industrial policy decisions to supranational authorities. European state aid policy was subsequently driven more by political realism than jurisprudence.[13] Indeed, it was not until 1984 that the Commission issued a negative decision against a Member State for issuing 'illegal' state aid.[14] With stagflation and high unemployment crippling European economies in the 1970s, neoliberal reformers argued that dirigistism was largely to blame. Moreover, European economies were facing heightened competition from Japan and the Asian 'tiger' economies, which were exporting superior but cheaper high-value industrial goods. These pressures created a perfect storm in which neoliberal reformers could push through stronger state aid measures.

European competition policy was considered a crucial tool for revitalising the single market by eliminating behind-the-border, non-tariff barriers to free movement of goods, capital and services. Competition Commissioner from 1985 to 1989, Peter Sutherland, argued that competition policy was 'the sole means of making the most of the potential offered by the completion of the large market'.[15] The Commission now put its monitoring and sanctioning authority to work in investigating state interventions that hindered market-based competition. It also introduced a State Aid Scoreboard that published annual state aid statistics across Member States, a softer 'naming, shaming, and faming' tool to incentive states to reduce state aid expenditures.[16] If political realism superseded jurisprudence in the previous era, in this neoliberal stage one could argue that jurisprudence was consistent with political realism. That is, Member States were committed to furthering the single market project and strengthening supranational capacity to enforce common rules were understood as essential to realizing this goal. Moreover, the neoliberal idea that market-based reforms were crucial to making

[12] H Buch-Hansen, and A Wigger, 'Revisiting 50 Years of Market-Making: The Neoliberal Transformation of EC Competition Policy' (2010) 17 *Review of International Political Economy* 20.

[13] M Ross, 'State Aids: Maturing into a Constitutional Problem' (1995) 15 *Yearbook of European Law* 79.

[14] W Davies, 'When is a Market not a Market? "Exemption", "Externality" and "Exception" in the Case of European State Aid Rules' (20130 32 *Theory, Culture and Society* 32. Case 84/82 *Germany v Commission* [1984] EU:C:1984:117

[15] P Akman and H Kassim, 'Myths and Myth-Making in the European Union: The Institutionalization and Interpretation of EU Competition Policy' (2010) 48 *Journal of Common Market Studies* 111, 117.

[16] See Commission, 'Scoreboard': www.ec.europa.eu/competition-policy/state-aid/scoreboard_en.

European economies more competitive and thus more prosperous was accepted, albeit to varying degrees, by most Member State governments during this period.

The 2005 State Aid Action Plan, with the headline 'less and better targeted aid', marked the beginning of a 'pragmatic' phase.[17] The Plan's reference to 'less' aid reflected continuity in the overarching principle that states should allow markets to allocate resources. 'Better targeted' acknowledged, however, that the market often fails to provide sufficient investment necessary to achieve the EU's overarching objective of promoting 'smart, sustainable and inclusive' growth. The Commission expanded the so-called 'General Block Exemption Regulation' (GBER) to exempt horizontal aid from prior notification and Commission approval, effectively steering Member States towards distributing 'good' types of state aid, such as investment in renewable energy or research and development. The Plan also exempted smaller amounts of aid from prior notification and approval, under the *de minimis* rule, on the grounds that it is expected to have negligible impact on competition. Bruszt and Vukov argue that EU state aid policy since 2005 can be characterised as supporting 'liberal developmentalism': applying rules equally to ensure an open and competitive single market (liberal), but with an awareness that states must intervene to assist domestic actors in harnessing the benefits of transnational market integration (developmental).[18]

The pragmatic stage also introduced some changes in state aid enforcement. The expansion of GBER, by exempting a large proportion of state aid from ex ante approval, effectively reduced the Commission's administrative burden. It also devolved more enforcement responsibility to national state aid authorities.[19] National state aid authorities were now responsible for advising their governments on GBER-compliant aid, keeping national public registers of individual aid awards to ensure transparency, and evaluating GBER aid schemes ex post. Other forms of 'vertical' aid – or, in other words, forms of government support targeted to one firm or sector – continued to require prior notification and approval, and the criteria became more technical. Assessing whether notified aid was permissible had long been left to Commission administrative officials specializing in European competition law. As criteria required the application of more methodologically rigorous analyses of market impact, such as the introduction of the Market Economy Investor Principle (MEIP), the Commission added economists to its state aid unit. This shift towards a more economic approach was consistent with broader trends within the Commission's competition unit, Directorate-General (DG) Comp. National governments responded in kind by adding economists to their state aid units, equipped with expertise to navigate the new Commission rules.[20]

[17] Commission, 'State aid action plan – Less and better targeted state aid: a roadmap for state aid reform 2005–2009' (Consultation Document) COM(2017) 107 final.

[18] L Bruszt and V Vukov, 'Making States for the Single Market: European Integration and the Reshaping of Economic States in the Southern and Eastern Peripheries of Europe' (2017) 40 *West European Politics* 663.

[19] Colombo, 'State Aid Control in the Modernisation Era' (n 11 above) 292–316.

[20] Buch-Hansen and Wigger, 'Revisiting 50 Years of Market-Making' (n 12 above) 35.

The 2008 global financial crisis put the Commission's ability to enforce state aid rules to the test due to the scale of many governments' rescue plans for their banking sectors and the speed with which they rolled them out. The Commission evoked the clause in the Treaties allowing aid 'to remedy a serious disturbance in the economy' and quickly processed applications, sometimes – in the case of the United Kingdom (UK) bailout of three large banks – approving millions in aid in just 24 hours.[21] In 2012 the Council passed the 'Modernisation Regulation' introducing additional changes to state aid rules.[22] It extended the GBER to exempt more categories of state aid, such as innovation, broadband infrastructure and culture and heritage conservation. It also integrated state aid into the Commission's new European Semester recommendations on economic, employment and fiscal policies, to 'improve the quality of public spending by discouraging aid that does not bring real added-value and distorts competition'.[23] Finally, it focused the Commission's priorities on investigating cases with the biggest impact on the single market. After taking over as head of DG Competition in 2014, Commissioner Margrethe Vestager put this change in practice by pursuing highly visible cases, such as ordering Apple to pay $14.5 billion in back taxes to Ireland.[24]

The COVID-19 pandemic poses another challenge to state aid policy. Member States have intervened massively in their economies to mitigate the negative effects of the pandemic. The European Commission responded by introducing special temporary measures that would ease the process of notification and approval.[25] Meunier and Mickus argue that the COVID-19 pandemic has reinforced moves already underway towards a more ambitious European industrial policy that envisions a more active role for the EU and its Member States in developing competitive and sustainable economies.[26] This does not necessarily mean, however, that the Commission is reverting back to practices during the post-war interventionist stage (when it turned a blind eye to enforcement and Member States were largely free to subsidize their economies as they wished). Instead, in many ways the Commission appears to have used the crisis to expand its authority over state aid. It has extended special instruments, such as Important Projects of Common European Interest (IPCEI), to aid economic recovery from the pandemic.[27]

[21] Davies, 'When is a Market not a Market?' (n 14 above) 52. Art 87 of the EC Treaty, now Art 107(3)(b) TFEU.

[22] Commission, 'Communication from the Commission – EU State Aid Modernisation (SAM)' (Communication) COM(2012) 209 final'; Council Regulation (EC) No 659/1999 of 22 March 1999 laying down detailed rules for the application of Article 93 of the EC Treaty [1999] OJ L83/1.

[23] Commission, 'Communication' (n 22 above) 23.

[24] Press Release, 'State aid: Ireland gave illegal tax benefits to Apple worth up to €13 billion': www.ec.europa.eu/commission/presscorner/detail/en/IP_16_2923.

[25] Commission, 'Communication from the Commission Temporary Framework for State aid measures to support the economy in the current COVID-19 outbreak 2020/C 91 I/01' (Communication) COM(2020) 1863.

[26] S Meunier and J Mickus, 'Sizing up the Competition: Explaining Reform of European Union Competition Policy in the Covid-19 Era' (2020) 42 *Journal of European Integration* 1077.

[27] Commission, 'Communication from the Commission Criteria for the analysis of the compatibility with the internal market of State aid to promote the execution of important projects of common European interest 2021/C 528/02' (Communication) [2021] OJ C528/10.

In sum, one could argue that post-COVID-19 European state aid policy is witnessing a change in emphasis in how the EU ensures a competitive free market: focusing more on helping European actors compete, both within and beyond the Single Market, than on strictly enforcing EU state aid rules. Put another way, EU state aid policy appears a bit more 'developmental' and a bit less 'liberal' in approach than the preceding pragmatic phase.

IV. Creative Compliance in Practice: Three Mechanisms

What does creative compliance entail within the evolving European state aid regime? Despite changes in state aid governance detailed above, its fundamental 'spirit' remains that supranational actors ensure that Member States comply with a common set of rules to foster free and fair competition. To comply creatively thus challenges these core principles by engaging in strategies to manipulate rules and enforcement mechanisms to advance a Member State government's interest. The following section examines three types of creative compliance. First, the 'exemption game', whereby potentially inadmissible 'bad' vertical aid is classified as 'good' horizontal aid in order to escape ex ante Commission scrutiny. Second, the 'Frankenstein' strategy, whereby national authorities assemble precedents to justify potentially inadmissible 'vertical' aid at the notification and investigation stages. Third, the 'two steps forward, one step back' strategy, whereby Member States avoid recovering state aid by making minor adjustments or pursuing appeals.[28] I argue that it is not enough for governments to want to engage in the three practices set out above; skilled national administrations with high levels of legal and economic expertise are required for governments to engage in successful creative compliance.

I illustrate how each of the three creative compliance strategies are used in practice through the case study of Hungary. Since taking power in 2010, Viktor Orbán has pledged to transform Hungary into an 'illiberal state'. That is, he promises to use the power and resources of the state to promote and protect domestic firms and industries against global competitive pressures along the lines of Russia and China.[29] Orbán combines this 'illiberal' rhetoric with Euroscepticism, arguing that Hungary must escape the control of Brussels to thrive economically and politically.[30] Hungary spends more on state aid as a proportion of Gross Domestic Product (GDP) than the EU-27 average, and higher than other comparable new

[28] L Bayer, 'How Orbán broke the EU – and got away with it', *Politico*, 24 September 2020: www.politico.eu/article/how-viktor-orban-broke-the-eu-and-got-away-with-it-hungary-rule-of-law/.

[29] P Krekó and Z Enyedi, 'Explaining Eastern Europe: Orbán's Laboratory of Illiberalism' (2018) 29 *Journal of Democracy* 39.

[30] A Bozóki and D Hegedűs, 'An Externally Constrained Hybrid Regime: Hungary in the European Union' (2018) 25 *Democratization* 1173.

Member States, levels that appear consistent with an illiberal model.[31] Puzzlingly, Hungary has spent a higher proportion of total aid on horizontal objectives and has received fewer negative decisions than average on its vertical aid schemes.[32] One would expect a Member State government that so openly pledges to defy European liberal rules and principles to openly spend more on vertical aid benefitting domestic firms and industries and blatantly ignore Commission enforcement measures. Yet overall Hungary appears highly compliant. I argue that one can account for this puzzling discrepancy by examining the different mechanisms of creative compliance outlined above.

A. The Exemption Game

As discussed above, the European Commission is tasked, as part of its broader competition portfolio, with prohibiting 'bad' vertical interventions – including direct subsidies, guaranteed loans or preferential tax arrangements – deemed to give an undue advantage to one firm or industry over others operating within the Single Market. Member states have been given greater scope since the 2000s to distribute, with less Commission scrutiny, 'good' horizontal state aid, such as research and development funding, considered to enhance national (and European) competitiveness.[33] Commission monitoring and enforcement practices have shifted accordingly: vertical aid continues to require ex ante approval, while horizontal aid, comprising an increasingly large proportion of Member States' total state aid, is monitored ex post. Reflecting on the promulgation of soft law measures in state aid, Blauberger cautions that 'the less precise the Commission's rules on admissible state aid, the easier it becomes for Member States to justify distortive aid on that basis'.[34] In other words, expanding the criteria for horizontal aid exempted from strict Commission oversight provides ample opportunities for Member State governments to make 'bad' aid 'good' through what I call an 'exemption game'.

Since 2005 the percentage of total state aid amongst the EU-28 declared as block exempt has steadily increased. By 2017, nearly 50 per cent of all total state aid spent across the EU-28 was declared covered by the GBER. On the one hand, we could interpret this data as governments simply doing what the 2005 Action Plan intended: targeting their aid away from vertical interventions and towards better horizontal objectives. On the other hand, the delegation of state aid monitoring

[31] J Hölscher, N Nulsch and J Stephan, 'State Aid in the New Eu Member States' (2017) 55 *Journal of Common Market Studies* 779.

[32] N Lindstrom, 'Aiding the State: Administrative Capacity and Creative Compliance with European State Aid Rules in New Member States' (2021) 28 *Journal of European Public Policy* 1789.

[33] M Cini, 'The Soft Law Approach: Commission Rule-making in the EU's State Aid Regime' (2001) 8 *Journal of European Public Policy* 192.

[34] Blauberger, 'Of "Good" and "Bad" Subsidies' (n 11 above) 735.

to national authorities raises more fundamental, but opaque, questions of the extent to which potentially distortive aid is being classified as block exempted aid. Not only does the Commission delegate to Member States the task of classifying and reporting different types of state aid; but, also, the ever-expanding list of GBER exemptions provides state aid authorities with more scope to classify aid as exempt. Motivations to classify potentially 'bad' aid as 'good' can include administrators' benign desire to avoid a lengthy and time-consuming process of receiving ex ante Commission approval. It can also be motivated by governments seeking to avoid Commission scrutiny, preferring the soft law guidance of GBER regulations. Whatever the motivation, national administrators must have sufficient experience and expertise to play the exemption game effectively.

We can examine how the exemption game works in practice in the case of Hungary. When Hungary entered EU accession negotiations in the late 1990s, like all applicant states it was required to transpose European state aid rules into relevant domestic legislation, develop legal and administrative competence to monitor state aid, and demonstrate a credible enforcement record. Although it was outside the single market and formal governance structures, Hungary still had to develop administrative capacity to enforce European rules.[35] In the case of state aid, applicant states are free to choose where they place their state aid units. Hungary, like many Member States, initially put its state aid unit, the State Aid Monitoring Office (SAMO), within the Ministry of Finance.[36] When Hungary became a full EU member in 2004 it became subject to Commission state aid monitoring and enforcement. Hungary shifted SAMO from the Finance Ministry to the Ministry of National Development in 2006 under a left-leaning government. Soon after Orbán won his second term in office in 2014, he moved the state aid authority to the Prime Minister's Office as part of a ministerial restructuring. By 2017 SAMO had grown in size to employ at least 20 full-time Hungarian lawyers and economists, many of whom had acquired degrees abroad.[37]

The relative size of national state aid administrative units, and their location in terms of proximity to the executive, can give us a broad indication of how governments approach state aid regulation. Making the exceptional move of placing the state aid monitoring unit in the Prime Minister's Office suggests that Orbán recognised the benefits of locating state aid advisors close to the centre of executive decision-making. However, we can dig deeper to understand how state aid administrators view their role. The 'spirit' of European state aid regulation is that state aid officials work closely with the European Commission to monitor and enforce European state aid rules. Colombo shows, for example, how the Commission has created an epistemic community made up of national authorities dealing with state aid on a day-to-day basis.[38] Hungarian state aid officials, conversely, appear equally

[35] Cremona, 'State Aid Control' (n 11 above) 265.
[36] E Hargita and Z Filep, 'State Aid Control in Hungary' (2004) 3 *European State Aid Law Quarterly* 6.
[37] Lindstrom, 'Aiding the State' (n 32 above) 1793.
[38] Colombo, 'State Aid Control in the Modernisation Era' (n 11 above).

or more aligned to their national governments than the Commission, defining their role as an 'advocate of aid granters'.[39] That is, they take a more proactive stance in advising the government whether its proposed aid could qualify as falling under block exemptions or be divided up in order to meet *de minimis* thresholds. Here it is important to note that block exempt aid is still subject to ex post Commission scrutiny. The exemption game must thus be played where classifications remain credible.

The exemption game is largely played behind the scenes. Occasionally it attracts public scrutiny. One such case involved the creation of a light railway connecting Orbán's home village to a neighbouring one in rural southwestern Hungary. The Hungarian government justified the investment of over two million euros as meeting the horizontal objective of boosting tourism in an underdeveloped region. The project was part of a larger EU structural and cohesion funding programme, which is subject to state aid rules. Critics argued that it was a vanity project with little prospect of achieving its proposed aims. They argued the main motivation was to line the pockets of local small businesses with close personal and political links to the ruling party. When Members of the European Parliament's Budgetary Control Committee travelled to Hungary in 2017 on a routine fact-finding trip and visited the railway, protesters held signs saying: 'Viktor Orbán became the richest Hungarian by stealing EU taxpayers' money. The thief is Orbán, not the people of Hungary!' The government argued that the Committee's fact-finding mission was politically motivated. 'I find it particularly outrageous', Orbán's chief of staff wrote to the committee chair, 'that out of thousands of co-financed investments you happen to attempt to examine a project implemented in the own village of the Hungarian prime minister'. One Estonian MEP travelling with the parliamentary delegation noted: 'At every meeting, you can feel the politicized character of the topic. We try to find as many hard facts as we can.'[40]

The politicisation of the European parliamentary committee's fact-finding mission, in which Hungarian leaders accused it of meddling in domestic affairs, illustrates the politicisation of state aid enforcement. The Commission has always faced what Doleys terms a 'dilemma of discretion': it is delegated authority to administer EU treaty state aid rules, but it must use discretion in how to interpret often imprecise language in both treaty and secondary legislation with respect to both the rules and its authority to enforce them.[41] The Commission increasingly faces a political dilemma. If, on the one hand, it intervenes in highly contentious domestic issues, such as the misuse of EU horizontal funds, governments can

[39] Lindstrom, 'Aiding the State' (n 32 above) 1795.

[40] L Bayer, 'In Hungary, big trouble over little train', *Politico*, 19 September. See also Directorate-General for Internal Policies of the Union, 'Fact-finding mission of the Budgetary Control Committee (CONT) to Hungary, 18–20 September 2017' (2017): www.europarl.europa.eu/cmsdata/126788/CONT%20mission%20to%20Hungary%20DRAFT%20programme%20reduced.pdf.

[41] T Doleys, 'Managing the Dilemma of Discretion: The European Commission and the Development of EU State Aid Policy' (2013) 13 *Journal of Industry, Competition and Trade* 23.

publicly accuse it of bias and overreach. On the other hand, if the Commission does not intervene, it risks being accused of absconding its responsibility for due diligence. Facing such a no-win situation, the Commission is more likely to turn a blind eye to the 'exemption game', depending on other European actors, from the European Anti-Fraud Office (OLAF) to the European Parliament's Budgetary Control Committee, to monitor horizontal aid. It has another tool at its disposal: applying conditions to special European funding, such as reinforcing anti-corruption tools and strengthening judicial independence, as a condition of receiving COVID-19 recovery funds.[42]

B. The Frankenstein Strategy

Creative compliance is also evident in the monitoring and enforcement of vertical state aid measures, such as direct subsidies, equity investments, loans or loan guarantees or special arrangements. When national state aid administrators prepare notifications to inform the Commission of any planned aid package, they must build a solid economic and legal case for permissibility and anticipate possible Commission objections. Much of the work putting together a solid notification is routine, such as demonstrating that a state aid measure does not confer an economic advantage on the recipient of the aid beyond that of a private investor. State aid administrators, like the scientist in Shelley's famous novel, can collect previous state aid decisions and assemble a case built on different precedents across Member States to justify a state aid measure. Like the novel itself, the 'Frankenstein strategy' can result in legal and political 'monsters' that take on a life of their own. This strategy can ultimately weaken the Commission's legitimacy over time and steer state aid policy away from its original objective. As Rui Tavares, a former Portuguese Member of Parliament (MEP), put it: 'Dr. Frankenstein built a monster, and the monster is made up of bits and pieces of other bodies that in themselves are not problematic. It's the mix that is problematic.'[43]

We can use a Hungarian case to illustrate the Frankenstein strategy in practice. Of all the vertical aid Hungary notified the Commission of granting from 2010, when Orbán took office, until 2018, the Commission conducted six investigations. One involved a Russian-financed nuclear power deal.[44] In 2014, the Hungarian government notified the Commission of its intention to form a new joint-stock company to construct two new nuclear reactors. Paks II would be funded by a 10-million-euro loan from the Russian government in addition to an estimated 2.5 million euros from the Hungarian budget. The reactors would be owned and

[42] E Zalan, 'EU may delay approval of Hungary's recovery plan', *EUObserver*, 13 July 2021: https://euobserver.com/news/152420.

[43] Bayer, 'How Orbán Broke the EU' (n 28 above) 1.

[44] Commission Decision (EU) 2017/2112 of 6 March 2017 on the measure/aid scheme/State aid SA.38454 (2015/C) [2017] OJ L317/45.

operated as part of a subsidiary of the Hungarian state-owned power company, MVM. Observers expected the Commission would object to the deal. The Russian-owned Rosatom won the no-bid contract to build the reactors, even though other companies, such as US-based Westinghouse Electric, had expressed interest. The Russian loan – at an interest rate above what Hungary was likely to secure from private markets – would be channelled through a Russian state-owned bank placed under EU sanctions. Moreover, the economic case for Paks II was questionable given the falling costs of electricity generation. The director of the Fiscal Responsibility Institute Budapest argued that Hungarian taxpayers and energy consumers would be left footing the bill for a premature deal. Finally, the EU was launching its clean-energy package that stressed smaller, decentralised, and renewable energy generation, the thrust of which went against construction of large nuclear reactors.[45]

The Commission under José Manuel Barroso had taken a hard line on Russian-financed energy projects, most notably opposing the South Stream gas pipeline project that would link Russian gas pipelines as far as Italy. Less visibly, but most relevant to the Paks II case, the Barroso Commission pressured another new Member State, Bulgaria, to sever ties with Rosatom's investment in Bulgarian nuclear power plants on the grounds that it violated EU competition rules.[46] The incoming President, Jean-Claude Juncker, remained relatively silent about the Paks II deal. His spokesperson insisted that it was a legal rather than political question, reiterating that 'regardless of the nationality of the investor in a public energy project, the Commission is called to assess each case by its own merits'.[47] The Commission considered objections to the no-bid deal and whether the project violated state aid rules, and eventually gave it the green light in 2016. When asked about the approval of this and other controversial Hungarian state aid cases, a European Commission state aid official reflected more generally on the quality of Hungarian state aid administrators: 'The Hungarian state aid authority is one of the best in the EU. The way in which they report state aid, and respond to our queries, is watertight in legal and economic terms.'[48]

The 'watertight' case for Paks II involved a kind of Frankenstein strategy that successfully assembled different rationales and precedents. When asked about Paks II, a Hungarian state aid official described how the state aid team 'took the Hinkley Point case and followed the same logic'.[49] Hinkley Point involved construction of a new nuclear reactor in southwest England with £19.6 billion funding from French and Chinese energy firms, in addition to UK government

[45] D Herzenhorn, S Stefanini and N Hirst, 'Shrugging Off Concerns, Europe Waves Through Hungary's Controversial Nuke Deal', *Politico*, 14 December 2016: www.politico.eu/article/europes-radioactive-embrace-hungary-russia-paks-ii-project-nuclear-reactors/.

[46] EURACTIV, Barroso warns Bulgaria on South Stream', *EURACTIV*, 28 May 2014: www.euractiv.com/section/energy/news/barroso-warns-bulgaria-on-south-stream/

[47] Herzenhorn, Stefanini and Hirst, 'Shrugging Off Concerns' (n 45 above) 1.

[48] Lindstrom, 'Aiding the State' (n 32 above) 13.

[49] ibid.

funding and guarantees. The Commission cleared the Hinkley Point project in 2014.[50] Austria and Luxembourg filed objections to the Commission's ruling, but the CJEU subsequently upheld the decision.[51] Hungary argued successfully that it was free to choose its energy mix under existing EU treaties.[52] It also argued that the development of nuclear energy is a valid public interest objective in providing Hungary with energy stability and security. Moreover, during the course of the proceedings it submitted its economic case, arguing that the plant would be profitable, even without a price floor on consumer electricity rates, an assessment that was endorsed by the German consulting firm Rothchild.[53] As for the no-bid deal, Hungary argued that Rosatom was the only firm that had the required specialised expertise.

One could argue that the strategy of piecing together different rules and precedents is simply compliance, or, in other words, what good legal counsel does routinely. What then makes creative compliance distinct? I argue that creative compliance assumes a certain degree of intentionality on the part of Member State governments to use legal expertise to escape the Commission's control by following the rules by form but defying their substance. Tibor Navracsics, Orbán's justice minister between 2010 and 2014 and later European Commissioner, explains his government's strategy: 'What we tried to do was to demonstrate to our critics by using comparisons that our solutions were not unique by far. Moreover, those policies criticised by the Commission could be found in other Member States as well.'[54] In the case of Paks II, one could argue that Hungary, in granting a no-bid contract to a Russian state-owned firm with expensive financing from a Russian-owned bank to build two Hungarian state-owned reactors, appeared to go against the spirit of European competition rules, in addition to diverging from many principles underlying a common European energy policy and foreign policy objectives in relation to Russia. It was simply the case that the Commission concluded that Hungary was technically in compliance. Like Frankenstein finding it difficult to control his creature once created, this form of technical Commission decision-making can have consequences. The Commission's 2020 proposals to create new instruments to control state aid involving state-funded foreign firms suggests it is now trying to re-level the playing field.[55]

[50] Commission Decision (EU) 2015/658 of 8 October 2014 on the aid measure SA.34957 (2013/C)) [2015] OJ L109/44.

[51] Judgment of 22 September 2020, C-594/18 P *Austria v Commission* [2020] EU:C:2020:742.

[52] Consolidated version of the Treaty on the Functioning of the European union (TFEU) [2012] OJ C326/47, Art 194(2).

[53] Herzenhorn, Stefanini and Hirst, 'Shrugging Off Concerns' (n 45 above) 1.

[54] Bayer, 'How Orbán Broke the EU' (n 28 above) 1, 2.

[55] S Meunier and J Mickus, 'Sizing up the Competition: Explaining Reform of European Union Competition Policy in the Covid-19 Era' (2020) 42 *Journal of European Integration* 1077. See also Proposal for a Regulation of the European Parliament and of the Council on foreign subsidies distorting the internal market COM(2021) 223 final.

C. Two Steps Forward, One Step Back

A final form of creative compliance relates to negative decisions on vertical aid. The Commission investigates a small proportion of state aid notifications it receives each year and issues negative decisions in a fraction of those cases. The potential costs of negative decisions are increasingly high. In legal terms, the Court of Justice of the EU can overturn Commission decisions, as it did in high-profile cases against special tax arrangements for Apple.[56] Negative decisions are also becoming increasingly political. Those who support the Commission taking a harder stance against governments granting preferential loans or tax exemptions to large multinational corporations have responded positively, arguing that the Commission has an important role to play in stopping a global race-to-the-bottom where footloose multinational firms can demand ever more attractive packages of government incentives as a condition of (re)locating their operations. Critics of intervention argue, on the other hand, that the Commission is overstepping its authority by intervening in what should be domestic economic decisions and, moreover, is making it difficult for Member States to compete against third countries.

Within this more politicized European state aid policy context, Member States receiving a negative decision from the Commission can use tools of creative compliance to delay or avoid penalties. We can turn again to the Hungarian case to illustrate. Since taking power in 2010, the Orbán government has received at the time of writing three negative Commission decisions.[57] Each involved the Fidesz-majority parliament levying special taxes on high turnover companies, namely advertisers, commercial food companies and tobacco distributors. In the advertising tax case, the German-based RTL group argued that the government's special tax on commercial broadcaster's advertising revenue discriminated against German-owned RTL, the largest commercial competitor to the Hungarian state-owned media.[58] RTL had become increasingly critical of the Orbán regime, both in its news division and in some of its serial productions that integrated criticisms into its story lines. RTL's chief executive in Hungary, Dirk Gerkens, argued at an international press briefing: 'We're the last major independent media company here and there's an attempt to raid us from the market.'[59] Arguing that opposition

[56] Judgment in the Case T-778/16 *Ireland v Commission* [2020] EU:T:2020:338, 15/07/2020.

[57] Commission Decision (EU) of 21 August 2015 – Health contribution of tobacco industry businesses (2015/NN) [2015] OJ C277/24; Commission Decision (EU) 2016/1848 of 4 July 2016 on the measure SA.40018 (2015/C) (ex 2015/NN) implemented by Hungary on the 2014 Amendment to the Hungarian food chain inspection fee C/2016/4056 OJ L282/63; Commission Decision (EU) 2017/329 of 4 November 2016 on the measure SA.39235 (2015/C) (ex 2015/NN) implemented by Hungary on the taxation of advertisement turnover [2017] OJ L49/36.

[58] M Banks, 'EU investigating whether Hungarian state aid spending is undermining media freedom', *The Parliament Magazine*, 26 October 2020: www.theparliamentmagazine.eu/news/article/eu-investigating-whether-hungarian-state-aid-spending-is-undermining-media-freedom.

[59] M Feher and V Gulyas, 'EU Commissioner: New Hungarian Tax Aimed at Chasing Broadcaster RTL Away', *The Wall Street Journal (internet edition)*, 28 July 2014.

to the advertising tax was fundamentally an issue of upholding the freedom of speech against Orbán's attempt to stifle dissent through amassing state control over the media, Gerkens threatened to take the case to the European Court of Human Rights. Vice-president of the Commission Neelie Kroes echoed this interpretation: 'Government control, monopoly and censorship belong to a different, darker period in Hungary's history: and no one should seek a return to it.'[60]

The Commission's state aid unit initiated an investigation of the advertising tax and, in 2015, came to a negative decision, with recovery.[61] In practice this meant that smaller the Hungarian government would collect payments from media companies, most of which were more loyal to Orbán, that they would have paid with a fixed rate of tax, and reimburse firms, namely RTL, who had paid more.[62] A Hungarian state aid official remarked about the case: 'I warned the government that the Commission was very likely to rule this illegal.' When asked why the government pursued the tax regardless, she replied simply: 'politics'.[63] The Orbán government brought before the General Court an action for annulment of the Commission's decision.[64] It made a treaty-based argument that the European Commission did not have competence over Member States' corporate taxation policies. It also argued that Hungary's progressive tax policy was not discriminatory in that it was transparently and consistently applied to all media companies operating in Hungary. The Hungarian government's reasoning was quite consistent with the CJEU decision on Apple and other cases involving corporate tax arrangements. While the appeal worked its way through the courts, the Hungarian parliament repealed the advertisement tax with retroactive effect in 2017.[65] However, it remains unclear whether the Hungarian government collected unpaid tax from the smaller state-owned and commercial broadcasters, who the Commission argued had unfairly benefited from advertising tax, or repaid the tax to those, such as RTL, who had been disadvantaged.

The Hungarian government thus managed to take two steps forward in exerting more state control over the media, even if it had to take one step back in eventually modifying its tax rules to address the Commission's concerns. On balance, the end result is that Orbán achieved his main aims. While Orbán did not manage to completely silence RTL – which continued operating in Hungary and with content critical of the government – Gerken, one of Orbán's most vocal critics, left his

[60] Feher and Gulyas, 'EU Commissioner (n 59 above).

[61] Commission Decision (EU) 2017/329 (n 57 above).

[62] Commission Decision (EU) 2017/329 (n 57 above). See also A Bátorfy and A Urbán, 'State Advertising as an Instrument of Transformation of the Media Market in Hungary' (2020) 36 *East European Politics* 44.

[63] Lindstrom, 'Aiding the State' (n 32 above) 13.

[64] Case T-20/17 *Hungary v Commission* [2019] EU:T:2019:448.

[65] General Court of the European Union, 'Press Release No 84/19 The General Court annuls the Commission's decision finding that the Hungarian advertisement tax was incompatible with the EU State aid rules': www.curia.europa.eu/jcms/upload/docs/application/pdf/2019-06/cp190084en.pdf.

post at RTL. Moreover, the tax advantages granted to other broadcasters are sunk costs difficult to recover. The Commission might prefer using formal infringement procedures to address alleged rule of law violations, calculating that it can provide a technical and less politicized alternative to Article 7 hearings. Critics, however, argue that such a strategy falls short in the Commission's fulfilling its responsibility to help protect the rule of law across the European Union.[66]

V. Concluding Remarks

European state aid policy is increasingly politicised. Some Member States are not only pushing back against the Commission's exclusive competence to enforce competition rules; they are challenging the free-market principles underlying the single market, as well as the extension of EU competencies in economic decision making, such as tax policy. This chapter examines the implementation stage of state aid policy in the context of increasing politicisation of European competition policy. It shows how some Member State governments are using strategies of 'creative compliance' to challenge the meaningful enforcement of state aid rules. It examines three creative compliance strategies across each stage of state aid enforcement: the 'exemption game' in the classification stage, the 'Frankenstein strategy' in the notification and investigation stage and the 'two steps forward, one step back' tactic in the recovery stage. The chapter suggests that it is not enough for Member State governments to want to evade meaningful Commission enforcement of state aid rules; creative compliance requires a sufficient degree of administrative capacity to play the game effectively.

One avenue for further research on creative compliance is the extent to which it can be generalized across Member States and policy areas. The case of Hungary shows how leaders of an avowedly 'illiberal' regime manage to achieve its objectives while ostensibly staying within formal EU rules. A pertinent question is whether creative compliance is used more frequently in Member States that are less likely to affect change at the EU level. As a leader of a new and more marginal EU Member State, Orbán might calculate, for example, that it is easier to achieve his objectives through creative compliance at the enforcement stage than through EU-level negotiations. If, however, an ambivalent 'rule-taker' like Hungary decides to become a 'rule-maker', it could likely find allies amongst more powerful EU members in changing the scope of EU competencies. A second question for further research is how the Commission is navigating its prescribed role as rule enforcer when those rules are subject to greater politicisation and change.

[66] See, for example, K McCourt, 'European Commission Lacks Tenacity on the Rule of Law: Rule of Law Report Lacks Consequences for Law Breaking', *Human Rights Watch*, 20 July 2022: www.hrw.org/news/2022/07/20/european-commission-lacks-tenacity-rule-law.

Fink suggests that the Commission is less likely to enforce state aid rules in Member States where levels of public trust in the Commission are lower. More research is required to consider when and how the Commission uses its discretion to enforce the rules it is tasked with upholding but maintaining legitimacy with those who demand more rigorous enforcement and those who advocate granting Member States more autonomy to grant state aid to address the myriad of economic and political challenges facing EU Member States.[67]

[67] VA Schmidt, 'Politicization in the EU: Between National Politics and EU Political Dynamics' (2019) 26 *Journal of European Public Policy* 1018.

Conclusions

CARLO MARIA COLOMBO, KATHRYN WRIGHT AND MARIOLINA ELIANTONIO*

I. Introduction

This book started from the premise that the present state of turbulence or polycrisis that is testing the EU's integration and socio-economic structures requires an analysis of how competition law, given its key position in the EU economic constitution, is transforming to respond to the emerging challenges. The existing debate has used primarily a sectoral perspective that focuses on specific areas of competition law and individual crises.[1] It has discussed the appropriateness of rules and their economic rationale for the multiple crises that are affecting the EU and has developed a number of proposals for how the limits could be overcome. However, competition law as an operational whole and as part of the broader EU institutional system is increasingly called upon to respond to the influence of these exogenous events affecting markets. It is therefore equally important to broaden the focus, address how substantive changes feed into the procedural and institutional aspects of EU competition law, and evaluate the extent to which the resulting system is in line with the fundamental principles shaping the EU constitutional framework.

* Carlo Maria Colombo is Marie Skłodowska-Curie Fellow at Sciences Po, France, and Assistant Professor of Administrative Law at Maastricht University, the Netherlands, carlo.colombo@maastrichtuniversity.nl. Kathryn Wright is a Senior Lecturer in Law, University of York, kathryn.wright@york.ac.uk. Mariolina Eliantonio is a Professor in European and Comparative Administrative Law and Procedure, Maastricht University, m.eliantonio@maastrichtuniversity.nl. Funded by the York-Maastricht Partnership and the European Union. Views and opinions expressed are however those of the author(s) only and do not necessarily reflect those of the European Union or the European Commission. Neither the European Union nor the European Commission can be held responsible for them.

[1] Eg on digitalisation: A Daly, Private Power, Online Information Flows and EU Law (Oxford, Hart Publishing, 2019); G Surblytė-Namavičienė, Competition *and* Regulation in the Data Economy (Cheltenham, Edward Elgar Publishing, 2020); B Lundqvist and MS Gal, Competition Law for the Digital Economy (Cheltenham, Edward Elgar Publishing, 2019). On environmental protection: A Gerbrandy, The Uneasy Relationship Between Sustainability and Competition Law (Oxford, Hart Publishing, 2021); S Kingston, Greening EU Competition Law and Policy (Cambridge, Cambridge University Press, 2011); J Nowag, Environmental Integration in Competition and Free Movement Laws (Oxford, Oxford University Press, 2017). On financial crisis: W-G Ringe and P Huber, Legal Challenges in the Global Financial Crisis: Bail-outs, the Euro and Regulation (Cheltenham, Hart Publishing, 2015).

Hence, the various analyses in this book broaden the purely substantive debates that have prevailed hitherto and collectively discuss how these transformations are redesigning the governance of EU competition law.[2] This concluding chapter gives an account of the emerging transformations, and the incipient constitutional questions, as they arise from the book's contributions. At the same time, it represents a starting point, as it proposes possible building blocks to expand this analysis on the institutional transformations involved in the post-modernisation shifts in competition law.

II. Powers and Aims

As repeatedly noted in the literature[3] and confirmed by many of the contributions in this book,[4] the competition rules set in the EU Treaties have remained unchanged since their inception. This is so even during the latest turbulent times, in which various crises have tested the rules' limits and responsiveness. The main reason for understanding this robustness hitherto lies in the flexibility of the EU competition law framework. This flexibility can be understood in two ways: as the ability of substantive rules, due to the open nature of their terms, to be interpreted and applied in an evolutionary way to new cases; and as the ability of the institutional structure to ensure sufficiently uniform and effective application of rules within a complex system of distributed competences.

In the first meaning, the flexibility stemming from the rules' broad formulation has given the Commission and national competition authorities (NCAs) the power to adapt the application of the substantive prohibitions and exceptions of competition rules across all areas to the new practices and dynamics emerging in markets as a result of the various crises affecting the EU.[5] In this sense, the present turbulence seems to unfold a trend towards the greater role of societal and public policy goals beyond pure market considerations in competition law

[2] See the Introduction to this book.

[3] See, among the many, A Gerbrandy, 'Rethinking Competition Law within the European Economic Constitution' (2019) 57 Journal of Common Market Studies 127, 129; A Biondi and E Righini, 'An Evolutionary Theory of EU State Aid Control' in A Arnull and D Chalmers (eds), The Oxford Handbook of European Law (Oxford, Oxford University Press, 2015) 670.

[4] See A Sikora-Kaléda, 'A Clash of Titans: EU Competition and State Aid Law and the Impact of the European Green Deal', Chapter 3 in this volume, P Nicolaides, 'The Response of EU Courts to Society's Digital and Green Challenges in the Field of Competition and State Aid', Chapter 8 in this volume, and CM Colombo and M Bonelli, 'Governing the Green Transition Through State Aid Control', Chapter 12 in this volume.

[5] P Van Cleynenbreugel, 'Digital Technology Disruptions and Competition Law: a Stress Test for the Existing Governance and Enforcement Frameworks?', Chapter 2 in this volume; F Costa Cabral, 'From Crisis Cartels to COVID-19 State Aid and Cooperation: The Non-Exceptionality of Crisis Management by EU Competition Law', Chapter 4 in this volume; O Stefan, 'Soft Law in EU Competition and State aid: an Imperfect Solution to Grand Regulatory Challenges', Chapter 10 in this volume; CM Colombo and M Bonelli (n 4 above).

responses to the crises. In the field of antitrust, agreements between companies can now be motivated due to 'sustainability reasons',[6] while collective agreements between self-employed workers of digital platforms regarding working conditions are allowed to rebalance their bargaining power.[7] More in line with the traditional approach, public policy interests, such as sustainability, are also playing a role in the compatibility assessment of State aid[8] and merger control.[9] In these instances, the principle of proportionality is used to tailor the allowed measure to the public policy objective pursued.[10] In addition to bringing competition law in line with the strategic direction of broader EU policy initiatives, this trend is not surprising.[11] As these crises are connected to societal challenges and transformations coming from outside competition law and affecting how markets operate, this opens the door to non-economic goals gaining a greater role in their evaluation than pure efficiency reasons connected to consumer welfare motivations.

This trend, however, does not speak of new exceptional competition law rules unfolding in the present turbulent era. Rather, the Commission has resisted calls to relax merger control rules to allow for the creation of national champions better able to withstand geopolitical pressures.[12] When it has used its broad discretion improperly, as it did when it used its power to review aid compatibility under Article 107(3)(c) TFEU to determine the common interest objectives that national State aid can legitimately pursue, the Court has intervened to restore the scope of the article, as in Hinckley Point.[13] Remarkably, this observation holds true even when EU competition law has been used to manage systemic crises such as that caused by the recent COVID-19 pandemic. Although such special circumstances may typically increase calls for suspending or relaxing rules, EU competition law, including its prohibitions and public policy justifications, appears to have been interpreted in a fairly consistent manner with past practice. While maintaining the general prohibitions of State aid in place, the Temporary Framework for State Aid[14] resorted to justifications defined and used previously, from more limited natural disasters and other serious disturbances, as well as the economic development that

[6] G Monti, 'Shaping the EU's Competition Law and Policy: Space for Multiple Actors?', Chapter 6 in this volume; Stefan (n 5 above).

[7] Stefan (n 5 above).

[8] Sikora-Kaléda (n 4 above); Colombo and Bonelli (n 4 above).

[9] Monti (n 6 above).

[10] M Hjärtström and J Nowag, 'General Principles of EU Law in EU Antitrust; For the General Role of Environmental Requirements' in KS Ziegler, PJ Neuvonen and V Moreno-Lax (eds), Research Handbook on General Principles of EU Law (Cheltenham, Edward Elgar Publishing, 2022). See also in this book, Sikora-Kaléda (n 4 above); Costa Cabral (n 5 above); Colombo and Bonelli (n 4 above).

[11] Among the many in this sense lately, see Gerbrandy (n 3 above).

[12] Monti (n 6 above).

[13] See Sikora-Kaléda (n 4 above); Costa Cabral (n 5 above); Nicolaides (n 4 above); Stefan (n 5 above); Colombo and Bonelli (n 4 above).

[14] Commission, 'Communication from the Commission, Temporary Framework for State aid measures to support the economy in the current COVID-19 outbreak' [2020] OJ C 91I, as amended.

justifies aid for undertakings in difficulty.[15] In the field of antitrust, the Temporary Framework for Cooperation,[16] while adopting a more conciliatory approach since the 2008 financial crisis to justify some limited agreements and mergers on public policy grounds (such as public health),[17] nevertheless seems to follow existing case law on the legitimate objectives that may justify the non-application of the Article 101(1) TFEU prohibition.[18] All this appears to speak to crisis management being an in-built feature of regular enforcement which is normatively coherent with its goals, principles and techniques.[19]

However, the use of flexibility in the substantive provisions of EU competition law does not mean that their role and scope in the current turbulent period is fully settled. Because of the way they are structured and operate, digital platforms may escape the traditional application of certain key concepts (market definition, concurrence of wills, abuse of dominance) and the economic theories used to interpret them to prove violations of Articles 101 and 102 TFEU.[20] Similarly, while sustainability has permeated all areas of EU competition law to justify practices that may limit their application, it remains uncertain how and to what extent it could allow competition and State aid rules to prohibit environmentally unsustainable conducts and enable the transformative change sought by the EU Green Deal to recalibrate the EU's economic model.[21] Similar debates emerge regarding the reliance on key elements of the EU Green Deal (eg, the Taxonomy Regulation[22] and the 'do no significant harm' principle) by competition law to promote the green transition,[23] as well as the boundaries of State aid control to prohibit support to environmentally harmful activities and the enforcement of environmental law infringements under Article 258 TFEU. Although a broad interpretation would seem to be in line with Article 11 TFEU, the interpretation given by the General Court seems to lean toward the opposite.[24]

At the same time, since their flexibility is not unlimited, EU competition rules may be unable to empower enforcers to adequately address these societal crises. This seems to be especially the case when disruptions and crises change market structures[25] and the reach of EU competition law proves inadequate to tackle

[15] Costa Cabral (n 5 above).

[16] See Commission, 'Temporary Framework for assessing antitrust issues related to business cooperation in response to situations of urgency stemming from the current COVID-19 outbreak' (n 14 above).

[17] Monti (n 6 above).

[18] Costa Cabral (n 5 above).

[19] Ibid.

[20] Van Cleynenbreugel (n 5 above).

[21] Sikora-Kaléda (n 4 above); Nicolaides (n 4 above); Colombo and Bonelli (n 4 above).

[22] Regulation (EU) 2020/852 of the European Parliament and of the Council of 18 June 2020 on the establishment of a framework to facilitate sustainable investment and amending Regulation (EU) 2019/2088 [2020] OJ L198/13.

[23] Sikora-Kaléda (n 4 above).

[24] Colombo and M Bonelli (n 4 above).

[25] Van Cleynenbreugel (n 5 above).

them. In response, at macro level a consideration of EU competition law's scope within the EU constitutional and institutional set-up, and how its gaps can be filled by other instruments, has emerged. Due to the disruptions caused by digital platforms to our democratic society, and the limits of competition law enforcement against these organisations, the EU recently approved the Digital Markets Act (DMA),[26] which introduces a logic of ex ante regulation, based on Article 114 TFEU.[27] Despite the risks associated with such a type of instrument, the aim of this regulation is to complement the deterrent effects of competition law enforcement, which follows the logic of ex post prohibition, and to ensure the contestability and fairness of the market in which gatekeepers operate.[28] At the same time, the outlined procedure largely resembles the competition law enforcement tool in Regulation 1/2003,[29] in particular, the Commission's enforcement powers (eg, requests for information, powers to take statements/interviews, powers to conduct inspections), remedial and sanctioning powers (interim measures, commitments and fines).[30] Similarly, to prevent distortions in the internal market caused by increased external competition from non-EU companies, which are particularly exacerbated by recent geopolitical tensions, the Commission has introduced the new Foreign Subsidies Regulation.[31] This new tool largely resembles existing enforcement mechanisms in the field of State aid that can address side effects on the domestic market as well as competition law beyond the EU's borders. However, these solutions, which are intended to complement and strengthen EU competition rules, are themselves prone to generate new challenges. The new DMA, for example, only covers certain behaviours that could lead to anticompetitive practices by digital gatekeepers based on cases that have been addressed in the past. Although this approach, applying to uncharted and rapidly evolving territory, is reasonable, there are doubts as to whether this regulatory instrument is future-proof.[32]

The second meaning of flexibility, regarding the institutional set-up of EU competition law introduced with modernisation, seems to have partly withstood the test of turbulent times. Nonetheless, periods of turbulence may heighten uncertainties about solutions and conflicting agendas about the role of competition law therein. In the complex enforcement landscape resulting

[26] Regulation (EU) 2022/1925 of the European Parliament and of the Council of 14 September 2022 on contestable and fair markets in the digital sector and amending Directives (EU) 2019/1937 and (EU) 2020/1828 (DMA) [2022] OJ L265/1.

[27] Van Cleynenbreugel (n 5 above); M Ioannidou, 'Unpacking Multilevel Elements in Digital Markets: Informing Effective Enforcement and Remedial Design in EU Competition Law', Chapter 11 in this volume.

[28] Van Cleynenbreugel (n 5 above); Ioannidou (n 27 above).

[29] Council Regulation (EC) No 1/2003 of 16 December 2002 on the implementation of the rules on competition laid down in Articles 81 and 82 of the Treaty [2003] OJ L01/1.

[30] Ioannidou (n 27 above).

[31] Regulation (EU) 2022/2560 on foreign subsidies K Wright, 'Levelling the Playing Field: EU Regulatory Extension Through Technocratic Cooperation', Chapter 5 in this volume; Monti (n 6 above); F Brito Bastos, 'Repurposing Administrative Procedures to Meet Novel Challenges in EU Competition Law', Chapter 9 in this volume.

[32] Van Cleynenbreugel (n 5 above).

from decentralisation,[33] various actors can address the same problem using different powers. The fact that the same behaviour of digital platforms may be subject to parallel investigations,[34] or to the concurrent application of regulation and competition law,[35] may lead to inconsistent decisions and different remedial approaches. This puts at risk fundamental EU constitutional values such as ne bis in idem,[36] legal certainty[37] and consistent and effective enforcement of EU competition law.[38] At the same time, national governments can use the leeway granted by their constitutionally protected powers to pursue their own policy agendas and reduce the scope of the Commission's powers in this area. Numerous thought-provoking instances emerged in the contributions. They range from Member States using their competence to develop industrial policy to put in place de facto anti-competitive practices that run afoul of EU merger rules,[39] or using their competence to determine the energy mix to grant State aid to polluting activities,[40] to national governments twisting the meaning of soft law developed for crisis management to prop up domestic firms in blatant violation of the fundamental principle of non-discrimination,[41] or creatively complying with Article 107 TFEU to circumvent EU State aid control.[42] Ultimately, these tensions pose obvious risks of fragmentation of the legal framework of the EU internal market and EU competition rules.

The EU law framework provides some key principles and tools to counter these tensions toward fragmentation. When the Commission decides to use them, the field seems, paradoxically, to return to its origins and abandon modernisation's trends toward greater centralisation and harmonisation of rules. In this sense, the DMA added a layer of centralised ex ante regulation against gatekeepers in the hands of the Commission, while the Foreign Subsidies Regulation builds on another 60 years of centralised State aid control in which the Commission alone has retained enforcement power.[43] At the same time, when centralisation is not possible, the 'glue' of greater cooperation among NCAs,[44] which is essential to resist outward tensions and avoid uneven enforcement, is promoted by imposing, within and outside the EU, common administrative decision-making rules and constitutional principles such as equivalence, transparency and requirements

[33] Ioannidou (n 27 above).
[34] Monti (n 6 above); Ioannidou (n 27 above).
[35] Van Cleynenbreugel (n 5 above); Monti (n 6 above); Ioannidou (n 27 above).
[36] Van Cleynenbreugel (n 5 above); Ioannidou (n 27 above).
[37] Van Cleynenbreugel (n 5 above); Monti (n 6 above); Ioannidou (n 27 above).
[38] Stefan (n 5 above).
[39] Monti (n 6 above).
[40] Nicolaides (n 4 above); Colombo and Bonelli (n 4 above).
[41] Stefan (n 5 above).
[42] N Lindstrom, 'Creative Compliance and the Politicisation of EU State Aid Implementation in Times of Crisis', Chapter 13 in this volume.
[43] Brito Bastos (n 31 above).
[44] C Harlow and R Rawlings, Process and Procedure in EU Administration (Oxford, Hart Publishing, 2014).

for independent regulators.[45] In this sense, the ECN+ Directive,[46] which aims to establish minimum harmonisation rules for the investigative and decision-making independence of NCAs, could be read as a response to the political pressures currently affecting the internal market that might otherwise bend the shortcomings of an imperfect, multilevel enforcement system to single Member States' own advantage.[47] Similarly, in EU external relations, EU institutions are increasingly exporting these values to other non-EU countries to ensure a level playing field and protect EU businesses from unfair external competition.[48] The question, however, is to what extent these principles and tools can resist the centrifugal pressures that are strong in turbulent times. Depending on the circumstances, the Commission may not use them, either purposely or due to legal limitations. To counter national policies contradicting EU competition law, the Commission could entrust stronger advocacy powers to NCAs with mutual support through the European Competition Network (ECN), or use Article 120 TFEU to require Member States to pursue their economic policies 'with a view to contributing to the achievement' of an open market economy with free competition. However, while the former instrument is not enshrined in the ECN+ Directive,[49] the latter has been carefully left unused by the Commission so as not to antagonise the Member States too much.[50] At the same time, Article 4(3) TEU, which imposes a duty of sincere cooperation, cannot be used when, as in the case of practices of digital platforms, there are overlaps between EU laws and national laws that pursue different objectives.[51] Ultimately, day-to-day technocratic cooperation among competition enforcers is essential, but it cannot be taken for granted.

III. Actors and Dynamics

European integration can be understood as a process of building an EU polity[52] as an institutionalised and constitutionalised structure with a collective identity. Drawing from its ordoliberal roots, EU competition law can contribute to this aim, not only by controlling distortions of competition, but also by ensuring

[45] Wright (n 31 above).
[46] Directive (EU) 2019/1 of the European Parliament and of the Council of 11 December 2018 to empower the competition authorities of the Member States to be more effective enforcers and to ensure the proper functioning of the internal market [2019] OJ L11/3.
[47] Monti (n 6 above); Brito Bastos (n 31 above).
[48] Wright (n 31 above).
[49] Monti (n 6 above).
[50] Ibid.
[51] Monti (n 6 above); Ioannidou (n 27 above).
[52] M Fichera, The Foundations of the EU as a Polity (Cheltenham, Edward Elgar Publishing, 2018); D Augenstein and M Dawson 'What Law for What Polity? Integration Through Law in the European Union Revisited' in D Augenstein (ed), 'Integration through Law' Revisited: The Making of the European Polity (Abingdon, Routledge, 2012).

welfare-maximisation, economic freedom and procedural justice. Embracing a direct link between competition and democracy as the normative underpinning of competition law may be negative, implying that distortions of competition might have a serious impact on a democratic polity and vice versa; or positive, where competition supports a democratic polity and vice versa.[53] In the face of turbulence, as the boundaries of competition law are challenged and redefined, so too are the roles of various actors and the dynamics between them. More traditionally studied actors, such as the Commission, NCAs, firms and courts, clearly continue to be important, albeit with some different roles. Alongside, we see the emerging or increasing relevance of less classic actors, such as third country governments and third country regulators, sector regulators and citizens beyond the role of 'consumer'.

As we set out in the introduction to the book regarding robustness, since turbulence is prone to generate the risk of political reaction and confrontation, robust responses require the input of expert knowledge and leadership capable of formulating transformative solutions, with the involvement of all affected interests. While the latter condition would imply more input from citizens, all three of these factors are reflected in the technocratic legitimacy model of competition enforcement. This model emphasises technocratic expertise and cooperation among independent authorities,[54] with the aim of improving credibility and ensuring the consistency of policy enforcement over time.[55] Given these benefits, independent authorities have been promoted among epistemic communities and across a range of EU policy areas as well as competition.[56] Additionally, there are efforts to network an epistemic community of competition professionals and independent authorities externally to mitigate substantive differences in national regulations with administrative cooperation, and requirements on the independence of authorities are exported through trade instruments to co-opt third country regulators.[57] The constitutional relevance of independent NCAs is highlighted in EU case law.[58] In terms of evolution, the independence from

[53] E Deutscher and S Makris, 'Exploring the Ordoliberal Paradigm: The Competition-Democracy Nexus' (2016) 11 Competition Law Review 186.

[54] H Kassim and K Wright, 'Bringing Regulatory Processes Back In: The Reform of EU Antitrust and Merger Control' (2009) 32 West European Politics 738; M Guidi, 'The Impact of Independence on Regulatory Outcomes: the Case of EU Competition Policy' (2015) 53 Journal of Common Market Studies 1195.

[55] G Majone, 'The Rise of the Regulatory State in Europe' (1994) 17 West European Politics 77; G Majone, 'Two Logics of Delegation: Agency and Fiduciary Relations in EU Governance' (2001) 2 European Union Politics 103; F Gilardi, Delegation in the Regulatory State: Independent Regulatory Agencies in Western Europe (Cheltenham, Edward Elgar Publishing, 2008); T Bull, 'Administrative Independence and European Integration' (2008) 14 European Public Law 275.

[56] Eg D Coen and M Thatcher, 'Network Governance and Multi-level Delegation: European Networks of Regulatory Agencies' (2008) 28 Journal of Public Policy 49.

[57] Wright (n 31 above).

[58] KJ Cseres, 'EU Competition Law and Democracy in the Shadow of Rule of Law Backsliding', Chapter 1 in this volume.

Member State governments and resourcing of NCAs was already identified when the ECN was established,[59] and was addressed to an extent post-modernisation in the ECN+ Directive.[60] However, it has taken on greater resonance with the rule of law crisis in particular Member States. In *Sped Pro*, this more recent post-modernisation case law goes further to affirm that NCAs must be independent in order to effectively protect firms and consumers', or indeed citizens', rights.[61] Further, the case establishes that independence is a condition for mutual trust between competition authorities.[62] To date trust has been built by protecting technocratic expertise in competition law and State aid,[63] supported through the principle of loyal cooperation and recognition of counterpart Member States' standards. However, the increased politicisation of the (non-)application of competition law tests the coherence and credibility of the system,[64] particularly the place of this technocratic model and trust between Member States.

Another significant theme emerging from the chapters is the potential impact of poly-crisis on the multilevel networked governance of EU competition law. This allows us to revisit issues of divergence/uniformity and centralisation/decentralisation raised in the modernisation debates. The evolving division of competences discussed above, particularly regarding regulation of big tech and data, raises implications for the division of tasks between the Commission, NCAs and sectoral regulators. In the antitrust field, there is some scope for NCAs to take different approaches to the same problem. On the one hand, this could lead to the fragmentation of (sector-specific) governance frameworks.[65] On the other hand, divergence, either through stricter solutions governing unilateral conduct[66] or through solutions taken outside competition law, can prove valuable in harnessing regulatory innovations addressing sustainability[67] and digital[68] concerns and, more generally, in setting the strategic direction for EU competition law.

This scope for regulatory innovation also raises the issue of policy leadership. A successful uniform competition policy has been built upon the Commission's leadership and the ECN as a policy space between the Commission and the NCAs. However, innovations are now also coming from the national level regarding several of the challenges in this book, such as environmental sustainability,

[59] Art 35 Council Regulation (EC) 1/2003 (n 29 above); Case C-53/03 Syfait v GlaxoSmithKline [2005] EU:C:2005:333.

[60] Brito Bastos (n 31 above).

[61] Cseres (n 58 above). See also Case T-791/19 Sped Pro v Commission [2022] EU:T:2022:67.

[62] B van Rompuy, 'Independence as a Prerequisite for Mutual Trust between EU Competition Enforcers: Case T-791/19, Sped-Pro v Commission' (2022) 13 Journal of European Competition Law & Practice 413.

[63] Colombo and Bonelli (n 4 above).

[64] Cseres (n 58 above); Lindstrom (n 42 above).

[65] Van Cleynenbreugel (n 5 above).

[66] Such as the 10th Amendment – German Competition Act. Van Cleynenbreugel (n 5 above); Monti (n 6 above); Ioannidou (n 27 above).

[67] Sikora-Kaléda (n 4 above); Colombo and Bonelli (n 4 above).

[68] Van Cleynenbreugel (n 5 above); Ioannidou (n 27 above).

e-commerce and big tech, using a range of enforcement tools (at least to respond to digital markets) based on national, rather than EU, competition law.[69]

Experimental governance could accommodate differences among Member States and would have the potential to enhance effective enforcement by testing different approaches.[70] These differentiated approaches could occur either through different interpretations of the competition rules, or by extending the possibility to apply national rules stricter than EU rules (as already allowed regarding unilateral practices under Article 3(2) Regulation 1/2003). In this way, Member States also have the potential to become policy leaders in competition law, reshaping the existing competences and division between the EU and national level and challenging the EU's primacy over the shape and scope of EU competition policy. By way of continuity, the ECN may be seen as the ideal forum to evaluate such differentiated approaches.

The use of such experimental governance structures would need to be underpinned by ex post evaluation and monitoring to assess the effectiveness of different approaches.[71] Regarding remedies, responsive remodelling would call for more effective coordination between enforcers, with greater participation of civil society and stakeholders. Remedial design would take into account the aims of deterrence, compliance and redress to promote more effective enforcement.[72]

Effective enforcement within the EU also needs to be matched with strategies to respond to external competition. The EU's external trade relationships test its influence on third State governments, competition authorities and other regulators and firms. In the context of Brexit and other trade agreements, technocratic cooperation has the potential to extend the EU's regulatory impact beyond its borders. Prohibitions on failing to effectively enforce laws and regulations in a way that would anticompetitively encourage trade or investment embed obligations in the domestic setting and affect the domestic regulatory architecture. The role of regulatory authorities is important not only in implementing regulatory commitments, but also in assessing and managing divergence, and in early resolution of potential disputes. These roles operate with the ultimate 'safety net' of governance mechanisms such as the rebalancing and enforcement mechanisms of bilateral FTAs and the Foreign Subsidies Regulation[73] when the 'soft power' of the

[69] Van Cleynenbreugel (n 5 above).

[70] Y Svetiev, Experimentalist Competition Law and the Regulation of Markets (Oxford, Hart Publishing, 2020); Y Svetiev, 'Networked Competition Governance in the EU: Delegation, Decentralization or Experimentalist Architecture?' in C Sabel and J Zeitlin (eds), Experimentalist Governance in the European Union: Towards a New Architecture (Oxford, Oxford University Press, 2010); G Monti and B Rangoni, 'Competition Policy in Action: Regulating Tech Markets with Hierarchy and Experimentalism' (2022) 60 Journal of Common Market Studies 1106; C Townley, A Framework for European Competition Law: Coordinated Diversity (Oxford, Hart Publishing, 2018). More broadly J Zeitlin, 'Experimentalist Governance in Times of Crisis' (2016) 39 West European Politics 1073.

[71] Wright (n 31 above); Monti (n 6 above).

[72] Ioannidou (n 27 above).

[73] Regulation (EU) 2022/2560 of the European Parliament and of the Council on foreign subsidies distorting the internal market [2022] OJ L330/1.

EU is not enough. These mechanisms explicitly aim to constrain or disincentivise regulatory competitiveness with the internal market.

Beyond networked governance on the enforcement side by technocratic institutions, the book also considered how companies, as the main subjects and targets of competition law, can contribute to the strategic reshaping of EU competition policy through different channels.[74] Notably, this can happen in the policy cycle as well as in the enforcement stage, through Commission consultations on legislative, regulatory and soft-law initiatives, such as the Digital Services Act package and the New Competition Tool.[75] Regarding merger control, non-economic arguments, such as environmental issues, can only be taken into account to the extent that they are put forward by the parties, and so firms play a role in initiating their consideration.[76] In enforcement, it is axiomatic that companies are the subjects of competition law (eg subject to investigation) and private watchdogs (ie as complainants and third parties in public enforcement, and litigants in private enforcement) given their ground level view of the market. Although the Commission retains discretion over whether to initiate proceedings,[77] companies play a role in identifying potential cases, including novel or disruptive issues. From a constitutional perspective, rights of defence and due process are relevant, and investigations and litigation may raise ne bis in idem issues for defendant firms.[78] Going beyond this traditional view of constitutional issues relating to firms, drawing attention to the principles of openness and stakeholder participation, the book highlights the importance of including firms in the transformation of competition law in response to societal challenges. This is important not only for the effectiveness of such transformation but also for its legitimacy.[79]

Further, courts have a significant role to play in upholding the constitutional framework, most evidently through judicial review. The classic approach of the Court allows a margin of appreciation to the Commission in complex economic assessments while not refraining from reviewing the Commission's interpretation of information of an economic nature, and whether it is capable of substantiating the conclusions drawn from it.[80] Various chapters of the book highlight the flexible use of the Commission's discretion.[81] This raises the question of whether

[74] F Pastor-Merchante, 'The Role of Companies in the Strategic Turn of EU Competition Law', Chapter 7 in this volume.

[75] Regulation (EU) 2022/2065 of the European Parliament and of the Council of 19 October 2022 on a Single Market For Digital Services and amending Directive 2000/31/EC (Digital Services Act) OJ L277/1; Commission, 'Single Market new complementary tool to strengthen competition enforcement'(2020):www.ec.europa.eu/info/law/better-regulation/have-your-say/initiatives/12416-Single-Market-new-complementary-tool-to-strengthen-competition-enforcement_en.

[76] Pastor-Merchante (n 74 above).

[77] Case T-64/89 Automec v Commission [1990] EU:T:1990:42.

[78] Raised by Van Cleynenbreugel (n 5 above) and Ioannidou (n 27 above), regarding digital market enforcement in different Member States.

[79] Pastor Merchante (n 74 above); Colombo and M Bonelli (n 4 above).

[80] Case C-12/03 P Commission v Tetra Laval [2005] EU:C:2005:87, paras 38–39.

[81] Both Costa Cabral (n 5 above) and Stefan (n 5 above) note the shift from legislative to executive intervention, implying greater discretion to executive authorities.

the EU Courts are, or should be, more or less interventionist in light of these new challenges and crises. In general, the Courts have endorsed the Commission's view – employing its margin of discretion – that existing EU competition policy is no obstacle to the digital and green transition, and supported the strict enforcement of competition rules as a facilitator of that transition. In some areas, however, there has been little case law to date, leaving avenues for future research. One open question is whether cooperating undertakings can rely on the exemption of Article 101(3) TFEU if the cooperation generates benefits for society as a whole (for example, environmental benefits) and not for the direct consumers of their product. This issue links with the broader concept of 'citizen' as opposed to 'consumer' welfare. The exemptions in antitrust and State aid appear flexible enough to incorporate improved environmental or digital performance as long as benefits for society outweigh the costs from the distortion of competition. However, the burden of proof on the Commission and companies for presenting credible theories of harm or benefit may be heavier.[82] There are of course other important functions of national courts (in addition to contributing to EU jurisprudence through preliminary references, since national courts are also EU courts[83]), some specific to EU competition and relevant to the challenges discussed: through judicial review at the national level, private enforcement (whether follow-on,[84] stand-alone or collective actions[85]),[86] recovering unlawful State aid, and in providing judicial remedies in public procurement procedures under the Foreign Subsidies Regulation.

A further aspect of the constitutional framework to be considered, if we conceive of the EU competition law as a system within the EU polity, is the role of citizens beyond the notion of consumer.[87] This includes new dimensions of workers in EU law in the context of collective agreements and the gig economy interacting with digital markets. From a substantive perspective this would require a wider conception of consumer welfare to 'citizen welfare',[88] implying that competition law could be used to promote the general well-being of EU citizens.[89] As the root causes of

[82] See Nicolaides (n 4 above).

[83] I Maher 'National Courts as European Community Courts' (1994) 14 Legal Studies 226.

[84] See the examples in Pastor-Merchante (n 74 above).

[85] Directive (EU) 2020/1828 of the European Parliament and of the Council of 25 November 2020 on representative actions for the protection of the collective interests of consumers and repealing Directive 2009/22/EC [2020] OJ L409/1; Directive (EU) 2014/104 of the European Parliament and of the Council of 26 November 2014 on certain rules governing actions for damages under national law for infringements of the competition law provisions of the Member States and of the European Union [2014] OJ L349/1.

[86] Pastor-Merchante (n 74 above); Ioannidou (n 27 above).

[87] Cseres (n 58 above).

[88] F Cengiz, 'The Conflict Between Market Competition and Worker Solidarity: Moving from Consumer to a Citizen Welfare Standard in Competition Law' (2021) 41 Legal Studies 73. See also Cseres (n 58 above).

[89] C Townley, *Article* 81 *EC and Public Policy* (Oxford, Hart Publishing, 2009) argued that this would involve requiring economic entities to promote general well-being and so participate in society as moral actors. See also F Cengiz, 'Legitimacy and Multi-Level Governance in European Union Competition Law: A Deliberative Discursive Approach' (2016) 54 Journal of Common Market Studies 826, arguing for citizens' involvement in decision-making.

crises lie in socio-political transformations outside of competition law, it operates within a wider democratic system. As implied at the start of this section, there is arguably a tension between insulating competition law from political interference, based on the technocratic legitimacy model and a purely economic effects-based approach, and greater democratic legitimacy. Notably, ordoliberal goals seem to be enjoying a resurgence in the Commission's decisional practice since 2013, alongside the emerging goals of environmental protection and sustainability, privacy and workers' protection and labour rights.[90] From a procedural perspective, this shift in substantive goals argues in favour of greater participation of citizens and other representative stakeholders, a point echoed in some of the contributions in Part III of the book.[91]

IV. Instruments and Procedures

The relationship between actors is mediated by instruments and processes, as explored in Part III. Several themes emerge. A key thread is the concept of continuity and change: continuity to uphold existing values, and change in attempts to future-proof responses to outstanding challenges. As reflected in the title of the book in 'times' of disruptions, several chapters allude to the temporal dimension of particular procedures or instruments. This is evident in the need to achieve the long-term goals of the EU Climate Law and EU Green Deal,[92] finding ways to align competition law with these green objectives[93] and in structuring responses to digitalisation.[94] In other instances, instruments – such as the use of soft law – represent short-term responses to sudden shock in the economy, such as the COVID-19 pandemic.[95] This raises consideration of the consequences of short-term and long-term responses to crisis (including in terms of legitimacy). In the short term, a sudden shock tends to necessitate an initial EU centralised response, but to be robust in the longer term may need greater involvement of a wider range of national authorities and other stakeholders.

The growing use of instruments for the green transition militate in favour of opening to a wider range of actors in the EU polity, despite State aid control

[90] K Stylianou and M Iacovides, 'The Goals of EU Competition Law: A Comprehensive Empirical Investigation' (2022) 42 Legal Studies 620.

[91] Colombo and Bonelli (n 4 above). Civil society organisations have asked for clarity from the Commission on the role of third parties (citizens, consumer bodies, and SMEs) in the implementation and enforcement of the DMA: www.beuc.eu/letters/clarity-urgently-needed-role-third-parties-implementation-and-enforcement-digital-markets.

[92] Regulation (EU) 2021/1119 of the European Parliament and of the Council of 30 June 2021 establishing the framework for achieving climate neutrality and amending Regulations (EC) No 401/2009 and (EU) 2018/1999 ('European Climate Law') [2021] OJ L243/1; Commission, 'Communication from the Commission, The European Green Deal' COM(2019) 640 final.

[93] Sikora-Kaléda (n 4 above); Colombo and Bonelli (n 4 above).

[94] Van Cleynenbreugel (n 5 above); Ioannidou (n 27 above).

[95] Costa Cabral (n 5 above); Stefan (n 5 above).

traditionally being structured around the Member State as grantor and Commission as enforcer. Indeed, the Aarhus Convention and the EU Green Deal, mainstreaming environmental protection throughout all EU policies, require greater openness to and participation of the public.[96] Further democratic issues arise in the implementation of State aid, where it is vulnerable to politicisation at the national level. Some Member States demonstrate 'creative compliance'. The case of Hungary demonstrates strategies whereby the letter, but not the spirit, of the law is adhered to, to the State's own benefit.[97] In the classification stage, this creative compliance is arguably a by-product of the Commission's discretion: less precise rules, more exemptions and delegation of classification to national authorities contribute to the Member State's ability to expand the criteria for exempted horizontal aid. Other examples include investment in legal advice and judicious use of legal precedents in the notification and investigation stage; and delaying or avoiding recovery of vertical aid by conceding tax modifications to achieve the government's aim of media control. This extent of creative compliance requires a sufficient degree of administrative capacity to be 'successful' from the Member State perspective. Notably, it also raises the dynamics between negotiation and implementation stages in EU policy-making more broadly, with implications for the scope of competences. Further, how does the Commission choose to exercise its discretion where some Member States demand greater enforcement, whereas others call for greater autonomy?

A further theme is the design of instruments. During periods of change or crisis, a mix of new and existing procedures and instruments can make the system more robust. As discussed in the introduction to this book, dynamic conservatism denotes how a system responds to heightened periods of crisis by creating innovative responses while simultaneously adapting the existing forms of governance to preserve fundamental goals, functions and values.[98] More significantly from a legal perspective, this mixing of new and existing procedures and instruments makes an important contribution to stability and legal certainty.[99] The idea of repurposing to maintain continuity arises in several contexts through the book, within and beyond the EU. Existing procedural models are applied to meet novel challenges – both horizontally, to new policy areas, and vertically, by mirroring in national administrations powers and processes originally held by the Commission. New instruments include the DMA, which itself mixes newer ex ante regulation with established ex post enforcement, and the Foreign Subsidies Regulation, extending elements of State aid. Elsewhere are examples of instruments employed in new contexts, such as the Temporary Frameworks, and Taxonomy Regulation in the green transition. This also affects the administrative frameworks required to meet

[96] See Colombo and Bonelli (n 4 above).

[97] Lindstrom (n 42 above).

[98] C Ansell, A Boin and M Farjoun 'Dynamic Conservatism: How Institutions Change to Remain the Same' in M Kraatz (ed), Institutions and Ideals: Philip Selznick's Legacy for Organizational Studies (Bingley, Emerald Publishing, 2015).

[99] Brito Bastos (n 31 above).

internal and external market challenges, including the ECN+ Directive and the Foreign Subsidies Regulation. Both instruments are designed to protect the integrity of the internal market. However, each instrument reflects a different legislative choice regarding allocation of powers between the EU and national administrations. The continuing decentralised system under the ECN+ Directive is a logical progression from the institutional set-up of modernisation under Regulation 1/2003. From a constitutional perspective, procedural repurposing may promote equal treatment of market actors which operate in substantially similar circumstances on the internal market, whether from Member States or third countries. In addition, it contributes to extending and strengthening the EU's regulatory governance territorially, as internal provisions on cooperation are mirrored in trade instruments.[100] In the case of the Foreign Subsidies Regulation, this centralised choice may be closely linked to the Commission's competence in trade as well as competition. Arguably in this area the Commission is prioritising its resources as guardian of the EU general interest.[101]

A key governance tool for flexible response to crises is EU soft law, developed largely in the context of EU competition and State aid law. In general, soft law instruments were previously used to signal how the Commission would manage its discretion and to give guidance to national authorities (to promote consistent application, sometimes codifying existing practice and case law) and firms (in the interests of legal certainty and legitimate expectations). Soft law is an imperfect solution to grand regulatory challenges.[102] In the post-modernisation phase, soft law instruments have been used to respond quickly to systemic crises. This is understandable due to their speed of adoption and flexibility. The 'emergency soft law' of Temporary Frameworks responding to the COVID-19 pandemic and the war in Ukraine, has suspended some competition rules. Substantively, this suspension challenges the more economic approach ushered in by the modernisation package. Procedurally, the adoption of emergency measures is by necessity subject to much lighter consultation. Competences are reshaped through soft law: initially, State aid guidance spilled over to regulate energy power; in recent times, more transparency for 'business as usual' competition and State aid soft law in the area of EU exclusive legislative competence, may not sufficiently compensate for regulating areas of shared competence such as energy and the environment.

Despite these concerns about overreach, State aid continues to be utilised as an important tool to govern the green transition. Although the case law is still developing,[103] the emphasis on environmental factors in the State aid compatibility assessment appears to be increasing. State aid control can also be used to impose conditions on Member States as a means of meeting wider decarbonisation commitments. These measures have the potential to improve greater

[100] Wright (n 31 above).
[101] Brito Bastos (n 31 above).
[102] Stefan (n 5 above).
[103] See Nicolaides (n 4 above).

monitoring and accountability of national policies. The increased use of finance as a governance and integration tool in EU policy, such as through the post-COVID economic recovery instruments and Next Generation EU green bonds, is evident. These instruments make use of the wider Taxonomy Regulation and 'do no significant harm' principle. In this way, while the EU Green Deal itself does not make explicit reference to competition policy instruments, those green transition tools may be used to recalibrate EU competition and State aid law.[104]

V. Moving Forward

In the introduction we defined governance in this context as the institutional eco-system of EU competition law, including the structures, processes and instruments used to coordinate actors' enforcement efforts, and how this is affected by its substantive rules. The various discussions in this collection provide a rich overview of how the governance of EU competition law is evolving to cope with the turbulent times Europe is experiencing, and how the resulting framework fits its role and constitutional limits with the EU Treaties. In addressing these questions, the book has engaged in a discussion that, while far from complete, provides important insights into how the role of competition law, as an operative whole, can be properly conceived within the EU constitutional framework.

First, dealing with crises whose causes are to be found in socio-political transformations has led to the resurgence of certain issues, such as the role of non-economic interests in the assessment of anticompetitive practices, or of competition law in a democratic system, or of citizens in competition law. Using the flexibility allowed by the rules, the main actors are responding to this period with robust responses that mix adaptation of existing tools with new solutions. Actors other than the classic ones are also gaining roles, making the adaptation of competition law and its processes to meaningfully involve them even more urgent.

Second, the book provided an initial assessment of how the field of competition law is using the leeway afforded by the EU constitutional set-up to cope with these turbulent times. A sense emerges from some of the contributions that EU and national institutions are using the constitutional and institutional flexibility of the field to cope with the poly-crisis affecting the EU. However, some contributions also seem to raise critical voices about the EU's responses to date, some of which fail to take full advantage of available tools or create problematic overlaps and conflicts.

Third, the collection considered how the constitutional role of competition law, in addition to ensuring protection of the competitive dynamics of the internal market, also encompasses promotion of democratic values and broader ambitions connected to the kind of society we want to become.

[104] Sikora-Kaléda (n 4 above).

In conclusion, three final remarks are relevant and may open the way for further research on the transformation of the governance of EU competition law in current times. First, one may ask whether the field of EU competition law is moving past modernisation and entering a new period of evolution in its historical development. Some aspects indicate continuity. The internal market and economic assessments still play an important role in the assessment of prohibited practices, while decentralisation, networking and an extensive use of soft law are still widely used to manage an increasingly complex and fragmented institutional set-up. Other trends, however, indicate a transformation and potentially the beginning of a post-modernisation era. The Commission is currently undertaking a review of EU competition law, whose scope appears to be unprecedented. Similarly, while public policy interests are acquiring an increasing role in antitrust assessment, decentralisation is being combined with (re)centralisation and expansion to other areas and new actors. Finally, the combination of soft(er) and hard(er) sources of law in the policy mix indicates that broad policy changes are ongoing. Second, this apparent crisis-driven approach taken by the Commission deserves a critical evaluation as to whether it is capable of producing effects and achieving the goals that competition law should pursue in the EU. For example, whether State aid through soft law as an emergency response to systemic crises is an appropriate response to keep the internal market afloat, or whether the long-term effects are too dangerous, seems yet to be fully explored and understood. All these aspects will be essential in assessing the strategic direction taken by the Commission. Third, there is some sense that the boundaries inside and outside the area of EU competition law are shifting, changing the role of actors, creating overlaps and conflicts. This suggests another fruitful strand of research to map any future divergence between enforcers.

INDEX

Aarhus Convention 267–9, 272, 306
abuse of a dominant position 9, 45–58
  burden of proof, reversal of 58
  companies, role of 154
  convergence 143–5
  cooperation, duty of 39–41, 126, 128
  Covid-19 and State aid 104–7
  crisis cartels 88, 101
  decentralisation 29–31
  digital transitions/disruptions 13, 45–58, 60–2, 173–6
    EU courts 174, 183–5, 191
    justification arguments 184–5, 191
    list of cases 184
    multilevel elements 242–4, 247
  enforcement 29–31, 39–42, 44–7, 54, 58, 61–2
  Foreign Subsidies Regulation 207
  green transitions/disruptions 70, 73–4, 153, 175
  Member States and EU, relationship between 146
  national competition authorities (NCAs) 39–42, 61–2, 64, 135–8, 139, 144, 169
  public interest 106–7
  Regulation 1/2003 27, 48, 61–2
  soft law 213, 218, 227–8
  State aid 88, 97–8, 103
abuse of economic dependence, rules on 240–1, 247, 252
access to justice 15, 254
access to the file 61
accession 1, 9, 19–20, 26–7, 117
accountability 14, 30–1, 132, 226, 273, 308
actors 3, 12–13 *see also* **companies, role of; institutions**
  dynamics 299–305
  multiple actors 133–51
  responsive remodelling 248–9, 252
  third parties, judicial protection for 266–8, 273
administrative procedures and instruments 195–211 *see also* **ECN+ Directive; Foreign Subsidies Regulation; soft law**
  allocation of powers 196–8
  Commission 14, 154
  companies 154–9
  comparative institutional analysis 196–7, 205
  continuity and change 205
  design 14, 195, 197–8, 211, 306
  digital transitions/disruptions 156, 157–9, 172
  European Supervisory Agencies (ESAs) 197–8
  evolvement of procedures and instruments 195–211
  finance, use of 308
  green transitions/disruptions 156–9, 172
  internal market 195, 199–200, 203–10, 307
  reuse of established legislative techniques 14, 196–8, 306–7
  soft law 155–8, 171
  stability 210–11, 306
  temporal dimension 305
advocacy gap 145–6, 150, 299
agriculture and State aid 76, 85, 86, 103
algorithmic collusion 53
Amazon 45–7, 59, 234, 239–43, 246, 248
anti-competitive practices
  burden of proof, reversal of 58, 64
  companies, role of 154
  convergence 143–4
  cooperation, duty of 39–41, 126, 128
  Covid-19 83–4, 86–7
  decentralisation 10, 29–31, 54
  digital transitions/disruptions 13, 45–8, 54–5, 58, 60–2, 64, 174–5, 296
  enforcement 10, 29–31, 39–42, 44–7, 54, 61–2
  Foreign Subsidies Regulation 207
  green transitions/disruptions 175, 177–83, 191, 192
    non-economic interests 73
    State aid 68, 70, 73–4, 78–9, 153

industrial policy 134
investigated companies in enforcement, position of 160–1
Member States and EU, relationship between 146
merger control 160–1, 298
national competition authorities (NCAs) 61–2, 64, 135, 137, 139, 144
non-economic interests 73, 308
public policy 9, 295–6
Regulation 1/2003 27, 48, 61–2
soft law 213, 218–19
State aid 83–8, 97–103
sustainability 177–83, 295

Apple 234, 239, 241–2, 244–5, 281, 289–90
artificial intelligence (AI), behavioural coordination by 53

backsliding *see* **rule of law backsliding**
barriers to entry 183, 191, 279
Big Tech 15, 234, 239–45, 302
damages actions 244–5
Digital Markets Act (DMA) 138
division of competences 301
enforcement 241–2, 252, 301
investigations 242–4
multiple actions 244–5
Platform-to-Business (P2B) Regulation 238–9
private enforcement 244–5
public enforcement 241–4
block exemptions
Commission 133
crisis cartels 100
de minimis rule 285
digital transitions/disruptions 187
General Block Exemption Regulation 10, 75–6, 158, 187–9, 269, 280, 281, 283–4
green transitions/disruptions 75–6, 187–9
soft law 217
State aid 10, 100, 103, 158
creative compliance 280, 281, 283–4
de minimis rule 285
green transitions/disruptions 75–6
technocratic cooperation, EU regulatory extension through 128
Temporary Framework for State Aid 93
Vertical Block Exemption Regulation 142
Brexit 6, 113, 278, 302
Brussels effect 115–16

cartels 32, 33–4, 98 *see also* **crisis cartels**
cease and desist non-compliance 60
Central and Eastern European countries (CEECs) 26–7
centralisation of enforcement *see also* **decentralisation of enforcement**
digital transitions/disruptions 59, 238
ECN+ Directive 202, 210
Foreign Subsidies Regulation 196, 203–4, 210, 298, 307
merger control 160
modernisation 298, 301
national competition authorities (NCAs) 38, 298
State aid 10, 255, 264, 269, 273, 298
certainty *see* **legal certainty**
Charter of Fundamental Rights of the EU (CFR)
defence, rights of the 127–8
effective judicial protection, principle of 41
ne bis in idem 62–3, 246–7
State aid 72, 258–9, 263
technocratic cooperation, EU regulatory extension through 127–8
China 113, 204–5, 275
citizen welfare 20, 21–2, 36–9, 43, 301, 304–5
CJEU *see* **EU courts**
climate emergency *see* **green transition**
collective agreements concluded by the self-employed, guidance on 219, 226
collusion 98, 177
comfort letters 104, 216, 220–1, 226–7
Commission 38–41 *see also* **national competition authorities (NCAs) and Commission,**
relationship between
block exemptions 133
burden of proof 304
centralisation 196, 203
comfort letters 104
commitment decisions 162–3
companies, role of 14, 154–9, 164–7, 172
competences 29, 245
'A Competition Policy Fit For New Challenges' 2, 7
complex economic assessments 303
cooperation 13–14, 114, 236–7, 246, 250, 252
court-like functions 40–1
Covid-19 and State aid 14, 83–7, 106–9, 147, 229
crisis cartels 101–3, 106, 146–7
decentralisation 133
DG Comp 25, 38–9, 120–1, 280
digital transitions/disruptions 14, 46–8, 51, 53–63, 174–7, 234–7, 251

enforcement 242–3, 252
EU courts 177, 183–5
European Green Deal 253, 257–9, 273
guidelines 187–8
soft law 223
discretion 295, 303–4
enforcement 86–7, 106–7, 108, 168
flexibility 303–4
Foreign Subsidies Regulation 207–8
green transitions/disruptions 183, 187–8
margin of discretion 93, 155, 183, 208, 303–4
soft law 9, 223–6, 307
State aid 92–3, 103, 108, 261–5, 166, 268, 285, 292, 306
tactical use 261
ECN+ Directive 14, 195–6, 198–202, 210
enforcement 138–42, 145, 151, 248–9, 257–8, 297
decentralisation 133
digital transitions/disruptions 242–3, 252
discretion 86–7, 106–7, 108, 168
European Green Deal 15, 257–8
Foreign Subsidies Regulation 298
investigated companies, position of 159–64, 303
national competition authorities (NCAs) 246, 252
State aid rules, creative compliance with 277, 284–5, 289–92, 306
third-party companies in enforcement, role of 164–7, 172
EU courts 25, 262
ex officio reviews 205–7
exemptions 133, 160, 276, 282, 283–6
flexibility 303–4
Foreign Subsidies Regulation 14, 124–6, 149, 196, 203–9, 298, 307
global financial crisis 2008 12, 147
green transitions/disruptions 14, 174–83, 187–91, 192
bilateral dialogue with Member States 266
European Green Deal 68, 71–2, 75–7, 80, 156–7
State aid 253–6, 266–73, 305–6
guidance/guidelines 93–6, 164, 182, 187–9, 191, 215–20, 223
harm, theory of 184–5
investigated companies in enforcement, position of 159–64, 303
investigations 165, 289–91
leadership 301
Member States and EU, relationship between 135, 146–50, 299
merger control 28–9, 47–8, 147–50, 160–2, 167, 295
monitoring 284–6
negative decisions 276, 282, 289–91
notification obligations 104, 206–7
ordoliberalism 305
precedents to justify State aid measures 276, 282, 286–8, 291
remedial powers 297
resources 9, 10, 144–5, 307
sanctions 297
soft law 84, 154, 215–27, 230, 307, 309
State aid 83–9, 91–3, 98–103, 159, 165
Code of Best Practices on State Aid, amendment of 268–9
Covid-19 83–7, 106–9, 147
creative compliance 275, 276, 277, 278–92, 306
discretion 92–3, 103, 108, 261–5, 166, 268, 285, 292, 306
exemption game 276, 282, 283–6
Frankenstein strategy 276, 282, 286–8, 291
green transitions/disruptions 68, 71–2, 75–7, 80, 253–6, 266–73, 305–6
precedents to justify measures 276, 282, 286–8, 291
soft law 222–5
State monopolies 146
third-party companies in enforcement, role of 164–8, 172
Trade Policy Review (TPR) 113
withdrawal of cases by Commission 139
commitment decisions 162–3, 227
Common Agricultural Policy (CAP) 85, 86, 103
common commercial policy (CCP) 131
common interest, objectives of 79, 91–5, 120, 295
companies, role of 153–72
accountability 14
administrative rule-making procedures 154–9
defence, rights of the 160, 162, 303
digital transitions/disruptions 156, 157–9, 172
green transitions/disruptions 156–9, 172
instrumental value of third-party companies 164–7
investigated companies in enforcement, position of 155, 159–64, 303

merger control 154, 160–6
national competition authorities (NCAs) and courts 168–71
participation 14, 154, 165–6, 171
soft law 155–8, 171
State aid 154, 158–60, 164, 165–8
subjects of competition law, companies as 154
third-party companies in enforcement of EU competition law, role of 155, 159, 164–71
transactionalisation of EU competition law 162–4
transparency 154, 171

compatibility assessments 69, 79, 259, 264–7, 272, 295, 307

competences
Commission 12, 29, 134
digital transitions/disruptions 15, 235, 245, 252
distribution 235, 242, 252, 294
division of competences 301
exclusive competences 8–9, 14, 131, 213, 223–4, 291, 307
green transitions/disruptions 271
industrial policy 298
merger control 31
parallel competences 29
shared competences 216, 224, 231, 307
State aid 284, 291

Competition and Markets Authority (CMA) 56, 120–1, 219

competition policy *see* **policy**

compliance *see* **creative compliance with State aid rules**

concentrations *see* **merger control**

conferral, principle of 254

constitutional framework 1–5, 8–13, 19–24, 43
'constitutional charter of EU law, competition law as 22–4
digital transitions/disruptions 46, 235, 245–7, 298
equivalence, principle of 298
flexibility 308
green transitions/disruptions and State aid 13, 65–6, 71–2, 254, 255–60, 270
independent regulators, requirement for 298–9
national competition authorities (NCAs) 43, 300
principles 14, 20, 29–42, 114, 121, 131–2, 214, 235, 278–9, 293, 298–9
quasi-constitutional rules 23
State aid
creative compliance 278–9
green transitions/disruptions 13, 65–6, 71–2, 254, 255–60, 270
technocratic cooperation, EU regulatory extension through 14, 114, 299

consultation
Commission 136
companies, role of 156–8, 171–2
Covid-19 158, 225
green transitions/disruptions 75, 156–9, 172
sectoral consultation 74
soft law 225, 231

consumer welfare 1, 21, 43, 70, 84, 99–101, 218, 295

convergence 122, 131–2, 136, 143–5

cooperation
administrative procedures and instruments 196–7
Commission 13–14, 39–40, 114, 236–7, 246, 250, 252
Covid-19 and State aid 83–4, 90, 103–7, 220, 296, 306
digital transitions/disruptions 235, 236–7, 251
ECN+ Directive 127–9, 196, 202
enforcement 217
green transitions/disruptions 176, 177–83, 191, 192
horizontal cooperation agreements 74
Horizontal Cooperation Guidelines 157, 218–19
investigated companies in enforcement, position of 163–4
national competition authorities (NCAs) 39–42, 202, 298
remedial flexibility 248
sincere/loyal cooperation, principle of 10, 39, 42–3, 137, 245, 299, 301
State aid 13, 83–4, 90
technocratic cooperation, EU regulatory extension through 13–14, 113–32
Temporary Framework for Cooperation (Covid-19) 83–5, 90, 98–100, 103–7, 296, 306

Copenhagen accession criteria 19, 26–7

corruption 22, 286

Court of Justice (CJEU) *see* **EU courts**

Covid-19 and State aid 6, 83–109 *see also* **Temporary Framework for State Aid (Covid-19)**

aggravating difficulties 93–4
agricultural products 85, 86, 103
cohesion funds 78
comfort letters 104
Commission 14, 83–7, 93–6, 104, 106–9, 147, 229, 281–2
consultation 158
cooperation 13, 83–4, 90
creative compliance 281–2
crisis cartels 103–6
crisis management 86–7, 89, 93, 96
direct damage 93–5, 97
efficiency 90, 104–7, 108
enforcement 85–7, 90, 96, 104–5
European Competition Network (ECN) 84, 87, 104–6
exceptional occurrences 83–9, 91, 94, 96, 104–5, 108
flexibility 224
guidance 93–6, 164, 215–18, 220
indirect damage 93–5, 97
integration 308
interpretation 89, 95, 295
judicial independence as a condition for recovery funds 286
justifications 86–7, 90, 93, 95, 105–6
modernisation 10, 84–5, 90, 104, 106, 108
multidimensional crisis, as 87
notification procedure 104
overcompensation, prohibition of 92, 94–5
public interest 86–7, 90, 106–7, 108
Rescue and Restructuring Guidelines (R&R Guidelines) 85, 93, 96
resilience 154
shortages 87, 104
soft law 14, 213–16, 217–18, 221–2, 224, 228–9
State aid 13, 83–5
strict application of competition law 147
suspension of rules 85–6, 104
Temporary Framework for Cooperation 83–4, 90, 98, 103–7
third-party companies in enforcement, role of 166–7
types of crises 87–90
urgency, degrees of 230
creative compliance with State aid rules 15, 276–92
administrative capacity, weakness of 278, 291, 306
block exemptions 285
Commission 278–92
discretion 285, 292, 306
enforcement 277, 284–5, 289–92, 306
exemption game 276, 282, 283–6
Frankenstein strategy 276, 282, 286–8, 291
investigations 289–91
monitoring 284–6
negative decisions 276, 282, 289–91
precedents to justify State aid measures 276, 282, 286–8, 291
Covid-19 281–2
de minimis rule 280, 285
enforcement 275, 276, 277–92
evolution of State aid policy 278–82
exemptions 283–6, 306
block exemptions 285
exemption game 276, 282, 283–6, 291
small amounts of aid from notification or Commission approval, from 280, 291
expertise 278, 280, 282, 284, 287–8
fragmentation 298
Frankenstein strategy 276, 282, 286–8, 291
fundamental rights 277
General Block Exemption Regulation (GBER) 280, 281, 283–4
global financial crisis 2008 281
horizontal aid 280, 282, 283–6, 306
Hungary 15, 275, 276, 282–91, 306
illiberal objectives 276, 277
ingenious disobedience, practice of 276
integration 279–80
internal market 15, 279–84
investigations 289–91, 306
justifications 276, 282, 286–8, 291
legal and economic expertise 282, 284, 287–8
monitoring 276, 279, 283–6
multinationals, negative decisions against 289
naming, shaming, and faming tools 279
national competition authorities (NCAs) 280, 306
negative decisions
multinationals, against 289
two steps forward, one step back 276, 282, 289–91
negotiations and implementation stages, dynamics between 306
neoliberalism 279–80
no-bid contracts 286–8
perpetual disintegration 276

policy 275, 277, 278–82, 306
precedents to justify state aid measures 276, 282, 286–8, 291
prevalence 276
rule of law crises 15, 275, 277, 291
size of national administrative units 284
soft law 276, 283–4
State Aid Action Plan 2005 280
State Aid Scoreboard 279
subsidies 276, 286
'take back control' 277–8
transparency 280
two steps forward, one step back 276, 282, 289–91
vertical aid
bad vertical aid classified as good horizontal aid 282, 283–6, 291
justification at notification and investigation stages of 282, 286–8, 291
negative decisions 276, 282, 289–91
precedents to justify aid 276, 282, 286–8, 291
crisis cartels
Covid-19 and State aid 103–6
efficiency 101–3
exemptions 88, 102–3
global financial crisis 2008 84–5, 147
industry restructuring 146
justifications 98, 101
social benefits 99–100
State aid 84–5, 88, 90, 98–106
crisis, definition of 88

damages 169–70, 215, 216, 244–5, 252
data protection
authorities, cooperation with 250–1
General Data Protection Regulation (GDPR) 136–7
personal data 45, 48, 52–3, 54
***de minimis* rule** 177, 228, 280, 285
decentralisation of enforcement 1, 29–31, 54 *see also* **centralisation of enforcement**
Commission 133, 137, 139–43
cooperation, duty of 39–40
country of destination principle 149
digital transitions/disruptions 54, 248, 298
effectiveness 39, 42
European Competition Network (ECN) 29–31, 118–19
ECN+ Directive 30–1, 196, 199, 202, 203, 210
enforcement 29–31, 248
Foreign Subsidies Regulation 203
institutions 309
merger control 27–8, 31, 161
modernisation 4, 301
mutual trust 39–40
national competition authorities (NCAs) 36, 39–40, 137, 139–43, 169–70, 202
public policy 309
Regulation 1/2003 29, 118–19, 139, 169, 216
soft law 215–16, 218, 220, 231
State aid 10, 256
defence, rights of the 61, 159–60, 162, 266, 303
democracy 13, 15, 19–28, 43, 300, 308
Copenhagen accession criteria 26–7
effects-based approach 305
Europeanisation of national competition laws 24–6
legitimacy 305
Ordoliberalism 37, 43
political capture 21–2
political institutions, integrity and impartiality of 20–1
populism 6–7
regulatory capture 21–2
deterrence 42, 236, 252, 297
Digital Markets Act (DMA)
Big Tech 138
centralisation 59, 238
cooperation and coordination between Commission and NCAs 236–7, 252
ECN+ Directive 210
enforcement 54, 58–63, 138–9, 236–8, 252, 306
ex ante regulatory tool, as 234, 236, 237, 297, 298, 306
gatekeepers 59, 139, 297, 298
inconsistent decisions, risk of 246
investigations 139, 237
legal certainty 64
multilevel elements 233–4, 235, 236–8, 252
national competition authorities (NCAs) 138–9, 236–7
Platform-to-Business (P2B) Regulation 238
Regulation 1/2003 237
sanctions 236–7
digital markets, multilevel elements in 14–15, 233–52
abuse of economic dependence, rules on 240–1, 247, 252
Big Tech 15, 234, 238, 239–45, 252
competences 15, 245, 252

constitutional challenges 235, 245–7, 298
cooperation 235, 236–7, 251
damages 252
deterrence 236, 252
Digital Market Act (DMA) 233–4, 235, 236–8, 246, 252, 297–8, 306
efficiency 51, 185, 187, 191
enforcement 234–6, 239–52
European Competition Network (ECN) 237, 248, 252
ex ante regulation 233–4, 236
fragmentation 235–8, 242, 246
gatekeepers 233–4, 235, 237, 297, 298
general principles of EU law 235
investigations 251
legislation 234, 235–9, 252
multiple actions 244–5
national competition authorities (NCAs) 234, 236–7, 239–41, 250–2
national courts 250, 252
national laws 234, 235–6, 238–41, 299
ne bis in idem 235, 246–7, 250, 252
parallel actions 241–4, 246, 298
Platform-to-Business (P2B) Regulation 235, 238, 239–41
remedial design 234–5
remedial flexibility 248–51, 298
responsive remodelling of competition law 15, 248, 249–52
sanctions 246–7, 250–1
unilateral conduct 237, 250

digital transitions/disruptions 6–7, 45–64, 153–4 *see also* **Big Tech; digital markets, multilevel elements in; EU courts' response to digital challenges**
2030 Digital Compass 156, 157
abuse of a dominant position 13, 45–8, 50–5, 57–61, 296
anti-competitive practices 13, 45–8, 54–5, 58, 60–2, 64, 296
artificial intelligence (AI) 53
behavioural challenges 13, 51–2, 64
Big Tech 301–2
burden of proof, reversal of 64
centralisation 59
CJEU, reviewable acts before the 61, 64
code of conduct, proposal for a 55–6
Commission 46–8, 51, 53–63, 157, 223
companies, role of 156, 157
competition for the market 50, 51
constitutional arrangements 46
consultation 157
decentralisation 54
Digital Markets Act (DMA) 54, 58–63, 64, 297
Digital Markets Board 57
Digital Markets Unit, creation of 55–6
divergence 52, 301
ECN+ Directive 195
enforcement 13, 46–8, 53–64, 297, 301
essential facilities, access to 52–3, 54
ex ante regulatory framework 13, 54, 61, 297
fines 46–8, 60–1
flexibility 296
foundational challenges 13, 52–3, 64
gatekeepers 59–63, 297
governance 46, 49–63, 64
intermediation services 46, 49–50
interoperability 59–60
interpretation 46, 51, 296
legislative modifications 55–7
long-term goals 305
market definition 50–1, 56
market-killing transactions 51–2
market share 50–1
media law, strengthening 55
merger control 45–8, 56–7, 60, 64
national competition authorities (NCAs) 51, 54, 58, 61–2, 64
ne bis in idem 62–3, 64
online platforms 13, 45–55
personal data, collection and monitoring of 45, 52–3, 54
Regulation 1/2003 52, 57, 61–2, 64, 297
right to be heard 61
sanctions 60, 63, 236–7, 250–1
self-employed 226
soft law 213, 219–21, 223, 229
Special Advisers' Report 2019 58
stress test for Commission's governance and enforcement frameworks 53–63
structural challenges 13, 49–51, 64
structural remedies 60
unilateral behaviour 57, 62, 64

dirigistism 279

discretion of the Commission 295, 303–4
enforcement 86–7, 106–7, 108, 168
flexibility 303–4
Foreign Subsidies Regulation 207–8
green transitions/disruptions 183, 187–8
margin of discretion 93, 155, 183, 208, 303–4
soft law 9, 223–6, 307
State aid 92–3, 103, 108, 261–5, 166, 268, 285, 292, 306
tactical use 261
Temporary Framework for Cooperation 105

discrimination 67, 228–9, 298
disruptions *see* **digital transitions/disruptions; green transitions/disruptions**
distribution agreements, regulation of 141
divergence
digital transitions/disruptions 52, 301
effectiveness, principle of 11
EU law and national competition law, divergence between 52
interpretation 141–2, 152
modernisation 301
national competition authorities (NCAs) 134
regulatory authorities 302
technocratic cooperation, EU regulatory extension through 113, 114, 121, 129, 132
do no significant harm principle 13, 66, 78, 79–80, 296, 308
dominance *see* **abuse of a dominant position**
dynamic conservatism 7, 306

ECN *see* **European Competition Network (ECN); ECN+ Directive**
ECN+ Directive 198–202, 307
accountability 30–1
allocation of powers 198, 210
centralisation 202, 210
Commission 14, 140, 144–6, 195–6, 198–202, 210
comparative institutional disadvantages, mitigation of 199–200
cooperation 127–9, 196, 202
decentralisation 30–1, 196, 199, 202, 203, 210
digital transitions/disruptions 195, 210
enforcement 14, 41, 195, 197–202, 203, 210–11, 299
harmonisation 199, 299
horizontal composite procedures 201–2
independence 30–1, 200, 301
information-gathering 199, 201
inspections 199, 201, 202
internal market 307
investigative powers 199
mutual recognition of national administrative decisions 196, 202
national competition authorities (NCAs) 134, 196, 198–202, 210, 299
accountability 30
Commission 140, 144–6
enforcement 30, 198–202, 203, 299
procedural design 14, 195, 198
recitals 199
Regulation 1/2003 196, 198–202, 307
reuse of established legislative techniques 14, 196, 198, 211
soft law 215, 216
economic activity, definition of 205
economic analysis, role of 256
economic assessments 231, 303, 309
economic crises 6–7, 146, 255 *see also* **global financial crisis 2008**
economic development 79, 86, 88, 92–4, 295–6
economic freedom 21–3, 300
economic rights 20, 21, 43
effectiveness, principle of
companies, role of 154
divergence 11
enforcement 20, 24, 29–44, 298, 302
European Competition Network (ECN) 10
institutions 294
judicial protection, principle of effective 41
State aid 256
technocratic cooperation, EU regulatory extension through 114–15, 127, 132
effects-based approach 1, 140, 302, 305
efficiency
common interest, objectives of 93
consumer welfare 84, 218, 295
Covid-19 and State aid 90, 104–7, 108
crisis cartels 101–3
digital transitions/disruptions 51, 185, 187, 191
energy 177–80, 187–8, 271
green transitions/disruptions 75, 177–82, 187–8, 253, 271
market efficiencies 1, 21, 84–5, 90, 96, 116, 135, 295
merger control 34–6, 99
public interest 34
resources, allocation of 134–5
State aid 93, 98, 102, 108, 256, 278
sustainability agreements 177–8, 180–2
Emissions Trading System (ETS) 229–30, 271
energy
1970s crisis 5, 215, 255
2020s crisis 6, 222, 229–30, 264, 271
Climate, Energy and Environmental Aid Guidelines (CEEAG) 75–6, 158, 229
Commission Toolbox on Energy Prices 229–30
decarbonisation goals, compliance with 75, 260, 265, 270–3, 307–8
ECN+ Directive 199

efficiency 177–80, 187–8, 271
energy mix 190, 265, 288, 298
guidelines 75–6, 99, 158, 187, 189, 191, 229, 231, 307
merger control 35, 99
nuclear energy 69, 190, 217, 260, 263–4, 286–7
renewable energy 188–9, 280
security 22, 87, 99, 217, 224, 288
State aid 76, 229–31, 264–5, 269, 298
2020s crisis 229–30, 264, 271
guidance 191, 307
nuclear energy 69, 190, 286–8
plans 257
renewable energy 280, 287
subsidies 176, 263
sustainability agreements 177–8, 180
enforcement 5, 15, 21, 39–43, 308 *see also* **centralisation of enforcement; decentralisation of enforcement; Regulation 1/2003**
abuse of a dominant position 29–31, 39–42, 44–7, 54, 58, 61–2
anti-competitive practices 10, 29–31, 39–42, 44–7, 54, 61–2
collective actions 304
Commission 138–42, 145, 151, 248–9, 257–8, 297–8
digital transitions/disruptions 242–3, 252
discretion 86–7, 106–7, 108, 168
European Green Deal 257–8
investigated companies, position of 159–64, 303
national competition authorities (NCAs) 246, 252
State aid rules, creative compliance with 277, 284–5, 289–92, 306
third-party companies in enforcement, role of 164–8, 172
consistency 199, 298, 300
cooperation 113–20, 123, 132, 217, 299, 300
Covid-19 and State aid 85–7, 90, 96, 104–5
deterrence 236
digital transitions/disruptions 13, 46–8, 53–63, 234–5, 238–45, 248–52, 297
Big Tech 241–2, 244–5, 252, 301
consistent and effective enforcement 298
Digital Market Act (DMA) 54, 58–63, 138–9, 236–8, 252, 306
European Green Deal 257–8
priorities 175–6
stress-testing 58–63
discretion 86–7, 106–7, 108, 168
ECN+ Directive 14, 41, 195, 197–202, 203, 210–11, 299
effectiveness 20, 24, 29–44, 298, 302
European Competition Network (ECN) 140–1, 248
ex post enforcement 10, 13, 124, 151, 161, 234, 306
flexibility 296–7
follow-on cases 163, 170, 245, 304
Foreign Subsidies Regulation 203–4, 298, 302
Free Trade Agreements (FTAs) 302
green transitions/disruptions 13, 15, 175–6, 254–8, 264, 267, 296
Hungary 282–91
investigated companies in enforcement, position of 155, 159–64
legal certainty 248–9
merger control 31, 42–3, 149, 164–6
multilevel enforcement system 30
mutual assistance 117–18
national competition authorities (NCAs) 30, 133–4, 280
Commission 138–42, 145, 151
digital transitions/disruptions 58, 234, 236, 248
ECN+ Directive 198–202, 203, 299
ne bis in idem 62–3, 246
Ordoliberalism 23
parallel actions 241–4, 248–9
priorities 175–6
private enforcement 169–70, 235, 238–9, 244–5, 250–2, 267, 303–4
public enforcement 238, 241–4, 250–2
soft law 215–17, 220
State aid 85–7, 90–1, 96, 104–5, 108–9, 275
creative compliance 275, 276, 277–92
green transitions/disruptions 13, 15, 254–8, 264, 267, 296
Hungary 282–91
stress-testing 58–63
sustainability agreements 178
technocratic cooperation, EU regulatory extension through 113–20, 123, 132, 299, 300
under-enforcement 31–6, 42, 44
enlargement 1, 9, 19–20, 26–7, 117
environmental protection *see* **green transitions/disruptions**
epistemic communities 11, 118–19, 123, 126, 132, 300
equivalence, principle of 114, 121–6, 131, 298
essential facilities, access to 52–3, 54

EU courts 173–92 *see also* **EU courts response to digital challenges; EU courts' response to green challenges**
Commission 25, 262
constitutional framework 303–4
convergence 144
Covid-19 and State aid 86
independence 40
Member States and EU, relationship between 144, 145
national competition authorities (NCAs) 40, 169–70
preliminary rulings 101, 174, 228, 304
soft law 225–6
State aid 86, 91–3, 262, 278, 289, 295
EU courts' response to digital challenges 61, 64, 183–5
barriers to entry 183, 191
block exemptions 187–8
Commission 14, 174–7, 183–5, 187–8
flexibility 303–4
harm, theory of 184–5
interpretation 173–5
market power 183
priorities for enforcement 175–6
reasons, duty to state 14
remote working 176
specificities of digital markets, rules to reflect the 176
standard of proof 14
State aid 14, 183, 186–91
taxation 186
EU courts' response to green challenges 173–83, 304
Commission 14, 174–83, 187–91, 192
exemptions 178–9, 186–9, 191, 192
fines 177
foreign subsidies 174, 176
greenwashing 176, 191
internal market 174–5, 187–91, 192
interpretation 173–5, 179
preliminary rulings 174
priorities for enforcement 175–6
reasons, duty to state 14
standard of proof 174
State aid 14, 176, 186–93
sustainability agreements 177–83, 191, 192
taxation 186
EU Merger Regulation (EUMR) 28, 45–8, 167
companies as main targets 154
Copenhagen accession criteria 27
decentralisation 31
digital transitions/disruptions 45–8, 60, 64
Foreign Direct Investment Screening Regulation 148–9
Foreign Subsidies Regulation 207
review 148
technocratic cooperation, EU regulatory extension through 128
European Arrest Warrant (EAW) 40
European Commission *see* **Commission**
European Competition Network (ECN) *see also* **ECN+ Directive**
advocacy gap 146, 150
Commission 10, 140–1, 144–6, 150
cooperation 120, 127–9, 237
Covid-19 and State aid 84, 87, 104–6
decentralisation 29–31, 118–19
differentiated approach 302
digital transitions/disruptions 62, 237, 248, 252
discussions, as a site for 141
enforcement 140–1, 248
European Green Deal and State aid 77
independence 301
national competition authorities (NCAs) 10, 140–1, 144–6, 150
policy-making 140
technocratic cooperation, EU regulatory extension through 120, 126–9
European Council 89, 107–8, 256
European Court of Justice *see* **EU courts**
European Economic Area (EEA) Agreement 117
European Green Deal (EGD) and State aid law 6, 65–81, 153, 254, 272
academic scholarship 68, 75
block exemptions 75–6
Charter of Fundamental Rights of the EU 72, 258–9
Climate Law of 2021 257–8, 269
climate neutrality 77, 80, 257–8, 260
Commission 68, 71–2, 75–7, 80, 156–7, 253, 257–9, 273
constitutional framework 13, 65–6, 71–2, 258–60
consultation 75, 156–7
do no significant harm principle 13, 66, 78, 79–80, 296, 308
enforcement 13, 257–8, 296
environmental agreements 78–9
environmental pressure within the EU legal order 71–7
European Hydrogen Bank (EHB) 76

green transition tools 13, 66
Guidelines on State Aid for Climate, Environmental Protection and Energy (CEEAG) 75–6
Important Projects of Common European Interest (IPCEI) 73, 76
integration 65, 67–73, 76, 258–9
intergenerational perspective 72
internal market 66–8, 71–4, 80–1, 259
interpretation 73, 79–80, 263–4, 296
legislative changes 73
Lisbon Treaty 67
long-term goals 305
mainstreaming clauses 259–60, 306
merger control 153
national climate and energy plans 257
national competition authorities (NCAs) 67, 76–7
national competition law 80–1
NextGenerationEU (NGEU) plan 258, 273, 308
notification requirements 75–6
novel instruments, transformation through 77–80
objectives 76, 258
Paris Agreement 257
polluter pays 68
proportionality 68, 75
socio-environmental dimension 67–8
soft law 71–2, 229
spillover effects 73
standards 78–9
State aid 109
sustainability 66–7, 71–9, 153, 258, 296
taxonomy 13, 66, 78, 258, 306
transformative character 258–60, 273
Treaties 67–80
European Hydrogen Bank (EHB) 76
European Pact on Immigration and Asylum 107–8
European Parliament 224, 286
European Semester 144, 281
European Supervisory Agencies (ESAs) 197–8
exemptions *see also* **block exemptions**
crisis cartels 88, 102–3
exemption game 276, 282, 283–6, 291
green transitions/disruptions 177–80, 186–7, 191, 192
State aid rules, creative compliance with 276, 280, 282, 283–6, 291, 306
experimental governance 302
experts
administrative procedures 197, 202
digital transitions/disruptions 55
dispute resolution 122–3
epistemic communities 123
green transitions/disruptions 122–3, 265, 272–3
networks 25, 118
political reaction and confrontation 8
State aid rules, creative compliance with 278, 280, 282, 284, 287–8
technocratic expertise 11, 37–8, 300–1
transformative solutions 300
external trade relations *see* **technocratic cooperation, EU regulatory extension through**

Facebook 45–6, 48, 51, 59–60, 136–8, 234, 239, 241
failing firm defence 98–9, 102–3
fairness 13, 90, 113, 127, 132, 238
financial crisis 2008 *see* **global financial crisis 2008**
fines
digital transitions/disruptions 46–8, 60–1, 234
ECN+ Directive 199
green transitions/disruptions 177
hardcore cartels 163
Member States and EU, relationship between 146
national competition authorities (NCAs) 41–2, 169
transactionalisation of EU competition law 162–3
flexibility 7, 9, 13–14
actors 308
Covid-19 224
digital transitions/disruptions 46, 296
discretion 303–4
enforcement 296–7
institutions 294, 297–8
polycrisis 308
remedies 248–51, 298
soft law 14, 213–14, 223–5, 307
State aid 13, 91, 108
foreign subsidies 174, 176 *see also* **Foreign Subsidies Regulation**
Foreign Subsidies Regulation 14, 174, 195–6, 203–10
allocation of powers 198, 210
bilateral agreements 125

centralisation 196, 203–4, 210, 298, 307
Commission 14, 124–6, 149, 196, 203–9, 298, 307
common procedural provisions 205–6
conclusion of administrative procedure, relevant issues throughout and after 208–10
ECN+ Directive 203
enforcement 203–4, 298, 302
ex officio reviews 205–7
formal investigations 207–8
information, provision of 124–5
inspections 209
interim measures 208
internal market 124–6, 149, 195, 203–10, 297, 303
investigations 125, 207–9
level playing field 123–4, 195
merger control 149, 205–8
national supervision authorities 203
notification obligations 124, 149, 206–7
open strategic autonomy 195, 204
preliminary examination stage 207
preliminary reviews 206–7
procedural design 14, 195, 198
proposed Regulation 196, 208
public procurement 205–8, 304
rebalancing mechanisms 302
recitals 203–4
redressive measures or commitments, decisions imposing 208
Regulation 1/2003 124, 203, 207–8
regulatory gap 123–4
repayment of subsidies 203
reuse of established legislative techniques 14, 196, 198, 206, 208–9, 211
State aid 123–4, 203–10, 298, 306
structure and conduct of administrative procedure 206–8
technocratic cooperation, EU regulatory extension through 121, 123–6, 297, 298, 307

fragmentation
digital transitions/disruptions 235–8, 242, 246
global trade system 13
governance 301
internal market 298
soft law 227–8
State aid rules, creative compliance with 298

France
abuse of a dominant position 48
abuse of economic dependence, rules on 240–1
national competition authorities (NCAs) 76, 243–4
primacy of competition law in the Treaties 146

Frankenstein strategy (State aid) 276, 282, 286–8, 291
fraud 286
Free Trade Agreements (FTAs) 114, 117–18, 121–3, 126–32, 302
fundamental rights *see also* **Charter of Fundamental Rights of the EU (CFR); participation rights**
economic rights 20, 21, 43
inspections 209
Ordoliberalism 24
privacy law 55
right to be heard61, 156, 165, 209
rule of law 39
State aid 254, 258–9, 277
Furman Report 55–6
future-proofing 61, 297, 305

gatekeepers 59–63, 139, 176, 233–4, 235, 237–8, 297, 298
general principles of EU law 68, 235
genetically modified organisms (GMOs) 198
Georgia, Russia's military action in 87–8
Germany 48, 136–8, 238–9, 252
Competition Act, amendments to 56–7
DG Comp 39
digital transitions/disruptions 56–7, 63, 238–9
European Green Deal and State aid 76–7
General Data Protection Regulation (GDPR) 136–7
hotels and online travel agents, regulation of agreements between 141
market tipping 238–9
ne bis in idem 247
Ordoliberalism 23, 37–9
price parity clauses 141–2
Regulation 1/2003 38, 57

gig economy 304
global financial crisis 2008 12, 89, 147, 173, 296
bank bailouts 281
crisis cartels 84–5, 147
Eurocrisis 2, 6

failing firm defence 99
green transitions/disruptions 257
Member States and EU, relationship between 145, 147
merger control 31
soft law 213–14, 221
State aid 84–5, 87–9, 107–8, 221–2, 257, 281

globalisation 25, 31, 100, 116, 210

Google 45–8, 59–60, 166, 168–70, 184, 234, 239, 241, 243–5, 251

governance, definition of 3, 308

Greece 76, 92, 145, 235

green transition 6–7 *see also* **energy; EU courts' response to green challenges; European Green Deal (EGD) and State aid law; State aid control, green transition through**
Clean Energy Package 224
Climate, Energy and Environmental Aid Guidelines (CEEAG) 75–6, 158, 229
Commission Toolbox on Energy Prices 229–30
companies, role of 156–9, 172
consultation 172
economic objectives of competition law 11–12
efficiency 75, 177–82, 187–8, 253, 271
Emissions Trading System (ETS) State aid guidelines 229–30
energy packages 229
environmental agreements 219
guidance letters 164
Horizontal Guidelines, revision of 157
Important Projects of Common European Interest 229
integration 8, 15, 65–73, 76, 254–60, 264–6, 271–3
national competition authorities (NCAs) 134
soft law 213, 219–21, 229
State aid 87, 109
sustainability 301
Ukraine, Russia's invasion of 222

guidelines/guidance 9, 213, 220–1
Climate, Energy and Environmental Aid Guidelines (CEEAG) 75–6, 158, 229, 261–2, 265, 268, 271
collective agreements concluded by the self-employed, guidance on 219, 226
comfort letters 227
Commission 93–6, 164, 182, 187–9, 191, 215–20, 223
companies, role of 155, 157–8
Covid-19 and State aid 93–6, 215–18, 220
digital transitions/disruptions 157
Emissions Trading System (ETS) guidelines 229–30
energy 75–6, 99, 158, 187, 189, 191, 229, 231, 307
green transitions/disruptions 157, 254, 261–2, 265, 268, 271
guidance letters 164
Horizontal Cooperation Guidelines 157, 218–19
Horizontal Merger Guidelines 99
informal individual guidance 220–1
Regional Aid Guidelines, consultation on 158
Rescue and Restructuring Guidelines (RR Guidelines) 85, 93, 96, 99
revision 217–18
State aid 75–6, 158, 224, 231, 261–2, 265, 268, 271
technocratic cooperation, EU regulatory extension through 114

hardcore cartel cases 163

harm, theory of 184–5

harmonisation
digital transitions/disruptions 235
ECN+ Directive 199, 299
maximum harmonisation 135
minimum harmonisation 30, 135–9, 299
modernisation 298
national competition authorities (NCAs) 30, 135–9, 140–2, 144–5, 150–1
standards 113
technocratic cooperation, EU regulatory extension through 114, 122

hotels and online travel agents, regulation of agreements between 141–2

human rights *see* **fundamental rights**

Hungary 13, 20, 33–4, 36–7, 41–2, 44
cartels 32–4
enforcement 34, 282–91
Euroscepticism 282
high level of compliance 283
illiberal state, as 13, 276, 282–3, 291
legal and economic expertise 284, 287–8
merger control, public interest exemption for 34–6
Ministry of Finance, State Aid Monitoring Office (SAMO) as within the 284
Ministry of National Development, move of SAMO to 284

monitoring 284–5
national economic interests, supporting 32
negative decisions 289–91
no-bid contracts 286–8
political power, accumulation of 32
Prime Minister's Office, move of State Aid Monitoring Office to the 284
protectionism 36
public procurement 32–4
rule of law 31, 275, 291
State aid rules, creative compliance with 15, 275, 276, 282–91, 306
strategically important sectors of the economy 31–2
taxation 289–91
under-enforcement of competition law 31–6
Watermelon cartel 32, 33–4

illiberal states 13, 276, 282–3, 291
Important Projects of Common European Interest (IPCEI) 73, 76, 281
independence 25, 298–9
Commission and NCAs, relationship between 134, 144
ECN+ Directive 30–1, 200, 301
EU courts 40
European Competition Network (ECN) 126, 301
merger control agencies 31
mutual trust, principle of 42, 126, 301
national competition authorities (NCAs) 30, 37–8, 41, 300–1
technocratic cooperation, EU regulatory extension through 121, 126–9, 131
uniformity 11
industrial policy
Industrial and Digital Strategies 158
Member States and EU, relationship between 134–5
merger control 147–8, 150, 298
national competition authorities (NCAs) 134
industry lobbying 144
information
asymmetries 79
defence, rights of the 160, 162
Foreign Subsidies Regulation 124–5
gathering 199, 201
third-party companies as sources of information 164–6, 172
inspections 140, 199, 201, 202, 209
institutions 4, 13, 15, 293 *see also* **Commission; EU courts; national competition authorities (NCAs); European Competition Network (ECN)**
autonomy 37–9
balance 69, 262
comparative institutional analysis 196–7, 199–200, 205
decentralisation 309
European Council 89, 107–8, 256
European Parliament 224, 286
flexibility 294, 297–8
formal and informal institutions 20
framing 7
gap-filling 297
green transitions/disruptions 254–5
integration 299–300
modernisation 297–8
post-modernisation 294
soft law 213, 309
State aid 15, 254–5, 267–9
technocratic cooperation, EU regulatory extension through 114, 115–21, 126–7, 131
uniformity 11, 294
Instagram 48, 51
instruments *see* **administrative procedures and instruments**
integration 20, 23, 25–6, 43–4, 100
access to justice 260
collective identity 299–300
democracy 22
green transitions/disruptions 8, 15, 65–73, 76, 254–60, 264–6, 271–3
institutions 299–300
negative integration 144, 255
positive integration 256
public procurement 67–8
State aid 254–60, 264–6, 271–3, 279–80
technocratic cooperation, EU regulatory extension through 119–20
interaction of crises 5–7
intermediation services 46, 49–50, 238
internal market 1, 4, 8, 11–12, 15, 309
administrative procedures and instruments 195, 199–200, 203–10, 307
Commission and NCAs, relationship between 136
digital transitions/disruptions 174–5
exclusive competence 8–9

Foreign Subsidies Regulation 124–6, 149, 195, 203–10, 297, 303
fragmentation 298
green transitions/disruptions 174–5, 187–91, 192
European Green Deal 66–8, 71–4, 80–1, 259
State aid 66–8, 71–4, 80–1, 253–6, 259, 262–3, 270
soft law 216–17, 221, 223
State aid 15, 85, 279–84
European Green Deal 66–8, 71–4, 80–1, 259
green transitions/disruptions 66–8, 71–4, 80–1, 253–6, 259, 262–3, 270
interpretation 9, 146–7, 303
Covid-19 and State aid 89, 95, 295
digital transitions/disruptions 46, 51, 173–5, 296
divergence 141–2, 152
flexibility 294
global financial crisis 2008 89
green transitions/disruptions 73, 79–80, 173–5, 179, 263–4, 296
national competition authorities (NCAs) 136, 141–2, 151–2
State aid 73, 79–80, 263–4, 296
investigated companies in enforcement of EU competition law, position of 155, 159–64
commitment decisions 162–3
cooperation 163–4
defence, rights of the 160, 162, 303
merger control procedures, special position of notifying companies in 160–4
State aid 159–60
strategic turn in competition law 161–2, 163, 172
third-party companies 159, 165
transactionalisation of EU competition law 162–4
investigations *see also* **investigated companies in enforcement of EU competition law, position of**
Commission and NCAs, relationship between 139
digital transitions/disruptions 139, 237, 242–4, 251
ECN+ Directive 199
Foreign Subsidies Regulation 125, 207–9
harmonisation 30
public participation 266
State aid rules, creative compliance with 289–91, 306
third-party companies in enforcement, role of 165

Japan-EU Economic Partnership Agreement 121–2, 123
judicial protection, principle of effective 41

leadership 8, 133, 143, 150, 300–2
legal certainty
administrative procedures and instruments 306
comfort letters 226
Commission and NCAs, relationship between 141, 143
digital transitions/disruptions 52, 64, 235, 242, 245, 248–9, 298
ECN+ Directive 201
soft law 223, 226–8
legitimacy 14, 23, 108, 223–6, 228, 277, 305
legitimate expectations 163, 227, 307
leniency programmes 144
level playing field 113–15, 121–6, 131–2, 184, 195, 254
liberal developmentalism 280, 282
lock-in effects 265, 270, 272
loyal/sincere cooperation, principle of 10, 39, 42–3, 137, 245, 299, 301

mainstreaming 259–60, 271, 306
market-killing transactions 51–2
market tipping 50
Market Economy Investor Principle (MEIP) 280
media
pluralism 35–6
state capture 36
strengthening media law 55
Member States and EU, relationship between 143–50
advocacy gap 145–6, 150, 299
Commission 135, 146–50, 299
competition policy, direction of EU 146–50
convergence 143–5
efficient allocation of resources 134–5
EU courts 144, 145
fines 146
global financial crisis 2008 145, 147
industrial policy 134–5
mergers, review of 147–50
open market economy principle 134–5, 150

merger control 9–11, 20, 27–31 *see also* **EU Merger Regulation (EUMR)**
centralisation 160
champions 10, 147–8, 150, 295
Community dimension 10, 28, 48, 60
compatibility assessments 295
decentralisation 27–8, 31, 161
defence, rights of the 160, 162
digital transitions/disruptions 45–8, 56–7, 60, 64
efficiency 34–6, 99
enforcement 31, 42–3, 149, 164–6
European Green Deal and State aid 153
ex ante control 28, 161
failing firm defence 98–9, 102–3
Foreign Subsidies Regulation 149, 205–8
industrial policy 147–8, 150, 298
information rights, limits on 160, 162
jurisdiction, allocation of 28–9
monitoring 28
national competition authorities (NCAs) 160–1
non-economic interests 303
notification obligations 60, 147, 160–4, 206–7
participation rights 160, 162, 165–6
procedure 160–4
public interest 9, 42–3, 99
public policy 9, 296
reviews 147–50
Siemens/Alstom merger 147–50
State aid 98–9, 102–3, 109
third-party companies in enforcement, role of 164–6
migrant crisis 87, 107–8
modernisation agenda 1, 4, 8–11, 133
centralisation 298, 301
convergence 143–4
Covid-19 and State aid 10, 84–5, 90, 104, 106, 108
crisis cartels 99–101, 103
decentralisation 4
Europeanisation 20
global financial crisis 2008 281
green transitions/disruptions 256–7
harmonisation 298
institutions 297–8
Modernisation Regulation 281
post-modernisation 7, 29–31, 294, 301, 309
Rescue and Restructuring Guidelines (RR Guidelines) 85
self-assessment system 104
soft law 215, 307
State aid 92, 99–101, 103, 108, 217, 281
Covid-19 10, 84–5, 90, 104, 106, 108
green transitions/disruptions 256–7
suspension of rules 307
monitoring 28, 276, 279, 283–6, 308
multilateral trade system 113, 115, 129
multinationals, negative State aid decisions against 289
mutual assistance 117–18, 202
mutual recognition principle 40, 114, 121, 196, 202, 301
mutual trust, principle of
independence 301
national competition authorities (NCAs) 199, 201
politicisation 301
rule of law 24, 39–40
technocratic cooperation, EU regulatory extension through 126, 301

national competition authorities (NCAs) *see also* **national competition authorities (NCAs) and Commission, relationship between**
accountability 30
advocacy gap 145–6, 150, 299
centralisation 38, 298
comfort letters 227
comparative institutional disadvantages, mitigation of 199–200
constitutional relevance 43, 300
cooperation 39–42, 202, 298
between NCAs 39, 250–2
Commission 236–7, 246, 250, 252
technocratic cooperation, EU regulatory extension through 114–15
court-like functions 40–1, 43
data protection authorities, cooperation with 250–1
decentralisation 39, 161, 169–70, 202
decision sections 38
digital transitions/disruptions 51, 54, 58, 234, 236–7, 239–41, 252
ECN+ Directive 30, 134, 196, 198–202, 210, 299
economic rights 20
economists to State aid units, adding 280
enforcement 58, 133–4, 234, 236, 280
comparative institutional disadvantages, mitigation of 198–202, 203, 299
effective 24, 30, 36–7, 39–40, 43–4
private 169–71
third-party companies in enforcement, role of 168–71

European Green Deal and State aid 67, 76–7
gatekeepers 235, 237
harmonisation of rules for investigation, decision-making and enforcement powers 30
independence 30, 37–8, 41, 200, 300–1
information-gathering 199, 201
inspections 199, 201, 202
merger control 42, 160–1
mutual trust 199, 201
one-stop shop principle 161
political standing 41
procedural and institutional autonomy, principle of 39
Regulation 1/2003 42, 200–2, 250–1
resources 301
rule of law 39–40, 43
safeguarding rights 39–40
soft law 219, 227
Sped-Pro judgment 24, 40, 43–4
State aid 67, 76–7, 170–1, 280, 306
sustainability agreements 219
technocratic cooperation, EU regulatory extension through 114–15
third-party companies in enforcement, role of 168–71
toolkit of powers 200
transparency 298–9
unilateral conduct 64

national competition authorities (NCAs) and Commission, relationship between 29, 36, 133–44, 301
abandonment of cases 140
allocation of powers 160–1
application of national competition law 134
competences 29, 245
consultation of Commission 136
contact with Commission, keeping in 139
convergence 136
cooperation 39–40, 236–7, 246, 250, 252
co-ordination mechanism 139
decentralisation 137, 139–43
decisions running counter to Commission decisions, prohibition on 139
Digital Markets Act (DMA) 138–9
distribution agreements, regulation of 141
divergent interpretation 141–2, 152
ECN+ Directive 196, 198–202
effects test 140
enforcement 138–42, 145, 151, 246, 252
European Competition Network (ECN) 140–1, 144–6, 150
executive competences, allocation of 134
harmonisation 135–9, 140–2, 144–5, 150–1
interpretation 136, 141–2, 151–2
investigations, advising Commission of 139
legal certainty 141, 143
legal framework empowering NCAs 135–9
non-infringement decisions, power to issue 140
Regulation 1/2003 29, 135, 137–42
resources 144–5
stricter competition rules, Member States with 135–9
sustainability agreements 141–3, 151, 219
third-party companies in enforcement, role of 168–71
uniformity of application of EU competition law 134
unilateral conduct, sanctioning 136
vertical restraints 141
withdrawal of cases by Commission 139

national laws 145, 238–41
Commission and NCAs, relationship between 134
digital transitions/disruptions 52, 234, 235–6, 238–41, 299
divergence between EU law and national competition law 52
European Green Deal and State aid 80–1
Europeanisation 24–6
State aid 9, 80–1
stricter national rules 302

national procedural autonomy, principle of 11

NCAs *see* **national competition authorities (NCAs)**

ne bis in idem 62–4, 235, 246–7, 250, 252, 298

neoliberalism 19–20, 279–80

New Competition Tool (NCT) 58–9, 157, 303

NextGenerationEU (NGEU) plan 258, 273, 308

no-bid contracts 286–8

non-economic interests 73, 218, 303, 308

non-regression commitments 114, 122

OLAF (European Anti-Fraud Office) 286

open market economy principle 134–5, 150

Ordoliberal School 19, 22–4, 37–9, 43, 299–300, 305

parallel actions 241–4, 246, 248–9, 298

participation rights *see also* **consultation**
companies, role of 14, 154, 171
Covid-19 166–7
defence, rights of the 160, 162

democracy 21
digital transitions/disruptions 250
green transitions/disruptions 254, 261, 266–9, 273, 306
investigations 266
merger control 160, 162
procedure 305
soft law 225
third-party companies in enforcement, role of 165–6
Platform-to-Business (P2B) Regulation 235, 238, 239–41
Poland, rule of law crisis in 275
policy 7–8, 24–9, 133 *see also* **public policy**
common commercial policy (CCP) 131
definition 154–9
European Competition Network (ECN) 140
green transitions/disruptions 260–73
leadership 301–2
Member States and EU, relationship between 135, 143–50
monitoring 308
soft law 213–14, 218–19, 229, 231
State aid 155–6, 256, 260–75, 277, 278–82, 291, 306
Trade Policy Review (TPR) 113, 115, 123, 129, 132
politics and politicisation 8, 39, 275, 305–6
administrative procedures and instruments 197
capture 21–2
coherence and credibility 301
democracy, preconditions for 23
distortions in the market 12
expert knowledge 8
institutions, integrity and impartiality of 20–1
interventions 38
mutual trust 301
national competition authorities (NCAs) 41
power, accumulation of 32
stability 21, 26–7
State aid, creative compliance with 15, 276–92, 306
polycrisis 2, 4, 6, 88, 108, 109, 293, 301, 308
populism 6–7, 13, 20, 29, 277
prices
Commission Toolbox on Energy Prices 229–30
crisis cartels 101
discrimination 185
energy 6, 215, 222, 229–30, 255, 264, 271, 288
fixing 30, 33–4, 88, 97, 100
gouging 88
increases 5, 97–9, 105, 181, 222, 229–30, 271
price parity clauses 141–2
reductions 103, 185
privacy law 55
private enforcement 169–70, 235, 238–9, 244–5, 250–2, 267, 303–4
procedure 11, 293, 305–8 *see also* **administrative procedures and instruments**
Aarhus Convention 267–9
fairness 127
formal examination stage 266–7
global financial crisis 2008 89
green transitions/disruptions 266–9
irregularities 171
justice 300
national competition authorities (NCAs) 39
preliminary stage 266
Procedural Regulation 206
proceduralisation turn in environmental law 267
safeguards 266–8
State aid 266–9
temporal dimension 305
third parties, procedural rights of 266
proportionality
Covid-19 and State aid 95, 106–7
European Green Deal and State aid 68, 75
inspections 209
ne bis in idem 247
public interest 107
public policy 100, 295
State aid 68, 75, 99–100, 217
technocratic cooperation, EU regulatory extension through 123
protectionism 31, 36, 150
public consultation *see* **consultation**
public interest 106–7
administrative procedures and instruments 197
crisis cartels 99
enforcement 42–3
European Green Deal and State aid 67
global financial crisis 2008 99
merger control 9
populism 29
proportionality 107
State aid 9, 85, 90, 108
public policy 5, 19, 294–6
Covid-19 and State aid 86, 107
European Green Deal and State aid 70
merger control 9, 296

proportionality 100, 295
State aid 9, 98, 100, 103
public procurement 32–4
Foreign Subsidies Regulation 304
integration 67–8
judicial remedies 304
soft law 230
technocratic cooperation, EU regulatory extension through 124, 126

reasons, duty to provide 14, 166–7, 226, 227
Rechtsstaat 37, 39
Recovery and Resilience Facility (RRF) 79, 174
Regional Aid Guidelines, consultation on 158
Regulation 1/2003
comfort letters 226
Commission and NCAs, relationship between 135, 137–42
Copenhagen accession criteria 27
decentralisation 29, 118–19, 139, 169, 216
digital transitions/disruptions 48, 52, 57, 61–2, 64, 237
ECN+ Directive 196, 198–202, 307
enforcement 41–3
European Competition Network (ECN) 127–8
Foreign Subsidies Regulation 124, 203, 207–8
heard, right to be 165
national competition authorities (NCAs) 42, 135, 137–42, 200–2, 250–1
Ordoliberalism 38
parallel actions 243
soft law 216, 226
technocratic cooperation, EU regulatory extension through 118–19, 128
transactionalisation of EU competition law 162
regulatory capture 21–2
regulatory gaps 123–4, 213
remedial powers 60, 234–5, 248–51, 297–8, 304
remote working 176
Rescue and Restructuring Guidelines (RR Guidelines) 85, 93, 96, 99
Research, Development and Innovation (RDI) framework 223
resources
Commission 9, 10, 144–5, 307
efficiency 134–5
national competition authorities (NCAs) 144–5, 301
technocratic cooperation, EU regulatory extension through 126, 128
responsive remodelling 15, 248, 249–52
restorative justice 249–50
reuse of established legislative techniques 14, 196, 198, 206, 208–9, 211
right to be heard 61, 156, 165, 209
rule of law 23–4, 26–7, 245 *see also* **rule of law backsliding**
rule of law backsliding
Central and Eastern Europe 6, 275, 291
checks and balances 31
decentralisation 39
European Competition Network (ECN) 301
green transitions/disruptions 267
Hungary 31, 275, 291
individual rights, safeguarding 39
media capture 36
national competition authorities (NCAs) 39–40, 43
neoliberalism 20
Poland 275
soft law 223
State aid 15, 223, 275, 277, 291
Russia *see also* **Ukraine, Russia's invasion of**
Georgia, military action in 87–8

sanctions
Commission 297
Covid-19 and State aid 87
crisis cartels 100
digital transitions/disruptions 60, 63, 236–7, 250–1
ne bis in idem 246–7
Ukraine, Russia's invasion of 222, 230
search engines 238
self-employed, guidance on collective agreements concluded by the 219, 226
Services of General Economic Interest (SGEI), economic advantage for 259
sincere/loyal cooperation, principle of 10, 39, 42–3, 137, 245, 299, 301
single market *see* **internal market**
societal contexts 9, 21, 23
cooperation between agreements 177–83, 191, 192
crisis cartels 99–100
social exclusion 67
socio-environmental dimension 67–8
soft law 9, 214, 218–19, 223–4

soft law 213–31 *see also* **guidelines/guidance; Temporary Framework for State Aid (Covid-19)**
accountability 226
adaptation 228
Atlanta doctrine 156
Better Regulation agenda 156
binding effects/non-binding effects 223, 224, 226
block exemptions 217
collective agreements concluded by the self-employed, guidance on 219, 226
comfort letters 216, 220–1, 226–7
Commission 84, 154, 215–27, 230, 307, 309
companies, role of 155–8
Covid-19 14, 229
discretion 9, 223–6, 307
companies, role of 155–8, 171
consultations 156–8, 225, 231
Covid-19 14, 213–18, 221–2, 224, 228–30
Damages Directive 215, 216
de minimis notice, revision of 228
decentralisation 215–16, 218, 220, 231
definition 213
digital transitions/disruptions 156–9, 213, 219–21, 223, 226, 229
ECN+ Directive 215, 216
emergency soft law 214, 221, 224, 225, 228–30, 307
enforcement 215–17, 220
environmental agreements 219
European Competition Network (ECN) 10, 155–6
evolution of EU competition law and State aid law 215–23
exclusive competences 213, 223–4, 307
flexibility 14, 213–14, 223–5, 307
fragmentation 227–8
global financial crisis 2008 213–14, 221
governmental intervention 215
green transition 213, 220–1, 229–30, 256
Clean Energy Package 224
companies, role of 156–8
Emissions Trading System (ETS) State aid guidelines 229–30
environmental agreements 219
European Green Deal 71–2, 156–8, 229
Important Projects of Common European Interest 229
guidelines 9, 213, 217–18, 220–1
hard law 213–18, 223–4, 228–30, 231
Horizontal Cooperation Guidelines 218–19
hybrid regulation 214, 215–23
institutions 213, 309
internal market 216–17, 221, 223
legal certainty 223, 226–8
legal orders of Member States, incorporation into 227–8
legitimacy 223–6, 228
merger control 155–6
modernisation 215, 307
national competition authorities (NCAs) 219, 227
New Industrial Strategy for Europe 156
non-discrimination 298
non-economic goals 218
notices 9, 213
participation 156, 225
policy choices 213–14, 218–19, 229, 231
principles, putting into abeyance established 228–30
public procurement 230
publication 225
qualitative level 214
quantitative level 214
reasons, duty to provide 226, 227
Regulation 1/2003 216, 226
regulatory gaps 213
societal issues 9, 214, 218–19, 223–4
soft law 14, 213, 221–5, 228–31
State aid 14, 213, 217, 221–5, 228–31, 256
Climate, Energy and Environmental Aid Guidelines, consultation on 158
companies, role of 155–6, 158
creative compliance 276, 283–4
European Green Deal 71–2
guidelines 158, 224, 231
Notice on the Notion of Aid 224
Regional Aid Guidelines, consultation on 158
State Aid Action Plan (SAAP) 217
sustainability agreements 219
transparency 221, 223, 225–6, 230–1
Ukraine, Russia's invasion of 87, 213–14, 217, 221–2, 225, 228–30
specialisation agreements 103
spillover effects 73
standards 11, 78–9, 116, 121–3, 131–2, 174
standing 165, 266–8
standstill clauses 170–1
State aid 9–11, 83–109 *see also* **Covid-19 and State aid; creative compliance with State aid rules; European Green Deal (EGD) and State aid law; State aid control, green transition through**

administrative procedures and instruments 203–10
block exemptions 103, 158
cartels, prohibition of 98
case law principles 91–3
centralisation 10, 298
classification 205
collusion 98
Commission 88–9, 91–3, 98–103, 108, 159, 165
  crisis cartels 101
  discretion 92–3, 103, 108, 206
  framing 13
  politicisation 275
  soft law 222–5
common interest objectives 92–3, 295
companies, role of 154, 164, 165–8
compatibility assessments 295
competences 9, 223–4, 291
Covid-19 13, 84–5, 228–9
crisis cartels 84–5, 88, 90, 98–103
crisis management 98, 108
defence, rights of the 159–60, 209
digital transitions/disruptions 14, 176, 183, 186–91
direct link between aid and damage 91–2
economic development 88, 92–3
efficiency 93, 98, 102, 108, 256, 278
emergency power, as a 5, 224
Emissions Trading System (ETS) guidelines 229–30
energy 76, 229–31, 264–5, 269, 271, 298
  guidance 191, 307
  nuclear energy 69, 190, 286–8
  plans 257
  renewable energy 280, 287
enforcement 10, 91, 108–9, 164–71, 217, 275
evolution of State aid law 215–23
exceptional circumstances 84–5, 88–92, 99
exclusive competences 9, 223, 291
flexibility within the rules 13, 91, 108
Foreign Subsidies Regulation 123–4, 298, 306
global financial crisis 2008 84–5, 87–9, 99, 107–8, 221–2
information rights, limits on 160
internal market 15, 85
investigated companies in enforcement, position of 159–60
justification 88, 91, 98, 102–3, 108
legitimacy safeguards 223–4
merger control 98–9, 102–3, 109
migrant crisis 87, 107–8
modernisation 10, 84–5, 92, 99–101, 103, 217
natural disasters 88, 91–2
Notice on the Notion of Aid 224
notification 90–1
overcapacity 102–3
participation rights 160, 165–7
policy 155–6, 256, 260–75, 277, 278–82, 291, 306
politicisation 15, 275–91
polycrisis 88, 108, 109
price increases 97–9
Procedural Regulation 206
proportionality 99–100, 217
public interest 9, 85, 90, 108
public policy 9, 98, 100, 103
recovery of State aid 304
Regional Aid Guidelines, consultation on 158
Rescue and Restructuring Guidelines (RR Guidelines) 85, 91, 93, 99
rule of law backsliding 15, 223, 275, 277, 291
sector crises 89–90
serious disturbance to the economy 90–1, 92–4
soft law 14, 155–8, 171, 213, 221–5, 229–31
specialisation agreements 103
standstill clauses 170–1
State Aid Action Plan (SAAP) 217
systemic crises 89, 92
Temporary Framework for Cooperation 84–5, 98–100
Temporary Frameworks for State aid 13, 84–5, 91
third-party companies in enforcement, role of 164–71
transparency 225, 230, 256, 280, 306
types of crises 87–90
Ukraine, Russia's invasion of 87, 222, 225, 228, 230, 307
State aid control, green transition through 253–73
  Aarhus Convention 267–9, 272, 306
  access to justice 15, 254
  advantage, definition of 255
  block exemptions 158, 256, 269
  centralisation 255, 264, 269, 273
  climate neutrality 260, 271
  Code of Best Practices on State Aid, amendment of 268–9
  Commission 187–91, 253–6, 261–73, 305–6

compatibility assessments 264–5, 267, 272, 307–8
compensatory justification principle 255–6
competences 187–8, 271
compliance checks 262–4
conditional State aid decisions 254, 261, 269–73
constitutional perspectives 254, 255–7, 270
decarbonisation goals, compliance with 75, 260, 265, 270–3, 307–8
decentralisation 256
defence, right of 266
discretion, exercise of Commission 261–5
Emissions Trading Scheme (ETS) 271
enforcement 254–8, 264, 267
EU courts 14, 173–83, 186–93
European Green Deal (EGD) 253–4, 257–64, 272–3, 306
Climate Law of 2021 257–8, 269
Commission 253, 257–9, 273
General Block Exemption Regulation, public consultation on 158
NextGenerationEU (NGEU) plan 258, 273, 308
exemptions 186–7
fundamental rights 254
Guidelines on State Aid for Climate, Environmental Protection and Energy (CEEAG) 261–2, 265, 268, 271
incentives for undertakings 186–91
integration 15, 254–5, 256, 258–61, 264–6, 271–3
internal market 187–91, 192, 253–6, 259, 262–3, 270
interpretation 263–4
lock-in effects 265, 270, 272
mainstreaming 271, 306
modernisation 256–7
notification requirement 256, 268–9
policy, evolution of State aid 260–73
procedure 266–9
proportionality 189
public participation 254, 261, 266–9, 273, 306
recovery orders 256
Services of General Economic Interest (SGEI), economic advantage for 259
soft law 256
standing 266–8
State Aid Action Plan (SAAP) 256, 262
subsidies 253, 259, 265
taxation 259
Taxonomy Regulation 265, 308
third parties, judicial protection for 266–8, 273
transparency 256, 306
Stern Review 71
Stigler Committee on Digital Platforms report 55
strategic turn in competition law 161–2, 163, 168, 171–2
stricter competition rules, Member States with 135–9, 302
subsidies *see also* **Foreign Subsidies Regulation**
creative compliance with State aid 276, 286
digital transitions/disruptions 174, 176
foreign subsidies 174, 176
green transitions/disruptions 174, 176, 253, 259, 265
suspension of application of competition rules 5, 86, 104, 170–1, 307
sustainability agreements 177–83
cooperation between undertakings, societal benefits from 177–83, 191, 192
de minimis agreements 177
efficiencies 177–8, 180–2
environmentally friendly distortions 178
environmentally harmful efficiencies 178
exemptions 177–80, 191
measurement of external benefits or harms 179–80
national competition authorities (NCAs) and Commission, relationship between 141–3, 151, 219
nature of effects 179
negative externalities 178–80
positive externalities 178–82
private benefits 178
soft law 219

'take back control' 277–8
taxation 186, 259, 289–91
taxonomy
classification of economically sustainable activities 78
European Green Deal and State aid 13, 66, 78–9, 258, 306
Taxonomy Regulation 78, 258, 265, 306, 308
technocratic cooperation, EU regulatory extension through 13–14, 113–32, 302
accession, conditionality requirements for 117
administrative cooperation 114
block exemptions 128
Brussels effect 115–16

Charter of Fundamental Rights of the EU (CFEU) 127–8
constitutional principles, export of 14, 114, 299
dispute settlement 114, 122–3, 129
divergence 113, 114, 121, 129, 132
effectiveness, principle of 114–15, 127, 132
enforcement 113–20, 123, 126–9, 132, 299, 300
epistemic communities 118–19, 123, 132, 300
equivalence, principle of 114, 121–6, 131
European Competition Network (ECN) 127–9
Foreign Subsidies Regulation (FSR) 121, 123–6, 297, 298, 302–3, 306–7
fragmentation of global trade system 13
Free Trade Agreements (FTAs) 114, 117–18, 121–3, 126–32, 302
globalisation 116
harmonisation 114, 122
independence 121, 127–8, 131
independent and effective authorities as counterparts 126–9, 301
institutions 114, 115–21, 126–7, 131
integration 119–20
inter-agency agreement 114
level playing field 113–15, 121–6, 131–2
merger control 128
modes of extension 115–21
mutual recognition principle 114, 121
mutual trust 301
national competition authorities (NCAs) 114–15
non-EU countries, extension of rules to 13
non-regression commitments 114, 122
politicisation 305
procedural fairness 127
proportionality 123
public procurement 124, 126
Regulation 1/2003 118–19, 128
regulatory clashes between jurisdictions 119
resources 126, 128
safeguarding measures 123
standards 116, 121–3, 131–2
territorial extension 116
third country regulators, cooperation with 13–14, 114
third State intervention 113
Trade and Cooperation Agreement (TCA) 114, 117, 120, 122–3, 127–31
Trade Policy Review (TPR) 113, 115, 123, 129, 132
transparency 115, 121, 127, 129–32
unfair trading conditions 13, 113, 132
Temporary Crisis and Transition Framework (Ukraine) 222, 225, 230
Temporary Framework for Cooperation (Covid-19) 83–5, 90, 98–100, 103–7, 296, 306
Temporary Framework for State Aid (Covid-19) 83–7, 90–7, 222
amendments 225
cooperation 220
crisis cartels 99–100
digital transitions/disruptions 174
European Parliament 108
expiry/phasing out 87, 176
flexibility 13, 257
justifications 295–6
proportionality 94–5
recapitalisation support 271
Rescue and Restructuring Guidelines (RR Guidelines) 93
reuse of established legislative techniques 306–7
Temporary Framework for State Aid (Ukraine) 87, 222, 228, 307
third countries *see* **technocratic cooperation, EU regulatory extension through**
third parties, judicial protection for 266–8, 273
annulment actions 266
green transitions/disruptions 266–8, 273
direct and individual concern 266–7
interested parties 266–8
State aid 266–8, 273
third-party companies in enforcement of EU competition law, role of 155, 164–72, 303
complainants, role of companies as 167–8
disruptive cases 166
duty of care 165–6
heard, right to be 165
information, third-party companies as a source of 164–6, 172
instrumental value of third-party companies 164–7
investigated companies in enforcement, position of 159
merger control 164–6
national competition authorities (NCAs) and courts 168–71
participation, right of 165–6
reasons, duty to give 166
State aid 164, 165–8

Trade and Cooperation Agreement (TCA) 114, 117, 120, 122–3, 127–31
Trade Policy Review (TPR) 113, 115, 123, 129, 132
transformations and constitutional challenges 1–5
transitions *see* **digital transitions/disruptions; green transitions/disruptions**
transparency
access to documents 129
comfort letters 226
companies, role of 154, 171
consultation 158
Covid-19 and State aid 108
digital transitions/disruptions 238
European Competition Network (ECN) 129
merger control 31
national competition authorities (NCAs) 298–9
peer review mechanisms 129–31, 132
professional or business secrecy 130
soft law 221, 223, 225–6, 230–1
State aid 225, 230, 256, 280, 306
technocratic cooperation, EU regulatory extension through 115, 121, 127, 129–32
Trade Policy Review (TPR) 129
travel agents, regulation of agreements between hotels and online 141–2
trust *see* **mutual trust, principle of**
two steps forward, one step back (State aid) 276, 282, 289–91
typologies of crises 6–7

Ukraine *see* **Ukraine, Association Agreement with; Ukraine, Russia's invasion of**
Ukraine, Association Agreement with 127–8, 130
Deep and Comprehensive FTA (DCFTA) 127
horizontal mergers 130
State aid 130
transparency 130
Ukraine, Russia's invasion of 173
Green Deal Industrial Plan 222
industry, resilience of 154
politicisation 275
public procurement 230
sanctions 222, 230
soft law 213–14, 217, 221–2, 225, 229–30
State aid 87, 222, 225, 228, 230, 307
Temporary Crisis and Transition Framework 222, 225, 230
Temporary Framework for State Aid 87, 222, 228, 307
unfair trading conditions 13, 113, 132
uniform application of rules 11, 134, 248–9, 294, 301
unilateral conduct 57, 62, 64, 136, 237, 250, 301

values and principles 24, 43 *see also* **effectiveness, principle of; fundamental rights; legal certainty; mutual trust, principle of; transparency**
compensatory justification principle 255–6
constitutional principles 14, 20, 29–42, 114, 121, 131–2, 214, 235, 278–9, 293, 298–9
equivalence, principle of 114, 121–6, 131, 298
general principles of EU law 68, 235
national procedural autonomy, principle of 11
Rechtsstaat 39
sincere/loyal cooperation, principle of 10, 39, 42–3, 137, 245, 299, 301
soft law 228–30
systemic values, upholding 7

WhatsApp 48

Milton Keynes UK
Ingram Content Group UK Ltd.
UKHW010228080224
437389UK00005B/220

9 781509 951796